Argumentation Library

VOLUME 10

Series Editors

ARGUING ON THE TOULMIN MODEL

New Essays in Argument Analysis and Evaluation

Edited by

DAVID HITCHCOCK
Mc Master University,
Hamilton, Canada

and

BART VERHEIJ
Rijksuniversiteit Groningen,
Groningen, The Netherlands

Springer

A C.I.P. Catalogue record for this book is available from the Library of Congress.

ISBN-10 1-4020-4937-4 (HB)
ISBN-13 978-1-4020-4937-4 (HB)
ISBN-10 1-4020-4938-2 (e-book)
ISBN-13 978-1-4020-4938-2 (e-book)

Published by Springer,
P.O. Box 17, 3300 AA Dordrecht, The Netherlands.

www.springer.com

Printed on acid-free paper

CONTENTS

ACKNOWLEDGEMENTS

The chapters in this volume have undergone peer review and were revised in the light of the resulting comments. We would like to thank the following referees and commentators for their help: Derek Allen, Richard T. W. Arthur, Peter Asquith, Mark Battersby, Trevor Bench-Capon, George Boger, Peter Cramer, Chris Eisenhart, James B. Freeman, Michael A. Gilbert, Tom Gordon, Leo Groarke, Dale Hample, Darrin Hicks, Anthony Hunter, Henrike Jansen, Ralph H. Johnson, James F. Klumpp, Christian Kock, Robert Kominar, Erik C. W. Krabbe, Ronald Leenes, Michael Leff, Ronald P. Loui, Peter McBurney, Daniel O'Keefe, Fabio Paglieri, Robert C. Pinto, Henry Prakken, Pedro Reygadas, Phyllis Rooney, Michael Scriven, Harvey Siegel, Guillermo Simari, Christina Slade, Robert G. Sullivan, Olaf Tans, Tim van Gelder, James Voss, Douglas Walton, Mark Weinstein, Joseph Wenzel, John Woods, John Zeleznikow.

We would also like to thank the Social Sciences and Humanities Research Council of Canada for its financial support of the conference in May 2005 at McMaster University on "The uses of argument", at which many of the papers in this volume were presented in preliminary form. The conference grant enabled us to hire an editorial assistant, Daniel Farr, to take care of the technical aspects of preparation of the manuscript of this book. Daniel was a reliable and capable editorial assistant, and we express our warm thanks to him for his dedication and professionalism.

For financial support of the May 2005 conference, we thank also McMaster University's provost and vice-president academic Ken Norrie, its vice president research Mamdouh Shoukri, its dean of humanities Nasrin Rahimieh, and the chair of its philosophy department Richard T. W. Arthur.

For their support of this project and their help in preparing the manuscript, we thank Anne-Marie Blaney, Publishing Editor in Ethics and Philosophy of Law at Springer; her assistant Natalie Rieborn; Gerrit Oomen, André Tournois and Joseph Albert André of the Springer production department; and Deborah Doherty of Springer Author Support.

We thank the editors of the journal *Argumentation* for permission to reprint eight articles from a special issue (vol. 19, no. 3, 2005) of that journal on "the Toulmin model today". The articles are the chapters by Andrew Aberdein, James B. Freeman, David Hitchcock, Ronald P. Loui, Henry Prakken, Chris Reed and Glenn Rowe, Bart Verheij, and James F. Voss.

Finally, we thank the editors of the journal *Informal Logic* for permission to reprint three articles from that journal. "Reasoning in Theory and Practice" by Stephen Toulmin was previously published in *Informal Logic* (vol. 24, no. 2, 2004), and is reprinted here with permission. "Toulmin's Model of Argument and the Question of Relativism" by Lilian Bermejo Luque was previously published in *Informal Logic* (vol. 24, no. 2, 2004), and is reprinted here with permission. "Evaluating inferences: the nature and role of warrants" by Robert C. Pinto was previously published in *Informal Logic*, and is reprinted here with permission.

CHAPTER 1

DAVID HITCHCOCK[1] AND BART VERHEIJ[2]

INTRODUCTION

[1]*Department of Philosophy, McMaster University, Hamilton, Canada L8S 4K1*
[2]*Artificial Intelligence, University of Groningen, Grote Kruisstraat 2/1, 9712 TS Groningen, The Netherlands*
E-mail: hitchckd@mcmaster.ca, b.verheij@ai.rug.nl

1. THE USES OF ARGUMENT

In *The Uses of Argument* (1958), Stephen Edelston Toulmin argued that the abstract and formal criteria of mathematical logic and of much twentieth-century epistemology had little applicability to the methods we actually use in everyday life to assess arguments. Toulmin called for a reform that would blend logic and epistemology into 'applied logic', focused on the structures of arguments in different fields and the corresponding differences in the standards for their appraisal. Its method was to be comparative, empirical and historical; it was to look concretely at the similarities and differences between ways of arguing and standards of proof in geometrical optics, historiography, civil litigation, morals and so forth, as these have evolved his torically.

Despite the pluralism of his title, Toulmin focused on one use of argument: to defend a claim made by asserting something. He noted certain field-invariant features of our doing so. First we present a problem, expressed in a more or less clear question. We have a certain opinion in mind as our solution to this problem; Toulmin is not concerned in this book with how we did or should arrive at it. We begin by acknowledging various candidates for a solution, candidates that are 'possible' in the sense that they have a right to be considered. Then we consider the bearing of information at our disposal on these suggestions, perhaps concluding that some are after all 'impossible', perhaps identifying one as most 'probable' in the sense of being most deserving of acceptance, perhaps identifying one as 'presumably' correct unless certain unusual or exceptional conditions apply.

During this process of rational justification, we throw up what Toulmin called 'micro-arguments' (Toulmin, 1958, p. 94), for which he proposed a field-invariant pattern of analysis designed to do justice to the process of defending a particular claim against a challenger. This pattern, which has come to be known as the 'Toulmin model' or 'Toulmin scheme', differed radically from the traditional logical analysis of a micro-argument into premisses and conclusion. First we assert

D. Hitchcock and B. Verheij (eds.), Arguing on the Toulmin Model: New Essays in Argument Analysis and Evaluation, 1–23.

something, and thus make a *claim* (C). Challenged to defend our claim by a questioner who asks, "What have you got to go on?", we appeal to the relevant facts at our disposal, which Toulmin calls our *data* (D). It may turn out to be necessary to establish the correctness of these facts in a preliminary argument. But their acceptance by the challenger, whether immediate or indirect, does not necessarily end the defense. For the challenger may ask about the bearing of our data on our claim: "How do you get there?" Our response will at its most perspicuous take the form: "Data such as D entitle one to draw conclusions, or make claims, such as C" (p. 98). A proposition of this form Toulmin calls a *warrant* (W). Warrants, he notes, confer different degrees of force on the conclusions they justify, which may be signaled by qualifying our conclusion with a *qualifier* (Q) such as 'necessarily', 'probably' or 'presumably'. In the latter case, we may need to mention conditions of *rebuttal* (R) "indicating circumstances in which the authority of the warrant would have to be set aside" (p. 101). Our task, however, is still not necessarily finished. For our challenger may question the general acceptability of our warrant: "Why do you think that?" Toulmin calls our answer to this question our *backing* (B). He emphasizes the great differences in kind between backings in different fields. Warrants can be defended by appeal to a system of taxonomic classification, to a statute, to statistics from a census, and so forth. It is this difference in backing that constitutes the field-dependence of our standards of argument. Ultimately, all micro-arguments depend on the combination of data and backing. In rare cases, checking the backing will involve checking the claim; Toulmin calls such arguments 'analytic arguments.' Most arguments are not of this sort, so that purely formal criteria do not suffice for their assessment; Toulmin calls them 'substantial arguments'. The sort of backing that is acceptable for a given substantial argument will depend on the field to which it belongs.

To illustrate the contribution of these constituents, Toulmin proposed the following diagram (p. 104):

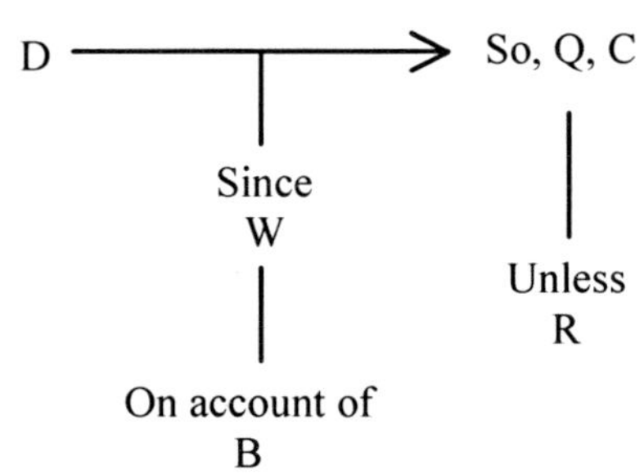

D for *Data* W for *Warrant*
Q for *Qualifier* B for *Backing*
C for *Claim* R for *Rebuttal*

Summarizing, in *The Uses of Argument* Toulmin emphasized a number of points that are by now familiar, but still deserve attention:

1. Reasoning and argument involve not only support for points of view, but also attack against them.
2. Reasoning can have qualified conclusions.
3. There are other good types of argument than those of standard formal logic.
4. Unstated assumptions linking premisses to a conclusion are better thought of as inference licenses than as implicit premisses.
5. Standards of reasoning can be field-dependent, and can be themselves the subject of argumentation.

Each of these points is illustrated by his layout of arguments. The rebuttal illustrates the first point, the qualifier the second point, and the warrant and backing the last three points.

2. RECEPTION OF TOULMIN'S BOOK

As Toulmin himself notes in his essay in this volume, which was delivered as an address in 2005, his fellow philosophers were initially hostile to the ideas in his book. They were taken up, however, by specialists in fields like jurisprudence and psychology, who found that they fit the forms of argument and reasoning that they were studying. And Toulmin's model was embraced by the field of speech communication in the United States, whose textbooks on argumentation now include an obligatory chapter on the Toulmin model of micro-arguments. More recently, the model has been appropriated by researchers in the fields of computer science and artificial intelligence, where it has been adapted for use in decision support systems, for instance in the domains of law and medicine. Work in these fields on topics such as defeasible reasoning, argumentation schemes and field-dependent standards of reasoning has roots in Toulmin's ideas. Toulmin has also strongly influenced the graphical representation of argument today, e.g. in software. And some philosophers have come to take Toulmin's ideas seriously, especially those working in what is called 'informal logic', the philosophical study of the analysis and evaluation of real arguments. In this sub-field, Toulmin's book is a post-war classic.

The present volume attempts to bring together the best current reflection on the Toulmin model and its current appropriation. All the essays were written in response to calls for papers for a special issue of the journal *Argumentation* (19: 3 [2005]) on "The Toulmin model today" and for a conference at McMaster University in May 2005 on "The uses of argument". They are a selection from the papers submitted, revised in the light of comments by referees and conference commentators, and in subsequent discussion. The chapters are not exegetical but substantive, extending or challenging Toulmin's ideas in ways that make fresh contributions to the theory of analyzing and evaluating arguments.

In the first chapter of the current volume, delivered as a keynote address at the McMaster conference, **Stephen Toulmin** acknowledges influences on his book from Dewey, Collingwood and (rather surprisingly) Lenin; recounts the history of its reception; and draws a moral conclusion from the historical relativity of our critical standards in various fields: we should be modest about our intellectual achievements, in the light of what has been and what will come after us. In the process, he reminisces about his teacher Ludwig Wittgenstein, who was clearly a formative influence.

As evidence for the influence of Toulmin's ideas, **Ronald P. Loui** turns to citation counts in his chapter 'A Citation-Based Reflection on Toulmin and Argument'. He reports that citations in the leading journals in the social sciences, humanities and science and technology put Toulmin and his works in the top 10 among philosophers of science and philosophical logicians of the 20th century. Thus, he concludes, Toulmin's *Uses of Argument*, and Stephen Toulmin's work in general, have been essential contributions to twentieth century thought.

Toulmin himself (1958, p. 1) claimed no finality for his ideas. And indeed his model has been reshaped in various ways, his claims have been contested by some and in response reformulated by others, and some but not all aspects of his approach have been incorporated in applications in different domains. The present volume testifies to these developments.

3. THE SPECTER OF RELATIVISM

For example, Toulmin's field-dependency thesis—that the standards for evaluating an argument are internal to the field to which it belongs—has been alleged to imply an unacceptable relativism, according to which 'anything goes' and nobody outside the specialists in a field can object to the standards that those specialists have developed for their intra-field arguments. The current volume includes four distinct attempts to rescue Toulmin's model from this allegedly dire consequence. To judge by Toulmin's 2005 address printed in this volume, they are trying to rescue Toulmin from himself. The reader will have to judge whether Toulmin ought to be rescued and, if so, which of the four attempts offers the best salvation.

Of the four attempts, perhaps the closest in spirit to Toulmin's own position is **G. Thomas Goodnight's** "Complex Cases and Legitimation Inferences: Extending the Toulmin Model to Deliberative Argument in Controversy". Goodnight's chapter responds to an objection by Jurgen Habermas (1981) that Toulmin does not draw the proper lines between accidental institutional differentiations of argumentation and forms of argumentation determined by internal structure. In response, Habermas introduces his own differentiatiation of argumentation into theoretical, practical, aesthetic, therapeutic, and explicative discourse and critique (1981, p. 23)—a differentiation that according to Habermas properly weights the validity and proof requirements of each form of argumentation. Goodnight proposes to defend Toulmin's notion that reasoning is grounded in fields by adding to Toulmin's model what Goodnight calls 'legitimation inferences'. A legitimation inference justifies the selection of backing to support a particular argument by justifying the choice of field in which to ground the argument. Such inferences, Goodnight argues, are of particular importance in what he calls 'complex cases'—cases where a number of reasons are potentially relevant but do not necessarily point in the same direction, and where a decision needs to be made to select some of them as grounds and discard others. Through the example of decision-making about risk, Goodnight argues that Toulmin's field-based approach, when supplemented by legitimation inferences, is superior to Habermas' proposed alternative.

A second attempt that, despite appearances, is close in spirit to Toulmin's own position is **Mark Weinstein's** "A Metamathematical Extension of the Toulmin Agenda". Weinstein accepts Toulmin's contextual, historical and field-dependent approach to understanding reasoning and argument in the sciences as exemplified by *Human Understanding* (1972). He notes that Toulmin presented a preliminary version of his model for the layout of arguments in his earlier work *The Philosophy of Science: An Introduction* (1953) and expresses admiration for his books on the history of science written in collaboration with June Goodfield (Toulmin and Goodfield 1961; 1962; 1965). But he is sensitive to a charge by Harvey Siegel (1987) among others that the absence of a foundation collapses Toulmin's theory of inquiry into an indefensible relativism. Weinstein argues that, although Toulmin is correct in his claim that formal models are of limited value as a way of expressing reasoning and argument in various sciences, there is an important place for formalism in the metatheory of such reasoning and argument. Conscious that Toulmin himself would be skeptical of such metatheoretical formalism, he nevertheless argues for what he calls a 'model of emerging truth' (MET) as an analogue of the metatheory of axiomatized mathematical theories. Unlike the metatheory of mathematics, which presupposes a domain of eternally existing objects and an assignment of once-and-for-all truth-values, Weinstein's proposed metatheory of the sciences allows for their historical development, both in terms of the embedding of one science in another and in terms of increasingly close approximations to an emergent truth. Truth, on Weinstein's model, becomes an ideal limit to which scientific inquiry can get closer as it develops. He advances his formal model as a way of providing a foundation for this Toulminian conception of scientific inquiry.

In "Toulmin's Model of Argument and the Question of Relativism" **Lilian Bermejo-Luque** points out that Toulmin himself criticized relativism, in his *Human Understanding* (1972), as a counterpart of the misconception of rationality as adherence to a deductivist ideal of knowledge. She notes that, despite this rejection of relativism, some scholars (e.g. Willard 1981) have read into Toulmin's theory of argument a deep relativism, according to which fields are independent sociological entities whose practices we can only describe—a view that she takes to imply that standards in different fields are incommensurable and incapable of appraisal from outside the field. She argues that this sort of relativism is unacceptable, and interprets Toulmin's model in such a way that it provides an antidote against it. She argues, first, that recognizing a piece of discourse as argumentation does not require us to recognize the field to which it belongs, only that a claim is being made and reasons offered in support of it. Thus argument analysis is not field-dependent. As for argument evaluation, she begins by arguing for a rather unusual interpretation of Toulmin's warrants as inference claims, of the form 'if D (data) then C (claim)', construed as a particular material conditional, i.e. as logically equivalent to the statement 'not both D and not C'. The modal qualifier appropriate to an argument's claim, on Bermejo-Luque's interpretation, is a function jointly of the truth-value or acceptability value of the reasons and the warrant. She argues that construing the warrant as a general justification of the inference from reasons to claim is a holdover from deductivism, which Toulmin opposes. On Bermejo-Luque's interpretation of Toulmin's warrants, the role of fields is to provide a stock of accepted truth-values for propositions. At the end of her chapter, Bermejo-Luque addresses the question of whether her interpretation corresponds to Toulmin's own understanding of his model. She concludes that, whatever the answer to this question, construing the value of an argument as a function of the value of its reasons and warrant leaves little room for relativism.

James B. Freeman, in "Systematizing Toulmin's Warrants: An Epistemic Approach", takes relativism to be one of four problems with Toulmin's notion of field. He claims that, if fields are understood as the discourse of a particular community, whose members would be free to set standards, Toulmin's thesis that standards of evaluation are field-dependent "raises the specter of relativism". Further, it is unclear what counts as a field, there is no explanation of why we are entitled to take for granted the reliability of certain warrants (as Toulmin claims we must, on pain of infinite regress), and it is difficult to assign some warrants to fields as Toulmin construes them. To solve these problems, Freeman proposes to classify warrants epistemologically, on the basis of how it is to be determined that they are reliable. He takes a warrant to be a generalization of the associated conditional 'If D, then C' of an argument; to be reliable, it must be capable of supporting counter-factual inferences: Data such as D would entitle one to infer a claim such as C. On this basis, he excludes empirical generalizations that are merely accidentally true, whether universally or for the most part. Lawlike generalizations capable of supporting counterfactual conditionals divide into four main types, corresponding to four distinct modes of intuiting their truth: *a priori*, empirical, institutional and evaluative. Freeman illustrates the distinction with a contrast between a warrant whose reliability is ultimately established by empirical intuition and one whose reliability is ultimately established by institutional intuition. Rather than being classified by fields in Toulmin's original sense, warrants will be classified by the type of intuition on which their reliability rests. Freeman notes that his proposal preserves Toulmin's insight that different kinds of warrant require different kinds of backing.

4. WARRANTS

The contributions by Bermejo-Luque and Freeman open up the question of how we are to construe Toulmin's warrants. Bermejo-Luque, rather unusually, construes them as particular material conditionals, of the form 'If D, then C'. Freeman, in contrast, construes them as lawlike generalizations of an argument's associated conditional, of the form 'In any (almost any/any normal) situation of which D would be true, C would be true.' Two other chapters in the current volume offer rival interpretations of Toulmin's warrants.

James F. Klumpp, in "Warranting Arguments, the Virtue of Verb" approaches the task of construing Toulmin's warrants from the point of view of Toulmin's aim of producing a 'working logic' that can be used on the fly by real people dealing with real arguments. He notes that students in his field of speech communication have great difficulty distinguishing data from warrants when they are asked to cast the components of an argument into propositional form. As a solution to this problem, Klumpp proposes to use the word 'warrant' not as a noun but as a verb, 'to warrant', thus capturing Toulmin's original dynamic presentation of the process of defending a claim against a challenger. Klumpp distinguishes seven different strategies that Toulmin uses in his chapter "The Layout of Arguments" to define 'warrant'. He finds unhelpful those strategies that characterize warrants in terms of their propositional form. More helpful, Klumpp maintains, are strategies that appeal to the function of warrants: to authorize the taking of data as proof of a claim. To warrant, according to the dictionary, is "to provide adequate grounds for; justify; to grant authorization or sanction to (someone); authorize or empower". So Toulmin's question, "How do you get there?", to which the answer is the warrant, should in Klumpp's view be rephrased as, "How do those data warrant the claim?" And the best way of understanding this functional construal is to present the constituents of Toulmin's model as arising in a conversational interchange, as Toulmin himself initially presented them. This functional construal of warranting, Klumpp argues, puts warranting at the heart of Toulmin's working logic, contextualizes micro-arguments, is much easier for students to apply, and gives rhetorical critics a richer vocabulary for dealing with the texture of argument.

In "Evaluating Inferences: The Nature and Role of Warrants", **Robert C. Pinto** takes Toulmin's warrants to embody a proposal to take generalizations that are not logical truths as rules of inference. He notes that such other philosophers as Peirce (1955), Wilfrid Sellars (1953; 1963), Hitchcock (1985; 1998), and Brandom (1994; 2000) make similar proposals. In discussing such proposals, in particular those by Hitchcock and Toulmin, Pinto is led to a novel position about the virtues arguments and inferences should have if their premisses are to be considered properly connected to their conclusion, i.e. to provide adequate reasons for the conclusion. He shifts from the usual criterion of truth-preservation to one of entitlement-preservation: arguments and inferences capable of justifying their conclusion are those in which premisses that it is reasonable to embrace make it reasonable to embrace the conclusion. The shift to entitlement-preservation in turn leads Pinto to appropriate from Toulmin's account of warrants a number of positions about the form statements expressing non-logical rules of inference should take: (1) Warrants when most candidly expressed take the form of granting an entitlement. (2) Warranting statements are general statements. (3) They should indicate the normative and action-guiding force of the warrant. (4) They should have a place for modal qualifiers, interpreted functionally. (5) When incorporated into the statement of a warrant, modal qualifiers should take the form of conveying entitlement to take a particular cognitive or doxastic attitude to a propositional content. (6) Warranting statements should acknowledge the existence of defeaters. (7) Determining whether a warrant has authority involves appeal not only to matters of fact but also to the goals and purposes of the reasoning that uses the warrant. On the basis of these principles, Pinto articulates an alternative account of warrants, an account that incorporates a qualitative 'evidence proportionalism' by licensing only doxastic attitudes toward conclusions that are appropriate to the evidence on which those conclusions are based. With this alternative account in hand, Pinto is then able to sketch an account of what makes a warrant reliable. He notes that such an account involves a critical appraisal of our inferential practices, as opposed to individual inference. Such practices, he holds, play certain roles in our lives, and their reliability is a function of how well they serve that role in the typical circumstances in which we rely on them. A reliable warrant is thus one that licenses a reliable inferential practice, and a reliable inferential practice is one that is objectively likely to produce an appropriate doxastic attitude in the typical circumstances in which we rely on it.

5. QUALIFIERS

Pinto's proposal to replace truth by doxastic and epistemic attitudes as the focus of arguments and inferences has far-reaching implications for our practice of argument evaluation. Additional arousal from our dogmatic slumbers comes from the defense by **Robert H. Ennis**, in his chapter entitled "'Probably'", of Toulmin's contextual definition in *The Uses of Argument* of this particular qualifier. According to Toulmin, "When I say 'S is probably P', I commit myself guardedly, tentatively or with reservations to the view that S is P, and (likewise guardedly) lend my authority to that view" (1964, p. 53). Thus the word 'probably' is given a speech-act interpretation. Ennis argues with great care that this interpretation not only is intrinsically plausible, but also fits the facts of our use of the term 'probably' better than its four current rivals: an objective specific numerical definition, an objective nonspecific numerical definition, an objective non-numerical definition, and a subjective numerical definition. Specifically, he subjects all five proposed definitions to three tests. Is a simple affirmative sentence containing 'probably' still meaningful enough in an argument-appraisal context when the proposed defining phrase is substituted for it? Does the proposed definition retain the inconsistency when someone asserts, "Probably *p*, but not *p*" for any proposition *p*? When one person says,"Probably *p*", and in the same situation another says, "Probably not *p*", does the proposed definition retain the inconsistency between the statements? Only Toulmin's speech-act definition passes all three tests. In addition, it fits definitions of 'probably' in good dictionaries. Ennis then deals at length with substitution-in-different-contexts objections by John Searle, in his *Speech Acts* (1969), that result in Searle's concluding that speech-act interpretations like Toulmin's commit a so-called "speech act fallacy". Ennis argues that Searle's objections do not stand up to critical scrutiny.

Ennis also urges that, if we are to give advice about argument appraisal to fellow human beings, our focus should be on real arguments, not artificial arguments composed solely of propositions; and holds that real arguments consist of commitments and committings of various sorts, none of which are propositions (although the commitments and committings can be to propositions). Because conceptions of the relationships of deductive validity and inconsistency that are current in contemporary logic, which successively are necessity and contradiction between *propositions*, these conceptions require adjustment. Ennis sees deductive validity in real arguments as a relationship between commitments, and uses 'inconsistency' in its everyday sense. Thus Pinto's construal of warrants as preserving entitlement to adopt a doxastic or epistemic attitude converges with Toulmin's and Ennis' focus on real arguments and a speech-act analysis of 'probably' to demand a radical shift in the concepts used to appraise arguments.

In agreement with Toulmin's situational emphasis, and in tune with the human judgment required to decide whether and how strongly to commit, Ennis urges the importance, not only of criteria and standards of argument appraisal, but also of sensitivity, experience, background knowledge, and understanding of the situation on the part of the arguer and the argument appraiser. He also suggests that the computerization of the appraisal of most real arguments, if they contain 'probably' in the conclusion, is doomed.

6. REBUTTALS

One of the distinctive features of Toulmin's model is its provision for rebuttals, exception-making conditions that undermine the authority of the warrant and may require retraction of the claim. In "The Voice of the Other: A Dialogico-Rhetorical Understanding of Opponent and Toulmin's Rebuttal", **Wouter Slob** uses Toulmin's understanding of the rebuttal as the basis for incorporating into contemporary dialectical logic a substantial role of the opponent. Because dialectical logic treats all arguments as supportive, Slob argues, it does not take seriously its own dialogical perspective. Rather than treating the opponent's role as simply that of requesting a proponent to defend a claim or an inference, dialectical logic should recognize that an opponent, in principle, can be called upon to defend a challenge as reasonable. Further, the counter-considerations that an opponent may introduce ought to be allowed to be of sufficient weight to justify such qualifiers of the conclusion as 'probably not' or 'certainly not'. Thus the conclusion would be the result of supporting considerations and rebutting forces brought forward by both proponent and opponent. Toulmin's rebuttal, Slob holds, allows for the introduction of counter-considerations. If we allow the rebuttal in Toulmin's diagram to be developed, with data provided in support of a claim that some exception-making circumstances obtain, we allow for a robust 'voice of the other'. Slob proposes an amplification of Toulmin's diagram to accommodate such a robust voice, an amplification that he argues is superior to that proposed by Freeman (1991). Rather than focusing on how well supported is the conclusion, as dialectical logic does, we should see arguments as interchanges of supporting and rebutting forces, in what Slob calls a 'dialogico-rhetorical' approach.

Like Slob, **Bart Verheij** wishes to extend Toulmin's conception of rebuttals so as to allow them to render a claim unsupported or defeated, despite the data offered in its support. In his chapter entitled "Evaluating Arguments Based on Toulmin Scheme", Verheij develops his account of rebuttals in the context of a formal reconstruction of Toulmin's scheme. He expresses the inference from data to claim by a conditional 'if D then C' that is defined only by the fact that one can apply modus ponens to it; it is not supposed to be a material conditional. The warrant in turn is expressed by a generalization of this conditional that covers the particular case mentioned in the data and claim. In both the inference claim and the warrant, the consequent can be qualified by any of Toulmin's qualifiers, which Verheij leaves uninterpreted. As Verheij notes, Toulmin in *The Uses of Argument* described the function of rebuttals in various ways: as setting aside the authority of the warrant, as contesting the applicability of the warrant, as defeating the claim. Verheij's formal reconstruction brings out that there are five possible targets in the data-warrant-claim part of Toulmin's model against which a rebuttal can be directed: the data, the claim, the warrant, the inference claim 'if D then C', and the inference from warrant to the inference claim 'if W, then if D then C'. Equipped with his formal reconstruction and his five types of rebuttal, Verheij constructs a theory of the evaluation status of the statements in an argument, according to which in relation to a given set of assumptions a statement can be either justified or defeated (contra-justified) or unevaluated. He provides for reinstatement of claims that have been defeated or left unevaluated. In his concluding remarks, Verheij notes that according to his formal reconstruction the main departure of Toulmin's model from standard logical notions is its introduction of the concept of rebuttal. Contemporary work on defeasible argumentation carries forward this novelty of Toulmin's approach.

7. EVALUATION

In *The Uses of Argument*, Toulmin gave no specific direction on how to evaluate arguments laid out according to his model. His subsequent co-authored textbook (Toulmin, Rieke and Janik 1979; 1984) proposed in summary form eight 'essential merits' of arguments: clarity on the kind of issues the argument is intended to raise, clarity on the underlying purpose of the argument, grounds relevant to the claim, grounds sufficient to support the claim, warrant applicable to the case under discussion, warrant based on solid backing, modality or strength of the resulting claim made explicit, possible rebuttals or exceptions well understood (1984, p. 238). But it did not elaborate. Verheij's "Evaluating Arguments Based on Toulmin Scheme" thus not only reconstructs Toulmin's account formally but also repairs an omission.

David Hitchcock in his "Good Reasoning on the Toulmin Model" likewise supplements Toulmin's analytical model with a scheme for evaluation. Toulmin himself proposed his layout as a tool for analyzing micro-arguments arising in a process of justifying a claim that articulated one's prior belief. He explicitly set aside the question of how someone might come to adopt the belief in the first place, as part of a process of inquiry. Hitchcock maintains, however, that one can apply Toulmin's model to inquiry as well, where one begins with a question to which one does not know the answer. He proposes criteria for reasoning that is directed at working out such an answer on the basis of information available to the reasoner. According to Hitchcock, good reasoning requires the fulfillment of four conditions. First, the grounds on which the reasoning is based must be justified. Hitchcock discusses the sources for such grounds. He notes that no sources for justified grounds are infallible and then provides a list of the most trustworthy ones: direct observation, observation records, memory, personal testimony, expert opinion, reference sources and previous good reasoning. Each of these sources is addressed from the perspective of a reasoner trying to answer a question. The second condition that must be fulfilled is that the reasoning is based on a justified, general warrant. As Hitchcock points out, good reasoning is not a function of the correctness of the warrant. What counts is whether the reasoner is justified in accepting the warrant at the given time and in the given context. This resource-awareness of Hitchcock's approach shows even more clearly in the third condition: the information used for the reasoning must be adequate. This adequacy includes the practical obtainability of the information, both in the sense of time and effort and in the sense of importance of the question to be answered. The fourth and final condition of good reasoning proposed by Hitchcock is that the reasoner must be justified in assuming that there are no exceptions to the warrant. This can for instance be the case when one knows of no exceptions, not even after a pragmatically justified search.

8. PRACTICAL REASONING

Toulmin claimed in *The Uses of Argument* that his model was invariant across fields. What varied, he thought, was the nature of the backing used to establish the authority of the warrants in a particular field. The field-invariance component of Toulmin's approach has come under attack from investigators of practical reasoning, especially legal reasoning. They point out that, in contrast to the single, static, established warrant of Toulmin's diagram, practical discourse—discourse that applies rules, principles and standards to decisions about what is to be done—needs to take account of a variety of sometimes conflicting rules and considerations.

Toulmin's diagram fits easy cases, where there is no controversy about which rule applies, how it is to be interpreted or what the facts of the case are. It does not fit hard cases where there is controversy about one or more of these questions. **Olaf Tans**, in "The Fluidity of Warrants: Using the Toulmin Model to Analyse Practical Discourse", argues however that, if we look beyond Toulmin's diagram to what he says in *The Uses of Argument* about the construction of micro-arguments, we can find the resources for a dynamic interpretation of how warrants unfold in practical discourse. On Tans's reading, Toulmin's theory accommodates three aspects of argumentation. First, we take steps from a foundation to a conclusion; these may include not only the familiar step from data to claim, but also an inference of the data from evidence or an induction of a preference for one warrant when two contradictory warrants are applicable. Second, we use backing, qualifier and rebuttal to test the authority of a given warrant. Third, as the argument unfolds, the warrant to be applied is tested, refined and adjusted to fit the case at hand. Tans finds this structure in the argumentation of the United States Supreme Court in a celebrated case involving the authority of the United States Congress to implement a treaty by regulating the killing of migratory birds. In the court's argument, Tans finds a sequence of three processes: initial construction of a warrant on the basis of the facts of the case and the relevant legal sources; refinement of the warrant in the light of backing, qualifiers and rebuttals; application of the warrant at a certain stage of this refinement process to the case at hand. Tans captures these three processes in a revised version of Toulmin's diagram, one that shows the data being used to generate an initial warrant, which in turn generates a refined warrant, which in turn generates an applicable warrant, which then authorizes the step from data to claim:

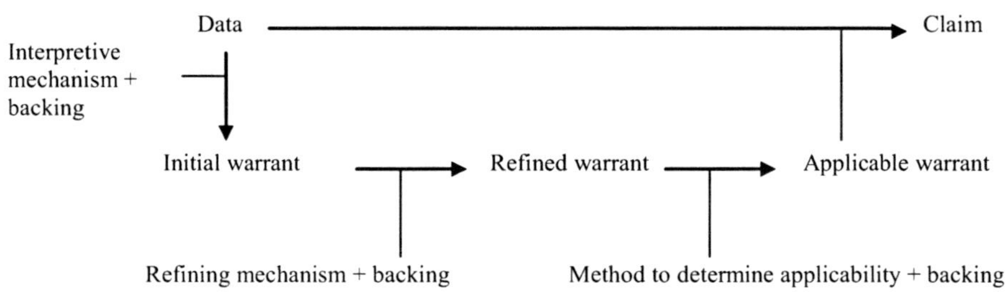

Tans points out a number of respects in which this analysis differs from the standard Toulmin model: the initial warrant is drawn from data; it undergoes change to fit the case at hand; the role of qualifier, rebuttal and backing is to help refine the initial warrant to make it applicable; and backing supports all the steps taken to arrive at an applicable warrant. Despite these differences, Tans regards his model as an elaboration rather than a refutation of Toulmin's theory, and indeed an elaboration foreshadowed by Toulmin himself in *The Uses of Argument* in the distinction between a warrant-using and a warrant-establishing argument.

Legal reasoning, of the sort that Tans discusses, has attracted the attention of researchers in artificial intelligence. In "Artificial Intelligence and Law, Logic and Argument Schemes", **Henry Prakken** explores the extent to which these researchers have taken to heart the lessons of *The Uses of Argument* for modeling legal reasoning. Prakken uses the perspective of argumentation schemes as they are studied in argumentation theory to discuss research into the application of artificial intelligence ideas to the field of law. Prakken notes that argumentation schemes can extend an approach to legal argumentation that is based on formal logic. Whereas logic focuses on form, argumentation schemes allow the specification of other considerations than purely formal ones, for instance epistemological or pragmatic. Prakken argues that much work on the application of artificial intelligence to the field of law can be regarded as taking an argumentation schemes approach. He divides legal problem solving into three main phases, viz. proof of the facts, rule interpretation and rule application, and subsequently shows how work dealing with these phases can be approached in terms of argumentation schemes. The chapter ends with a discussion of the extent to which the main lessons of Toulmin's work have been taken into account in the field of artificial intelligence and law. Prakken notes that especially Toulmin's points that argument premisses can play different roles, that arguments are defeasible and that evaluation criteria are field-dependent are adhered to.

Christian Kock points out in his "Multiple Warrants in Practical Reasoning" that both Toulmin in *The Uses of Argument* and the pedagogical applications of his theory focus much more on arguments in support of the truth of some proposition than on arguments in support of a policy. Brockriede and Ehninger, in their influential Toulminian typology of warrants (1960; 1963), distinguish only one type of warrant, a 'motivational' warrant, as available to support practical claims about what course of action to pursue. Kock argues that we need to distinguish different types of motivational warrants, because they belong to different and incommensurable dimensions—a feature of our practical reasoning on which Toulmin did not focus. In his co-authored textbook (Toulmin, Rieke and Janik, 1979), for instance, there is no distinction among warrants for practical claims. Kock finds the resources for a typology of practical or 'motivational' warrants in what is probably the oldest rhetorical handbook in the western tradition, the *Rhetorica ad Alexandrum*. The author's dictum as to what one must show when one exhorts an audience to do something constitutes, on Kock's interpretation, an inventory of the incommensurable dimensions relevant to deciding what to do: justice, lawfulness, expediency, nobility, pleasure, ease of accomplishment, necessity, practicability. With no calculus available to weigh up these incommensurable values against one another, we must support our preferred ranking with rhetorical appeals to analogy, to difference and to examples, as well as with rhetorical devices of amplification and diminution.

Toulmin himself proposes a qualitative weighing approach to such situations, an approach also endorsed by the 17th century philosopher Leibniz. **Txetxu Ausín** argues in "The Quest for Rationalism without Dogmas in Leibniz and Toulmin" that

Leibniz shares the situated approach to practical reasoning exemplified in Toulmin's attack on 'the tyranny of principles' (1981) and his promotion of a 'new casuistry' (Jonsen and Toulmin, 1988). Like Toulmin in *Return to Reason* (2001), Leibniz wished to strike a balance between the legitimate demands of formal models of rationality and the lessons of a historically and socially situated practice. Also like Toulmin, he turned to jurisprudence as his model for reasoning about contingent matters. Ausín notes the gradualism of Leibniz, which permits degrees of licitness or illicitness, and suggests that both Leibniz and Toulmin could endorse fuzzy logic as appropriate for a working logic of such nuanced verdicts. Leibniz and Toulmin, he concludes, share a soft rationalism, open to difference, pluralism and controversy—a 'rationalism without dogmas'.

9. APPLICATIONS

As the saying goes, the proof of the pudding is in the eating. In this context the proof, or test, of Toulmin's model is in the results of its application in various fields. The just-mentioned contributions have revealed a need to extend the model when it is applied to legal and other practical argumentation, while at the same time retaining the core of Toulmin's insight that real argument uses material warrants as rules of inference and is defeasible.

How does Toulmin's model fare when applied in other fields? In their chapter "From Arguments to Decisions: Extending the Toulmin View", **John Fox** and **Sanjay Modgil** report on their adaptation of the Toulmin model to provide computational decision support for clinical decision-making in the field of medicine. Their research is based on a varied methodology, which is imperative given the admirable multidisciplinarity of their research context. They have systematically observed medical professionals, they have designed and tested decision support software for the medical domain and they have done foundational work in argumentation theory. In the course of this research, a Logic of Argument has been developed, in which several elements of Toulmin's model are recognizable, in particular warrants, backings, rebuttals and qualifiers. In Toulmin's spirit, they specify several possible backings that can provide justification for the warrants underlying medical argumentation, as follows: general medical knowledge and scientific principles; objective evidence from clinical observations and trials; the authority of professional organizations; a local hospital policy; and the clinical judgement of an individual doctor. Fox and Modgil pay special attention to the occurrence of competing claims with several arguments for and against them. This requires the assessment of the relative confidence in such claims, a topic not addressed by Toulmin. Fox and Modgil discuss a set of qualifiers in terms of argument relations. For instance, they take 'P is possible' to mean that there is an argument that supports P and no argument that rebuts it. As an illustrative parallel, they mention the standardization of risk categories by the International Agency for Research on Cancer concerning claims of the form 'Chemical X causes cancer', where for example the qualifying term 'probable' stands for 'There is better evidence than merely recognition of possible carcinogenic activity'. A further topic treated by Fox and Modgil is what they call stopping rules. Stopping rules provide criteria for answering the question: when can argumentation safely stop and commitments be made? In practical domains such as medicine, the safety that should be assured by stopping rules is especially tangible. Fox and Modgil discuss an epistemic and a utilitarian stopping rule. They have applied their research to the assessment of suspected breast cancer, to the prescription of drugs for common conditions, and to the assessment of genetic risk of cancer.

Another area where the Toulmin model has been applied is the law. The starting point of **John Zeleznikow**'s "Using Toulmin Argumentation to Support Dispute Settlement in Discretionary Domains" is the need to deal with discretionary decision-making when developing software support in the domain of law. Whereas the positivist aspects of legal decision-making, i.e. those determined by legal sources such as legal statutes, can be fruitfully modeled in by now classical rule-based expert systems, discretionary decision-making requires another approach. Zeleznikow explains that he and his coworkers have selected neural network technology to allow for the modeling of discretion. They noted certain problems with this approach, and turned to Toulmin's argument model in an attempt to deal with these problems. In one of the projects that Zeleznikow describes (Split-up, dealing with software that supports decision-making about the distribution of marital property), the connection between data and claim in Toulmin's model is implemented by a neural network trained on the basis of existing decided cases. The neural network plays the role of a so-called 'inference warrant', and the training of the network is its backing. Which data are relevant for determining a conclusion is determined by 'relevance warrants', which can be backed by statutes and cases. Zeleznikow describes a number of other projects in which he and his group continue on this approach. Zeleznikow and his group have for instance addressed eligibility for legal aid, evaluation of eyewitness evidence, refugee law and sentencing. He also reports on the use of Toulmin argument structures to build an online dispute resolution environment with the goal to provide software that can help to avoid litigation.

James F. Voss reports in his chapter entitled "Toulmin's Model and The Solving of Ill-Structured Problems" on the use of Toulmin's model to study how experts solve ill-structured problems. Ill-structured problems differ from well-structured problems in having a vaguely stated goal, requiring retrieval of constraints from outside the problem statement, admitting a variety of ways of representing the problem and working out a solution, having plausible or acceptable solutions rather than right or valid ones, typically eliciting supporting argument for a proposed solution along with arguments against alternative solutions, not admitting final solutions, and needing a database that makes simulation difficult. The argumentative and rhetorical features of solutions to ill-structured problems made them suitable for analysis using the Toulmin model. In their study, Voss and his co-investigators used the Toulmin model to analyse written transcripts, generally about 10 paragraphs long, of tape-recorded oral responses by experts on the Soviet Union to the problem of how to improve agricultural productivity in that country. In order to model the highly developed arguments found in their transcripts, Voss and his co-investigators found it necessary to make six extensions to the Toulmin model. First, they allowed the claim of one argument to be the datum of another, thus permitting the chaining of arguments together. Second, they introduced an explicit definition of an implied warrant. Third, they allowed the backing to be an argument. Fourth, they allowed such backing arguments to have a rebuttal. Fifth, they allowed the qualifier to be an argument. Sixth, they allowed the rebuttal to be an argument. With these extensions, the investigators were able to code the components of a complex line of argument using Toulmin's terminology. But it was difficult to tell whether a given statement was datum or backing, and they almost never found a stated warrant. Furthermore, Toulmin's model did not provide information concerning the problem-solving process as a whole, for the analysis of which the investigators used another model. Toulmin-type argumentation thus turned out to be embedded in a higher-level problem-solving process.

We find another specific application of Toulmin's model in the chapter by **Manfred Kraus** entitled "Arguing by Question: A Toulminian Reading of Cicero's Account of the Enthymeme". Cicero in his *Topics* describes an argument from contraries, called by rhetoricians an 'enthymeme', which he says "springs from" the third undemonstrated argument of Stoic propositional logic. He gives as an example a line in iambic verse: "Do you condemn this woman whom you accuse of nothing?" Such compressed rhetorical questions can be reconstructed as valid arguments of the form: Not both p and q; q; therefore not p. The example would have the form: Not both you condemn this woman and you accuse this woman of nothing; you accuse this woman of nothing; therefore, you do not condemn this woman. The logical form is impeccable, but Cicero's formal analysis fails to bring out how dubious such rhetorically framed arguments are, and thus needs to be supplemented. Toulmin's model, Kraus argues, provides exactly what is needed. The conclusion is the claim, and the second premiss the datum. The negated conjunction is the warrant. But this warrant must be interpreted as postulating some incompatibility between the conjuncts, in order to have some basis independent of the truth of the conclusion to be proved. And the alleged incompatibility will require backing, which as Toulmin says will be field-dependent. As it turns out, in every one of Cicero's examples, the available backing does not support an unqualified universal warrant. Hence the negated conjunction requires qualification and the conclusion must be accompanied by acknowledgement of a potential rebuttal. The weakness of the warrant explains why the argument is phrased as a rhetorical question. A rhetorical question puts strong psychological pressure on the addressee to provide the anticipated response, and thus compensates for the epistemological weakness of the warrant. In Cicero's examples, Kraus finds a small number of topical argumentative patterns that constitute the backing for the incompatibility warrants in a rhetorical enthymeme. Once these topical patterns are detected, it is easy to detect the appropriate rebuttals. Kraus's analysis demonstrates the insight that can be gained by applying Toulmin's model as a supplement to a formal analysis.

Toulmin explicitly characterized his model as a jurisprudential one focused on procedure, rather than a mathematical one focused on a quasi-geometrical ideal (1958, p. 95). It would be easy, then, for a casual reader to think that his model was not intended to apply to mathematical proofs, which were the focus of the logical tradition against which he was setting himself. But **Andrew Aberdein** argues, in "The Uses of Argument in Mathematics", that Toulmin's layout of arguments can represent the structure of arguments in mathematics. A 'critical' argument in mathematics, i.e. one that challenges a prevailing mathematical theory or seeks to motivate an alternative, is an argument about mathematics rather than in it, and so is just as amenable as any other critical argument to analysis on the Toulmin model. Aberdein cites as an example a Toulminian analysis of a critical argument by Ernst Zermelo and others for admitting the axiom of choice as an axiom of set theory. The challenge is to see how well Toulmin's layout models 'regular' arguments in mathematics, i.e. mathematical proofs. Aberdein finds quite satisfactory Toulmin's own use of his model to represent the proof by the ancient mathematician Theaetetus that there are exactly five platonic solids (Toulmin, Rieke and Janik, 1979). Further, Aberdein notes that Toulmin's qualifier permits the analyst to represent which steps in a non-constructive classical proof are constructive, thus flagging those components that are problematic from a constructivist point of view. He also considers the charge by some critics that the abstraction of diagrams like Toulmin's makes different and even incompatible reconstructions possible. For a number of proofs where different reconstructions are possible, he shows that these differences reflect ambiguity in the original text, and thus provide a useful service of clarification. A particularly difficult challenge comes from two competing reconstructions using the Toulmin model of the proof of the four colour theorem, the theorem that four colours may be assigned to the regions of any planar map in such a way that no two adjacent regions receive the same colour. The proof of this theorem is so long that no human being has ever reviewed all its steps; instead, a computer has constructed the lengthiest part of the proof on the basis of an algorithm produced by a human being. Aberdein attributes the difference in the reconstructions of the proof to the fact that one of them restricts itself to the only sort of defeater recognized by Toulmin, a rebuttal that shows that the conclusion is false, whereas the other allows an undermining defeater (Pollock, 1987) showing that the conclusion does not follow. Since all defeaters of mathematical proofs are undermining defeaters, whether or not they also rebut the conclusion, Aberdein proposes to add undermining defeaters to the rebuttals that Toulmin recognized, in order to recognize as a potential defeater of the proof of the four-colour theorem an error in our human mathematical reasoning or in the hardware or firmware on which the algorithm establishing the data has been run.

10. COMPARISONS

Diagramming is a standard technique for representing the structure and content of arguments, both in pedagogical contexts and in certain professions such as law. But diagramming on the Toulmin model is not the only available method. A popular alternative is the sort of box-and-arrow diagram introduced by Beardsley (1950). As **Chris Reed** and **Glenn Rowe** point out, in their chapter entitled "Trans lating Toulmin Diagrams: Theory Neutrality in Argument Representation", each diagramming technique involves deep assumptions about the nature of argument. Thus translating diagrams of one sort into diagrams of the other is more than a technical task of transforming pictures: it involves the integration of the two underlying theories. In their chapter, Reed and Rowe report on how they have accomplished this integration and implemented it computationally in their software Araucaria. In the process of doing so, they provide a comparison of Toulmin's theory of argument structure to the theory underlying box-and-arrow diagrams, which they call the 'standard treatment'. Reed and Rowe took as their objective to work out theoretically and implement computationally a system of storing in a common interlingua diagrams constructed using either theoretical framework, in such a way as to make possible a consistent and deterministic conversion, without input from the user, from one type of diagram to the other, with no impact on analysts working within one theoretical framework of the idiosyncratic features of the other. They report that the atoms recognized by the two theories, such as a Toulminian datum and a standard treatment premiss, are the same. They argue that a Toulminian datum-warrant-claim (DWC) structure corresponds to a standard treatment structure of a linked argument with two premisses. A standard-treatment linked argument with more than two premisses corresponds, they hold, to a Toulminian DWC structure with a single datum and multiple warrants. To permit translation into a Toulminian diagram of the complex argument structures recognized by the standard treatment, they propose to allow any of the five ancillary components in a single Toulmin argument (data, warrant, backing, qualifier, rebuttal) to be a claim in another Toulmin argument; the resulting recursive definition allowing for Toulmin arguments of arbitrary complexity has been widely adopted in computational implementations of the Toulmin model. Analogously, they allow multiple Toulminian components in support of a single claim. Toulmin's qualifiers correspond to a degree of support used in the standard treatment to label an arrow between two argument components. The backing in Toulmin's model is difficult to distinguish from the data offered in support of a warrant that is supported by a sub-argument; if the distinction has meaning in Toulmin's framework, it disappears on translation into the standard treatment. On translation back from a standard treatment analysis to Toulmin's framework, the default decision is to translate premisses offered in support of a warrant as data in a new argument with the warrant as its claim. The most troublesome and theoretically interesting component of Toulmin's model for translation purposes is his rebuttal. Unlike Aberdein, Reed and Rowe treat Toulmin's rebuttal as what Pollock (1987) calls an 'undercutter'. They consider four ways of translating rebuttals into a standard treatment diagram, and opt for representing it as a counter to an implicit premiss, e.g. that no exceptional condition obtains, which in the standard treatment might be part of an argument scheme. The two frameworks thus handle undercutters in distinctively different ways, Toulmin's by identifying multiple forms of inference and the standard treatment by treating them as counters to implicit premisses within a basically deductivist model. Reed and Rowe store analyses couched in either theoretical framework in an Argument Markup Language (AML), whose scheme is thus the 'deep structure' from which various kinds of analyses can be generated.

Fabio Paglieri and **Cristiano Castelfranchi** undertake a comparison of a different sort in their chapter entitled "The Toulmin Test: Framing Argumentation within Belief Revision Theories". Their focus is the relation between theories of belief revision and theories of argumentation. In their delineation of the terms, Paglieri and Castelfranchi regard belief revision theories as dealing with an agent changing his mind in the light of new information and argumentation theories as being about agents trying to persuade other agents to believe something. The main goal of the chapter is to start the investigation of how belief revision and argumentation are systematically related. The method underlying the chapter is to apply what Paglieri and Castelfranchi call the 'Toulmin test' to two theories of belief revision, namely the canonical Alchourrón-Gärdenfors-Makinson version of belief revision (AGM) and their own Data-oriented Belief Revision (DBR). The Toulmin test is whether one can map Toulmin's argument model onto a belief revision theory. They argue that AGM belief revision fails the test in two ways. First it cannot distinguish between new information that comes to be believed and new information that fails to be believed. This is related to the so-called, much-debated, success postulate underlying the original AGM approach: new information simply is believed after a belief change. The second and more severe failure of AGM belief revision is that it does not distinguish structure in doxastic states, and this prevents it from encoding even the simplest forms of argumentation. For instance, there is no notion of beliefs being reasons for other beliefs. DBR belief revision fares better on these points. The success postulate is left behind by considering belief change as a two-step process: new information directly affects an agent's data structure (to be distinguished from his belief set), which in turn can lead to a change in the agent's beliefs. Whether a belief change occurs is determined by structural relationships with other data and by a process of belief selection. The belief selection process uses relevant properties of data, for instance their relevance, credibility, importance and likeability, to assess whether they are believed or not. Paglieri and Castelfranchi discuss how elements of Toulmin's model can be implemented in their DBR approach and discuss some extensions. They treat the topic of focusing in argumentation and include a discussion of plausibility.

11. REFLECTING ON TOULMIN

In the final chapter in this volume, "Eight Theses Reflecting on Stephen Toulmin", **John Woods** engagingly confesses that he himself was part of the early resistance among philosophers to Toulmin's ideas. Influenced by developments in computer science, cognitive psychology and logic in the last 40 years, Woods now recants that resistance. His eight theses are stimulated in part by Toulmin's theoretical approach, and in part by his example.

Woods defends his first thesis, that validity is nearly always the wrong standard for real-life reasoning, on the ground that the cognitive limitations and situatedness of human beings make the necessary truth-preservation that is the hallmark of validity the wrong standard in most situations: it is unattainable and too brittle. Here Woods endorses Toulmin's recognition that our warrants, and thus our claims, are often qualified—an endorsement that virtually all the contributors to this volume share.

Woods' second thesis is that the probability calculus distorts much of probabilistic reasoning. In contrast to mathematical theories of perspective and continuity, he argues, the mathematical theory of probability developed by Pascal does not supersede and displace the pre-mathematical treatment of it. In fact, Woods notes, we often use the word 'probable' as a synonym for the non-quantitative term 'plausible'. This residue of our earlier usage, not covered by Pascalian probability, has its own place. Woods' third thesis is that scant resources have a benign influence on human reasoning. In support of this thesis, he notes that individual human beings do not have enough information, time, computational capacity, infrastructural support and money to adhere on their own to standards of deductive or inductive reasoning. For an individual human being, falling short of those standards is not a fault, but to be expected. Recognition of our resource constraints implies a fallibilist epistemology, one that allows for defeat of previous reasoning by new information. Woods' fallibilism accords with the universal recognition by our contributors of the role of defeaters in argumentation, a role first made widely popular through the concept of rebuttal in Toulmin's model.

Woods' fourth thesis is that conceptual change drives scientific advancement, a thesis that he finds subtly defended in Toulmin's *The Philosophy of Science* (1953). Woods' fifth thesis is that logic should attend to the cognitive aspects of reasoning and arguing. Although there is no place for psychology in set theory, model theory, recursion theory or proof theory, there is a place for psychology in the logic of agent-based reasoning, which must attend to how human beings actually do reason. Woods' thesis chimes with Toulmin's call in *The Uses of Argument* for an applied logic that the man in the street can use (1958, pp. 1, 254-255), though Toulmin himself was averse to introducing psychological considerations into the study of argument. Woods' sixth thesis is that ideal models are unsuitable for determining normativity. The fact that something is analytically true in a certain model (e.g. that in rational decision theory the best option in a situation of decision-making under risk is the one that maximizes expected utility) does not make it true. To get our normative bearings, Woods argues, we do better to look to our actual practice rather than to an ideal model, because we know that by and large our practice enables us to survive and flourish. Woods' call to base our norms on how human beings actually reason and argue is reflected in Toulmin's field-dependency thesis, according to which the backings for our warrants, and thus the standards by which our arguments are to be appraised, are the standards of the argument's field as they exist at the time.

Woods' seventh thesis is that what he calls the 'Can Do Principle' should be applied with caution. The Can Do Principle is to use what we can do to deal cognitively with a new situation; for example, if we have an axiomatized probability theory, we apply it to everyday reasoning about probabilities. Toulmin's lifelong emphasis on the contextuality and situatedness of our reasoning corresponds exactly to Woods' note of caution about the Can Do Principle; to impose abstract schemes on complex realities without regard for their complexities is both anathema to Toulmin and a violation of Woods' thesis. Woods' eighth and final thesis is that domain-specific logics are as welcome as they are unavoidable. Woods points out the difficulties that have faced the project of constructing a logic that is a universal foundation of the sciences, for example in applying it to quantum mechanics. He thus warmly embraces Stephen Toulmin's idea that logically correct reasoning be made sensitive to disciplinary peculiarities.

12. SYNTHESIS

When we look back at the chapters in this volume, what can we say in general about the contemporary appropriation of the Toulmin model? The first and most obvious point to make is that Toulmin's model has had, and continues to have, an enormous influence on the study of argumentation. The citation indexes consulted by Loui put this point beyond doubt. It is reinforced by the number, scholarly excellence, geographical range, and disciplinary breadth of the contributions to this volume. Here are 24 substantial articles by 27 scholars from 10 countries on three continents, working in an interdisciplinary domain ranging from artificial intelligence via philosophy to speech communication—all of them addressing directly Toulmin's work on argument, especially his famous model. And they are doing so from the perspective of their contemporary work, not from a purely historical perspective.

Part of the explanation for the influence of Toulmin's 'layout of arguments' is its simplicity. As Toulmin himself says in this volume, it was never intended to be a comprehensive theory of argumentation. It formed part of Toulmin's case, made against the background of British analytic philosophy of the 1950s, for a new turn in logic. Precisely because it was so incomplete, it has leant itself to varying interpretations, extensions and amendments. An obvious extension, exhibited in several chapters in this volume, is to allow the chaining together of Toulmin argument structures by transforming into the claim of a new argument any of the six elements in a given argument—even its claim, for which a new independent argument can be made. Another extension, exhibited for example in the chapters in this volume by Verheij, Aberdein and Slob, is the development of Toulmin's ambiguous conception of a rebuttal into a comprehensive doctrine of argument defeaters, including at least the distinction between rebutting defeaters and undercutting defeaters (Pollock, 1970). A third extension, exhibited in textbooks by Brockriede and Ehninger (1963) and by Toulmin himself and his collaborators (Toulmin, Rieke and Janik, 1979), as well as in chapters in the current volume by

Freeman and Kock, is the development of a taxonomy of warrants, which may be grounded sociologically, epistemologically or in some other way. Typologies of argumentation schemes, with their associated critical questions, may be interpreted as taxonomies of warrants, even though the concept of an argumentation scheme stems from a different source, *The New Rhetoric* of Chaim Perelman and Lucie Olbrechts-Tyteca (1958/1969). A fourth extension, articulated in different ways by Olaf Tans and Thomas Goodnight in the current volume, is to allow argumentative development of a warrant appropriate for the issue at hand, thus making warrants dynamic. A fifth extension, illustrated in the current volume by the chapters of Freeman, Verheij and Hitchcock, is to develop a system for evaluating arguments when they are analyzed on the Toulmin model.

Not everything in Toulmin's simple model has stood the test of time, but much has. Virtually all contributors to the current volume accept that rules of inference can have material content, and can be modally qualified. The latter shows most explicitly in Woods' remarks about our concept of the probable, in Ennis's defense of Toulmin's speech-act interpretation of the word 'probably', and in Fox and Modgil's qualitative interpretations of Toulmin's qualifiers. With qualification comes the possibility of defeaters, i.e. what Toulmin called 'rebuttals'. And with all this apparatus comes inevitably the recognition of different roles for the premisses of traditional logic: data supporting a claim, backing for a warrant, counters to potential rebuttals. Further, though Toulmin's field-dependency thesis has its critics, and can be given different interpretations, the idea that standards of logical appraisal vary by field is accepted by a good number of contributors to the current volume, and has received computational implementation in the decision support systems referred to in the chapters by Fox and Modgil and by Zeleznikow.

In his 1958 volume, Toulmin decried the mathematical logic of his day and called for an applied logic that would combine logic and epistemology. A striking development since then has been an increasing rapprochement between Toulmin's ideas and formal logic. We can see this in all the work in artificial intelligence that uses argumentation, work illustrated in the current volume by the contributions of Fox and Modgil, Paglieri and Castelfranchi, Prakken, Reed and Rowe, Verheij and Zeleznikow. It is evident as well in the chapter by Woods, which is explicitly a recantation of Woods' earlier expressed skepticism, and in the attempt of Weinstein to give Toulmin's contextualized and historicist philosophy of science a meta-mathematical foundation. Those with a visceral antipathy to formalisms of all kinds may decry these developments. Those who appreciate the precision of formal treatments, with their externalization of components often left implicit in natural language communication, will welcome them.

Two related issues in particular stand out from this volume as being part of ongoing debate. The first is what if anything to do about the apparent relativism involved in making standards for the appraisal of argument dependent on what the practitioners in the relevant field have come to agree upon at a particular time. Toulmin himself in his introductory chapter seems to counsel: do nothing, because the relativism is not pernicious. But be modest about what you think you have

accomplished in your work in your own discipline. Other contributors to this volume are not so insouciant. Goodnight, Weinstein, Bermejo-Luque and Freeman each propose a distinctive route to firmer ground.

The second issue is how to interpret Toulmin's warrants. This volume includes proposals to take them as singular essentially truth-functional conditionals (Bermejo-Luque), as generalizations of conditional inference licenses (Hitchcock), as generalizations of singular defeasible conditionals (Verheij), as law-like generalizations supporting counter-factual claims (Freeman), as authorizations of entitlements (Pinto), and as acts of authorizing (Klumpp).

A novel development in these chapters is a reclassification of the claims that we support by argument. Pinto in his chapter construes the presentation of an argument as justifying a certain doxastic attitude to a proposition, rather than the proposition itself. A similar idea emerges quite independently from Ennis's defense of Toulmin's speech-act analysis of the meaning of the word 'probably'. It is the idea that the conclusion of an argument is not a proposition, or a sentence, or a statement—in a word, not something that can be true or false—but an act. According to Toulmin, "When I say 'S is probably P', I commit myself guardedly, tentatively or with reservations to the view that S is P, and (likewise guardedly) lend my authority to that view" (1964, p. 53). If we accept this analysis, then a conclusion like 'The raccoon will probably not bother you' is a speech act, and its acceptance would be, as Pinto claims, the adoption of a certain doxastic attitude to the embedded proposition. If so, we need a wholly new approach to the analysis and the evaluation of arguments. We predict that this development will continue.

How can we sum up Toulmin's distinctive contribution? He has consistently defended the local and the particular over against the decontextualized universal. His most recent book *Return to Reason* (2001), for example, celebrates the renewed contemporary appreciation of 'the reasonable' in preference to 'the rational', in the sense of the abstract a priori rationality that has dominated modern thinking since Descartes. The present volume gives evidence of a wide appreciation for Toulmin's celebration of the reasonable. But the attraction of the universal understandably remains very strong. In fact, the search for the universal has given us deep and important results. But while we dream of the universal, we should never forget about the particular that's before us here and now.

CHAPTER 2

STEPHEN E. TOULMIN

REASONING IN THEORY AND PRACTICE

University of Southern California, Los Angeles, California
E-mail: toulmin@usc.edu

ABSTRACT: As my book *The Uses of Argument* pointed out, we must look and see how our critical standards vary from one area or activity to another—e.g. from politics to aesthetics. Hence we need to explore how these critical standards evolve, and how the most reflective and best-informed people in any area of experience refine those standards. We cannot understand where we are now unless we understand how we got here, even in a field like mathematics. Hence we must modestly recognize that the best we can do now is the best we can do *now*; and that those who come after us will move beyond our ideas. There is much contingency in these historical developments.

KEYWORDS: Argument; R. G. Collingwood; communication; critical standards; John Dewey; fields; history; Lenin; Stephen E. Toulmin; *The Uses of Argument*; Ludwig Wittgenstein

Note: The following is a revised version of an address given at McMaster University in Hamilton, Ontario on May 19, 2005, at a conference on the uses of argument sponsored by the Ontario Society for the Study of Argumentation.

1. ACKNOWLEDGEMENTS

Let me begin with a word of gratitude to John Dewey, whose book *Essays in Experimental Logic* was regarded with some contempt by my colleagues in Britain, but which is very much to his merit. Long before most of us, he saw the need to consider how reasoning enters, not only into technical life, but also into everyday life, so that the ways in which we express ourselves and—more important—the activities within which we express ourselves, set the stage without which judgments of soundness and acceptability can never be formulated or put to work.

Let me add two more acknowledgements.

One of them will come as no surprise to anybody, and that is my debt to R. G. Collingwood. Collingwood made me see the importance of viewing ideas from a historical point of view, something that Wittgenstein never understood. Wittgenstein has a comment in his First World War diary, "What is history to me? Mine is the first and only world." – a reflection of the fact that he was at that stage a solipsist, a position which (thank God) he finally broke with after his conversations with Friedrich Waismann around 1930.

D. Hitchcock and B. Verheij (eds.), Arguing on the Toulmin Model: New Essays in Argument Analysis and Evaluation, 25–29.

Another debt which will come as more of a surprise is to Lenin. Lenin in his *Materialism and Empirio-Criticism* argues that this preoccupation with formalism at all costs is a way of distracting the intelligent young from social problems, to the extent that higher education is a way of reinforcing the prejudices of the existing order and so, as Allan Bloom misguidedly called it, achieving "the closing of the American mind".

2. RECEPTION OF *THE USES OF ARGUMENT*

That said, when I wrote *The Uses of Argument*, the last thing I thought I was doing was producing a theory of rhetoric. I wrote the book as part of a polemical debate within analytical philosophy, as it existed in Britain around the year 1960. The initial reception of the book was uniformly hostile—Peter Strawson dismissed it out of hand in the BBC's weekly publication, *The Listener*, my colleague Peter Alexander at Leeds called it "Toulmin's anti-logic book", and my director of research, Richard Braithwaite, was deeply distressed, seeing me as abandoning the standards he had set up in the philosophy of science. One way or another, I concluded that—like Hume's *Treatise of Human Nature*—the book would "fall still-born from the press". So I was amazed to find that it continued to sell, for reasons which I discovered only when I came to the United States for the first time in the next year, and discovered that it was being used up and down the Mississippi Valley as a theory of communication. I was at first surprised by this, but I am now highly grateful. It is the only one of my books that has never gone out of print. My first book, *Reason in Ethics,* was in print for 39 years, had a brief revival in paperback, but is now remaindered. *The Uses of Argument* continues to sell, and the royalties come in handy.

When my wife was taking her law courses at DePaul University in Chicago, she sat next to a young man who found her surname familiar, because his girlfriend was studying communication, and she said, "Oh yes, I am married to him". The next week he came back, and said, "Oh, no, my girlfriend said that was quite impossible. Toulmin lived shortly after Aristotle". Well, I knew I was old, but I didn't know I was quite as old as that.

To come to the heart of the matter, when *The Uses of Argument* appeared, Otto Bird wrote of the book as "a rediscovery of Aristotle's topics". I didn't understand this allusion at the time, and only since I engaged more intensively in my own first-hand study of Aristotle have I come to see that he was right. Aristotle—a doctor and the son of a doctor—had a strong feeling for the practicality of reason, and was in some ways a pioneer of medical ethics. He introduced a useful distinction between "general" and "special" topics. General topics covered such things as metaphor, simile, analogy and the like, which are equally to the point regardless of the subject matter and activity in the context of which we make use of the terms. Special topics are those which have a bearing and a use only within the framework of one activity

rather than another—theoretical physics, say, rather than criminal law, rhetoric rather than aesthetics, and so on—you can make up whatever combinations you like. In these cases we have to look and see how the standards vary from one area to another. Those of us who follow legal cases know the difference between proof beyond reasonable doubt, clear and convincing evidence, and the rest: distinctions which were absolutely crucial in the O. J. Simpson case, where, although he was bizarrely found not guilty of murder, he nevertheless had to pay a lot of money to the dependents of those whom he was credibly believed to have killed.

3. THE EVOLUTION OF STANDARDS OF CRITICISM

So we need to explore further—and it is to all your credit that you have been doing so—the ways in which the standards of criticism evolve, and the ways in which the most reflective and best-informed people in any particular area of experience refine those standards. As Imre Lakatos points out in his book, *Proofs and Refutations*, even the standards of rigour in mathematics themselves have a history. What Theaetetus regarded as rigorous would be quite unacceptable to Gauss, in the early 19th century, or Bourbaki, in the 20th. Our whole way of thinking about what gives acceptability to mathematical arguments is itself part of cultural history, so that we can fully understand mathematics only if we understand the *history* of mathematics. We can't understand where we are now, without understanding how we got there.

And of course, once we recognize the need to understand how we get to a particular point, we have to recognize also that the work of our successors will supersede our own ideas, and we must be modest in recognizing that the best we can do is indeed the best we can do. The best we can do, that is, is to consider when we live, where we live, how we live, what the most reflective and best-informed experience of our colleagues in different areas has been, and what options are open in the future for the people who will come after us, and will revise and move beyond our ideas.

If Albert Einstein had not had a visual imagination, the whole range of options in theoretical physics would not have taken the form they did during the 20th century. From the time of Newton up to the time of Einstein, the central conceptions of mathematical physics were essentially Cartesian, not in the sense of demanding certainty, but in the sense of being—in a narrower sense which I won't bother to define—*mechanical*. Leibniz would not have regarded a computer as a machine. It has no cog-wheels, there is no engagement of forces. That was one of the reasons why Leibniz deeply objected to Newton's theory of gravitation. He saw no mechanical connection between the Sun and the Earth. We may have better ways of understanding how gravitation works, even though *gravitons* remain one of the more mysterious features of the physical world. But at any rate we do not see it as a matter of cog-wheels, which is to say - as my Yugoslav friend Stefan Dedijer commented—what we have here is "the subversion of historical materialism by science": a recognition that the world of ideas is, in its own way, as powerful as the world of forces and attractions and, in particular, *collisions*.

Henri Poincaré's great essay in *Acta Mathematica*—which won a prize from Oscar VII of Sweden—was an analysis of the foundations of mathematics in which he showed that there are indeed always liable to be critical interactions which defeat the possibility of prediction, regardless of how small the limitations of our demands are. There are always liable to be what he calls "chocs"—interactions whose consequences are intrinsically unpredictable. If this were not so, then the possibility of predicting in advance exactly what the content of Beethoven's *Choral Symphony* was going to be would turn Beethoven himself into a plagiarist: he was merely writing down what we ourselves had previously predicted that he would write down. One of Karl Popper's better essays, *On Clouds and Clocks*, makes the point that when two human beings meet—eye to eye—the question is who will act first: Who's to say? Can we tell? We just have to wait for the outcome.

4. HUME'S KANTIANISM

To move on one step, let me offer a re-interpretation of Hume and Kant. I read *A Treatise of Human Nature* as saying the following: "Oh, so all we have is sensory inputs and Euclidean deductions, is it? Well, let's see where this gets us". The answer, of course is: it gets us nowhere. The result is what misguided teachers of philosophy call "Humeanism": namely, the conclusion that we don't know anything, and can't legitimately claim to know anything, and this makes the World *unintelligible*. But, in Book III of the *Treatise*, Hume goes on to argue that we can't make sense of the World unless we bring certain ideas of causality, morality, and the like to bear on our understanding of the World. Without these, we can't make sense of anything.

Immanuel Kant on the other hand took it for granted that Hume was indeed a "Humean" in the fashionable sense; and he thought that his own distinctions between percepts and concepts were purely original; whereas, if I am right, they were ones which in a schematic way Hume had already anticipated.

5. CONCLUSION

Finally, a few concluding comments. Firstly, about the work of my former teacher Ludwig Wittgenstein. When we went to his classes in Cambridge in the years immediately after the Second World War, he seemed to us to be a purely original genius, and the passages at the end of the *Tractatus* about the skeptic, who climbs a ladder which he kicks away, seemed, to us, to have come down from heaven. Unfortunately, they come from Sextus Empiricus. If you look at the *Adversus Mathematicos*, the last paragraphs are the source from which anybody could have got this particular image. Wittgenstein was himself never one for giving page references, or indeed acknowledgements at all.

The only person to whom Wittgenstein recognized his debt was G. E. Moore, who was responsible for a lot of improvements in the work of the *Philosophical Investigations*. When I lived with my first wife at the bottom of G. E. Moore's garden, the only person that Dorothy Moore allowed to come to see Moore—who was then in retirement—was Wittgenstein. He was allowed to come for two hours on Thursday afternoons, and he soon found that, if he presented Moore with an argument about which Moore said, "Well, I don't see how that could *possibly* be right", there must be something wrong with it. So he would go away, reformulate it, and present it to Moore again, and if Moore then nodded his head Wittgenstein would go back to his room at Trinity College at the top of the gateway on Jesus Lane where he had his classes, and where a large trestle table stood, with all the slips that later formed the collection known as *Zettel*, and many of which were incorporated into what I was personally exposed to: namely, the material in the second part of the *Philosophical Investigations*.

Where did he get these ideas from? Well, as a Viennese scholar has pointed out, Wittgenstein didn't go to a public high school. He was tutored at home by graduate students working with Fritz Mauthner, who wrote a *Sprachkritik* about which Wittgenstein wrote in the *Tractatus*, "All philosophy is a critique of language, but not in Mauthner's sense". Mauthner may have differed with him about exactly in what sense philosophy is a critique of language, but there is little doubt that his students were hired by Wittgenstein's father, who was of course the Mellon or Carnegie of the Hapsburg Empire—a steel magnate and a leading member of the local *Evangelisch* community. At his parties in the *Argentinastrasse*, Gustav Mahler and Bruno Walter would have conversations.

To add a final point: The success of *The Uses of Argument* is largely due to the fact that I chose colloquial words (grounds, backing, and so on) which everybody understands. So too did Aristotle. His "four causes" are the "from what", the "who did it", the "what sort it is", and the "in aid of what". (The terms *essential cause*, *material cause*, *formal* and *final cause*, were mediaeval Latin introductions, which confused rather than elucidated his meaning.)

So I welcome this occasion for a creative and constructive discussion of all these issues: in particular, the relationship between what there is left for us to do under the heading of "philosophy", and what you yourselves are engaged in doing under the heading of "the analysis of argumentation". Are these purely distinct activities, or are they ones which blend into one another at the margin? This for me is the central question with which we are, and will continue to be, concerned for the rest of this week, and I look forward very much to hearing what you have to say about it.

Thank you very much.

CHAPTER 3

RONALD P. LOUI

A CITATION-BASED REFLECTION ON TOULMIN AND ARGUMENT

Washington University, Campus Box 1045, One Brookings Drive, St. Louis, Missouri 63130-4899, USA
E-mail: loui@wustl.edu

ABSTRACT: This article considers Toulmin's recent impact on scholarship by comparing his citation counts with those of other celebrated philosophers. Toulmin is found to be in good stead, in fact better cited recently than many of the great names at the intersection of philosophy of science and philosophy of logic.

KEYWORDS: Stephen E. Toulmin; argumentation; intellectual history; philosophy of logic; philosophy of science; citation counts

Intellectual history has always appealed to certain kinds of scholars. The prospect of being vindicated by future thinkers can compensate for the difficult struggle that many original thinkers experience when they take risks, attempt fundamental change, or simply have difficulty communicating their ideas to contemporaries. Especially in today's intellectual din, where the fast pace of technology and science and the rise of new disciplines can make it hard to hear traditional voices, where scholars are under pressure to produce short-term and conventionally valuable thoughts, there is merit in what the intellectual historian does.

The new tool in intellectual history is the citation count. Today, there are numerous ways to gauge the impact of a publication because there are numerous citation databases that are maintained, both by professional organizations and by companies in the business of providing high quality indexes. Online databases make comparative study possible across an entire discipline.

For Stephen Toulmin, intellectual history is a relevant question. Toulmin is known widely as a seminal author, is appreciated in many disparate intellectual communities, and continues to grow in stature. By all accounts, Stephen Edelston Toulmin has done things in an academic career that only few will do. He stands as an important twentieth century thinker, whether one thinks he is a logician, a philosopher of science, a rhetorician, a popular writer, or even an intellectual historian himself. His work reaches the most improbable corners of the academic landscape. I have been approached by many people wanting to discuss the Toulmin diagram, by scholars from every continent, for dozens of purposes, whether they use the diagram formally or

D. Hitchcock and B. Verheij (eds.), Arguing on the Toulmin Model: New Essays in Argument Analysis and Evaluation, 31–38.

informally, whether they are technologists or Luddites, whether they know a lot about Stephen Toulmin or nothing at all. Meanwhile, the depth of Toulmin's work has always been under suspicion, its technical importance questionable; and one can even quarrel whether there are precedents for his views. Toulmin is one of the scholars most in need of objective standards for placement in intellectual history.

So how well is Toulmin cited? Which of Toulmin's works is the most cited? Which work has had the most impact? Of course the last two questions are not the same. *Wittgenstein's Vienna* by Allan Janik and Toulmin, which I have never personally seen cited, has had more impact on me personally than *The Uses of Argument*, which my research community cites regularly. Still, we can measure the citation counts, and the relation between impact and citation count is tangible. In *Origins of Genius*, Dean Keith Simonton goes so far as to equate genius with achievement (a dubious move which I do not endorse) and to assert that citation is the best contemporary measure of the latter (a claim I find more agreeable).

Readers of this volume would probably be surprised if it were not the case that *The Uses of Argument* were Toulmin's most cited work. In fact, it is. But the surprise is just how close is the count. The Institute for Scientific Information (ISI, http://isiwebofknowledge.com/) numbers, in Summer 2005, ignoring unusual citation forms such as foreign language variations of titles, are as follows:

776	USES OF ARGUMENT
668	HUMAN UNDERSTANDING
344	COSMOPOLIS
266	FORESIGHT AND UNDERSTANDING
182	INTRODUCTION TO REASONING
158	PHILOSOPHY OF SCIENCE
122	RETURN TO COSMOLOGY

This means that of the millions of journal articles that have appeared in the past decade and a half, in the leading journals in humanities, social sciences, and science and technology, 776 distinct articles cited Toulmin's *The Uses of Argument* in some form or another. The database begins in 1988, so one may calculate that nearly four dozen journal articles per year cited *The Uses of Argument*. This number needs to be given some meaning. But first, it is worth remarking on the distribution.

It is unusual today even for a philosopher to have lead publications that are all books. This is consistent with our understanding of Toulmin as that special kind of academic who can make a career on a few deeply considered and generously crafted publications. He is clearly an academic of a purer time, when writing was a valued part of authorship. In short, Toulmin wrote books, not articles, and there are few pure academics who can afford that luxury today. That pattern is only observed today among very popular authors, for example, Daniel Dennett and Douglas Hofstadter. It is unusual for such authors to have ideas that are precise enough to be useful to technical authors in a discipline who are writing journal papers, and even more unusual for the pattern of citation to identify a particular idea. Toulmin's argument diagrams are unusual in this respect.

Second, the rate at which *The Uses of Argument* is being cited is growing. If one looks at the citations by year, with a two-year sum to smooth the year-to-year variations, it seems clear that Toulmin's book is becoming more popular. In fact, at the time of this writing, the half-year citation count for 2005 is 30, which is on pace to be the best year for the book (60 cites projected for 2005) (See Table 1, Figure 1.)

It is true that the number of journal articles indexed each year is growing, so one may expect growth in citations for a publication which is actually remaining constant in its impact. But compare, for example, Chaim Perelman's *New Rhetoric*, which seems to be falling in yearly citations, at least among English language authors (Table 1).

Toulmin's *Uses of Argument*			Perelman's *New Rhetoric*		
	year	2-year		year	2-year
2004	47	100	2004	25	52
2003	53	92	2003	17	38
2002	39	73	2002	21	44
2001	34	63	2001	23	50
2000	29	55	2000	27	45
1999	26	53	1999	18	46
1998	27	61	1998	28	49
1997	34	69	1997	21	54
1996	35	67	1996	33	71
1995	32	70	1995	38	58
1994	38	72	1994	20	45
1993	34	55	1993	25	50
1992	21	52	1992	25	50
1991	31	50	1991	25	47
1990	19	35	1990	22	66
1989	16	38	1989	44	78
1988	21		1988	34	

Table 1: Citations for Toulmin's *Uses of Argument* and Perelman's *New Rhetoric*

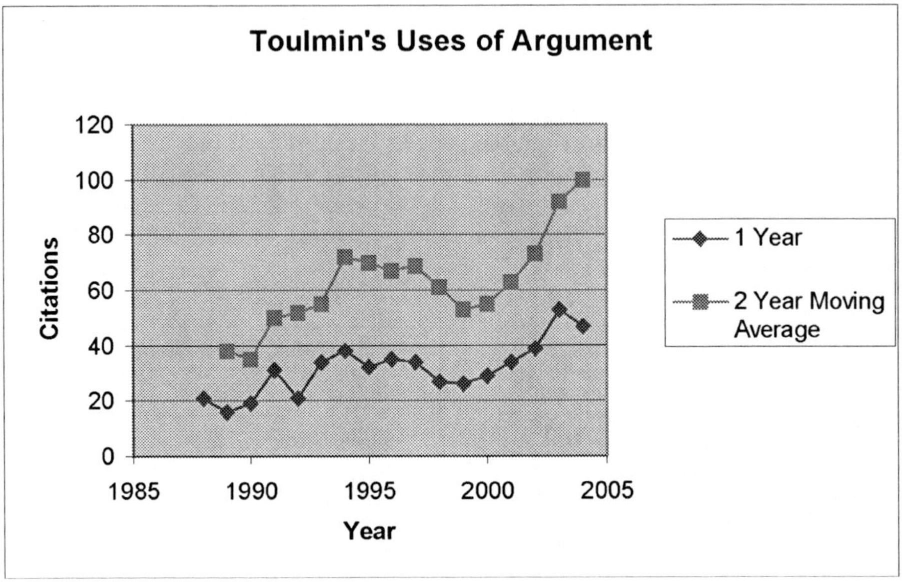

Figure 1. Citations of Toulmin's *Uses of Argument.*

Perhaps it is not new to point out that Toulmin has been a special intellectual whose recognition is growing. How big has he been, and how big is he now?

If we compare Toulmin to other philosophical logicians and philosophers of science, Toulmin's numbers shine. Counting any journal article published in 2004 that cites some work of an author, Toulmin fares well on a list of related and celebrated authors (Table 2).

One can argue about who ought to be on such a list. It is hard to decide which works of Popper, Russell, or Chomsky to include, for example, and which to exclude. Similarly, should Foucault or Polanyi be included? Turing or Wittgenstein? The list of excluded names that would challenge for the top of the list is probably quite small.

In any case, it should be satisfying to those who admire Toulmin's work to see Toulmin so high on such a list. Toulmin appears solidly ahead of many of the great names in philosophy of logic and philosophy of science.

Celebrated Philosophers of Science & Philosophical Logicians Year 2004 journal citations for all works
1. 870 l zadeh
2. 543 t kuhn
3. 271 w quine
4. 262 h putnam
5. 224 j austin
6. 182 s kripke
7. 139 a tarski
8. 130 s toulmin
9. 123 a whitehead
10. 113 j girard
11. 112 j barwise
12. 112 i lakatos
13. 111 m bunge
14. 107 r carnap
15. 99 c hempel
16. 95 h reichenbach
17. 94 n rescher
18. 88 p gardenfors
19. 87 r stalnaker
20. 80 j hintikka
21. 79 p feyerabend
22. 79 n cartwright
23. 77 p suppes
24. 72 a ayer
25. 61 g vonwright
26. 58 m fitting
27. 56 s kleene
28. 50 a church
29. 47 p geach
30. 47 i levi

Table 2: Citations for Toulmin and related authors

If we rank each author by the total number of citations (1988-2004), for the most popular work of the author (counting only the most common citation forms seen in 2004), then Toulmin does just as well (Table 3).

Total journal citations best cited work, ISI abbreviated title
1. 12364 t kuhn, structure science
2. 6085 l zadeh, inform contr
3. 2197 i lakatos, criticism growth kno
4. 1975 j austin, how do things words
5. 1853 w quine, word object
6. 863 h putnam, reason truth hist
7. 854 c hempel, aspects of sci expl
8. 851 p feyerabend, against method
9. 669 s toulmin, uses of argument
10. 640 s kleene, intro metamath
11. 636 j girard, theoretical computer
12. 540 a whitehead, sci modern world
13. 477 j barwise, situations attitudes
14. 463 s kripke, naming necessity
15. 432 a tarski, pac j math
16. 407 j hintikka, knowledge belief
17. 404 h reichenbach, elements symbolic lo
18. 390 p gardenfors, knowledge flux
19. 366 g vonwright, explanation understa
20. 362 m bunge, treatise basic phil
21. 300 n cartwright, how laws physics lie
22. 287 p martinlof, inform control
23. 276 c alchourron, j symbolic logic
24. 251 p suppes, probabilistic theory
25. 248 i levi, enterprise knowledge
26. 244 n rescher, many valued logic
27. 236 a church, j symbolic logic
28. 231 r carnap, meaning necessity
29. 215 a ayer, language truth logic
30. 198 b chellas, modal logic intro

Table 3: Citations for most popular works of Toulmin and others

Perhaps few would anticipate that Toulmin has been larger than Carnap, Church, Tarski, and Russell-Whitehead, in the past decade and a half. In fact, after a handful of colossal ideas: paradigm shifts and methods, fuzzy logic, illocutionary force, the analytic-synthetic distinction, supervenience and deductive-nomological explanation; Toulmin diagrams must be mentioned next. This has to be impressive and surprising to any intellectual historian.

The picture of Toulmin's work is a bit different in my mind, even with the evidence of these citation counts. To me, Toulmin's *The Uses of Argument* is no more courageous than H.L.A. Hart's introduction of the term "defeasible" to philosophical logic and analytic philosophy (see also Loui, 1995). Although Hart does not use the word "argument" much, it has always seemed to me that Toulmin's position is highly derivative from Hart's. To me, Toulmin does not give sufficient attribution to Hart's related thought. Toulmin's exact and only textual reference is:

> These distinctions [analytic versus substantial arguments], will not be particularly novel to those who have studied explicitly the logic of special types of practical argument: the topic of exceptions or conditions of rebuttal, for instance – which were labeled (R) in our pattern of analysis – has been discussed by Professor H.L.A. Hart under the title of 'defeasibility,' and he has shown its relevance not only to the jurisprudential study of contract but also to philosophical theories about free-will and responsibility. (It is probably no accident that he reached these results while working in the borderland between jurisprudence and philosophy.) (1958, p. 142; see also p. 260)

Toulmin moves immediately to Sir David Ross's prima facie qualification of moral rules and never returns to Hart. Once one has conceived of the defeasible connective, it is not much of a leap to consider connections among defeasible rules and tree-shaped derivations as arguments.

But Toulmin's 1958 work is essential in the history of argumentation.

First, Hart appeared to abandon the position, or in any case, refused to defend it. Dialectical logical form resided in one place only: in the hands of Toulmin, for nearly two decades, as deductive logicians spread their dogma. This is of tremendous intellectual historical importance. I think of nascent mammalian life hiding in caves while pre-Cambrian life dominated the surface of the earth. Toulmin provided a lone outpost of resistance, a single place where the fire burned during a long winter, where dialectical travelers of the logical landscape could stop for a rest. Some would re-discover the defeasible conditional as a contortion of deductive conditionals, but there has been a long and respectable development of argumentative form and its ramifications, awaiting the return of mathematical logicians.

Second, Toulmin's penchant for reaching non-specialists in his broad writing, the "informal logicians", and the teachers of good writing style, was essential to the growth of the study of argumentation. There are no competing sources of argument in rhetoric. Not the elegance of Chaim Perelman's French, nor the accessibility of Ronald Munson's texts, nor the prolixity of Doug Walton's meditations can compare to the common, democratic, plain-faced, singularly cogent appeal of Toulmin. I believe that Rescher, with his brevity and scholarship, eclipses Toulmin in his *Dialectics*, which is almost a poetic work. But the 1977 timing of Rescher's monograph was not good, and the little Rescher book had little impact. Meanwhile, everyone associated with scholarship in rhetoric, dialectic, or informal logic seems to have read Toulmin's *The Uses of Argument.*

Finally, Toulmin's suggestion of a method of diagramming argument was fortuitous indeed! It is a method which we can all find slightly comical in its simplicity. I remember thinking how naive it seemed in the hands of University of Colorado-Boulder Computer-Supported Collaborative Work (CSCW) technologists in the late eighties. But it is a diagram that has survived all competitors, and which delivers its underlying philosophy unmistakably. One cannot draw a Toulmin diagram without understanding that an argument is not a proof, and this understanding immediately elevates the discussion above deductive logical misunderstandings. One can even argue philosophical and logical fine points in the deployment of these modest box and arrow primitives. In retrospect, Toulmin's diagrams make Peirce's Venn-like diagrams and Frege's skewed branching trees seem vulgar and confining.

In time, argumentation should overcome even fuzzy predication and fuzzy connectives as the most important nondeductive development in the history of logic. I don't know how long it will take for citation counts to show this as a fact. Probably it will take a long time for scholars to come to this position, and citation counts may soon lose their meaning, as publication and citation habits change. Nevertheless, the student of argument must take heart in the citation evidence that is already available for comparative impact. I had approached this article by preparing all kinds of apologies for the seminal philosophical logician, relative to the mathematical logician or technically nonstandard logician. I had expected mathematical uses of logic to be more numerous than references to logical styles of reasoning. I had expected that AGM belief revision or modal deontic logic, as two examples, would be bigger than Toulmin's argument in the citation databases. I am happy to report that I was unduly pessimistic. We can claim that Toulmin's *The Uses of Argument*, and Stephen Toulmin's work in general, have been essential contributions to twentieth century thought, and the citation counts are clearly there as grounds for the claim.

Acknowledgements

I would like to acknowledge that some of the numbers were provided by Alex Schiller, who did the counts for "famous authors" in philosophy of science.

CHAPTER 4

G. THOMAS GOODNIGHT

COMPLEX CASES AND LEGITIMATION INFERENCE: EXTENDING THE TOULMIN MODEL TO DELIBERATIVE ARGUMENT IN CONTROVERSY

Annenberg School for Communication, University of Southern California, Los Angeles, CA 90089-0281, USA
E-mail: gtg@usc.edu

ABSTRACT: A warrant may be grounded in personal testimony, technical method, or public consensus. The justified choice of a field, in authorizing the warrant and providing further extension of support constitutes a legitimation inference. Complex cases evolve when a surplus of good reasons appear as potential support for a claim, and a choice must be made either to select a single ground for the claim or to advance independently valid reasons, differentially grounded, as support. Complex cases enter the realm of controversy when not all relevant grounds offer the same degree of support or point in the same direction, and a choice to select some grounds and discard others must be justified. The justification of the selection of grounds constitutes a legitimation warrant—a missing inferential element of the Toulmin model.

KEYWORDS: controversy; Stephen E. Toulmin; legitimation; field; complex case; deliberation

1. INTRODUCTION

The Toulmin model (1958/2003) opened the door to the recovery of practical reason, the development of informal logic, and the advances of critical thinking into the realms of the everyday uses of argument. An alternative to positivistic reasoning, the model provided a basic outline that called attention to the ordinary communicative practices that lend support to claims for a reason. This intuitive idea of argumentation is at the basis of Habermas's own notion of the "form of argumentation" where: "We try to support a claim with good grounds or reasons; the quality of the reasons and their relevance can be called into question by the other side; we meet objections and are in some cases forced to modify our original positions" (1981, p. 31). Thus, Habermas follows Toulmin into more complex observations, reaffirming the distinctions between the general schema of reasoning which is more or less field invariant and the much more elaborate "field-dependent rules of argumentation which are constitutive for the

D. Hitchcock and B. Verheij (eds.), Arguing on the Toulmin Model: New Essays in Argument Analysis and Evaluation, 39–48.

language games or life-orders of law, medicine, science, politics, art criticism, business enterprise, sport, and so on" (1981, pp. 31-32). To appreciate an argument, then, it is necessary to understand the sort of enterprise "that is supposed to be advanced through argumentation", and to appreciate the enterprise, one follows the rules of thumb of argument general to all practical engagements and special to the authorized moves and certified standards of a field.

The fields of argument explored by Toulmin, Rieke and Janik include science, law, management, art criticism, and ethics (1979, pp. 203-338). The fields are said to differ along "varied" constellations of complex procedures. The categories for assessing the requirements of argument for fields include: (l) degrees of formality ranging from informal turn taking to ritual advocacy, (2) degrees of precision ranging from mathematical exactitude to more common ballpark estimates, (3) alternative requirements for completion or resolution that range from mutual agreement producing consensus to impartial judgment effecting a verdict, (4) diverse goals that are linked to "*what is at stake* within the forum involved" (p. 198). In this last respect, the goals of argument will reflect the "general purposes" and "practical demands" placed upon argument by the practices of a field and the objectives of the interlocutors. It is at this juncture that Habermas raises an objection, namely that Toulmin "doesn't draw the proper lines between *accidental institutional differentiations of argumentation,* on the one hand, and the *forms of argumentation* determined by internal structure on the other" (p. 35). In other words, the categories of formality, precision, resolution mode, and purpose are insufficient descriptors to differentiate between those "validity claims" (assertions of the worthiness of an argument to be recognized or trusted) that are grounded in routines of practices and those that are core to sustaining the integrity of an institution or form of life. At this point, Habermas leaves field theory behind and introduces his own well-known theory that differentiates argumentation into theoretical, practical, aesthetic, therapeutic, and explicative discourse and critique (1981, p. 23). The advantage of Habermas's system is that it properly weights the validity and proof requirements of each form of argumentation.

The purpose of this paper is to extend the original Toulmin model, with its intuitive focus on practice, and its tantalizing promise to find grounds for practical reasoning in the warrant-using and warrant establishing work of reasoning authorized by the forms and practices of reasoning within fields. I will argue, contra Habermas, that argumentation is best served by repairing rather than abandoning Toulmin's field-grounded reasoning. The major repair I offer is the addition of "legitimation inferences", that is justifications of the selection of backing to support a given argument. I will endeavor to show how the addition of such components permits the understanding of complex cases, where grounds may or may not point unequivocally in a single direction for conclusion. Finally, the modern predicament between practical and technical reasoning will be explored around the issue of risk in order to illustrate the uses of a repaired Toulmin model in analyzing contemporary controversy. In the end, the reconsidered Toulmin model may help answer Habermas's objection that Toulmin's field analysis cannot differentiate between essential and accidental features of a field in authorizing a warrant.

2. LEGITIMATION INFERENCES

The Toulmin model is missing a critical component: a legitimation warrant. Unnoticed by any of its many interpreters, readers and critics, Toulmin is able to make the case convincingly that the selection of grounds for establishing a warrant or support is a natural connection between argument and context (1958, p. 103). Indeed, in Toulmin, Janik and Rieke, the choice of the grounds for an argument is circularly defined because an argument and its purpose are the same thing: legal reasoning contextualizes legal argument, the purpose of ethical argument is ethical decisions and so forth (1979). The problem with this notion is that it begs the question as to why any specific argued-claim is legitimately appropriate, judicable, proper, or even relevant to a given field. Further, since practitioners can borrow standards analogically from another field, or supplement the reasoning of one field with the arguments of another (presumption moves from the law to science in setting proof standards), the establishment of a claim within the ambit of a field does not always establish what standards of argumentation offer proper certification. The justification of a decision to ground a particular argument in a field I have called elsewhere a "legitimation inference" (1991).

The choice of backing to certify the authority of a warrant requires a special kind of inference. Like any other part of the model, the choice of grounding is criticizable; yet, the selection of backing is not another item of support, a reservation, qualifier, or claim. Neither is the selection of backing reducible to the warranted relationship linking support to claim. When called upon to justify the crucial choice to develop an argument out of a certain interpretation of the authority, relevance, and acceptability of a field, an interlocutor may be asked to show sufficient and necessary reasons for the selection of that field—that is to legitimate the assumed or explicit connection. In a warrant-using argument, legitimation inferences impart sufficient reasons for the selection of a field to ground and develop support, warrants, qualifiers and reservations. In a warrant establishing argument, legitimation is a complicated process that balances competing choices among fields in the interests of rendering an overall judgment that the connections among different fields of backing, while somewhat novel, are none the less reasonable.

Typically, the legitimation inferences are left in the background. There are different reasons for this, depending upon whether a "field" is constellated as informal practices of communicative reasoning, professional decision-making, or political advocacy. In everyday argumentation, we disagree with one another without having recourse to either an etiquette coach or a rule book because it is appropriate to ground our discussion in the informal conventions of conversation and common opinion. In a court of law, members of the forum itself—with its formidable symbolism, rituals, trained advocates and justices—collaborate to put on a trial where reasons tend toward questions of justice. Likewise in other forums, from science to religion, the rules of reasoning appear as imminent within a situated discourse, and the situation a production of the practices, procedures, and issues of the interlocutors. Finally, in politics, the nature of a deliberation grounds discussion in questions of power and expediency by virtue of the time toward which decisions are tending to come to a vote or a head. In other words, the social rules, institutional fora, and eventfulness of argument lend cues as to the field from which reasons should be developed and from which standards should be borrowed to inform tests of reasoning or the outcomes of judgment. The personal, technical, and public fields within which the same (or similar) claims may be grounded suggest that the deliberative exigencies of situated argument are typically enmeshed in complex case making. The following section distinguishes complex cases that evolve from warrant-using argumentation, and those that typically evolve from warrant-establishing reasons.

3. THE COMPLEX CASE

A complex case is a situated argument where the settlement of a disagreement depends upon the resolution of multiple points of disagreement. This section divides complex cases into two types: first, those cases where the process of reasoning is well-established and shaped into coherent case-making. Type I complex cases equate the procedure of arguing with the essential nature of the enterprise, and reflect warrant using strategies. Type II complex cases are those that cobble together justifications for assembling a complex set of reasons, drawn from diverse fields, to support deliberative reasoning. The latter cases do not rest on any inherent equation of form and purpose, but often give rise to novelty.

Type 1 Complex Cases

Classical rhetoric defines the complex case in terms of stasis theory. Questions of fact are deployed around a contested conjectural stasis. Questions of definition are procedurally argued through a definitional stasis. Questions of the justice or expediency of the act are argued through a qualitative stasis. And questions of jurisdiction fall under a translative stasis (Burton, 2004). In the classical paradigm, the levels of disputation distribute the burden of proof, such that to affirm the guilt of an accused a prosecution need establish the preponderance of evidence at all levels, while the defense need only successfully wage dispute on one. As is well-known, should the facts, definition, quality, or place not be successfully established, a case cannot be made; on the other hand, should all of these claims be put in order, then the force of reason places a demand for a ruling by a judge or a call to render a verdict by the jury. Indeed in discussion prior to trial, a judge may inquire of potential jurors as to whether they are capable of making decisions upon weighted evidence and of following basic rules of rational conduct presupposed by the jurisprudential model of argument. Such a model offers a complex case insofar as multiple issues are potentially in play anytime the prospect of a legal dispute arises; participants in the trial are trained to see in the particular case a field of potential arguments weighted and categorized along the lines of potential issues for an overall contest between positions; and, a mode of coming to terms with the diverse issues are invested in a procedure that makes sense on its face.

The complex case constituted by forensic stasis is an exception to, rather than a paradigm of everyday argumentation where decisions of choice and expediency, means and ends, risks and outcomes prevail. In every situation where probable argument is in play aimed at choice and avoidance, there is no assurance that (l) there will be a finite number of levels at which arguments may statiate, (2) that all engaged in a dispute will agree upon criteria of relevance to discern what issues need be resolved, or even discussed, to properly resolve an issue, and even should there be an agreement as to relevance (3) that the claims involved will bind together in a neat way such as to distribute the burdens of proof, determine sides of an argument, and provide a coherent route to adjudication. Nor is it even the case that a normative model of deliberation which prescribes levels of stases for rendering sound, practical judgments will get the advocates closer to a resolution.

In practical argumentation, models have focused on evolving various schemes that appear as a fitting counterpart to forensic stasis. One common model is the ill-solution paradigm. In making a choice about medical care, one would need to know: if there were an illness, how serious it was, what the cause of the illness would be (to discover if there were any incidental changes that would eliminate the problem), the effectiveness of a cure, and whether side-effects would do more harm than the solution good. This complex case is like forensic stasis insofar as it offers a coherent, reasonable model of argument that aims at a decision by distributing the burden of proof. Just as in forensics, if there is any one of the levels of the claims that cannot be established, there is no reason to go forward with a positive judgment.

The difference that is lurking here is that whereas the question of justice is constitutive of reaching a legal decision, the complex case underwriting public deliberation is analogical. In Habermas's terms with which we began, the illness-cure model is an accident or variation on deliberative reasoning, whereas forensic stases are constitutive of justice. Indeed, the medical model is not necessarily appropriate to political activity, and itself rests on the unexamined bias at the bottom of Western medicine as a field: "do no harm". One can imagine a prudential model of complex case-making that would envision government as an initiator of action, with a duty to search out and mitigate social problems—where outcomes were in the interests of compensation for past wrongs, present inequities, or future legitimacy. This would put presumption on the side of change. In other words, the model of deliberation—the narrative within which case-construction is articulated—is not a necessary part of deliberative argument, but only a preference to frame a context in a particular way in the service of an overall view of how deliberation best proceeds for citizens.

Type II Complex Cases

In a pluralistic society, deliberation is complicated because the contexts within which arguments are made are not obvious, authoritative, or relevant to all who have a right to a say as citizens and members of the society. Type II complex cases typically engage what Toulmin calls "warrant-establishing" arguments. In such cases, it is not enough to determine the likely truth or falsity of a well-established series of claims that regulate the production of proof and inference bearing upon a claim. The act of placing a claim within a given field requires assembling a case where more than one ground must be addressed. The relative weighting of different grounds in an overall decision makes for quite complex deliberative argument, indeed. If complexity offers less security in linking argument to grounds, it also offers the potential benefit of forming a more robust consensus—more on this later. At this point, I would like to enter a simple example to illustrate the use of legitimation inferences in an instance of complex case-making.

Suppose that you are at the pharmacy and are evaluating the reasons that go into a decision to take a new product "*Nexia*", to fight "acid reflux disease". At a personal level, you have what seems like an upset stomach, hoping that the pain signals digestion issues with "something you ate", (+l) but you also know that there are worse maladies that afflict others in your family (–1). At another level, you are aware of the chemistry of traditional remedies for gas (+l), but are also interested in the ability of research to provide more effective "relief" (–1). At a third level, you have heard a congressional investigation condemn "direct to market advertising" (–1) as preying upon the gullible but you are also aware that the FDA regulates efficacy (+1). Do you buy "*Nexia*" or not? How do the arguments "add up" in deliberating a reasonable decision?

A complex case could be rendered by simply adding and subtracting positive and negative reasons, and a reasonable purchase could be defined by the preponderance of affirmative or negative evidence. Probability theory would render calculations somewhat more complex should the degree of confidence be measured in the strength of an affirmative or negative judgment, but the principle of determining the outcome would be relatively the same. Indeed, should all the reasons for or against a claim be vectored in the same direction, then a decision is rendered transparent: it would not make sense to ignore the conclusion. If all the reasons favored "*Nexia*" or all the reasons were opposed to the decision, then further deliberation is not necessary.

Deliberation is never in principle a closed matter, however, and the search for disconfirming or countervailing reasons may continue. In the above example, one might introduce questions of price and availability of resources at the end of an evening; so, a lack of available cash might settle the argument. A consensus emerges, however, when all claims at the different levels of argumentation *independently* support a central claim. Purchasing product *Nexia* is a good idea because of personal experience, technical information, systemic trust, and financial availability. What happens, however, when the field of argument relevant to a reasoned decision fails to become transparent?

A genuinely complex case arises where reasons point in multiple, relevant, different directions in supporting and contesting a claim that must be resolved before a reasonable decision can be rendered. This complexity forces a reasoner into a second-order set of questions about the comparative relationship among the grounds that are positioned in support of or opposition to the claim. Questions arise as to the relative weight of reasons that point independently in opposite directions. Even the assumed independence of relationships among independently grounded reasons, relating to the case, may come into question.

The comparison of relative weight among alternative grounds arises most often when a single ground does not provide a self-evident context, and a reasoner is forced to think over what groundings are fitting for the specific choice in question. Such reflection is provoked when multiple lines of support are available, conflicting, and relatively equal in attributed rational force. Thus, whether to rely on personal experience, technical reasoning, or public trust opens a question in a particular case, where advice conflicts, as to what constitutes a legitimate decision.

Formally, two kinds of arguments apply: first, the contention that a particular ground should be discounted as non-determinative in the decision; second, the reason why a particular grounds (or combination) should trump countervailing argumentation. The discounting of, and preference for, alternative grounds for argumentation ideally should be isomorphic, but may not be the same. When the preferences for one kind of ground over another become a rule that is generally applied, then a complex case may be said to have evolved through a "warrant-establishing" argument; namely, reasons have been discovered for settling upon grounding a claim in a conflicted context. These warrant-establishing warrants may or may not form authoritative precedents for selecting one sort of ground over another in situations of a particular type.

Complex case-making of this sort (Type II) occupies a substantial portion of everyday argumentation in pluralistic societies, I believe, because modern living teams with a surplus of reasons for decision, and deliberation requires sorting through the multiple sources that aspire to guide, if not determine, the grounds upon which rational conduct is deliberated. The routine requirements of complex case-making are well-illustrated in contrasting the personal field of risk assessment, prudential reasoning, to its technical counterpart in science. The question of how to square practical and scientific justifications when they evolve as opposing grounds for a decision is a core question of modern deliberation within the practice of everyday life, as well as a site for the continuing evolution of controversy.

4. RISK AND LEGITIMATION CONTROVERSY

A traditional view of practical decision-making involves the element of chance or fortune in all decisions. Chance is that element of a decision that speaks to a gap between one's grounded expectations and the actual outcome of an endeavor. The practice of deliberative argument assumes that humans are fallible, that they make errors and can learn from mistakes by sifting causes and consequences relating choice to activity. The element of chance recognizes that in spite of the best reasons, outcomes of actions can exceed or disappoint expectations. The intervention of chance into human affairs creates a deliberative space where risks can be appraised and evaluated, their consequences anticipated and hedged. Type I cases emerge when a deliberation draws upon a single field to make a case for taking a chance; Type II cases emerge when multiple fields are in play, offering something less than fully commensurable reasons.

Traditional views of practical reason acknowledge that chance intervenes into human affairs. There are three elements that always accompany portrayals of the goddess *Tyche* (luck for the Greeks) and *Fortuna* (fortune for the Romans). The goddess is displayed holding a cornucopia, representing abundance, standing on a stream or a ball, indicating impermanence, and nearby is a rudder, indicating steering or intent. The symbolic field is rather unambiguous insofar as the elements of luck enter into human actions in the pursuit of fruitful enterprises. Occasionally, fortune is blind representing that she is indifferent to whether the person pursuing an end is deserving or not; at other times, fortune is shown by a wheel, cautioning or encouraging reasoners to remember that chance has its up and down cycles. The goddess of fortune has been figured as present at great events such as battles or at personal ones like childbirth. In any event, the relation between risk and reason appears to be a staple acknowledgement in the Western tradition. Douglas and Wildavsky (1983) argue that all notions of risk are culturally bound. So the limits of practical reasoning occasioned by fortune have underwritten the limits of prudential reasoning and conduct for millennia.

Prudential argumentation counsels that fortune visits those who are prepared, who do not take incautious risks, who learn from experience, and who draw from general wisdom to guide principles of conduct. In everyday argumentation, risks are evaluated from the standpoint of personal experience—not from an objective calculus. Experience with risks, the intensity of revulsion to a bad outcome, bad publicity, and personal preference all combine to make up a cautionary field where rules of thumb are evolved to guide whether an action should be undertaken or a choice made. While preferences may vary, some risks can be avoided, others can be framed as not worth taking, and a few may constitute appropriate gambits, if losses are not important or could be recouped. A common sense approach to risk-taking depends upon practical reasoning to draw from the field of experience a connection between cause and effect of an action, thus advising whether or not a risk should be taken. Further, common understanding of risk provides a mode of reception for unplanned events that are either windfalls or downfalls, depending on the circumstances. When fortune intervenes, little can be done.

Modernity has changed the reasoning through which risk is appraised. Multiple, scientific models now underwrite the scientific assessment of risk (Renn, 1992). Science makes the appraisal of risk in relation to deliberation quite difficult by introducing relatively unique, even counterintuitive measures of understanding. Several of these will be mentioned.

Latency is the idea that a risk may be encountered at some point and its harms only evolve years later. Latency removes the idea that risks are knowable at the time they are encountered and that precautions can be taken in a timely fashion.

Multiple causality is the idea that no one factor may engender a risk, but that a combination of unique circumstances may accumulate so as to bring about an undesirable set of affairs. Thus, to eliminate one potential cause of a problem (smoking) may do nothing for another (genetic predisposition). In many cases, to solve one cause of a problem may cause other undesirable risks.

Threshold reasoning argues that low level risks may remain without consequence for years, only to suddenly accumulate at unknown points and cross the line into a harmful condition. A car may travel for many miles with proper maintenance before its engineering tolerances are crossed all at once. In some cases, the direction of activity which approaches a harmful threshold is not known.

Uncertainty is a measure of probability of success or failure of a chosen outcome. A general domain of uncertainty, however, says nothing about the individual case. When making a decision, say, to have a medical procedure, the range of estimates must somehow be translated into individual judgments. Further, uncertainty itself rests on the unknown; that is, any scientific probability is only valid in the limited sense that it has yet to be disproved by other factors yet to be taken into account and potentially relevant.

Complex cases evolve where practical reasoning and scientific reasoning are both relevant to a decision, but neither is determinative. In many, if not most cases, a particular claim may find internally contradictory evidence within the field of personal risk taking and within the field of science, too. In such a complex case, the choice of which arguments within field X + Y+Z to compare with contrary arguments in the field X + Y + Z create the potential for thorough-going controversy. At a minimum, if practical and scientific reasoning conflict, the choice to ground a risk decision in one field or the other has to be accounted for in the specific case. In a case of maximum controversy, the configurations of practical, scientific, and political reasons from alternative fields create a complex case that balances the argumentative force of fields (and subfields) against one another. The legitimation inferences that evolve to subordinate one field to another, discounting opposing reasons, create new warrants for argumentation or involve interlocutors in the painful process of finding no reasonable guidance to crucial questions. Legitimation inferences that set precedents reconfigure the relationships among fields, or contestation within and among fields, by answering the question of justified choice among the grounds of reason.

5. CONCLUSION

In the beginning of the essay, I promised to redeem Toulmin from the criticism of Habermas by showing how the Toulmin model could be adapted to seek out those argumentative situations where standards for reasoning essential to a field evolve. This can be done, but only if the model is made sensitive to the crucial area of justification that constitutes a legitimation inference. The justification of a choice of grounds forces reflection upon why a specific backing should count in this case, for this choice, in a specific deliberative context. Subjecting the constellating body of authority to scrutiny generates a justification for that particular field, as an essential guideline to authorizing a warrant as credible, trustworthy, reliable, or believable. Thus, the choice of field grounding permits discrimination between relevant grounding and accidental features of an enterprise. Tables were turned on Habermas's own view of argumentation that rests reasoning in distinct categories by virtue of independent sources of validity claims. It is true, that cases that are rendered complex by multiple reasons may be simplified by constitutive stases, such as in questions of justice. On the other hand, in deliberation complex cases evolve because personal, technical, and political fields may all be relevant but point in alternative directions. The arena of risk was explored to illustrate the challenge of evolving coherent justifications for combinatory grounds in making important choices in modern life. In the end, argumentation theorists are called to study controversies where the unsettled relationships among fields and good decisions give rise to arguments over the appropriate choice or revision of backing. Such disputes engage us critically in the study of legitimation controversies.

CHAPTER 5

MARK WEINSTEIN

A METAMATHEMATICAL EXTENSION OF THE TOULMIN AGENDA

Educational Foundations, Montclair State University, Montclair, NJ 07043, USA
E-mail: weinsteinm@mail.montclair.edu

ABSTRACT: Toulmin is famously seen as a progenitor of informal logic and is first among many who seek to move the study of argument away from its roots in formal, especially mathematical, logic and towards its place in inquiry. Toulmin's efforts, however, have been criticized for lack of foundation. I will argue that although Toulmin is correct in rejecting mathematical logic as a theory of argument and logical empiricism as the philosophy of science, there is a significant role for metamathematics in the normative foundation of argument. The core is a metamathematical account of truth and entailment based on physical science rather than arithmetic.

KEYWORDS: Stephen E. Toulmin; metamathematics; truth; argument; epistemology; entailment; warrant; backing; philosophy of science; inquiry; formal logic

1. INTRODUCTION

Stephen Toulmin begins the *The Uses of Argument* by distinguishing his project from traditional logical theory, which, following Aristotle, maintains that "logic should become a formal science—an *episteme*" (2003, p. 3). His project, the 'practical assessment of argument' leads to the alternative 'jurisprudential model' that is the hallmark of his contribution to argumentation theory. Similarly in *Human Understanding*, his *Philosophy of Science*: *An Introduction,* and his splendid volumes on the history of science written with June Goodfield, Toulmin develops an alternative to the then fashionable logical empiricist accounts of science. Toulmin's work however, has been substantively criticized by Harvey Siegel (1987) among others, for failing to offer the sort of foundation that, according to Siegel, even Toulmin sees to be required lest the theory of inquiry fall to impotent relativism. I will argue, that although Toulmin is correct in rejecting mathematical logic as an adequate theory of argument, and logical empiricist constructions as an adequate basis for the philosophical understanding of science, there is a significant role for metamathematics in the new logic. In particular, I will show how a model of truth and entailment, based

D. Hitchcock and B. Verheij (eds.), Arguing on the Toulmin Model: New Essays in Argument Analysis and Evaluation, 49–69.

on mature physical science rather than arithmetic, provides the support that Siegel calls for, affording a normative basis for Toulmin's account. The paper indicates a radical extension of Toulmin's agenda, one which requires an analysis of central logical concepts utilizing a technical treatment that draws upon the very metamathematical tradition that Toulmin is most often seen to reject.

Toulmin's discussion is more complex than the focus on the familiar model of warrant, grounds and backings might indicate. Toulmin introduces the model in the first chapter of *The Uses of Argument*, 'Fields of Argument and Modals', and although the issue of fields, among the more discussed aspects of Toulmin in the literature, warrants significant discussion, much of the chapter is focused on the modalities, an issue less common in discussions of Toulmin's work.

Both concerns, however, are essential, and as the structure of the chapter indicates, they shed light on each other. The modalities of claims reflect the strength of the warrants and the standards of the backing, features that result from embedding of arguments in fields. Toulmin's discussion is rich and includes issues of probability addressed in a detailed and technical manner, offering arguments against the then standard views of Carnap and Kneale. But from our point of view the main contribution of his alternative view is the general requirement that: "If we are to keep clear in our minds about knowledge and probability, we must remember always to take into account the occasion on which a claim is being judged, as well as that on which it is uttered" (2003, p. 57). Sensitivity to the occasion is required by the embeddedness of the argument in a context of prevailing assumptions, the field from which the argument is drawn, and the purposes for which the argument is being advanced (e.g. Toulmin distinguishes between "warrant-using and warrant-establishing" arguments (p. 118)). Concern with the occasion of use requires attention to guarded assertions such as estimations of the likelihood of supporting evidence, limitations, counter-arguments and open questions, factors that qualify the force of the argument.

Toulmin rejects both the standard model for categorical assertions, what he calls 'analytic arguments', as well as any account of inductive reasoning that requires a definitive estimate of the likelihood of the evidence to be required for the estimation of probabilities. "The fundamental mistake is to suppose that the evidence in the light of which we estimate the likelihood of some view must be written into the estimate we make, instead of being kept in the background and alluded to only implicitly" (p. 75). The reason for this is the ever-changing context of knowledge, commitments shifting under the pressure of argument. Arguments point towards the "occasion on which claims are to be judged", and thus, "a statement will have to be attributed as many truths as there are possible bodies of evidence bearing on it" (p. 75). This creates the essential challenge for a theory of argument adequate to Toulmin's agenda. For issues of likelihoods and the support of claims at varying levels of analysis and argumentation require that distinctions among levels and kinds of support be indicated with sufficient clarity and cogency that philosophical intuitions can be applied to the underlying logical and epistemological issues. And for this, I would argue, there is no substitute for the richness and transparency of metamathematics.

Toulmin, in his rejection of formal logic and the analytic entailments that determine its practical applications as well as its metatheory, contrasts "technical logic" to what he refers to as "practical assessment of arguments" (p. 2). Distancing himself from the tradition that sought to develop a 'science of logic' he explores key concepts in logical theory in terms of another perspective on argumentation one that looks at "practical questions about the manner in which we have occasion to handle and criticize arguments in different fields" (p. 2). It is in the analysis of practical argument that the jurisprudential model has its sway. But is that the only place to draw a line? For there is an equally fundamental distinction, that is, between practical arguments engaged in within political and ordinary affairs, and argumentation within specialized fields of inquiry. Except when seen in contrast to technical logic, there is reason to question whether such disparate contexts of argumentation share logical structure (Weinstein, 1990). I will argue that although the "field-invariant" apparatus envisioned by Toulmin (p. 33) might be usefully applied with appropriate modification to both sorts of contexts, deep concepts in logical theory are better derived from specialized argumentation in disciplined inquiry. And, perhaps paradoxically, that an adequate conception of such argumentation permits a significant metamathematical treatment. As we shall see, tying the notion of entailment to a set-theoretic model of truth yields an epistemological foundation for Toulmin's much contested notions of warrant and backing. And as importantly, it shows a direction for advancing Toulmin's truncated project in *Human Understanding.*

2. TOULMIN AND METAMATHEMATICS

As should be apparent, the notion of truth available from the study of mathematics within standard formal languages suffers from its inapplicability to situations that do not share three essential aspects of mathematics as logically represented: clarity of model relations captured in exhaustive and exclusive extensional definitions, the identification of truth as satisfaction within an available model (e.g. arithmetic), and logical necessity as truth in all possible models. Without substantive argument to the contrary, it seems obvious that the concepts used in practical argument are not readily reconstructed to fit the mathematical ideal without significant distortion. Many concepts are not definable in extensional terms, criteria for membership are not explicitly defined, there are overlaps and 'bushes' in the tree structures that represent conceptual relations and membership frequently cannot be decided in any effective way. An intended model is rarely available antecedent to the inquiry at hand and necessity is frequently limited to a range of models, as in physical necessity defined in terms of physical constraints on logically possible models. But it is not merely the rigor of the mathematical ideal that renders it misleading. Mathematical logic construes truth as a univocal property of statements. This obscures the complexity with which truth functions in extra-mathematical contexts. This is clear in *The Uses of Argument.* Argumentative support requires more than the truth of premises and abstract rules of inference. Among the premises we need to distinguish the grounds (a relevant basis in fact or other information to support the claim at the appropriate level of abstraction) from the warrants (statements or rules sufficiently general in respect of the ground and claim that support the inference). And most crucially, the backing, a context of interpretation and understanding that sets standards for rigor, relations among claims, grounds and warrants, and a domain of primary application which determines modality commensurate with the strength of the warrants.

If we accept this much, it seems arguable that the mathematical logicians' notion of truth is irrelevant to most situations that require human beings to determine the facts of the matter. Traditionally, this has been construed as the distinction between deductive and inductive logic. But, given the central role of deduction in science and other empirical procedures (Magnani, 2001), that line must be drawn elsewhere. But where? Without the anchor of a priori necessity exemplified by the well-understood domain of arithmetic, from where will we draw an alternative normative paradigm? Toulmin's concern with human understanding points away from the mathematical paradigm to the broader concerns of inquiry and especially to science. But disciplined inquiry in science might not support Toulmin's rejection of 'scientific logic'. For short of a disciplinary based relativism of the sort that Siegel (1987) has shown to be inadequate for normative understanding, the disciplines require the same sort of foundational grounding that was traditionally sought in the foundations of arithmetic. From a logical point of view, understanding of the normative foundation of disciplined knowledge requires an account of the essential logical triad of truth, entailment and relevance.

I would argue that it was the traditional concern with the foundation of arithmetic that renders formal logic problematic in many contexts of argumentation, rather than the scientific nature of meta-logical inquiries. That is, it was the image of arithmetic in the underlying logic and especially in the theory of truth associated with Tarski, rather than the metamathematical turn, that creates many of the problems that Toulmin sees so clearly. Constructing a metamathematical foundation does not require abandoning the essential contribution to logic that the focus on argumentation, 'the uses of argument', affords. Nor is it to question the enormous value of Toulmin's concern with 'evolution of concepts' as exemplified in scientific inquiry. And I especially include the historical work with June Goodfield. It is rather to assert that description, no matter how compelling, needs to be grounded in a normative philosophical enterprise that attempts the traditional task of understanding the central logical concepts as used.

The connection I will make between logic and inquiry rests on my conjecture that metamathematical models of key logical concepts can be drawn from the structure of inquiry in physical chemistry, seen as the prototype for disciplined inquiry that yields knowledge at the highest level of epistemological warrant consistent with its a posteriori nature. If the model is noetically compelling the further task is to see whether it may serve as a metaphor for analogous images of truth and entailment in less epistemologically demanding domains, ultimately serving as the basis for the general theory of truth in argument and a consequent theory of entailment.

In the case envisioned, as in much of inquiry, what is required is an account of the dynamics of propositions seen as interconnected by various relationships of support, which both reflect and afford estimates of likelihoods, estimations of vulnerability to challenge in light of competing positions, degree of relevance to the issues at hand as a function of consequences across the field of commitments, and so on. Logic adequate to inquiry must be sensitive enough to take practical and theoretic account of such a range of considerations. It is among Toulmin's most salient contributions to epistemology, especially in *Human Understanding*, that he sees this as the essential philosophical project.

Toulmin has a lot to say about how disciplinary practice grounds the epistemic enterprise, both in *Human Understanding* where he offers insights into the underlying epistemological structures in rather abstract philosophical terms and in the deeply indicative volumes in the history of science with telling historical and methodological detail. Although the historical texts have been overlooked in the discussion even by Toulmin (there is a bare mention of his work with Goodfield in *Human Understanding*), they characterize the richness of the dialectic in disciplined discourse in a manner that permits the arguments to stand out. Using the frames of large areas of science (physical chemistry, astronomy and time-bound disciplines such as history and evolutionary biology) he is able to reconstruct a plausible account of how the problem situation is constructed and resolved through theoretic and practical advance (Toulmin and Goodfield, 1961; 1962; 1965). This is the sort of data that a theory of inquiry can be built from. *Human Understanding* attempts this while arguing for the centrality of the description of practice to an adequate philosophical account of inquiry-based understanding as against alternative philosophical models.

This sets the task. For participants in the discipline the level and kind of support are more or less apparent in the claims made and challenges refuted. Students of a subject matter acquire the sense of familiarity that supports such complex judgments as the result of long study and assimilation into a community of argument. It is for the student of the logic of argument to make the underlying structure of these complexes transparent both in their functioning and in their noetic plausibility. And this transcends description. It requires a normative account that captures what the description contributes in a noetically transparent manner. This seems to me to require metamathematical precision and reach. It also seems to me to require changes in the logical foundation.

Toulmin's study of argumentation in science makes the emergent nature of truth evident, for truth is an essential outcome of inquiry and other critical dialogues, when viewed from an epistemological perspective. But the role that truth plays in such essential dialogical activities requires normative stability, in that, as Harvey Siegel (1987) reminds us, relative truth is no truth at all. An immediate problem for an emergent theory of truth is to offer an account of stability sufficient to meet the test of non-relativism while admitting the evolutionary nature of truth, an account of truth that has the robustness typical of the standard account, while permitting an image of truth far different from that envisioned heretofore. In the standard account the model, as in arithmetic, is available independent of the inquiry. If we take physical chemistry as the paradigm, the model against which truth is to be ascertained emerges from inquiry (Weinstein, 2002a). The scientist must wait upon science to see if his or her conjectures are true.

In addition and in contrast to the mathematical, truth based on the paradigm of mature physical chemistry, like most of physical science, requires ambiguity in evolving model relations. Both relations within models and relations among models permit approximations, and it is the history of these approximations that determine the progressive nature of an inquiry. Truth, in the final analysis, will be identified with the progressive appearance of a model that deserves to be chosen. So both the intuitions of correspondence and coherence are saved. The ultimate model emerges as a function of increased coherence and it stands as an ideal object against which correspondence could be ascertained. It is, as in Pierce's view, "the ideal limit to which endless investigations would tend" (Hartshorne and Weiss, 1960, 5.565). It is the substance of how judgments of epistemic adequacy are made antecedent to the truth predicate being defined that is the main contribution of the construction, the Model of Emerging Truth (MET) offered in this paper. Finally, in place of strict implication contrasted with induction in its various senses, MET permits degrees of necessity reflective of the extent of model relations, that is, it permits inferences within models to be reassessed in terms of the depth and breadth of the field of reducing theories from which models are obtained. That is to say, MET yields a theory of entailment that permits of degree.

But why metamathematics? Whatever the failings of mathematical logic as an object language, that is a language in which arguments are to be couched; mathematical logic has excelled as a meta-language—that is, as a language for exploring such complex systems as arithmetic. The classic example of such success is Peano Arithmetic in which a set of axioms and a logical basis, including the specialized procedures of mathematical induction, permit the properties of the axiom set to be provably preserved through permissible operations. That is to say, the axioms define the system and implicitly identify the truth predicate as truth in the intended model, and permitted operations are logical implications, that is, are true in all models (Mostowski, 1966).

The association of mathematical logic with the logic of arithmetic exposes an ambiguity in Toulmin's demarcation of scientific from practical logic. Formal logic has been applied as a practical tool for analyzing argument in mathematics and those other areas of argument that rely on truth functional, extensional or categorical relations as in propositional and syllogistic arguments. And it is also a basis of the meta-structure that yields the wealth of knowledge of logical systems hard won over the past century. It enabled the foundation of arithmetic to be displayed in a meta-language that developed and sustained the highest standards of noetic clarity and systematicity. Metamathematical arguments appeal to the deepest philosophical intuitions while exhibiting well-regulated developments that enable deep results about logic to be conjectured, proved or rejected. This is a great deal to give up in logical theory. The weakness of formal logic as a vehicle for the construction and evaluation of much of argumentation does not require abandoning metamathematics as a framework for the logical aspects of the theory of argument. But there is another concern. Rigor has been more often achieved in metamathematics than relevance. One root cause may be the failure to see the ambiguity just mentioned. Traditional metamathematics, drawing from concern with its traditional domain of application, arithmetic, was stymied in its ability to afford useful analyses of actual argument by limiting its purview to arguments that satisfied the criterion of adequacy natural to arithmetic, but patently inadequate for most arguments elsewhere, that is, logical necessity. For mathematical systems, in so far as they are epistemologically a priori, are deemed to require logical necessity, as do arguments based on analytic principles, such as the categorical arguments that are characteristic of syllogistic. But in the overwhelming majority of the topics for which argumentation is central, logical necessity is too high a demand and so we are looking for a logical construction of a very different sort.

Metamathematics gives us direction as to how to proceed. Entailment and related notions of truth have been at the core of a number of elaborations and extensions in attempts to offer logical images of aspects of human thought, from the epistemological to the ethical (Hintikka, 1969). Such attempts give a synoptic image that connects the issue at hand with the procedures developed within meta-theory. These yield transparent definitions and regularized procedures that permit of reasoned assessment at the highest levels of rigor. To write a metamathematical construct is to invite such scrutiny. This in itself is enormous dialectical yield. But rigor without purpose is mere show. A metamathematical image most show persuasive structural elements that give a noetically satisfying account of logical properties. It must be adequate to the phenomena that it attempts to portray and indicative of deep philosophical clarifications.

As in many non-standard analyses of truth and entailment, MET is sensitive to the preponderance of evidence and changes in the evidence (it is non-monotonic in that additional premises may confute a seemingly valid inference). Relevance is a complex function of the other two. Following Govier (1985) the relevance of a proposition is determined by its effect on the truth of other propositions. And I would add a particular concern with propositions that have broad impact upon truth such as warrants and other aspects of backing. This points to truth, warrant and backing as a precondition for determining relevance. And it is to backing, warrant and truth that we will turn our attention. As in all formal models, the contribution is one of systematicity and transparency. Whatever the difficulty of initial understanding, MET, once understood, wears its virtues and vices on its face. In particular, it provides a systematic way to organize, articulate and evaluate changes in the theories used to interpret and explain the evidence for a claim. It identifies the underlying notion of truth and indicates how entailments support inference within such a complex truth structure. As indicated, professional training develops competence in using field-specific principles of inference and strategies for estimating the weight of evidence.

Philosophical understanding, illuminating the normative force of such principles and strategies, requires an account which is rich enough to capture the phenomena but transparent enough to be evaluated theoretically

MET has at its core the specification of two different sorts of functions. First, fairly standard functions that map from a theory, construed as a coherent and explanatory set of sentences, onto models. That is, sentences that describe events or that offer generalizations as explanations of these events are assigned objects, relations or ordered-relations in a defined domain, which constitutes what the theory may be taken to be about. Second, a much more powerful set of functions maps from other theories onto the theory, thereby enormously enriching the evidentiary base and furnishing a reinterpretation now construed in relation to a broader domain. That is to say, a theory may have its domain reinterpreted when its descriptions and explanations are seen to be instances of some broader and more encompassing domain, as in seeing chemical processes to be the result of molecular interactions. This is the insight that reflects the choice of a physical science as the governing paradigm. Mature physical science reconstrues experimental evidence, laws and theories in the light of higher-order, more abstract, theories, which unify heretofore-independent domains of physical inquiry. These unifications, or 'reductions', offer a massive reevaluation of evidentiary strength and theoretic likelihood. It is the weight of such reconstruals in identifying the ideal domain that grounds the truth predicate that MET attempts to capture. MET shows how we find out what our theories are really about, ontology in a sense that resonates with Pierce as alluded to above.

Mature physical science is also characterized by the open textures of its models and the approximations within which surrogates for deductions occur (in the standard account idealizations and other simplifications). The construction here attempts to make sense of the need for approximations and other divergences among models at different levels of analysis and articulation by offering intuitive criteria for assessing the epistemic function of the approximation in light of emerging data and the theoretic surround.

The key contribution of MET is that it enables us to construe epistemic adequacy as a function of theoretic depth and the increase of explanatory adequacy as inquiry progresses, rather than, as in standard accounts, as conformity to pre-existing models or predicted outcomes. This changes the logical structure of truth and entailment as compared to the arithmetic ideal and to the positivist accounts that take, for example, models of data as fulfilling an analogous role to models in arithmetic in the standard account. That is, they both serve as a template against which a claim is evaluated. In the once standard account of scientific inquiry, the model that yields confirmation is available prior to the inquiry; the relation between theory and data is a function mapping expectations onto outcomes. But, as Toulmin shows us, epistemic adequacy requires something more. It requires concern with the epistemic context, that is the body of information deemed relevant on an occasion of argumentation. MET includes a function that maps from a deep explanatory base onto the theories upon which expectations are based. This would allow, among other things, choosing between alternative theories even where expectations converge, and, with an elaborated metric, grounding the assignment of prior probabilities and other estimations of likelihood.

3. THE MODEL OF EMERGING TRUTH

We begin with an explanation relation constructed to resist manifest irrelevancies of the sort that plagued Hempel and others who worked with the D-N model of explanation. The standard move against the D-N model was to construct logically equivalent but irrelevant alternative explanations, thereby showing that a formal model could not distinguish plausible from obviously inadequate explanations. Counter moves included tightening the explanation relation to block irrelevant insertions. Omer (1970) offers a comprehensive summary and a useful suggestion that affords a logical block on such relations. The explanation relation, immediately below, modifies Omer's logical block with a pragmatic one. The construction envisions a set of sentences displayed for maximal clarity; (a) through (d) are standard conditions on explanation and (e) guards against the inclusion of logically innocuous but irrelevant constructions by requiring the explanans to be as close as possible to the explanandum. The determining phrase in (e) "available within the set of sentences accepted by the discourse community" is the first of a number of pragmatic turns in MET. A logical exclusion is not possible since Craig's Interpolation Lemma guarantees that a sentence of the sort the condition (e) seeks to preclude, an interpolation sentence, can always be constructed (Robbin, 1969). An intuitive metaphor for interpolations is that if p implies q, p implies s and s implies q for arbitrary sentence s. Craig's Lemma accounts in a deep way for the irrelevance of formal logic to argument, by showing that logically innocuous yet manifestly irrelevant sentences can always be added to a proof. We guarantee relevance pragmatically by only accepting the closest explanation available from the actual explanations available within a field of inquiry

A more systematic version of MET is available in Weinstein (2002a). The following is an indicator of the essential elements. I have attempted to make the formalism more available by forgoing the usual array of Greek letters, italics and the like. Lower case letters name individual functions, models or sentences; upper case letters are (ordered) sets of such items; double upper case letters are (ordered) sets of such (ordered) sets. Ordered sets are indicated by angle brackets. All indices, asterisks etc. are written on the line. An item is often used as its name; use/mention should always be clear in context. By 'field' we mean a structured set of sets, with various elements ordered in a variety of ways. Ordered sets enable us to keep track of items and discuss relations among them.

1. T is a set of sentences, {t1,...,tn}. The explanandum, s, is a sentence. The explanans, Tc is the longest sequence, tc1,...,tcm, of truth-functional components of T whose conjunction is logically equivalent to T. We say that T explains s, in symbols, T|-e s, just

when:

a) Tc implies s,
b) Tc does not imply not-s,
c) for some tci in Tc, tci is a nomic generalization,
d) for any tci in Tc, neither tci implies s, nor s implies tci, and
e) there is no sequence of sentences r1,...,rk, available within the set of sentences accepted by the discourse community that accepts T, such that, for some sequence of tc1,..., tcj in Tc
   i) tc1,...,tcj implies r1&,...,&rk,
   ii) r1,...,rk does not imply tc1&,...,&tcj,
   iii) upon replacing tc1,...,tcj in Tc by r1,...,rk, in symbols Tcr, Tcr implies s.

Since our concern is with physical science there is an obvious constraint that a substantial number of the tci's will describe experimental or other empirical phenomena. As required by condition (c), some of these are nomic generalizations. No attempt to resolve the many issues involved in characterizing nomic generalization will be made. But the account of scientific structures, immediately below, shows how the intuition that nomic generalizations hold across a range of selected models can be given mathematical content.

We now move to the substance of MET, what we call a 'scientific structure'. We move from restricted implication relations to semantic entailment. Semantic entailments are the analogue of implications in standard logics such as the first order predicate calculus where it is provable that: p implies q iff all models of p are also models of q (completeness) (Mendelson, 1964). The fundamental semantic relationship is of a sentence being true in a model, that is, there is an assignment of n-tuples of objects in a model to n-ary predicates in a sentence. We say a sentence, s, is true in a model, m (m ||-s) just when there is an assignment from s onto the domain of m. (van Fraassen, 1971). Intuitively, m exhibits what s asserts. An obvious example would assign to the predicate 'greater than' the set of pairs of integers, m, n such that m is greater than n. A model requires the specification of a domain, in traditional logic the domain is frequently the integers. Truth in a model is easily generalized to sets of sentences by modeling their conjunction. In what follows we will be interested in models of T. We will be most interested in the history of model relations that is, we will look how closely an empirical model (for example, a model of data) satisfies some selected model (frequently the intended model) of the theory (Suppes, 1969). Such intended models are most often idealization, as in the properties of gases in the Boyle-Charles' Law, which includes statistical assumptions that disregard physical effects such as deformation on impact (Nagel, 1961). So we will be looking at how closely a series of models are approximating the theoretic expectations, that is the degree of isomorphism between actual empirical models and ideal models. This is possible, in general, because of the availability of a definable range of near isomorphisms such that a model is in an appropriate approximation to some selected (intended) model (Apostel, 1961). An example would be a series of measurements approximating a theoretic value. We intend a level of approximation consistent with the practices of the scientific discourse frame within which a scientific structure is sustained. The level of appropriate approximation is a posteriori, and we refrain from any attempt to legislate, a priori, what it should be. This is the second pragmatic turn. It is, among other things, the progress of near isomorphisms over time across sequences of models that reflects normativity. Science is rarely perfect, but it is expected to improve.

2. We define a scientific structure as an ordered triple, TT = <T, FF, RR>, with or without indices, primes, asterisks, etc., where:
   a) T is the syntax of TT, that is, a set of sentences that are the linguistic statement of TT. The set T is closed under a restricted consequence relation, Con, where Con(T) = {s: T |-e s}.
   b) FF is a field of sets, F, such that for all F in FF, and f in F, f(T) = m for some model, m, such that, either:
      i) m ||- T, or
      ii) m is a near isomorph of some model, n, and n ||- T.
      FF is closed under set theoretic union: if sets X and Y are in FF, so is X U Y.
   c) RR is a field of sets of functions, R, such that for all R in RR and every r in R, there is some theory T* and r represents T in T*, in respect of some subset of T, k(T). We close RR under set-theoretic union as well.

FF includes primary evidence based on what T predicts or explains. RR includes secondary evidence based on the 'reduction' of T to another theory T*. The notion of reduction relies on the availability of 'effective representing functions', a purely syntactic operator that maps formulas and variables of some theory, one to one, onto formulas and variables of another theory, and, in addition, preserves identity. An effective representing function, r, represents T in T* in respect of a subset k(T), of expressions of T, such that for every expression e of k(T), if e is in k(T) then r(e) is an expression e* in (T*). An important property of such representing function is: r reduces T to T* is equivalent to, for every model m of T there exists a model m* of T* such that, for every sentence s of k(T), s is true in m if and only if r(s) is true in m* (Eberle, 1971).

This enables us to define key notions, articulating the history of T under the functions F in FF and R in RR. The basis is a model chain.

3. We define a model chain, C, for theory, T, as an ordered n-tuple <m1,...,mn>, such that for each mi in the chain, mi = <di, fi,> for domain di and function fi, and for each i and j, i< j≤ n, di = dj and mj is a realization of T later in time than mi.

A realization can be thought of as an experimental array or other set of data acceptable in the light of the standards in the field of inquiry that T sits in. We say ‘realization’ because the various mi’s may not be models of T, rather, near enough approximations. This is a consequence of the pragmatic turn.

3.1. Let m* be an intended model of T, making sure that f(T) = m for some f in F, and that m||-T. We then say that C is a progressive model chain if:

a) for every mi in C, mi is isomorphic to m*, or

b) for most pairs mi, mj in C, i,j, $i < j \leq n$, mj is a nearer isomorph to m* than mi.

The notion of a progressive model chain permits us to formalize the intuition that a progressive theory furnishes closer theoretic interpretations to the range of phenomena within its domain of application. The basic interpretation is the intended model. Thus, theories have epistemic virtue when all models are substantially interpretable in terms of the intended model, or are getting closer to the intended model over time. We say ‘most’ since we cannot assume that theoretic advances are uniformly progressive. Frequently, theories move backwards without being, thereby, rejected. We are looking for a preponderance of evidence or perhaps, where possible, a statistic. We do not define this a priori. What counts as an acceptable rate of advance is a judgment in respect of a particular enterprise over time. This is another aspect of the pragmatic turn.

A related, but distinguishable notion, a theory being model progressive, begins with the intuition that theories transcend their initial domain of applications as they move from limited conjectures to effective explanatory theories. This notion defines a sequence of models that capture increasingly many aspects of the theory.

3.2. Let T’ be a subtheory of T in the sense that T’ is the restriction of the relational symbols of T to some sub-set of these. Let f’ be subset of some f in F, in some realization of TT. Let <T’1,...,T’n> be an ordered n-tuple such that for each i,j, $i < j \leq n$, T’j reflects a subset of T modeled under f’ at some time later than T’i. We say that T is model progressive under f’ if:

a) T’k is identical to T for all indices k, or

b) the ordered n-tuple <T’1,...,T’n> is well ordered in time by the subset relation.

3.3. Let < C1,...,Cn > be a well ordering of the progressive model chains of TT, such that for all i,j, $I \leq j \leq n$, Cj is a later model chain than Ci. TT is model chain progressive if the n-tuple <C1,...,Cn> is well ordered in time by the subset relation.

The intuition should be clear. A theory’s models in the sense of the sets of phenomena to which it is applied must confront the logical expectations the theory provides. That is to say, as the range of application of a theory moves forward in time and across a range of phenomena, the fit between the actual models and the ideal theoretic model defined by the intended model is getting better or is as good as it can get in terms of its articulation. The model history of a theory T, enables us to evaluate the theory as it stands. By examining T under RR we add the dimension of theoretic reduction. The key intuition here is that, under RR, models are donated from higher-order theories. Theories under RR form a strict partial order (transitive, irreflexive and asymmetric) but with constraints on transitivity since we are dealing with approximations. The models (or near models) of T donated under functions in R are differentiated from models of T under functions in F by their derivational history and by the particulars of the members of RR. Similar constructions offer a precise sense of progressiveness under RR. This will enable us to offer essential definitions resulting in a principled ontological commitment in terms of the history of the theory and its relations to other essential theories with which it comports. MET enables us to distinguish particular models and their history across the field, giving us criteria for preference among them. The ex post facto selection of an ontologically significant model from among the intended models in light of their history will be seen to ultimately yield a truth predicate in the Tarskian sense. The main contribution of the construction put forward in this paper is a substantive description of how judgments of epistemic adequacy are made before such a truth predicate is defined. MET elucidates the criteria for model choice in terms of the history of the scientific structure, TT, within which a theory sits. That is, we define plausible desiderata, not only upon the theory and its consequences (its models under functions in F), but also in terms of the history of related theories that donate models to the theory under appropriately selected reduction relations (sets of functions in R). It is the structure of the field under these reduction relations, and in particular the breadth and depth of the model chains donated by interlocking reducing theories, that determines the epistemic power of the theory.

4. We now turn our attention to the members of RR. Recall that the members of R represent T in T* in respect of some subset of T, k(T). Let <k1(T),...,kn(T)> be an n-tuple of representations of T over time, that is, for i < j, kj(T) is a representation of T in T* at a time later that ki(T). We say that TT is reduction progressive if,

   a) k(T) is identical to Con(T) for all indices, or
   b) the n-tuple is well ordered by the subset relation.

4.1. We call an n-tuple of theories, RC = < T1,...,Tn > a reduction chain, if for all i,j there is a ri in Ri such that ri represents Ti in Tj in respect of k(T)for all i < j ≤ n. RC = < T1,...,Tn > a deeper reduction chain than RC' = < T'1,...,T'j >, if Ti is identical to T'j for all i ≤ j and j < n.

4.2. We call a theory reduction chain progressive if T is a member of a series of reduction chains, <RC1,…,RCn> and for each Rci + 1, RCi + 1 is a deeper reduction chain than Rci.

This leads to an even more profound extension under RR.

4.3. T# is a branching reducer if there is a pair (at least) T’ and T* such that there is some r’ and r* in R’ and R*, respectively, such that r’ represents T’ in T# and r* represents T* in T# and neither T’ is represented in T* nor conversely.

4.3.1. B = <TT1,TT2,...,TTn > = < < T1, F1, R1 >, < T2, F2,R2>,..., < Tn, Fn,Rn >> is a reduction branch of TTn if Tn is a branching reducer in respect of Ti and Tj, i,j ≥ 2; j ≤ n.

4.4. We say that a branching reducer, T is a progressively branching reducer if the n-tuple of reduction branches <B1,...,Bn> is well ordered in time by the subset relation.

5. Let TT# = <TT1,...,TTn> be an ordering of scientific structures seriously proposed at a time. Let <<T1,F1,R1>,...,<Tn,Fn,Rn>> be their respective realizations at a time. We say that a set of models M, M = <m1, m2,...,mn> is a persistent model set if for domains, d,

a) M = <<m1= <d1,f1>, m2 = <d2,f2>,..., mn = <dn,fn>> and for all i, j di = dj, or

b) M is a persistent model set in a set of ordered subsets of TT#, such that the sequence is well ordered in time by the subset relation.

Intuitively, M contains the ordered models that define what the theory can be seen to *really* be about. At each level in the ordering a model of what the theory is about has shown itself to be adequate over time and available for reinterpretation and integration with other adequate models. Physical chemistry tells the tale. We live in a world of substances, which are indicative of chemical processes, which are indicative of molecular structure, which are indicative of atomic structure, which is what chemistry may be seen to be about in reality. If particle physics ever gets truly sorted out, there will be another layer. I stop with the Periodic Table of Elements as the most coherent and pragmatically effective picture of the ‘architecture of matter’ that we have. That is, I take the Periodic Table of Elements to be true, in the sense elaborated below (6-6.33) even though changing and evolving.

The intuition behind MET may be stated boldly: true theories ramify. A theory, whatever its initial intended models, takes its ontological commitment in light of how the theory fares in relationship to other theories whose models it incorporates under reduction. That is, we fix reference in light of the facts of the matter, the relevant facts being how the theory is redefined in the light of its place in inquiry as inquiry progresses. The awareness by inquirers of the history of success of scientific structures enables them to set standards for model choice rationally, in terms of plausible criteria based on successful practice. The formal model enables us to look at the history of approximations to the original interpretations of the theory (intended models) in terms of their goodness-of-fit, and most crucially the relations between ontologically relevant models donated from above (from reducing theories) reinterpreting or even replacing intended models. That is, it enables us to look at how intended models fare under the impress of higher-order reducing theories. Finally, it permits a natural definition of truth internal to the scientific structure (Weinstein, 2002a). Truth, as we shall see below, is defined as an ideal outcome as in Pierce but with mathematical content as in Tarski. Truthlikeness becomes a quantifiable metric as the theories in the structure move towards truth. That is, as the intended models of reducing theories substitute for intended models of reduced theories, increasing the confirmatory basis and the depth of explanatory adequacy. The confirmatory basis is increased since under reductions confirming evidence of theories connected via reduction to a theory indirectly confirms that theory as well. MET could be modeled with actual assignments of physical properties and relations. The model chains and their relations could be displayed, weighted and evaluated. Designing such an array would require a period of testing and adjustment, possibly through computer simulations of fragments of physical theory organized according to MET. The yield would be a rational reconstruction of argumentation in a substantive field of inquiry. But even in the abstract, the power of MET is in its logical clarity. The construction displays what one can mean by 'ramify'. And it offers an available formal metaphor for increasing truthlikeness as the outcome of inquiry of the sort found in physical chemistry, our presumptive candidate for a naturalist ontology.

4. BACKING AND WARRANT

Toulmin's views on warrant and backing are too well known in general to require much more than mention. In what follows I will be extending these notions in ways that, given his antipathy to mathematics, Toulmin would be unlikely to welcome as his own. Therefore, I won't try to justify the constructions in relation to any of his specifics, rather work with the ideas in a general sense that I take to be consistent with the basic understanding of his work.

Backing is the framework within which warrants are to be seen. It constitutes the justificatory ground for the warrants in use and shows them to respect the relevant methodological demands, frequently differing in different domains of inquiry. In physical science such methodological items include such diverse things as experimental apparatus, broadly construed, typical use of language with special vocabularies, and clearly formulated procedures for using concepts in the widest variety of ways, from identifying instances to deep theoretic explanations. But if we take the intuition behind metamathematics seriously, whatever can be described, can be described in some language, whence the syntax T in TT. And given a syntax we can define functions from that syntax onto models. Models are guaranteed by the deepest, yet most optimistic result in modern logic, every consistent set of sentences has a model. Further, every consistent set has a countable model, the notorious Löwenheim-Skolem Theorem (Kleene, 1950). The paradoxical consequences of Löwenheim-Skolem are well known; a denumerable model of the real numbers is available, but this model cannot possibly be the intended model of the real numbers, which are provably non-denumerable (Putnam, 1983). Given our construction this is a welcome consequence, for following Putnam, the paradox implies that models are not inherent but rather selected (Weinstein, 2002a). A scientific structure, TT, is defined by syntax and procedures for model choice. And so for my purposes TT and its history indicates the backing for T through the various sets of functions included in RR and FF. The relevant history is that of the changing and evolving array of functions mapping sentences onto models under interpretative functions in the various F's in FF, intuitively, the interpretations of the sentences in various models, and the members of the reduction functions R in RR that offer a new set of interpretations along the chain that reflects theoretic connections with T. The guiding intuition is that the principled reinterpretation of a predicate (concept) in a theory as an instance of a predicate (concept) from a higher-order reducing theory determines what the theories may be seen as *really* about. The most obvious case would be the reduction of the enormous variety of chemical reactions known empirically to the molecular description of the underlying process that explains the reaction—the stuff of Chemistry 101. The commitment to the ontology of molecules and atoms is, in my view, a consequence of the power of the reductions, available as the theory exhibited in the Periodic Table of Elements became better understood, coupled with the veritable explosion of chemical knowledge that followed in its wake.

Despite the formalism, MET is an extension of Toulmin rather than of Tarski. This results from the 'pragmatic turn.' The various functions are all a posteriori. The sets of models are to be of actual empirical and explanatory models that constitute the substance of the field of inquiry represented by the scientific structure. The functions in F reflect the specifics of experimental rigor and measurement. Explanation is no longer all or nothing as in the D-N model. We can be satisfied with near isomorphs to the intended model leaving open how closely experimental outcomes and other observations need to conform to the intended model to serve the purposes of inquiry at a time. And similarly for the scope of the representing functions in R. Representing functions, recall, represent only a selected subset of the reduced theory. That is, a reducing theory may fail to accommodate all aspects of the reduced theory based on disciplinary standards of principled rather than ad hoc limitations. Both sets of functions can be broadened or restricted as more models become available whether through new experiments, new applications, and especially through newly available reductions. What counts as near enough or broad enough is for the members of the field to determine. As is the pace of advance, that is how much stasis or even backward movement is tolerable as inquiry proceeds. Such modifications capture at least some part of Toulmin's notion of rebuttal for they require that claims based on scientific structures be hedged with caveats that reflect an informed sense of issues such as goodness of fit, range of application and estimations of the potential for progress. What is a priori normative is the requirement that isomorphisms are getting tighter over time. And that the reductions are progressive and the chains in which they sit are progressively deeper and broader as inquiry advances. Scientific structures are assessed in terms of general a priori standards such as increase in descriptive and explanatory power, but are given substance by being grounded in the working standards of the field of inquiry. Thus, both the methodology and the underling epistemology are naturalistic as in Toulmin's vision in *Human Inquiry*, but normativity is noetically transparent, precisely presented and open to philosophical challenge.

An immediate yield is in the theory of warrants. What I see as the key insight that drives Toulmin from mathematical logic is the idea that our warrants are limited and presented as limited when used, and so deductive connections are just too strong to make sense of argumentation. And, of course, in conjunction with the rejection of a probabilistic interpretation of the weakening of deductive entailments. The key that enables a general theory of warrant to be constructed on the model of entailment is the insight of David Hitchcock (1998) that warrants are substantive generalizations, that is, constructed by generalizing over content expressions of whatever logical type. In my earlier work. I saw this by analogy to Carnap's L-true in Beta, that is, true by virtue of meaning postulates (Weinstein, 1991). But this proved intractable since meaning postulates are just too strong to capture the variety of warrants in use, ranging from logically true to mere rules of thumb (see Pinto, 2001) for a discussion of the variety of doxastic attitudes that supports such a view). Thus, what we want from a theory of entailment is a principled account of the strength of the relationship between premises and conclusion in accord with the underlying inference structure. A first approximation to strength can be read directly from MET.

As a basis, a generalization, w, is a putative warrant if there is a T such that T|-ew. Whence, w is in T since T is closed under the consequence relation. A putative warrant is, thus, a consequence of some accepted body of codified knowledge so constructed as to include near models and with controls on irrelevance. We then develop strength as a measure of the theory T as seen within a structure TT. There are three levels of strength, although each can be internally complex as in the Richter Scale, for example, the levels of warrant in the paragraphs that follow can be internally structured through a metric on the history of progressive model chains and similarly for reductions.

At the first level, a putative warrant, w*, is available as a warrant in T, if the models of T under functions in F form a progressive model chain (3.1). The intuition is clear. A warrant must rest within a body of knowledge that is either adequate to the intended model or moving progressively towards it. Intuitively, a generalization serves as a warrant where there is reason to expect that generalization to be adequate to the phenomena it purports to describe or increasingly so.

We then add strength in two significant ways, first in terms of models generated by functions in F and second in terms of models donated from functions in R. A warrant in T, w*, is strong if the model chains for T are model progressive (3.2) It is stronger if the model chain, C*, for T is model chain progressive (3.3). The intuition is that strong warrants are adequate to an increasing range of similar phenomena and stronger if they are increasingly so. Again, physical chemistry yields numerous examples. We are confirmed in a chemical analysis in terms of molecular structure when, initially, the empirical values are increasingly close to theoretic demands. We are reinforced in our commitment to the analysis when other chemical phenomena yield analogous results. Accounting for chemical properties through the construct of chemical valence is not only effective in particular cases, but it is broadly applicable to an ever-broadening range of chemical phenomena as new chemical substances and their reactions are discovered or invented, often with increasing yield in precision as instrumentation and our theoretic understanding improves (Langford and Beebe, 1969).

The next level of strength reflects deep theoretic connections, so a warrant in T, w*, is super strong if T sits in a progressive model chain C* and where C* is supported by deeper underlying theories (4.1). That is to say, C* sits in a reduction chain RC* which is reduction progressive (4.2). Super strong warrants are the best indicators of ontology internal to a theory. But for the ontological commitment to be broadly warranted the progressive reduction chains must themselves branch. This is clear in physical science. Ontology, and the connection with truth in some sense approaching correspondence, in conjunction with internal realism (and to the exclusion of instrumentalism), requires the grand unifications, the major reductions: electricity and magnetism, chemistry and physics, physical chemistry and biology and possibly psychology and biochemistry. That is, they are branching reducers (4.3) and ultimately, progressively branching reducers (4.31). The broadening theory ramifies under the impact of new conceptions (models) available from the reducing theories, which expose deep connections and permit intuitions of underlying unity.

5. TRUTH AND ONTOLOGY

The outcome of the discussion so far is what I have called, following Putnam, "internal realism" (Weinstein 2002a). That is, the commitment within a scientific structure as to how reality is to be construed. That takes us some way into ontology, but not nearly far enough if our internal ontology is to be a candidate for ontology in the broader philosophical sense, that is, a general commitment to the character of being. I take the intuition behind scientific realism to be that the ontology of a theory is general in respect of acceptable scientific structures across the board. This view was abandoned along with the unified science movement of the mid-century

(Hardcastle and Richardson, 2003). But the view still resonates in various forms of modern materialism, particularly in the hope that mental predicates can be reduced to states of the nervous system (Churchland, 1988). The view of reduction presented here helps to make sense of such a view, since not all we include in a reduced theory (of the mind) needs to be represented (by a physical correlate). Rather, the physicalist enterprise of reducing mental predicates to physiological states just needs to be progressive in the various senses indicated above.

Not surprisingly, we attempt to capture ontological commitment in the connections among the various scientific structures TT, We define criteria for a candidate ontology in the broad sense starting where we left off with the a persistent model set. Recall:

5. Let TT# = <TT1,...,TTn> be an ordering of scientific structures seriously proposed at a time. Let <<T1,F1,R1>,...,<Tn,Fn,Rn>> be their respective realizations at a time. We say that a set of models M, M = <m1, m2,…,mn> is a persistent model set if for domains, d, if,
   a) M = <<m1 = <d1,f1>, m2 = <d2,f2>,..., mn = <dn,fn>> and for all i, j di = dj, or
   b) M is a persistent model set in a set of ordered subsets of TT#, such that the sequence is well ordered in time by the subset relation.

5.1. M is an ontic set for TT#.

5.2. We say that a ontic set, O, is a favored ontic set if:
   a) O is the set of intended models of a theory, T, standing at the head of a progressive reduction chain. (Notice, O is thus the ontic set of all of the theories in the chain.)
   b) the members of the reduction chain are themselves reduction progressive.
   c) T is a progressively branching reducer.

Notice that the set consisting of an ontic set and the sets that it generates (the set of sets under the reduction relation) form a persistent model set. An interesting yield of the notion of persistent model set is that it explains instrumentalism in theoretically primitive or dubious contexts. Without a theory that donates models, the most persistent models are models of the data, whence instrumentalism or other brands of positivism. Of course, working with mature physical science our concern is with theoretic coherence. Which, although requiring that functions map onto models of data or other empirical models, takes its ontology from the deeper theoretic commitments as a function of reduction. For the scientifically informed, the world is really made up atoms and molecules, even though exactly what atoms and molecules will come to be seen as waits on the progress of science.

We now define the ideal of truth emergent.

6. TT is progressive if:
   a) TT is model progressive (3.2).
   b) TT is model chain progressive (3.3).
   c) TT is reduction progressive. (4).
   6.1. We call T a progressive reducer if:
      a) T is reduction chain progressive (4.2).
      b) T is a progressively branching reducer (4.4).
   6.2. We say T is a favored reducer, if:
      a) TT is progressive (6).
      b) T is a progressive reducer (6.1).
   6.3. T is a most favored reducer if T is a maximally progressive reducer, that is, T is the nth member of a reduction chain such that for all Ti, $1 < i < n$, Ti is a favored reducer. (Notice, Tn is not reduction progressive, since it stands at the head of the longest reduction chain.)
      6.3.1. The set, O, of ontic models of Tn, is thus, a favored ontic set in respect of every Ti in the reduction chain.
      6.3.2. If Tn is a most favored reducer, and O is its favored ontic set than O is the ontology of scientific structure TT.
      6.3.3. An ideal truth predicate for TT can then be constructed in a fairly standard Tarskian manner as: 's is true' for s in Tn in TT, iff O||-s where O is the ontology of TT and Tn is the most basic theory of all.

6. FINAL THOUGHTS

Formal models such as MET, whatever their intuitive appeal, stand or fall on the clarity with which they expose the logical basis of what Ralph Johnson has taught me to call 'information structures', of which scientific structures are a paradigmatic example. This requires that actual exemplifications of MET, formalized fragments of physical chemistry, be reconstructed and their adequacy to the historical phenomena determined. My intuition is that this could be exhibited through a computer model that relied on the architecture sketched here strengthened by metrics across TT, reflecting expert knowledge in chemistry. It could then be determined whether such a model affords insights sufficient for a rational reconstruction of crucial arguments in the history of physical chemistry. Such a rational reconstruction would show how warranted decisions are made in light of a relatively stable but changing structure of fact and theoretic adjudication. More saliently, perhaps, MET can be seen to reflect the intuition that lies behind the notion of "a web of belief", informally indicated by Quine but unarticulated in precise logical constructions (Quine and Ullian, 1978). It also offers an image of "entrenchment" (Goodman, 1965) that is to say, depth of commitment measured as a function of degree of connectedness within a system.

As always in the formal tradition, what is offered, although an idealization, is a precise root metaphor. The test is to see whether the root metaphor once articulated has essential consequences in the elaborated structure that it generates and most pertinently, whether the elaborated structure offers a philosophically compelling image of the fundamental concepts it encapsulates. That is, the metaphor should be articulatable so that it makes sense of actual practices while affording a noetically available normative account of the logic of those practices. The purpose of formalism is to show that fundamental, yet impressionistic, ideas can be given precise mathematical content, and so, show they are no longer suspicious on the grounds of vacuity. Metaphors, similar to the web of belief, 'belief stores', 'oracles' and 'commitments', abound in the argumentation literature. Absent a clear sense of model, internal relations within such constructs remain obscure. It remains to be seen whether something similar to MET can be usefully translated into the many amorphous contexts of ordinary argumentation—a project for a community not an individual. But whatever the outcome of such a project, MET attempts to afford a metaphor for those areas of human inquiry that have served us best, our understanding of the natural world through broadly relevant and deeply warranted theories, a project with which Toulmin should have profound sympathy.

Acknowledgements

Acknowledgement is owed to the editors for their enormous efforts in detecting unclarities and other infelicities.

CHAPTER 6

LILIAN BERMEJO-LUQUE

TOULMIN'S MODEL OF ARGUMENT AND THE QUESTION OF RELATIVISM

Department of Philosophy, University of Murcia, Campus de Espinardo 30071, Murcia, Spain
E-mail: lilianbl@um.es

ABSTRACT: In *The Uses of Argument*, Toulmin proposed a distinction between field-dependent and field-invariant standards for argument appraisal that gave rise to a relativistic understanding of his theory. The main goal of this paper is to show that epistemological relativism is not a necessary consequence of Toulmin's model of argument. To this end, I will analyze the role that fields are to play within this model, given a proposed conception of one of its key elements: the warrant of an argument.

KEYWORDS: Toulmin model; relativism; warrant; argument fields; criteria for argument evaluation

1. TOULMIN'S MODEL OF ARGUMENT

In *Human Understanding*, S. E. Toulmin criticised not only dogmatism, but also relativism, as the counterpart of the same misconception of rationality, namely, rationality as adherence to a deductivist ideal of knowledge. In 1958, Toulmin had already developed an alternative to deductivism in *The Uses of Argument*. In this work, Toulmin proposed a new conception of logic based on the distinction between field-dependent and field-invariant criteria for argument evaluation. Despite Toulmin's aim, the idea of field-dependent criteria gave rise to a relativistic reading of his theory of argument. The main goal of this paper is to show that epistemological relativism is not a necessary consequence of the model of argument that Toulmin proposed in 1958. I wish to show that, rather, it is a good way to fight it.

According to Toulmin, every argument is composed of a *claim*, the *reason*[1] for that claim and the *warrant* that licenses the step from this reason to that claim. In principle, this is the simplest form of argument. But Toulmin observes that in everyday arguments, we can also distinguish three more elements: *backings*, *rebuttals* and *modal qualifiers*. Backings are defined as "other assurances" that stand "behind our

[1] What I call "reasons" were named "data" in Toulmin (1958), and "ground", in Toulmin, Rieke and Janik (1979).

D. Hitchcock and B. Verheij (eds.), Arguing on the Toulmin Model: New Essays in Argument Analysis and Evaluation, 71–85.

warrants" (1958, p. 103). And rebuttals are "circumstances in which the general authority of the warrant would have to be set aside" (1958, p. 101).

About modal qualifiers, Toulmin says that they are "an explicit reference to the degree of force which our data confer on our claim in virtue of our warrant" (1958, p. 101). Although he observes that many arguments do not contain this explicit reference, this would not necessarily prevent him from holding that such a reference must be present, at least implicitly, for something to be an argument. In fact, following Toulmin's considerations about logic and their consequences for his non-deductivist conception of justification, we can take it that, in his model, to argue is to try to establish the modality of a claim. Consequently, despite Toulmin not being explicit regarding this question, we can consider that, according to his model, to evaluate an argument is to determine which modal qualification is appropriate for the claim, given the reason adduced for it, or whether the modal qualification provided by the arguer is correct or not. A claim, then, is a proposition modally qualified; and to argue for a claim is to argue for a positive modal qualification like "probably *p*", "necessarily *p*", "*p* (is true)", "*p* (is highly acceptable)", etc.

In order to determine the appropriateness of a modal qualification, we should first determine the meaning of the corresponding modal terms. Indeed, this is Toulmin's first goal in *The Uses of Argument*: in its very first pages, he analyses the meaning of 'impossible' by attending to the different uses of expressions like 'cannot'; and he concludes that they can all be reduced to the following pattern: "P being what it is, you must rule out anything involving Q: to do otherwise would be R, and would invite S" (1958, p. 29).[2]

Observing this pattern, Toulmin distinguishes two aspects of the meaning of modal terms: the force and the criteria of their use. The force of a modal term is the practical implications of its use (1958, p. 30), and it is field-invariant: for example, whenever we say that something is 'possible' we are pragmatically meaning that it is worth considering. Following Toulmin's conception, we obtain that these pragmatic consequences of modal terms are *necessary* because they *cannot* be avoided: that is, to say that something is possible and then not take it into account is performatively inconsistent, and this is something to rule out when we try to make accessible our verbal behaviour to others. According to his notion of the meaning of 'impossible', we would say: "pragmatic conditions for the use of modal expressions being what they are, you must rule out anything involving their violation; to do otherwise would be to attribute/commit a performative inconsistency and that may render incomprehensible your/other's verbal behaviour".

On the other hand, the criteria of the use of a modal term are " . . . the reasons by reference to which we decide in any context that the use of a particular modal

[2] Toulmin remarks that this kind of pragmatic definition of modal terms does not stand for an ontological characterisation, but rather for a functional one. In fact, Toulmin thinks that it is senseless to try to develop ontological characterisations of modal terms because their only role in language is just to qualify our assertions, given the "strength of the backing which we have for the assertion, evaluation or whatever" (1958, p. 90).

term is appropriate" (1958, p. 30). These criteria determine the meaning of modal terms as much as the pragmatic consequences of their use. But they accomplish this function by bringing about the qualification that modal terms are able to bear. In Toulmin's view, things are not impossible, possible, necessary, probable, etc *simpliciter*, but they are morally, pragmatically, legally, economically, linguistically, logically, etc impossible, possible, necessary, probable, etc. As I will argue in due course, this is the sense in which Toulmin would say that the criteria for the use of modal terms are field-dependent.

2. THE RELATIVISTIC READING OF TOULMIN'S MODEL

But the idea of field-dependent criteria gave rise to a relativist reading of Toulmin's proposal. In this reading, the nature of fields and their role in argument appraisal were at the core. Indeed, the very notion of field appears as a matter of controversy. For example, C. Schroeder (1997) criticises that there exists a "general tendency towards relativism within the Toulmin approach", and he characterises fields as follows:

> [T]he concept of argument fields . . . refers to the modes used by a person to assess arguments, the standards by reference to which a person assesses them, and the manner in which a person qualifies her or his conclusions about them. (p. 98)

B. Burleson (1979) says that fields provide the *substantive context* of an argument, which:

> . . . either implicitly or explicitly, provides the criteria against which the merits of an argument should be evaluated. Each language game is a locus of communally shared and tested standards of intelligibility, truth, sincerity and correctness-the components of rationality which all good arguments must meet. (p. 147)

For J. F. Klumpp (1981), fields are subject matter and they determine what types of data can be used to support a claim. And D. Zarefsky (1982) considers that Toulmin "proposed that, for any given field, there are accepted standards for judging the worth of arguments" (1982, p. 191).[3]

---

[3] This interest in argument fields is alien to *The Uses of Argument*. There, Toulmin is hardly concerned with a proper characterisation of the concept, rather he seems to use it in a loose way. This should have induced at least some doubts in those who took fields to be the cornerstone of argument appraisal: if this concept were intended to have such an important role, the author that introduced it would have been more concerned with its definition and the way fields manage to provide those standards. On the contrary, in *The Uses of Argument*, the clearest account of fields is the following definition: "two arguments will be said to belong to the same field when the data and conclusions in each of the two arguments are, respectively, of the same logical type: they will be said to come from different fields when the backing or the conclusions in each of the two arguments are not of the same logical type" (1958, p. 14). This

The view that fields provide standards for argument appraisal is bound to at least a moderate epistemological relativism: the justificatory power of arguments becomes a property to be decided "intra-field". But authors like C. A. Willard have extracted deeper relativistic consequences from this idea.

In "Argument Fields and Theories of Logical Types", Willard argues that we should conceive of fields as "sociological entities" if we do not want to make them "redundant to studies of language and logic" (1981, p. 137). In his view, the appraisal of argumentation is a matter of different sets of practices belonging to fields as sociological entities (1981, p. 141). These sociological entities provide their own standards for the practice of argumentation, but these very standards cannot be further justified: they stand at the basis of any protocol of argumentation within a given practice. Rather, they are "conventions" that hold for those particular fields and their argumentative practices. Consequently, in "Argument Fields", he proposes "an embryonic theory of argument fields" as the cornerstone of a wider proposal on argumentation theory as a merely explicative endeavour (1982, p. 75). Such conception is further developed in *Argumentation and the Social Grounds of Knowledge* (1983).[4]

My concern in this paper is about the idea of *field-dependency*. I want to show that a misconception of field-dependency gives rise to an unacceptable relativism regarding argument appraisal. So let me recall at this point that in *The Uses of Argument*, Toulmin's main interest is in the way "we actually assess the soundness, strength and conclusiveness of arguments" (1958, p. 1). At the end of this paper, I will try to show that there is a sense of field-dependency related to the rhetorical dimension of argumentation that should play a role in Argumentation Theory. But in arguing against the alleged relativistic consequences of Toulmin's model, my point is just to show that fields do not actually provide standards to determine the way "we actually assess the soundness, strength and conclusiveness of arguments".

Yet my task is slightly more complicated, because the logical and rhetorical dimensions of argumentation are deeply interwoven. If we wish to deal with real, everyday argumentation, we have to be able to interpret certain speech acts as argumentation. The way arguments should be assessed within a given practice would determine the sorts of things that count as attempts at rational persuasion within a given field. But this is tantamount to determining what counts as argumentation within that field.

In that sense, we should observe that the sort of relativism that Willard endorses is the ultimate one because it implies incommensurability. The moral from Willard's

---

definition could induce us to believe that fields are "logical types", but according to Toulmin's examples, we should understand that Euclid's *Elements*, statistical reports about the Swedes, or the *Nautical Almanac* constitute logical types, and this is such a peculiar concept of "logical type" that it is not of great help in shedding light on the concept of field and its role for argument appraisal.

[4] However, in *A Theory of Argumentation* (1989), Willard has proposed a more nuanced account of fields. My concern in this work is on the way the concept of *field-dependency* can give rise to a treacherous form of relativism, and Willard's cited views just play the role of providing a good example.

thesis is not only that "argument goodness" is a property to be decided "intra-field", but also that the very idea of argument evaluation is pointless: we would have no reason to rule out any discourse, for it would always be possible that it belongs to a field whose standards of rationality are alien to us. The point of Argumentation Theory would be just to try to explain these communicative practices within their corresponding fields.

To be more precise, I think we can distinguish two levels of incommensurability in Willard's conception: On the one hand, insofar as standards for argument appraisal could only be applied within their corresponding fields, it would be senseless to try to establish their intrinsic value as standards: to that end, we should produce an argument to be sanctioned either by these very standards or by other standards. In the first case, we would have circularity, in the second, infinite regress. Thus, it would be impossible to compare the quality of the standards of different arguments' fields. As a consequence, for example, we would have no reason to prefer Psychology to Astrology. At this level, incommensurability means incomparability between fields, and also between argumentation belonging to different fields.

But Willard would also establish incommensurability as the structural impossibility of deciding on certain arguments: the idea that argument appraisal depends on those standards that determine the practice of argumentation within a given field implies that we cannot decide on arguments belonging to fields which are alien to us because their standards are also alien. At this level, incommensurability is not only a thesis about appraisal but also about interpretation, because to be alien to a field's standards for argument appraisal is tantamount to being unable to understand its related practices as argumentation.

In what follows, I will try to show that this position is untenable in itself and also that Toulmin's model is not committed to this sort of relativism, but rather it could represent an excellent antidote against it.

3. *REASON*, *WARRANT* AND *CLAIM* AS CONSTITUTIVE ELEMENTS OF ARGUMENTATION

The Speech Act of Arguing: *Reasons* and *Claims*

The normativity involved in our use of the concept 'argumentation' implies that, whichever the field, we distinguish argumentation from other types of speech acts by stressing two main features. First, when we argue we do not merely try to communicate beliefs, but also try to induce certain beliefs. And secondly, that inducement is conducted by reasons. Because of that, argumentation is usually defined as an attempt at rational persuasion, that is, persuasion by means of reasons.[5] Thus, in order to interpret a piece of discourse as argumentation, we have to recognise, at least, the belief to be induced and the reason by means of which this belief is aimed to be induced, whether or not either of them is explicit in the actual performance of the discourse. In this sense, to say that a given discourse is argumentation implies that we already interpret that discourse as instantiating, at least partially, the form "reason, so claim". That is, we do not "discover" reasons and claims after acknowledging a piece of discourse as argumentation. Rather, we interpret a piece of discourse as argumentation because we interpret it as an attempt at persuading someone of a claim because of a reason. In that sense, *reasons* and *claims* are constitutive elements of argumentation. Whenever we take it that two propositions play respectively the role of a claim and its reason in a given discourse, we are interpreting that discourse as argumentation.

On the other hand, to acknowledge something as a claim or as a reason does only require being able to acknowledge certain intentional attitudes, namely, claiming and supporting a claim, whether or not this support seems sound to us. Otherwise, we would only be able to acknowledge reasons when they seem good to us. But then, we would only acknowledge arguments when they seem good to us, and the question of relativism would vanish from its very beginning: there would be no argument which is good within a field but bad within another. Therefore, if we do not want to rule out relativism too quickly, we must agree that we are able to recognise reasons even if they are not good reasons. But this means that we recognise reasons and claims, not because of their logical function in argumentation, but rather because of their communicative function in discourse, namely, that of accomplishing the intentional attitudes of claiming and supporting a claim.[6] Therefore, what enables us to interpret a piece of discourse as argumentation is not our acquaintance with the field the argument comes from and its standards for justification. It is our ability to recognise reasons and claims in the above sense.

But this does not suffice for assuring the possibility of argument appraisal, and this is the other aspect of the relativist challenge. We will need another element that is also constitutive of argumentation and that enables us to explain its justificatory power: the *warrant*.

A Proposed Conception of *Warrants*

Toulmin defines *warrants* as "general, hypothetical statements which can act as bridges (between datum and claim) and authorise the sort of step to which our

---

[5] In Bermejo-Luque (2004) I have argued that this is the only intelligible meaning of "rational persuasion".

[6] In Snoeck-Henkemans (2002) and Houtlosser (2002), there are interesting analyses of the ways English speakers can perform/recognise intentions of claiming and supporting a claim.

particular argument commits us" (1958, p. 98).[7] In order to distinguish *warrants* from *reasons*—something that is particularly significant for his proposal—Toulmin also says that reasons "are appealed to explicitly, warrants implicitly" (1958, p. 100).[8] So it seems that generality and implicitness are two key features of *warrants*.

On the other hand, he says that the difference between *warrants* and *backings* is that "statements of warrants . . . are hypothetical, bridge-like statements, but the backings for warrants can be expressed in the form of categorical statements of fact" (1958, p. 105). Yet, as D. Hample has pointed out, grammatical differences do not necessarily amount to functional ones (1977, p. 2). Pointing to a functional distinction, D. Hitchcock explains that "the warrant is the person's justification for inferring the claim from those grounds. [By contrast] a challenger may ask for justification of the warrant, to which the answer will be a proposed backing for the warrant" (2003b, p. 485).

But I find this attempt at providing a functional distinction between *warrants* and *backings* rather problematic: which sort of "justification for our inferences" would provide warrants? It could only be epistemic justification: someone may be morally justified in inferring whatsoever because of his sorrow, but this by no means is a way to warrant his claims. So, if warrants justify the inferences, not the acts of inferring, they should be reasons for the corresponding inference claims. But, if warrants "justify" our inferences in this sense, every argument contains another argument, namely the argument "warrant, so inference claim". But then, we would need a new warrant to justify our inference from our warrant-reason-for-the-inference to our inference claim, and this warrant would be another reason with a new warrant to bridge the new gap, and so on. Thus, we would never be entitled to infer a claim from a reason if warrants, as bridges between reason and claim, should bridge the gap as justifications for our inferences.

Actually, why should any justification of the inference, as an inference rule or as a general statement, stand necessarily implicit in arguments?

The inference claim is not a justification of the step from reason to claim, but the explicitation of this step. When the inference claim is true (or highly plausible, etc), the argument justifies a claim that *p* is true (or highly plausible, etc) because its

---

[7] Toulmin says that *warrants* can be written as the corresponding conditional of every argument that renders it formally valid, but he considers that the proper way to make them explicit is: "Data such as D entitle one to draw conclusions, or make claims, such as C" (1958, p.98). Hitchcock among others has objected that "Toulmin equivocates on whether a warrant is a statement or a rule", but he considers that "the equivocation is harmless, since a warrant-statement is the verbal expression of a warrant-rule" (2003b, p. 484).

[8] Hample (1977, p. 1) takes the following citation from *The Uses of Argument* to show that Toulmin himself would not seem to consider implicitness as an essential feature of warrants: "any argument can be expressed in the form 'Data; warrant; so conclusion' and so become formally valid" (1958, p. 119). But Hample's argument does not work: nothing prevents Toulmin from saying that this is a new argument which has another warrant, a formal one as it corresponds to a formally valid argument—namely, *modus ponens*—which is, again, implicit in it.

reason is true (or highly plausible, etc). When we use a warrant, what we do is to infer a claim from a reason.

Following a well known argument by L. Carroll (1895), W. Grennan has shown that inference claims are necessarily implicit in arguments because they cannot be incorporated in them without changing the meaning of the former argument. As argued above, any argument would shape the form "reason (A), so claim (B)", thus, for any argument:

> . . . the inference claim is "if A then B". Now suppose we add "if A then B" to the original argument, in an attempt to make the inference claim explicit. The argument form is now "A, if A then B; so B". But the inference claim for the revised argument is "if A, and if A then B, then B". If we now add this, we change the stated argument again, generating a new inference claim. Thus, an infinite regress begins when we try to make it explicit in the argument. (Grennan, 1997, p. 69)

Contrary to inference claims, general rules are not "bridges" between reasons and claims. One reason is that there are several rules of inference suitable for any given argument. Take a well-known example by M. Scriven (1976, p. 166): "She's red-haired, so she's probably quick-tempered". As Scriven observes, the general rule "if a person is red-haired, then that person will probably be quick-tempered" is not the only one that could justify the argument's inference: for example, "if a woman is red-haired, then she will probably be quick-tempered" could do it as well. Indeed, there are many more possible candidates: "if someone has something red in his body, then that person will probably be quick-tempered", "if someone belongs to a minority because of the colour of his hair, then that person will probably be quick-tempered", etc. This will depend on the aspect of the reason on which the general rule would pivot.

In addition, every general rule can have conditions of rebuttal applicable to the particular case stated by the argument. For example, the rule "if a woman is red-haired then she will probably be quick-tempered" may fail to justify our inferring that someone is quick-tempered because she is red-haired, if she is not a woman but a baby, or if she is dead, or a calm person, etc.

For both reasons, general rules are not direct licenses to obtain the claim from the reason. Rather, they behave as reasons for inference claims.[9] When they are good reasons, they justify the inference, but they are not "bridges" in the sense that inference claims are.

---

[9] That is, they may constitute arguments' backings as much as "categorical statements of fact" because, as Hample pointed out, grammatical differences do not necessarily amount to functional ones. Within this picture, the backing, as a reason for the inference claim, can be either a general rule or a categorical statement of fact, and it is required when the inference itself is challenged. Analogously, a rebuttal would turn out to be a defeater of the backing as a reason for the inference claim.

The Appraisal of Arguments

As inference claims, warrants are not only necessarily implicit, but they are also constitutive of arguments. Thus, having a warrant is not a property just of good arguments: every argument has a warrant insofar as every argument patterns the form "reason, so claim". The difference between good and bad arguments is not that good arguments have warrants, but rather that good arguments have warrants that are true, or highly acceptable (and reasons of this sort too, so that the arguments justify their claims that a target proposition is true, highly acceptable, etc), whereas bad arguments have false or insufficiently acceptable warrants and/or reasons. Thus, the values of reason and warrant determine which is the modal term that should qualify the claim for which we argue, and consequently, they also determine the justificatory power of the argument. In that sense, reasons and warrants supply the field-dependent criteria that regulate the use of a particular modal term, whereas the force of this modal term specifies the pragmatic role of the claim within its context.

Following Toulmin's analysis of modal qualifiers, we can say that the value of a proposition corresponds to the degree of force of the modal term that should qualify this proposition when asserted (in our case, either as a reason, as a warrant or as the conclusion of the argument). Actually, according to Toulmin's pragmatic account of modal terms in general, and of the truth-operator in particular (see, for example, (1958, p. 81)), we may assume that the value that corresponds to a proposition because of the modal term that should qualify the corresponding assertion is a truth-value, i.e. a measure of the pragmatic force that we are entitled to allot on this assertion.

According to this interpretation, the modal qualification that corresponds to a claim *c*, i.e. the degree of force that we are entitled to assign to the corresponding proposition when it is presented as the claim for which we argue, would be the resulting value of a function whose variables are the values of the reason *r* adduced for *c* and the value of the warrant that makes of *r* a reason for *c*. This function can be specified in different ways, but its role is to make explicit the meaning of each modal qualifier as "an explicit reference to the degree of force which our data confer on our claim in virtue of our warrant" (1958, p. 101).

But how should we determine the value of a warrant, so conceived? In my view, we should interpret the warrant as the corresponding material conditional, which is to be valued under the argumentative conditions in which it arises, namely, that the reason alleged in the argument (whose content is the antecedent of the conditional) is supposed to be true or highly acceptable, and also that we have not already independently determined the real value of the claim for which we argue (whose content is the consequent of the conditional). These conditions suffice to free us from the paradoxes of material implication when appraising warrants. To determine the truth-value of a material conditional under these conditions is to determine the degree of positive relevance of the antecedent for the consequent. And to accomplish this task, general rules as much as general statements of fact can be of great help as reasons for this conditional. If, according to them, the conditional happens to be true or highly acceptable, the warrant will correspondingly authorise our inference to such and such degree.

A Holdover from Deductivism

I am not very sure about Toulmin's own position regarding the features of warrants, for he frequently insists that warrants are general. But he also characterises them as necessarily implicit, and as bridging the gap between reason and claim. Moreover, as I will try to show in this section, the idea that warrants are justifications for inferences is a holdover from deductivism, the epistemological position which is at the core of Toulmin's criticisms in *The Uses of Argument*. In order to give priority to this aspect of his work, I propose to conceive of warrants as the corresponding inference claim of each argument, that is, as the particular conditional that licenses the step from a particular reason to a particular claim. In my view, then, a good reason to favour a conception of warrants as inference claims is to be faithful to Toulmin's goal of fighting deductivism.

Why do we need justification for our inferences? The obvious answer is that we need it in case they are challenged, and this answer is perfectly sound. By contrast, the idea that good arguments need justified inferences is a holdover from deductivism. Within this epistemological model, to justify a given proposition is not only to show that this proposition is true because of a given reason, but also to show that this proposition will always be true if the reason is true, no matter how the world happens to be. This demand was accomplished by demanding a necessarily true inference claim, usually, an inference claim that is true in virtue of its form. Accordingly, cogent non-valid arguments were supposed to have implicit premises that would render them valid; usually, formally valid, in virtue of a self-evident true inference claim like *modus ponens*, or *universal instantiation*.

The abandonment of deductivism meant not to demand necessarily true inference claims. But still, we might feel that our claims are not sufficiently justified if our inference claims are not themselves justified. Yet, the truth is that, in order to justify our claims, we do not need our inference claims to be necessary, or justified. We just need them to be true, or highly plausible. The inference claim enables us to pass from reason to claim; if it is true, or highly plausible, the claim will be justified because of the reason. Second-level justification may be desirable in certain cases, but it does not prevent us from falsity. On the one hand, we can always demand third-level justification, fourth-level justification, and so on. On the other hand, deductivism just postpones the problem: the question of determining the truth-value of the inference remains open, whether we take it to be a warrant or a missing premise.

4. THE RHETORICAL ROLE OF FIELDS WITHIN ARGUMENTATION THEORY

Fields as Providers of Truth-values

According to the view proposed in this work, *reason*, *claim* and *warrant* are constitutive of argumentation, and the justificatory power of arguments depends on the truth-values of their reasons and warrants. All we need in order to appraise an argument is to determine these truth-values.

Our acquaintance with an argument's field may make much easier the task of determining certain propositions' truth-values: for example, if we are physicians, it may be easier to determine the truth-value of P: "Inherited mutations in the bone morphogenetic protein receptor 2 gene are associated with primary pulmonary hypertension"[10] But according to the present account, there would be no structural impossibility for a non-physician to decide on this proposition. The non-physician will probably have more difficulty in determining its truth-value, he will need some more information, new arguments, explanations or whatever. But they all must be available because they are the means by which others—for example, certain physicians—came to know that P is true.

In any case, 'difficulty' is not 'structural impossibility', rather the opposite: only that which is possible can be difficult to get. The field of Medicine provides the truth-values of certain propositions, but it does not provide standards for argument appraisal in any sense whatsoever. The non-physician is not in need of standards that he cannot achieve because he is alien to the field; he is only in need of information. Thus, strong relativism, which conceives fields as providers of standards for appraisal, and thus, is committed to incommensurability as the structural impossibility of deciding on certain arguments, loses its grounds.

Two Rhetorical Roles of Fields as Providers of Truth-values

Consider J. Wenzel's view (1982): "A field of argument is an integrated complex of concepts, propositions and arguments, persisting over time, directed to shared explanatory goals, embodying shared judgmental standards, held consensually by initiates of a discipline" (p. 211). I think that this conception is perfectly acceptable. Yet, obviously, not every argument would have a field in this sense. Thus, according to this conception, fields would not provide standards for argument evaluation; otherwise those arguments without a field could not be appraised.

We can assume that arguments belong to fields insofar as fields are subject matter, intellectual disciplines, or, in general, systems of propositions. According to this characterization, fields would accomplish a rhetorical role in Argumentation

[10] This proposition may justify inference claims like "if John has a mutation in the bone morphogenetic protein receptor 2 gene, then he will probably develop pulmonary hypertension".

Theory. They would play this role at two levels. The first level would have to do with the determination of the persuasive power of arguments. In this respect, to assign a given argument to a certain field would make possible its appraisal according to the truth-values that the audience normally addressed in that field attributes to its reason and warrant. For example, if we are interested in the effectiveness or suitability of a given argument for a particular audience, namely, the normal audience of a given field, it might be useful to appraise this argument according to the beliefs commonly held by that audience. These beliefs will likely be accessible by reference to the things the field, as a system of propositions with an ascription of truth-values, has established.

Consequently, when someone determines that a given argument belongs to a given field, this very assignment usually determines the truth-values that she attributes to the propositions involved in the argument. In those cases, the field behaves as the matrix to which the question of further justifications is addressed, and where these questions are supposed to be solved—either at the present, or in the future. This assumption does not imply that the field provides standards for appraising the argument; it only means that the matters that constitute the field are the subject matter of the argument. If we do not assign the argument to any field, or if the very field is in question (for example, if we disregard its attribution of truth-values), we will have to determine the truth-values of the propositions involved independently of the field. In this case, we would only lack a given assignment of truth-values, not standards to appraise the argument.

This aspect of fields as providers of truth-values would explain Zarefsky's observation that "scientists might dismiss certain data or claims as unscientific while another discipline might embrace the very same data and claims" (1982, p. 195). This disagreement would not point to a set of different standards for argument evaluation, but only to a divergent assignment of truth-values for the propositions involved in it.

The second level of the rhetorical role of fields within Argumentation Theory is a heuristic one. In this respect, an assignment of an argument to a given field determines the interpretation of the argument itself. In particular, it may enable us to understand which are its real claims and reasons. For example, it is much easier to determine what is going on if we realise that a certain debate about medical practices is not legal but moral. The reason is that many terms, like 'good' or 'advisable', also have force and criteria of use. And these criteria, that is, the reasons that justify our use of such terms, vary according to the field: something might be advisable for legal reasons, but not for moral ones. In certain circumstances it may be advantageous to pretend that a given reason has moral consequences when, in fact, it just has legal ones.

In this respect, T. Goodnight's article 'The personal, technical and public spheres of argument: A speculative inquiry into the art of public deliberation' (1982) provides insightful examples of the strategic importance of assigning a piece of discourse to a given field. According to my account, this effect may be a consequence of two causes. On the one hand, when we determine that a given argument belongs to a given field, we point to the way we should understand it. On the other hand, such an assignment also determines the alleged audience that is to evaluate it, i.e. those experts who are supposed to know what the truth-values of the propositions involved are.

Toulmin's Views on Fields as Providers of Standards for Argument Appraisal: Logical versus Epistemological Normativity

But what about Toulmin's own views about field-dependency as actually outlined in *The Uses of Argument*? As I have tried to show, the idea of field-dependency regarding the criteria for the use of modal qualifiers would just mean that, in order to say that a claim is morally or physically necessary, we have to give reasons (with their corresponding warrants) belonging to the field of morals, or to the field of physics, respectively. Yet, at the end of *The Uses of Argument*, Toulmin seems to identify the idea of field-dependency regarding the criteria for the use of modal terms with the idea of field-dependency regarding the standards for argument evaluation. I think that this identification results from what Toulmin takes to be one of the main consequences of his criticism of traditional logic as a normative theory of argument, namely, the need for a "rapprochement between logic and epistemology, which will become not two subjects but one only" (1958, p. 254). It is because of this idea that he would come to the view that field-dependency regarding the criteria for the use of modal terms, i.e. the fact that the reasons for our modally qualified claims may belong to fields, shows that argument goodness is a matter of field-dependent standards.

According to the conception of warrants proposed above, Toulmin would have shown indeed that inference goodness is a matter of content, not a matter of form. That is, he would be grounding a non-formal conception of logic as a normative theory of inference, pointing out that formal inference is just a particular case of material inference. But this result would not imply by itself a rejection of the distinction between a normative theory of inference, i.e. logic as traditionally understood (whether formal or not), and a normative theory of argument, i.e. epistemology as traditionally understood. For example, Toulmin's analysis of modal qualifiers would constitute a means to determine epistemological normativity because to determine that a claim has been correctly qualified requires judging the support that the reason adduced for this claim is able to confer on it, and this is not only a matter of the truth-value of the warrant, but also of the truth-value of the reason.

Nonetheless, Toulmin identifies 'validity', which is, in principle, just a logical concept, with 'argument goodness'. Because of that, he says that "what has to be recognised first is that validity is an intra-field, not an inter-field notion" (1958, p. 255). That is how, at the end of *The Uses of Argument*, his well-grounded idea that the criteria for the use of modal terms are field-dependent turns into the idea that validity is an intra-field notion. From that view, there is just a little step to the view that fields provide "standards" for the appraisal of arguments.

On the other hand, in *Human Understanding* Toulmin characterised fields as rational enterprises, or more specifically, as intellectual disciplines. Consequently, in his view, there would be arguments that do not belong to any field, namely, those arguments that can hardly be said to belong to an "intellectual discipline". But this does not seem to pose a problem respecting the possibility of their appraisal. Consequently, it would seem difficult for Toulmin to work out a role for fields as providers of standards for argument evaluation. Anyhow, I rather think that such a conception of fields coheres with the idea that fields constitute sets of propositions with an assignment of truth-values. The truth-values attributed to each proposition can be either the result of those arguments that, through time, have constituted the *corpus* of the field, or a matter of stipulations, axioms or primitives of this field as an intellectual discipline.

5. CONCLUDING REMARKS

According to my proposed reading of *The Uses of Argument*, Toulmin's distinction between the force and the criteria of use of modal terms would just stress the fact that, in order to determine that a claim is legally plausible, we have to give reasons belonging to the fields of law and jurisprudence, whereas in order to determine that a claim is mathematically impossible, we have to give reasons belonging to Mathematics. The criteria that determine the particular use of a modal term may vary from field to field, but this does not mean that each field provides its own standards for argument appraisal, it only means that the reasons that credit a particular modal qualification of a claim belong to fields. Consequently, it would make no sense to conceive of fields as (incommensurable) sets of standards for rationality.

Thus, the field-dependency of arguments would mean that the reasons supporting our modally qualified claims may belong to fields as established sets of propositions with an assignment of truth-values. Additionally, for an assertion to count as a reason for a target claim we must make sense of a warrant licensing the step from this assertion to the claim. This warrant may also belong to a field, and its truth-value would determine the extent to which the argument is *logically* good. In that sense, the whole point of stressing *field-dependency* would be to give an account of *validity* as a material, rather than as a formal matter. This is something which, in my view, is at the core of Toulmin's criticism of classical logic as a tool for argument appraisal.

In any case, if we agree that the value of an argument is a function of the value of its reason and warrant, it seems difficult to find room for relativism: our assignments of truth-values to the corresponding propositions can only be justified by further arguments. Indeed, whatever the field, it is both our duty and our inclination as rational beings to do so.

Acknowledgements

I wish to thank Professor Joseph Wenzel for his interesting and detailed comments on the first version of this paper. I was very pleased to have him as the commentator of this paper at the 2005 OSSA Conference. In subsequent exchanges, I have also had very good comments and suggestions from Professor David Hitchcock and Professor Robert Pinto. They all greatly helped me to improve that first version and to clarify my position. On the other hand, that version won the Blair Essay Prize and for this reason, it was published in the journal *Informal Logic*, whose editors have kindly given me permission to publish the present revised version in this volume. Finally, the work presented in this article has been financially supported by a fellowship from the Spanish Government, Ministerio de Educación y Ciencia, FPU programme.

CHAPTER 7

JAMES B. FREEMAN

SYSTEMATIZING TOULMIN'S WARRANTS: AN EPISTEMIC APPROACH

Department of Philosophy, Hunter College of The City University of New York, 695 Park Avenue, New York, NY 10021, USA
E-mail: jfreeman@hunter.cuny.edu

ABSTRACT: Relevance of premises to conclusion can be explicated through Toulmin's notion of warrant, understood as an inference rule, albeit not necessarily formal. A normative notion of relevance requires the warrant to be reliable. To determine reliability, we propose a fourfold classification of warrants into *a priori*, empirical, institutional, and evaluative, with further subdivisions possible. This classification has its ancestry in classical rhetoric and recent epistemology. Distinctive to each type of warrant is the mode by which such connections are intuitively discovered and the grounds on which we ultimately justify them. The classification of warrants is thus epistemic. We illustrate the difference by contrasting empirical physical with institutional intuition, and argue for the advantages of this approach over Toulmin's conception of field dependence.

KEYWORDS: Warrant; backing; relevance; intuition; reliability; presumptive reliability

1. INTRODUCTION

We hold with many in informal logic that for an argument to be cogent, its premises must be acceptable, relevant to its conclusion, and constitute grounds adequate for accepting the conclusion. Toulmin's model suggests an explication of relevance. To ask the warrant generating question—How do you get there?—of information put forward as data to support a claim is to ask in the first instance why those data are relevant to the claim. An apropos answer Toulmin calls a warrant.

2. WARRANTS, PREMISE RELEVANCE, AND PROBLEMS

Toulmin's notion of warrant, however, is problematic. Warrants are "rules, principles, inference-licences, ... general, hypothetical statements, which can act as bridges"

D. Hitchcock and B. Verheij (eds.), Arguing on the Toulmin Model: New Essays in Argument Analysis and Evaluation, 87–101.

(1958, p. 98).[1] But rules and inference licences are not statements (although corresponding to an inference rule is a generalized hypothetical statement). In this paper, a warrant is an inference rule, albeit not necessarily formal, demonstrative, deductively valid. This accords with Toulmin's indication that to state a warrant more explicitly than just "If D, then C", one may cast it in the form: Given data such as D, one may take it that claims such as C, (1958, p. 98) i.e. as an inference rule. Given this understanding of warrant, we can begin to explicate the notion of premise relevance. As a first approximation, we may say that a premise is relevant to a conclusion just in case there is a warrant which licences the move from the premise to the conclusion. This will not do. For given any premise P and conclusion C, what is to prevent one from simply formulating the inference rule,

Given that a premise such as	P,
One may take it that a conclusion such as	C?

On this explication, any premise will be relevant to any conclusion—just formulate the inference licence associated with the argument. Considerations such as these led us to argue in (1992) that we should regard relevance as a ternary relation between a premise, a conclusion, and a set of inference rules. P is relevant to C with respect to **I** if and only if there are inference rules in **I** licencing moves from P (together perhaps with members of a set **S** of statements) to intermediate conclusions, and from these to C in some finite number of steps. If **I** contains a rule allowing us to get from P alone to C in one step, we say that P is immediately relevant to C with respect to **I**. Should taking P together with certain other statements or taking several steps be necessary, given the contents of **I**, P is mediately relevant to C with respect to **I**.

In (1992), we regarded both senses of relevance as descriptive. Saying that P is relevant to C with respect to **I** makes no comment on whether the inference rules in **I** are valid or reliable. Not all of them need be. A set of inference rules may contain the fallacy of affirming the consequent. For P to be "really" relevant to C, the inference rule or rules to which one appeals to licence the move must all be reliable in one sense demanding explication. Toulmin recognizes this in presenting his model, when he acknowledges that although one may see why the proffered warrant explains relevance, one may question whether in general from data such as D, one make take it that C. One may then ask for backing for the warrants, "other assurances, without which the warrants themselves would possess neither authority nor currency" (1958, p. 103).

The first point that Toulmin makes after presenting this characterization of backing in (1958) is that backing is field dependent. In different fields, warrants will be backed in different ways.

---

[1] In (1996, pp. 126-129), Johnson discusses and documents the confusing variety of ways that Toulmin *et al* characterize warrants in (1984) and its accompanying *Teaching Guide*.

> 'A whale will be (i.e. *is classifiable as*) a mammal', 'A Bermudan will be (*in the eyes of the law*) a Briton', 'A Saudi Arabian will be (*found to be*) a Muslim'—the words in parentheses indicate what these differences are. One warrant is defended by relating it to a system of taxonomical classification, another by appealing to the statutes governing the nationality of people born in the British colonies, the third by referring to the statistics which record how religious beliefs are distributed among people of different nationalities. (1958, p. 104, italics in original)

The issue of field dependence is a problematic feature of Toulmin's model for several reasons. First, identifying what field a warrant (and so its backing) belongs to may be problematic, as Johnson complains.

Given that	*x* is a society that conducts its public affairs in the style of a surrealistic painting,
One may take it that	*x* can be regarded as worse than totalitarian.

(Compare Johnson, 1996, p. 131.) What is worse, Johnson urges, is that the whole notion of a field is vague.

> Law and science qualify, of course. Does astrology? Does common sense? Does philosophy? And what happens when, as is often enough the case, an arguer provides grounds from different fields? Obviously no one warrant will suffice to link the grounds with the claim, unless the already nebulous concept of a field is to be extended to allow for *super-fields*! (1996, p. 134)

Part of the problem may involve the connotations of "field". Is a field what in (2005a) we called an authority-conferring field, a formal or informal body of received knowledge and technique, (Compare Coady, 1992, pp. 278-279.), open to revision, capable of being transmitted to others who could then be certified as achieving a level of competence in that field? Branches of science and skilled trades would count as fields in this sense. But what about morals or more generally issues of evaluation, which may not be generally recognized as an authority-conferring field? In (1958, p. 104), Toulmin speaks of the field of morals.

Beyond these problems with the notion of field is Toulmin's emphasis that we need to look to a field to legitimize warrants used in arguments within that field. The standards for argument evaluation are field dependent. Toulmin makes this plain in (1958, pp. 36-38), where he contrasts force with criteria or canons: "All the *canons* for the criticism and assessment of arguments...are in practice field-dependent, while all our terms of assessment are field-invariant in their *force*" (1958, p. 38, italics in original). We may expect that warrants in different fields are backed in different ways. How then do we assess whether a warrant is properly backed? Are there canons for this? Are those canons themselves field-dependent or field-transcendent?

Toulmin indicates another potentially problematic feature of warrants and backing. Just as the warrant is implicit in a move from data to claim, but may be made explicit, so the backing for a warrant made explicit may and in some cases properly will be left implicit. As he notes, if one were to demand backing for every warrant, then should Jones present an argument employing warrant W_1, that warrant would be challenged. In a supplementary argument for W_1, Jones employs a warrant W_2. That in turn is challenged.... To avoid an infinite regress, "Some warrants must be accepted provisionally without further challenge", taking for granted "the existence of considerations such as would establish the acceptability of the most reliable warrants" (1958, p. 106). A stock of provisionally accepted field-dependent warrants seems a far cry from seeing logic as involving canons for argument appraisal recognized as correctly certifying arguments as deductively valid or inductively strong antecedently to evaluating arguments within a given field. That we must accept certain warrants provisionally, taking for granted that the most reliable warrants can be shown acceptable raises some significant epistemological questions. Do we simply provisionally accept certain warrants or are some warrants accept*able* in a basic way, analogous to acceptable basic premises? If the acceptable warrants are those most reliable, how do we recognize these warrants?

Given these problems with the notion of field, we propose a distinctly different approach to warrant reliability, an epistemic approach. We ask first whether we may sort warrants in an epistemically fruitful way. In (2000) and (2005a), we propose a fourfold typology of statements: necessary statements, descriptions, interpretations, and evaluations. The ancestry of the description/interpretation/evaluation distinction is in classical rhetoric (See Kruger, 1975, p. 137.). We add the category of necessary statements to honor Kruger's case that analytic statements should be accorded their own separate classification (1975, p. 138), but find necessary statements to accord a properly broader category. We may apply this classification to warrants with one modification. We understand descriptions and interpretations both to be contingent statements. Descriptions are extensional while interpretations are intensional.[2] This has implications for how we understand universally generalized conditionals. Where such a statement is a description, it does not support a subjunctive conditional, whereas an interpretation does. Consider an arbitrary warrant. The associated generalized conditional is not simply asserting that there is no case in which one is given premises of the sort $P_1, P_2, \ldots, P_n$ and one may not take it that a conclusion of the sort C. Rather, it is making the much stronger assertion that *were* one given premises of the sort $P_1, P_2, \ldots, P_n$, one *would* be entitled to take it that a conclusion of the sort C. The associated generalized conditional is subjunctive and the statement thus an interpretation. The category of description then does not apply to warrants.

---

[2] Thus we recognize many types of modalities, not just alethic.

Our classification of statements is epistemically suggestive. Clearly in many instances one comes to know a necessary truth in a manner different from one's coming to know a moral truth or an empirical truth supporting a subjunctive, such as a causal law. This has a moral for warrants also, as we shall develop shortly. How does one then come to acquire warrants, i.e. to make inferences according to a certain pattern? This may happen in three ways. First, one might receive the warrant on the word of someone else, as one might receive personal testimony. Such a mode of acquiring warrants may seem less than satisfactory. Ordinarily, when we take a step from premises to conclusion, we "see" how the premises are connected to the conclusion. If we were simply to accept an inference pattern on someone's word, however, we need have no such insight. If we do, such insight may be a matter of immediate intuitive recognition, as when one recognizes the legitimacy of an elementary deductive inference rule. Immediate acceptance upon intuitive apprehension of an inferential connection is the second way one may acquire a warrant. By contrast, upon the suggestion of a connection, one may defer acceptance until the warrant is somehow properly defended, which amounts to defending the associated generalized conditional properly. Accepting the warrant upon defense is the third way of acquiring warrants.

How does the mechanism by which one acquires a warrant bear on its reliability? Taking one's word, under certain circumstances, is a reliable warrant-generating mechanism. If the proponent has reliably come to make inferences according to the pattern of the warrant–i.e. the mechanism forming this inference habit is overall reliable and no defeaters are operative in this case–and if the recipient has reliably received his vouching for the warrant, i.e. she recognizes that he is sincerely vouching for the warrant, that there is a presumption of reliability for his having acquired this inference habit, she understands what the proponent has said and accepts the inference licence on this basis[3], there is a presumption for the reliability of the warrant from her perspective. But for the proponent to come to hold the warrant reliably, he must have either reliably intuited the inferential connection which the warrant expresses, seen that the warrant is properly defended, or reliably received the warrant from someone else. Obviously, the transmission chain is finite. So at some point, we shall reach a proponent who has either accepted the warrant immediately or on the basis of an argument. Under what circumstances would the proponent have reliably acquired the warrant? As we have already suggested, the mechanisms generating beliefs properly classifiable as necessary statements, interpretations, or evaluations are distinct. Clearly the same should be true for necessary, interpretive, and evaluative warrants. Obviously, for each type, we have two cases to consider. The case of immediate intuitive grasping is primary, however. Of those warrants grasped, i.e. discovered in a certain way, in some cases the immediate grasping may be sufficient to establish that the warrant is reliable or at least that one may presume it reliable. In other cases, argumentation may be

[3] We have discussed these issues in much greater detail for acquiring beliefs in Chapter 10 of (2005a), especially sections 10.1-10.3.

necessary to justify reliability. If we classify warrants according to their mode of immediate apprehension, we can later subdivide the classification according to needed justification. We have carved nature at a joint. We hold that more than three types of immediate or intuitive apprehension are involved. This means that we can provide a more fine grained classification of warrants than just necessary, interpretive, and evaluative. We present our subdivision in the next section.

3. TYPES OF WARRANT AND TYPES OF INTUITION

Let us agree to call modes of immediately apprehending general connections, be they expressed in generalized conditionals or warrants, modes of intuition. We hold that we may distinguish types of intuition according to the types of warrant they grasp. Within interpretive warrants, we hold that we may distinguish two types involving radically distinct epistemic conditions. Consider

Given that	x is a beam of electrons moving perpendicularly to a magnetic field,
One may take it that	x is deflected.

(Compare Burks, 1951, p. 367.) This is an empirical warrant reflecting an empirically discerned causal connection. By contrast, consider

Given that	x has been bequeathed a sum of y dollars in z's will,
One may take it that	x will receive y dollars in due time after z's demise.

This warrant rests not on a connection one might discern by observation, but upon one's understanding a connection brought about through statute law. Systems of statute law include systems of constitutive rules. As opposed to regulative rules which specify limits within which certain already defined acts or practices may be appropriately performed, constitutive rules define those practices. What is it to score a goal in soccer, to be a British subject, to be classifiable as a mammal within a certain system of taxonomy? These are constituted by the rules of soccer, the statutes defining British nationality, the specifications of the system of taxonomy itself. Searle calls such systems of constitutive rules institutions (1969, p. 51). We call such warrants institutional. It should be clear that the empirical intuition involved in grasping empirical warrants is distinctly different from the institutional intuition involved in grasping institutional warrants. The former is based on discovering connections in the external world, while the latter is based on learning sets of constitutive rules.

We may further subdivide empirical warrants, since they need not concern only connections in the inanimate physical world.

Given that	*x* has a strong commitment to human rights,
One may take it probably that	*x* actively supports some human rights organization

concerns a connection in the empirical world, but one based on a conscious intention of a human being. We may classify these as personal as opposed to physical warrants. However, for the purposes of this paper, we need not be concerned with this further distinction. Also, we need not here concern ourselves with whether the class of necessary warrants needs to be further subdivided, for example into formal, semantic, and mathematical. We likewise need not inquire here whether the class of evaluative warrants needs to be subdivided in a way including intrinsic, deontic, aretaic, and aesthetic warrants. The four types of warrants–necessary, empirical, institutional, and evaluative–clearly involve different epistemic mechanisms for their apprehension.

We thus hold that corresponding to each of these types of warrants is a distinct type or mode of intuition. Hence we distinguish *a priori*, empirical, institutional, and evaluative intuition. We believe that for each of these types of intuition, we may identify conditions under which it grasps warrants in a presumptively reliable way, certifying these warrants as presumptively reliable. Although we are issuing a promissory note on this claim at this point, for our collateral we note that we have argued the parallel claim for necessary, empirical, institutional, and evaluative generalizations in (2005a, Chapters 6-9). Warrants grasped through these presumptively reliable employments of intuition are properly basic on analogy with properly basic beliefs such as those of sense perception in the absence of defeaters. We also hold that in certain cases, although intuition may grasp a suggested connection, one may also recognize that this intuitive grasping is not in itself sufficient to presume the reliability of the warrant and thus defense or argumentation for the warrant is required. But in each of these cases, the type of warrant involved determines the type of argument appropriate and the conditions necessary to establish a presumption for the reliability of the warrant. Limitations of space prohibit our discussing each mode of intuition. However, in the next section, we shall contrast empirical physical intuition with institutional intuition over their grasping of warrants, and over the conditions indicating when such grasping is properly basic and if not, what sort of argumentation is required.

4. PHYSICAL VERSUS INSTITUTIONAL INTUITION

I believe we may analyze the operation of physical intuition as the imposition of an interpretive category on a recognized incidence of covariation. The paradigm case is efficient causation. Experience presents us with instances of one property, condition, state of affairs uniformly, standardly, or at least frequently being associated with another property, condition, or state of affairs. A match's being struck is standardly accompanied by its lighting. This is covariation. By imposing the category of efficient causation, physical intuition formulates a causal hypothesis, seeing the antecedent events constituting the independent variable and the consequent events as the dependent variable. Corresponding to this causal hypothesis, physical intuition also grasps a warrant—in this way it draws the moral from the observed covariation—allowing us to project or infer from the presence of the independent variable to the presence of the dependent variable. The observed covariation is the input for physical intuition, which is thus empirical.

Grasping a nomic connection by imposing the category of efficient causation is a creative act generating a new belief. This new belief is not inferred from reports of the observed covariation. Such observations pertain to the context of discovery, although they could be included within the context of justification. Thus the causal hypothesis is a basic belief and the corresponding warrant is also basic. However, neither belief nor warrant are properly basic. Although one may intuit a connection of causal dependency, ordinarily there will be a number of other relevant independent variables which might explain the occurrence of the dependent variable. Without ruling out the operation of those variables, one is not justified in accepting the causal hypothesis or inferring according to the corresponding warrant. But notice that this employment of physical intuition determines the nature of the argument for the acceptability of the causal hypothesis and the reliability of the corresponding warrant.

Does physical intuition ever generate properly basic beliefs or warrants? Consider the case where physical intuition imposes the category of natural kind. Experience presents us with a number of properties or conditions clustering together. Being an apple involves having a skin of a certain texture, flesh of a certain type, seeds of a certain appearance, a typical shape, and size within certain parameters. This also is covariation. By imposing the category of natural kind, some of these covariant properties will be deemed consequences of the causal "essence" of the natural kind. Hence one may infer from an object's being an instance of that kind to its having these properties, e.g.

Given that	x is an instance of the natural kind water,
One may take it that	x is odorless.

In (2005a),[4] we presented Kornblith's argument in (1993) for the reliability of certain features of these inferences. Presenting his argument is beyond our scope in this paper. But we do need to comment on how apprehending certain features of a natural kind as essential to the kind leads to making inferences based on those features. Kornblith quotes the psychologists Medin and Ortony, who claim that "people act as if their [natural kind] concepts contain essence placeholders that are filled with 'theories' about what the corresponding entities are" (Medin and Ortony, 1989, p. 186; quoted in Kornblith, 1993, p. 106). In filling in what is essential to the kind, these theories identify determinable features which are universal to the kind, for example mode of nutrition (as opposed to color) for a species of living thing. One identifies the actual determinate mode of nutrition associated with a given species by empirical observation of a few members of that species. Once ascertained, that determinate is projected, i.e. we make inferences according to the warrant that from something's being an instance of that natural kind we may take it that it has this particular determinate mode of nutrition.

Why do we regard natural kind warrants as basic? Consider: Do we reason from premises that the property is a determinate of a certain determinable, that the determinable is an essential property of the natural kind, and that the observed instances displaying this determinate are instances of this natural kind to the claim that if something were an instance of this kind, it would satisfy that determinate? We might adapt Hitchcock's argument against reconstructing enthymemes as arguments with missing premises here (1985, pp. 94-95). Such a reconstruction is not faithful to the phenomenology of the situation. We do not entertain such arguments. In seeing that something is an instance of a natural kind, one is seeing a pattern in what one views, a pattern involving an essence which identifies the observed determinate as belonging to the essence of the kind. Our apprehension that this determinate is projectable seems a basic, intuitive apprehension.

Are warrants thus grasped presumptively reliable? The reliability of the warrant is a function, at least in part, of the accuracy or verisimilitude of the theories filling the essence placeholder. (Compare Kornblith, 1993, p. 106.) A more reliable theoretical understanding of the natural kind will result in more reliable warrants. But in many cases, I believe we can presume the reliability of the theories filling the essence placeholder, for in many cases these theories will reflect current common understandings deriving from some combination of common knowledge and scientific opinion, and thus may have a significant degree of verisimilitude. In these cases warrants grasped intuitively through the imposition of a natural kind concept are presumptively reliable to a significant degree.

Institutional intuition, by contrast, grasps warrants by intuiting an inferential moral upon understanding a certain constitutive rule. To defend the view that a form of intuition operates to grasp at least some institutional warrants immediately and presumptively reliably, we need to ask how we learn such rules. This happens in two primary ways. We may assimilate such rules informally by tentatively engaging in

[4] See Chapter 8.6, 'Physical Subjunctives and Physical Intuition'.

the practice they constitute, having our understanding refined through the reinforcement or correction of others—we learn the rules of soccer by actually playing soccer. By contrast, we may consult some authoritative formulation of the rule—we learn who is a British subject by consulting the British Nationality Acts. Surely in many cases we informally learn constitutive rules immediately or intuitively. For example, we find by experience that certain moves are accepted as having scored a goal and by reflection come to apprehend what sort of performance constitutes scoring a goal.

The proper test for having informally learned the constitutive rules of a practice successfully is being able to engage in that practice correctly or recognize that others are correctly engaging in that practice. One need not be able to state the rules explicitly. To informally learn the rule is to acquire the warrant. Surely, from having learned the rule constituting scoring a goal in soccer, one would project from Jones' having kicked the ball into the net from the field that Jones had scored a goal. One's learning the rule and acquiring the warrant would be one and the same. Surely if one has learned the rules correctly, one's warrant is reliable. Better yet, the warrant is reliable to the degree that one has learned the rule correctly.

Again, it would seem that our learning some constitutive rule through our encountering some authoritative formulation of the rule would in many cases be immediate, as long as our understanding of the rule was immediate and straightforward.

Consider Toulmin's classic warrant

Given that	*x* was born in Bermuda,
One may take it that	*x* is a British subject.

To back this, as Toulmin points out, one may consult the relevant sections of the British Nationality Acts. Should those statutes include that those born in British crown colonies are British subjects, which seems quite unambiguous, given adult language comprehension, we understand the relevant clauses when we read them and grasp the corresponding warrant immediately, i.e. intuitively.

Under what circumstances is that warrant reliable? More modestly, under what circumstances may we presume that the warrant is reliable? According to Searle's speech act theory, the written formulation of the rule that one consults is an assertive. It asserts that certain constitutive rules have been agreed to or that certain provisions have been legally enacted. The assertive thus reports that another speech act has taken place, a declaration. According to Searle, a declaration "brings about the correspondence between the propositional content and reality, successful performance guarantees that the propositional content corresponds to the world" (1979, pp. 16-17). For the warrant to be reliable, the assertive must be true. One may presume the assertion true if one may presume that the source making the assertion is trustworthy. But the warrant must also reflect the propositional content of the declaration. In grasping the warrant, one must understand the declarative correctly. But for sentences in general, according to Searle, to understand a sentence is to know its meaning and "the meaning of a sentence is determined by rules, and those rules specify both conditions of utterance of the sentence and also what the utterance counts as" (1969, p. 48).[5] But these rules are constitutive rules of a language and its semantics, many of which we learn simply by picking them up, as we learn the constitutive rules of other practices.

Our understanding of a declarative is ordinarily immediate. We do not on the basis of some utterances make inferences about their meaning to the conclusion that it has been declared that *p*. Rather, ordinarily we understand the declaration, including its implications for making projections according to its associated warrant. That warrant will be reliable to the extent that we have understood the declarative. We may presume that warrant is reliable to the extent that we may presume we understand the declarative. But if we are able to communicate successfully using the language in which the declarative is expressed, there is a presumption that we have mastered these rules to an adequate degree. Our grasping the warrant is not only basic but properly basic.

Although understanding a legislative declarative is many times immediate, this will not always be the case. As is well known, a legislature may intentionally leave the wording of a statute vague, so that courts may later make it precise in accord with then prevailing conditions. Even one who has successfully mastered the constitutive semantic rules of the language can then ask what that statute means. When supplemented with a court ruling, one presumably will have an answer. But then statute + court ruling will back certain warrants recognized immediately through institutional intuition. Likewise if a statute contains an ambiguous expression, a court may need to rule on which sense is indicated. But then, barring further problems with meaning, the statute should be understandable given mastery of the constitutive rules of the language.

If the court's rulings are not to be simply a judicial exercise of legislative authority, a declaring of a more precise statute, it is incumbent on the justices to argue that the statute should be properly construed as having the meaning they have assigned to it. This, if you will, is a hermeneutical argument. Should an institutional warrant need defense, its immediate grasping not be sufficient to presume its reliability, and the question be not simply whether some proper legislative authority made some declaration, such a hermeneutical argument is required. Although giving an account of such hermeneutical arguments is clearly beyond the scope of this paper, we expect that such arguments would include basic premises concerning meaning, meaning connected with basic legal principles, and perhaps the meaning of other statutes which have been made precise in ways analogous to those proposed for this statute and whose acceptance as precised constitutes a precedent for the proposed precising of this statute. In this way, we may have justificatory backing for an institutional warrant, as we could have justificatory backing for physical warrants.

---

[5] Searle discusses rules of reference and predication in (1969), Chapters Four and Five.

5. AN EPISTEMIC CLASSIFICATION OF WARRANTS

If the argument of the preceding section is cogent, empirical and institutional intuition are distinct, grasping different sorts of connections, suggested or discovered in different ways, and backed or justified by different sorts of considerations. Clearly, necessary connections and evaluative connections of supervenience constitute two further types of connections, grasped by distinct modes of intuition. Hence, we have identified four modes of intuition–*a priori*, empirical, institutional, and evaluative, allowing that there can be further subdivisions within these modes, such as distinguishing physical from personal empirical intuition or distinguishing particular types of evaluative intuition. Our proposal is to classify warrants according to the mode of intuition which discovers them and to replace Toulmin's notion of warrants belonging to fields with warrants classified in this way. What are the advantages of this proposal?

This classification preserves Toulmin's insight on the field dependency of warrants but without the problematic notion of field. Different warrants will be justified or backed in different ways, and we must look to the type of warrant to determine how this is done properly. But we do not classify warrants according to fields. Earlier we raised four problems for fields. First, what counts as a field? By contrast, that we may distinguish these four proposed types of intuition, that their epistemic modes of operation are distinct, seems straightforward. If several different types of warrants are used within an argument, we need not puzzle over what field is involved. Second, Toulmin's notion of field raised the specter of relativism, with field-dependent standards of evaluation. The problem becomes more acute if fields are understood as the discourse of a particular community, whose members would be free to set standards. By contrast, that different types of connections are apprehended through different modes of insight or intuition and may require different types of evidence for their backing does not entail that there are no objective standards for determining when a statement of that connection is properly defended and the corresponding warrant reliable, at least to a certain degree. Presenting a full case that there are indeed such objective standards in connection with each of the four types of intuition discussed is beyond the scope of this paper.

A third problem for Toulmin's field-dependent account concerns the need simply to take for granted the reliability of certain warrants. On our account, certain warrants are properly basic, the mode of intuition presumptively reliable when grasping the underlying connection. This is not a matter of assumption. We are able to give a case for the presumptive reliability of intuition in this employment.[6]

Finally, the issue of assigning a warrant to a field seems to be problematic–at least in some cases. Can we readily determine to which of our four broad categories a warrant belongs? Consider the hard case above:

---

[6] We present such cases in (2005a), Chapters 6-9, in connection with the issue of basic premise acceptability.

Given that	*x* is a society that conducts its public affairs in the style of a surrealistic painting,
One may take it that	*x* can be regarded as worse than totalitarian.

Consider the property constituting the conclusion. On a simple level of analysis, this predicates intrinsic badness. The premise, to the extent that we can determine some cognitive meaning for it, asserts an interpretation, that the manner in which the society conducts its public affairs manifests certain dispositions. The warrant is straightforwardly evaluative, based on intuiting that intrinsic disvalue supervenes upon certain set patterns of societal behavior. A deeper level of analysis is possible, but beyond our scope here. Such deeper analyses may on occasion show that warrants are of mixed type but the types will be resolvable into our scheme.

Here are some further warrants which have been posed as test cases for our classification scheme.[7]

1)	(W1)	If anything is red, it will not be black.
2)	(W2)	A man who is proved to have driven more than 30 mph in a built up area can be found to have committed an offence against the Road Traffic Acts.
3)	(W3)	A Saudi Arabian will be found to be a Muslim.
4)	(W4)	Basketball teams that have a stronger defense and have the psychological edge will prevail in a best of seven series.

Casting (W1)-(W4) in the canonical form of warrants is straightforward. (W1) is an *a priori* warrant, and one we take to be properly basic, reflecting the structure of our color concepts. (W2) is an institutional warrant, grasped by institutional intuition upon understanding the specific provisoes in the Road Traffic Acts. We question whether (W3) should be regarded as a warrant, since we understand it to express a descriptive empirical generalization. (W4) is a causal and thus empirical interpretive warrant, involving in part psychological causation. It is grasped by empirical intuition, which is not to say that this employment is presumptively reliable.

Sometimes it may be more problematic to cast something in the canonical form of a warrant than to categorize the warrant when cast. In illustrating a warrant within the field of science and engineering, Toulmin *et al* propose that for the purpose of "designing a bridge that must be capable of carrying twenty-ton trucks", an engineer "has at his disposal certain established equations linking the dimensions of steel girders of various shapes to their breaking strength, or shear" (1984, p. 50). A

---

[7] Ralph Johnson has posed these cases in his commentary on the version of this paper presented at the Ontario Society for the Study of Argumentation conference on the Uses of Argument, May 20, 2005. Johnson has taken (W1), (W2), and (W3) from Toulmin (1958, pp. 98, 99, 103).

general formula relating breaking strength to shape and dimensions will be the warrant of the engineer's argument for a particular type of girder. We should be able to present this formula in the canonical form:

Given that	*x* is a steel girder of dimensions *y*,
One may take it that	*x* has a breaking strength greater than the minimum necessary. (1984, p. 50)

This is an empirical physical warrant, ultimately backed by causal investigations. We leave the remaining examples Toulmin *et al* present as exercises for the interested reader.[8]

6. EPISTEMIC CLASSIFICATION, RELIABILITY, AND RELEVANCE

Our epistemic classification of warrants gives us a way to assay determining warrant reliability. Determine first what type of warrant is involved. The conditions of reliability will be different for different types of warrant. For *a priori* warrants, this condition is validity. In some cases, recognizing validity will be immediate. In other cases, a proof of validity is required. However, as we pointed out in (1992), at least for the formal species of *a priori* warrants, providing such proofs is a matter of applying apropos principles of settled logical theory. Notice that the warrant is valid if and only if its associated conditional is logically true. Basically the same argument providing backing in Toulmin's sense establishes the validity of the warrant and the logical truth of the associated conditional. This gives us the clue to understanding what reliability means for empirical, institutional, and evaluative warrants. These are reliable if and only if the associated generalized conditional is properly justified. Such justification will show that the associated generalized conditional, if not true, is at least verisimilitudinous to a certain degree.

In some cases, as we have already argued, recognizing the reliability of the warrant and the verisimilitude of the associated conditional is immediate, given the evidence upon which the appropriate intuition discovers the connection expressible either as the warrant or as its associated conditional. In other cases, the associated conditional must be justified, the justifying argument also constituting backing for the warrant. In (1992), we indicated how for empirical warrants we could give such a justifying argument, drawing on work of L.J. Cohen (See 1992, p. 226 for references.) and how to devise on this basis a properly normative definition of relevance for statements whose relevance would be explained by empirical warrants. It remains first to adapt that discussion to empirical warrants as understood in this paper and further to adapt that discussion or provide alternative accounts of when

---

[8] Toulmin *et al.* present their discussion of warrants in Chapter 5 of 1984 (pp. 45-59).

the generalized conditionals associated with institutional or evaluative warrants are properly justified. We then need to determine the extent to which the definition of relevance can be extended to statements whose relevance would be explained by institutional or evaluative warrants, or again to develop alternative definitions of relevance for these statements. Such adaptations and extensions are subjects for future research. In this paper, we have established the epistemic framework for that research.[9]

[9] We wish to thank Prof. Ralph H. Johnson for his extensive comments on a preliminary version of this paper, both his formal commentary at The Uses of Argument Conference and as a referee for *Argumentation*. We wish also to thank a second anonymous referee of *Argumentation* and David Godden for their comments on preliminary versions.

CHAPTER 8

JAMES F. KLUMPP

WARRANTING ARGUMENTS, THE VIRTUE OF VERB

Department of Communication, University of Maryland, College Park, MD 20742-7635, USA
E-mail: jklumpp@umd.edu

ABSTRACT: *The Uses of Argument* presented Stephen Toulmin's call for a working logic and the classical statement of his layout of argument. In chapter 3, which explicated the model, each element was defined using multiple strategies. Toulmin presented his terminology both as a category system for labeling statements or propositions and as a functional vocabulary to describe "what … is involved in establishing conclusions by the production of arguments" (1964, p. 97). These two uses of the vocabulary did not come together seamlessly in his account, however. Nor have they done so in subsequent work. Interpretations and elaborations of the Toulmin model, including Toulmin's own with Rieke and Janek in *An Introduction to Reasoning*, have tended to characterize the overall model functionally but have defined and illustrated the elements as different kinds of statements. This paper calls for more attention to a definition for the 'warrant' element that emerges from the dialogue strategy of definition: 'to warrant' as a verb capturing the movement between the data and the claim. The paper argues that the result of this perspective is a more functional and thus rhetorically-based statement of the Toulmin model.

KEYWORDS: Stephen E. Toulmin; warrant; argument; working logic; fields of argument

1. INTRODUCTION

In the opening paragraphs of *The Uses of Argument* (1964), Stephen Toulmin commits himself to understanding "the canons and methods we use when, in everyday life, we actually assess the soundness, strength and conclusiveness of arguments" (p. 1). There are a number of interesting if not novel elements entailed in this commitment. At its heart is an assertion that assessment of argument is a central practice in day-to-day language use. Toulmin designates the dimensions of this assessment soundness, strength and conclusiveness. Furthermore, the raising of the issue of how we *actually* assess arguments gives the reader the hint of the differentiation Toulmin will introduce between the idealized logic of traditional perspectives and his effort to study working logic: reasoning as it takes place in 'everyday life'. Finally, the commitment posits a discernible system of assessment knowable through the study of people arguing.

Toulmin's commitment in those opening paragraphs first attracted me to his ideas. As a student of rhetorical argument—the ways in which people draw upon the

D. Hitchcock and B. Verheij (eds.), Arguing on the Toulmin Model: New Essays in Argument Analysis and Evaluation, 103–113.

resources of language to understand their world and cajole each other to cooperative participation in that endeavor—I found that Toulmin's task captured my own. Indeed, in my home discipline of speech communication Toulmin became the standard framework for explaining and teaching microargument.

The spirit of Toulmin's commitment in those opening paragraphs carries into the third chapter of his treatise: 'The Layout of Arguments'. If a layout is to aid description and assessment, then its terms and characteristic moves must permit the casting of the arguments that surround us every day into its framework. Rhetorical critics must be able to draw upon the layout to open up the strategic dimensions of arguments. Everyday users—including our students—must be able to develop their abilities to use the layout *on the fly*, as it were. Over the years, the success of Toulmin's layout for these tasks has been modest. Occasionally, rhetorical critics have drawn on the layout to map arguments, but it cannot be said to have totally captured their loyalty. Toulmin's layout is the pervasive choice in textbooks for argumentation and even in public speaking, yet those with whom I converse about teaching and those I supervise in my department's courses in argumentation report that their students suffer great difficulty in casting argumentative exchanges within the layout. 'Is this statement data or a warrant?' is still guaranteed to glaze eyes. In fact, it is that move—the obligation to recast uttered statements into an expressive form complying with the linguistic characteristics of data or warrant—that diminishes the utility of the layout.

Many years ago, in rereading *The Uses of Argument*, I was struck by the novelty of Toulmin's first definition of the terms of the layout: a conversation between two interlocutors built around the claims of the first and the skeptical challenges of the second. I observed that seldom was this schema employed when teaching the Toulmin layout or conceptualizing argument with its terminology. I committed to doing so. The result has been a profoundly more useful layout that focuses on the act of arguing rather than the propositional form of premises.

My task in this essay is to explicate this approach to the layout. I argue that the key to this interpretation is to recognize that 'to warrant' is a splendid English verb that perfectly captures the dynamic movement of reasoning in the Toulmin layout. I will argue that the reconceptualization of argument embodied in the Toulmin model reaches its full potential to move from an idealized to a working logic when the requirement to cast arguments into propositions is also left behind and the layout deployed as a method of portraying the underlying movement of reasoning. Thus, presenting the key term of the layout—the warrant—as a verb, the part of speech capturing movement, best actualizes the working logic.

2. TO WARRANT AN ARGUMENT

In the chapter 'The Layout of Arguments' Toulmin offers at least seven strategies for defining 'warrant'. These various strategies are not inconsistent, but if one seeks to fully appreciate the difference between the new working logic that Toulmin champions and the geometrically based logics that he seeks to displace, certain strategies emerge as more effective in assisting the "man-in-the-street" to achieve "application to his practice" (p. 1).

Some of these definitions link the concept of warrant with the major or middle premise of traditional syllogisms. Following a reprisal of the famous syllogism establishing Socrates' mortality, Toulmin works toward a similar argument about the Swede Petersen's Protestantism (pp. 108-110). He is exploring the differing expression of arguments in which backing replaces stated warrants. In case we miss the link to syllogistic logic he proffers: "The relevance of our distinction to the traditional conception of 'formal validity' should already be becoming apparent" (p. 110). We do not, of course, want to lose sight of the purpose of the strategy on these pages: drawing upon the syllogistic analogy permits the clearest statement of the distinction between the syllogistic or analytic argument and substantial argument. In this example Toulmin is making the point that in everyday discourse it is most often the backing to the warrant that is stated, not the warrant itself.

Unfortunately to my mind, Toulmin loses much of the uniqueness of a working logic the farther he goes toward developing this example. His rather awkward prose rendering of the argument translates easily into his layout, but at the price of insight into the generalization of his procedure to natural prose expressions. The same problem continues as universal premises are explored in observations about our club-footed friend Jack (pp. 113-118). Taken together with the next section, which draws together arguments about the Bermudan Harry and Jack's sister Anne's red hair to make the distinction between substantial and analytic arguments (pp. 118-24), Toulmin's treatment returns the effort at distinction to the old strategic problem of casting arguments into proper expressive form as an avenue toward testing their logical validity. Thus, the search for a working logic returns to the characteristic moves of the idealized logic. This confusion has led many to see Toulmin's model as less than novel or, as Brockriede and Ehninger (1960) put it, as "a syllogism lying on its side" (p. 47).

A second definitional strategy exploits a different analogy—the law courts. Toulmin compares the warrant to points of law.

> This distinction, between data and warrants, is similar to the distinction drawn in the law-courts between questions of fact and questions of law, and the legal distinction is indeed a special case of the more general one—we may argue, for instance, that a man whom we know to have been born in Bermuda is presumably a British subject, simply because the relevant laws give us a warrant to draw this conclusion. (p. 100)

In the end, this statement dissolves the analogy into an argument by division. The important confusion to me is that the argument's reference to the power of relevant laws to supply a warrant, combined with the specific to more general reasoning (or vice versa), leaves behind the impression of warrants as *formal* statements of relationship contextualized within general principles.

I find this characteristic unfortunate, but Toulmin does not. Although he repeatedly makes the point that in working logic "data are appealed to explicitly, warrants implicitly" (p. 100), he often offers warrants in propositional form. In the analogy to the law, the reference is to positive or written law. There are, in the law books, written specifications that *are* (in the force of this statement of the analogy) the implicit warrants of the argument.

Having this point fresh in our minds, it is a propitious time to introduce a distinction that sorts Toulmin's strategies. In the two strategies we have just considered, warrants are propositional. They have substance which they lend to the argument. Is the propositional nature of legal statutes a characteristic generated from their special character and carried to the general character of warrants, or is the propositional character in fact what sets them apart? Read in context, what makes them special is that they are in the field of law. Thus, we are led to believe that all warrants have tacit, but fundamental, propositional character. Shortly I will suggest that other definitional strategies release us from this propositional form to emphasize, in preference to their propositional quality, the power of warrants to authorize the movement from data to claim.

Perhaps the propositional definitions reach their most troubling manifestation in a third strategy of definition: "general, hypothetical statements, which can act as bridges, and authorise the sort of step to which our particular argument commits us. These may normally be written very briefly (in the form 'If D, then C')" (p. 98). Despite the fact that Toulmin goes on to complicate this propositional expression, the simple statement of the hypothetical—if D, then C—is too often taken to be the field-invariant propositional form of a warrant, only the content being field-dependent. Today I encounter teachers adopting this simple definition of warrants and encouraging students that warrants are as simple as stating: if D, then C. This, of course, trivializes the function of warrants. As a working logic it makes it easy to express warrants, but leaves us without what Toulmin points to as the problem required to move beyond the trivial case: the requirement that the hypotheticals be authenticated.

It is the search for authentication that takes us away from the propositional statements, for now the emphasis shifts from the form of the proposition to its function. The fourth strategy of definition is transitional: "warrants ... correspond to the practical standards or canons of argument" (p. 98). There is, of course, considerable difference between 'canons' and 'practical standards'. The former imply a refined sort of knowledge in which contemplation and careful sorting elevate certain propositions to a level of acceptance that others do not achieve. Canons are socially authorized in an extended process of refinement. Practical standards seem to receive their status through a more commonly enacted day-to-day refinement of experience.

The movement to practical standards I take as significant, for Toulmin with this simple move carries us from a formal refinement by experts—perhaps even by idealized logicians—into a socially functioning everyday practical activity in which normal blokes acquire a practical knowledge of what data warrants important claims. In this pair Toulmin gives us our first glimpse of his later distinction between warrant-using and warrant-establishing arguments. Warrants have become the product of socially constructed argumentative processes—formal and informal. The conjunction Toulmin has constructed portrays the broad assertion that the social processes of warrant husbandry mark scientific and other academic disciplines, the law, and ordinary day-to-day interaction. Practicality drives canonized and non-canonized reasoning.

This ambiguous functionality also marks the fifth definition of warrant: "propositions of a ... kind: rules, principles, inference-licences, or what you will" (p. 98). 'Rules' suggests the kind of carefully performed sifting that canons of argument suggests. Principles transcend the process of canonization, seemingly signifying products that have attained a status generally recognized. The more infrequently encountered term 'inference-licences' expresses the full functional perspective on the warrant. Licenses convey the attained authority, in this case the authority of data to establish claims. The warrants remain propositions, but they now become warrants not by virtue of their form but by virtue of their power, their authority. The imprecision of the last phrase in Toulmin's definition— 'or what you will'—indicates more clearly that this list of terms communicates not the status of the propositions but their function to authorize the move from data to claim.

This move to the functional becomes explicit in a sixth definition of warrant. Toulmin observes: "The question will be asked, how absolute is this distinction between data, on the one hand, and warrants, on the other". The problem he posits is the bane of those trying to teach ordinary arguers—including students—to differentiate propositions that are claims, from those that are data, from those that are warrants. He answers:

> By grammatical tests alone, the distinction may appear far from absolute, and the same English sentence may serve a double function: it may be uttered, that is, in one situation to convey a piece of information, in another to authorise a step in an argument, and even perhaps in some contexts to do both these things at once. (p. 99)

Here is the ultimate problem of sorting propositions into the layout and what ultimately differentiates the layout and its working logic from idealized logic. The form of the sentence does not permit the separation. You cannot simply look at a sentence and tell the function it is serving. Gone are the possibilities of readily seeing the form 'if D, then C' and saying, 'Aha! a warrant'. Propositions are warrants as they perform the *function* of warrants, as they authorize the taking of data as proof of a claim. They turn the pedagogic attention from teaching students to recognize the form of statements to recognizing the way in which statements function in the generation of faith in a claim.

In my judgment, Toulmin's seventh strategy (and, by the way, the earliest strategy presented in the essay) is the most fruitful in teaching the layout of argument. This is the conversation, the narrative of accomplished argument. I quote at length:

> Let it be supposed that we make an assertion, and commit ourselves thereby to the claim which any assertion necessarily involves. If this claim is challenged, we must be able to establish it—that is, make it good, and show that it was justifiable. How is this to be done? Unless the assertion was made quite wildly and irresponsibly, we shall normally have some facts to which we can point in its support: if the claim is challenged, it is up to us to appeal to these facts, and present them as the foundation upon which our claim is based....
>
> We already have, therefore, one distinction to start with: between the *claim* or conclusion whose merits we are seeking to establish (C) and the facts we appeal to as a foundation for the claim—what I shall refer to as our *data* (D). If our challenger's question is, 'What have you got to go on?', producing the data or information on which the claim is based may serve to answer him; but this is only one of the ways in which our conclusion may be challenged. Even after we have produced our data, we may find ourselves again asked further questions of another kind. We may now be required not to add factual information to that which we have already provided, but rather to indicate the bearing on our conclusion of the data already produced. Colloquially, the question may now be, not 'What have you got to go on?', but 'How do you get there?'. To present a particular set of data as the basis for some specified conclusion commits us to a certain *step*; and the question is now one about the nature and justification of this step. (pp. 97-98)

Toulmin has posited the archetypal case of argument as a conversation in which an interlocutor challenges the grounds of our making a claim. The challenges are of different types because the questions asked are different questions. One seeks information, the other expresses the skepticism that the information provided satisfies the demand for support for the claim. By casting the process in the form of a conversation rather than in the form of propositional layout Toulmin has refocused our attention on the function our statements serve in arguing.

I now reach the edge of Toulmin's treatment in 'The Layout of Arguments' and go further than he goes. I ask: Why should the response to this second question be labeled 'warrant'? The answer is found in the English verb, 'to warrant': "to provide adequate grounds for; justify; to grant authorization or sanction to (someone); authorize or empower" (American Heritage Dictionary). The question, rephrased in our terminology becomes: *How does that data warrant that claim?*

The verb form removes even the last vestiges of the requirement that the form of the warrant be propositional. The functional is the essence. To be sure, propositional statements may be generated to satisfy the warrant challenge, but the warrant function is the relationship between the data and the claim: the authorization of the step.

3. WARRANTING AS A WORKING LOGIC

The functional emphasis transforms the warranting concept into the synthetic heart of the working logic. To the arguer, the key choice is the selection of information (data) to support (warrant) the claim. The geometry of the argument becomes linear, but linear with multiple and complex vectors. Arguments emerge out of the assertions and challenges as interlocutors negotiate the warranting of the claim. Warranting challenges may be met by the selection of alternative information (data), by the assertion of the authority of the information to prove the claim (backing), or by the generation of chained arguments in which the arguer makes claims about the relationships of data and claim—in Toulmin's terms warrant-establishing arguments. The dialogue that marks the skeptical relationship of the interlocutors is the search for data that warrant the claim. When the strength of the warranting relationship is successfully challenged, the options of identifying special limiting conditions (rebuttal) and recognizing the shading of probabilities (qualifiers) provide other options for the arguer negotiating the strength of his/her argument with the interlocutor.

The functional emphasis also expands the scope of argument by placing the individual microargument into a judgment contextualized beyond its own terms. This expansion results from the idea that the warranting power of data transcends the individual argument. An arguer selects data that s/he anticipates will warrant the claim. That power—that authority—lies in the complex warrant-establishing process. The licensing quality of warrants that Toulmin describes grows from the transcendent, socially constructed, authority of a field. The social complex that makes arguments go has the sensitivity to the warranting power of information at its heart.

The power of warrants thus lies at the intersection of two dimensions: the pragmatic and the social. A working logic is the product of argumentative language acts that refine and work through a kind of Darwinian testing of the quality of warrants. Warrants that lead to faulty decisions—decisions that lead to unwise actions—have their authority eroded in their pragmatic use. Warrants that show wisdom have their authority reinforced. This evaluation is carried in the social knowledge that resides in the field of the interlocutors.

In describing this central role for warrants, we have touched on the major elements that set Toulmin's working logic apart from idealized logic: the secondary triad, the idea of warrant-using and warrant-establishing arguments, the context of fields as active elements of argument. So the functional definitions carry the virtues of Toulmin's critique. The synthetic power of functional definitions captures the multiple dimensions that shape an argument in the Toulmin system.

4. THE ADVANTAGES OF THIS VIEW OF ARGUMENT

I began this exploration of a functional view of warrant with a very pragmatic diagnosis of the Toulmin model: my students could not readily analyze an argument—discuss its working with the Toulmin terminology and then think through its weaknesses to refute or strengthen its argumentative power—measurably better than they could with other ways of treating argument. Nor was the terminology particularly dominant as a language for rhetorical critics who are so often interested in argument.[1] So I return now to a bald claim: my students work more easily with a functional notion of warrants, and I find the synthetic character of the functional definitions much more conducive to the full understanding of argumentative complexes.

I cannot generate any systematic data to support my claim for the students' ease of use, but I can report my long experience in the classroom. Furthermore, I think I understand why the process is so much easier. First, for students the most difficult part of logical analysis is turning normal English sentences into propositional form. In the functional deployment of the layout, they need not do so. They simply need to understand the three functions at the heart of the model: claiming, supporting, and warranting. What is your claim? What data will you offer to support it? Why do you think that data warrants that claim? Consider a simple and actual example:

> Bonnie: I am afraid you will not be able to graduate in May.
>
> Jeremy: Why not?
>
> Bonnie: You failed to file the Application for Diploma form by the February deadline.
>
> Jeremy: I thought they were fairly lenient with deadlines on this paperwork?
>
> Bonnie: Generally they are, but not with that form. Long experience tells us that is the one deadline you better not miss.

No need to work through translation problems here. Bonnie's claim is clear. She is shown responding to Jeremy's doubt with a fact explaining his problem. His effort to doubt the authority of her fact to warrant her claim is met with a sophisticated response: backing and rebuttal.

No doubt part of the secret here is the conversational model. In deciding the strategy to present this view of argument, I pondered whether the proper stress was on the warrant as a verb or on the conversation as a paradigm case of argument. Toulmin's standard conversation and the specific variations on it present the interplay of assertion and skeptical challenge that constitutes the dialectic of

---

[1] There are exceptions that employ the verb form to great insight. See, for example, McKerrow (1990); Simosi (2003); Bates *et al.* (2005). Although all these employ the notion of warranting claims with data, they generally do not exploit the visual layout in doing so.

argument. The conversation stresses that the notion of 'making an argument' as the expressive assertion of a single arguer oversimplifies the more subtle calculation of interactional awareness that we stress in talking about rhetorical argument. Indeed, one message I often deliver to students terrified about the possibility of debate, where an interlocutor could actually tell them their argument was not convincing, is that the debater is the lucky one: she knows where her interlocutor's resistance is. The public speaker must arrive at the issues of resistance in the face of silence.

Of course, one may object that insisting that translation into a conversation be substituted for translation into propositions is still translation into an alternative form with the attendant difficulties. Even though a conversational form might be preferable because it is a more natural form for a working logic, the real advantage is that the conversational model teaches differently than the propositional. The conversational model is a pedagogic strategy for teaching the interactive function of claim, data, and warrant. That lesson learned, the analysis of individual arguments ought to feature an appreciation for the functioning of the argument without translation into conversational form. In propositional analysis, on the other hand, translation into propositions is a necessary step. Indeed, the probative power of propositional analysis lies in the translation into propositions. It is translating ordinary discourse into propositional form that allows *formal* assessment to proceed.[2] Thus, the essential lesson provided by Toulmin's working logic to teach ordinary arguers is the functional relationships in argument, not the conversational form.

Furthermore, the emphasis on the functional recognizes that although the conversational form may more directly record many cases of working logic, other cases are in non-conversational formats. A few paragraphs ago I highlighted my claim that students found the functional approach easier to employ. I acknowledged a characteristic of our shared field as I anticipated the interlocutor's expectation that I might produce systematic evidence of this greater ease. But I rejected that strategy for warranting my claim, asserting instead the rather vague authority of my experience. Indeed, this is an argument where the backing is explicit and the data implicit in the argument. In re-presenting that argument I have not cast it into the conversational form (although I have used that metaphor a bit in this paragraph to describe my strategic choices). I have instead featured the ways the various statements of the argument relate functionally to each other in producing my argumentative effect.

Still another advantage students demonstrate in learning the model functionally is their greater ability to think through the options defined by the central role of the warrant as a synthetic pivot of assertion and challenge. When the authority of warranting is challenged, they can see the catalog of moves open to the arguer. They develop a feel for the nature of the challenge and the appropriateness of alternative data, backing, rebuttal, qualification, or chain argument.

---

[2] Charles Arthur Willard (1976) argues that translation is endemic to diagrammatic strategies for treating arguments and that translation into propositional form is the essence of Toulmin's argument.

The centrality of warranting in the functional definition also facilitates students' ability to use the model in assessment. They quickly perceive the context of the argument in a field. The social test—Is that the data that warrants that sort of claim in that field?—comes more naturally as a question. But if that question is answered skeptically, the question turns to: Why not? If not, how might the claim be warranted? What are the restrictions of the field? How does that field establish warrants? Are there possibilities to strengthen the argument?

The result is a more consistent pedagogy of argument. Students work more easily with the ultimate questions of perceiving, testing, challenging, and strengthening arguments. But they also perceive argument as a fundamental language activity through which humans negotiate their daily lives.

I also asserted that to a rhetorical critic the synthetic power of warranting arguments permitted a fuller vocabulary for dealing with the texture of argument. I would point to the Bush administration's arguments for the Iraqi war as illustrative (Klumpp, 2005; 2006). The justification for the Iraq War is a search for warranted justification set into the framework of American war-making. Issues surrounding the erroneous data to support arguments for war suggest full exploration of warranting options and how they were developed.

Arguments surrounding the recent drama in the United States over the fate of Terry Schiavo also illustrate the explanatory power of operating with functional and field-centered perspectives on argument. Schiavo had been severely impaired in a medical crisis many years before. Her physicians had diagnosed her as being in a persistent vegetative state from which she would never recover. Citing her own indications that she would not want to be artificially supported in such a scenario, her husband asked the courts for permission to suspend extraordinary life support. Her parents objected. Following several court decisions, the case was embraced by particular political groups in the United States to support their 'right to life' beliefs. Before Schiavo's wishes were carried out, the Congress of the United States had intervened and adjudication by the Supreme Court had been sought. The loud and splintering texture of public argument over the fate of this unfortunate woman and its implications for fundamental issues of life and death opened in so many ways to a rich consideration of issues of warranting. The contrast of argument in the legal field to argument in the streets; the technical involvement of Congressional action; the role of the field of medicine versus the human connection of a mother and father; differences in the acceptable evidence of meaningful life; all of the bypassing that constituted the differing positions on these issues took on apparent texture at the intersection of various fields of argument and the warranting practices that define each. While the constraints of this essay do not permit a full elaboration of this episode, consider only the bypassing over the question of Terry Schiavo's responsiveness to those around her. American media played repeatedly a videotape containing a visual of Schiavo and the disembodied voice of her mother. The legal system relied on the diagnosis of medical experts to warrant its conclusion that Schiavo existed in a 'persistent vegetative state'. The medical profession has specific criteria for such a state, and telemetry and specific diagnostic techniques provided data to experts trained in medicine with which they warranted their claim in court testimony. The streets saw instead a videotape of Schiavo with eyes aimed in the direction of the disembodied voice of her mother. Connectedness was perceived in the image constituting the human responsiveness that parents perceive in their children as love. Clearly the medical/legal and media/popular interpretations drew upon two different fields. The latter did not constitute evidence for the court, nor was medical testimony relevant to the street. Indeed, an interesting moment occurred when Senator Bill Frist, Senate majority leader and a trained and licensed physician, attempted to bridge these fields by asserting his medical credentials and claiming diagnosis via the videotape. His statement was met with doubts about medical personnel who would diagnose via videotape. Clearly the issues of what warrants claims of human responsiveness and the contrasting contexts of fields accepting claims only by their own acceptable warranting helped to define the bypassing that marks the conflict between the courts and the streets.

5. A FINAL THOUGHT

To the best of my reading Toulmin never explains his choice of the term 'warrant' for the bridging element of his layout. The most common definition of the noun 'warrant' points to the legal document issued by a court authorizing action by the court's officials. That kind of image of formal proceedings to authorize action distorts the more informal sense of appropriateness captured in a working logic. To me, the more straightforward definition of 'to warrant'—'to provide adequate grounds for; justify; to grant authorization or sanction to (someone); authorize or empower'—better achieves the distinctiveness of a working logic. I propose a change of emphasis, a tilting from one definitional strategy in 'The Layout of Arguments' to another. I frankly admit that I propose an elaboration toward rhetorical argument with its focus on explaining the argumentative workings of everyday arguers and away from the validity concerns of logicians. Thus, I urge diminished urgency for the search for the propositional linkages of data to claim. Instead, I believe that a greater concern for the functional relationships that define the layout of argument promises a more vital approach to the working logic that Toulmin and I seek.

CHAPTER 9

ROBERT C. PINTO

EVALUATING INFERENCES: THE NATURE AND ROLE OF WARRANTS

Department of Philosophy, University of Windsor, Windsor, Ontario N9B 3P4, Canada
E-mail: pinto@uwindsor.ca

ABSTRACT: Following David Hitchcock and Stephen Toulmin, this paper takes warrants to be material inference rules. It offers an account of the form such rules should take that is designed (a) to implement the idea that an argument/ inference is valid only if it is *entitlement preserving* and (b) to support a *qualitative version* of *evidence proportionalism.* It attempts to capture what gives warrants their normative force by elaborating a concept of *reliability* tailored to its account of the form such rules should take.

KEYWORDS: warrant; inference rule; material inference; evidence proportionalism; entitlement preserving inference; inferential practice; reliability; David Hitchcock; Stephen E. Toulmin

1. INTRODUCTION

This paper explores two ideas:

1. That there are *material inferences* — i.e. inferences whose "validity" does not depend on logical form.[1]
2. That rationality is a matter of making our *attitudes* toward propositions or propositional contents *appropriate to the evidence* which shapes them — developed in what might be called a *qualitative* version of evidence proportionalism.[2] Though I think this conception of rationality can be applied in

[1] Trudy Govier (1995, p. 178) distinguishes between *formal validity, deductive validity* and what she calls *umbrella validity.* She defines umbrella validity as follows: "An argument is valid if and only if its premisses are properly connected to its conclusion and provide adequate reasons for it. It is invalid otherwise". When in this paper I refer without qualification to validity, it is *umbrella validity* that I am referring to.

[2] I am particularly interested in this idea as an alternative to the approach to argument in Goldman (1999, chapter 5) — an approach dominated by the idea that the social value of argument lies principally in its potential for disseminating *true* beliefs. (Goldman defends the primacy of truth as an epistemic virtue in (2002).) My dissent is motivated *in part* by my Popperian conviction that what it is reasonable to aim for in many if not most situations is something other than literal truth — it is closeness to the truth (Popper famously called it *verisimilitude*) — and that rationality requires that our doxastic attitudes reflect this fact.

D. Hitchcock and B. Verheij (eds.), Arguing on the Toulmin Model: New Essays in Argument Analysis and Evaluation, 115–143.

a very general way to illuminate the rationality of decisions and of such things as preferences, this paper will consider only how it can be worked out with respect to *cognitive* attitudes, and more specifically with reference to *doxastic* attitudes.[3]

The discussion that follows will be framed by an examination of two closely related versions of the proposal that we take certain generalizations which are not "logical truths" to be rules of inference (where 'logical truth' is unpacked after the manner of Quine (1953, pp. 22-23)) — the versions offered by David Hitchcock and Stephen Toulmin, respectively. For the most part, I will ignore other attempts to

---

Goldman (1988, pp. 89-93) challenges the centrality of the idea that "credal states" must be appropriate to the strength of evidence — a view he calls "evidence proportionalism". He principally has in mind the view that the "degree of belief" one has in a proposition ought to be proportioned to the strength of the evidence which supports that proposition — usually with the assumption that numeric values can be assigned both to degrees of belief and to strength of evidentiary support. The idea I am interested in might be described as a *qualitative* variant on evidence proportionalism — the idea is that the *sort* of doxastic attitude one adopts toward a proposition should be *appropriate* to the evident reasons which favor it (where doxastic attitudes are assumed to be type-identified by the functions they allow propositions to play in our cognitive lives). Goldman's criticism of evidence proportionalism is quite explicitly framed so as to apply to views like the one I am interested in, views which don't involve assigning numeric values to belief and to support (he says on p. 90 that he will "assume whatever repertoire of credal states the evidence proportionalist wishes to postulate..."). Goldman's criticisms turn on the claim that "proportioning" belief to evidence is not a sufficient condition of epistemic justification, since either (i) the proportioning may have occurred by accident or else (ii) the belief may have been arrived at by a valid method which the believer has no reason to suppose is a valid method.

In the exposition that follows, I attempt to sidestep the issues Goldman raises by simply bracketing the question of when an individual is "subjectively justified" in adopting a conclusion or a particular attitude toward it. My rationale for this strategy is that in this paper I am trying to address the following two issues: (i) what should a rule of inference look like and (ii) when is such a rule "objectively" a good rule.

[3] In my paper 'Generalizing the notion of argument' (reprinted as chapter 2 of Pinto (2001)) I urged that the study of argument should be broadened to include, not just reasons for adopting doxastic attitudes, but reasons for adopting conscious attitudes generally. In Pinto (2003b) I proposed classifying conscious attitudes as cognitive, conative and evaluative — a classification which reflects Rescher's recognition (Rescher, 1988, p. 3) of three types of rationality: cognitive rationality (whose "product" is factual contentions or beliefs), practical rationality (whose product is action recommendations or injunctions), and evaluative rationality (whose product is evaluation or appraisal). In Pinto (2003b, pp. 6-7) I recognized three distinct categories of *cognitive* attitude toward propositions: (a) *doxastic* attitudes (belief and belief-like states such as presuming, expecting, etc.), (b) *acceptance* attitudes (which concern whether one is prepared to use a proposition as a premiss from which to draw conclusions in a given context) and (c) *degrees of confidence* (perhaps as measured by the odds at which we are willing to bet on the truth of a proposition). *Acceptance* attitudes (and maybe degrees of confidence as well) are *context-dependent*, but *doxastic* attitudes are not (see, 2003b, Appendix B).

deploy the idea of material inferences — in C. S. Peirce,[4] Wilfrid Sellars,[5] or Robert Brandom,[6] for example.

There are three questions that arise when one attempts to deploy the notion of "rules of inference" which are not logical truths, questions whose significance becomes salient when Hitchcock's and Toulmin's accounts are compared:

1. What *form* should the statements that express such rules take? For example, in Hitchcock's account, they typically have the form of a certain kind of "covering generalization" which contains no explicitly normative expressions. In Toulmin, when warrants are "made more explicit" (1958, p. 98; 2003, p. 91) they contain normative expressions.
2. What *virtues* must *arguments and inferences*[7] have if they are to be considered valid? Should we say that they must be truth-preserving? But then what about good arguments that aren't deductively valid and which have true premisses and a false conclusion? Can we say that they must at least be such that it's unlikely that their conclusions are false given that their premisses are true? But what about the possibility of "practical" arguments and inferences whose conclusions are intentions or prescriptions — things whose "propriety" does not consist in their being true? Or perhaps we can accommodate both defeasible inferences and practical inferences by saying, with Brandom,[8] that what matters about inferences is whether they preserve

---

[4] See for example the notion of a "guiding principle" in 'The Fixation of Belief' (Peirce, 1955, p. 8ff.) and the entry entitled 'What is a leading principle?' in Peirce (1955, pp. 129-34).

[5] Most notably see Sellars' discussion of "material inferences" in 1953 ('Inference and meaning') and in 'Some reflections on language games' (which originally appeared in 1954, but is reprinted as chapter 11 in Sellars (1963)).

[6] See Brandom's insistence, following Sellars on the importance of "material inferences" in chapter 2 of Brandom (1994) and chapter 1 of Brandom (2000). Note his suggestion that "the notion of formally valid inferences is definable in a natural way from materially correct ones, but there is no converse route" (2000, p. 55). Though Brandom's discussion of material inferences is quite explicitly derivative from Sellars, and though material inferences play an essential role in Brandom's project, he does not follow Sellars in associating them with lawlike statements and subjunctive conditionals. Brandom (1994, p. 634) observes that although "the difference between inferential connections among concepts that are counterfactually robust and those that are not is an important one . . . nothing is made of it here. This is partly because the notion of nomologicality and counterfactual reasoning, important though they are in other contexts, has not been reconstructed in scorekeeping terms as part of this project . . ." On p. 635 he explains in greater detail why he chooses not to do so.

[7] Following Pinto (2001, pp. 36-37), I take arguments to be invitations to inference and I take the "logical appraisal" of an argument to consist in the appraisal of the inference it invites. The arguments and inferences whose virtues I'm asking about are limited to what Blair (2003, pp. 1-2) calls *atomic arguments* and to the sorts of inference that are invited by atomic arguments.

[8] Brandom (1994, chapter 3) introduces *commitment* and *entitlement* as normative or deontic statuses (p. 159), and distinguishes between inferences which are commitment-preserving and those which are entitlement-preserving (p. 168ff.). In chapter 4, entitlement gets linked to the "being justified" that makes for knowledge as opposed to mere belief — (p. 201), but see all of Section I of chapter 4 (pp. 199-206). The concept of an entitlement-preserving inference came into focus for me from my reading of Brandom. However, Brandom's views are controversial, and I am certainly not in full agreement with everything he

"normative statuses" — for example, whether they are entitlement-preserving. But then what sorts of "entitlement" must be preserved by inferences that are valid and how is such an idea to be implemented?

3. What virtues must *rule statements* have if they are to have *normative* force, if they are to be *fit* to serve as norms for arguments and inferences? The significance of this question will emerge, I hope, in Parts 3 and 6 below.

2. WHAT FORM OUGHT WARRANTS TO TAKE? HITCHCOCK'S ACCOUNT

Building on work by Rolf George (1972; 1983) and beginning with his 1985 paper 'Enthymematic Arguments', Hitchcock has been developing a "general theory of inference appraisal" (Hitchcock, 2002, p. 1):

> According to a current version of this theory, a conclusion follows (conclusively, provisionally, etc.) from premisses adduced in its support if and only if some covering generalization of the argument is non-trivially acceptable (always, provisionally, etc.).

Hitchcock himself has come to identify "the covering generalization of the argument" with Toulmin warrants quite explicitly (Hitchcock, 1998, p. 27; 2003a).[9]

Key Features of Hitchcock's Theory

The *core* of Hitchcock's theory — carefully articulated and argued for in Hitchcock (1985) and (1998) — offers an account of what it is for a conclusion to follow "conclusively" from its premisses.[10] The general theory arises from the core theory by relaxing the requirement that the covering generalizations described in the core theory must be *universal* generalizations.

---

says. Accordingly, nothing in this paper presupposes the truth of any of Brandom's views, and I've written the paper so that it does not presuppose familiarity with his views.

[9] As I see it, the key papers in this series are Hitchcock (1985; 1992; 1994; 1998; 2003a). In addition, Hitchcock (2002; 2005a) contribute additional perspectives on the issues in the five papers that constitute the main series. It is worth noting that even in the first paper in this series, Toulmin is mentioned several times as holding a view similar to the view that Hitchcock is developing (see especially, 1985, p. 94). The identification of covering generalizations with Toulmin warrants becomes most explicit and most prominent in the papers from 1998 and 2003.

[10] Hitchcock (1992, p. 112) says that "arguments where we look for truth preservation between premisses and conclusion" may be called "conclusive arguments". See also Hitchcock (1994, pp. 58-59) where he says that such arguments exhibit 'conclusive validity'. It is worth noting that the official topic of Hitchcock (1985) is "enthymematic arguments" and in its opening paragraphs it explicitly exempts from consideration arguments "appropriately appraised by a non-deductive standard". Hitchcock (1998) does not explicitly exclude such arguments from consideration, but it is clear that so-called "non-deductive arguments" would not qualify as arguments in which the conclusion follows from the premisses on the "revised generic conception of consequence" formulated on p. 26 of that paper.

The theory has two components.

1. The first component is a method for identifying, in the case of arguments that would typically be considered enthymemes, "the assumption" which the argument requires or presupposes (what has often been called its "missing premiss" or "implicit premiss").
2. The second component is the claim that the identified assumption should not be considered a *premiss* of the argument, but should be considered a rule of inference that licenses the move from the explicit premiss or premisses to the conclusion.

The method for identifying "the assumption" of an argument is roughly as follows:

1. Form the argument's associated conditional (a conditional statement whose antecedent is the conjunction of the argument's premisses and whose consequent is its conclusion).
2. Form a universal generalization with respect to at least one "repeated content expression" — where a "content expression" is defined in such a way that the standard logical particles are not content expressions and where a content expression is "repeated" if and only if it occurs more than once in premisses and/or conclusion. At least one of the content expressions over which one generalizes must occur in both premisses and conclusion[11] — though not every content expression over which one generalizes need occur in both premisses and conclusion.[12]

Hitchcock calls a proposition formed in this way a *covering generalization* of the argument. For example, to use a stock example, the argument

A1 Socrates is a man.

---

[11] Hitchcock offers two reasons why the "assumption" of an enthymematic argument must generalize over a content expression occurring in both premisses and conclusion. (1) According to (1985, p. 87), unless there is a repeated content expression common to premisses and conclusion, the premisses will not be "topically relevant" to the conclusion and the argument will be a non-sequitur. (2) According to Hitchcock (1992, pp. 111-112), we ought (following Bolzano) to rule out "trivial cases in which there is no counter-example because no substitution could make the premisses true or no substitution could make the conclusion false". So he adds the requirement that at least one substitution on the variable content makes the premisses true and at least one substitution makes the conclusion false. "A consequence of these added requirements is that an argument with a good inference has a content expression repeated in a premise and the conclusion" (1992, p.112).

[12] Hitchcock envisages cases where we would *also* want to generalize over additional content expressions that occur only in the premisses – see the marijuana/alcohol example that occurs in Hitchcock (1985, pp. 92-93).

Therefore Socrates is mortal.

has just one covering generalization, and it may be expressed as follows:

For any value of x, if x is a man then x is mortal.

Hitchcock (1985, p. 89) formulates a *universal generalization thesis* to the effect that

> . . . an enthymematic argument implicitly assumes the truth of a universal generalization of its associated conditional with respect to at least one repeated content expression.

But of course if there is *more than one* repeated content expression in an argument, there will be several propositions that count as covering generalizations. Moreover, in some cases there can be concerns about the class over which we are generalizing.[13] Accordingly Hitchcock (1985, pp. 93-94) formulates a "fully qualified" version of the universal generalization thesis which provides guidance in picking out a universal generalization that might be called *the* generalization which an argument assumes.

Hitchcock suggests that the universal generalization thesis is confirmed by the fact that, to a considerable extent, the propositions it picks out as an argument's "assumption" coincide with or are logically equivalent to the propositions that we would intuitively pick out as its assumption. Thus it is significant that if asked for the assumption on which A1 depends almost nobody would offer the "logical minimum" ("If Socrates is a man, then Socrates is mortal"), and almost everybody would choose "All men are mortal" or something close to it.

Later presentations diverge from the 1985 paper with respect to covering generalizations in at least three respects.

1. They do not attempt to pick out one of the possible covering generalizations and call it *the* assumption of the argument. There is no need to do this if our aim is evaluation, especially if we construe the covering generalization as a rule of inference rather than as a premiss. For we can say that an argument is *valid* (or that its conclusion follows from its premisses) whenever it has *at least one* covering generalization which is true or acceptable.
2. Later presentations include an important restriction on covering generalizations not included in the 1985 paper (or in the 1994 paper) — that

[13] With reference to an example on (1985, p. 93), Hitchcock says, "The context of utterance of the argument indicates that we should generalize the associated conditional only over the class of words ending in '-ing'. Doing so we get the sentence, 'For any word ending in '-ing', if it is the subject of the sentence then it is a gerund' or, in more standard English, 'Every word ending in '-ing' which is the subject of a sentence is a gerund'". That is to say, formulating a covering generalization for an argument may require making certain considerations *explicit* which are not explicit in the text with which we are working but whose bearing may be inferred from features of the context from which that text is drawn.

the truth or acceptability of the covering generalization must be non-trivial.[14] Roughly, some substitution of repeated content expressions in the argument with which we started produces true premisses, and some substitution produces a false conclusion (see, for example, 1998, pp. 24-26).

3. Finally, although the *core* theory presented in Hitchcock (1985) and (1998) requires or assumes that covering generalizations are *universal* generalizations, less restrictive accounts are offered in Hitchcock (1992, esp. p. 112), (2003a, esp. p. 80) and (2005a, p. 205), which states, "The requirement that the warrant be general is not a requirement that it be *universal*" [italics mine].

Hitchcock (1985, pp. 94-95) offers two lines of argument for construing the covering generalizations as rules rather than as premisses.

1. He points out problems that arise if we construe them as premisses and we also say that a premiss is either (a) a statement an arguer offers in support of her conclusion or (b) a proposition which the arguer "had in mind" in offering her argument. For there are enthymemes that appear to be perfectly good arguments, and in many cases the arguer doesn't actually have the covering generalization in mind.
2. He points to the method of criticizing an argument by counter-example as evidence that we can evaluate an enthymematic argument without stating an implicit assumption.

In (1998, p. 31) he lists five benefits to be derived from regarding them as inference licenses rather than as premisses.

Significance of Hitchcock's Theory

Hitchcock's theory is worthy of note for three reasons.

1. It provides a principled way to identify a small list of potential rules (or warrants) for any argument or inference in which there is at least one content term that occurs in both premisses and conclusion.
2. Its generality and (if I may call it that) austerity enable Hitchcock to formulate clearly the question of whether certain "assumptions" are best conceived of as premisses or as inference rules (warrants), and to do so in a way that permits him to develop plausible arguments for conceiving of them as warrants.

---

[14] Hitchcock has communicated to me that he considers the omission of this point from the published version of the 1985 paper to have been an unfortunate oversight.

3. Its generality and austerity will enable us to highlight issues I want to raise in this paper about the virtues arguments should possess, about the virtues inference rules should possess and about the form we should expect warrants or rules of inference to take.

To see both the appeal of Hitchcock's proposal, as well as the questions that arise concerning the virtues arguments should possess, consider the way Hitchcock formulates his "revised generic[15] conception of consequence" (1998, p. 26):

> There is some *general feature of the argument* which is *incompatible with the argument's having true premisses and a false conclusion*, even though that feature is compatible with the argument's having true premisses and compatible with the argument's having a false conclusion. [italics mine]

Suppose for a moment that the principal virtue to be prized in arguments is that they be *truth-preserving* (i.e., that they do not lead from true premisses to a conclusion that's not true). A universal covering generalization which is true picks out a "general feature" of an argument on account of which it will have that virtue. Thus an evaluator, who wants to know whether an argument is truth-preserving, can assure herself that it is if she can find a universal covering generalization for that argument which is true. Notice also that, if an evaluator is in a position to *know* — of some covering *generalization* for the argument — that it is true, she can make this determination without having first to determine the truth of the conclusion.[16]

3. WHAT VIRTUES SHOULD ARGUMENTS AND RULES OF INFERENCE HAVE?

But now let's ask what virtue such *covering generalizations* (CGs) should possess.

Covering Generalizations of the Core Theory

Begin by considering the CGs of the core theory, which are *universal* generalizations and which accordingly will be truth-preserving.

---

[15] The phrase "generic theory of consequence" appears only in the 1998 paper. That paper recognizes five conceptions of logical consequence (the deducibility conception, the modal conception, the substitutional conception, the formal conception and the model-theoretic conception). In previous papers (e.g., (1985) or, in part, (1994)), Hitchcock had tended to couch his points in substitutional terms. The "official" formulation in Hitchcock (1998, p. 26) is phrased so as to be applicable to three of the five conceptions (the substitutional, the formal and the model-theoretic) — hence the phrase "generic conception of consequence".

[16] Hitchcock (1985, pp. 86-87) had suggested that an argument is a *non-sequitur* if the only way to show that its associated conditional is true is by showing that its conclusion is true.

Notice that there are different "variants" on the idea that the principal virtue of arguments and inferences is truth-preservation. Thus we *might* say that to qualify as a rule of inference it suffices

1) That a universal CG be true with respect to the actual world.

Or, alternatively, we might demand some more stringent requirement. Thus, availing ourselves of "possible worlds" talk, we might opt for one or another of the following requirements:

2) That a universal CG be true in all "logically" possible worlds (i.e. worlds whose description would not be inconsistent with any *logically* true statement — where 'logical truth' is defined after the manner of Quine).
3) That a universal CG be true in all "semantically" possible worlds (i.e. worlds in describing which no "meaning postulate" — e.g. that 'colored' applies to everything to which 'red' applies — is violated).
4) That a universal CG be true in all members of some interesting subset of semantically possible worlds — for example, the possible worlds in which what we currently believe to be laws of nature obtain.[17]

Thus on one occasion Hitchcock held that for an argument to be valid, its CG must be "lawlike" (1994, p. 59) — a view which we might take to commit him to something like (iv). One motive for opting for something like (iv) might be this: we want our principles of inference to include principles we can employ in reasoning from suppositions that are, or may turn out to be, contrary to fact. And generalizations that aren't lawlike don't "support" contrary-to-fact conditionals.[18]

A quite different approach to the virtue inference rules should have can be found in Toulmin, who typically says that warrants must be *reliable* and that they derive their "authority" from backing which shows that they are reliable. It may well turn out to be the case that not all rules which are truth-preserving are fit to be relied upon, and that not all inferences which are fit to be relied upon are truth-preserving. Part 6 of this paper will offer a sketch of what we might take such reliability to consist in.

---

[17] If we make the kinds of moves made in Sellars (1953) and especially chapter 11 of Sellars (1963), the possible worlds in which *our* laws of nature hold will coincide with the set of semantically possible worlds (where the "meaning postulates" or p-rules that pick them out are the meaning postulates of *our* language). In a very early paper ('Concepts as involving laws and inconceivable without them' — Sellars (1948)), he had considered and rejected the possibility of making sense of nomically necessary conditionals by construing them as true in some subset of possible worlds. The alternative that emerged several years later is the sort of view set out in Sellars (1953) and in chapter 11 of Sellars (1963) (which had first appeared as a paper in *Philosophy of Science* in 1954).

[18] See for example the arguments for the need to recognize "material inferences" in Sellars (1953) — those arguments rest on the need for subjunctive conditionals in empirical science.

Covering Generalizations of the General Theory

Notice that none of (i)-(iv) in the preceding section is going to work for good arguments/inferences that are not "conclusive" — inferences of the sort sometimes called "inductive" or (in a happier phrase) inferences in which the support that premisses lend to a conclusion is recognized as defeasible. The norms by which such inferences are assessed ought not to be rules that are truth-preserving, since such inferences can be good even when their premisses are true and their conclusions false. Hitchcock extends his core theory to handle such cases by loosening the requirement that covering generalizations be *universal*, and suggesting that a CG may be "possibly qualified as holding 'generally' or 'presumably'" (2003a, p. 80), or that it is "non-trivially acceptable (always, provisionally, etc.)," or that it "can be modally qualified, as holding for the most part, or *ceteris paribus*, or even just sometimes" (2005a, p. 205). Perhaps the clearest example of what he has in mind by such qualifications is to be found in Hitchcock (1992, p. 112), where he formulates a "conception of good inference" in the following terms:

> The argument contains one or more repeated content expressions on which uniform substitutions within a category or subcategory sometimes make the premises true, sometimes make the conclusion false, and <u>either always, mostly, or provisionally make the conclusion true when they make the premises true</u> [underlining mine].

The virtue which good arguments exhibit on this account is formulated *with reference to truth*, and we might say such arguments are good just when the truth of their premisses is *indicative* of the truth of their conclusions. [19] But such formulations raise several questions which Hitchcock himself has not attempted to answer.

1. It is not clear exactly what it *means* to say that of a set of substitutions that they *"provisionally* make the conclusion true" (Hitchcock, 1992) or that a covering generalization can be qualified as "holding presumably" (Hitchcock, 2003a). This is something that needs to be spelled out in greater detail.[20]

---

[19] In another context, Mark Weinstein (2002b, pp. 166-167) has proposed, for example, that we recognize a "range of entailment kinds" from logical entailments to "weak entailments that are no more than suggestive", and that "we might expect for each entailment kind a linked implication relation based either on an appropriately modalized warrant, or alternatively, on appropriately characterized inference tickets". He has, he says, "explored in detail how such a relationship could be given rigorous metamathematical content for entailments that depend on theoretic depth and breadth, modeled on the entailments within mature physical sciences". Weinstein (2002b) only broaches these ideas in summary fashion, but see the references there to five of Weinstein's papers where they are developed more fully.

[20] Consider, for example, the claim that a CG (for example, of the form: for any x if Fx then Gx) holds only *presumably* or *presumptively*. That can't be taken to mean that we may *presume that* for any x if Fx then Gx. As soon as one discovered an object that was F but not G, one would no longer be entitled to make such a

2. Though what it means to settle for "mostly" instead of "always" in the formulation of a covering generalization is clear enough, the *implications* of doing so need to be assessed. (a) Such "weakening" of criteria for the acceptability of a conclusion might well give rise to the sorts of problems associated with the attempt to formulate a purely probabilistic criterion of acceptance, such as the lottery paradox (see Pinto, 2001, pp. 106-107, especially footnote 5). (b) And chaining together a series of inferences that are not truth-preserving can lead to "untoward" results, and as a result it may turn out to be necessary to introduce epistemic operators into the consequent of covering generalizations (see the second of the two considerations formulated on pp. 127-28 below).

In Part 5 of this paper, following up on ideas suggested by Toulmin which Hitchcock himself doesn't draw on, I will attempt to work out a way of conceiving *exactly* how a CG may be qualified as holding only generally or presumably or provisionally which addresses the issues raised in points (1) and (2).

Practical Arguments and Inferences

Finally, we should note that even the more relaxed idea that arguments and inferences need only be truth-*indicative* isn't going to shed light on forms of argument that culminate in *prescriptions* or on forms of inference that culminate in a *decision* or an *intention*, since prescriptions, decisions and intentions don't have truth-values (i.e. their "direction of fit" is not word-to-world, but is world-to-word — see Searle (1979, pp. 3-4) and section 32 of Anscombe (1957)).

Epistemic Status

In recent years Hitchcock has come to insist that CGs possess an additional sort of virtue. In (2001, p. 1) he says that an argument's conclusion follows from its premisses if and only if it has some covering generalization that is "non-trivially acceptable (always, provisionally, etc.)", adding that a CG is acceptable if and only if it "deserves to be accepted by the appraiser". In (2003a, p. 80) he says that an argument's conclusion or claim follows from its ground

> . . . if and only if there is some *justified* covering generalization of the argument, possibly qualified as holding "generally" or "presumably" [italics mine].

---

presumption. Presuming cannot be "applied to" the CG *as a whole* — the universal quantifier cannot occur within the scope of the presumption. Rather, *the reference to presumption must fall within the scope of the universal quantifier*. One must modify the CG to say something like: for any x, if Fx then x is presumably a G. But that, I think, will come down to saying: if you know something is an F, then you may presume it to be a G — in which case, one's CG will turn out to be the sort of warrant that I describe in Part 5 of this paper.

See also the discussion of "justified applicable warrant" in Hitchcock (2005a). These texts all imply that a warrant must meet some sort of *epistemic* criterion.

I want to distinguish between the *content* of a rule or warrant, and the epistemic status which that content has for a particular person at a particular time. And, as I've already indicated in note 2 above, I want to set aside (or abstract from) questions about the *epistemic* status rules of inference must have for persons making an argument or drawing an inference, or for those appealing to the rule in the course of evaluating an argument or inference. I propose to deal here only with questions about the "content" of warrants – both (a) the *form* the content should take and (b) material features the content must have if it is to be *fit* to serve as a rule. And I want to press such questions especially in connection with cases in which the support licensed by such rules is defeasible.

4. AN ALTERNATIVE CONCEPTION OF ARGUMENT VIRTUE

Entitlement-preserving Inferences

A common idea about arguments and inferences is that they provide *justification* for their conclusions. Of course *bad* arguments and inferences don't justify their conclusions, only good arguments do. It's possible to think of the justificatory potential of good arguments as simply a *by-product* of their meeting the criteria for being good.[21] But it's also open to us to think that *what makes an argument good* is precisely its *having justificatory potential.* Let's try to make sense of the justificatory potential of arguments and inferences along the following lines:

> An *argument* justifies its conclusion if and only if it *shows* — i.e. *makes it apparent* — *that it is reasonable* to embrace (perhaps to assert) that conclusion, given its premisses.
>
> An *inference* justifies its conclusion if and only if it *makes it reasonable* to embrace (perhaps to accept) that conclusion, given its premisses.

If we follow up on these thoughts, we're led to a conception of argument virtue quite different from the conceptions just considered in Part 3. Let us endorse the idea that an argument is good only if it is *reasonable* to embrace its premisses.[22] Then arguments or inferences with justificatory potential will be those in which premisses

[21] E.g., one might hold that good arguments are the ones that are truth-preserving and that arguments can justify their conclusions just because they are truth-preserving.

[22] I take it to be relatively uncontroversial that "acceptability" epistemically understood is a *necessary* condition of premiss adequacy. For a defense of the idea that it is also a *sufficient* condition of premiss adequacy, see Pinto (2001, pp. 23-26; 2002).

which it is *reasonable* to embrace render a conclusion *reasonable* to embrace. Such arguments need not be *truth*-preserving, but they will be *entitlement*-preserving.

In Part 5 of this paper, I am going to try to extract from Toulmin's account of arguments a rudimentary way of conceiving rules of inference consonant with the idea that the principal virtue of arguments is some sort of entitlement-preservation. But before attempting to do that, I want to provide motivation for the shift from truth-preserving norms to entitlement-preserving norms.

Why Conceive of Good Inferences as Entitlement-preserving Inferences?

Why shift from a truth-preservation conception of argument virtue to an entitlement-preservation conception? Such a shift has potentially radical consequences, since it invites a move away from an approach to arguments and inferences that reduces to *logic* as traditionally conceived, toward an approach that will have to be grounded in *epistemology*. 'Reasonable' is not a word that belongs to the vocabulary of logic as traditionally conceived; it is a term whose elaboration will, almost inevitably, have to take place within an epistemological perspective.

In the case of good arguments which are "conclusive" and have "factual" premisses and conclusions, the shift to an epistemological perspective *might* turn out to be optional. But I want to suggest two reasons why such a shift may well be inevitable for any satisfactory treatment of *defeasible* arguments and inferences.

1. Contemporary discussions of good arguments that aren't deductively valid highlight the fact that they are *defeasible* and attempt to conceptualize the relationship of such arguments to the considerations that "defeat" them — to the *defeaters*. But the notion of a defeater is, I submit, an ineluctably *epistemic* notion. Let *r* be a consideration which can play the role of a defeater in connection with an inference from *p* to *q*. *r* does not defeat the inference from *p* to *q* by being *true.*[23] Rather, *a defeater defeats an inference only in virtue of having a certain epistemic status* — paradigmatically, by being or becoming *known* to be true — or what amounts to an epistemic status (e.g. being "in the database" or being derivable from what's "in the database"). Defeasible support for a conclusion is undermined or overridden by defeaters that have *come to light*.
2. Even though we "accept" the conclusions of defeasible inferences, we must have some way of *marking* the fact that they are conclusions of defeasible inference — that they are, to put it crudely, "less than completely certain". Otherwise, we run the risk of stringing together a series of defeasible inferences

[23] At least if we're thinking of what Pollock (2001, p. 235) calls *rebutting* defeaters and what I (2001, p. 28) call *overriding* defeaters. For whenever an argument has true premisses and a false conclusion, there will be a host of *true* propositions which "rebut" its conclusion — i.e. from which the negation of its conclusion follows or could be inferred. Hence, on the assumption that the mere truth of a rebutter defeats a defeasible inference, virtually every defeasible inference with a false conclusion will turn out to be defeated.

> with "untoward" results. Suppose we let p lead to the acceptance of q, where propositions like q are true 60% of the times at which propositions like p are true; and suppose we also we let q lead to the acceptance of r where propositions like r are true 60% of the times at which propositions like q are true. Then we will let p lead to the acceptance of r, when the probability of r given p *may* be no more than .36 — and that is an untoward result. The problem that threatens is not avoided by increasing the percentages — no matter how high the percentages get, stringing together such inferences "degrades" the support our initial premiss gives to our terminal conclusion and raises the possibility that a sufficiently long chain of such inferences will have an "untoward" outcome. It becomes essential therefore to *mark* the conclusions of defeasible inferences as such — which is, I think, what words like 'probably', 'presumably', 'possibly', or 'almost certainly' are in fact doing when they're used to qualify our conclusions. The presence or absence of such markers will indicate when and how it is *reasonable* to use those conclusions as the premisses of further arguments. But to do *that* is just to perform the function which the vocabulary of epistemic evaluation performs.

These considerations are by no means conclusive. But I think they are enough to make it worthwhile to elaborate the idea of entitlement-preservation in greater detail. That's what I'll try to do in the remainder of this paper.

5. THE FORM OF WARRANTS REVISITED: AN ALTERNATIVE ACCOUNT BASED ON FEATURES OF TOULMIN'S TREATMENT OF ARGUMENTS

One place we might look for examples of entitlement-preserving principles is in the accounts Chisholm used to give of epistemic principles. For reasons I won't pursue here,[24] I think it will prove more instructive to extract explicitly entitlement-preserving principles from ideas and suggestions sketched in Toulmin (2003/1958) and Toulmin, Rieke and Janik (hereafter Toulmin *et al.*) (1984/1979). Accordingly, I'm going to construct an account of the form of warrants by picking and choosing from among elements of Toulmin's story. I take full responsibility for the result, but I acknowledge Toulmin as the source or inspiration of much (though clearly not all) of what I say.

[24] For one thing, Chisholm (1957; 1966; 1977) works with a small number of such principles, few of which throw much light on the "material" inferences I'm interested, whereas Toulmin warrants — as Hitchcock has recognized — hold out the promise of illuminating such inferences. For another, Chisholm's account of the *authority* of such principles leads either to the claim that they are synthetic *a priori* propositions (see the hint of this in Chisholm, 1957, p. 112) or to something that resembles Moore's various attempts to defend common sense (see Chisholm on the "problem of the criterion" in (1966, chapter 4) and (1977, chapter 7).

Key Features of Toulmin's Account

There are six features of Toulmin's account of arguments that I think any account of the form of warrants should incorporate or make provision for. They are as follows:

1. Toulmin often formulates warrants as straightforward statements about objects ("Scarcely any Swedes are Roman Catholics") and says they may be written in the form "If D, then C". But he says that "they can profitably be expanded, and made more explicit" by putting them in a form such as "Data such as D entitle one to draw conclusions, or make claims, such as C" (1958, p. 98; 2003, p. 91) [underlining mine]. Note two things about the second of the forms just quoted:
   (i) It quite *explicitly* takes the form of granting an *entitlement*, as does another "expanded" statement form suggested in the very same passage: "Given data D, you may take it that C".[25]
   (ii) It construes warranting statements as *general* statements — it is data *such as* D that entitle one to make a claim *such as* C (see Hitchcock, 2003a, pp. 73-74).
2. Toulmin clearly distinguishes warrants from the "backing" which gives them authority by pointing to the *normative* and *action-guiding* force or function of warrants. Explaining the relation of backing to warrant with an example turning on a British statute, he says about the example (1958, pp. 105-106; 2003, p. 98):

   > Though the facts about the statute may provide all the backing required by this warrant, the explicit statement of the warrant itself is more than a repetition of these facts: it is a general *moral* of a practical character, about the ways in which we can safely argue in view of these facts [underlining is mine].

3. He recognizes a crucial role for *modal qualifiers* ('probably', 'possibly', 'certainly', 'presumably') in the presentation of arguments (1958, pp. 100ff; 2003, pp. 93ff). More importantly, he offers what I would call a *functional interpretation* of those qualifiers (2003/1958, chapters 1 and 2) — his insistence that the "field-invariant" *force*[26] of such qualifiers is to be found

---

[25] In fact this last form of words echoes the way in which rules of inference are standardly formulated in expositions of classical formal logic — as far back, at least, as the Preface to the second edition of the *Principia Mathematica*.

[26] Toulmin wants to distinguish between the *force* of such terms, which is "field invariant", and the *criteria* for their use, which varies from field to field. Since there are notorious difficulties in pinning down the meaning of the "field" (Toulmin's definition in terms of "logical types" (1958, p. 14; 2003, p.14) isn't much help, and moreover doesn't fit what he often seems to have in mind when he himself uses the term — namely disciplines.) One might do better to say that the force of such terms is context independent, while the criteria for their use will vary from context to context.

"in the practical implications of their use" (p. 28).[27] Thus on his interpretation, the force of saying "Possibly *p*" is to accord to *p* the "right to considered". And the force of saying "S is probably P" is to "commit myself guardedly, tentatively or with reservations to the view that S is P, and (likewise guardedly) lend my authority to that view"[28] and he observes that the addition of the modal qualifiers "has the effect of indicating what *sort* of reliance the supporting material entitles us to place on the claim, C" (Toulmin *et al.*, 1984/1979, p. 87).

4. In the Toulmin model, modals occur principally as *qualifying the conclusion* of an argument. However, Toulmin occasionally includes elements that correspond to such modal qualifiers *in his formulation of warrants themselves*. On the few occasions he does so, he uses expressions which convey explicitly that we are *entitled to adopt a particular cognitive or doxastic attitude* toward a propositional content. For example, in formulating a warrant whose backing consists of information about statutes, he chooses the following form of words: "*If* a man was born in a British colony, he *may be presumed to be* British" (1958, p. 105; 2003, p. 98). So phrased, the warrant recognizes an entitlement to adopt one particular cognitive attitude — presuming — toward a propositional content.[29]

There is a range of such attitudes — presuming that *p*, expecting that *p* and being certain that *p*, for example — and I believe that each can be type-identified by reference to the *functional* role in our cognitive lives that it bestows on their contents. For example, an *expectation* that X will occur or

---

[27] Note especially his remark that the modal operators "are best understood...by examining the functions they have when we come to set out our arguments" (1958, p. 18; 2003, p. 17).

[28] Lurking in the background here is the account Austin gives in 'Other minds' of what we do when we say "I know". "When I say 'I know', I give others my word: I give others my authority for saying that 'S is P'" (Austin, 1970/1946, p. 99). By virtue of lending my authority unguardedly, I make myself liable for criticism should what I lent my authority to prove false — in that event I am "liable to be rounded on by others" (p. 100). But if I lend my authority guardedly — if I say only "I am sure" and do not say "I know", then according to Austin I'm not liable to be "rounded on". Something analogous is true in Toulmin's account of "Probably S is P" (see, 1958, pp. 57-62; 2003, pp. 53-57). Though I don't endorse Toulmin's account of 'probably' in all its details, I do hold a view that is similar to it (see the final sentence in note 29 below.)

[29] When discussing the modal qualifiers, Toulmin makes it quite clear that employing them does not yield sentences which *refer to* doxastic attitudes: "saying 'S is probably P' is *not* saying 'I am fairly confident, but less than certain, that S is P', for 'probably' does not belong to this series of words . . . When I say 'S is probably P', I commit myself guardedly, tentatively or with reservations to the view that S is P, and (likewise guardedly) lend my authority to that view" (1958, pp. 52-53; 2003, p. 49). However, he concedes (to the proponent of the "subjective" interpretation of probability) that "He [the subjectivist] has noticed one thing (perhaps the only one) which is always the case whenever the word 'probably', or one of its derivatives, is used correctly: everyone who says and means 'Probably *p*' does *believe confidently* that *p*" (p. 59). In this regard, he is adopting a view about 'probably' that my co-authors and I adopted in Pinto, Blair and Parr (1993, pp. 95-97) — that 'probably' is an "assertion qualifier" and that, although in saying 'Probably *p*' we may in some sense be *expressing* our "belief attitude" toward what we are claiming, the claim we are *putting forward* or *asserting* is *p*.

has occurred provides a basis of inferences and actions that would normally be successful only if X will occur or has occurred. Someone who *expects*, but is not *fully certain*, that X has occurred or will occur can base actions or inferences on that expectation, but if she's not fully certain she will make backup plans to cover the eventuality that X might turn out not to be (or to have been) the case. Thus a reasonable person can expect (indeed be quite confident) that her lottery ticket won't win, and will make plans and undertake commitments on the assumption that it won't win, but can still hold on to the ticket because she knows it *might* be a winning ticket after all.

5. Under the heading of "rebuttals" Toulmin recognizes the role of defeaters in argument and inference. He seldom if ever includes a reference to rebuttals in his formulation of warrants, but rather treats them as matters which affect the *applicability* of warrants (1958, pp. 101-102; 2003, pp. 94-95; see also Toulmin *et al.*, 1984/1979, chapters 10, 11, and especially 13).[30] The existence of defeaters needs to be acknowledged in the *formulation* of warrants, and though I won't purse the matter in this paper, a full account of warrants will have to shed light on the relationship of defeaters to the warrants whose force they defeat.

6. Toulmin treats the issue of whether a particular warrant has "authority" as (i) an issue whose resolution typically involves appeal to matters of fact (which make up the backing of the warrant) but also as (ii) an issue that must be addressed in light of the *goals* and *purposes* alive in the context of the reasonings that are to be assessed on the basis of that warrant.[31]

An Alternative Account of the General Form of Warrants

I want to make the idea of warrants for entitlement-preserving arguments and inferences more concrete. In order to do so, I offer a first sketch of the form such warrants might take. The sketch is a preliminary one, since it leaves a number of loose ends unresolved. But here are instructions for how to create a warrant of the sort I'm interested in. The process has five steps.

1. Given an argument or inference, construct a covering generalization for it after the manner of Hitchcock. For simplicity's sake, assume the result is of the form

   H1 (x) If x is F then x is G.

[30] Section 4 of Hitchcock (2005a) accommodates defeaters in essentially the same way.

[31] In Toulmin's account, the authority of warrants — considered as "general morals of a practical character" (1958, p. 106; 2003, p. 98) — arises from their backing. But — as I read Toulmin — that authority is also rooted in the goals they are to serve (see Toulmin *et al.* (1984/1979, pp. 274-276), and at various junctures in chapters 26-30 of that work).

Of course, if there were more than one "repeated content expression" in the argument with which we started, we might choose to replace more than one of them with variables and prepend more than one universal quantifier.

2. Next enhance H1 by inserting the phrase 'it is reasonable to suppose that' as follows:

W1 (x) If it is reasonable to suppose that x is F then it is reasonable to suppose that x is G.

I am using *supposing* as a generic concept in relation to which believing, being almost certain, presuming, expecting, etc., stand as species. Notice that for quantification to work here, we have to be talking about *de re* supposing, not *de dicto* supposing. This should pose no problem, since supposing is something like believing, and we know how to manage with the distinction between *de re* and *de dicto* ascriptions of belief.

3. But of course if supposing is anything like believing, what it's reasonable for one person to suppose can be quite different from what it's reasonable for another to suppose. So we need to complicate things a bit further, and include a reference to the *person* for whom a supposing might or might not be reasonable, and the *time* at which it is reasonable.

W2 (S) (t) (x) If it is reasonable at t for S to suppose that x is F then it is reasonable at t for S to suppose that x is G.[32]

4. Since we're taking supposing to be a *generic* expression of which presuming, expecting, being certain, etc., are forms or species, let us write our formula in such a way that it can accommodate a variety of different "species" of supposing, by introducing subscripts as follows

W3 (S) (t) (x) If it is reasonable at t for S to suppose_i that x is F then it is reasonable at t for S to suppose_j that x is G.[33]

The intent is that in formulating a potential warrant for a particular argument or inference, we may specify one form of supposing in the antecedent of the warrant and specify either the same or a *different* form of supposing in the

[32] The idea that the principles in terms of which we evaluate arguments and inferences should be relative to persons (and also to times) is consistent with the views about argument appraisal defended in my early paper "Logic, epistemology and argument appraisal," first presented in 1989 and reprinted as chapter 3 of Pinto (2001). Notice also that the form I'm proposing would leave us the option of restricting the domain of values which the quantificational variables might take. We might, for example, restrict the applicability of a warrant to the members of one or another professional community.

[33] It is not difficult to see how to enhance this preliminary account of the form of warrants to make provision for arguments and inferences with two or more premisses towards which an individual might have different doxastic attitudes — for example, someone drawing an inference about whether Reilly is married might *be quite sure* that Reilly is a Catholic priest, but only *presume* that he is not an Eastern rite priest. The need for antecedents with more than one "it is reasonable for S to . . ." clauses will also arise if we should want to have warrants that take us from a desire and a belief to an intention. See the last paragraph of part 6 on p. 134

consequent of the warrant. This provision will enable us to provide what I earlier called a "qualitative" equivalent to the idea that *belief should be proportioned to the evidence.*

5. Finally, we need to include a qualification that recognizes the role that defeaters play in our reasoning about most matters. I propose to do that by including such a qualification, as follows:

> W3a (S) (t) (x) If it is reasonable at t for S to suppose$_i$ that x is F then, in the absence at t of undermining or overriding evidence, it is reasonable at t for S to suppose$_j$ that x is G.

The underlined phrase is a "dummy" clause that, in effect, recognizes the existence of a set of problems which need to be solved.

Significance of the Alternative Account

The result is a form of warrant which

1. Is consistent with the idea that good arguments are *entitlement preserving;*
2. Construes the entitlements in question as *epistemic* entitlements;
3. Incorporates a qualitative version of "evidence proportionalism" by enabling us to license only doxastic attitudes toward conclusions that are appropriate to the evidence on which those conclusions are based;
4. Makes explicit provision for defeasible arguments and inferences.

W3 and W3a are of course elaborations of an idea originally drawn from Hitchcock. But elaborating Hitchcock's idea in the way that I have brings us to something that's closer to the way Toulmin sometimes expresses his warrants. Recall for instance the example quoted in the previous section:

> *If* a man was born in a British colony, he *may be presumed to be* British.

To recast that in the form of W3 we need only construe the word "may" as granting *epistemic* permission, and make it explicit that what creates the epistemic permission to presume is the *knowledge* that a man was born in a British colony.

Rules like these are quite different from the sorts of rules that logicians formulate. To understand their significance, I suggest we recall the "maxim of shallow analysis" that Quine (1960, p. 160) says should govern our paraphrases into "canonical systems of logical notation":

> expose no more logical structure than seems useful for the deduction or other inquiry at hand.

If rules whose form is captured by W1 through W3a are to be commended, it is because often *not enough structure is exposed* in the canonical notations of more traditional logics to enable us to offer *nuanced evaluations* of the arguments and inferences that interest us. Indeed, we might want to observe a modified version of Quine's maxim:

> move up from rules of the form of H1 toward rules of the form of W3a only when, and to the extent that, it is useful to expose more structure in order to achieve an appropriately nuanced evaluation.

Two final notes about the "general form of warrant" that W3 and W3a represent.

1. Observe that warrants in which the "species of supposing" referenced in the antecedent and the consequent are the *same* will form a special case of this more general form — they will be "entitlement-preserving" in a narrow sense. Where a single premiss is known to entail its conclusion, for example, warrants will usually be entitlement-preserving in that narrow sense. But arguments and inferences that are not "deductively valid" will usually require warrants which are entitlement-preserving only in a broader sense captured by the general form of W3. What is preserved is these cases is reasonableness — but the kind of "doing" which is pronounced reasonable in the antecedent (e.g. being sure that) is a different kind of "doing" from that pronounced reasonable in the consequent (e.g., expecting).
2. Notice also that we *could* make the form of warrant I'm proposing more general still by recasting it to accommodate propositional attitudes other than (but in addition to) doxastic attitudes — e.g. conative and evaluative attitudes such as *desiring it to be the case that, intending that, fearing that*, etc. See for example my 1990 paper "Generalizing the notion of argument," reprinted as chapter 2 of Pinto (2001). Doing so would yield an even more powerful tool, one which would enable us to conceptualize the role of *reasons* in the constitution of emotions, in the formation of values and of intentions, and in the deliberation that issues in our practical choices.

6. WHAT VIRTUES SHOULD WARRANTS HAVE?

Taking my cue from Toulmin's frequent reference to the *reliability* of warrants, I want to offer a sketch of the virtue such warrants should have by offering an account of what we might take the reliability of a warrant to consist in. Though I think the account that follows is *consistent* with many of the things Toulmin says about how warrants acquire their authority, the account is quite specific to the conception of warrants sketched in Part 5 of this paper and in its details is almost certainly not anything which Toulmin himself ever actually had in mind.

Rules and Inferential Practices

I'll use an example of a type of inference my spouse taught me to make. She's fond of Courtland apples, and often asks me to pick up a few when I shop for groceries. The first time I did, she complained that the apples I brought home were sour — she only likes the sweet ones. When I asked how I could tell whether a Courtland is sweet, she said something like the following, pointing to a Courtland apple she'd just taken out of the refrigerator:

> Look at the coloring of the skin. If there's a fair amount of red in its skin, as there is in this one, you can assume that it's sweet.

She warned me that although this works with Courtland apples; it doesn't work for every kind of apple. A bit of probing revealed that she had discovered this technique herself by trial and error, and that she continues to use the technique because it works for her. Probing also revealed that, although she is aware that not all Courtland apples with this sort of coloring are sweet, she has no idea what proportion of them are sweet. Moreover, she doesn't know whether this technique works with Courtland apples *generally*; she only knows that it works in the places where she shops for apples.

It's also worth noting that although she uses this technique in deciding which Courtlands to *buy*, before she'd serve Courtland slices to guests, she would actually *taste* a slice from each apple to "make sure" that slices from that apple aren't sour. In other words, she treats the expectation arising from her inference as sufficient for some purposes (buying) but not for others (serving to guests).

My spouse had supplied me with a rudimentary "rule of inference" which, at the risk of pedantry, we can formulate as follows:

> If you know (i.e. have the right to be sure) that the skin of a Courtland apple has a coloring similar to a particular sample, then it is reasonable for you to expect that it will be sweet.

Notice the following things about this "rule":

1. It *endorses* an inferential practice in which my wife engages, and which she has taught me to engage in.
2. That practice is sustained or reinforced because it regularly gets my spouse and me where we want to go, and it would be extinguished if it ceased regularly getting us where we want to go — if we started to find more than occasionally that the Courtlands we brought home weren't sweet.
3. The possibility of such reinforcement and extinction depends on the fact that we have *other ways of finding out* whether an apple is sweet — by biting into them, etc. But those other ways of finding out also have an "inferential dimension" (does this apple taste sour because it actually *is* sour, or am I coming down with a bug in virtue of which *nothing* would taste sweet to me)

— that is to say, those *other* ways of finding out are sustained by *other* inferential practices. Inferential practices face the tribunal of experience not singly but as corporate bodies, somebody might say.

4. The rule which endorses our inferential practice is not a rule that my spouse or I need to formulate explicitly or to follow *consciously* when we draw conclusions about the sweetness of Courtland apples in the store. In Sellars' happy phrase (1968, pp. 75-77), it is not a rule for *doing*, it's a rule for *criticizing*. In cases like this, the practices may come first, the rules may get formulated in our attempt to get a "reflective hold" on them — perhaps for purposes of evaluating the practice or some instance of the practice.
5. In cases like this one, finding a rule involves finding a *description* which fits one or another of our inferential practices — which is something that Hitchcock's technique for generating covering generalizations enables us to do, and which my elaboration on Hitchcock's technique also enables us to do. But acknowledging such a description as a *rule* involves, in addition, a decision to *endorse* one or another of our practices and to endorse it *under some such description.*

We can begin to understand the *authority* of such norms – and the *virtues* to be expected of them when they are formulated as rules – by reflecting on the considerations that should lead us to *endorse* one or another of our practices *under a rule-like description of it.*

The Context of Rules: Critical Practice

I suggested in the preceding section that inferential practices like those in my example are *reinforced* or *extinguished* depending on whether they regularly "get us where we want to go". Now reinforcement and extinction may be reasons *why* we engage in or cease to engage in inferential practices, but they are not reasons *for* engaging in such practices.

Reasons *for* engaging or not engaging in a practice begin to emerge only when we start to reason *about* our practices. To reason *about* our inferential practices, we need to get some kind of "reflective hold" on what they are. And formulating a *rule-like* description is *one* way of doing that — we can say, for instance, that we often *behave as though* we were following a rule that *permits* us to do X when Y obtains. But then the decision to *endorse* a practice can take the form of deciding (or perhaps finding out) whether following (or conforming to) such a rule would be a good thing to do.

Even though we may never have had any such rule actually in mind when engaging in an inferential practice — and even if we never *start* having it in mind at such times — the rules we reflectively endorse can become *rules of criticism* to which we can revert when evaluating what an actual person does on a particular occasion.

The emergence of a practice of reasoning *about* our inferences and our inferential practices changes things in important ways (see Sosa for a similar point[34]). It institutes a new kind of practice — a *critical* practice[35] — in which we evaluate individual performances by measuring them against rules we've reflectively endorsed. Moreover, and perhaps most importantly, it permits us — as Brandom points out[36] — to *discuss the merits* of the practices we engage in and to ask for and give reasons for endorsing them. Finally, the reflective practice of reasoning *about* our inferential practices introduces *a new kind of "reinforcement" and "extinction"*: the *realization* that our practice would be better if it were changed in a certain way gives us reasons *for* changing our practices that can become reasons *why* they change.

---

[34] Sosa's insistence on the importance of "reflective knowledge" can be seen as a partial recognition of this point, or a first step in its direction. See "Knowledge and intellectual virtue" in Sosa (1991, pp. 225-244, esp. pp. 239-242) and also "Intellectual virtue in perspective" in Sosa (1991, pp. 270-293, esp. p. 290).

[35] In "The relation of argument to inference," I attempt to trace a possible evolution of the concept of inference through a series of 6 steps (Pinto, 2001, pp. 42-43). What I've just pointed out corresponds to steps 2 and 3 of that process. That paper recognizes further stages in the evolution of critical practice and in our concept of inference — most importantly, a step in which "[w]e move . . . to a broadened conception of criticism, one not tied quite so closely to logical rules or material principles of inference, but modelled in part on the discussions of the probative value of evidence that occur in contexts where articulable rules are not available". I'm still inclined to think that our critical practice extends beyond the realm for which we are able to formulate anything like rules of inference — a realm in which nevertheless "the value of [our] inferences is not something that is just arbitrarily accepted; rather it is something open to discussion and rational evaluation". Quotations are from Pinto (2001, p. 43).

[36] Brandom has insisted on the "expressive" role of logical vocabulary. Thus he has recently said:

> Instead of seeing conformity with logical truths as what rationality consists in, one can see logical vocabulary as making possible the explicit codification of meaning-constitutive inferential relations. On such an expressive view of the function of logic, the task characteristic of logical locutions as such is to let us *say,* in the form of explicit claims, what otherwise we could only do - namely, endorse some material inferential relations and reject others. Prior to the introduction of the conditional, for instance, one can implicitly take or treat the material inference (in any of the three senses botanized above [commitment-preserving, entitlement-preserving, and inferences reflecting incompatibility relations]) from *p* to *q* as a good or bad one, endorsing or rejecting it in practice. Once a suitable conditional is available, though, one can explicitly *claim that p* entails *q*. And explicit claims are the sort of thing we can *reason* about, ask for *evidence* or *arguments* for. The expressive job of specifically *logical locutions* is to make inferential relations explicit, to bring them into the game of giving and asking for reasons as things whose own rational credentials are available for inspection and criticism. (2002, p. 9)

Brandom's overall project, which is — to put it crudely — to model all intentional states and statuses on what is required to make sense of linguistic performances, while taking assertion to be the prototypical speech act. The *content* of an assertion is to be understood in terms of (a) what other assertions it *commits* us to (downstream, in his terms) and (b) what other assertions (upstream, in his terms) can *entitle* us to it (i.e. can be offered as reasons for it). Since *assertion* is an on/off concept, his account does not lend itself to "reconstructing" the functionally type-identified variations in doxastic attitude that are central to my account. At this point, it is not at all clear to me what the effect would be on Brandom's project if you tried to include in it the recognition of functionally type-identified varieties of "guarded" assertion. It might amount to a fairly minor addition or emendation; but then again, it might upset the applecart.

Reliability

So we find ourselves staring at the question: what would *reasons* for endorsing an inferential practice have to look like? Or — and this is not *quite* the same question — what would make an inferential practice a *good* one? The issues here are very much like the issues raised in Parts 3 and 4 about the virtues of arguments and inferences, but we're now playing in a slightly different key – we're asking about the virtues of *inferential practices*. Shifting into this key, two sorts of consideration now become possible.

(A) What *role* does one or another practice play in the broader scheme of things?
(B) How *well* do the "outputs" of a practice serve the role or roles which that practice plays?

Identifying the *role* of a practice provides an *objective* basis or criterion for making a value judgment about the outputs of the practice – in light of something like the principle that it's *good* when something serves its purpose and *bad* when it fails to serve its purpose.[37]

The purposes served by the sorts of inferential practices I'm considering in this paper must, in the nature of the case, be purposes which require the adoption of a doxastic attitude toward a propositional content. They must be purposes which require the *fixation of belief* about some matter, as it were. Now *some* purposes served by the adoption of doxastic attitudes are *insensitive* to whether the propositional content of the doxastic attitudes serving them are *true* or *close to the truth* — for example, loyalty to a friend may perhaps require that I believe him to be innocent of some charge *irrespective* or whether or not he is. Such purposes can indeed give rise to "reasons for belief" of a special sort — which I have elsewhere called pragmatic reasons[38] — but they are not the sorts of purposes in relation to

[37] Since I'm *not* about to claim that any such principle is "true by definition", no "naturalistic fallacy" lurks in the bushes here. Moreover, my view is that using the word 'good' without scare quotes to characterize something which serves a purpose is *appropriate* only if one *endorses* the purpose which it serves. It is only in virtue of a *positive evaluative attitude* toward a purpose that characterizing the "means" to it as 'good' has genuine *normative* force. This is, I think, the fundamental insight of prescriptivism — though the point need not be developed in quite the same terms as those in which prescriptivists have developed it.

Moreover, one's evaluation of a means as good is *reasonable* only if one's evaluative attitude toward the purpose it serves is itself reasonable. It is a component of my view of reasons that there can be *reasons* for such evaluative attitudes — see Pinto (2003b) for this point — and that therefore such attitudes can be, or fail to be, reasonable.

[38] In the paper 'Reasons' (2003a, pp. 7-8), I distinguished between *reasons* for believing or accepting something and *grounds* on which we do or might accept it. I called attention to "pragmatic reasons" for believing (represented, for example, by the argument in Pascal's wager), and suggested that the mark of such pragmatic reasons is that they don't contain *grounds* for belief or *evidence* for what is to be believed.

which the reliability of *inferential* practices ought to be judged. Accordingly, I assume that any purpose in light of which the reliability of an *inferential* practice is properly judged must be a purpose

(a) which requires the adoption of a cognitive (e.g. doxastic) attitude, and
(b) whose realization is sensitive to whether the propositional content of the required cognitive attitude is true or close to the truth.

Thus, for any inferential practice whose outputs belong to a particular series of doxastic attitudes (*being certain* that *p*, *presuming* that *p*, *expecting* that *p*, for example), typical purposes won't be served unless there is a substantial likelihood that *p* is true or close to the truth in the range of occasions in which the practice is appropriate.[39] For inferential practices whose outputs belong to a *different* series of doxastic attitudes (for example, *suspecting* that *p*, *treating p as a "live option"*), typical purposes will require only that there be a non-negligible likelihood that *p* is true or close to the truth in the range of occasions in which the practice is appropriate.

In Pinto (2003a) I argued for the claim that rational decisions about whether to *accept* a proposition as a basis for further inferences, though made in light of evidence, are also dependent on epistemic and non-epistemic goals and purposes — since (among other things) the "strength" of evidence needed to warrant acceptance of a premiss will depend in part on what's at stake in the reasoning which will be based on that premiss.[40] Something similar is true with respect to the rationality of adopting *doxastic* attitudes toward propositional contents. The purposes requiring the fixation of belief on a given matter can be either "practical" or "theoretical", and in either case are relevant to determining whether a given constellation of evidence warrants adoption of a given doxastic attitude.

Moreover, when the purposes served by an inferential practice require a substantial likelihood of truth or verisimilitude, the doxastic attitude issuing from the practice should *also* serve the purposes of the practice *even when truth or verisimilitude is not achieved.* Suppose that the output of an inference is an expectation or a presumption in which what is expected or presumed proves *false*. In *many* (perhaps all) such cases in which the expectation or presumption is *reasonable*, it will still have served my broader purposes well despite its content having proved false. If I plan a picnic because I *expect* it will be sunny, but make backup provisions for the eventuality that it might rain (because I only *expect* it will

---

Although in that paper I contrasted *pragmatic* reasons with reasons *containing grounds* for believing, I did not there explain the basis of the distinction between the two sorts of reasons. I will say here that "pragmatic reasons" for a belief are reasons which serve purposes that *don't* require that what is believed be true, close to the truth, or likely to be true.

[39] I.e., the occasions on which the antecedent of the "rule" which captures the practice would apply.

[40] See the examples in Pinto (2003a, pp. 5-6, and pp. 13-14). For a similar or related point, see Freeman (2003) (which draws on ideas to be found in Clarke (1989)), and Freeman (2005a, p. 62).

be sunny and am not certain of it), my doxastic attitude will have served me well even when it rains. Without an *expectation* of some sort concerning the weather I would have made no plans at all. Even in matters theoretical, a presumption — for example, the *presumption* that the gauges I'm employing in my experimentation are functioning properly — can serve me well even if it "fails" (e.g. if the gauges don't function properly). For the *variation in the type of reliance* I place on different elements of my experimental design gives me a "plan of attack" when the results I'm getting don't add up (I check the gauges first, before I start questioning the second law of thermodynamics). And without some such presumption there would have been no experiment in the first place, and hence no second iteration in which the problem with the gauges has been taken care of.

But if considerations like these put us in a position to make objectively based, *nuanced* assessments of inferential outputs, they put us in the position to ask the following question about an inferential practice:

> (C) How *reliably* does the practice yield outputs that serve the role that it is playing?

This question must be interpreted as equivalent to something like the following:

> (C') What is the objective likelihood that the output of the practice will be a good output, where goodness is judged in light of the role that the practice is playing?

The very idea that a practice is *reliable* — is *fit* to be relied upon — already contains the idea of the objective likelihood of a *good* output.

Now it is important to note that an objective likelihood can only be calculated with respect to a *reference class*.[41] I submit that the appropriate reference class for determining the objective likelihood of successful outcome for an inferential practice must be fixed by reference to the typical circumstances in which that practice has been or will be relied upon.

As a result, the reliability of an inferential practice — for example, of expecting a Courtland to be sweet when we know that its skin exhibits a certain color pattern — will depend on an objective likelihood. But the objective likelihood on which it depends *will not be identical with the objective likelihood that a Courtland is sweet given that its skin exhibits a certain color pattern.* Rather it will be the objective likelihood of (i) arriving at an *appropriate* *doxastic attitude* when (ii) relying on the practice *in the typical circumstances in which it has been or will be relied upon.*

A reliable warrant can be defined as one which licenses a reliable inferential practice.[42]

---

[41] Compare Brandom's use of a similar point in his assessment of reliability theories of perceptual knowledge — for example in chapter 3 of Brandom (2000).

[42] I am trying to characterize what the "objective virtue" of a rule of inference consists in. I am not attempting here to give an account of how we *know* — or how we can have *reason to believe* — that a proposed rule is reliable in the sense defined. But let me point out that, if this account of the "objective

Significance of This Account

The upshot of these points is an account which makes the "fitness" of a rule to serve as a warrant depend *in part* on the non-epistemic values of those whose reasoning is to be evaluated by reference to them, as well as on the sorts of situations in which the inferential practices it licenses will actually be exercised. The account therefore makes the reliability of warrants highly context-sensitive. For these two reasons it might be called a pragmatic account of the virtue of rules of inference. But the position I'm defending is *not a "subjectivism" about warrants*, since it makes the authority of warrants depend on the objective likelihood of good outcomes and it makes the evaluation of outcomes depend on objective considerations. Moreover, even though it makes the authority of warrants depend *in part* on the non-epistemic values served by inferential practices, it does not do so in a way that runs afoul of Siegel's critique of the "means-ends conception of rationality",[43] nor is it subject to Siegel's arguments against those who construe epistemic normativity as a crude form of instrumental rationality.[44] Finally, because the position carefully distinguishes between *entitlement*-preserving rules and *truth*-preserving rules, it can *embrace a pragmatism about rules*

---

virtue" of warrants is correct, we are in a position to *know* that a proposed warrant is reliable only if we are in a position to *estimate the order of magnitude of certain objective likelihoods. One* way of getting in a position to do *that* is to carefully tally the relative frequency of success resulting from the application of the rule (and to *infer* that the *relative frequency* in our sample reveals the order of magnitude of the *objective likelihood* required for reliability). It is my impression, however, that we seldom base our estimates of objective likelihood on careful tallies of relative frequencies, and that we *almost never* do so when deciding which inferential practices or strategies are good ones. It is essential to remember, therefore, that although having a careful tally of a relative frequency may be a *sufficient condition for* having a reason for adopting an estimate of objective likelihood, it is not *a necessary condition* for having such a reason.

[43] See the Postscript to Siegel (1988, pp. 127-137), which develops two principal objections to a means-ends conception of rationality: (i) that it is unable "to assess the rationality of ends" (p. 130) and (ii) that it "threatens to rule out some sorts of reasons in favor of prudential or efficiency considerations" (p. 131). I agree with Siegel on both these points. However, they do not apply to the position I am defending here. With regard to (i), see note 37 above concerning the position I take with respect to means-end evaluations. With regard to (ii), my current position is that ends are indeed constitutive for the existence of reasons (the existence of reliable rules of inference is a necessary condition for the existence of reasons, and rules can be judged reliable only in relationship to the ends that inferential practices serve). However, it does not follow from that position that every reason is of the means-end variety — i.e. it does not follow that the propositional content of the antecedent of every rule of inference concerns a means-end relationship.

[44] Siegel (1996) deals with attempts by Giere and Laudan to reduce specifically epistemic normativity to instrumental rationality. My view is not subject to the arguments Siegel advances against Laudan and Giere in that paper. For one thing, my view recognizes rules of inference which take the form of "categorical" epistemic norms, and is therefore not subject to the central argument Siegel advances, which turns on whether all epistemic norms take the form of "instrumental" reasons. For another, the view propounded here simply does not reduce to a "crude" or "whatever works" pragmatism with respect to epistemic goodness, since the goals or purposes which ground the reliability of inferential practices are to consist in purposes which (a) require the adoption of doxastic attitudes to propositional contents and which (b) are sensitive to whether those propositional contents are true.

without embracing a pragmatist account of truth and *without foreswearing a realist account of the contents of our doxastic commitments.*

7. CONCLUSION: DIRECTION OF FURTHER RESEARCH

What I've presented here is an initial sketch of a possible way of doing things. There are at least three respects in which this way of doing things needs to be elaborated by offering much more detailed accounts of elements that it invokes.

First, the account depends crucially on the concept of *functionally type-identified doxastic attitudes*, and I haven't done much more than hint at how attitudes like expecting, presuming, being certain, suspecting, etc., can be characterized and differentiated from each other in functional terms. Until I show that such a characterization is realizable in sufficient and compelling detail, it will remain unclear whether the variant on "evidence proportionalism" I'm attempting to float here fares any better than the more traditional forms of evidence proportionalism which require us to assign numeric values to degrees of support and degrees of belief.

Second, in trying to sketch the form that warrants should take, I wave my hand in the direction of *defeaters* by including the clause "in the absence of undermining or overriding evidence" in W3a. That's a *little* better than saying "other things being equal", but not much! It remains to be demonstrated that this clause can be unpacked in a coherent manner that is both consistent with the overall story I'm telling and is not objectionably circular.

Finally, my discussion of *the authority and reliability of warrants* offers no more than a very preliminary sketch of a complicated topic. My principal example was of an inferential practice that is quite local, does not exhibit "field dependence" as that term has come to be widely understood, and is known to be reliable because it has worked in practice for a few individuals (and not by appeal to the sort of backing which Toulmin typically cites as lending warrants their authority). In those respects, my example is far from typical.

Moreover, in appealing to the purposes served by inferential practices, I have left it open whether the standard appealed to should be the purposes which, on one or another occasion, motivate *individuals* to rely on an inferential practice or whether it should be the purposes which motivate a *cognitive community*[45] to institute or endorse an inferential practice.

A fully satisfactory account of the authority and reliability of warrants would need:

---

[45] Weinstein (2002b, pp. 178-179) has raised important questions about the use I tried to make of the notion of cognitive communities, and their relation to critical practice, in chapter 13 of Pinto (2001). A satisfactory account of the purposes served by inferential practices would require me to address those questions in a systematic way. It would also require me to deal with the relationship of the norms that hold sway *within* the cognitive communities associated with specific disciplines both (a) to individual practical reasoning outside those disciplines and (b) to argumentative discourse in the public sphere.

1) to consider the differences between the "casual" or "occasional" sort of warrant that served as my example and the "standing warrants" which tend to be "field dependent,"
2) to examine carefully the variety of specific ways in which warrants are and should be scrutinized when doubts are raised about their authority, and finally
3) to address the question of when the output of an "objectively" reliable inferential practice is "subjectively" justified.

Acknowledgements

I'm indebted to David Hitchcock, Harvey Siegel, Ralph Johnson and David Godden for critical comments on earlier versions of this paper.

CHAPTER 10

ROBERT H. ENNIS

'PROBABLY'[1]

University of Illinois, UC
3904 Trentwood Place, Sarasota, Florida 34243, USA; E-mail: rhennis@uiuc.edu

ABSTRACT: From a real-argument point of view, Ennis defends Stephen Toulmin's speech-act contextual definition of 'probably' by considering and rejecting alternative hypotheses, by noting a dictionary distinction between 'statistical' and non statistical senses of 'probability', by indicating the plausibility of the definition as exhibited in Toulmin's practical examples, and by showing how the thesis survives standard contemporary challenges. These challenges arise from the expectations that the content of arguments be limited to propositions that have truth conditions, that the study of argument appraisal focus on contextless arguments, that actions performed by the use of a term be not part of the term's meaning, and that a term retain the same meaning in different contexts. Consequences of the thesis and its defense include strong reservations about computerizing the process of appraising real arguments containing 'probably' in the conclusion, a need for courses in critical thinking and informal logic to emphasize the importance of Sensitivity, Experience, Background, Knowledge, and Understanding the Situation (SEBKUS), and the desirability of including deductive logic in courses in critical thinking and informal logic.

KEYWORDS: Probably; probability; probable; subjective probability; argument; qualified reasoning; soundness: ordinary language; speech act; illocutionary act; deductive validity; critical thinking; informal logic

1. INTRODUCTION

The Thesis

My thesis is that Stephen Toulmin was basically right in his speech-act contextual definition of the word 'probably', which is, "When I say 'S is probably P', I commit

[1] My thanks to Derek Allen, Jennie Berg, John Canfield, Sally Ferguson, David Hitchcock, and Kirk Ludwig for helpful comments. I am especially indebted to Professors Allen and Ludwig for having shown me that my approach differs more from much contemporary thinking than I had previously realized. Previous versions of this essay were presented and discussed at an OSSA conference on Toulmin's *The Uses of Argument* at McMaster University, Hamilton Ontario, May 18-21, 2005, and at a meeting of the Florida Philosophical Association in Cocoa Beach, FL, November 12, 2005.

D. Hitchcock and B. Verheij (eds.), Arguing on the Toulmin Model: New Essays in Argument Analysis and Evaluation, 145–164.

myself guardedly, tentatively or with reservations to the view that S is P, and (likewise guardedly) lend my authority to that view" (1964, p. 53). In characterizing it as a speech-act definition, I mean that to use 'probably' in that simple context is to perform a speech act—in the popular sense of 'speech act'. More technically, I might call it an illocutionary act that is not merely an affirmation (Austin, 1962). Strictly speaking, all affirmations are speech acts and make a commitment, but the particular non-affirmation speech act here is the guarding, the reserving. 'Guardedly committing' actually represents two speech acts, committing and guarding the commitment, but for convenience I shall treat them as one speech act, which I shall call 'guardedly committing'.

Note that the definition in the interpretation that I shall defend is not of the closely-related 'probable',[2] nor the distantly-related 'probability' which calls for a number. So an attempt to test this thesis by automatically translating 'probably' into some other term would not count as a test without adequate justification of the translation. Furthermore, the interpretation I shall defend is about stand-alone (unembedded) affirmations of sentences of the form, 'S is probably P', or 'Probably S is P'. So my thesis is a delimited version of Toulmin's hypothesis. A contextual definition does not commit us to automatic generalization to all other contexts because it does not by itself contain sufficient rules for such generalization. Embedded occurrences of 'S is probably P', as in indirect speech, are discussed later under "Substituting the Performance of the Act of Guardedly Committing for 'Probably'", as are non-affirmation occurrences of 'probably', as in questions like, 'Is S probably P?'

Practical Application

There are at least three practical contexts in which this thesis is relevant: 1) attempts to computerize reasoning, 2) argument appraisal as taught in critical thinking and informal logic courses, and 3) decisions about the inclusion of deductive logic in critical thinking informal logic courses. I shall elaborate.

Attempts to Computerize Reasoning in Real Arguments

People trying to computerize reasoning that contains occurrences of the qualifier, 'probably', might well find it inviting to convert the qualifier to a number (such as, .80, or 80%), or a range or distribution (stated as numbers), so that mathematics can be done in deciding whether an argument containing the word is a good argument, and in deciding the meaning, acceptability, and application of a statement containing the word. Nicholas Rescher (1976) and John Pollock (1995) are sympathetic to this idea. One implication of the arguments in this essay is that such conversion is not legitimate in real arguments.

---

[2] I suspect that a similar case can be made for a different speech act definition of 'probable'.

Argument Appraisal

Strategy. In 'Argument Appraisal Strategy: A Comprehensive Approach' (2001), I offered an approach to appraisal of real arguments, in accord with which, instead of classifying an argument (as deductive, inductive, etc.) before appraising it, one should bypass classification (because that process has fatal flaws), and successively apply legitimate sets of argument standards. An argument that satisfies at least one set is to be judged acceptable. An argument that satisfies no legitimate set of standards is to be judged unacceptable. (There are of course various shortcuts that enable an argument appraiser to avoid the full application of some sets of argument standards.)

One example of a set of argument standards is soundness standards (which require deductive validity and true premises). But the application of soundness standards to good arguments that have the word 'probably' in the conclusion leads to problems. The following argument, in which I was trying to reassure a friend, is a typical case (called 'RA' for 'raccoon argument'):

> RA: Raccoons rarely attack a human when they do not feel threatened and do not feel that their young are threatened. The raccoon that is ambling across the yard does not feel threatened by us, and it does not feel that its young are threatened—its young are not around. So the raccoon will probably not bother you.

As I argued in 'Applying Soundness Standards to Qualified Reasoning' (2004), RA (which is typical of many real arguments) was not deductively valid in the context in which it was offered because of conflicting possibilities, such as frothing at the mouth, suggesting rabies. So it was not sound. I also believe that it satisfied no other commonly-applied set of standards, requiring me (by the approach outlined above) to judge it unacceptable, although I believe it to have been a good argument in the context in which it was presented.

So I suggested loosening soundness standards for such qualified reasoning by *stripping* the qualifiers (here 'rarely' and 'probably')[3], checking for deductive validity, and if, and only if, deductive validity holds, continue by replacing the qualifiers and making a human judgment about the acceptability of the reasons, and ultimately the conclusion, with sufficient *Sensitivity, Experience, Background Knowledge, and Understanding of the Situation* ('SEBKUS', pp. 35-37). In this particular case, I needed to make a human judgment with sufficient SEBKUS about whether to commit myself guardedly to the proposition that the raccoon will not bother my friend. Note that SEBKUS is a set of criteria that the argument appraiser should satisfy in appraising the argument. The satisfaction of these criteria does not guarantee a justified judgment by the appraiser. The assumption is that the satisfaction of SEBKUS makes it more likely that the judgment will be justified.

---

[3] Stripping 'rarely', because it is negative in its direction, results in its replacement by 'never'. Stripping qualifiers like 'rarely' and 'usually' results in universalizing. Stripping 'probably' consists of its elimination.

The delimited Toulmin hypothesis requires the above-mentioned human judgment in appraisal of a real argument if the conclusion is an unembedded sentence of the form, 'S is probably P' or 'Probably S is P'. Accordingly, the delimited Toulmin hypothesis requires sufficient SEBKUS, if the decision about the conclusion is to be made reasonably.

I advocate the teaching of the SEBKUS approach in attempts to improve the decision-making and statement-appraising prowess of our students and fellow citizens of the world, including attorneys, bricklayers, homemakers, judges, mechanics, politicians, and the unemployed.

Stance. This approach incorporates a stance toward arguments that focuses on appraisal of real arguments – in the context of human interaction (which includes one's own interaction with oneself) – that are offered when trying to identify and formulate a defensible position (as opposed to a persuasive one). This real-argument stance differs from the more-limited stance of concern only with propositions, truth conditions, and contextless arguments. In concluding, "The raccoon will probably not bother you", assuming the delimited Toulmin hypothesis, I was, among other things, performing an action of guardedly committing to (or affirming) the view that the raccoon will not bother my friend. This raccoon conclusion is not a proposition in the philosophical sense of 'proposition' (although it could become a proposition with the removal of the word 'probably' and the elimination of the committing). Propositions do not contain actions, though they might be about them.

Furthermore, the raccoon conclusion does not have a set of truth conditions in the standard philosophical sense. It does not make sense to speak of the truth conditions for an action, though there might be truth conditions for a claim about whether an action has been performed, and for a claim about whether the raccoon was going to bother my friend. (However, I do believe that it makes sense to apply the words 'true' or 'false' to the conclusion—a qualification I shall not defend in this essay, though I probably[4] shall do so at some other time.)

In sum, the concerns in this appraisal-of-real-arguments stance extend beyond propositions, truth conditions, and contextless arguments. In so saying, I am not disavowing interest in propositions, truth conditions, and contextless arguments. These are useful elements in deciding about deductive validity, a type of decision that is part of the approach I recommend.

These introductory comments about stance are made in advance in order to notify those who are interested primarily in propositions, truth conditions, and contextless arguments that the topic here is broader than those to which they are accustomed. Accordingly they should be cautious in trying to make all the views in this essay fit into their ideas about propositions, truth conditions and contextless arguments.

---

[4] Note how well the Toulmin definition fits this use of 'probably'. I guardedly commit myself to elaborating the qualification at some other time.

The Inclusion of Deductive Logic in Critical Thinking Courses

One of the problems in the application of soundness standards is the paucity of arguments that actually satisfy soundness standards, resulting from the scarcity of deductive validity in real arguments. Even though there are many arguments in real life that approach deductive validity, many of them fail to be deductively valid because of the implicit or explicit inclusion of qualifying terms like 'rarely', 'probably', 'generally', 'probable', '*ceteris paribus*', and '*prima facie*' (the latter two almost always being implicit). The scarcity of deductive validity in real life is sometimes offered as a reason to reduce drastically the amount of deductive logic taught to students in attempts to teach them to think critically. For example, Michael Scriven, among others, speaks scornfully of the role of deductive logic in critical thinking and informal logic courses (2003, p. 22).

Defenders of the utility of the teaching of deductive standards ought, I believe, to welcome my remarks because the suggested procedure for loosening soundness standards makes the applicability of our teaching of basic deductive standards[5] useful in evaluating many more real arguments than is now the case under strict soundness standards.

2. THE ARGUMENT IN SUPPORT OF THE THESIS

The argument in this essay is an ordinary-language argument, as is appropriate when we are trying to interpret the language of real arguments because ordinary language is generally the language used in real arguments. The thesis about 'probably' is an empirical claim about how the word is currently used in this culture. Hence the thesis probably has its best chance of survival when judged by best-explanation standards, according to which a thesis basically gets its support from its ability to explain the data, the inconsistency of its competitors with the data, its consistency with the data (especially in the face of challenges), and, usually, its plausibility. The data are what we would say under certain circumstances. I am aware that people sometimes differ in their beliefs about 'what we would say' and that this problem was one of the problems of the ordinary-language movement, but I think that readers will agree with what I claim we would say.

In the rest of this essay, I shall offer an extended argument in support of my thesis, the delimited Toulmin hypothesis. The first part of the argument indicates the initial plausibility of the thesis, and examines certain problems with prominent alternative views. The second part of the argument consists of responses to some challenges to the thesis.

---

[5] For an approach to deduction that does not involve the paradoxes of material implication and their cohorts, see Ennis (1969; 1981; 1996).

Initial Plausibility

Toulmin supported his view by noting its plausibility in two everyday contexts, a little boy's dilemma, and the language of weather prediction (1964, pp. 47-52). The boy's dilemma was that his young female friend wondered whether he would return for another visit the following day, but he knew that there was a possible trip to the zoo. He did not want to say 'No' because the possible trip might not occur or interfere, and he could not "decently" come unexpectedly. He did not want to say 'Yes', because he did not want to risk her feeling that he let her down. So at his mother's suggestion, he said 'Probably', resolving his problem. The appropriateness of his reply is explained by the thesis. The boy committed himself guardedly, tentatively, with reservations.

In the weather-prediction context, Toulmin quotes a weather forecast: "Cloudy conditions now affecting Northern Ireland will spread to N. W. England during the day, probably extending to the rest of the country in the course of the evening and night" (p. 50). Again the appropriateness of using 'probably' in that context is explained by the thesis, assuming the forecaster wants to hedge the claim about the extension of the cloudiness.

Competitive Alternative Hypotheses

Given recent thinking, four primary alternatives to the delimited Toulmin hypothesis occur to me. They are embodied in the following roughly-stated definitions:

1. *The objective specific numerical definition (specific probability below 1.0 and above 0.5):* To say 'S is probably P' is to say that the objective probability of S's being P is X, where 'X' is a specific number below 1.0 and above 0.5 (such as 0.80),[6] or some specific range below 1.0 and above 0.5 (such as between 0.7 and 0.95), or some specific probability distribution with a mean below 1.0 and above 0.5 (such as a normal distribution with a mean of 0.80 and a standard deviation of 0.05).
2. *The objective nonspecific numerical definition (nonspecific probability, substantially above 0.5, but less than 1.0):* To say 'S is probably P' is to say that the probability that S is P is less than 1.0 but substantially greater than 0.5.[7]
3. *The objective non-numerical definition (*using *'probable').* To say 'S is probably P' is to say that it is probable that S is P.

---

[6] Probabilities are assumed to range from 1.0 (certain) to 0.0 (impossible).

[7] This is an improvement, suggested by David Hitchcock (2005, email communication), over the alternative I originally suggested. Actually, he also included the phrase, "relative to the available evidence", which I have omitted here because, as I have argued elsewhere (2004), using that phrase avoids the responsibility that accompanies a guarded commitment that does not include the phrase.

4. *The subjective numerical definition (subjective probability):* To say 'S is probably P' is to say that the subjective probability of S's being P is a number, X, below 1.0 and above 0.5 (such as 0.8), or a range below 1.0 and above 0.5 (such as 0.5 to 0.99), or a distribution with a mean below 1.0 and above 0.5 and a standard deviation of, say, 0.05. This means that the speaker's degree of belief that S is P is that number, range, or distribution.

In appraising these four hypotheses, I shall consider 1) their possibility of providing a substitute for 'probably' in the raccoon conclusion; 2) their retention of a speaker's inconsistency; and 3) their retention of an inconsistency between what two people say. I shall then consider the reports of my favorite dictionaries about 'probably', 'probable', and 'probability'.

Making Sense of a Substitution for 'Probably'

If any of these four hypotheses is correct, then it should provide in the three examples so far considered a way to replace the word 'probably' with its hypothesized interpretation. For example, given the delimited Toulmin definition, the raccoon conclusion can be replaced by 'I guardedly commit myself to the view that the raccoon will not bother you.' I shall argue that not only the delimited Toulmin definition, but the second and third alternative definitions as well, satisfy this test. But the first and fourth alternative definitions do not satisfy it because they require a number or numbers that are just not available.

1. *The Objective Specific Numerical Definition.* This definition, the first alternative hypothesis, which treats 'probably' as an objective term precisely indicating the way things are, is impossible to apply to RA because it fails to tell us where (between 1.0 and 0.5) the number, range, or distribution is. One could invent a number, or numbers, but since we are evaluating real arguments, there would be no assurance that the one picked is the one the arguer has in mind. There certainly is no reason to think that a particular number is justifiably attachable to 'probably' in everyday arguments. So the first hypothesis fails the substitution test.

   This difficulty makes it impossible to objectively computerize the evaluation of real arguments containing 'probably' (in its ordinary sense) in the conclusion when it is not in the premises or reasons. There are other difficulties as well, including the rest of my argument in this essay that the numerical senses of 'probability' do not define 'probably'.

   In noting this impossibility, I am assuming that '"S is P" is certain' does not imply 'S is probably P'. To assume otherwise would be to neglect the guarding in 'S is probably P'.
2. *The Objective Nonspecific Numerical Definition.* This definition, the second alternative hypothesis, does not require that 'probably' be precisely defined in terms of a specific number, range, or distribution. It says "substantially

above 0.5", so it enables a substitution that makes sense: 'The probability that the raccoon will not bother you is less than 1, but substantially above 0.5.' That makes sense and would give us some positive indication (but not certainty) that the raccoon is not dangerous. So this definition passes the first test.

3. *The Objective Non-Numerical Definition (Using the Word, 'Probable').* Similarly the third definition passes this test: 'It is probable that the raccoon will not bother you' makes sense.
4. *The Subjective Probability Numerical Definition.* Identifying a number for the fourth alternative definition (the subjective numerical sense) cannot be done, although by hypothesis it is above 0.5. Others, in appraising RA, do not know what specific number or numbers to insert as my degree of belief. So the fourth definition fails this test.

Thus the first and fourth alternative definitions fail the test. The second and third, along with the delimited Toulmin definition, pass it. That is, they enable the appraisal of RA to proceed.

Retention of a Speaker's Inconsistency

Assume a situation in which I have rolled a pair of honest dice, but no one saw the result. However, an automatic camera did record the result, which was boxcars (two sixes). We have just learned the result by viewing the photo. The chances of not getting boxcars were 35 out of 36. Suppose I then say, 'I probably did not roll boxcars, but I rolled boxcars.' This pair of statements is inconsistent. How can I say that it probably did not happen if I believe that it happened? The proposed speech-act hypothesis explains and retains the inconsistency. If you make a commitment, you are inconsistent if you concurrently commit yourself in the opposite direction, even if the first commitment is guarded.

However for all four alternative hypotheses the inconsistency disappears:

1. *The Objective Specific Numerical Definition.* 'The probability that I did not roll boxcars was 0.97222...[35/36], but I rolled boxcars.' That is consistent.[8]
2. *The Objective Nonspecific Numerical Definition.* 'The probability that I did not roll boxcars was substantially above 0.5 though less than 1.0, but I rolled boxcars.' That is consistent.
3. *The Objective Non-Numerical Definition (Using the Word 'Probable').* 'It was probable that I did not roll boxcars, but I rolled boxcars.' That is consistent.
4. *The Subjective Numerical Definition (Subjective Probability).* 'My degree of belief that I did not roll boxcars was 0.97, but I rolled boxcars.' This is consistent.

---

[8] Assuming frequency probability for 1 and 2. If one assumes an interpretation of logical probability that assigns either 1 or 0 when the result has already occured but before the dice photo is revealed, counterexamples to 1 and 2 will be exhibited when the situation is described in the present and future tenses.

That these four alternatives are all consistent counts against the corresponding alternative definitions of 'probably' because the boxcars statement containing 'probably' is inconsistent.

Retention of Inconsistency between the Statements of Two People

So far, the first and fourth alternatives failed both tests. The second and third, the objective non-specific numerical and the objective non-numerical (using the word 'probable') passed the first, but failed the second.

As I shall next argue, the third test, the retention-of-inconsistency test, is failed by the fourth alternative definition (the subjective probability definition), though the three objective definitions pass this third test. The test is whether the hypothesis retains the inconsistency between statements made by A and B when A says, 'The raccoon will probably not bother you', and B says, 'The raccoon will probably bother you.' They cannot both be right. The inconsistency is retained by the delimited Toulmin definition, because A and B are expressing opposing commitments.

1. *The Objective Specific Numerical Definition.* A says, 'The probability that the raccoon *will not* bother you is greater than 0.5', while B says, 'The probability that the raccoon *will* bother you is greater than 0.5'. These two statements, as interpreted in the objective numerical way, retain the inconsistency. They cannot both be right, even though each is lacking specificity.
2. *The Objective Nonspecific Numerical Definition.* A says, "The probability that the raccoon *will not* bother you is substantially higher than 0.5", while B says, "the probability that the raccoon *will* bother you is substantially higher than 0.5", retaining the inconsistency. They cannot both be right.
3. *The Objective Non-Numerical Definition (Using the Word, 'Probable').* A says, 'It is probable that the raccoon will not bother you'; B says, 'It is probable that the raccoon will bother you'. They cannot both be right. It cannot be that it is both probable that the raccoon will not bother you and probable that the raccoon will bother you. The expressed inconsistency is retained.
4. *The Subjective Numerical Definition.* Suppose A says, 'My degree of belief that the raccoon *will not* bother you is 0.95', while B says, 'My degree of belief that the raccoon *will* bother you is 0.95'. Both statements *can* be right because they are not about the likelihood of being bothered, but rather are statements about A's and B's degrees of belief. A can readily agree that B's degree of belief that the raccoon *will* bother you is 0.95, while A holds that A's degree of belief is 0.95 that the raccoon *will not* bother you. Both A and B can readily and consistently believe both statements just as the rest of us can readily and consistently believe both statements. Although A and B probably do disagree with each other about what is likely to happen, the subjective

probability definition has made their statements compatible. The original statements using 'probably' could not both be right. But the statements produced by the subjective probability definition could both be right. This is a serious problem for subjectivist interpretations of 'probably'. There was an inconsistency between A's and B's statements when put in terms of 'probably', but the subjectivist hypothesis incorrectly implies the elimination of the inconsistency between the statements.

Dictionary Definitions

Support for rejecting the first, second, and fourth (the numerical) hypotheses, is to be found in my favorite dictionaries, the Random House dictionary and the *OED*.[9] They do not give a "statistical" or "math" (numerical) sense for 'probably', though they do for 'probability'. However, other than by noting the grammatical difference (adverb vs. adjective), they do not differentiate between 'probably' and 'probable', so they do not support the rejection of the third hypothesis. Interestingly enough, they do give a meaning in terms of the adjective 'probable' for a non-numerical noun, 'probability', according to which 'probability' is "the quality or fact of being probable".[10] Presumably they would extend this to 'probably' as follows: To say that S is probably P is to say that the probability is that S is P. However, this equation would fail the same test (the second test) as the third alternative definition, the one using 'probable'.

Additional support for the Toulmin hypothesis is this part of the OED's definition of 'probably': "As a qualification of the whole statement....Now the ordinary use"[11] However, coming out in 1991, as it did, it might have been influenced by Toulmin's hypothesis.[12]

Summary of the Evidence So Far

In sum, all four alternative hypotheses about 'probably' have failed at least one of the three linguistic tests, while the speech-act thesis about 'probably' has passed all three tests. Furthermore the numerical hypotheses (#1, #2, and #4) have failed the dictionary test—the distinction between "statistical" and non-statistical meaning, the former not applying to 'probably'. Because I am unable to think of any other significantly different hypotheses that are likely to be seriously advanced and that would not fail one or more of the tests, and because the delimited Toulmin hypothesis is plausible as shown by his examples and the dictionary support, we now have considerable support for the delimited Toulmin hypothesis. So let us look at some major challenges.

---

[9] Urdang (1968), p. 1055; Simpson & Weiner (1991), Vol. 12, pp. 534-536.

[10] Ibid.

[11] Simpson and Weiner (1991), p. 536.

[12] The earliest appearance of which, to my knowledge, was in Toulmin (1950a).

3. RESPONSES TO CHALLENGES TO THE THESIS

In discussions that followed presentations of earlier versions of this essay,[13] I have encountered two sorts of challenge that are relevant to the delimited Toulmin hypothesis: 1) those arising from the failure of what I have said and argued to fit into a structure that sees argumentation in terms of propositions, truth conditions, and contextless arguments; and 2) those arising from attempts to substitute the speech act mentioned in my thesis for 'probably' in a variety of contexts, including past tense claims, indirect speech, quoted speech, conditionals, imperatives, questions, wonderings, and agreeings and disagreeings.[14]

Propositions, Truth Conditions, and Contextless Arguments

Those who are committed to limiting our concerns to propositions, truth conditions, and contextless arguments probably disapprove of some assertions I have made. They look for truth conditions for propositions, and assume that the conclusion, "The raccoon probably will not bother you" is a proposition. So they hold that the raccoon conclusion should have truth conditions. But I have claimed that there is an *action* of committing and of guarding in the conclusion of that real argument. And there are no truth conditions for actions (though there are for a claim that an action has been performed). Committing myself and guarding that commitment are actions, for which it does not make sense to request truth conditions.

Deductive Validity and Inconsistency. They feel that questions of deductive validity can be raised only about relations between propositions. If this is so, then my raising questions about the deductive validity of RA does not make sense, given that I hold the conclusion to be an action of committing and guarding the commitment, and given that propositions do not contain actions.

In more depth, one standard test for deductive validity calls for inconsistency between the premises and the negation of the conclusion. If the inconsistency is there, the argument is deductively valid. But 'inconsistency' is taken by many to mean contradiction between propositions. If the conclusion is not a proposition, the test does not apply. So for real arguments containing commitments and other actions, a broader notion of deductive validity is needed.

Here is a reasonable one: A real argument is deductively valid if, and only if, a commitment to the premises necessarily requires a commitment to the conclusion. Under this commitment conception of deductive validity, RA is deductively invalid because a commitment to the premises is not inconsistent with a lack of commitment to the conclusion. The possible frothing at the mouth makes the point.

---

[13] See footnote #1.

[14] There were other challenges in the discussions, but because I believe that they do not challenge what is in the current essay, I shall not mention them here, though I do appreciate the role of all the challengers in helping me sharpen the interpretation and defense of the thesis.

Note that I have used the word 'inconsistent' in the ordinary sense, not in the technical sense of 'contradictory' which requires propositions. If A guardedly commits himself to a conclusion, and also guardedly commits himself to its denial, A is inconsistent, though his commitments do not contradict each other in the technical sense that requires contradictory propositions. For example, if A says, 'Probably S is P, and probably S is not P', A is inconsistent, though neither statement is a proposition because each includes an action, making the pair of statements not contradictory in the technical sense.

This commitment conception of deductive validity obviously needs further development. One important part (that handles the contextless argument cases with which we all are so familiar) would be that a commitment to specified propositions necessarily requires a commitment to another proposition if and only if that other proposition follows deductively from the specified propositions.[15]

Meaning. Some feel that giving the meaning of something that is said calls for saying what is said, not what is done, suggesting that in saying something one can not also be doing something that is part or all of the meaning of what is said. I see no reason for holding such a narrow notion of meaning. For example, I cannot tell you what was said when I said, "I nominate A for the Vice Presidency", without explaining the meaning in terms of the action I performed in saying that. Nor can I tell you the meaning of the word 'I' without saying what speakers do with that word, that is, refer to themselves.

Relevance and Responsibility: SEBKUS. Concern with real arguments requires expanding the set of things for which we are responsible in evaluating an argument, so that we are responsible for sufficient attention's having been given to finding and appraising the value and bearing of relevant factors. Thus one who draws a conclusion in most real arguments becomes responsible for much more than the contextless deductive validity, including whether the premises are true or probably so, whether an adequate search for alternatives has occurred, and whether the sources are credible. Sensitivity, experience, background knowledge, and understanding of the situation (SEBKUS) become important, as we could see in judging RA. Responsible committing (often guarded) is required.

For some of us (including me) to transition from considering only proposition-containing, contextless arguments to focusing on real arguments is difficult, I believe because of our lengthy period of dealing with contextless arguments. However, there is no doubt that real arguments should be the ultimate focus, if we want to be truly relevant to human concerns.

---

[15] For the general idea here, I am indebted to David Hitchcock (2005, email communication).

Substituting the Performance of the Act of Guardedly Committing for 'Probably'

There are several types of context in ordinary speech in which the word 'probably' is not used to perform an act of guarded committing. For example, my friend said, "Ennis said that the raccoon would probably not bother me." In using 'probably' in this report, my friend was not guardedly committing himself to his not being bothered; he was reporting my having performed that speech act. So not all uses of the word 'probably' are performances of the speech act. This would be a legitimate cause for concern if we assume that every non-ambiguous word should mean the same thing in every context and if we feel that performance of the act is at least part of the meaning of 'probably'.

Types of allegedly problematic contexts include past-tense statements, indirect speech (exemplified in the previous paragraph), quoted speech, conditionals, imperatives, questions, wonderings, and agreeings and disagreeings. These types of contexts have been offered as challenges in discussions of earlier versions of this essay. [16] Most were also considered by John Searle in a section of his *Speech Acts* (1969) that he called "The speech act fallacy". In that section, Searle, appealing to several different principles of meaning that he formulated, challenged four speech act interpretations of key words: R. M. Hare's account of 'good' (1952), P. F. Strawson's of 'true' (1949), J. L. Austin's of 'know' (1946), and Toulmin's of 'probably' (1950a).[17]

Searle's putative counterexamples deal with 'good', though he said, "Similar counterexamples will refute the speech act analyses of 'true', 'know', 'probable',[18] etc." (p. 139). For citations of principles and some comments, I shall use Searle's presentation (rather than the informal comments of discussants) because his comments and principles are published. Any questions about what was actually said and the context in which it was said can then be more readily answered by anyone in the world. However, all the indicated contexts are current topics of discussion.

Contexts of concern can be grouped under three headings: 1) the past tense, 2) contexts in which there is a guarded committing—though not by the speaker, and 3) contexts in which there is as yet no guarded committing. Let us begin with the easiest to handle, the past tense.

The Past Tense. Searle said, "If [sentences containing the speech act term] are in the past tense, then the act is reported in the past tense" (p. 138). For this claim about the past tense, Searle offered no defense except the soon-to-be-quoted RP, for which he offered no defense. This past-tense claim is satisfied by the verb 'promise', to which Searle has devoted considerable study, but not by 'good' and 'probably'.

Searle reports that Hare claims that "the word 'good' is used to commend" (Searle, 1969, p. 137). As a putative counterexample to Hare's view, Searle offers a pair of sentences that should be equivalent if Hare's view and Searle's claim about

---

[16] Mentioned in footnote 1.

[17] Essentially the same essay as appeared as a chapter in *The Uses of Argument* (1964).

[18] Apparently he felt that 'probable' and 'probably' are interchangeable.

the past tense are correct. Searle said, "'This used to be good' is not equivalent to 'I used to commend this'" (p. 139). Searle is right that the two sentences are not equivalent, but wrong in thinking that, according to the speech act interpretation of 'good', they should be equivalent. If 'good' is used to perform the speech act of commending, the commending occurs when the word 'good' is uttered, although in this case the thing commended is what used to be. To be fair to Hare, the second sentence of the pair should read, 'I now commend how this used to be', a revision that is in conflict with Searle's past tense claim, but which does result in equivalent sentences, given Hare's view. Thus the counterexample fails; Searle's claim about the past tense is incorrect.

Searle did not explicitly deal with 'probably'. He only said, "Similar counter-examples will refute the speech act [analysis of 'probably'] (p. 139). However, the response for 'probably' is similar to the response for 'good'. If I now say, 'The raccoon was probably not going to bother him,' I am not reporting a past action of guarded committing by me. Instead I am guardedly committing myself now to the proposition that the raccoon was not going to bother him. It is a guarded commitment, made at the time of utterance, to a proposition about how things were previously. So there is no reason for special concern about past-tense sentences containing 'probably'.

Guarded Committing—though Not by the Speaker. Consider next the contexts in which the use or mention of the word 'probably' by someone does not imply the performance of a guarded committing by that person even though there is a reported guarded committing by someone. An example is the indirect speech assertion uttered by my friend, "Ennis said that the raccoon would probably not bother me". Searle offered a principle of meaning, which he deemed "obvious" (p.137), that applies to this case. Let us call this principle 'OP', for 'original principle':

> OP: Any analysis of the meaning of a word (or morpheme) must be consistent with the fact that the same word (or morpheme) can mean the same thing in all grammatically different kinds of sentences in which it can occur. (p. 137)

He later offered a revised principle, 'RP', and still later another principle, 'AP', both of which I shall soon quote. If OP is correct, my friend's use of 'probably' in the indirect speech context is a counterexample to the claim that 'probably' is used to perform the speech act of guarded committing, if the claim is taken to be an analysis of the meaning of 'probably'.

My friend used the word 'probably' in reporting my act. But my friend obviously did not perform the act of guarded committing about the raccoon. So either the principle is wrong, or the Toulmin definition is wrong if it is an analysis of the meaning of 'probably'. However, the same problem would exist for the speech acts of promising (Searle's specialty) and nominating. For example, if in response to the question, 'What did A and B say?' I say, 'A said that he [A] promises to support the essay contest', and I say, 'B said that she [B] nominates A'. I am not performing the speech acts. I am reporting them, although I use the words 'promises' and 'nominates'.

According to Searle's OP, these indirect-speech reports of speech acts are counterexamples to the speech act interpretations of 'probably', 'promise', and 'nominate', assuming they are analyses of meaning. According to OP, as I interpret it, 'probably', 'promise', and 'nominate' must be able to mean the same thing in performances of their act as in the indirect speech statements I just reported. But they can not mean the same thing because no such performance by the speakers (my friend in the 'probably' report, and me in the 'promise' and 'nominate' reports) occurs in these reports.

How can it be that 'probably', 'promise', and 'nominate' are not able to mean the same thing in all contexts? Perhaps instead we should ask, 'Why should we expect them to do so, given that language is an exceedingly complex institution?' Assuming that the speech acts are part of the meaning of these terms when used by speakers in simple unembedded statements, in such form as, 'I promise that X', 'I nominate A', and 'S is probably P', why should the use of the key words ('promise', 'nominate', and 'probably') in other contexts, like indirect speech, be able to be a performance of the same acts? Obviously, these words are not used to perform these acts by the speaker in indirect speech. So OP is questionable. I suspect that Searle realized this fact, motivating his subsequent offering of another principle (RP), soon to be quoted.

Given the speech act assumption about the meaning of these three terms in unembedded assertive contexts, let us think of what they reasonably could mean in these reported-speech-act contexts. It is reasonable for our language to contain a way for us to report the performance of an act by someone else. A reasonable way to do that is to present something in the form of a report that tells what happened—without our actually doing what we report someone else to have done. So in such reports, the speech act words would not have exactly the same meaning that they have in unembedded affirmation contexts, that is, they would not be used by the speaker to perform the action. In order to be useful in giving a report, they would have a closely related meaning – that the action was performed. In the 'probably' case, it is reasonable for my friend to report, "Ennis said that the raccoon would probably not bother me" meaning, 'Ennis guardedly committed himself to the proposition that the raccoon would not bother me'. If I were building a language, that is how I would build it.

I have not just now proved that the speech act interpretations are correct. I have only shown that if they are correct for unembedded affirmation cases, the lack of the speaker's performing the act in indirect speech contexts is not unreasonable. It is to be expected, given the context.

With direct quotations, the reporter of the direct quotation reports the words used, without necessarily making any commitment about, or even understanding, their meaning. So if the delimited Toulmin hypothesis is correct, direct quotes containing a speech-act word provide more conflict with OP. A statement by my friend, "Ennis said, 'The raccoon probably will not bother you'", contains an embedded occurrence of 'probably'. When my friend said the word 'probably' in that embedded occurrence, my friend was not performing the action of guarded affirming. But when I used 'probably' when I said, "The raccoon probably will not bother you", I did perform such an action. Again I have not proved that the delimited

Toulmin hypothesis is correct. I have only shown that if it is correct for unembedded affirmation cases, its not holding for direct-speech quotations is reasonable and to be expected. That is how I would build a language.

No Guarded Committing—Yet. The remaining contexts mentioned above (conditionals, imperatives, questions, wonderings, and agreeings and disagreeings) are somewhat different. In these contexts the act might not be performed at all. For example, in the following conditional, even though there are two occurrences of 'probably', the act of guarded committing is not performed—by anyone:

> C: If the raccoon probably will not bother her, then she can probably safely turn her back on the raccoon.

Given that the conditional context permits no actions of guarded committings within either the antecedent or the consequent, a plausible meaning for the antecedent here is 'A guarded commitment to the proposition that the raccoon will not bother her is justified'. Given a corresponding meaning for the consequent, the conditional means, 'If a guarded commitment to the proposition that the raccoon will not bother her is justified, then a guarded commitment to the proposition that she can safely turn her back on the raccoon is justified'.

Suppose we are wondering whether to commit ourselves to the antecedent of this conditional in order to help us decide whether to commit ourselves to the consequent. Thus we are wondering whether to commit ourselves to the statement that a guarded commitment to the proposition that the raccoon will not bother her is justified. Suppose we do commit ourselves to the statement that the raccoon will probably not bother her. Then we must be committed to the antecedent, that is, the statement that a guarded commitment to the proposition that the raccoon will not bother her is justified. Otherwise we had no right to perform the act of guarded committing.

Then, given a commitment to the conditional, we would be committed to the consequent in the conditional, 'A guarded commitment to the proposition that she can safely turn her back on the raccoon is justified'. If we are committed to this consequent, then we are committed to a guarded commitment to the proposition that she can safely turn her back on the raccoon because we are committed to the guarded commitment's being justified. Thus we are committed to the statement that she can probably safely turn her back on the raccoon. In sum, given a commitment to the conditional, and given a commitment to the antecedent, 'The raccoon will probably not bother her', we are committed to the statement that she can probably safely turn her back. That does not necessarily mean that we perform the act of guarded commitment, only that we are committed to doing so.

This is reasonable. We should not expect an action to follow necessarily from premises that justify it. Actions are performed. A commitment to the conclusion is the best we can reasonably expect to follow necessarily. However, given a commitment to that conclusion, it would be reasonable to perform the action, that is, it would be reasonable to say, "She can probably safely turn her back", unless there are good practial reasons for not doing so, such as, hiding a surprise from her that she might see if she turns around.

Thus, given the delimited Toulmin hypothesis, and given the context of a conditional, interpreting the embedded 'S is probably P' as 'A guarded commitment to the proposition that S is P is justified' is to be expected because it is the reasonable thing to do. Among other things, this interpretation enables our maintaining an action version of the intuitively plausible 'affirming the antecedent' form of reasoning. This elaboration of the action version of affirming the antecedent is one small step in the development of a commitment conception of deductive validity.

As in the contexts of indirect and direct speech reports, the interpretation in a conditional context is a function of the combination of the context in which the term appears and the delimited Toulmin hypothesis. Again it would make sense to build the language this way.

Similarly, the meaning of occurrences of 'probably' in imperatives, questions, wonderings, and agreeings and disagreeings is reasonably taken to be some rendition of 'guarded commitment is justified', and is a function of those contexts. Here are examples:

'Please make sure that the raccoon probably will not bother her' means 'Please make sure that a guarded commitment to the proposition that the raccoon will not bother her is justified'. This interpretation is reasonable given the delimited Toulmin hypothesis and the imperative context. To satisfy the imperative on this interpretation of it, I must arrange things so that a guarded commitment to the proposition that the raccoon will not bother her is justified. Then someone can justifiably say, 'The raccoon will probably not bother her', unless there are good practical reasons for not doing so.

Questions and wonderings are similar to each other, so I shall deal only with questions. It is reasonable to expect that 'Will the raccoon probably not bother her?' means 'Is a guarded commitment to the proposition that the raccoon will not bother her justified?' For me to answer 'Yes' to this interpretation of the question is to commit myself to the statement that a guarded commitment to the proposition that the raccoon will not bother her is justified, which requires me to commit myself to a guarded commitment to the proposition that the raccoon will not bother her. Actually the strength of the verbal endorsement, "Yes", entitles one to assume that I have in effect performed the action of saying 'The raccoon will probably not bother her'.

For me to answer negatively in the question context implies that a commitment to a guarded commitment that the raccoon will not bother her is not justified. This could be because I think that not even a guarded commitment is justified, in which case I might say 'No, the raccoon might well bother her'. Alternatively I might answer negatively because I think that it is certain that the raccoon will not bother her (so the guarding is overruled). In the latter case, I might well say, 'No, it is certain that the raccoon will not bother her'.

The last contexts I shall consider are agreeing or disagreeing, as in saying, "It is true (or false) that S is probably P", "I believe (or do not believe) that S is probably

P", etc. These can be handled like the previous ones, in which the embedded 'S is probably P' means 'A guarded commitment to the proposition that S is P is justified'. For example, saying "It is true that the raccoon will probably not bother her" means 'It is true that a guarded commitment to the proposition that the raccoon will not bother her is justified.' Given these contexts and the central unembedded affirming meaning of 'saying that S is probably P', it is reasonable for the action not to be directly perfomed in saying that S is probably P in these embedded contexts. But it is reasonable to treat the action as in effect perfomed in the agreeing contexts like 'It is true that..', 'I believe that..', etc.

Basically the idea for all the contexts in the 'Guarded Committing-though Not by the Speaker' and 'No Guarded Committing-Yet' categories is that in saying that S is probably P the action is not perfomed at all, or not directly perfomed, for contexts in which the unembedded affirmation delimitation is not satisfied. However, for the 'No Guarded Committing-Yet' category, the action is lurking in the institutional background, so to speak, waiting to be performed. Furthermore it is in effect performed in the embedding affirmation contexts (e.g., "Yes", "true", and "I believe").

The meaning in the unembedded affirmation context (for example, the conclusion of RA) is the central one. The other meanings are a function of the combination of the delimited Toulmin hypothesis and the context in which the term 'probably' appears.

Other Principles. Searle's revised principle (RP) might or might not be compatible with the function claims that I have offered, depending on his interpretation of the word 'function':

> RP. Literal utterances which are not performances of the act A [should] stand in a relation to performances of A in a way which is purely a function of the way the sentences uttered stand in relation to the standard indicative sentences, in the utterance of which the act is performed. (p. 138)

It is not clear from the words in RP how to tell what way it is that is the "function of the way the sentences uttered stand in relation to the standard indicative sentences". There is an almost unlimited number of possible functions. So it is not clear from those words whether the particular function-of-the-context explanations I have offered are in accord with his principle. But perhaps it does not matter. He offered no defense of RP, nor any other-than-RP defense for the mistaken past-tense claim considered earlier that appears immediately after RP and is apparently believed by Searle to be an implication of RP. Furthermore, two pages after RP (which seemingly is a successor to OP), he presents AP, which is more inscrutable than, partly because it seems to be in conflict with RP.

> AP: If someone offers an analysis of the meaning of a word, then what he offers must hold true of all literal occurrences of the word where it has that literal meaning. (p. 140)

This seems to say that where we have the literal meaning, we must have the literal meaning.

In sum then, in the present section I have shown first and foremost that the suggested meanings of occurrences of 'probably' that in the contexts considered are not used to perform the act of guarded committing are a function of the contexts and are reasonable and to be expected, given the delimited Toulmin hypothesis, making resolvable the apparent problems with indirect speech, quoted speech, conditionals, questions, wonderings, and agreeings and disagreeings. I have also shown that there is no problem with past tense sentences containing 'probably'. Lastly, I have exhibited puzzlement about what interpretable justifiable principle Searle really meant to offer to justify his claim that the speech-act interpretations of 'good', 'true', 'know', and 'probably' are fallacious. Incidentally, in this section I generally avoided shorthand and symbols for fear that such things might hide crucial assumptions.

Actually Searle mentioned, but apparently did not endorse, a fourth principle, its source being "the speech act analysts" (p. 138). It suggests that the nonperformances of the speech act be explainable in terms of the "primary use" of the speech act terms. My reasonableness approach is compatible with this explainability approach. The nonperformances are explainable because they are the reasonable things to expect in the nonperformance contexts.

4. SUMMARY AND COMMENT

In the context of the appraisal of real arguments, and within that context, the consideration of qualified but otherwise deductively-valid arguments, I have presented and defended a delimited version of Toulmin's speech-act contextual definition of the qualifier, 'probably': "When I say 'S is probably P', I commit myself guardedly, tentatively or with reservations to the view that S is P, and (likewise guardedly) lend my authority to that view".

Four leading possible alternative definitions of 'probably' are inconsistent with some evidence or have some sort of problem, while the contextual speech-act definition is consistent with and appears to explain or help explain the evidence offered. The four alternatives are the objective specific numerical definition (probability with a number above 0.5 and less than 1.0), the objective non-specific numerical definition (probability substantially above 0.5, but less than 1.0), the objective non-numerical definition ('probable'), and the subjective numerical definition (subjective probability above 0.5 and below 1.0). Three tests used to judge the value of these definitions are making sense of a substitution for 'probably', retention of a speaker's inconsistency, and retention of inconsistency between the statements of two people.

Good dictionaries constitute a fourth type of evidence, and support the rejection of the numerical hypotheses. However, these dictionaries do not draw an other-than-grammatical distinction between the adjective 'probable' and adverb 'probably', a fact that bears further investigation at some other time. The plausible explainability of the use of 'probably' in Toulmin's little-boy and weather examples is a fifth type of evidence. A sixth type of evidence is the ability of the thesis and its defenses to withstand two sorts of challenge:

1. The problem with the contextless-argument, truth-condition, proposition approach is that it is too narrow to accommodate real life arguments and interactions, which incorporate actions and commitments.
2. Some putative counterexamples have arisen from the use of 'probably' in contexts other than present-tense unembedded affirmations. One type of context is the past tense, which turns out not to be a problem at all when we realize that using 'probably' in a past-tense statement does not put the performance of the act in the past. The second type of context is that in which the act is performed, although not by the speaker. Examples are indirect and quoted speech, which are simply reports of the performance of an act of guarded commitment. The third type of context is that in which the act is not yet explicitly performed or performed at all. Conditionals, imperatives, questions, wonderings, and agreeings and disagreeings are examples. In these contexts the word 'probably' is not part of an unembedded affirmation. The reasonable thing for 'S is probably P' to mean in these contexts is 'A guarded commitment to the proposition that S is P is justified'. If a commitment to the statement, 'A guarded commitment to the proposition that S is P is justified', develops or is present, then, from the committer's point of view, it is reasonable to perform the lurking speech act, unless there are good pratical reasons for not doing so.

In the process of responding to these challenges I proposed some basic tenets for a commitment approach to deductive validity, but more elaboration is needed.

The thesis and its defense have three significant practical consequences:

1. Attempts to computerize real-argument reasoning containing 'probably' will generally fail because there is no number that is connected to 'probably' in the ordinary sense in which 'probably' is used in real arguments.
2. The SEBKUS-associated weakening of soundness standards to handle qualified reasoning is helpful. 'SEBKUS' is an acronym for *Sensitivity, Experience, Background Knowledge, and Understanding of the Situation.* Critical thinking courses should emphasize 'SEBKUS' because its elements are factors that help an arguer and an argument appraiser decide whether to perform the action of guarding a committing, as well as whether to accept the reasons in an argument.
3. There is a role for deductive logic in critical thinking and informal logic courses at least because of its role in appraising a stripped argument in the application of qualified soundness standards.

A theoretical consequence is that if the thesis and its defense stand the tests of time and scrutiny, it might be appropriate to reconsider the speech-act theories of 'true', 'know', and 'good'.

CHAPTER 11

WOUTER H. SLOB

THE VOICE OF THE OTHER: A DIALOGICO-RHETORICAL UNDERSTANDING OF OPPONENT AND OF TOULMIN'S REBUTTAL[1]

Rijksuniversiteit Groningen, Theological Department, Oude Boteringestraat 38, 9712 GK, Groningen, The Netherlands
Het Oelbred 7, 9472 WK Zuidlaren, The Netherlands
E-mail: whslob@hotmail.com

ABSTRACT: Although contemporary dialectical logic recognizes an important role for the opponent in argumentation, it remains loyal to the idea that arguments are supportive. In this paper, it is argued that because of this dialectical logic does not take seriously its own dialogical perspective. Without acknowledging a substantial role for rebutting factors in argumentation, the role of the opponent remains secondary. Toulmin's understanding of the rebuttal suggests a way to incorporate such a substantial role of the opponent.

KEYWORDS: Dialectical logic; Stephen E. Toulmin; rebuttal; dialogical rhetoric; opponent; burden of proof

1. INTRODUCTION

A negative conclusion is also a conclusion. It is normal scientific practice to test hypotheses and negative results are as important as positive ones—albeit perhaps not always as exhilarating. For some reason, however, contemporary logic seems to overlook the negative conclusion. It is preoccupied with supporting conclusions and acknowledges only positive results. This is surprising. Classical logic, we will remember, was by definition focused upon supportive arguments. But since logic made a *dialectical* shift, one would expect a different approach. The dialectical shift, resulting from the work of C.L. Hamblin, the Erlangen School, Barth and Krabbe, and with Stephen Toulmin and Chaim Perelman as important precursors, acknowledges not only proposition, but also opposition. In fact, opposition to a claim is what gives argumentation its sense. Only when there is an opponent who does not as yet accept the claim, does it makes sense for the proponent to defend it.[2] Dialectical theory

---

[1] This article is a revision of a paper read at the OSSA-conference 2005: The Uses of Argument. I thank the audience for stimulating remarks and especially Fabio Paglieri for insightful comments.

[2] The logical roles are known by different names: van Eemeren, Grootendorst and Kruiger (1984): protagonist/antagonist, Freeman (1991): proponent/challenger, Johnson and Blair (1983): arguer/doubter

D. Hitchcock and B. Verheij (eds.), Arguing on the Toulmin Model: New Essays in Argument Analysis and Evaluation, 165–180.

thereby analyzes argumentation as verbal exchanges between proponent and opponent with the purpose "to establish whether the protagonist's [proponent's] standpoint is defensible against the critical reactions of the antagonist [opponent]" (van Eemeren, Grootendorst and Kruiger, 1984, p. 17).

Despite this important role of the opponent, it seems that in the resulting conclusion her influence is only marginal. Her counter-considerations may only *modify* the conclusion; they can never overturn it. James B. Freeman for instance argues that any conclusion is always a qualified conclusion, because of possible counter-considerations. Yet his 'modality' is always a positive one, ranging from 'possibly' to 'certainly' (cf. Freeman, 1991, p. 111). Apparently, although in a modified form, dialectical logic is just like classical logic concerned with supportive arguments. In that sense, the argument remains a matter 'of the proponent' and serves to support his position. Dialectical logic may not be as dialogical as it wants to be. Is the opponent nothing more than a stooge in a monological act?

In this contribution, I intend to investigate the reasons for this feature of dialectical logic and propose a way of granting the voice of the other a more substantial role in the conclusion of arguments. Stephen Toulmin's layout of arguments will be shown to be useful for doing so.

2. DIALECTICAL CRITERIA FOR GOOD ARGUMENTS

Dropping the formal-logical criterion of soundness—truth of the premises combined with validity of the inference[3]—dialecticians apply three basic criteria of good reasoning: *acceptance*, *relevance* and *adequacy*. These three criteria correspond to three different types of questions that might be asked by an opponent. The first question concerns the premises. If support is to be derived from them, it is clear that they must be accepted. The second type of question concerns the relevance of the reasons provided. Even if the premises are undisputed, they must also be relevant to the matter in discussion. Relevance concerns the link between the premises and the conclusion: it tells why these premises yield this conclusion. The third type of question is somewhat less straightforward, as it brings forward possible weaknesses of a given argument. For several reasons, even an argument that is acceptable and relevant may not be adequate. The evidence may only be slim, or there are possible reasons that might overrule the argument, or there may actually be counterevidence. At issue is: does the argument hold in the light of possible counter-considerations?

Together, the three basic questions of acceptance, relevance and adequacy determine the strength of the argument. Clearly, this is seldom an all-or-nothing matter. Whereas formal logic knows no shades, applying these criteria yields

---

(questioner), Walton (2003): proponent/respondent. For convenience, I apply Barth and Krabbe's (1982) proponent/opponent throughout.

[3] Ralph Johnson takes the rejection of formal-logical soundness as defining characteristic of 'informal logic' (cf. Johnson, 1995). The differences he observes between dialectical and informal logic are not on this point: "it appears that the rules of pragma-dialectics embody the force of the criteria used by the informal logic approach" (p. 241).

nuances. All three allow for degrees, and taken together a definite conclusion will almost never be reached. Precisely for that reason, dialectical logic is more apt than its formal counterpart to apply to actual argumentative practice.

3. ARGUMENTATIVE RESPONSIBILITIES

In the dialectical view, the opponent and the proponent have distinctive argumentative responsibilities. By means of a question the opponent initiates the argument because any 'why' challenges the proponent to defend the claim and to bring forward supporting reasons. Barth and Krabbe (1982) accordingly define the proponent and opponent by stating: "P[roponent] opposes none of the statements in the (pure) conflict, and O[pponent] is neutral to none of them" (p. 59). Barth and Krabbe want to present a normative orientation rather than a description of an actual situation, but it is clear that the respective roles of proponent and opponent are different with respect to the burden of proof involved. Only the proponent is called to defend his position if called for.

Of course, all dialecticians admit that the opponent may not only be critical of a claim of the proponent, but may have a standpoint herself. If so, however, the discussion is to be considered 'mixed' and should be treated as a complex argumentative situation: "[a] set[s] of simple conflicts superimposed upon each other *without interfering with one another*" (Barth and Krabbe, 1982, p. 74, italics original). Analyzing mixed discussions as separate discussions in which the argumentative responsibilities are reversed, allows one to keep the two responsibilities clear. The burden of proof remains to be seen as a matter incumbent upon the proponent only.

In the meantime, the opponent has no obligation to defend her position; questions can be asked at any time and the proponent is obliged to answer them. It is telling that according to the pragma-dialecticians van Eemeren and Grootendorst only the proponent ('protagonist') can violate rule number two of their ten commandments: "a party that advances a standpoint is obliged to defend it if the other party asks him to do so" (van Eemeren and Grootendorst, 1992, p. 208). Probably the idea is that whoever claims must defend. This is in itself a quite acceptable maxim, but it neglects two things. Firstly, allowing the opponent to ask away without even attributing burden of proof for her challenges invites filibustering (a fallacy seldom acknowledged by theorists). As the opponent does not have to justify her position in the discussion, she is free to obstruct the process, which in certain circumstances may be an appealing strategy. Secondly, if the opponent has no obligation to defend her position, she cannot be forced to accept any conclusion. In particular, she cannot be asked to defend stubborn opposition in the face of all the support the proponent has provided. Dialectically, there is nothing wrong with an opponent who keeps repeating: "Can you give me another reason? (And don't ask me why I am not impressed by the reasons you have given me; I have no obligation to tell you, remember.)"

Barth and Krabbe suggest that one might object to this asymmetry in burden of proof out of a 'feeling of justness',[4] but that is not my concern. Rather, my point is that if we cannot force the opponent to give up unreasonable resistance we have not improved much upon formal logic in terms of understanding normativity. Such a logical tool is as useless to contribute to actual argumentation as formal logic is.

If the opponent is attributed burden of proof for her position in the discussion, we can better see how actual discussions work, what is involved in them and how the discussants are in fact reaching compelling conclusions. Attributing to the opponent burden of proof does not only concern the situation in which she defends a standpoint of her own, but also concerns her opposition as such. Clearly, it is not a wise policy for any proponent to confront the opponent in an early stage of the discussion with this option. Any opponent asking "Why should I accept your claim?" will not be convinced by the counter-question "Why not?". But what is wrong with this strategy is precisely its strategy, not the fundamental impossibility to ask for the reasonableness of the position of the opponent.

Walton and Reed acknowledge that some critical questions bring along burden of proof. Sometimes, they argue, "the critical questioner has to provide some additional evidence to supplement the question" (2003, p. 210). The reason for this is that merely posing a question does not suffice to "cast the burden of proof back on the proponent" (idem). What they seem to suggest is that in some cases the proponent can *too easily* answer the opponent. Only when the opponent has supported her question, is a more substantial question required. As an example they discuss the appeal to expert opinion. Several critical questions can be asked. Some of them force the proponent to give evidence, or fail to answer adequately. For instance the 'field question' ("Is the expert an expert in the relevant field?") requires the proponent to show that this is indeed the case. Other questions, Walton and Reed argue, are not by themselves sufficient to provoke a substantial answer. In particular the 'trustworthiness' and the 'consistency' questions (asking respectively for the bias of the expert and the consistency with other experts) are supposed to require argumentative support to demand an answer. Walton and Reed fear that the trustworthiness question 'is the expert reliable' can simply be answered by 'yes', and that evidence for the untrustworthiness of the expert is required from the opponent to get a better answer than this. It is hard to see, however, how such a sharp distinction can be made between different critical questions. It seems to me that also the 'field question' can easily be answered by a 'yes', without providing more evidence for the argument. And, clearly, a 'yes' to such a question is not as such conclusive. (Was Einstein's expert opinion not to use the atomic bomb relevant? Obviously, he was an expert in the working of the atomic bomb, but certainly not in strategic-political considerations.) Contrariwise, I see no reason why some proponent would not be inclined to give evidence when asked the trustworthiness question; it would certainly strengthen his case. We do not need such an artificial distinction, however, when all questions in principle bring along burden of proof. How heavy a particular burden is in any given case, depends not on the type of question, but on the

[4] Cf. Barth and Krabbe (1982): "if the reader has qualms about the fundamental asymmetry in simple conflicts of opinions and feels that everything has to be symmetrical in order to be 'just', ..." (p. 75).

situation and in particular on the demands of the interlocutor. Some questions are answered right away, but others need support to be taken seriously. In contrast to the pragma-dialectical rule number 2, therefore, I do not think that all questions as such deserve serious attention. We may see it as a variant of Aristotle's dictum "not to enter into discussion with everybody" (*Topica*, VIII, 14, 164b). Also a question must be reasonable, and it is up to the opponent to defend this, if asked to do so.

4. WHAT IS AT ISSUE IN ARGUMENTATION?

The distribution of the burden of proof is intimately connected to the question as to what constitutes an argument. Generally, an argument is conceived as given reasons that support a claim: "argumentation comprises the whole constellation of utterances advanced in defense of a standpoint" (van Eemeren and Grootendorst, 1992, p. 14). If this is indeed what is at stake in a discussion, it is no wonder that only supportive reasons are taken into account. Is this, perhaps, what James Freeman calls a "monological view of argument" (1991, p. xiii), and which he contrasts with a dialogical view in which argument is seen as an "interchange between two or more persons" (idem)? Probably not what either Freeman or van Eemeren and Grootendorst intend. Yet, emphasizing the supportive function of argumentation alone, and disregarding counter-indicative aspects, does suggest a semi-monological approach.

Walton and Krabbe more consistently elaborate on the dialogical outlook, and distinguish between different kinds of discussions. Different types of discussions have different goals (as well as different rules), and hence different kinds of argumentative responsibilities (Walton and Krabbe, 1995, pp. 65-121). Without discussing these in detail here, we can say that this suggests that the participants have a mutual[5] interest in the outcome of a discussion. This implies, however, that the logical role of the opponent must be more substantial than merely triggering the discussion. Freeman acknowledges this, to a certain extent: the questions of the opponent may weaken or soften the conclusion so that a qualification is in place. Still, Freeman also wants an argument to be supportive. The role of the opponent is only to nuance the conclusion. A negative conclusion should be analyzed as a(nother) thesis for which the opponent becomes proponent.

If, however, an argument is really an interchange between argumentative interlocutors, why not think of the claim at issue as a conclusion to which both participants contribute substantially? The proponent provides supporting reasons, but possible counter-considerations are as important to come to a balanced conclusion. Typically, the opponent embodies the countering, rebutting, side of the discussion.

This suggestion puts the understanding of what an argument is in a different light. Rather than giving support for the claim, argumentative interchange is now seen as determining the relative weight of the conclusion, for which not only supporting but also rebutting forces are important. This implies that any conclusion

[5] Not necessarily: shared. The interlocutors may have different motivations to participate.

is always, just as Freeman maintains, a qualified conclusion, but in contrast to Freeman, it can also involve the qualification becoming negative. The range is from 'certainly', via 'possibly', to 'unlikely' or 'certainly not'.

If this approach is taken, the relation of the logical roles within a discussion changes as well. As long as only one of the participants faces burden of proof, it makes sense to distinguish sharply between proponent and opponent in a rather adversarial way. The moment both participants contribute to the conclusion, there is no need to apply such a sharp distinction, nor indeed, to postulate such an adversarial understanding of argumentation. The burden of proof shifts during the discussion back and forth between both participants and the question is not who faces the onus, but whether or not (s)he meets it.

5. TRUTH OR COMMITMENT?

Although the issue is rarely discussed, we may suspect an epistemological motive behind the preoccupation to regard arguments as supportive. The idea presumably is that the conclusion must reveal some truth, as for instance Ralph Johnson (1996) says: "an argument is an attempt to persuade someone (even oneself) on rational grounds of the 'truth' of some controversial thesis" (p. 262). I will leave aside here what 'rational grounds' exactly comes down to, and shall refrain from discussing the rather complicated issue of understanding truth, just to remark that truth is generally considered an all or nothing matter. Either a claim is true, or it is not. Obviously, this puts the idea of qualified conclusions under pressure: what does it mean to qualify something that is not supposed to have any shade? Freeman argues that qualifications are not part of the conclusion, but indicate the connection between premises and conclusions. In a rather classical fashion he remarks that "the truth of the premises guarantees the truth of the conclusion" (Freeman, 1991, p. 118). Still, as the connection between premises and conclusion is argumentatively based on evidence, and depends upon the acceptance of specific participants in the discussion, the truth of the conclusion remains underdetermined. I take this to say that acknowledging the qualification of the conclusion is a matter of epistemological discomfort, resulting from the human predicament of necessarily having only a limited view. In this view, the truth of the conclusion per se is an all or nothing matter, but the limitedness of human perspective calls duly for epistemic modesty. This assumption would clarify why arguments must be supportive; it makes no sense to qualify a conclusion negatively that in itself is supposed to be true. Indeed, this could only be concluded by a positive qualification of its denial. But in that case, the truth of the negation would be at issue.

It is questionable, however, whether truth understood in this way is useful in the study of argumentation. We may suggest an alternative understanding of the status of the conclusion. Not as reflecting truth in any sense, but as providing commitment of the participants. The predicament of human limitedness is obviously acknowledged, but it is not considered a matter of discomfiture. In fact, limited conclusions are all we can have and there is no reason to complain about that. It involves the modesty that all claims are tentative in the sense that counter-considerations may overturn even our deepest convictions in due course, but until then, we shall have to act according to our best knowledge. Conclusions, then, are not supposed to reflect all-or-nothing matters such as truth, but indicate the degree of commitment resulting from specific exchanges of arguments. There is hence no reason to object to the idea that argumentative qualification belongs intrinsically to the conclusion, and there is no reason to object to negative qualifications.

In this line of thought it may be remarked that what we are after in argumentation is not belief, or belief-change. Rather is it acceptance, in the sense that the opponent takes up epistemic responsibility for the disputed thesis, and hence makes it 'premissible', "sentences that he can use as his premises for inference and action" (Tuomela, 2000, p. 127). Rather than a mental state, or even a disposition, acceptance is a matter of communication. But communication in the widest sense: not only linguistic, but also in relation to the world around us.[6]

6. DEVELOPING COMMITMENT

If argumentation is about yielding commitment for some claim, it should be made clear how positive and negative aspects come together and how commitment is welded from both of these forces. I propose to see the conclusion as the vector-like result from supportive and rebutting forces brought forward by both participants. In this view, the proponent contributes the supporting force, whereas the opponent contributes the rebutting force. We are not interested primarily in linking premises and conclusion, but in transferring commitment. In rhetorical terms, the proponent wants to 'win over' the opponent. As the proponent is ready to defend his thesis, he is committed to it himself. Considering the opposition of his interlocutor, she is not (as yet). We may understand the attempt of the proponent to 'win over' the opponent as an attempt to bring her to drop the opposition and to accept commitment to the claim. On the other hand, the opponent may have good reasons to keep her reservations, or may even have compelling reasons why the claim should not be accepted. She, in other words, is committed to a neutral or negative attitude towards the claim and is ready to defend her position.

An argumentation may be understood as the interchange between those two positions. The point now is how commitment is transferred to the other side. Clearly, any reason that is proposed, even if it is only a strategic move, brings along commitment. But if a reason is accepted within a particular context, then not only the proponent but also the opponent has acknowledged commitment.

---

[6] The relationship between beliefs and acceptances is an important issue, but cannot be discussed here at length. The difference, though, may be misconceived. Raimo Tuomela (2000) argues that "the main difference between belief … and acceptance would seem to be the connection to language and reasoning which acceptance has and belief does not have" (p. 128). In Slob (2002a), I argue that belief also is an aspect of communication. If so, however, distinguishing beliefs and acceptance would lose its sense.

Regarding commitments, Walton and Krabbe (1995, p. 186) distinguish between assertions and concessions.[7] The former, but not the latter, involve burden of proof. Both these kinds of commitments, however, may contribute to the conclusion. It should be noted, therefore, that the opponent must be on his guard, and should not too readily allow for advanced arguments of the proponent. If she does not want to allow for a specific move, she should refuse her commitment by expressing her reservations, or indeed, her rejection. This is as much as saying that argumentation not only involves burden of proof, but also burden of questioning. When a reason passes unquestioned, it may very well be considered accepted. Walton (2003) deals with this matter and shows how it is linked to the question of retraction. The opponent must be allowed to retract commitment, if the full implication of some commitment becomes clear while the discussion is in progress. I shall not here enter into discussing this issue extensively. What is important, however, is that acknowledging the burden of questioning is a way to make both participants responsible for the outcome of a discussion and hence helps us to understand the transference of commitment.

If, either by advancing or by accepting, both participants are committed to any given reason, I shall call it *established* within the context. Cleary, not all reasons are easily established. Sometimes an elaborate sub-argument, satisfying the demand for acceptance, relevance and adequacy, is required to win over the interlocutor. But if the interlocutor finally accepts the conclusion of the sub-argument, commitment to its role in the bigger context is also established.

From this perspective, whether or not a reason is established depends upon the acceptance of the reason by the interlocutor. It should be seen that nothing more is required. In particular, no external perspective of some neutral arbiter is required. We can do without it, because the participants themselves can guard the process of accepting and rejecting reasons. As long as the opponent has reasonable questions, the proponent is still called to answer them. But if the opponent is satisfied, the argument reaches closure because without any questions left, the reason for arguing has disappeared.[8] If, after all, questions induce to argumentation, the discussion comes to an end when no questions are left.

Still, whether or not the opponent accepts the reasons presented does not depend upon her good- or ill-humouredness, as if she is completely free to do as she likes. The proponent can enforce it, when the opponent has no longer any reasonable

---

[7] They also acknowledge so-called 'dark-side' commitments, a very interesting though somewhat underdeveloped type of commitments. Dark-side commitments concern silent assumptions and are interesting because they may account for argumentative 'perforation': commitments that transcend the limits of a specific discussion and that are binding in other discussions as well. Acknowledging this makes 'argumentative negotiation' understandable. For a more elaborate discussion cf. Slob (2002a, p. 104).

[8] Argument-closure is still a matter in dispute. Walton (2003) remarks that "in principle, the dialogue could go on and on …", but also says that "there is nothing to prevent some limits being imposed on the length of such critical questioning intervals" (p. 31). To my mind, *we* do not need to worry. It is up to the respective interlocutor to impose limits; as long as (s)he is prepared to continue the dialogue, questions and answers are being exchanged. This leaves the dynamic of dialogue fully in the hands of the participants and rejects in particular any reference towards a 'rational' anchor-point, such as Freeman seems to seek by appealing to 'intuitions' (cf. Freeman, 2005b, 105f). The trouble in both approaches may lie in the shared idea that we need rules to regulate dialogues. I think that interlocutors suffice.

doubts. It is here that the double burden of proof pays out. Not only the proponent, but also the opponent can be called to defend her position. Just as the proponent is supposed to convince the opponent of his position, so it is the proponent who is the main audience for the opponent. In other words: both participants should convince their respective interlocutor and hence should orient their reasons to each other. In this process, nothing more is required than applying reasons that are convincing for the interlocutor, and accepting commitment that results from advancing them. In this 'balance of powers' the proponent is most times the one who wants to win over the opponent and is strategically advised not to call the opponent too quickly to defend her position. But at some point, for instance when more than sufficient good reasons have been given, the opponent may be called to defend further opposition. In this way, accepting reasons is a matter that can be enforced by the proponent: if the opponent, given the reasons presented, still refuses to accept the conclusion, she must bring up good reasons herself. Or become unreasonable (as far as the proponent is concerned).[9]

As the opponent also faces burden of proof, and may defend her position in the discussion, it is very well possible (even likely) that her rebutting input is relevant for the overall conclusion. But this can be so only when her reasons are established. That is, when her interlocutor (the proponent of the main argument) accepts the reasons of the opponent, he is to be considered committed to this rebutting force. As the opponent herself has advanced the rebutting input, she is committed to it already.

In this way, dialogical rhetoric conceives of argumentative normativity as a balance of standards of both interlocutors. Both participants should orient their arguments mutually to each other in order to defend their respective positions and thereby establish reasons. To the extent that the respective interlocutor accepts the reasons, they are established and influence the final conclusion. Supporting and rebutting factors add up and together lead up to the conclusion. Both participants are committed to this conclusion, because both are committed to all the ingredients.

7. TOULMIN'S DIAGRAM

Not being merely illustrative, diagrams help to show the structure of an argument and serve as a strategic tool. Toulmin's proposals in *The Uses of Argument* (1958) are useful here, especially because they allow us to incorporate the three basic criteria of argument evaluation in the distinguished elements of argumentation.

As is well known, Toulmin distinguishes between Data, Warrant, Backing, Rebuttal, Qualifier and Conclusion. The basic line goes from data to conclusion. The warrant is added because it indicates why the data are relevant for the conclusion. Backing is added to support the warrant itself. The rebuttal is added because there may be counter-considerations to reckon with. The rebutting force may qualify the conclusion.

---

[9] For a discussion on 'unreasonableness' in this understanding, cf. Slob (2002b).

In a diagram, Toulmin's layout of arguments looks like this:

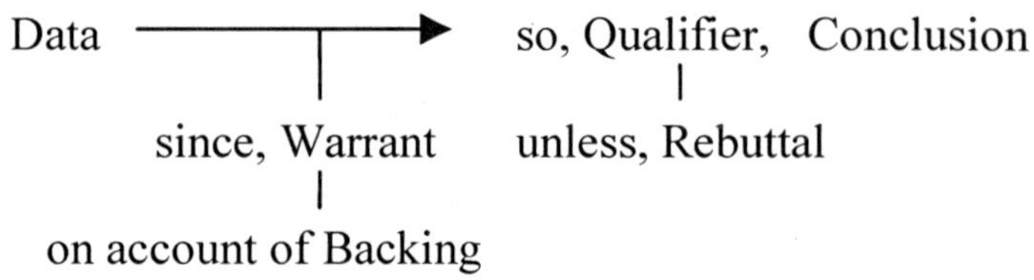

Figure 1. Diagram of Toulmin's layout (1964, p. 104).

Toulmin's scheme serves well to show how the three basic questions of dialectics, acceptance, relevance and adequacy, contribute to the development of an argument. Being called to defend a claim, a proponent brings forward a reason, in Toulmin's scheme the data. If this is as such accepted, the reason is without further ado established and leads unobstructedly to the conclusion. If so, the discussion will be over because the opponent has no further objections. But obviously, she may have some hesitations. First, she may question the acceptability of the data itself. This simply calls for support, which results in a sub-argument. The argument is extended, so to speak, with a 'deeper', subordinated layer.

Beside the acceptability of the data, the opponent may also ask for the relevance of the reason: why does the data lead up to the conclusion? The question of relevance seeks some kind of bridging between data and conclusion, and this is precisely what Toulmin's notion of warrant brings about. A warrant licenses the inference from data to conclusion and typically consists of a rule. Toulmin considers it important to support warrants with the special element of backing, but when we allow that the main argument by a sub-argument can be extended 'sideways' as well this element becomes superfluous.[10]

The third question concerns possible counter-considerations, and asks for the adequacy of the reasons given. Although the data presented may be both acceptable and relevant, there can be compelling reasons why the conclusion does not follow. These counter-considerations can collectively be headed as the rebuttal. When it is recognized that counter-considerations may undermine the conclusion, to some extent, we must also accept the qualifier.

8. STRETCHING THE REBUTTAL

Toulmin's rebuttal may qualify, but cannot overrule the conclusion. This is also the way dialectical logicians perceive of counter-considerations. If argumentation is considered to be supportive of the conclusion, then it is obvious that the qualifier must

[10] Verheij (2002, §2.3) makes the same observation but does not drop the backing.

be positive. If so, counter-considerations can be allowed to modify the conclusion, but cannot be acknowledged to outweigh the support. In fact, as the overall argument is required to be supportive, it is even better when the counter-considerations can be shown to be neutralized. If so, the neutralized rebuttal gives in fact extra strength to the conclusion: "...counterrebuttals support conclusions by ruling out possible rebuttals..." (Freeman, 1991, p. 163). Acknowledging the rebuttal as a separate element of argumentation is therefore not designed to lend the voice of the other an ear, but serves dialectically the purpose of supporting the conclusion in an indirect way.

Allowing that rebuttals can be overruled so that the conclusion is strengthened rather than weakened is in fact rebutting the rebuttal. This is more than a funny observation, for it means that we can ask for the adequacy of the rebuttal. If so, presumably, we can also ask for the acceptability and the relevance of the rebuttal. In other words, just as the data could be questioned for further support, yielding a 'deeper' argument, and just as the warrant could be asked for support, extending the argument 'sideways', so it seems that we can ask for the liability of the rebuttal, extending the argument 'sideways' as well (but in the opposite direction, so to speak, than the warrant). In order to be able to draw the diagram, I propose to order the elements of Toulmin slightly differently. We literally must make room for the sub-arguments, but positing warrant and rebuttal in opposing positions indicates their mutual relation within the argument aptly as well.

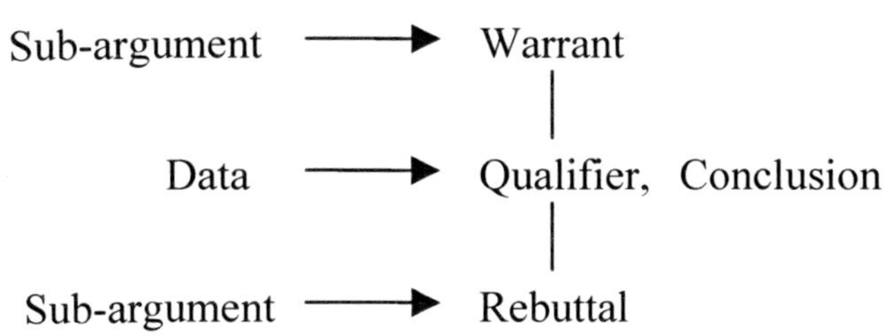

Figure 2. Toulmin's layout, with sub-arguments.

Now a difficulty occurs. The sub-arguments regarding data and warrant can both be understood as supportive for the conclusion, but this is not the case with the rebuttal. Only if rebutted itself is the conclusion supported. Support for the rebuttal itself means in effect an undermining of the conclusion. If we allow the rebuttal to be developed within the structure of the main argument, it means that we are not only acknowledging supportive, but also rebutting forces. In such a proposal, the voice of the other begins to speak up.

As will be clear by now, I think there is ample reason to incorporate rebutting factors within argumentation. This will mean that we have to adjust the diagramming technique also. Not only because diagramming is a valuable tool to gain insight in the structure of argument, but also because vice versa: diagrams show important features of argument analysis. And they may show possible weaknesses perhaps more clearly than words alone can do.

9. FREEMAN'S DIAGRAMS OF REBUTTING THE REBUTTAL

James B. Freeman, in his *Dialectics and the Macrostructure of Arguments* (1991), gives an impressive adjustment of Toulmin's basic scheme of the layout of arguments. From a dialectical point of view, he develops Toulmin's ideas and thereby makes an important contribution to our thinking about argument structure and analysis. Still, his proposals leave us with several questions and difficulties. If diagrams turn out to be unclear and contrived, this may be an indication that its theoretical basis is muddled. To my mind, some of Freeman's diagrams indeed bring to light questionable aspects of the dialectical approach.

One of the problems concerns the role and position of the opponent within argumentation. Diagrammatically this problem concentrates on understanding the rebuttal. In line with the general dialectical approach, Freeman thinks that conclusions are strengthened by the fact that the rebuttal is countered and neutralized. Hence, a counter-rebuttal is to be considered as a supporting premise for the main argument. Unfortunately, however, a counter-rebuttal cannot simply be added to other premises, because only in relation to the rebuttal can it make sense. Freeman, therefore, proposes the following diagram:

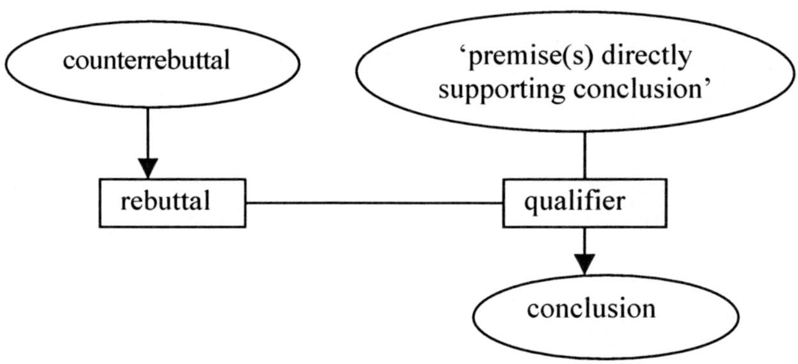

Figure 3. Freeman's proposed diagram (1991, p. 164).

Freeman (1991) thinks that this diagram can "display the unique role of the counterrebuttals quite perspicuously" (p. 163). I cannot agree. The diagram suggests that there are two types of premises: those that directly support the conclusion, and those that do so indirectly (counterrebuttals). Far from being perspicuous, this picture yields several questions: how do direct and indirect premises relate? For instance, are they coordinatively compound or multiple? This question is considered important because it concerns the strength of the argument: multiple arguments are supportive independently of each other, whereas coordinatively compound arguments have strength only collectively.[11] If direct and indirect premises are multiple, the logical position of the counterrebuttal is undermined. It is supposed to neutralize the force of the rebuttal, but it is hard to see how in multiple argumentation rebuttals affect the direct premises in the first place; they are supposed to be independent. Yet, if the two types of premises are coordinatively compound, we face another problem. It is always and at all stages possible to come up with rebuttals, even the most farfetched and irrelevant ones. Clearly, farfetched and irrelevant rebuttals are easily countered. But if we are dealing with coordinatively compound argumentation, we *must* counter all possible objections, because only collectively does a coordinatively compound argument have strength.

Diagrammatically, Freeman's proposal is downright unclear. The counterrebuttal is supposed to support the conclusion, but it is not even connected to it! Freeman (1991) claims that "the arrow from the counterrebuttal premise does ultimately point to the conclusion. But it points through the rebuttal box to indicate that the rebuttal is non-operative in this case" (p. 164). As far as I can see, however, nothing of such kind is indicated at all. There is no pointing through the rebuttal box, and there is no indication that the rebuttal is not operative. Rather, the diagram reads as if the counterrebuttal in fact supports the rebuttal!

Clearly, this is not what Freeman wants. But he does acknowledge that it is possible to support the rebuttal.[12] Figure 4 represents this idea in a diagram.

What we have here is not merely a rebuttal, but a counterargument.[13] Freeman (1991) asks how the counterargument is integrated within the main argument and gives the following revealing answer: "to answer this question, we must ask how

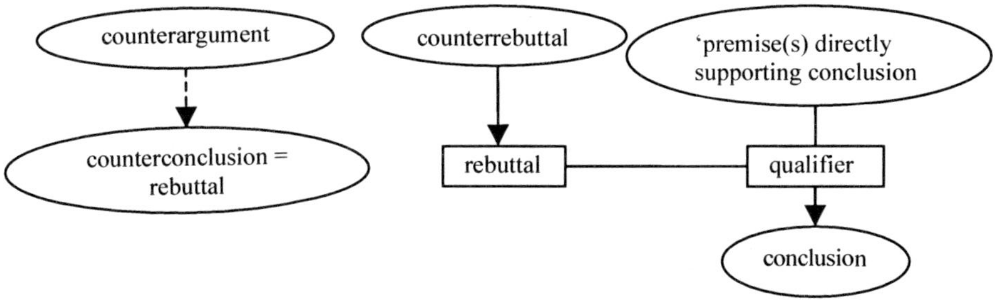

Figure 4. Freeman's diagram, with support for rebuttal.

---

[11] Cf. van Eemeren and Grootendorst (1992, p. 164). For an elaborate discussion of the difference between those two structures, cf. Snoeck Henkemans (1997).

[12] Cf. Freeman (1991, 193/194).

[13] Or rather: a counter-sub-argument.

arguers may reply to the objections" (p. 194). The counterargument itself is given no place within the main argument, but is only acknowledged to the extent that the main arguer replies to it. Anxiously, so it seems, a monological picture is preserved.

We should see that it is odd to acknowledge the counterargument only as a neutralized rebuttal. The main reason to introduce the qualifier was to absorb the rebutting force of counterconsiderations. We now see that rebuttals are recognized only when they are neutralized. In such circumstances, it is hard to see what rebutting force is left to qualify the conclusion in the first place. If rebuttals have any genuine force, they should be fully integrated within the structure of the main argument.

Freeman's diagram shows that this is not at all the case. Argument and counterargument are separated. It keeps the burden or proof of proponent and opponent neatly apart, and thereby remains within the limits of the dialectical approach. But obviously, both arguments have bearings upon each other, and it is strange that this cannot be made clear in a diagram.[14] More troublesome is that this separation of argument and counterargument makes the interference between arguments pro and contra invisible. It is not clear how premises either pro or contra relate to each other and how they interfere with the opposing line of argument.

We may see how the dialectical approach leads to contrived consequences when we look at the way that Freeman eventually proposes to integrate the counter-argument within the structure of the main argument. Consistently, a supported

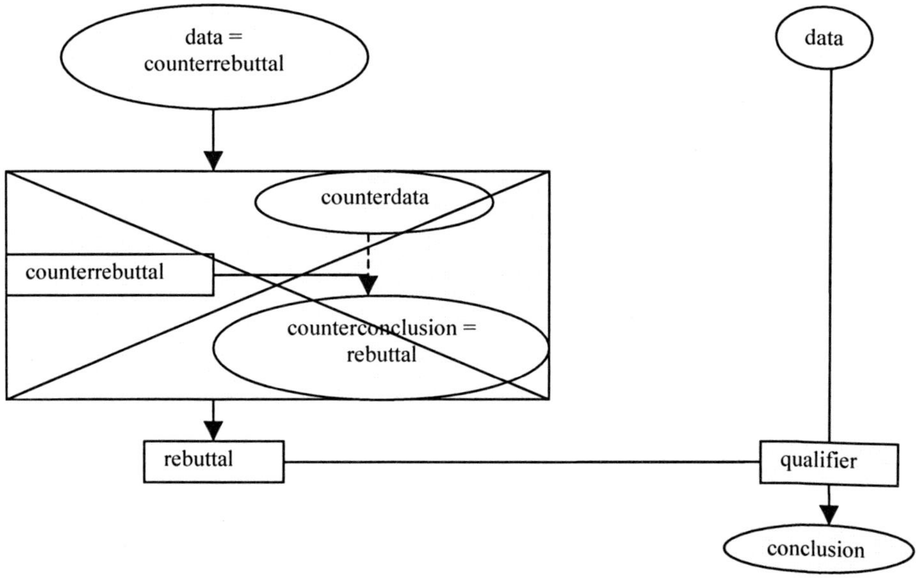

Figure 5. Freeman's diagram, support for rebuttal neutralized.

[14] All the more so, because Freeman (1991, p. 168) criticizes Scriven for the very same problem.

rebuttal is only interesting if it is neutralized in the main argument. To achieve this, Freeman proposes to 'box' the counterargument, and then diagrams it accordingly: counterrebuttals neutralize, as indirect premises, the force of the rebuttal which is indicated by crossing the box.[15] Figure 5 puts this idea in a diagram.

The diagram is far from clear. Introducing the box brings in several argumentative elements that are not accounted for. Not merely acknowledging data, rebuttal, qualifier and conclusion, Freeman also seems to acknowledge counter-data, counter-rebuttal, counter-qualifier, counter-conclusion. Freeman also introduces two different arrows: the main arrow, going from data to conclusion and the dotted counter-arrow, going from counter-data to counter-conclusion. As far as I can see, all Freeman really needs is a counter-rebuttal: if the rebuttal is effectively rebutted, the conclusion is not threatened by its negative impact. But in order to be able to acknowledge an effective rebuttal-rebuttal it is necessary to acknowledge real discussion within the structure of the main argument and this involves a substantial role of the other.

It seems to me that recognizing the voice of the other allows one to diagram the requirements of argumentation in a much more straightforward way. Counter-considerations can be incorporated as extensions of the main argument. In fact, the possibility that the main argument can be extended both 'deeper' and 'sideways' was already suggested above. What we get is shown in Figure 6.

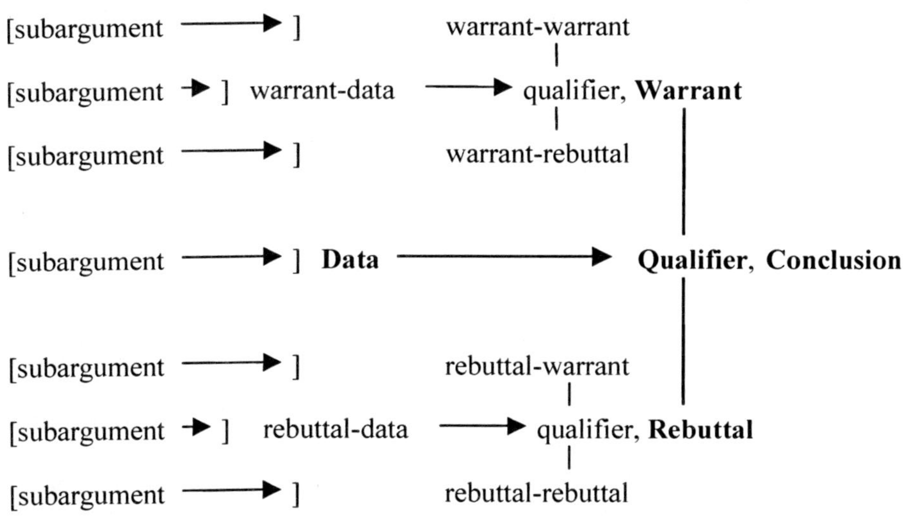

Figure 6. Toulmin's diagram, extended wider and deeper.

[15] Cf. Freeman (1991, 198ff).

This picture, however, is not possible in a dialectical understanding. The sub-arguments regarding data and warrant can both be understood as supportive for the conclusion, and hence fit the dialectical scheme. But this is not the case with the rebuttal. Only if rebutted itself, is the conclusion supported. Support for the rebuttal itself means in effect an undermining of the conclusion. If we allow the rebuttal to be developed within the structure of the main argument, it means that we are not only acknowledging supportive, but also rebutting forces. This requires that the opponent must have substantial impact within the main argument itself.

10. CONCLUSION

In a sense, I have not done much more than argue that all participants in a discussion are accountable for their own position, and should defend their respective position if called for. Why should this be controversial for dialecticians? Indeed, why is this not simply the default position?

There is a reason: dialectically, argument analysis serves argument evaluation. The main question is: is the conclusion sufficiently supported? This means that the dialectical approach is primarily focused upon the product of argumentation: only a clear-cut and orderly argument can be judged properly. Dialogical rhetoric, by contrast, follows the argumentative process and sees arguments as interchanges of supporting and rebutting forces. In my proposal, argument analysis does not serve evaluation, but serves the mapping of established reasons. Evaluation is no longer at stake in argument analysis, because a reason is only established when both discussants have in fact accepted it and thus have evaluated it positively. The map of established reasons forms a vector that leads up to the conclusion. Data form the basic ingredient, warrant forms the positive force of the argument and the rebuttal the negative counterpart. Argument analysis shows these two forces and display their relative contribution to the conclusion.

Lending the voice of the other an ear is acknowledging the substantial function of counterconsiderations. They may not only defeat an argument, but indeed bend it in an opposite direction. Clearly, the rebuttal in the main argument is the prime focus of this function. But also in the sub-arguments of the data and the warrant counterconsiderations can be given.[16] Both data and warrant may be extended to sub-arguments with rebuttals of their own. It is clear that the rebuttal-rebuttal is in fact a reason of the proponent of the main thesis and supports the claim as it undermines the rebuttal. Still, which of the elements derive originally from either the proponent or the opponent is for argument-analysis not a main interest. What is important is to map the established reasons and both participants are committed to these. In this way, a suitable conclusion is reached that both participants not only should, but will, accept.

[16] Verheij (2002) sums up five different types of rebuttals: against 1: datum, 2: claim, 3: warrant, 4: 'first implicit conditional', 5: 'second implicit conditional'. The data-rebuttal concerns 1, the main-rebuttal concerns 2 and 5, and the warrant-rebuttal concerns 3 and 4.

CHAPTER 12

BART VERHEIJ

EVALUATING ARGUMENTS BASED ON TOULMIN'S SCHEME

Artificial Intelligence, University of Groningen, Grote Kruisstraat 2/1,
9712 TS Groningen, The Netherlands
E-mail: b.verheij@ai.rug.nl

ABSTRACT: Toulmin's scheme for the layout of arguments (1958) represents an influential tool for the analysis of arguments. The scheme enriches the traditional premises-conclusion model of arguments by distinguishing additional elements, like warrant, backing and rebuttal. The present paper contains a formal elaboration of Toulmin's scheme, and extends it with a treatment of the formal *evaluation* of Toulmin-style arguments, which Toulmin did not discuss at all. Arguments are evaluated in terms of a so-called dialectical interpretation of their assumptions. In such an interpretation, an argument's assumptions can be evaluated as defeated, e.g. when there is a defeating reason against the assumption. The present work builds on recent research on defeasible argumentation (cf. e.g. the work of Pollock, Reiter, Loui, Vreeswijk, Prakken, Hage and Dung). More specifically, the author's work on the dialectical logic DEFLOG and the argumentation tool ARGUMED serve as starting points.

KEYWORDS: Stephen E. Toulmin; defeasible argumentation; argument evaluation

1. INTRODUCTION

In his book *The Uses of Argument*, Stephen Toulmin (1958) has argued that arguments need to be analyzed using a richer format than the traditional one of formal logic in which only premises and conclusions are distinguished. He has proposed a scheme for the layout of arguments that in addition to *data* and *claim* distinguishes between *warrant*, *backing*, *rebuttal* and *qualifier*.

As an illustration, Toulmin discusses the claim that Harry is a British subject. The claim can be supported by the datum that Harry was born in Bermuda. That there is a connection at all between datum and claim is expressed by the warrant that a man born in Bermuda will generally be a British subject. In turn, the warrant can be supported by the backing that there are certain statutes and other legal provisions to that effect. The warrant does not have total justifying force, so the claim that Harry is a British subject must be qualified: it follows presumably. Moreover there are possible rebuttals, for instance when both his parents were aliens or he has become a naturalized American.

D. Hitchcock and B. Verheij (eds.), Arguing on the Toulmin Model: New Essays in Argument Analysis and Evaluation, 181–202.

Schematically, the result is as in Figure 1 (Toulmin, 1958, p. 105). Toulmin *et al.* (1984) give many further examples.

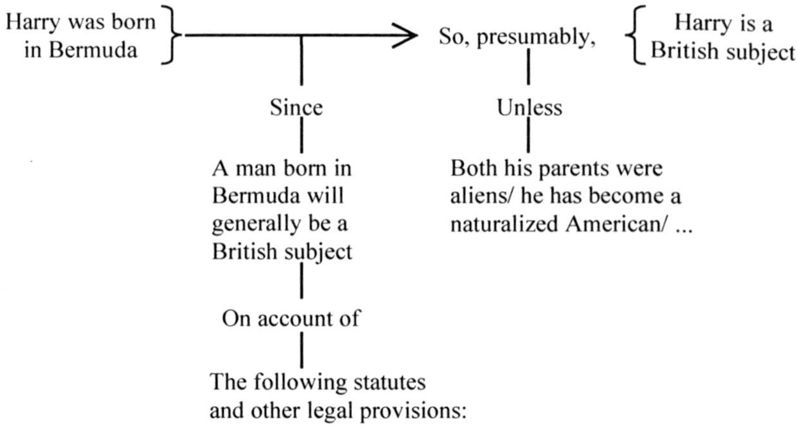

Figure 1. An example of Toulmin's scheme for the layout of arguments.

Toulmin's scheme for the layout of arguments has had a continuing influence on argumentation researchers (cf., e.g. van Eemeren *et al.*, 1996, pp. 129-160; Bench-Capon, 1997). Its general form is shown in Figure 2 (Toulmin, 1958, p. 104):

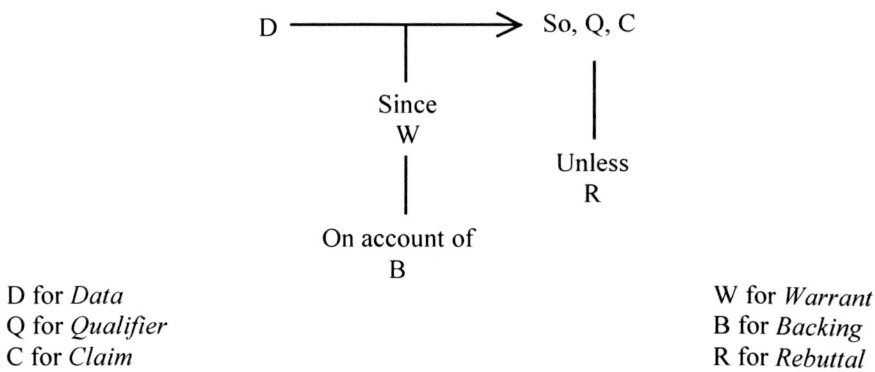

Figure 2. The general form of Toulmin's scheme for the layout of arguments.

The Data consist of certain facts that support the Claim. The Warrant is an inference license according to which the Data support the Claim, while the Backing provides in turn support for the Warrant. A Rebuttal provides conditions of exception for the argument, and the Qualifier can express a degree of force that the Data give to the Claim by the Warrant.

Good points of Toulmin's work were his emphasis on the following:

1. In argumentation, the warrants of arguments (in the sense of inference licenses) can be at issue and their backings can differ from domain to domain.
2. Arguments can be subject to rebuttal in the sense that there can be conditions of exception.
3. Arguments can have qualified conclusions.
4. Other kinds of arguments than just those based on the standard logical quantifiers and connectives (for all x, for some x, not, and, or, etc.) need to be analyzed.
5. Determining whether an argument is good or not involves substantive judgments and not only formal.

Since the appearance of Toulmin's book, all of these points have found increasing support in different research communities (under the direct influence of Toulmin or independently).

Notwithstanding Toulmin's critical stance towards formal logic,[1] in the present paper, a *formal* elaboration of Toulmin's central ideas will be given. It is shown that Toulmin's central ideas can well be set out in a formal way by the use of techniques of today's formal logic.

It goes without saying that the game of formalization is here not played for mathematical pleasure. The main reason for formalization is that it allows the repair of an omission in Toulmin's work. Toulmin's omission is that he has only discussed the *structure* of arguments (in terms of the roles of the different kinds of elements of arguments), but has not paid attention to the *evaluation* of arguments. In other words, he does not provide an analogue of logical validity as an evaluation criterion for arguments - perhaps because he does not believe there to be one.

This is a major omission, especially in view of the role of rebuttals in his scheme: clearly a rebuttal can influence the evaluation of an argument for a particular claim. Using Toulmin's example above, whether the datum that Harry is born in Bermuda justifies the claim that he is a British subject depends on whether Harry's parents were aliens. Assuming that Harry's parents were aliens, the datum does *not* justify the claim, while assuming that they weren't aliens, the datum will normally justify the claim (unless there is another rebuttal, such as that Harry has become a naturalized American). As stated previously, perhaps Toulmin did not believe there to be an evaluation criterion analogous to logical validity. Here it is shown that there is such a

[1] Toulmin's recent book *Return to Reason* (Toulmin, 2001) can be regarded as an elaboration of this critical stance. He speaks of a centuries-old imbalance in our pursuit of knowledge and defends reasonable judgment (grounded on practical experience) against the dominance of rationality (based on theory).

criterion by providing one: it is based on the idea of *dialectical interpretation* (cf. Verheij, 2003a; 2003b; 2005b). Briefly, the statements in an argument are evaluated with respect to the argument's assumptions. Statements can be justified (e.g. when there is a justifying reason for them), defeated (e.g. when there is a defeating reason against them) or neither.

Of course it is impossible to retain all of Toulmin's central ideas in their exact original form - some ideas will be adapted and extended. The task set here is one of reconstruction with a contemporary eye, and thus by necessity involves an *interpretation* of Toulmin's ideas. Still the goal is that the elements of Toulmin's scheme will find a recognizable place in the present elaboration.

The starting point for the reconstruction of Toulmin's scheme is a particular theory of dialectical argumentation, called DEFLOG. It is related to my work on argument assistance software (see, e.g. Verheij, 2003a; 2005b on the ARGUMED system). In the present paper, the relevant parts of DEFLOG are introduced alongside the reconstruction of Toulmin's scheme. For a more extensive account of DEFLOG, the reader may want to consult Verheij (2003b; 2003c). The present work builds on research on defeasible and dialectical argumentation (cf. e.g. the work of Pollock, 1987; Reiter, 1980; Loui, 1998; Vreeswijk, 1997; Prakken, 1997; Hage, 1997; and Dung, 1995). An earlier version of this paper was presented at the OSSA 2001 conference (Verheij, 2002).

There are many relations of the points discussed in this paper with work in the field of argumentation theory. For instance, the treatment of warrants in this paper is related to argumentation schemes (see, e.g. Walton, 1996b; cf. also Verheij, 2003c) and Hitchcock's use of covering generalizations (1998). Such cross-connections between formal and informal approaches to argumentation deserve further attention, but fall outside the scope of this paper. The book *Argumentation Machines. New Frontiers in Argument and Computation* (2003; edited by Reed and Norman) is a useful resource in this respect.

2. ELABORATING ON TOULMIN'S SCHEME FOR THE LAYOUT OF ARGUMENTS

In the following, the elements of Toulmin's scheme for the layout of arguments will be reconstructed, in a way that is formally explicit. A step-by-step strategy will be followed. Simple arguments will be analyzed in terms of primitive notions like statements, justifying reasons etc.

A graphical representation will be used that arranges the elements of Toulmin's scheme in a different way than in Toulmin's original. The reason for this is a pragmatic one: in this way it becomes possible to use the ARGUMED software described by Verheij (2003a; 2005b). ARGUMED is argument assistance software that can graphically represent arguments and evaluate the status of the statements involved. It can be downloaded at http://www.ai.rug.nl/~verheij/aaa/.

Figure 3 shows Toulmin's original arrangement on the left and the new arrangement on the right. For reasons that will become clear below (in section 3, notably Figure 10), the element of rebuttal has been left out here. Note also that in Figure 3 some of Toulmin's lines (e.g. between Backing and Warrant) have been replaced by arrows. The reason for this adaptation is that in the formal treatment below each of the arrows corresponds to a conditional sentence.

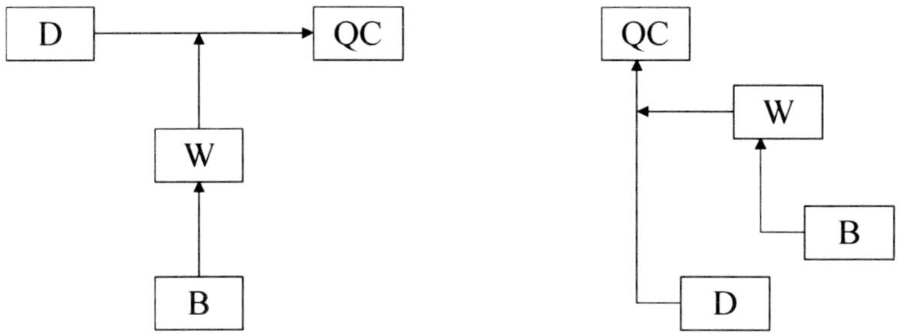

Figure 3. Toulmin's original arrangement (without rebuttal; on the left) presented differently (on the right).

The main difference between the original arrangement and the new one is that reasons appear below their conclusions. For instance, the data D appear below the qualified claim QC (why the qualifier and the claim are taken together is explained below) and the backing B appears below the warrant W. Other differences will be explained when they become relevant.

Data and Claim

The first step in the present reconstruction is to consider Data and Claim. In Toulmin's (1958) own words, we have

> one distinction to start with: between the *claim* or conclusion whose merits we are seeking to establish (C) and the facts we appeal to as a foundation for the claim - what I shall refer to as our *data* (D). (p. 97)

Let's look at Toulmin's example: if we seek to establish the claim that Harry is a British subject, we could for instance appeal to the datum that Harry was born in Bermuda. In an ordinary language argument this could be expressed thus:

> Harry was born in Bermuda. So he is a British subject.

Already at this early stage, it is convenient to adopt some conventions that elaborate on Toulmin's. The first is the convention that arguments are constructed from one or more *statements* expressed by *sentences*.[2] In the example we find the two statements that Harry is a British subject and that Harry was born in Bermuda, expressed by the sentences 'Harry is a British subject' and 'Harry was born in Bermuda', respectively.

The second convention is to distinguish between two different *roles* of statements in arguments: some are the argument's *assumptions*, others its *issues*. An argument's assumptions are the foundation on which the argument is built, whereas an argument's issues can be regarded as the topics or themes of the argument. A peculiarity of this convention is that an argument can have the effect that an issue of the argument can be settled by the argument (and hence is not 'at issue'). This occurs when the evaluation of the argument shows that an issue of the argument is justified or defeated.

In the example, it is assumed that Harry was born in Bermuda, and an issue that Harry is a British subject. If it were assumed that Harry is a British subject, there would be no need to provide a reason for it. If the datum were itself not assumed, i.e. if it were an issue that Harry was born in Bermuda, that issue would have to be established by further argument.

The third convention concerns the *evaluation* of the statements in an argument. The idea is that the statements in an argument can be evaluated, depending on the information expressed in the argument. For instance, the assumption that Harry was born in Bermuda is - since it is an assumption - taken to be justified. Also the argument's issue that Harry is a British subject is evaluated as justified, but only since there is a reason justifying it, viz. that Harry was born in Bermuda. At present, two evaluation statuses are distinguished: statements can be justified or they can be unevaluated. If for instance the statement that Harry was born in Bermuda were itself an issue, that statement and the statement that Harry is a British subject would not be justified. (Later we will also distinguish statements that are defeated. See section 3).

This brings us to the fourth convention, which concerns *support by reasons*. One point of an argument like 'Harry was born in Bermuda. So he is a British subject' is that it expresses that the statement that Harry was born in Bermuda *supports* the statement that he is a British subject. It not only expresses the assumption that Harry was born in Bermuda and the issue that Harry is a British subject, but also that there is a support relation between the two statements. In other words, the argument implies that there is a conditional relation between the two statements, that can - for instance - be expressed by the compound sentence 'If Harry was born in Bermuda, he is a British subject'.[3]

---

[2] It is more precise to say that *the propositional content* of statements is expressed by sentences. Statements can be regarded as a kind of speech act (cf. Austin, 1962; Searle, 1969).

[3] David Hitchcock has informed me that the claim that an argument 'Data, so claim' implies the conditional statement 'If data, then claim' can be given historical support by reference to the Stoic interpretation of conditional propositions, as reported in Diogenes Laertius, *Lives and Opinions of the Eminent Philosophers* 7.71: '... the conditional connective 'if' .. declares that the second [i.e. the consequent] follows from the first [i.e. the antecedent].'

The conditional 'If ..., (then) ...' is here not construed as the notorious material conditional of standard logic. One important reason for this is that a material conditional is truth-functional: its truth value is determined by the truth values of the conditional's antecedent and consequent. Cf. Haack, 1978; Hage, 1997; Prakken, 1997; Verheij, 1996. The conditional 'If D, then C' implied by an argument 'D. So C' should however intuitively reflect some relation between D and C that is not captured by the truth values of D and C alone.

In order to prevent confusion with the material conditional, a dedicated arrow ~> is used here. A conditional D ~> C only validates Modus ponens. There is no way of deriving a conditional D ~> C on the basis of logic alone; deriving D ~> C will always be based on premises. For instance, D ~> C does not follow from a deduction of C from D.[4] Still D ~> C can follow, namely when it is the consequent of another conditional, e.g. W ~> (D ~> C). See the next subsection on warrant.

Statements expressed by sentences of the form 'If ..., (then) ...' can themselves be assumed or an issue, just like all other statements. For instance, an argument like 'Harry was born in Bermuda. So he is a British subject' can be considered to imply the assumption that if Harry was born in Bermuda, he is a British subject. A conditional assumption of this form can be referred to as the *associated conditional* of the argument (cf. Hitchcock, 1985).[5]

According to the present conventions, the argument 'Harry was born in Bermuda. So he is a British subject' implies the following:

> It is assumed that Harry was born in Bermuda.
> It is an issue that Harry is a British subject.
> It is assumed that if Harry was born in Bermuda, he is a British subject.
> It is justified that Harry was born in Bermuda.
> It is justified that Harry is a British subject.
> It is justified that if Harry was born in Bermuda, he is a British subject.

The issue that Harry is a British subject is justified, since the statement that Harry was born in Bermuda is a justifying reason for it. In general, a statement D is said to

---

[4] In terms of the jargon associated with the rules of inference of natural deduction: ~> has the standard elimination rule for conditionals (viz. *Modus ponens*), but lacks the standard introduction rule. In fact, there is no rule of inference introducing ~>. I have introduced the term 'primitive implication' for such a conditional (Verheij, 2003b).

[5] The associated conditional of a data-claim argument is a 'minimal' commitment implicit in the argument, viz. simply the conditional that connects data and claim. In argumentation theory, the generalization of such a conditional to a rule statement (in our example the rule that those born in Bermuda are British subjects) is also often referred as the implicit assumption of an argument (van Eemeren *et al.*, 1996, p. 14 and elsewhere). Those generalizations are here referred to as the warrants of an argument. See the next subsection on warrant and the last paragraph of section 1 of this paper. Hitchcock's associated conditional of an argument (1985) is construed as a material conditional. There are other types of implicit assumptions (see, e.g. Ennis, 1982).

be a *justifying reason* for another statement C if the statements that D and that if D, then C are both justified.

The above can be summarized in a graphical representation of the argument (cf. Verheij, 2003a; 2003b) (Figure 4).

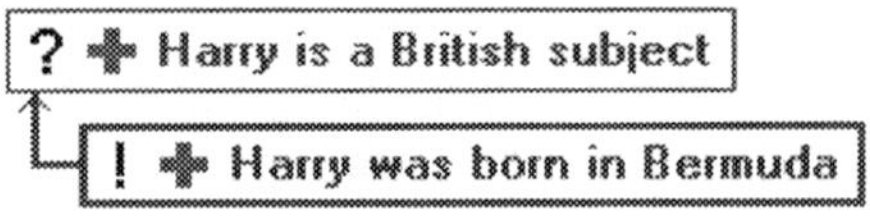

Figure 4. An elementary argument.

The exclamation mark indicates an assumed statement, the question mark a statement that is an issue. The associated conditional (that if Harry was born in Bermuda, he is a British subject) is depicted by the arrow. That the two elementary statements are justified is indicated by the plus signs and the dark bold font.

Figure 5 shows what happens if it were an issue that Harry was born in Bermuda.

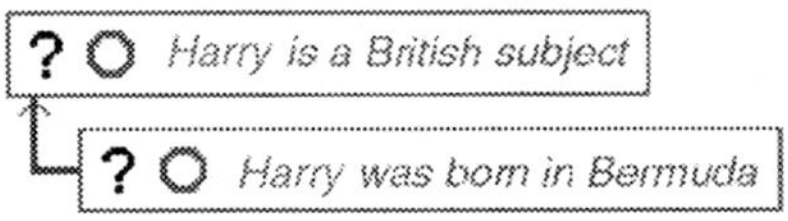

Figure 5. If the datum were an issue.

Now both elementary statements are unevaluated (as is indicated by the light italic font and the zero sign) since for neither is there a justifying reason. The dark colour of the arrow indicates that the corresponding conditional statement is a justified assumption.

By the present conventions an argument like 'Harry was born in Bermuda. So he is a British subject' is closely linked to the following formal derivation based on Modus ponens (From φ and $\varphi \sim> \psi$, conclude ψ):

$$\frac{\text{Harry was born in Bermuda. Harry was born in Bermuda} \sim> \text{Harry is a British subject.}}{\text{Harry is a British subject.}}$$

The two premises of the derivation correspond to the two assumptions of the datum-claim argument (one of them the associated conditional), the conclusion of the derivation to the issue. The Modus ponens form of the derivation makes explicit how the evaluation status is transferred from the assumptions to the issue: when the statements that φ and that $\varphi \sim> \psi$ are both justified, then the statement that ψ is also justified.

It is tempting to read the Modus ponens-derivation itself as the following informal argument:

> (*) Harry was born in Bermuda. If Harry was born in Bermuda, then he is a British subject. So he is a British subject.[6]

However, this informal argument is clearly *another* argument than the example 'Harry was born in Bermuda. So he is a British subject' (one relevant difference being that while the shorter example could occur in an ordinary argumentative text, the extended version (*) only occurs in logic-oriented texts). (See also Carroll's dialogue 'What the tortoise said to Achilles', reprinted in Hofstadter (1980), that shows how adding the 'If..., then ...'-assumption underlying an argument leads to an infinite regress.)

Until now, we have for convenience omitted the qualifier in Toulmin's example. In the example, the datum 'Harry was born in Bermuda' does not support the claim 'Harry is a British subject' in an unqualified manner, but only *presumably*. Concerning such *qualifiers* as Toulmin distinguishes in his scheme, we will here be very brief. A qualifier is simply thought of as some kind of modal operator on statements. As a result, Toulmin's qualifier will be considered as being a *part* of the sentence that expresses the claim supported by the data. In Toulmin's example, we will take it that the datum supports the claim 'Presumably, Harry was born in Bermuda'. As a result, the relevant conditional is 'If Harry was born in Bermuda, then presumably he is a British subject' instead of the one used above. No semantic assumptions about the qualifiers are assumed here, in style with Toulmin's loose treatment. For instance, he seems to use the qualifiers 'presumably' and 'generally' more or less interchangeably (even though the former suggests an epistemological and the latter an ontological point of view).

There is much more to say about qualifiers (for instance, Peter McBurney has suggested that a proper treatment of qualifiers will lead to a richer set of rebuttals than discussed in section 3), but this falls outside of the scope of this paper.

Warrant

The next step is to consider the *warrants* of arguments. Toulmin (1958) describes warrants as "general, hypothetical statements, which can act as bridges [between data and claim, BV], and authorise the sort of step to which our particular argument commits us" (p. 98). In other words, warrants are inference licenses that express that certain claims follow from certain data. The warrant of Toulmin's example on British subjecthood is the statement 'A man born in Bermuda will generally be a British subject'. Toulmin thinks of warrants as *general* inference licenses: not only if *Harry* was born in Bermuda, he is a British subject, but also if *John* was born in Bermuda, he

---

[6] Such a reading of logical derivations as informal arguments is the basis of many textbooks that connect logic with informal argument. Here logical derivations play a related, but more modest role, viz. as explications of the transfer of evaluation status from assumptions to issues.

is a British subject, etc.[7] It seems that for Toulmin the statement 'A man born in Bermuda will generally be a British subject' is equivalent to a scheme like the following, where *Person* stands for any person:

> If *Person* was born in Bermuda, then generally *Person* is a British subject.

Here '*Person* was born in Bermuda' and '*Person* is a British subject' can be taken as a *generic* datum and claim, respectively. The apparent equivalence for Toulmin between rule statements like 'A man born in Bermuda will generally be a British subject' and conditional schemes like the one above is for instance suggested by his emphasis on the bridge-like character of warrants (e.g. p. 98 as cited above, and p. 105, where he discusses the difference between warrants and backings). The discussion of the formal validity of arguments of the type 'D. W. So C' (p. 118f., especially p. 119), where D stands for the data, W for the warrant and C for the claim, strengthens this suggestion. The formal structure of such an argument could be made explicit in the following way:

> D(t). D(x) ~> C(x). So C(t).

Here x is a variable instantiated by t. (In general, there can be several variables.) Toulmin mentions a variant of this formal structure in the style of classical syllogisms:

> X is an A. All A's are B's. So X is a B.

Somewhat confusingly, Toulmin is not fully consistent in his discussion of warrants: occasionally, he seems to refer to an *instance* of a conditional scheme (like the one above) as a warrant, for instance when he mentions the short form 'If D, then C', where D and C are particular (and not a generic) data and claim (p. 98). However, as stated previously, at other places Toulmin unambiguously emphasizes the generality of warrants (e.g. in the description of warrants cited above, p. 98, but also on p. 100, where he states that warrants certify the soundness of all arguments of the appropriate type).

Summarizing, it is convenient to distinguish the following three:

(1) A man born in Bermuda will generally be a British subject.
(2) If *Person* was born in Bermuda, then generally *Person* is a British subject.
(3) If Harry was born in Bermuda, then generally he is a British subject.

The first is the ordinary language expression of a warrant. It is a rule statement that connects certain kinds of data to certain kinds of claims. It is these that in the present paper will be referred to as warrants (which is in agreement with Toulmin's conception of warrants and with most of Toulmin's examples).

---

[7] It has been argued that a given data-claim argument can have different warrants, dependent on the scope of the generalization (cf. Hitchcock, 1998).

The second is the conditional scheme that is the formal explication of the bridge-like connection resulting from warrants. In a sense (and, as stated previously, apparently according to Toulmin) an ordinary language warrant like (1) above is equivalent to a conditional scheme such as (2): it may be taken that each implies the other. Moreover, it seems straightforward to write algorithms that translate the one to the other (at least for significant subsets of ordinary language examples of warrants, e.g. for simple generic sentences like 'Bermudans are British subjects' and 'Thieves are punishable'). It should be noted however that in ordinary language argument, the conditional schemes will themselves never occur. They are merely convenient constructs in order to summarize the range of particular argument steps as they are licensed by the generic warrant that corresponds to the scheme.

The third, 'If Harry was born in Bermuda, then generally he is a British subject', is the associated conditional that expresses that a particular datum implies a particular claim. Conditionals such as (3) are the instances of the conditional schemes like (2) that correspond to ordinary language warrants (1).[8]

The only formal connection between the three that will be used below is that between the warrant (in the sense of an ordinary language rule statement) and the associated conditional that forms the bridge from datum to claim. It can be expressed as the nested conditional 'If W, then if D, then C', or formally as W ~> (D ~> C).[9] The nested conditional expresses that it follows from the warrant that the claim follows from the datum. This nested conditional is normally left implicit in an argument, just like the conditional 'If D, then C'.

The result is graphically represented in Figure 6.

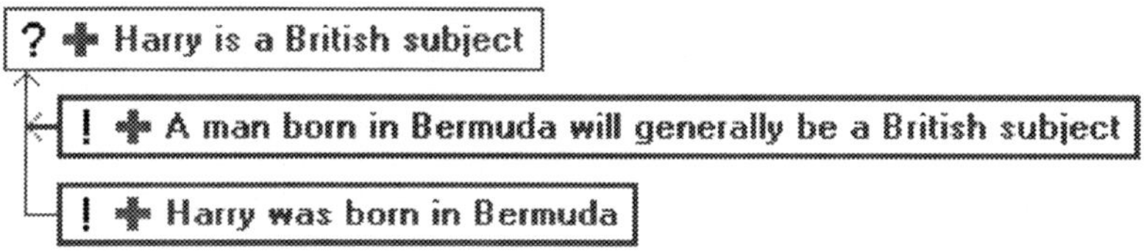

Figure 6. Datum, claim and warrant.

[8] It may be noted that our treatment has the effect that warrants, conditional schemes and their instances all use the same qualifier (unlike in Toulmin's example where the qualifier in the warrant is 'generally' and the qualifier of the claim is 'presumably'). The 'generally' in 'If Harry was born in Bermuda, then generally he is a British subject' refers to the class of (real or hypothetical) cases or situations in which Harry was born in Bermuda. Cf. also the remarks on qualifiers as modal operators in the preceding subsection on data and claim.

[9] We use these conditionals here since DefLog and ArguMed (as described by Verheij 2003a; 2003b; 2005) do not have variables and variable instantiation. If these would be added to DefLog, the present treatment using conditionals W ~> (D ~> C) could be replaced by stipulating equivalences between warrants W and conditional generalizations D(x) ~> C(x) and then deriving instances D(t) ~> C(t) of D(x) ~> C(x).

That the statement that a man born in Bermuda will generally be a British subject, is a warrant is visualized by an arrow pointing to an arrow: here the arrow from the warrant statement points to the arrow representing the associated conditional that if Harry was born in Bermuda, he is a British subject. The warrant justifies the connection between datum and claim.

The transfer of evaluation status from assumptions to issues can be made explicit as the two-step Modus ponens derivation shown in Figure 7.

$$\frac{D. \qquad \dfrac{W. \quad W \sim> (D \sim> C).}{D \sim> C.}}{C.}$$

Figure 7. A two-step Modus ponens derivation.

D, W and W ~> (D ~> C) are assumptions of the data-claim-warrant argument. In Figure 6, W ~> (D ~> C) is shown using a thicker line than D ~> C in order to show that the former is an assumption of the argument instead of an issue.

Backing

The next important element of arguments distinguished by Toulmin is that of the *backing* of warrants. Backings provide support for warrants. They become relevant when a warrant is challenged. This occurs when the legitimacy of the range of arguments as licensed by a warrant is challenged. In Toulmin's example, the warrant that a man born in Bermuda will generally be a British subject, is supported by appeal to particular statutes and legal provisions (which are not explicitly mentioned by Toulmin). Formally, the relation between backing and warrant is the same as the relation between datum and claim,[10] and requires nothing new. An argument 'B. So W' (where B is a backing of some warrant B) can be analyzed just like an argument 'D. So C'. In the former case, the associated conditional has the form 'If B, then W'. In the example, it becomes 'If the statutes and other legal provisions so-and-so obtain, then a man born in Bermuda will generally be a British subject'.

Even though datum and backing formally play a related role, Toulmin notes a relevant difference between them: there are arguments containing data but without explicit backing (as in 'D. So C'), while there are no arguments containing backing

[10] As a result, the warrant of an argument 'B. So W' (where B is a backing of a warrant W) can again be challenged and require further backing. When the warrant W* of the argument 'B. So W' is backed by B*, the warrant of the corresponding argument 'B*. So W*' can in turn be challenged, and so on, *ad infinitum*. As Toulmin remarks, *some* warrants must be left unchallenged (p. 106), just as some data for that matter. See e.g. Hage (2000) for a recent discussion of (amongst other topics) the resulting problem of justification (with an emphasis on the context of legal reasoning).

but lacking data. According to Toulmin, the occurrence of a backing *presupposes* the occurrence of data (and claim).[11] Toulmin also emphasizes the difference between backing and warrant: backings can be categorical statements of fact just like data, while warrants always are general bridge-like statements (cf. p. 105). A central point in Toulmin's book is that different kinds of backings occur in different fields of argument. Among Toulmin's examples of backings are statutes and acts of Parliament, statistical reports, appeals to the results of experiments and references to taxonomical systems. All can provide the backing that warrant the arguments as they are acceptable in particular fields.

The graphical representation of an argument involving a backing is shown in Figure 8.

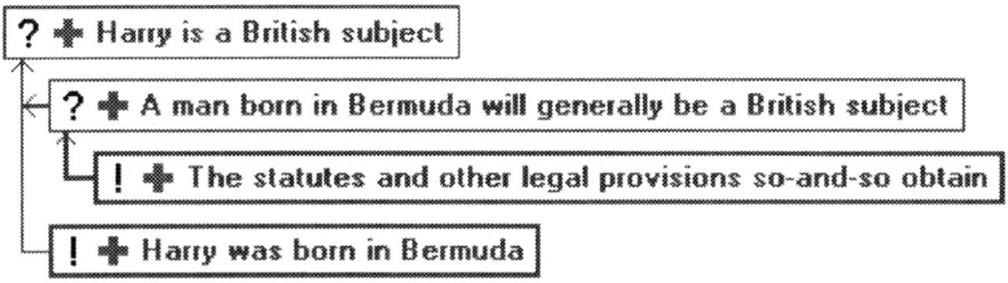

Figure 8. Adding the backing.

If the backing were itself an issue, we would get what is shown in Figure 9.

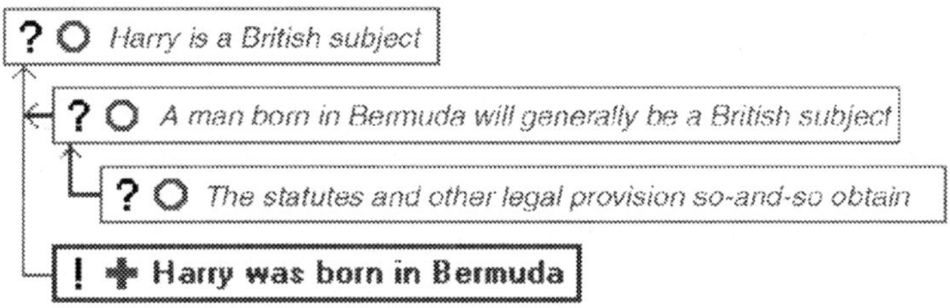

Figure 9. If the backing were an issue.

[11] Whether Toulmin is right here is arguable. For instance, in the law it is common to argue about the validity of legal rules, even outside the context of a concrete case to apply the rule to. This would correspond to an argument concerning the backing of a warrant (the legal rule), without having concrete data (the case facts) and claim (the legal consequence) in mind.

Neither the statement that Harry is a British subject nor the warrant statement that a man born in Bermuda will generally be a British subject, is now justified since there is no justifying reason for them. Note however that the arrows from backing to warrant and from warrant to the arrow from datum to claim are justified assumptions. The arrow from datum to claim is now an unevaluated issue (while it was a justified issue in Figure 8).

It should be noted that the reconstruction of Toulmin's analysis of arguments with data, (qualified) claim, warrant and backing as above is hardly a deviation from standard logical notions, though perhaps a different use of them. This is in contrast with Toulmin's claims. As has been noted by others, the distinction of data, claim, qualifier, warrant and backing can be dealt with in a way that is not too far from standard logic, while retaining the differences between them. In the present reconstruction, the technical tools used are essentially a Modus ponens-validating conditional and variables (plus the unelaborated suggestion to consider modal operators for the qualifiers). The main differences between Toulmin's treatment and standard logic arise from differences in emphasis with respect to philosophical and argumentation-theoretical starting points (such as the mentioned field-dependency of the backings of warrants and the distinction of different roles of statements in an argument).

3. REBUTTAL

A genuine and radical deviation from standard logic is required by Toulmin's notion of *rebuttals*. However, Toulmin hardly elaborates on the nature of rebuttals.

Kinds of Rebuttals

As Toulmin puts it, rebuttals involve conditions of exception for the argument (p. 101). Apparently, for Toulmin, rebuttals can have several functions. For instance, rebuttals can 'indicate circumstances in which the general authority of the warrant would have to be set aside' (p. 101), but can also be (and for Toulmin apparently equivalently) 'exceptional circumstances which might be capable of defeating or rebutting the warranted conclusion' (p. 101). On p. 102, he also speaks about the applicability of a warrant in connection with rebuttals. In other words, Toulmin speaks of the defeat (or rebutting) of the conclusion, of the applicability of the warrant and of the authority of the warrant, in a rather loose manner, without further distinction. Toulmin is unclear about the relation of these seemingly different situations. Here the three will be distinguished, in a way that naturally fits the reconstruction of the other elements of Toulmin's scheme above, as follows. If we look at the warrant-data-claim part of Toulmin's scheme (which in our reconstruction includes the qualifier), there are five statements that can be argued against:

The data D.
The claim C.
The warrant W.
The associated conditional 'If D, then C' that expresses the bridge from datum to claim.
The associated conditional 'If W, then if D, then C' that expresses the bridge between warrant and the previous associated conditional.[12]

Reasons against any of these statements can be seen as a *kind of rebuttal* of an argument that consists of warrant, data and claim (Figure 10).

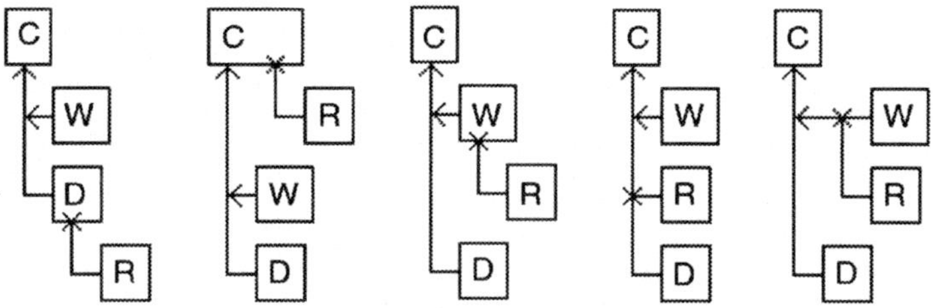

Figure 10. Five kinds of rebuttal.

The first three speak for themselves, and are clearly all different. An argument against the datum that Harry was born in Bermuda (for instance by claiming that Harry was born in London) differs from an argument against the claim that Harry is a British subject (for instance by claiming that Harry has become a naturalized American) and from an argument against the warrant that a man born in Bermuda will generally be a British subject (for instance by claiming that those born in Bermuda are normally French).

An argument against the fourth kind of statement (the first associated conditional), can be regarded as an attack on the connection between data and claim. Such attacks have been dubbed *undercutting defeaters* by Pollock (1987).[13] Harry having become a naturalized American could be an argument against the connection between Harry being born in Bermuda and Harry being a British subject.

An argument against the fifth kind of statement can be regarded as an attack against the warrant's applicability: normally the warrant can justify the conditional that connects data and claim, but since there is a rebuttal, the warrant does not apply. In other words, when the associated conditional if W, then if D, then C, is not justified, the warrant, which normally gives rise to a bridge between data of type D

[12] Including variables and variable instantiation as suggested in note 9 would affect this fifth statement.

[13] The second kind of rebuttal is related to what Pollock (1987) calls rebutting defeaters. We do not elaborate on these here because that would involve technical detail that is not relevant here. Cf. e.g. Hage, 1997; Prakken, 1997; Verheij, 1996 on priorities and weighing reasons.

and claim of type C, does *not* give rise to such a bridge for the actual data D and claim C at hand. For instance, Harry's parents both being aliens could well be an argument against the applicability of the warrant that a man born in Bermuda will generally be a British subject.[14]

The three situations to which Toulmin attaches the term rebuttal (defeat of the conclusion, of the applicability of the warrant and of the authority of the warrant) are among these five kinds of rebuttals, viz. the second, fifth and third, respectively. The other two kinds of rebuttals of a warrant-data-claim argument, viz. that of the first and fourth kind, are apparently not mentioned by Toulmin.

The Effect of Rebuttal on Argument Evaluation

We now turn to a major omission of Toulmin's discussion: a topic he does not address is the *effect* of rebuttal on the evaluation status of the statements in an argument. Interestingly, this has turned out to be a notorious, but rewarding topic for logical study (cf. the work on formalizing defeasible and dialectical argument; see e.g. Chesñevar *et al.*, 2000; Prakken and Vreeswijk, 2002).

In the present approach, a third evaluation status is introduced in order to analyze the effect of rebuttal on the evaluation status: statements can not only be justified or unevaluated, but also *defeated.*[15] The latter status applies when there is a defeating reason against the statement. A defeated statement is 'contra-justified'. For instance, in the example, it can be defeated that Harry is a British subject in light of the reason against it that he has become a naturalized American, even though Harry was born in Bermuda. (See Verheij, 2003a; 2003b; 2005b for a discussion of technical difficulties of the evaluation of arguments.)

One difficulty is the fundamental *nonmonotonicity* of the resulting logic: when assumptions are added it can occur that previously justified statements are no longer justified (cf. in a more general logical setting Gabbay *et al.*, 1994). In standard logic, when sentences are added to an initial set of sentences the truth of which is assumed, the set of implied truths never gets smaller. Additional assumptions normally allow more conclusions to be drawn, and never fewer. In contrast, in a context of reasoning with pros and cons, as for instance in Toulmin's analysis of argument, where there is not only support but also attack, statements that are initially justified with respect to a set of assumptions can become defeated (or unevaluated) in light of additional assumptions.

Toulmin's example can be used as an illustration: when it is not assumed or otherwise justified that Harry's parents were aliens or that he has become a

[14] Especially in the law, the applicability of rules (which play a role similar to Toulmin's warrants) is often at issue. Cf. Hage, 1997; Prakken, 1997; Verheij, 1996. In Hage's and Verheij's work, it is also discussed how the *weighing* of reasons for and against a conclusion can be formally treated.

[15] It depends on one's taste whether this approach is regarded as a three-valued interpretation of the whole of a logical language (in terms of the values j, d and u for justified, defeated and unevaluated) or as a two-valued interpretation of a part of the language (in terms of the values j and d, with possibly some sentences of the language left uninterpreted).

naturalized American, etc., i.e., when the possible rebuttals are not effective, it is justified that Harry is a British subject on the assumption that he was born in Bermuda and that a man born in Bermuda will generally be a British subject. However, when one of the rebuttals is effective, e.g., when it is assumed that Harry's parents were aliens, Harry being a British subject no longer follows as a justified statement, but is unevaluated (given that there are no *other* reasons for or against it).

Just as justifying reasons for a statement can make an issue justified, defeating reasons against a statement can make it defeated. Formally, it is convenient to distinguish statements of the form 'It is defeated that ...', where the dots indicate a sentence expressing another statement. In this way, *attack by reasons* can be dealt with by analogy with support by reasons (cf. section 2). Whereas the support relation between data D and claim C is expressed by the associated conditional 'If D, then C', the attack relation between a rebuttal R and a claim C is expressed by the statement 'If R, then it is defeated that C' (for a rebuttal of the second kind above). The latter will formally be denoted as R ~> xC (where xC expresses that it is defeated that C and ~> is the conditional used to express support)[16] or more briefly as R ~x C. In general, a statement R is said to be a *defeating reason* against another statement C if the statement that R, and the statement that if R, then it is defeated that C, are both justified (cf. the notion of a justifying reason in section 2).

It can now be defined which statements are supported by a set of assumptions (using the simple logical language with connectives ~> and x as used above) and which attacked. A statement S is *supported* by the assumptions if the statement S is itself an assumption or follows from the assumptions by the repeated application of Modus ponens (From φ and φ ~> ψ, conclude ψ). A statement S is *attacked* by assumptions if the statement that the statement is defeated (i.e. the statement that xS) is one of the assumptions or follows from the assumptions by the repeated application of Modus ponens. When a set of assumptions is *conflict free*, i.e., when there are no statements that are both supported and attacked by the assumptions, it is now easy to define the *evaluation status* of statements with respect to the assumptions, as follows. A statement is *justified* (with respect to the conflict-free set of assumptions) when it is supported by the assumptions. A statement is *defeated* (with respect to the conflict-free set of assumptions) when it is attacked by the assumptions. Any other statement is *unevaluated* (with respect to the conflict-free set of assumptions).

Evaluation in the more important general case of possibly conflicting sets of assumptions is subtle (and those who are not formally inclined may want to pass over this). The definition for conflict-free sets does not work since when there is a conflict there are statements that are both supported and attacked by the assumptions. Therefore in the general case, the assumptions are considered to be *defeasible* in the sense that not all statements assumed to be justified need also turn

---

[16] The sentence 'It is defeated that C' expresses the *dialectical negation* of the statement that C. Dialectical negation expresses the denial that a prima facie justified assumption is justified. See Verheij, 2003a; 2003b; 2005. An omission that I hope to fill in future work is that I did not yet provide a good explanation of the relation between ordinary negation and dialectical negation.

out to be evaluated as justified when the whole set of assumptions is evaluated. The idea is that some of the assumptions are themselves defeated since they are attacked by other assumptions. As a result, a set of prima facie justified assumptions Δ is divided into two parts: the justified part and the defeated part. In words, the justified part is a maximal conflict-free subset of Δ that attacks all elements of the defeated part. Such a justified part is said to *dialectically interpret* Δ.

The formal definition is as follows:

> Let Δ be a set of sentences defeasibly assumed to be justified, and let J be a subset of Δ (possibly equal to Δ). Then J *dialectically interprets* Δ when the following hold:
>
> 1. J is conflict free.
> 2. Any statement in Δ that is not in J is attacked by J.
>
> A *dialectical interpretation* of Δ is a pair of sets (Supp(J), Att(J)), where J dialectically interprets Δ, Supp(J) consists of the statements supported by J, and Att(J) consists of the statements attacked by J. The statements supported by J are said to be *justified* in the dialectical interpretation of Δ corresponding to J, while those attacked by J are said to be *defeated.*

There is a close formal connection between this definition of dialectical interpretation and Dung's argumentation frameworks (1995). Other related work has for instance been done by Pollock, 1987; Reiter, 1987; Loui, 1998; Vreeswijk, 1997; Prakken, 1997; Hage, 1997.

There is a lot to say about this definition of dialectical interpretation. For instance, while some theories have a unique dialectical interpretation, others have none or several. For further information, the reader is referred to Verheij (2003a; 2003b, 2005b) and the software that can be downloaded at http://www.ai.rug.-nl/~verheij/aaa/. Here we will confine ourselves to examples related to Toulmin's scheme.

Toulmin's Example

Let's again consider Toulmin's example concerning Harry. Assume as datum that Harry was born in Bermuda (D) and as rebuttal that Harry has become a naturalized American (R). It is an issue that Harry is a British subject (the claim C). For simplicity we first forget about warrant and backing. The relation between datum and claim is implicitly assumed, and can formally be expressed as D ~> C. The relation of the rebuttal with datum and claim is assumed to be of the *fourth* kind above, i.e. as an attack against the associated conditional that If D, then C. Therefore the relation is expressible as R ~> x (D ~> C). Formally, the set of assumptions Δ consists of four sentences, viz. D, R, D ~> C and R ~> x (D ~> C). The set contains a conflict: D ~> C is both supported (since it is an assumption) and attacked (by applying Modus ponens on R and R ~> x(D ~> C)). The set of assumptions has a dialectical interpretation however: in it, the assumption D ~> C is defeated, while the other three are justified. The claim C is unevaluated since it is neither justified nor defeated in the dialectical interpretation. This is in accordance with the intuition that there is neither a justifying reason for C, nor a defeating reason against it. It can be checked that this is the *only* dialectical interpretation.[17]

Graphically, we get Figure 11 for the case that the rebuttal is assumed.

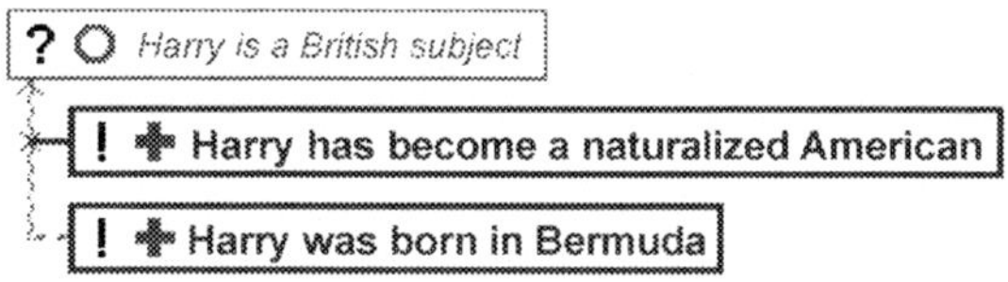

Figure 11. A rebuttal.

The arrow ending in a cross indicates that the rebuttal attacks the associated conditional that if Harry was born in Bermuda, he is a British subject. It is now not justified that Harry is a British subject since it is an issue for which there is no justifying reason. (Nor is it defeated.) The associated conditional is defeated (indicated by the dotted line) since there is a defeating reason against it, viz. the rebuttal.

If it were an issue that Harry has become a naturalized American, Figure 12 would be the result.

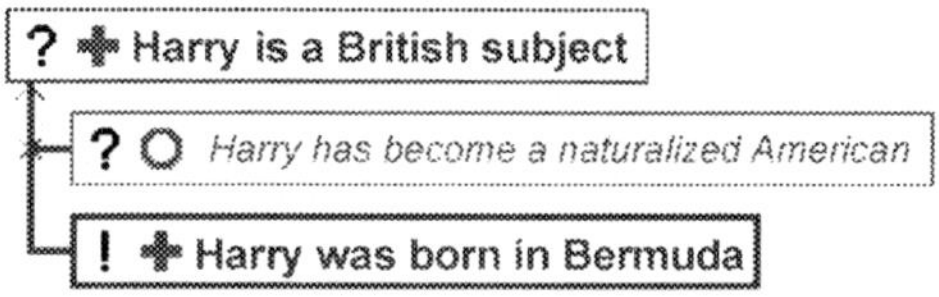

Figure 12. If the rebuttal were an issue.

Now it is justified that Harry is a British subject, since the rebuttal does not have effect and the associated conditional is not defeated, but justified. The graphical representation clearly demonstrates that rebuttals can have a decisive

[17] In this case, a straightforward, but tedious approach would be to check *all* 16 subsets of the set of four assumptions. When Δ gets larger, this quickly becomes impossible in practice. A shorter argument for the present example goes as follows. Let Δ consist of the four assumptions D, R, D ~> C and R ~> x (D ~> C). Δ attacks only one sentence, namely D ~> C since only the dialectical negation x (D ~> C) of that sentence follows by *Modus ponens* from Δ. Hence only D ~> C is a candidate for being defeated in a dialectical interpretation of Δ. As a result, there are only two subsets that might dialectically interpret Δ, namely Δ itself or Δ minus D ~> C. Δ itself cannot be a dialectically interpreting set since it is not conflict free. Δ minus D ~> C is a dialectically interpreting set since it is conflict free and attacks D ~> C.

effect on the evaluation of arguments and the statements in them: when the rebuttal is an issue, the claim is (prima facie) justified, but when the rebuttal is assumed, the claim is not justified.

Recall that Toulmin did not distinguish between kinds of rebuttals. In the previous paragraphs, the rebuttal R that Harry has become a naturalized American was considered to be a rebuttal of the fourth kind. Let's now analyze the example considering R as a rebuttal of the *fifth* kind, i.e. it attacks the applicability of the warrant in Harry's case. Formally, this is denoted thus: R ~> x (W ~> (D ~>C)). In other words, if the rebuttal R is justified, then it is defeated that the conditional that if D then C, follows from the warrant W. As a result, in case of R, W does not imply that D can support C. The following are assumed:

D:	Harry was born in Bermuda
W:	A man born in Bermuda will generally be a British subject
R:	Harry has become a naturalized American
B:	The statutes and other legal provisions so-and-so obtain

It is an issue that Harry is a British subject (C). The assumed logical connections (that are normally left implicit) are as follows:

B ~> W
W ~> (D ~> C)
R ~> x (W ~> (D ~>C))

The set of assumptions contains a conflict: the nested conditional W ~> (D ~> C) that expresses that W implies that D can support C, is both supported (as an assumption) and attacked (since its defeat follows from R and R ~> x (W ~> (D ~>C))). In the unique dialectical interpretation, only W ~> (D ~> C) is defeated (by the defeating reason R against it), while the other six assumptions are justified. As a result, the statements that D ~> C and that C are unevaluated since there is no justifying reason for them.

Assuming that the rebuttal is of the fifth kind, we get the graphical representation shown in Figure 13.

The arrow ending in a cross indicates that the rebuttal that Harry has become a naturalized American attacks that the conditional that if Harry was born in Bermuda, he is a British subject, follows from the warrant statement. It is now neither justified nor defeated that Harry is a British subject since there is neither a justifying reason for it nor a defeating reason against it.

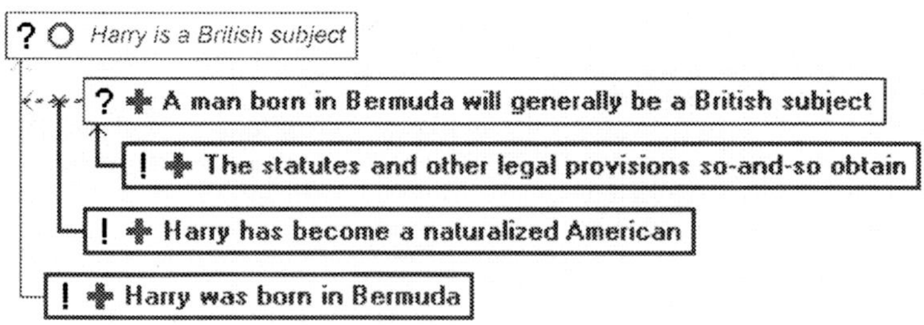

Figure 13. Rebuttal of the fifth kind.

If the rebuttal were itself an issue, the evaluation would be different, and it would be justified that Harry is a British subject (Figure 14).

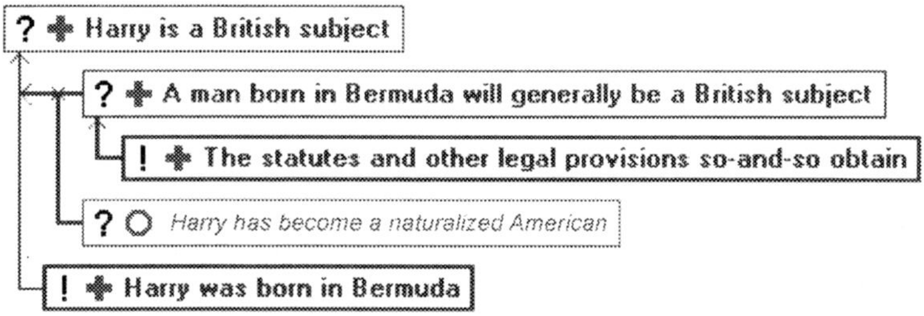

Figure 14. If the rebuttal were an issue.

The Reinstatement of a Claim

An important phenomenon related to the evaluation of arguments as discussed above is the *reinstatement* of a claim. This occurs when a claim is at first justified, for instance in the light of an argument without rebuttal, subsequently unjustified, for instance when a rebuttal is added, and finally again justified, when the rebuttal is in turn shown to be unjustified. The latter might occur when the rebuttal is itself the claim of a scheme that is extended by a rebuttal.

Toulmin does not discuss this phenomenon of reinstatement (simply because he does not discuss the evaluation of arguments at all). An example based on Dutch tort law is the following. It may be claimed that someone has committed an unlawful act on the basis of the datum that he has violated a property right. An example of the violation of a property right is the breaking of someone else's window. In Dutch tort law, a warrant could be that violations of property rights are unlawful, which can be backed by article 6:162 of the Civil Code. If the argument is limited to the present information, the claim can be thought of as justified (on the basis of the argument). It can subsequently be argued that there is a rebuttal: there is a ground of justification for the act since the person obeyed an official's command. (Note that the rebuttal is here the claim of a second scheme with the obeying of the official's command as datum.) At this stage, the claim that an unlawful act has been committed is no longer justified on the basis of the argument involved. The argument can further be extended by adding a rebuttal to the second scheme: the official giving the command was unauthorized to do so. As a result the claim of the second scheme (viz. the existence of a ground of justification) is no longer justified. Since it is at the same time the rebuttal of the first scheme, it loses its rebutting effect in that scheme, and the claim that an unlawful act has been committed is again justified.

Verheij (2003a; 2003b) gives more examples of the evaluation of arguments and the reinstatement of statements. A full theory of dialectical arguments is presented in which statements (including conditional statements corresponding to support and attack) can be supported or attacked by any number of other statements and in which support and attack can be chained (thus for instance allowing the attack of an attacking statement).

4. CONCLUSION

In the present paper, Toulmin's scheme for the layout of arguments has been formally reconstructed. An important omission of Toulmin's treatment has been repaired by providing an account of the evaluation of Toulmin-styled arguments. It has been discussed how the evaluation status of the statements in an argument is determined by a dialectical interpretation of the assumptions of the argument. In such an interpretation, assumptions are taken to be defeasible, so that they need not all be evaluated as justified in an interpretation: some can be defeated, viz. when they are attacked by a defeating reason against them. In order to achieve this, Toulmin's scheme for the layout of arguments has been interpreted in terms of a theory of dialectical arguments (Verheij, 2003a; 2003b).

It can be concluded from the present work that the main deviation from standard logic of Toulmin's scheme is the element of rebuttal. Since Toulmin, the logic of rebuttal has deservedly received widespread attention (under the name of defeasible argumentation). The present paper is a continuation of that line of research.

Another important point of Toulmin's work is the field-dependency of the backings of the warrants underlying arguments. Toulmin has stressed that the rules of argument can vary from domain to domain. This raises a fundamental and a practical question. The fundamental question is what remains of logic when the rules of argument are variable. The practical question is to determine the rules of argument in particular domains. Both questions still require substantial research. Beginnings of answers to these important questions can be found in the works of Girle *et al.*, 2003; Hage, 1997; McBurney and Parsons, 2000; Verheij, 1999; 2003c; Walton, 1996b.

Acknowledgements

I thank Peter McBurney and David Hitchcock for their attentive, clever and scholarly comments.

CHAPTER 13

DAVID HITCHCOCK

GOOD REASONING ON THE TOULMIN MODEL

Department of Philosophy, McMaster University, Hamilton, Canada L8S 4K1
E-mail: hitchckd@mcmaster.ca

ABSTRACT: Some solo verbal reasoning serves the function of arriving at a correct answer to a question from information at the reasoner's disposal. Such reasoning is good if and only if its grounds are justified and adequate, its warrant is justified, and the reasoner is justified in assuming that no defeaters apply. I distinguish seven sources of justified grounds and state the conditions under which each source is trustworthy. Adequate grounds include all good relevant information practically obtainable by the reasoner. The claim must follow from the grounds in accordance with a justified general warrant. If this warrant is not universal, the reasoner must be justified in assuming that no exception-making circumstances hold in the particular case to which it is applied.

KEYWORDS: Adequacy; good reasoning; justified conclusion; justified premiss; reasoning; Stephen E. Toulmin

1. INTRODUCTION

Stephen Toulmin (1958/2003) advanced his model for the layout of arguments without providing criteria for evaluating arguments so laid out. Some criteria are given in his co-authored textbook based on this model (Toulmin, Rieke and Janik, 1979/1984). On page 238 of the 1984 edition, for example, the authors prescribe eight "essential merits" of arguments: clarity on the kind of issues the argument is intended to raise, clarity on the underlying purpose of the argument, grounds relevant to the claim, grounds sufficient to support the claim, warrant applicable to the case under discussion, warrant based on solid backing, modality or strength of the resulting claim made explicit, possible rebuttals or exceptions well understood. But these conditions are underdeveloped. The textbook focuses rather on the structure of arguments and on the forms their components take in different fields.

Toulmin's model applies not only to arguments, whose authors address verbalized reasoning to someone else, but also to solo verbal reasoning, in which reasoners draw conclusions for themselves from information at their disposal. I shall propose guidelines for such reasoning, from the perspective of someone about to engage in it rather than of someone critically evaluating it after the fact. Solo verbal reasoning as I understand it must have some verbal components (merely thought, spoken aloud, written, signed, etc.) but can have non-verbal components. For

D. Hitchcock and B. Verheij (eds.), Arguing on the Toulmin Model: New Essays in Argument Analysis and Evaluation, 203–218.

example, its grounds can include non-verbal perceptual stimuli or non-verbal symbolic artefacts such as figures and drawings. In what follows, I shall use the unqualified term "reasoning" as a convenient abbreviation for "solo verbal reasoning" as just defined. I shall assume that the Toulmin model and its components (claim, grounds, warrant, qualifier, rebuttal, backing) are known, and shall propose criteria for good reasoning in terms of the components of this model. I shall use "conclusion" as a synonym of "claim" and "premisses" as a synonym of "data" or "grounds"; the latter usage reflects my position, argued elsewhere (Hitchcock, 2003a), that the warrant of an inference is not a premiss but an inference-license. Although I shall not discuss solo non-verbal reasoning, I make no assumption about whether the Toulmin model applies to such non-verbal reasoning.

Goodness of a kind is relative to function. A good eye is one that has characteristics that are sufficient for seeing well. A good bread knife is one that has characteristics that are sufficient for cutting bread well. Similarly, good reasoning is reasoning that has characteristics that are sufficient for accomplishing well the function of the reasoning. Reasoning in fact has many functions, for each of which there will be a correlative account of its goodness. I shall focus on one common function of reasoning: to arrive at a correct answer to a question whose answer is not immediately obvious to the reasoner but may be inferred from information at the reasoner's disposal. The question may be purely theoretical: Why did the aeroplane hijackers who attacked the World Trade Centre choose September 11 as the date of their attack? Or it may be practical, or practically oriented: What possible difficulties do I need to be aware of before starting to install a central vacuum system in my house? How long will it take to get to a place I plan to go to tomorrow? What is the best way of handling my two-year-old's temper tantrums? Sometimes the answers to such questions are obvious, but when they are not, and we have or can get information from which to work out an answer, reasoning is appropriate. Naturally we want to arrive through this reasoning at a correct answer.

There is of course no litmus test or gold standard for correctness of conclusions. We cannot write the conclusion on a piece of paper, dip it in a liquid, and determine from the colour of the paper whether the conclusion is correct or incorrect. We are not infallible visionaries, but human beings, working with incomplete information of less than perfect quality. Instead of correctness or truth, we must make do with the next best alternative: justification by the best practically obtainable evidence. This is why many warrants hold in most or some cases rather than in all cases, why we qualify our conclusions with such words as "probably" or "possibly", and why we acknowledge potential rebuttals.

Our immediate goal, then, is to reach the answer that the best relevant practically obtainable evidence justifies us in accepting. I propose four individually necessary and jointly sufficient conditions for reasoning that reaches this goal. First, we must be justified in accepting the ultimate grounds on which we base our reasoning. Second, our grounds must include all the relevant justified practically obtainable information. Third, the conclusion must follow in virtue of a justified warrant. Fourth, if the warrant is not universal, we must be justified in assuming that in the particular case there are no defeaters that rule out application of the warrant. I propose these conditions for reasoners to apply to their own reasoning, thus abstracting from consideration of the audience and dialogical context when reasoning is verbalized to others. Let us now consider each of these conditions in detail.

2. JUSTIFIED GROUNDS

It is perhaps self-evident that good reasoning with a function of arriving at a previously unknown correct answer to a governing question must start from grounds that we are justified in accepting. Correct conclusions can follow from incorrect premisses, but it is an accident if they turn out to be correct. To have some assurance of reaching our goal, we need justification for our starting-points.

There are many sources of justified premisses. The most trustworthy ones appear to be direct observation, written records of direct observation, memory of what one has previously observed or experienced, personal testimony, previous good reasoning or argument, expert opinion, and appeal to an authoritative reference source. None of these sources is infallible. Further, the list is open to emendation; in particular, it makes no special allowance for evaluative or normative ultimate premisses.

Direct Observation

In general, the most basic source of justified premisses is direct observation. Seeing the thick black clouds getting ever larger in the western sky is good justification for believing that thick black clouds are forming in the western sky. Hearing the screaming of one's two-year-old rapidly diminish in loudness after he is put into his room alone is good justification for believing that the temper tantrum faded away after he was put in his room alone. The smell of smoke is good justification for believing that there is smoke in the air one is breathing in. Observation includes not only such witnessing by the human senses but also the reception of information by some sensory apparatus like a telescope; Norris (1979) identifies observation with determining by the use of human or other sensory apparatus on some specific occasion what is happening or what state something is in, Shapere (1982) with reception by an appropriate receptor of information transmitted without interference from the observed entity. Observation so defined depends logically on a theory of the source of the information, a theory of its transmission and a theory of its receptor; if an observation is to be credible, such well-established theories must apply and the observer must at least know of their existence and applicability (Kosso 2001). But such background theories are not a part of the observer's reasoning. Rather, the observation is the starting-point, and it is used as the basis for further inferences, which in general will be less reliable than the observation (Norris, 1979). As physical knowledge increases, and new sensory receptors are invented and improved, the range of what can be observed expands; an extreme example of such expansion is the observation of the centre of the sun by the detection of neutrinos a mile beneath the earth's surface, discussed in a well-known paper by Shapere (1982).

Thus observation is not a passive reception of ready-made facts. Rather, it involves description and justification, description in expressing informational content in an observation report (possibly to oneself) and justification in that it must be possible to show that the report is about something (the source of the information, the observed object) and that it is accurate (Kosso, 1992, p. 113).

When is an observation justified? Norris (1984) has proposed criteria for observing well, for reporting observations well and for appraising observation reports; the latter criteria incorporate those proposed by Ennis (1962, p. 90) and by Norris (1979, pp. 18-20) and by Norris and King (1984, p. 7). Such lists are derived from common-sense experience, from the practice of scientific observation, from the results of psychological experiments, and from treatment of eye-witness testimony in law courts; and are subject to correction from these sources. Synthesizing the work of Ennis and Norris with reports by Loftus (1979) and by Loftus & Doyle (1992) of the results of psychological studies, we can say that, in general, an observation is justified to the extent that the following conditions are met:

1. *Well-established background theories* of the source of the information, its transmission and the receptor show that the receptor in such an observational situation accurately receives information from the source under normal conditions.
2. *The sense or sensory apparatus being used* (e.g. sight, hearing, photographic plates, radar equipment, neutrino detectors) *is in good condition and functioning properly*. In particular, a human observer should be functioning at a moderate level of emotional arousal, neither so torpid as to be only dimly aware of the surroundings nor so highly stressed as to be incapable of observation of the complexity required (Loftus, 1979, pp. 33-36; Loftus and Doyle, 1992, pp. 29-33).
3. *The conditions for observation are adequate*. If the observer is using a human sense, the event must be within the observer's perceptual range: bright enough, loud enough, close enough to be picked up by the ordinary senses (Loftus, 1979, p. 22). Also, the medium of observation should not systematically distort the observed characteristic. Also, the more time there is to make the observation and the more opportunities there are to make the observation, the more likely is it that the observation is accurate (Loftus, 1979, pp. 23-25).
4. *The information being received is of a sort that is generally accurately detected by the receptor*. This condition can be made more specific for human sense perception, as follows. The observed state of affairs should be salient, in the sense that it would be mentioned without prompting if the observer were to report immediately on what had just been observed (Loftus,

1979, pp. 25-27). Humans should be generally accurate at observing the type of fact being observed; for example, the duration of an event is *not* usually accurately observed, but is typically overestimated, particularly when an observer is feeling stress or anxiety (Loftus, 1979, pp. 27-31). If the observation concerns details of an event, the event should not be emotionally loaded (Loftus, 1979, pp. 31-32; Loftus and Doyle, 1992, pp. 24-29).

5. *The observer takes care to notice accurately.* Observation tends to be more accurate if the observer actively uses one or more senses to take in details of what is observed, rather than just attending to one aspect of the situation (Loftus, 1979, pp. 48-49).
6. *The observer, if human, is primed to observe accurately.* The observer should not be biased by previous expectations (cultural, personal, experiential or temporary) of what is going to be observed (Loftus, 1979, pp. 36-48; Loftus and Doyle, 1992, pp. 36-40). Observation tends to be more accurate if the observer has information before the observation that indicates the importance of correct observation in the situation (Loftus, 1979, pp. 49-51).
7. *The observer has whatever expert knowledge is required to use any instruments involved* (e.g. a telescope) *and to interpret what is observed.*
8. *No other justified information contradicts the observation.*

An observation that meets the just-mentioned criteria may nevertheless turn out to be incorrect. Things formerly taken to be observed accurately can later be discounted as due to defects in sensory equipment or to mistakes in some theory used to interpret the equipment's output. Here, as elsewhere, justification is not truth.

Written Records of Direct Observation

A second source is written records of direct observation. Such records are important in many professional contexts where the content of observations must be available and accurate long after the observation is made, such as scientific research, police investigation and medical examination. Written records make it possible to restore previous observations without depending on the vagaries of memory, which is notoriously plastic and unreliable (Schacter, 1995). Norris (1984, p. 136) proposes the following criteria for good records of observations:

1. The observation should be reported no more precisely than can be justified by the observational technique that was used.
2. The record should be made close to the time of observing.
3. The record should be made by the observer.
4. The record should be made in the same environment in which the observation was made.

Memory

A third source is memory of what one has previously observed or experienced. Human memory is basically accurate; we would not cope as well as we do if we did not remember accurately how to get from A to B, where we left something we now want, and so forth. But it is subject to decay and error. As the work of Elizabeth Loftus (1979) among others has shown, distortions and failures can occur not only at the initial acquisition stage (the observation) and at the later retrieval stage, but also during the intervening retention stage—human memory is plastic. In *The Seven Sins of Memory*, Daniel Schacter (2001) classifies the causes of inadequate human memory. Three of his seven "sins" are sins of omission, causing failure to retrieve the desired information: absent-mindedness (lack of attention resulting in failure to store the information in the first place), transience (the fading of memory over time), and blockage (inability to retrieve something that is still stored in our memory). Another three "sins" are sins of commission in which we retrieve distorted information: misattribution (assigning what is remembered to the wrong source, even to reality rather than fantasy), suggestibility (implantation by leading questions, suggestions or comments at the time of retrieval), bias (editing of our remembered past in the light of current beliefs). The seventh "sin" is a source neither of failure nor of distortion, but of unwanted intrusion: persistence involves repeated recall of disturbing information that we would prefer not to think about. Schacter argues somewhat speculatively (2001, pp. 184-206) that these seven inadequacies are by-products of otherwise adaptive features of human memory.

Schacter's sins of commission warn us to attend to factors that reduce the accuracy of human memories. In particular, episodic memories decline in accuracy with the passage of time (Loftus, 1979, pp. 53-54; Schacter, 1995, pp. 25-26). Subsequent information or misinformation, especially when delayed or about peripheral details, can distort one's memory, even to the extent of adding non-existent objects to one's memory of an episode or changing the type, colour or subjective impression of observed objects (Loftus, 1979, pp. 54-78; Loftus and Doyle, 1992, pp. 61-66). One's own thought processes–one's biases, one's labelling, one's guessing what one observed, one's verbalizing of a recollection–can affect how one stores in memory an observed episode (Loftus, 1979, pp. 78-87). Memories are in general less accurate about peripheral or unimportant details than about emotionally salient and central facts (Schachter, 1995, p. 16). False episodic memories can be produced in neurologically unimpaired adults by association with actual stimuli, by inferences from misinformation about the stimuli, by leading questions, by post-event misinformation, by previous forced guessing, by hypnosis, by emotional arousal at the time of observation (with respect to peripheral details), or by an incongruent mood (Schacter, 1995). The presentation of false post-event information commonly distorts memories in four circumstances: much time has elapsed, the false information is embedded in a subsidiary part of an information-seeking question, the observed event was violent (thus disrupting the initial storage of information in memory), and there is no warning immediately before receiving a post-event message that the message may contain misinformation (Loftus and Doyle, 1992, pp. 68-70). The information one retrieves from memory can be affected by whether the retrieval environment is the same environment in which the original observation was made; if the information is retrieved in response to questions, it can be affected by what types of questions are asked, how they are worded and who is asking them (Loftus, 1979, pp. 88-99). One's confidence in the accuracy of one's memory is not necessarily a good guide to how accurate it is (Loftus, 1979, pp. 100-104; Loftus and Doyle, 1992, pp. 75-77). Thus reasoners need to be careful about relying on memory alone. Loftus and Doyle cite experimental evidence, however (1992, pp. 81-83), that one can improve one's memory of an episode by taking oneself through the four stages of a so-called "cognitive interview": reinstate mentally the context of the episode, report everything, recall events in different orders, recall the episode from different perspectives.

Personal Testimony

A fourth source is personal testimony of what has been directly observed or experienced. Such testimony is no better than the observation or experience on which it is based. It must be scrutinized in terms of the criteria mentioned earlier for observation, written records, and memory. For example, testimony based on distant memories is suspect if unsupported by written records made at or near the time of the observation. Even apparently honest reports of current experiences must be evaluated for accuracy, since they can be unclear or involve questionable interpretation. Criteria for evaluating observation reports can be found in Ennis (1962, p. 90), Norris (1979, pp. 18-20; 1984, p. 137), and Norris and King (1984, p. 7).

It is particularly important in evaluating testimony to be on guard against second-hand, third-hand, or more distant testimony. As the game of "telephone" dramatically shows, the quality of messages passed from one person to another tends to deteriorate with each transmission. An additional complication in evaluating testimony is the possibility that its author may distort the truth through a careless or intentionally deceptive formulation. Self-deception, faulty interpretation, and sloppy verbalization are more common than intentional deception.

Previous Reasoning or Argument

A fifth source is previous good reasoning or argument. The reasoner may already have reached a relevant conclusion by previous reasoning, for example that the date of September 11 is likely to have had some significance for the cause promoted by the attacks on the World Trade Center. Alternatively, the reasoner may have been convinced by someone else's argument to accept a relevant conclusion of that argument. If the relevant conclusion was justified by the earlier reasoning or argument, it becomes a justified premiss of the new reasoning.

Expert Opinion

A sixth source is expert opinion, such as the opinion of a qualified electrician on the adequacy of a circuit for a particular appliance. In some cases, it is possible and desirable to scrutinize the reasoning by which the expert arrived at the opinion in question. In other cases, however, it is either impossible or undesirable to undertake such scrutiny, and the acceptability of the expert's opinion must be judged indirectly.

Ennis (1962, pp. 196-197) proposed criteria for evaluating expert opinion. Modifying his list in the light of reflection on the ways in which experts' opinions might be mistaken, we can say that, in general, expert opinion justifies a claim to the extent that the opinion meets the following seven conditions:

1. The opinion in question must belong to some subject matter in which there is expertise. An opinion can belong to an area of expertise even if the expertise is not based on formal education; there are experts on baseball and on stamps, for example.
2. The author of the opinion must have the relevant expertise. It is important to be on guard against "expert fixation", accepting someone's opinion because that person is an expert, when the expertise is irrelevant to the opinion expressed.
3. The author must use the expertise in arriving at the opinion. The relevant data must have been collected, interpreted, and processed using professional knowledge and skills.
4. The author must exercise care in applying the expertise and in formulating the expert opinion.
5. The author ideally should not have a conflict of interest that could influence, consciously or unconsciously, the formulated opinion. For example, the acceptance of gifts from the sales representative of a pharmaceutical company can make a physician's prescription of that company's drug more suspect.
6. The opinion should not conflict with the opinion of other qualified experts. If experts disagree, further probing is required.
7. The opinion should not conflict with other justified information. If an expert opinion does not fit with what the reasoner otherwise knows, one should scrutinize its credentials carefully and perhaps get a second opinion.

Sometimes we do not know directly whether these seven conditions are met, and we must judge by inference. The track record of an expert in the relevant field of expertise is good evidence, positive or negative, about the trustworthiness of that expert's new opinion. Awareness by the expert that others will subject the opinion to scrutiny counts in favour of its trustworthiness.

Authoritative Reference Source

A seventh source is an authoritative reference source, such as an encyclopedia or the *Handbook of Chemistry and Physics*. Authoritative reference sources differ from expert opinions in that they contain generic information, whereas expert opinions apply expertise to a particular situation. Ideally, authoritative references embody the best available evidence at the time they are composed.

General Remarks

No matter how one's premisses are justified, it should be kept in mind that being justified is not the same as being correct. A premiss justified by direct observation, or by a written record of a direct observation, or by an authoritative reference source, may later turn out to be false. The friend one "sees" across the road may turn out on closer inspection to be someone else who looks like one's friend. The secretary taking notes at a meeting may have misheard or misinterpreted what was said. An entry in a reputable encyclopaedia, general or specialized, can be superseded by subsequent research or world events. The moral is: One should always be prepared to revise one's opinion in light of compelling new evidence to the contrary.

3. ADEQUATE INFORMATION

If one is trying to answer a question correctly on the basis of obtainable information, one needs to take into account all the good relevant information that is practically obtainable. Relevant information is information that could make a difference to the answer one reaches. That is, a justified warrant links it, in combination with other already obtained or obtainable information, to an answer to the question that could be different than the one justified by the information already obtained. In many contexts–such as medical diagnosis, police investigation, military and other intelligence work, scientific research, interpretation of such symbolic artefacts as written texts or works of art or musical compositions, adjudication, consumer choice—different pieces of information often point to a different answer to a given question. Hence, if in such a context one considers only information that supports one answer, and ignores information that points to a different answer, one is more likely to reach an incorrect conclusion than if one considers everything. A common human failing is to close prematurely on a particular answer, then seek supporting evidence for this answer, while failing to seek (or even ignoring) evidence that points in a different direction. Indeed, high school English teachers often teach their students to write essays this way: Adopt a thesis, then assemble evidence to support it. This is a fallacy of empirical investigation known to psychologists as "confirmation bias" (Klayman, 1995). Both experimental-critical and historical-textual empirical investigators of human reasoning have concluded that the most common flaw of informal reasoning is the failure to consider lines of argument supporting conclusions contrary to the one reached (Finocchiaro, 1994). The mass media occasionally report examples of such failures in detective and intelligence work: convictions for murder are sometimes reversed on the basis of DNA evidence, and intelligence estimates of a foreign country's military preparations sometimes prove wildly inaccurate. Confirmation bias occurs in a subtle way in the publication in scientific journals of experimental results that are tested for their statistical significance. Since the best journals are distinguished by the strictness of their criterion, accepting only results that are significant at the .01 level (as opposed to the .05 level or .10 elsewhere), the published evidence relevant to a given empirical question can be a biased sample of the evidence actually obtained by researchers.

In working out the correct answer to a question, one needs to consider only information that is good, relevant to the question, and practically obtainable. In other words, one can ignore information that is either bad or irrelevant or not practically obtainable.

Information used to arrive at an answer to one's question must be good information, in terms of the conditions previously mentioned for justified premisses. There is no point in taking bad information into account, still less in devoting time and effort to acquiring it.

Information used to arrive at an answer to one's question must be relevant, in the sense that taking it into account might make a difference to one's answer. Relevance is thus a function of context. Suppose the question is whether all swans are white. We have a justified assumption, well supported by direct and reported observation of birds of both sexes in many species, that birds of a single sex in a single species have uniform colouring; for example, all male cardinals have the same bright red colouring. Suppose that we are aware of observations of swans of both sexes in each of many species: mute swans, trumpeter swans, whistling swans, and whooper swans. Suppose that all observed swans of these species were seen to be white. Then observing more swans of any one of those species, of either sex, is irrelevant; we have strong reason to believe that no such additional observation will produce a different answer to our question. But then we hear reports that there are different species of swans in the southern hemisphere. Observing swans of those species is relevant. Once we become aware of observations of the "black swans" of Australia and New Zealand, which are as black as their name implies, then no further observations of swans is relevant; we have conclusive proof in the last observations of a negative answer to our question: not all swans are white. In general, if the justified premisses at one's disposal support an answer to one's question that no additional evidence can overturn, then no such further additional evidence is relevant. Of course, if further information casts doubt on one or more of those justified premisses, then the situation can change.

Finally, information used in arriving at a correct answer must be practically obtainable. The word "practically" implies relativity both to the time and effort required to obtain the information and to the importance that one answer the question correctly and to the urgency of arriving at an answer. If it will take a two-minute Internet search to get relevant information of good quality, and one has the two minutes to spare, and it is important that the answer be correct, and one can wait two minutes before closing in on an answer, then one ought to do the Internet search. If the question is whether to quarantine a patient with symptoms like those of sudden acute respiratory syndrome (SARS), a contagious viral infection with a 15% mortality rate, and it takes a week to get the result of a "gold standard" test of the patient's blood sample, then one quarantines the patient first (unless one can immediately exclude a diagnosis of SARS) and reviews the quarantine decision after receiving the result of the blood test. There is of course no general algorithm for balancing considerations of time, effort, urgency and importance of correctness in deciding whether it is practical to obtain a certain piece of good relevant information. Judgement is required. There may however be algorithms for determining in specific domains whether it is practical to obtain good relevant information.

4. JUSTIFIED WARRANT

If one's reasoning is to justify one's conclusion, that conclusion must follow from one's premisses in accordance with a justified general warrant.

The phrase "*in accordance with*" means that the warrant actually applies to the inference. In other words, the warrant is semantically equivalent to some generalization of the reasoning's associated conditional "if p_1 and ... and p_n, then c", where p_1, ..., p_n stand for the premisses and c for the conclusion (with qualifiers and rebuttals removed). The requirement that the warrant actually apply to the inference should be obvious. A subtle danger in reasoning, which reasoners may not notice, is the use of a generalization of the converse of the associated conditional. For example, one may reason from hearing a train-like whistle that a train is in the vicinity. Reflecting on why one thinks this follows, one might propose the generalized warrant: If a train is in the vicinity, then I hear a whistle like the one I just heard. But this is the converse of the required warrant, which is rather: If I hear a whistle like the one I just heard, then a train is in the vicinity. This warrant may not be justified; for example, one may be aware that one has a neighbour who is a train aficionado addicted to playing recordings of trains at high volume and that there are no train tracks in one's vicinity. (If the conclusion is qualified by the word "possibly", then a generalization of the converse may support the inference, in so-called abductive reasoning, i.e. reasoning from some observed phenomenon to a hypothesis that may explain it. But the generalization of the converse seems to be in Toulmin's terminology backing for the warrant, rather than the warrant itself. The warrant is: whenever someone hears a train-like whistle it may be produced by a nearby train. The backing for this warrant is: If the driver blows the whistle of a nearby train, it makes a sound like the sound I just heard.)

In addition to being applicable, the warrant must be *general*. No conclusion follows in just one particular case; if it follows in one case, it follows in parallel cases. An applicable warrant picks out a class of such cases. It is important to realize that there may be several ways of doing so. In general, warrants generalize over the repeated content expressions of one's reasoning, and they must generalize over at least one content expression that occurs both in a premiss and in the conclusion (Hitchcock, 1985). If more than one content expression is repeated, then the reasoning has several potential warrants for the inference. Furthermore, the extent to which one generalizes over a given content expression is variable. In the example just mentioned of the train-like whistle, one might generalize over the implicit time constant "now" to all times, to a given time of day, or to a given time interval like the current calendar year. These three generalizations produce three different warrants: whenever I hear a whistle here that sounds like this a train is in the vicinity, whenever at about 7 p.m. I hear a whistle here that sounds like this a train is in the vicinity, whenever in the current calendar year I hear a whistle here that sounds like this a train is in the vicinity.

The requirement that the warrant be general is not a requirement that it be universal. Warrants, as Toulmin pointed out, can be modally qualified, as holding for the most part, or *ceteris paribus*, or even just sometimes. Such qualifications, along with qualifications of the epistemic status of the warrant, imply imperfect support for the conclusion, which may or may not be explicitly marked in one's reasoning.

Finally, the warrant must be *justified*. It is neither necessary nor sufficient that the warrant actually hold, i.e. that the generalization is correct (whether universally, for the most part, or *ceteris paribus*). Correctness of the warrant is not sufficient, because reasoners need to draw inferences in accordance with warrants of which they are actually aware. Thus, for example, a logic student in the 1920s who considered axiomatized Peano arithmetic could not use the correct generalization that no consistent axiomatization of arithmetic is complete to draw the conclusion that axiomatized Peano arithmetic is incomplete, because this generalization had not yet been shown to be true. Correctness of the warrant is not even necessary, for the same reason that it is not necessary that the premisses of good reasoning be true. Fallible human reasoners with limited resources have no direct access to truth, or more broadly to correctness; they must make do with what at any given time they are justified in accepting. The corollary of this fallibility is that good reasoners must be ready to revise their cognitive commitments, including the warrants in accordance with which they reason, in the light of new good evidence.

In Toulmin's model, warrants are justified by backing. His conception of backing, and his distinction between warrant-using and warrant-establishing arguments, is linked to his strong field-dependency thesis, about which reservations have been expressed, for example in several chapters of Norris (1992). In fact, there seems no reason to postulate a sharp difference in kind between warrant-using reasoning and warrant-establishing reasoning. If one is reasoning to a conclusion that will later serve as a warrant for further reasoning, the conclusion is one's claim and the "backing" for that claim constitutes one's grounds; the inference from grounds to claim will have its own warrant. In good medical reasoning, for example, conclusions about individual patients are reached using so-called "evidence-based" generalizations about risk factors, diagnosis, prognosis or treatment. The evidence that justifies such generalizations tends to take the form of clinical trials and other analytical studies, the conclusions from which are incorporated through meta-analysis and systematic review into authoritative clinical guidelines and references. Reasoning from the results synthesized in a systematic review to a clinical guideline is, in Toulmin's terminology, another instance of reasoning from grounds to a claim, only at a higher level than reasoning that applies a clinical guideline to the observed circumstances of a particular patient.

5. JUSTIFIED IN ASSUMING NO DEFEATERS APPLY

A well-known feature of Toulmin's model is that many warrants come with rebuttals, or exceptional conditions under which the warrant lacks authority or is inapplicable, or the conclusion is false; Verheij (2002/2005a) has clearly distinguished these various types of rebuttals, which Toulmin lumps together. If the warrant that justifies one's inference is not universal, one must be justified in assuming that no exceptional condition in the particular case rules out application of the warrant. Such exceptional circumstances include not only circumstances that show that the conclusion is incorrect but also circumstances that show that the warrant is inapplicable to a particular situation, even though the conclusion may be correct. The former type of exceptional circumstance, one that shows the conclusion to be incorrect, may be said to *override* (Pinto, 1999) or *rebut* (Pollock, 1970) the warrant; a standard example is the circumstance that a bird is a penguin, which overrides the warrant that birds fly (since penguins do not fly). The latter type of exceptional circumstance, one that shows the warrant to be inapplicable even though the conclusion may nevertheless be correct, may be said to *undermine* (Pinto, 1999) or *undercut* (Pollock, 1970) the warrant; a standard example due to Pollock (1995) is the undermining of the warrant that things that look red are red by the circumstance that the object one is looking at is illuminated by a red light. The distinction between overriding defeaters and undermining defeaters was first made by Pollock in his (1970); there may be other types of defeaters. Verheij (2002/2005a) has added two other types to Toulmin's three types of defeaters, and has developed a subtle theory of the way in which the justification status of the components of the Toulmin model changes as defeaters of various sorts are acknowledged, including defeaters of defeaters. For the warrant in particular, the central point is that, if one is not justified in assuming that a warrant lacks defeaters in the particular case, then one's conclusion about that case is obviously unjustified.

The condition that one is justified in *assuming* that no defeaters apply is weaker than the condition that one has a justification (i.e. proof) that no defeaters apply. To require a reasoner using a non-universal warrant to have a justification that no defeaters apply is to impose too great a burden of proof on the reasoner. The non-existence of a defeater is not a ground from which the reasoner arrives at a given conclusion; if it were, the reasoner would need to have as good a justification for it as for any ground. Rather, defeaters are something to be aware of as a possibility; in many cases, there are indefinitely many possible defeaters, and it would paralyse reasoning to require a reasoner to have a justification for excluding each and every one of them.

What does it take to be justified in assuming that no exception to a warrant applies to the particular case about which one is reasoning? In some situations, institutional and legal requirements impose obligations to determine whether anything about a particular case defeats the warrant. For example, a detective must ensure that the evidence that can be presented in court will be sufficient to prove beyond a reasonable doubt that the suspect is guilty of a criminal offence. A physician has a duty to conform to recognized standards of care. Such institutional requirements can be given a consequentialist justification.

More directly, in the absence of such institutional requirements, one can take a directly consequentialist approach. *First*, one must know of no exception to the warrant in the particular case. *Second*, if an exceptional condition has serious consequences and one can find out without too much difficulty whether it is present in the particular case, one must find out whether the exceptional condition is present. For example, it is generally safe to start across an intersection when the light turns green, but not if another vehicle is running a newly red light on the cross street. Since it takes only a brief look in each direction to find out if any vehicle is running the red light, an appropriately careful driver will look in each direction as the light turns green. (The example is a bit artificial, since the behaviour of experienced drivers in such routine situations is a matter of automatic habit, but reasoning can be used in forming such habits, for example, in driving instruction.) The more serious the consequences of an exception, the more effort one should be prepared to put into finding out if it is present. It is a matter of judgement where to draw the line. *Third*, if one knows of no exception and one's pragmatically justified investigation has not discovered an exception, one can draw one's conclusion *as if* there is no exception. But one should be alert to the possibility of discovering at a later time some exceptional circumstance pertaining to the particular case. If one's observation of a clock leads one to conclude that the time is 10:15, and shortly after one sees another clock which reads 11:20, then one should suspend judgement as to what time it really is until one finds out which of the two clocks is correct.

6. SUMMARY AND COMPARISON

The four conditions—justified grounds, adequate information, justified warrant, justification in assuming no exceptions apply—are individually necessary and jointly sufficient for good reasoning. If any one of the four conditions is absent, the reasoning is not good; it does not justify the conclusion. If they are all present, the reasoning is good; it does justify the conclusion.

Only two of the four conditions are intrinsic to the parts of the reasoning: justified grounds and justified warrant. The other two—adequate information and justification in assuming no exceptions apply—are characteristics of the activity of reasoning. They concern whether one has investigated and reasoned enough, and so belong to the pragmatics of reasoning. Toulmin himself already distinguished in *The Uses of Argument* the phases in such a process of investigation (1958, pp. 15-22). Jean Goodwin has suggested, in a commentary on a version of this paper, that one could find the materials for a pragmatics of reasoning in the talk in civic debates about whether debaters have met their probative obligations.

Justification is not the same as truth, or correctness. Even bad reasoning can, by a lucky chance, arrive at a correct conclusion. And even good reasoning can, by an unlucky chance, arrive at an incorrect conclusion. The reason for preferring good reasoning to bad reasoning is that, on the whole, one is more likely to arrive at the correct answer to one's question through good reasoning than through bad reasoning.

The Toulmin-type approach to the evaluation of reasoning and arguments can be usefully compared and contrasted to an approach through the concepts of argument schemes (or argumentation schemes) and their corresponding critical questions, pioneered by A. C. Hastings (1962) and developed among others by Manfred Kienpointner (1992), Douglas Walton (1996b), Wayne Grennan (1997) and J. Anthony Blair (1999; 2001). An argument scheme is a general pattern of argument, e.g. from a sign to that of which it is a sign. The patterns so identified are typically so general that conformity to the pattern creates not even a presumption that the conclusion is to be accepted if there is justification for accepting the premisses. The critical questions relevant to a given argument scheme include questions about the premisses or grounds (are they true/acceptable/justified?), questions about the warrant, and questions about defeaters, generally posed in a way that does not differentiate between these functions. As Pinto (1999) points out, an argument scheme's critical questions about the acceptability of the premiss(es) and about the truth, sufficiency or contextual appropriateness of the warrant need to be answered positively before a particular argument conforming to the scheme can be treated as one that even creates a presumption that its conclusion is to be accepted. Such critical questions ought to be, but often are not, distinguished from critical questions about exceptional circumstances in the particular case that override or undermine the inference. The Toulmin-based approach described in the present paper makes the distinction clear. The approach of the present paper is also less restrictive than most of the literature on argument schemes about the types of argument schemes (i.e. warrants) to which reasoning and arguments can be expected to conform. That is a virtue, because random sampling of argumentative texts turns up many passages that are difficult to bring under the comparatively brief list of types recognized in the argument scheme literature (Hitchcock, 2002); Van Eemeren and Grootendorst, for example, recognize only three main types (1992, pp. 94-102). Grennan (1997) is an exception in having a quite lengthy and systematically generated list of argument schemes, and also in acknowledging the difference between presumption-creating critical questions and presumption-defeating critical questions. The present paper also differs from the argument scheme literature in focusing on reasoning rather than argument. But all argument schemes can also be treated as reasoning schemes, as Blair (2001) for example notes.

Acknowledgements

This chapter adapts material from Milos Jenicek and David Hitchcock's *Evidence-Based Practice: Logic and Critical Thinking in Medicine* (pp. 41-49; copyright 2005, American Medical Association; material used with permission). The second paragraph of the "Summary and Conclusions" section adapts points from Jean Goodwin's insightful commentary at a conference at McMaster University in May 2005 on a presentation of this paper; I thank her for this commentary. For helpful comments on previous versions, I thank Jonathan E. Adler, Mark Battersby, J. Anthony Blair, Robert H. Ennis, James B. Freeman, Trudy Govier, Nicholas Griffin, Ralph H. Johnson, Robert C. Pinto, Bart Verheij and Mark L. Weinstein. I thank as well the referees, James B. Freeman and Bart Verheij, for their careful and perceptive comments.

CHAPTER 14

OLAF TANS

THE FLUIDITY OF WARRANTS: USING THE TOULMIN MODEL TO ANALYSE PRACTICAL DISCOURSE

University of Amsterdam, Faculty of Law, Department of Constitutional Law, P.O. Box 1030 1000BA, Amsterdam, The Netherlands
E-mail: o.j.tans@uva.nl, olaf.tans@wanadoo.nl

ABSTRACT: This contribution seeks to understand the dynamic nature of practical arguments on the basis of an alternative reading of Toulmin's theory. The essence of this alternative reading is that warrants are conceived of as unstable elements of practical logic: they evolve as arguments are unfolded in, for example, legal decisions. Using this insight, a judgement by the US Supreme Court is analysed and shown to go through various phases of warrant-construction. Finally, the Toulmin scheme is adapted in order to capture this dynamic aspect of practical reasoning.

KEYWORDS: Stephen E. Toulmin; practical discourse; legal reasoning; warrant; construction; dialectic

1. INTRODUCTION[1]

The complexity of arguments used in practical discourse keeps scholars searching for new theories and models. The main difficulty lies in the fact that in practical discourse we try to order our social environment on the basis of normative standards such as rules, principles and values, but these standards are not easy to apply to concrete cases. On the one hand, these standards always have to be interpreted in the light of the ever-changing world they are supposed to keep in order. On the other hand, even when it is crystal clear what a certain standard means in the light of a certain case, it always remains to be seen whether other standards or considerations stand in the way of its application. As MacCormick puts it: "There are background principles always available to qualify, defeat, or even override a discourse couched in terms of rules" (MacCormick, 1978, xii).

This contribution argues that the Toulmin model can help to understand and analyse this complexity of practical discourse. This may come as a surprise, because the Toulmin model is often criticised for not being suited to deal with complex

[1] The author would like to thank Henrike Jansen, Marc Loth and Bob Brouwer for their useful comments.

D. Hitchcock and B. Verheij (eds.), Arguing on the Toulmin Model: New Essays in Argument Analysis and Evaluation, 219–230.

argumentative structures. Allegedly, this model is too simple and static to capture the nuances of practical reasoning: it over-simplifies arguments, forcing them into a so-called 'single-claim, single-ground, single-diagram mode', whereas in practice arguments have a more complex structure (Gasper and George, 1998, p. 376). It will be argued, however, that the Toulmin model has more to offer than this line of criticism wants us to believe. Although it may indeed appear to be quite static, the Toulmin model is in fact very useful where it comes to analysing the arguments that appear, for instance, in the practice of legal decision-making. This potential can be revealed if we let go of the standard diagram and return to the theory from which it sprang, as set out in *The Uses of Argument.*

More concretely, this contribution takes the following route. First, it discusses the limitations of the standard Toulmin scheme when it comes to understanding the complexity of practical discourse. Secondly, a more dynamic reading of *The Uses of Argument* will be presented, making this theory more sensitive to the complexity of practical reasoning. Thirdly, a decision of the U.S. Supreme Court will be analysed so as to reveal a certain evolution in its argumentative structure. The essence of this analysis is that, whereas the standard Toulmin scheme forces one to conceive of warrants (rules) as solid, stable authorisers of argumentative steps, they can also be seen as flexible and evolving. Complex practical arguments can be explained as the products of discursive processes in which warrants (rules) are repetitively altered in order to become a satisfying justification.

2. THE LIMITATION OF THE STANDARD TOULMIN SCHEME

Before discussing the limitation of the standard Toulmin-scheme, it may be wise to explain what is meant by the term 'practical discourse', and how legal decision-making relates to it. To keep it simple, in this article practical discourse is understood as argumentation about normative statements, such as statements about what values should be pursued, what rules should guide behaviour, and which norms are binding (Raz, 1990, p. 10). Legal decision-making is considered to be a 'special case' in that it observes a number of specific procedures and constraints in arguing about normative statements, but it is not fundamentally different from general practical discourse (Alexy, 1989, p. 179). On the contrary, this article joins those theorists who believe that, because of its special nature, legal decision-making provides fruitful cases for the study of practical discourse.[2]

[2] Feteris points out, for example, that legal decisions are taken in a social and institutional environment that demands justification (1997, p. 355). Others have stressed that the public character of legal decisions, combined with the fact that they tend to draw attention, stimulates the explicitness and completeness of arguments. Toulmin himself, finally, illustrates the relevance of legal decision-making to the study of practical discourse with his famous jurisprudential analogy.

Toulmin is one of those theorists. In *The Uses of Argument* he argues that, to understand the structure of arguments in general, it is useful to make a comparison with the legal process (Toulmin, 1958, pp. 7, 96). When we argue we try to convince an imaginary 'Court of Reason' that poses questions similar to the ones posed when legal cases have to be solved: what is the claim; what is the ground; how is the step from the ground to the claim warranted; why would we accept this warrant; are there no exceptions? If, for example, we want to argue that a person by the name Harry is a British subject, our argument will have the following well-known structure (Toulmin, 1958, p. 105):

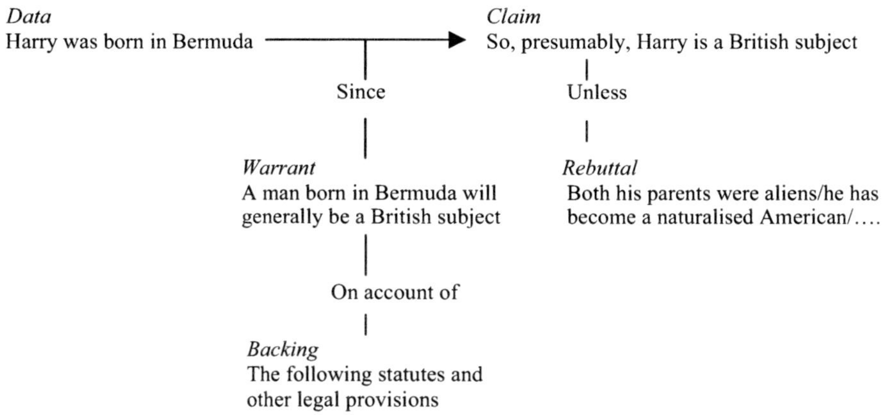

Although this is one of the most cited theories about argumentation, it is at the same time widely regarded as having a limited ability to explain the complicated discursive patterns that occur in, for example, legal practice. The easiest way to describe this limitation is to say that, in this form, it can only explain so called 'easy' cases. In legal theory, the easy case is considered to be a legal decision focusing only on the internal justification of the conclusion on the basis of certain premises (Alexy, 1989). This means that there is no controversy (at least not one acknowledged by the decision maker) about the interpretation of rules or classification of facts, or about the truth, and that the decision is based on a fairly simple deductive argument (MacCormick, 1987, p. 199). As in Harry's case, the decision maker appears to be confident that certain statutes and provisions indicate the existence of a certain rule and that this rule is applicable to a certain case, provided that the exceptional circumstance does not occur.

It may come as no surprise, however, that the main focus of attention by those who try to explain the structure of legal reasoning, and more generally by those who try to explain the nature and the development of the law, are so-called 'hard cases'. In hard cases, the decision also focuses on the external justification, which means that apart from the deductive operation from certain premises to a certain conclusion, the premises themselves are put to the test. In Harry's case, for instance, we might wonder why the text of a certain statute should be taken to express the rule that a man born in Bermuda will generally be a British subject, or why that statute is more important than an international treaty regulating nationality, or how we can be sure that Harry was in fact born in Bermuda.

Hard case situations occur for social rather than logical reasons. More specifically, they occur when the decision maker perceives a gap in the law: "...the realization that there is ambiguity, vagueness, penumbra, or obscurity in some legal provision seen as applicable to the disputed case or upon which the interpreting court has been requested to make an interpretative decision" (Bengoetxea, 1993, p. 219). One could also say that hard cases lead us to go beyond the formal account of a legal system, and force us to deal with those aspects of the law that cannot be explained as simple rule-application. In yet other words: it is mainly in hard cases that the law reveals what Toulmin calls its 'working logic' (Toulmin, 1958, p. 146). As it stands, however, the Toulmin scheme seems too simple to offer a satisfying explanation.

3. TOWARDS A MORE DYNAMIC USE OF TOULMIN'S THEORY

There have been many attempts to adapt the Toulmin scheme to the complexities of practical argumentation. Hambrick, for example, proposes a more 'field-specific' approach, which means that he seeks to analyse the nature of grounds, warrants and backings specific to policy arguments (Hambrick, 1974). Gasper and George, furthermore, try to transcend the standard Toulmin model by using multiple diagrams to avoid oversimplification (Gasper and George, 1998, p. 382). Patterson, finally, tries to capture the nuances of constitutional decision-making by adding extra warrants and backings to the standard Toulmin scheme (Patterson, 1996, pp. 169-179).

Applying such theories, the writer of this article has been trying to reconstruct the logic of a number of decisions by constitutional courts. It turned out that by using multiple diagrams and field-specific accounts of data, claims etc., it was indeed possible to capture the complexity of these legal decisions. Nevertheless, this type of reconstruction proved to be unsatisfying in two ways. First, it results in diagrams containing so many elements and logical relations that it does not yield a coherent insight in the logical structure of arguments. More precisely, this type of reconstruction does not add to what the original legal decisions already make clear, namely that we are dealing with highly complicated forms of practical reasoning. Secondly, the reconstruction remains artificial, in the sense that a dynamic phenomenon - a legal argument that is gradually unfolded in a written text - is reduced to a static diagram of functional elements and their logical relations.

As will be argued in the remainder of this article, Toulmin's theory can be used in such a way that a more meaningful understanding of the dynamic of practical discourse is gained. Before this alternative reading is presented it may be wise to state that it is not claimed to be in accordance with the author's intentions. Although it is difficult to see a reason why the following would imply a parting with

Toulmin's theory, one cannot rule out the possibility that someone else does. In that (latter) case, the following is to be regarded as an attempt to overcome some of the limitations of the Toulmin scheme.

With that reservation, this article proposes the following reading of the theory set out in *The Uses of Argument*, consisting basically of three components.[3] The first component is that argumentation is characterised by the fact that one (group of) statement(s) can function as a basis for another statement, that we take steps from a foundation to a conclusion. In this respect, Toulmin focuses on the step from *data* to *claim*, but one argument can contain more types of steps. It may, for instance, be necessary to infer the data from given evidence, or to induce a preference for one warrant in case two contradicting warrants are applicable.

The second component is that we try to justify these steps by giving support. According to Toulmin this involves the use of a warrant on the one hand and the use of backing on the other, but here it is argued that it is all about the warrant. More precisely, this contribution adheres to the thought that backing, qualifier and rebuttal are all discursive procedures to somehow test the authority of a given warrant. As van Eemeren, Grootendorst and Kruiger remark (1987), one could say that these are sub-arguments of a compound argumentation (pp. 203-204). A backing, for example, is in fact a new argument to defend the authority of the warrant.[4]

Thirdly and most importantly, this implies that although warrants tend to be presented as static authorisers of argumentative steps, they are in fact changing as practical arguments are unfolded. As shall be illustrated, this means that practical arguments are not logically stable: they are not characterised by a steady, regressive support-structure (backings supporting warrants, warrants supporting these backings, etc.), but rather by an *evolving* support-structure, a logic that develops as the argument progresses. In this way, even the most complicated practical arguments can be based on one single warrant. The crux, however, is that this single warrant can be subject to a complicated procedure of testing, refinement and adjustment, in order to make it 'fit' the case at hand.

In the next sections, a decision by the US Supreme Court will be analysed to illustrate how this works out in practice. Although a similar pattern was found in a number of other legal decisions, it must be stressed that the following analysis is not intended to be statistically relevant. Rather, it is a theoretical experiment. In order to improve the plausibility of the analysis, however, I can refer to a number of studies that describe a more or less similar phenomenon, though not in terms of Toulmin's theory. According to Sunstein, for example, the meaning of principles is established in a confrontation with the circumstances and the facts of cases to which they are applied (Sunstein, 1993). Brewer explains that this confrontation involves an adjustment of general normative principles in the light of specific examples (Brewer, 1996). As we shall see, a Toulmin analysis can help to understand this discursive process.

---

[3] This reading of Toulmin's theory is inspired by: Heidt (1968, p. 101), and Trent (1968, pp. 252-259).

[4] An extensive analysis of the concept of 'warrant' can be found in Hitchcock (2003a).

4. THE INITIAL CONSTRUCTION OF A WARRANT

In 1916 the governments of the United States and Canada signed a treaty prohibiting the killing, catching, or selling of migratory birds. In order to effectuate this agreement, the American Congress adopted the Migratory Bird Treaty Act (MBA) of 1918, according to which it was no longer allowed to engage in 'wild games' involving migratory birds. The state of Missouri, where these games were very popular, considered the MBA to be in conflict with the tenth amendment to the Constitution, which reads: 'The powers not delegated to the United States by the Constitution, nor prohibited by it to the States, are reserved to the States respectively, or to the people.' Missouri claimed that only the states had the power to legislate in matters of wild life protection, as the Constitution did not explicitly attribute that power to the federal government. It sued Mister Holland, a federal functionary in charge of enforcing the MBA, and the case went all the way to the US Supreme Court.[5]

As in most legal arguments, the decision first focuses on selecting written rules that can provide a warrant to decide the case at hand. Apart from the tenth amendment, there are also Constitutional provisions that help the case of Mr. Holland, that is, the federal government's case. Article 2.2 states that the President has the power to make treaties, and article 6 prescribes that treaties are 'the supreme law of the land'. Hence, the Supreme Court was dealing with written rules pointing in different directions: legislative autonomy of the states versus governmental supremacy where it comes to subjecting the states to rules laid down in treaties. In other words, the Court had to construct a warrant on the basis of ambivalent legal material.

How does one deal with this aspect of the argument in terms of Toulmin's theory? Judging from the example of Harry who was born in Bermuda, we would have to localise the process of legal warrant-construction in its relation to a backing of statutes and other legal provisions. At first sight, this seems adequate, for statutes and provisions are indeed often presented as the reason for the relevance of a certain rule. There are, however, two objections to this analysis. First, the argumentative process is over-simplified by stating that legal warrants are simply backed by written rules. As mentioned, the 'jump' from written rules to legal warrants can involve complicated interpretive processes constituting the major part of legal decisions. Secondly, it can be argued that instead of playing the role of the backing of legal warrants, written rules function as data. Actors in legal practice generally operate on the theory that there would be 'sources' of law; that legal warrants are drawn from objectively existing documents with a legal status. Imagine the Supreme Court posing the question Toulmin uses to discover the data of an argument: 'What have you got to go on?' It seems inevitable that the answer of the state of Missouri contains some reference to the tenth amendment, and that this provision thus functions as data.

[5] *Missouri v. Holland*, 252 U.S. 416; 40 S. Ct. 382; 64 L. Ed. 641 (1920).

We can improve our understanding of the argument by taking account of the fact that it comes about in various steps, the first of which concerns the initial construction of a legal warrant on the basis of the following sub-argument:[6]

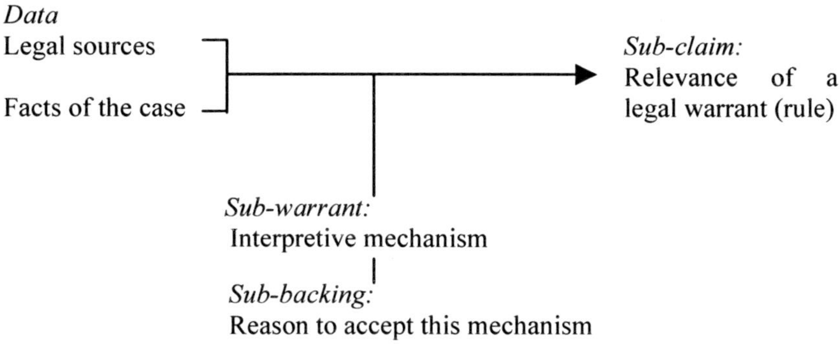

In *Missouri v. Holland* the Supreme Court decides that, although there seem to be conflicting legal sources, the relevant legal warrant is that treaties are the supreme law of the land, even when the tenth amendment applies. This is a sub-claim used as the starting point for the rest of the argument. The Court justifies its sub-claim by referring to the 'language' of the Constitution, which means that it relies on a so-called textual or grammatical interpretive mechanism. The reason for using this mechanism is not specified; we can only guess why the Supreme Court chooses this particular method of interpretation.

5. REFINING THE INITIAL WARRANT

By nature, rules force a decision maker to draw a conclusion when certain facts are the case (if p then q), but that does not guarantee actual rule-application. Hage, for instance, argues that reasoning with (legal) rules involves two steps. In accordance with the foregoing, the first step consists of identifying relevant rules (warrants) on the basis of legal sources. The second step consists of weighing the reasons for and against application of those relevant rules (Hage, 1997, pp. 123-124). In the same way, Schauer remarks that rules have a degree of force. In principle, they determine an outcome in a given situation, but they can be challenged by so called 'competing considerations' (Schauer, 1991, pp. 112-118).

Although it is very likely that judges weigh reasons for and against the application of given rules, or test their force in the light of competing considerations, they rarely make it explicit in their rulings, probably because they are expected to strengthen our belief in the legal system rather than to cast doubts on the problem-solving capacity of its rules. Therefore, they tend to keep up the appearance that they

[6] This scheme is partly based on: Hage (1997, p. 97).

are simply applying the rules and use more subtle ways to adapt this application to the circumstances of specific cases. In this respect, Toulmin's theory may be more realistic: after establishing a warrant, the step from data to claim can be qualified by adding potential rebuttals to the structure of the argument (Toulmin, 1958, p. 101).

The point, however, is that all these theorists seem to disregard a crucial fact, namely that this testing, or weighing, or qualification, does not leave the original warrant untouched. In theory, it may be possible to say that warrants are first established and then embedded in a more complicated logical structure, but in actual discourse this occurs more gradually and recursively. Take *Missouri v. Holland.* After the Supreme Court has identified the relevant rule, it opens the door to potential competing considerations by stating:

> The language of the Constitution as to the supremacy of treaties being general, the question before us narrowed to an inquiry into the ground upon which the present supposed exception is placed.

At first sight, this manoeuvre fits well in Toulmin's theory of argumentation: the Supreme Court qualifies the step from data to claim by adding a potential rebuttal to the structure of the argument. As we shall see, however, this manoeuvre is the beginning of a development of the argument altogether. In *Missouri v. Holland*, the Supreme Court moves on to qualifying the warrant that treaties are the supreme law of the land as follows:

> With regard to that, we may add that when we are dealing with words that also are a constituent act, like the Constitution of the United States, we must realize that they have called into life a being the development of which could not have been foreseen completely by the most gifted of its begetters. It was enough for them to realize or to hope that they had created an organism; it has taken a century and has cost their successors much sweat and blood to prove that they had created a nation. The case before us must be considered in the light of our whole experience, and not merely in that of what was said hundred years ago. The treaty in question does not contravene any prohibitory words to be found in the Constitution. The only question is whether it is forbidden by some invisible radiation from the 10th Amendment.

These few lines are indicative of the evolution of arguments in practical discourse. In the process of discussing potential qualifications or rebuttals to the original warrant, the Supreme Court has at the same time altered the warrant itself. This is clearly expressed in the last sentence, which implies that the effect of the tenth amendment has to be reconsidered, thus indicating that the initial warrant is susceptible to refinement. In other words, the argument goes through a second phase of warrant-construction, in which the original warrant is reformulated and adapted in the light of competing considerations:

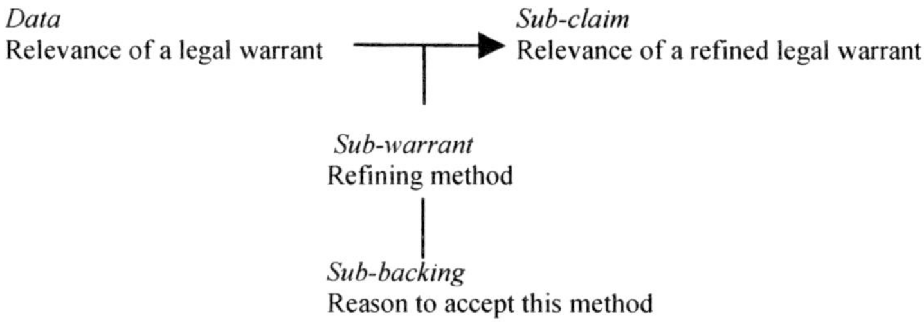

Although this development is now portrayed as a fairly straightforward argumentative step, it can involve a manifold and reciprocal heuristic process. In this respect, Verheij (2001) speaks of legal decision-making as a kind of 'dialectical theory construction' (p. 1). In the same vein, Ashley speaks of a 'dialectical relationship between legal cases and normative principles'. Interestingly, this author also gives some empirical evidence of the fact that refinement of warrants takes place on a wider scale. After a systematic study of a set of ethics cases written by a professional association's board of ethical review, he concludes: "The abstract principles inform the analysis and decision of the specific cases, but the decisions of the specific cases can specify the meanings of the abstract principles and change the ways in which they are applied in future cases" (Ashley, 2004, p. 1).

With regard to *Missouri v. Holland*, this specification of meaning can be reconstructed as follows. The original warrant was that treaties are supreme law of the land, even when the tenth amendment applies. In the course of the argument, this has changed into: treaties can be forbidden by an invisible radiation of the tenth amendment. The relevancy of this warrant is a sub-claim that will be the starting point of the last step in the argument. The specification is authorised by a sub-warrant according to which there can be exceptions to the general applicability of legal rules. The reasons to accept this sub-warrant are clearly explained in the quotation: a constitution is like an organism, it grows, and its rules can therefore acquire new meaning.

6. THE APPLICATION OF THE WARRANT

The essence of practical reasoning is that it gives answers: concrete solutions to concrete problems of social order. This means that the process of refining and adjusting warrants cannot go on forever. At some point, the decision maker will have to apply them to bring clarity to a certain case. According to the standard Toulmin scheme, a backing supports this final move from data to claim. As the foregoing analysis illustrates, however, this functional element can play a role in all the phases of practical reasoning, just like all the other functional elements.

In contrast to a standard Toulmin analysis, therefore, this article argues that the conclusion of a practical argument is not characterised by giving a final backing. Rather, this conclusion is characterised by the fact that the decision maker puts an end to the discursive process of refining the warrant by deciding that it now 'fits' the facts and considerations of the case. In other words: the warrant is ready to be applied. This step is the result of yet another sub-argument, in which the warrant can still undergo change:

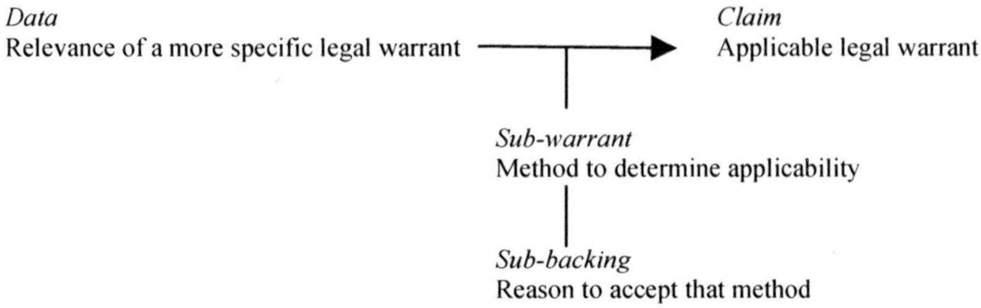

In *Missouri v. Holland*, the following statement marks the entrance of the conclusion of the argument:

> We must consider what this country has become in deciding what that amendment has reserved.

Again, we can say that the warrant has evolved, in that the 'invisible radiation' from the tenth amendment that was introduced earlier, is now to be deduced from 'what this country has become'. This new criterion modifies the warrant drastically and paves the way for a series of more general legal and sociological observations, leading to the conclusion that the tenth amendment cannot be taken to 'radiate' a rule that the government cannot sign treaties with regard to the protection of migratory birds.

Finalising the argument, the Supreme Court decides that the MBA is valid. Apparently, it was of the opinion that the warrant had been sufficiently developed and was ready to be applied to the case of *Missouri v. Holland.*

7. A MODIFICATION OF THE TOULMIN SCHEME

Combining the three phases that have been analysed in the preceding paragraphs, the following scheme captures the layout of the argument in *Missouri v. Holland* all together:

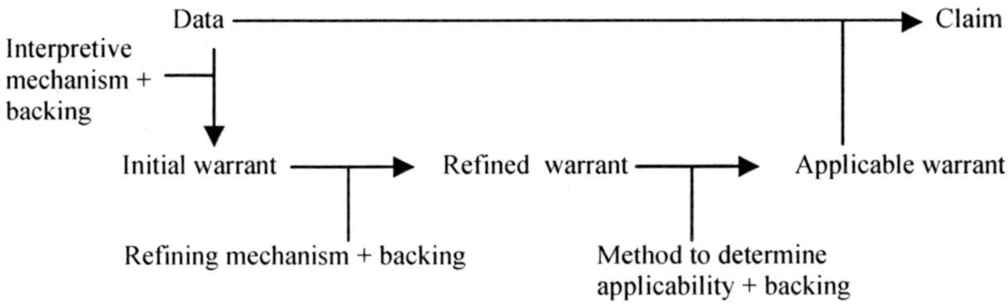

This analysis exhibits a number of differences from the standard Toulmin scheme. First, the initial warrant is considered to be drawn from data: legal rules are 'found' in sources of law. Secondly, this warrant is taken to undergo change as the argument unfolds: it is gradually moulded into a shape fitting the case at hand. Thirdly, the other functional elements (qualifier, rebuttal, backing) are considered to be discursive procedures that play a role in this ongoing warrant-construction, rather than playing a role in supporting the eventual step from data to claim. According to Toulmin, for example, a qualifier indicates "...a degree of force which our data confer on our claim in virtue of our warrant" (Toulmin, 1958, p. 101). In the model presented above, this boils down to a refinement of the warrant itself. Fourthly, the element of backing is considered to play a role in supporting all these steps that are taken to arrive at an applicable warrant.

Despite these differences, this modification is to be seen as an elaboration rather than a refutation of Toulmin's theory. It is striking, for example, that although *Missouri v. Holland* shows a complicated line of practical reasoning, we can still say its final claim is the result of a fairly simple step based on certain data: given the facts of the case and the valid rules, the Federal government was entitled to issue the MBA. This was also the case in the other legal decisions that were analysed. Furthermore, Toulmin's theory is reinforced by the fact that it appeared to be possible to understand the logical structure of a number of complicated legal decisions by analysing their six functional elements. This article only theorises that, in practical arguments laid down in the text of legal decisions, these elements work together more dynamically than the standard Toulmin scheme suggests.

Moreover, it must be stressed that Toulmin himself seems to indicate the possibility of such an elaboration. After setting out his famous scheme in *The Uses of Argument*, the author moves on to discuss some specific themes, among them the contrast between 'warrant-using' and 'warrant-establishing' arguments (Toulmin, 1958, p. 120). A warrant-using argument involves deduction, which means that established warrants are applied to fresh data to derive new conclusions. One can think of the example of Harry being a British subject, in which the acceptability of the warrant is taken for granted. A warrant-establishing argument involves induction, which means that we use our observations as the backing for creating a new warrant. According to Toulmin (1958): "In this type of argument the warrant, not the conclusion, is novel, and so on trial" (p. 120).

In this light, the foregoing analysis explains how both types of argument cooperate in legal decisions. On the one hand, the Court reaches its conclusion by means of a deductive, warrant-using argument. To put it more generally, what lawyers are doing "...is simply maintaining the legal system by the means of an apparent normative argument" (Calhoun, 1988/1989, p. 409). On the other hand, before the Court reaches the point of deduction it first engages in a more or less inductive, warrant-establishing line of reasoning, or rather, a line of reasoning in which an already established warrant is put to the test and transformed in order to fit the case at hand.

8. CONCLUSION

Using Toulmin's theory of argumentation, this contribution has tried to get a grip on the dynamic structure of arguments produced in the practice of legal decision-making. The upshot is that these arguments can be explained as products of a discursive process in which warrants are tested, refined and adjusted in the light of additional considerations, in order to construct acceptable deductions. This process is reconstructed as going through three phases. First, warrants are drawn from legal sources and identified as being relevant to the facts of a case. Secondly, they are further developed and modified under the influence of the specific circumstances and considerations regarding the case. Thirdly and finally, they are regarded as fitting the case and applied to reach a conclusion. Legal arguments, one may say, are based on warrants that are gradually moulded into a satisfying shape.

To conclude, a brief remark about where this analysis may lead. Primarily, it aims to lead to a better understanding of the structure of single arguments that are produced in concrete situations. This is the 'micro-perspective' that seems to dominate the study of practical discourse, and that has also dominated this contribution. It is conceivable, however, that the foregoing analysis could also lead to insights regarding the totality of legal or practical arguments and how they constitute what Toulmin calls a 'field' of argument. In this macro-perspective, we may attempt to analyse the development of, for example, the legal field of argument by analysing how warrants are first constructed in one case and then re-used and further refined in the other, etc. We might, in other words, start to get a grip on the law as a warrant-recycling system. This, however, is an entirely new theme, to be discussed in another contribution.

CHAPTER 15

HENRY PRAKKEN

ARTIFICIAL INTELLIGENCE & LAW, LOGIC AND ARGUMENT SCHEMES

Department of Information and Computing Sciences, Utrecht University, and Faculty of Law, University of Groningen, P.O. Box 80.089, 3508 TB Utrecht, The Netherlands
E-mail: henry@cs.uu.nl

ABSTRACT: This paper reviews the history of AI & Law research from the perspective of argument schemes. It starts with the observation that logic, although very well applicable to legal reasoning when there is uncertainty, vagueness and disagreement, is too abstract to give a fully satisfactory classification of legal argument types. It therefore needs to be supplemented with an argument-scheme approach, which classifies arguments not according to their logical form but according to their content, in particular, according to the roles that the various elements of an argument can play. This approach is then applied to legal reasoning, to identify some of the main legal argument schemes. It is also argued that much AI & Law research in fact employs the argument-scheme approach, although it usually is not presented as such. Finally, it is argued that the argument-scheme approach and the way it has been employed in AI & Law respects some of the main lessons to be learnt from Toulmin's *The Uses of Argument*.

KEYWORDS: Argument schemes; legal reasoning; defeasible reasoning; nonmonotonic logic; warrants

1. INTRODUCTION

In the early days of Artificial Intelligence & Law research there was a sometimes heated debate about the suitability of logic for modelling legal reasoning. Logic, it was said, could not cope with the vagueness, indeterminacy and adversarial nature of the law (e.g. Berman and Hafner, 1987). Now we know that this criticism was not justified and that logical methods can also be applied when arguments for opposite conclusions are possible. For instance, techniques from nonmonotonic logic have been used to model reasoning with hierarchies of possibly conflicting rules (see Prakken and Sartor, 2002, for an overview) and even to model aspects of reasoning with precedents (e.g. Prakken and Sartor, 1998; Prakken 2002). However, even if these modern techniques are used, a logical approach still has some limitations and it needs to be supplemented with other elements. The point is that the notion of a logical inference is very abstract. The logical validity of an inference purely depends on the meaning of some structural words involved in the inferences, such as the connectives (and, or, if, not, . . .) and the quantifiers (all, some, most, . . .).

D. Hitchcock and B. Verheij (eds.), Arguing on the Toulmin Model: New Essays in Argument Analysis and Evaluation, 231–245.

However, sentences that are indistinguishable from a logical point of view can very well play different roles in an argument. This point was perhaps first stressed by Toulmin (1958), who in his famous scheme for arguments distinguished a *claim* connected to *data* by a *warrant* on account of a *backing,* and subject to exceptions specified by a *rebuttal.* Perhaps more important than Toulmin's particular scheme is his general observation that the various elements of an argument can play different roles, which leads to different standards for evaluating arguments.

Consider by way of illustration the following sentences:

All Dutch men are tall.

All email addresses are personal data.

From a logical point of view, both sentences are universally quantified implications. However, from an epistemological point of view they are clearly different. The first sentence is an empirical statement about a certain class of animals, while the second sentence is a legal rule interpreting a certain legal concept. Someone who disagrees with the first sentence will use different ways of attacking it than someone who disagrees with the second sentence. Attacks on the first sentence will typically refer to empirical observations ("Yesterday I saw a short Dutchman") or to empirical methodology ("Your sample is biased"). By contrast, attacks on the second sentence will usually refer to a legal source (relevant statutes), to legal authority ("The Dutch supreme court ruled otherwise") or to principle or policy ("Regarding email addresses as personal data allows the use of privacy protection laws against spam"). Sometimes arguments about empirical statements are also source-based ("How do you know that all Dutch men are tall?" "Henry told me, and he is Dutch, so he is in the position to know". "But Henry often lies".). However, even within the class of empirical statements there are clear differences. Compare

Dutch men usually like soccer.

Witnesses usually speak the truth.

Both sentences are empirical generalisations but the second one is more, since it also expresses a source of knowledge while the first does not. Because of this difference, the second statement can be attacked in ways that do not apply to the first. For instance, it can be attacked on the grounds that a witness is biased, or has malfunctioning senses. Of course, debates about the first sentence could also evolve into a debate about sources, if it is asked what the source is of this generalization. But the sentence itself does not express a source of knowledge.

The general point of these examples is that the use of sentences in arguments does not only depend on their logical form but also on other things, such as their epistemological or pragmatic nature. Logic, with its abstract definition of logical validity (whether deductive or nonmonotonic), is blind to such differences, and should therefore be supplemented with a so-called "argument-scheme" approach. In line with Toulmin (1958), such an approach can identify the different roles that the various elements of an argument can play and thereby paves the way for a field-dependent notion of validity of arguments. The reason is that different types of premises have different ways of being critically examined and, since different fields can have their own typical argumentation schemes, the criteria for evaluating arguments will differ for each field.

Argumentation theory is the only research area where the notion of argument schemes (or "argumentation schemes") is explicitly studied as such. However, in this paper I want to argue (following Gordon, 2003) that much AI & Law research in fact also employs the argument-scheme approach and thus takes some of Toulmin's main lessons to heart. In doing so, it is not my aim to give a comprehensive overview of AI & Law research. Rather, I will use a select set of examples from the AI & Law literature to illustrate the argument-scheme approach.

The rest of this paper is organised as follows. In Section 2 I explain the notion of an argument scheme as it is studied in argumentation theory, followed by a brief discussion in Section 3 of how argument schemes can be formalised in AI models of commonsense reasoning. In section 4 I briefly sketch the main phases of legal problem solving, viz. proof of the facts, rule interpretation and rule application. In the subsequent sections (5-7) I then discuss some of the main argument schemes used in each of these phases and some of the AI & Law projects modelling these schemes. In Section 8 I discuss some limitations of the argument-scheme approach to legal reasoning and in Section 9 I conclude by discussing how this work in AI & Law can be seen as developing the research program suggested by Toulmin (1958).

2. ARGUMENT SCHEMES

In this section I sketch the main ideas behind the argument-scheme approach in argumentation theory. The notion of argument schemes is one of the central topics in current argumentation theory. For a recent overview see Garssen (2001). Important contributions to the study of argument schemes have been made by Douglas Walton (e.g. 1996b). As conceived by him, argument schemes technically have the form of an inference rule. Consider, for instance, the following scheme from epistemic reasoning of "arguments from the position to know" (Walton, 1996b, pp. 61-63):

Person W says that p.
Person W is in the position to know about p.
Therefore (presumably), p.

(Note the resemblance to our example "witnesses usually speak the truth" from the introduction. In fact, the latter sentence is an instance of this scheme.) Or consider the following scheme from practical reasoning, of "arguments from consequences" (Walton, 1996b, pp. 75-77):

If A is brought about, then good (bad) consequences will (may plausibly) occur.
Therefore, A should (not) be brought about.

Our "all email addresses are personal data" example from the introduction may be transformed into an argument from good consequences:

> *If the term "personal data" of the Dutch Data Protection Act is interpreted to include email addresses, then legal measures against spam become possible, which is good.*
> *Therefore, the term "personal data" of the Dutch Data Protection Act should be interpreted to include email addresses.*

Argument schemes are not classified according to their logical form but according to their content. Many argument schemes in fact express epistemological principles (such as the scheme from the position to know) or principles of practical reasoning (such as the scheme from consequences). Accordingly, different domains may have different sets of such principles. Argument schemes come with a set of critical questions that have to be answered when assessing whether their application in a specific case is warranted. Some of these questions pertain to acceptability of the premises, such as 'is *W* in the position to know about *p*?' or 'is the possibility to use legal means against spam really good?". However, other questions point at exceptional circumstances in which the scheme may not apply, such as 'is *W* sincere?' or "are there better ways to bring about these good consequences?". Clearly, the possibility to ask such critical questions makes argument schemes defeasible, since negative answers to such critical questions are in fact counterarguments, such as "Person *W* is not sincere since he is a relative of the suspect and relatives of suspects tend to protect the suspect". Another reason why argument schemes are defeasible is that they may be contradicted by conflicting applications of the same or another scheme. For instance, a positive instance of the scheme from consequences can be attacked by a negative instance of the same scheme, such as by "interpreting email addresses as personal data also has bad consequences, since the legal system will be flooded with litigation, so the term "personal data" should not be interpreted to include email addresses". Or one person in a position to know (say an eyewitness) may have said that the suspect was at the crime scene while another eyewitness may have said that the suspect was not at the crime scene. Or a witness testimony may be rebutted with an argument from another scheme, such as an argument using camera evidence.

Above I said that argument schemes are classified according to their content. However, from a logical point of view they can be transformed into instances of logical inference rules by adding the connection between premises and conclusion as a conditional premise. Since as just explained most argument schemes are defeasible, this conditional will also be of a defeasible nature. For instance, the scheme from the position to know can be transformed into:

> *Person W says that p.*
> *Person W is in the position to know about p.*
> *Persons who are in the position to know usually speak the truth.*
> *Therefore (presumably), p.*

And the scheme from consequences can be transformed into

> *If A is brought about, then good (bad) consequences will (may plausibly) occur.*
> *If bringing about A will (may plausibly) result in good (bad) consequences then, other things being equal, A should (not) be brought about.*
> *Therefore (presumably), A should (not) be brought about.*

Thus both schemes become an instance of the *defeasible modus ponens* rule, which is formalised by many systems of nonmonotonic logic (for an overview see Horty, 2001):

> *P.*
> *If P then usually Q.*
> *Therefore (presumably), Q.*

This scheme can be attacked by arguing that there is an exception to the rule that *if P then usually Q* (for instance, *P & R* and *If P & R then usually not-Q*). However, the fact that such a logical reconstruction of argument schemes is possible should not be taken to mean that the notion of argument schemes has no point. The point is that the two argument schemes above are typical ways in which the inference scheme of *defeasible modus ponens* can be instantiated, each with their own typical ways of critical testing, and that they therefore merit independent study instead of merely as instances of this abstract inference scheme.

3. A FORMAL FRAMEWORK FOR REASONING WITH ARGUMENT SCHEMES

I will now briefly outline a formal framework for modelling reasoning with argument schemes. It especially draws on work of myself and others on argument-based approaches to so-called nonmonotonic reasoning. This outline also illustrates the remarks made in the introduction that (new) logical tools exist that can cope with uncertainty, disagreement and exceptions. The logical account of argument schemes outlined in this section was first proposed by Prakken *et al*. (2003). Independently, Verheij (2001) suggested a similar account in the context of his "Deflog" logic and developed it in Verheij (e.g. 2003c).

The fact that argument schemes leave room for counterarguments naturally points at an argument-based approach to the formalisation of reasoning with such schemes. To this end, so-called logics of defeasible argumentation are in principle very suitable. Such logics were developed in AI to formalise commonsense reasoning (for an overview, see Prakken and Vreeswijk, 2002) and they have been popular in AI & Law as a way to formalise the adversarial nature of legal argument (see e.g. Gordon, 1995; Prakken and Sartor, 1996; 1998; Bench-Capon, 2003; Verheij, 2003c). Essentially, such logics define arguments as trees of deductive and/or defeasible inferences (such as deductive or *defeasible modus ponens*) and they allow for attacks on the defeasible inference steps of an argument (such as attacking defeasible modus ponens by arguing that there is an exception to the rule). For present purposes the work of the philosopher and AI researcher John Pollock (e.g. 1995) is especially relevant, since he classifies defeasible inference rules according to general principles of epistemology and practical reasoning. He calls his defeasible inference rules *prima facie reasons*. One such reason is the perception principle:

Having a percept with content p is a prima facie reason to believe p.

Other *prima facie* reasons studied by Pollock are, for instance, the statistical syllogism (a probabilistic version of *defeasible modus ponens*) and principles of memory, induction and temporal persistence.

As in all systems of logic, in Pollock's system an argument can be attacked by denying one of its premises (in fact I am ignoring some technical complications here). In addition, Pollock allows arguments to be attacked in two ways. An argument can be *rebutted* with an argument for the opposite conclusion, and it can be *undercut* with an argument why a *prima facie* reason does not apply in the given circumstances. Intuitively, undercutting attacks do not argue that the attacked conclusion is false, but only that the conclusion is not sufficiently supported by its premises. Note that thus Toulmin's notion of a rebuttal in fact corresponds with Pollock's notion of an undercutter. An example of an undercutter is that if somebody perceives an object of red colour, then an undercutter of the perception principle is that the object is illuminated by a red light. For an example of an undercutter in a legal context, consider the argument "The suspect was at the murder scene at the time of the murder since witness John saw the suspect there" (applying the *prima facie* reason from perception; note that this reason can be applied only if it is first argued with a position-to-know argument that John saw this because he says that he saw it.). This argument is undercut by "It was too dark, so John could not have made a reliable identification" (applying an undercutter of the perception scheme).

How does Pollock's system relate to the argument-scheme approach? Essentially, the answer is that argument schemes can be formalised as prima facie reasons, that applications of schemes resulting in opposite conclusions can be regarded as rebuttals, while negative answers to critical questions about exceptional circumstances correspond to undercutters. The possibility that arguments can be defeated accounts for the defeasibility of argument schemes (recognised by Toulmin in his notion of a "rebuttal"), while the notion of undercutters allows for field-dependent standards for evaluating arguments, since each scheme has its own undercutters.

This is not all there is to say about argument-based logics. Given a set of conflicting arguments, it must be determined whether some of these arguments prevail. This is done in two steps. Firstly, standards can be used for comparing conflicting arguments to see which one is stronger than the other, if any. For instance, in case of two conflicting arguments from good consequences, one might (other things being equal) prefer the argument about the consequences that are judged the most important (e.g. in our example one might prefer the value of protecting the legal system against too much litigation over the value of fighting spam). Next, when all relations of relative strength between conflicting arguments are determined, the dialectical status of an argument is defined, to identify the defeasibly valid inferences. An important phenomenon here is *reinstatement*: suppose that argument *B* is stronger than argument *A* but that *B* is itself attacked by a stronger argument *C*; in that case *C* reinstates *A*. Consider again our rebutting arguments based on two conflicting witnesses (call them John and Bob). Even if we would prefer Bob's testimony given that, say, he is an adult and John a child, the argument using Bob's testimony may be undercut by a third argument *C* "Bob's testimony is unreliable since he has a strong reason to hate the suspect".

An intuitive way to define the defeasible validity of arguments is in the form of an *argument game* between a proponent and an opponent of an argument. Proponent starts the game with the argument to be tested and then the players take turns, each attacking the preceding argument. Opponent's arguments must be at least as strong as their targets while proponent's arguments must be stronger than their targets. A player has won if the other player has run out of moves. Now an argument *A* is defeasibly valid if the proponent has a winning strategy (in the game-theoretic sense) in a game beginning with *A*, i.e. if he can make the opponent run out of moves no matter how she plays.

In sum, argument-based logics conceive of argumentation as a tree of trees: individual arguments are trees in which statements are linked with each other by inference rules, and the dialectical status of arguments is determined by forming a dialectical tree of all possible ways to play an argument game for this argument. An argument is defeasibly valid if the proponent can choose his arguments in the dialectical tree in such a way that he always ends in a leaf with one of his own arguments.

4. A BRIEF SKETCH OF LEGAL PROBLEM SOLVING

Let us now take a closer look at legal reasoning, to identify some of the main argument schemes used in it. (The analysis in this section is not meant to be original; it merely serves as a basis for the further discussions.) I will take my starting point in the phenomenon of a statutory rule that has to be applied to the facts of a case. A typical legal rule is of the form

If Conditions then Legal consequence.

A legal rule connects the factual world with the normative world. Consider the following paraphrase of a legal rule from the Dutch Data Protection Act:

> *If personal data is reused without the subject's permission for means irreconcilable with the aims for which the data were collected, then the reuse is not allowed.*

Consider now the following (entirely real) case. Somebody claims, firstly, that Utrecht University has given the addresses of all their students without their permission to the local police in order to enable the police to start a campaign against bicycle theft (a very common criminal offence in Dutch university towns) by sending all students a letter to warn them that buying a stolen bicycle is itself a criminal offence. The person also claims that this was not allowed since this goal is irreconcilable with the aim for which these addresses were collected, viz. to manage the university administration with respect to their students. Now if such a case is taken to court, at least four questions have to be answered.

The first question is whether all these events indeed happened. This is a matter of evidence. It will be decided on the basis of the available 'sense data', such as, for instance, the letter of the police and further documentary evidence (e.g. a letter of request from the police to the university board) and/or witness testimonies (e.g. a statement by a police officer that they obtained the addresses from the University).

Suppose that on the basis of this evidence the court is convinced that the events indeed occurred. Then a second step has to be taken to classify the events under the conditions of the rule, viz. interpreting the rule's conditions to decide whether it subsumes the events as proven by the 'sense data'. A well-known problem here is that often there are no clear criteria for this decision, because of the vagueness or open-texturedness of the rule's conditions. This is the question to which most of the AI & Law research on legal argument is devoted.

Suppose now that the court has decided that the events as proven indeed classify as an instance of the rule's conditions, for example, on the grounds that preventing theft of bicycles has nothing to do with running the university administration. Then two further questions have to be answered. The first is whether the rule is legally valid, i.e. whether it is from a legally recognised source of law. This question must be answered independently of the facts of the case. This is different for the final question to be answered, viz. whether the rule must be applied to the case at hand, or whether there are circumstances that prevent the rule's application (e.g. a conflicting rule also applies, or applying the rule would be manifestly unjust or unreasonable). Perhaps the university could argue that the negative consequences for its students and employees are so small and that the problem of bicycle theft in Utrecht is so serious while no other measure has worked that applying the rule in this case is unreasonable. Perhaps the university can even cite a precedent where the rule was set aside in a similar case.

In sum, statutory rule application involves (at least) four steps: proving that the facts to which the rule is claimed to apply have indeed occurred (evidence), deciding that the facts as proven are subsumed under the rule's conditions (classification/

interpretation), deciding that the rule is valid law (rule validity) and deciding that the rule ought to be applied (rule application).

It should be noted that this four-step process is in general not sequential. For instance, the choice of facts to be proven is determined not only by the available evidence but also by the possible rules that may fit the facts once proven. If a university student in our example thinks that a claim on the basis of breach of contract is more promising than a claim on the basis of privacy violation, she might select different facts-to-be-proven, such as that a contract exists, and she might accordingly search for different items of evidence. Modelling this process of reinterpreting the facts to fit a certain rule has so far proven too hard for AI & Law research (cf. e.g. Branting, 2003).

Let us now have a closer look at each of the four steps, discussing some of the main argument schemes involved and some of the AI & Law research on modelling these schemes.

5. SCHEMES FOR REASONING ABOUT EVIDENCE

Until the 2003 Conference on AI & Law in Edinburgh, reasoning about evidence was a largely neglected area of AI & Law research. One exception was Lutomski (1989), who presented an early application of the argument-scheme approach to evidential reasoning at ICAIL-1989 in Vancouver. His system, which was implemented but, to my knowledge, never used in practice, was meant to assist an attorney in dealing with statistical evidence in the domain of employment discrimination. The system stored typical arguments based on statistics in a Toulmin structure, together with typical critical questions (for instance, "have all and only relevant data been collected?").

At ICAIL-2003 a considerable number of papers addressed the topic of evidential reasoning. One of them was my paper with Chris Reed and Douglas Walton (Prakken *et al.*, 2003), in which some first steps were taken to develop an explicit argument-scheme analysis of evidential reasoning. This work was further developed in Bex *et al.* (2003) and Prakken (2004). In this section I briefly summarize this work.

The basic idea is to formalise evidential argument schemes in John Pollock's framework (see Section 3) as *prima facie* reasons and to regard the critical questions attached to the schemes as pointers to undercutting defeaters. Some of Pollock's own reasons directly apply to evidential reasoning, such as the perception principle discussed in Section 3 and principles based on memory, induction and the statistical syllogism. The latter principle is Pollock's probabilistic version of *defeasible modus ponens*. I paraphrase it in a version without numbers:

> *'c is an F' and 'F's are usually G's' is a prima facie reason for 'c is a G'.*

This principle drives reasoning with empirical generalisations. The main undercutter is subproperty defeat, which captures exceptions to a generalisation:

> *'c is an F&H' and 'it is not the case that F&H's are usually G's' is an undercutter of the statistical syllogism.*

For example, an argument using "Dutch men usually like soccer" may be undercut by an argument using "It is not the case that Dutch men with a PhD degree usually like soccer". Applying both generalisations to the author of this paper results in a defeated argument that Henry likes soccer, although no argument for the opposite conclusion can be built.

In addition, Bex *et al.* (2003) discuss argument schemes for applying witness testimonies (essentially a variant of the scheme of arguments from the position to know), expert testimonies (another variant of this scheme) and temporal persistence. The latter reason can be used to argue from the fact that a fact *F* is true at a time *T1* that *F* is still true at a later time *T2,* if there is no evidence that *F* became false between *T1* and *T2*. Temporal persistence is an important aspect of evidential reasoning. For instance, in civil cases the usual way to prove that one has a legal right (e.g. ownership) is to prove that the right was created (e.g. by sale plus delivery). The other party must then usually prove later events that terminated the right. Prakken (2004) also discusses several ways to attack empirical generalisations that do not employ the subproperty defeater but that attack the sources of the generalisations (such as 'common sense' or 'science'). Bex *et al.* (2003) applies the approach of Prakken *et al.* (2003) to a small part of Kadane and Schum's (1996) reconstruction of the famous Sacco and Vanzetti case (viz. their Chart no. 4). The arguments that resulted from this reconstruction turned out to be based on Pollock's reasons from memory, perception, temporal persistence and the statistical syllogism and on the "position to know" scheme as reconstructed as an instance of the statistical syllogism (cf. the end of Section 2 above). The counterarguments that were not rebuttals could all be analysed as undercutters of these schemes.

This work is still preliminary. One direction of future research is attempting to formalise the schemes that practicing lawyers use in their cases. For common-law jurisdictions interesting sources of such schemes exist, viz. manuals for trial advocacy, such as Bergman (1997). By and large, this manual (implicitly) follows the argument-scheme approach, listing typical evidential arguments and typical ways to attack them. Another valuable research direction is capturing the available knowledge about the reliability of eyewitness testimonies in a knowledge-based system (cf. e.g. Bromby and Hall, 2002).

6. SCHEMES FOR RULE APPLICATION

Applying a legal rule to the facts is perhaps the central element of legal problem solving. One of the most elaborate AI & Law accounts of what it takes to apply a legal rule is given by Hage and Verheij in an application of their "reason-based logic" (see e.g. Hage, 1997; Verheij, 1996). Their central claim is that applying a legal rule involves much more than just applying the logical inference rule of *modus ponens* (whether defeasible or not). Their account of rule application can be briefly summarised as follows. First it must, of course, be determined whether the rule's conditions are satisfied (the interpretation question). If this hurdle is cleared (see also Section 7), it has to be determined whether the rule is legally valid (for instance, by arguing that it is from a certain legally recognised source). Then it has to be determined whether the rule's applicability is not excluded in the given case (for instance, the Dutch Data Protection Act does not apply to the police). If this is the case, it must finally be determined that the rule can be applied (i.e. that no conflicting rules or principles apply). Interestingly, while Hage and Verheij mainly discuss how rule application can be blocked by legal principles, the CABARET system of Skalak and Rissland (1992), only allows rule application to be blocked by citing a precedent where the rule was not applied (see also Section 8). CABARET's approach is based on Gardner's (1987) point of view that if a legal principle or value justifies setting aside a rule, this will usually have been decided in a precedent.

Both Hage and Verheij and others (such as Gordon, 1995; Prakken and Sartor, 1996) have shown how arguments about these issues can be formalised in nonmonotonic logics. Among other things, these techniques can model the fact that in legal practice the validity and applicability of legal rules is usually presumed, a presumption which can be overturned only by an argument that it does not hold. The details of the techniques used are beyond the scope of the present paper, except for the remark that they in fact formalise and further develop Toulmin's notion of a rebuttal; see Prakken and Sartor (2002) for an overview of the various techniques. For present purposes the main conclusion is that the argument scheme for rule application involves various steps and that each of these steps can be attacked in stereotypical ways.

7. SCHEMES FOR PRECEDENT-BASED REASONING

In the previous section I briefly mentioned that most AI & Law research on the modelling of legal argument concerns the interpretation of legal concepts. This is a very hard research problem, since often a large gap exists between the concrete nature of the facts of a case and the abstract nature of legal concepts. This induces legal uncertainty in (at least) two ways.

The first way is the existence of conflicting interpretation rules (based, for instance, on opinions of legal experts, on commonsense interpretations of natural language, or on the rationale of a precedent). For instance, one judge (or legal scholar) may say that email addresses are always personal data since when combined with an IP address of a computer they enable the identification of the user, while another judge or legal scholar may argue that an email address is not personal data if the left part of the address does not resemble the user's name. These are simply conflicting if-then rules, and any suitable technique from nonmonotonic logic can be used to formalise reasoning with such rules (see again the survey in Prakken and Sartor, 2002). This is essentially the approach taken by Gardner (1987). Her (implemented) system, which investigated whether a contract was created by offer and acceptance, stored possibly conflicting interpretation rules derived from legal experts, commonsense and case law, and applied these rules in *modus-ponens* style, using a priority mechanism to give precedence to case law rules over conflicting expert or commonsense rules.

However, sometimes interpreting a legal concept is not a matter of simply formulating or selecting a suitable interpretation rule. Sometimes all there is, is a set of different factors, possibly with different magnitudes, that somehow have to be weighed in each particular case to determine its outcome. A well-known AI & Law example is HYPO's modelling of the American precedent-based domain of trade secret law (Ashley, 1990). However, this phenomenon is not confined to common law jurisdictions. For instance, the Dutch Data Protection Act, when defining the concept of irreconcilable reuse of personal data, states five factors that "at least" have to be taken into account, without stating how they should be combined in a given case:

1. The similarity between the aim of the reuse and the original aim for which the data were collected;
2. The nature of the data involved;
3. The consequences of the reuse for the person to whom the data pertain;
4. The manner in which the data were obtained;
5. The extent to which suitable measures are taken to protect the privacy of the person to whom the data pertain.

In such 'factor-based' domains, a decision in a new case is often made by referring to past decisions, i.e. to precedents. However, as shown by e.g. Ashley (1990), the rationales of precedents often do not directly apply to a new case since different cases often have different constellations of the relevant factors and their values. Therefore, the rationales must often be adapted to fit the new case. A typical way to do so is to point at the similarities to a precedent with the desired outcome, to argue that because of these similarities the same decision should be made in the new case. And two typical ways to attack such an argument are, firstly, distinguishing the precedent by pointing at the differences and, secondly, pointing at a counterexample, i.e. at another precedent that is at least as similar and that has the opposite outcome. All this (and more) is modelled in the HYPO system. It is interesting to note that HYPO uses such precedent-based arguments in the context of an argument game (see Section 3 above) between a plaintiff and defendant in a certain case. In fact, the disputes thus generated by HYPO are at most three moves long (plaintiff-defendant-plaintiff) but nothing prevents a generalisation to disputes of arbitrary length. Thus

HYPO illustrates that reasoning with precedent-based argument schemes can be modelled as a logical argument game.

The HYPO system is now more than 15 years old and much research has followed it. Most of the subsequent research consists of enriching HYPO's scheme for representing precedents and exploiting the added expressiveness for generating new kinds of arguments and counterarguments. While HYPO just distinguishes sets of pro-plaintiff and pro-defendant factors and a simple decision (plaintiff won or defendant won), in the CATO system (Aleven, 1997) hierarchies of more and less abstract factors can be defined so that, for instance, a distinction can be downplayed by arguing that at a more abstract level the cases are still similar. Consider the following example in the context of Dutch privacy law, where one case is about a single sending of a warning letter by the police to students while another case (also entirely real) is about a single sending of a fund raising letter by the university to their students and employees. The cases could be distinguished at this factual level but the distinction could be downplayed by arguing that both cases are about one-time letters about matters of public interest. Others, e.g. Prakken (2002), Bench-Capon and Sartor (2003) and Atkinson *et al.* (2005) have tried to represent the values that are advanced or endangered by deciding a case in one way or another, resulting in the modelling of new, teleological argument schemes, related to Walton's argument scheme from consequences. For instance, in Prakken's (2002) approach a distinction can be emphasised by saying that because of the differences between the precedent and the current case, following the precedent in the current case will not advance the same values as were advanced by the precedent's outcome.

8. LIMITATIONS OF THE ARGUMENT SCHEME APPROACH

Concluding this brief overview of AI & Law research, we have seen that an argument-scheme approach to the modelling of legal argument is a useful supplement to a purely logic-based approach. In particular, an argument-scheme approach can model the different roles that the various statements in an argument can have and thus allow for different standards for evaluating arguments. We have also seen that much AI & Law research in fact employs the argument-scheme approach, although it usually is not presented as such.

Perhaps at this point the reader has the impression that all that modelling legal reasoning is about is modelling the relevant argument schemes and associated critical questions, and using them in a logical argument game as explained in Section 3. However, this would be a severe simplification of legal reasoning, and much interesting work in AI & Law goes beyond this simple approach.

For instance, CABARET (Skalak and Rissland, 1992) defines strategies and tactics for using and combining rule- and precedent-based schemes for certain dialectical purposes, such as confirming or discrediting a rule. Thus CABARET in fact defines rational strategies for playing an argument game. And part of the HYPO and CATO systems are mechanisms for interpreting existing material before using it in an argument. For instance, CATO still uses HYPO's simple case representation scheme but CATO's factor hierarchy can be used to generate different arguments about why a case was decided the way it was, by suggesting different 'paths' from the factors to the decision through the hierarchy. The idea of reinterpreting precedents was further developed by Loui and Norman (1995), who model five ways to reinterpret the (precedent-based) arguments of one's opponent in order to reveal new attacking points so that they can be better attacked. One way is to argue that in the precedent the outcome was based on choosing between two conflicting arguments, and that in the new case the winning argument does not apply since one of its premises is missing in the new case, so that the argument that was overruled in the precedent should now prevail. Finally, Bench-Capon and Sartor (2003) have addressed the problem of theory formation, by modelling constructors for theories that explain a certain set of precedent decisions. All this is very important work but it goes beyond the argument-scheme approach. Either it provides the material from which arguments can be built (CATO, Loui and Norman, Bench-Capon and Sartor) or it defines tactics and strategies for how an argument game can be played (CABARET, Loui and Norman).

9. AI & LAW AND TOULMIN

Finally, it is interesting to discuss how all this AI & Law work respects the observations of Toulmin (1958). To start with, the reader might wonder why AI & Law has not made more direct use of Toulmin's argument scheme. Here Toulmin's own reflections on his 1958 work are relevant. In the preface of his second edition (Toulmin, 2003) he expresses his surprise that many regarded his 1958 scheme as a proposal for a theory of argumentation while his aim had been different, viz. to criticise the view that all arguments can be put in deductive form. We should therefore not be surprised that subsequent research has replaced Toulmin's original single argument scheme with revised and more refined classifications of schemes. In line with this, it seems more worthwhile to investigate how AI & Law has taken the general lessons of Toulmin (1958) to heart than to discuss how AI & Law has used Toulmin's particular scheme.

In my opinion, AI & Law has taken to heart the following three of Toulmin's (1958) lessons. Firstly, Toulmin stressed that premises of an argument can have different roles. We have seen that AI & Law has identified many argument schemes with stereotypical roles for premises. Secondly, Toulmin stressed that everyday arguments are defeasible, which he captured in his notion of a rebuttal. It has been argued many times before that the field of nonmonotonic logic has formalised and further developed this aspect of Toulmin's scheme, and the logical account of reasoning with argument schemes outlined in Section 3 illustrates this point. Finally, Toulmin stressed that the standards for evaluating arguments are field-dependent.

His original argument scheme captured this by allowing for different backings of warrants. The account of Section 3 illustrates that it is possible to capture similar distinctions in a system of formal logic (be it a nonmonotonic logic), if the logic allows for the formalisation of different argument schemes, each with their own set of typical premises. Then the field-dependency of the standards can be captured by identifying the schemes employed in a certain field and formulating the undercutters that correspond to the critical questions of these schemes. Since different fields can have their own typical argumentation schemes, the criteria for evaluating arguments will thus differ for each field.

Concluding, while AI & Law has replaced Toulmin's original argument scheme with more refined analyses, it has done so fully within the spirit of Toulmin's challenge to develop an account of the validity of reasoning that applies to everyday argument. What is especially exciting is that AI & Law has shown that such an account can still be formal and computational.

Acknowledgements

An earlier version of this paper was presented at a session on Artificial Intelligence and Law of the International Congress of Comparative Cultures and Legal Systems, Mexico City, 9-14 February 2004. I am indebted to Trevor Bench-Capon and Thomas Gordon for illuminating discussions about the topic of this paper.

CHAPTER 16

CHRISTIAN KOCK

MULTIPLE WARRANTS IN PRACTICAL REASONING

Department of Media, Cognition, and Communication, University of Copenhagen, 2300 Copenhagen S., Denmark
E-mail: kock@hum.ku.dk

ABSTRACT: The concept of warrant reflects Toulmin's general insights that validity in reasoning comes in many forms, and that reasoning in most fields cannot possess the necessity and certainty that attract many thinkers to the 'Rationalist' paradigm. However, there is a scarcity of concepts in one part of Toulmin's theory of argument. While the pedagogical applications of Toulmin's model offer a fine-grained system of warrant types for propositions (sign warrants, causal warrants, etc.), they have only one category of warrant for practical claims (proposals for action) – the 'motivational' warrant. Fortunately, ancient rhetorical thinking can help us correct this insufficiency. For example, the author of the rhetorical textbook used by Alexander the Great proposed a typology of practical warrants. His approach highlights what I propose to call the 'multidimensionality', and hence what modern moral philosophers call the 'incommensurability' of warrants—the absence of a common measure allowing for a 'rational' balancing of conflicting warrants. The widespread occurrence of multidimensionality in practical argument lends support to Toulmin's general anti-rationalist view of reasoning. Moreover, while multidimensionality prevents 'rational' balancing, it legitimizes and even necessitates the use of rhetoric in practical reasoning.

KEYWORDS: Stephen E. Toulmin; warrant; argument model; rhetoric; practical reasoning; multidimensionality; incommensurability: Joseph Raz; Martha Nussbaum; Isaiah Berlin; Rhetorica ad Alexandrum

For over 50 years, Stephen Toulmin has consistently argued that validity in reasoning comes in many forms dependent on field, function, and context. Just as energetically, he has argued that most of all these forms of validity are different, each in its own way, from the paradigm set up in the 17th Century in the wake of Descartes' rationalism and Newton's universal mechanics—the paradigm in which validity in reasoning meant geometrical certainty, universality, and necessity. Toulmin's first book, *An Examination of the Place of Reason in Ethics* from 1950, was also his first to strike this theme. Here, he argued that what constitutes good reasoning in the field of ethics follows different rules than good reasoning in other fields, e.g., mathematics, physics, or aesthetics. Indeed, reasoning in ethics is at least two separate things, both distinct in function and form.

D. Hitchcock and B. Verheij (eds.), Arguing on the Toulmin Model: New Essays in Argument Analysis and Evaluation, 247–259.

Toulmin's fundamental insight into the multiform, non-universal and non-necessary nature of validity in reasoning was inspired, no doubt, by the later Wittgenstein's teaching at Cambridge. This insight, at any rate, is bound up with an unmistakably Wittgensteinian view of language, several years before the actual publication of the later Wittgenstein's thinking, as in this statement: 'Speech is no single-purpose tool. It is, in fact, more like a Boy Scout's knife' (p. 83).

The idea that good reasons are many kinds of things, while anticipated in 1950 and reiterated to this day, was stated in its most explicit form in *The Uses of Argument* in 1958. The idea underlies the famous 'argument model', whose centerpiece is the notion of 'warrant'. The main difference between Toulmin's model and traditional formal models, beginning with the Aristotelian syllogism, is that warrants are not premisses about the issue in question but assumptions we rely on about the kind and degree of argumentative weight we may assign to the grounds offered. And the underlying insight here is precisely that there are, depending on field and context, many kinds and degrees of argumentative weight.

So Toulmin's main point in introducing the notion of warrant is to highlight the variety of ways and degrees in which the step from grounds to claim may be justified. There is no one universal and timeless way in which reasoning takes place. From first to last, the main thrust of Toulmin's thinking about reasoning is against the assumed uniformity of warrants, and against the idea that reasoning in all fields of human reasoning proceeds from premisses to conclusions in a certain, deductive, and universal manner. The relations between grounds and claims in human reasoning may be warranted to varying degrees and in any number of ways; and, to adopt a phrase from Toulmin's latest book, *Return to Reason*, this is why we now need to abandon the dream which ties 'certainty, necessity, and rationality into one single philosophical package' (2001, pp. 205-206). This entrancing dream, the intellectual program of Modernity, as Toulmin calls it, sprang from seeds planted in the 17th Century in reaction against the rampant irrationality of the religious wars and in exultation over the triumphs of universalist, geometrical reasoning as demonstrated by Newton. Only in the last decades, Toulmin argues, are Western intellectuals waking up from this dream.

Further, one might say that Toulmin is above all concerned with the epistemology and history of science, and his master insight is that even science is not describable by the mathematical paradigm of certainty, necessity, and rationality. There is no unitary Royal Road to certain knowledge of what is the case.

The centrality of this concern in Toulmin's thinking perhaps explains the curiously subdued part played by practical reasoning, i.e., argumentation over political and social *action*, in most of his theoretical work. As shown by all his examples in *The Uses of Argument* (including the classic assertion 'Harry is a British subject'), Toulmin's theory of argumentation tends to dwell on arguments over propositions, i.e., claims about what is the case, and it rarely looks at claims regarding policy, i.e., proposals for action, whether in the political or the personal sphere. Toulmin's main concern is with the epistemology of reasoning and hence with those fields primarily where the Rationalist paradigm has in particular made its seductive bid for supremacy—e.g., the sciences, economics, and philosophical ethics. That a geometrical or Rationalist account of political argumentation is illusory is far more obvious to most, even philosophers.

The fact that Toulmin in *The Uses of Argument* dealt so cursorily with practical reasoning may explain why the pedagogical applications of Toulmin's model also have had little to say about it. Wayne Brockriede and Douglas Ehninger (1960) were the pioneers in using Toulmin's model as a pedagogical tool. It is from them that we have the most common typology of warrants. They base it on the Aristotelian concepts of logos, ethos, and pathos, respectively:

> (1) an arguer may carry data to claim by means of an assumption concerning the relationship existing among phenomena in the external world, (2) by means of an assumption concerning the quality of the source from which the data are derived; and (3) by means of an assumption concerning the inner drives, values, or aspirations which impel the behavior of those persons to whom the argument is addressed. (1960, p. 48)

Arguments of type (1) are called *substantive*, of type (2) *authoritative*, and of type (3) *motivational*. Of these main types, only substantive arguments are further subdivided—by means of a 'commonly recognized', six-fold ordering that includes arguments based on *cause*, *sign*, *generalization*, *parallel case*, *analogy*, and *classification*. No further distinctions are introduced concerning 'authoritative' or 'motivational' arguments. Instead, Brockriede and Ehninger cross-tabulate the types they have defined with a typology of claims based on the ancient *stasis* system, which renders four categories: *designative claims* (whether something is), *definitive claims* (what something is), *evaluative claims* (of what worth it is), and *advocative claims* (what course of action should be pursued). The resulting table shows, among other things, that 'motivational' arguments are applicable only to evaluative and advocative claims. Conversely, about the warrants that may be invoked in support of advocative claims, we only learn that they are motivational.

The net result is that in the applications of Toulmin's model to the teaching of argument there is a surprising shortage of concepts to describe warrants relevant to advocative claims, i.e., practical reasoning. The solitary term 'motivational' is little help, in fact it might mislead us into thinking that only *pathos* appeals have a role here, or even that their only role is here.

This omission is serious not only because it keeps us from understanding that there are different types of 'motivational' warrant. Even more, it is serious because if we do not understand and consider the variety of warrant types invoked in arguments about action, neither do we understand why these arguments so often involve the amount of controversy that they do, and why they necessarily involve rhetoric rather than geometrical demonstration.

This neglected reason for the 'rhetorical' rather than demonstrative or rational nature of practical argument has to do with what I have proposed to call the *multidimensionality* of such arguments (Kock, 2003). The main reason why we should distinguish between types of motivational warrants is that these belong to different *dimensions*; and this fact again explains why practical arguments are the province of rhetoric, not demonstration.

The point in choosing the term 'dimensions' for different types of warrant is that dimensions are not reducible or translatable to one another; for the understanding of a multidimensional complex, each dimension is necessary.

The issues that cluster around the notion of multidimensionality have been discussed by philosophers for the last 25 years or so under other headings such as *incommensurability* and *incomparability*.

Perhaps the most articulate and convincing spokesman of the notion of incommensurability in recent years has been Joseph Raz. He defines the condition of two reasons for action being 'incommensurate' in the following way:

> Two competing reasons (for specific actions on specific occasions) are incommensurate if and only if it is not true that one defeats the other, nor that they are of equal strength or stringency. They are incommensurate in strength, that is, reason does not determine which of them should be followed, not even that there is equal reason to follow either. When reasons are incommensurate, they are rendered optional, not because it is equally good (or right or reasonable) to choose the option supported by either reason, but because it is reasonable to choose either option (for both are supported by an undefeated reason) and it is not unreasonable or wrong to refrain from pursuing either option (for both are opposed by an undefeated reason). (2000, pp. 102-103)

Raz sees his position, including his belief in the widespread occurrence of incommensurate reasons, as an instantiation of what he calls a 'classical' stance, as against a 'rationalist' one. Interestingly, then, Raz joins Toulmin in the ranks of the self-styled anti-rationalists. There are, according to Raz, three crucial differences between the two conceptions:

> First, the rationalist conception regards reasons as requiring action, whereas the classical conception regards reasons as rendering options eligible. Second, the rationalist conception regards the agent's own desire as a reason, whereas the classical conception regards the will as an independent factor. Third, the classical conception presupposes the existence of widespread incommensurabilities of reasons for action, whereas the rationalist conception, if not committed to complete commensurability, is committed to the view that incommensurabilities are relatively rare anomalies. The three differences come down to a contrast between the rationalist view that generally rational choices and

> rational actions are determined by one's reasons or one's belief in reasons and are explained by them, as against the classical conception that regards typical choices and actions as determined by a will that is informed and constrained by reason but plays an autonomous role in action. (2000, pp. 47-48)

To simplify, what characterizes the 'rationalist' is his belief that reasons for one action are necessarily stronger than those for another, and hence 'require' or 'determine' that particular action. Raz, like Toulmin, is sceptical of such determinism. As we saw, the crucial insight in Toulmin is his rejection of necessity and certainty in human reasoning. And that, in Toulmin, goes for human reasoning of all kinds, not just for moral or practical reasoning.

But Raz, I suggest, has insights that might supplement Toulmin's. This is because he is more consistently concerned than Toulmin with the particular complexity inherent in practical reasoning as a result of the simultaneous presence of incommensurate reasons. To go a step further, I suggest that the main reason to reject necessity in practical reasoning is not the epistemic complexity of any individual single warrant (this is the issue that has always been Toulmin's central concern), but the multidimensionality and hence incommensurability (Raz's main concern) of the *set* of warrants that may be invoked in each case.

It should be noted here that the multidimensionality and incommensurability we are talking about here is not the same concept as the incommensurability that Thomas Kuhn pointed to in *The Structure of Scientific Revolutions* in 1962. What Kuhn meant was the inability of two competing epistemic paradigms to accommodate each other's viewpoints—the kind of incompatibility that, according to Kuhn, would precede a scientific revolution. Instead, what we are talking about here is the issue that has been a constant concern of moral philosophers at least since it was highlighted by James Griffin in the article 'Are There Incommensurable Values?' (Griffin, 1977). It is the problem that may arise for anyone facing a practical decision because a certain value or warrant argues for a certain action A, whereas another value or warrant, incommensurate with the first, argues against A. As a paradigmatic example, we might cite the British debate over fox-hunting, where the 'cruelty to animals' argument against this practice relies on a bio-ethical warrant, whereas pro-fox-hunting arguments rely on economic and social warrants about livelihood and 'hallowed traditions'. Or again, there is the ongoing debate in many countries over criminal legislation; here left-wingers rely on a social utility warrant when they point out that severe punishments are costly and do not prevent crime, whereas right-wingers tend to rely, among other things, on a 'justice' warrant in demanding that victims' sentiments be respected.

In each of these two exemplary issues, incommensurate warrants are at play. In both cases, both sides have arguments that carry *some* weight. The problem is one of deliberation—a word that etymologically means the weighing of alternatives against each other on a scale. To decide which alternative has the weightier arguments in its favour, one would seem to need one common measure or warrant that could put the grounds arguing for the two alternatives on a common denominator and calculate the net result in a deductive, i.e., necessary way. No such common denominator exists, and, as I have tried to show elsewhere (Kock, 2003), no matter how one would try to define it, it would involve arbitrariness and hence not be necessary.

Yet numerous philosophers beginning with Plato have felt the need for such a common measure and have suggested what it might be. Martha Nussbaum in *Love's Knowledge* has discussed the Greeks' need for such a 'value monism' that reduces all values, whether physical beauty, scientific truth or moral goodness, to one and the same, thus saving humans from facing the disturbing complexities of ethical and practical decisions. Toulmin himself has pointed to the distinctly mathematical inspiration behind Plato's epistemology and ethics (2001, pp. 18-19). Against the Platonic monism Nussbaum sets Aristotle's belief that each virtue and good is a particular thing, so that in regard to "honor, wisdom, and pleasure, just in respect of their goodness, the accounts are distinct and diverse" (*Nicomachean Ethics*, 1096b). But the monistic urge in philosophy has been strong, as witness, e.g., John Stuart Mill's belief in the necessity of setting up utility as an 'umpire' in the clashes between incompatible moral demands:

> If utility is the ultimate source of moral obligations, utility may be invoked to decide between them when their demands are incompatible. Though the application of the standard may be difficult, it is better than none at all: while in other systems, the moral laws all claiming independent authority, there is no common umpire entitled to interfere between them; their claims to precedence one over another rest on little better than sophistry, and unless determined, as they generally are, by the unacknowledged influence of considerations of utility, afford a free scope for the action of personal desires and partialities. (*Utilitarianism*, Ch. 2)

However, in spite of all such attempts, a growing number of moral philosophers nowadays are convinced, like Raz, that incommensurability and hence optional choices, rather than required choices, are a condition of our moral and practical life.

But what that means is only that there is no necessary, deductive and certain algorithm telling us what is required when a moral or practical choice has grounds that argue for different actions and invoke different warrants or values. However, the existence of incommensurability and optional choices does *not* mean that we do not weigh alternatives and make choices. We do make choices, and we do so because we have debated reasons and weighed them against each other. Only we do not have a common measure or umpire that will render an indisputable, algorithmic verdict, in the way that a pair of scales renders an objective, physical verdict as to which scale has most weight on it.

This description of the situation for anyone faced with a choice between incommensurate reasons is similar to the description faced by Chaïm Perelman when, in concluding his project *De la justice* in 1945, he realised that he could find no rationally binding justification of the values underlying human laws. When

Perelman found that such a value rationalism was not viable, he did not, as is well known, opt for complete scepticism or relativism. Instead, he acknowledged that people do in fact argue about the values they cannot prove. And he decided to investigate *how* they argue.

This, as is also well known, led to his 're-discovery' of rhetoric. Perelman and Toulmin, in the same year, both made a pioneering case for the claim that in most human matters no necessity or certainty is achievable, yet for precisely that reason argumentation is possible and indeed necessary. But they both concentrated on the uncertainty of our reliance on any single warrant or value on which we wish to step from grounds to claim; neither of them gave their full attention to the particular difficulty caused by the simultaneous presence of several incommensurate values or warrants.

It is a fact not often remarked upon that 1958, the year which saw the publication of both Perelman's and Toulmin's groundbreaking works on argumentation, was also the year in which Isaiah Berlin's thinking on value pluralism was first fully articulated in his inaugural lecture at Oxford, 'Two Concepts of Liberty'. As in the case of Toulmin, Berlin's seminal idea springs from a view that there is no single and universal criterion of meaningfulness for all domains of human knowledge or science. But more explicitly than Toulmin, Berlin takes his pluralist reasoning into the realm of ethics and politics, shaping (if not inventing) the notion of incommensurability.

Toulmin, of course, was not unaware of it. He had commented on the type of quandary it presents as early as in *Reason in Ethics*:

> Given two conflicting claims ... one has to weigh up, as well as one can, the risks involved in ignoring either, and choose 'the lesser of two evils.' Appeal to a single current principle, though the primary test of the rightness of an action, cannot therefore be relied upon as a universal test: where this fails, we are driven back upon our estimate of the probable consequences. (1950, p. 147)

Here we have Toulmin's characteristic rejection of the universal supremacy of any single principle, and we also have the understanding that a weighing must take place. The appeal to a principle and the estimate of consequences, by the way, are the two different types of reasoning in ethics that may both be valid, depending on the situation. But what Toulmin does not go into is the fact that the weighing of consequences will lack determinacy when the conflicting claims rest on warrants belonging to different dimensions, e.g., honour and utility in the guises of, respectively, bio-ethics and livelihood.

Many years later, Jonsen and Toulmin in *The Abuse of Casuistry* were acutely aware that humans may face moral problems "beyond the reach of universal principles and general theories, and require them to strike equitable balances between varied considerations in ways relevant to the details of each particular set of circumstances" (1988, p. 306). "At any stage in the development of a people and culture, experience brings them to adopt certain general opinions about the *scope*, *force*, and *relative priority* of different kinds of moral considerations" (p. 325). The crucial terms here, seen from our angle, are 'equitable balances' and 'relative priority'. Similarly, as one of the main reasons for the difficulty of applying concepts 'outwardly' to the world of concrete objects, Jonsen and Toulmin mention that "parallel arguments often point to different presumptions the practical implications of which have to be reconciled" (p. 327). However, even in this work of practical ethics, by far the most attention is given to the other main reason that mere principles are insufficient, the epistemic reason, i.e., the consideration that "presumptive conclusions can have 'certitude' only when the relevance of the concepts or terms involved is not in doubt" (p. 327).

This epistemic difficulty militating against determinism in reasoning clearly is and always was Toulmin's main concern. The paradoxical requirement in practical decisions to strike a balance between warrants lacking a common measure is one that he does not explore in similar depth. In *An Introduction to Reasoning*, the textbook that Toulmin co-authored with Rieke and Janik (1979), we find fine-grained distinctions between warrant types for factual propositions, very similar to those in Brockriede and Ehninger (sign warrants, causal warrants, etc.), but again there is no comparable attempt to distinguish between warrants for practical (advocative) claims.

Ancient rhetoric, however, had more to offer here. From its beginning in so-called sophistic teaching, rhetoric was centrally concerned with argument about action. We need only go to what is probably the very oldest extant textbook on rhetoric in the West, the *Rhetorica ad Alexandrum*, a work whose author—one Anaximenes—we do not know, but which is believed to have been written for the rhetorical training of the young Alexander the Great.

This book has had a strange fortune in the history of rhetoric. We do not know whether young Alexander actually used it, but we know that it has been either ignored or roundly condemned by commentators ever since. The classicist Manfred Fuhrmann, for one, who edited a modern text of this work, has also written an introduction to classical rhetoric in which he calls it 'radically relativistic', condemning its 'barefaced opportunism' and 'eely routine' (1984, p. 29). The kind of teaching that brings down this abuse on the author's head is exemplified in the following enumeration:

> He who persuades must show that those things to which he exhorts are just, lawful, expedient, honourable, pleasant, and easy of accomplishment. Failing that, when he is exhorting to that which is difficult, he must show that it is practicable and that its execution is necessary … It is for these qualities … that those who seek to persuade or dissuade must look. (1421b)

What hostile critics appear to feel about such advice is that the author is telling us to claim indiscriminately that any proposal we advocate is *all* these things. However, we may also read 'Anaximenes' as saying that the following are the warrants which are in fact invoked in arguing about actions. Such actions—so arguments might go—should be executed because they are one or more of the following:

1. just (*dikaia*)
2. lawful (*nomima*)
3. expedient (*sympheronta*)
4. honourable (*kala*) (a better translation than Rackham's might be 'noble')
5. pleasant (*hēdea*)
6. easy of accomplishment (*rhaidia*)

Where difficult actions are concerned, we may further invoke the warrants that they are

1. practicable (*dynata*) and
2. necessary (*anankaia*).

Suddenly, it becomes clear that what 'Anaximenes' presents is an inventory of the warrants available for practical reasoning. In arguing over practical issues, people essentially invoke warrants found in this list. They do so because they have to. What alternatives can we cite that do not really fall under one of these headings? On the other hand, can any items be stricken from the list? Even if we did made minor corrections of that kind, we still have here a helpful synopsis of the *dimensions* of practical reasoning. The point about dimensions, please recall, is that they are all necessary; they are not reducible or translatable to one another. An action may be 'honourable' but not very 'expedient'; it may be 'just', but not 'lawful'; etc. Even disregarding the epistemic uncertainty of applying these attributes 'outwardly' to the world of concrete objects, we are still faced with the second difficulty: that of weighing incommensurate warrants on the same scale, for example, just so much 'honour' against so much 'expediency'. We lack the common measure that will enable us to do this with 'certainty, necessity, and rationality'.

This second difficulty undercutting rationality in practical reasoning has, I suggest, only had passing attention in Toulmin's work. It is this kind of 'incommensurability' that Raz and other moral philosophers have explored. But while Raz can thus be said to take his analysis a step further than Toulmin, he too stops short. It is not enough to say that two competing courses of action, relying on incommensurate reasons, are 'optional'. It is true that we cannot weigh them with certainty and necessity, as the rationalist would; but we humans *do* weigh such options and make choices anyway.

Perelman and 'Anaximenes' are among the thinkers who have realized how we do that. Since a number of incommensurate warrants may be invoked, and since there is no logical or philosophical way to measure which one takes carries most weight in any given case, we are left with the resources of rhetoric to help us decide, or—if that is our aim—to win the adherence of others for a given choice. We cannot measure. 'Demonstration', to use Perelman's term, is not applicable; but rhetoric is.

Among the resources we can use to help us weigh alternatives whose weight cannot be measured are, according to 'Anaximenes', *analogies*, *opposites*, and *examples*. By emphasizing likenesses and/or differences between the action under consideration and other, paradigmatic ones, we may bring ourselves and others to decide that the reasons arguing for that action are weightier than those arguing against.

Essentially, the resources we are directed to here are the same that Perelman and Olbrechts-Tyteca found in the empirical project which became *The New Rhetoric*. Moreover, these resources constitute the method of 'casuistry' which Jonsen and Toulmin explored in their book, and which Toulmin has in effect advocated from the start of his career. Instead of universal principles, casuistry deals in analogy or 'parallel arguments': Practical arguments, they state,

> draw on the outcomes of previous experience, carrying over the procedures used to resolve earlier problems and reapplying them in new problematic situations ... the facts of the present case define the *grounds* on which any resolution must be based; the general considerations that carried weight in similar situations provide the *warrants* that help settle future cases...[and] so the resolution of any problem holds good *presumptively*; its strength depends on the *similarities* between the present case and the precedents; and its soundness can be challenged in situations that are recognized as *exceptional*. (1988, p. 35)

By 1988, Jonsen and Toulmin had realized that argumentation as they see it and rhetoric are largely synonymous terms: "Practical moral reasoning today still fits the patterns of topical (or 'rhetorical') argumentation better than it does those of formal (or 'geometrical') demonstration" (p. 326). But this was not always Toulmin's understanding of what the term 'rhetoric' means. As a philosopher, he seems to have been taught that rhetoric is the strategic effort to win compliance in one's audience by any means; in *Reason in Ethics* the phrase 'rhetorical force' refers to properties which are "useful in forwarding ... particular policies" (1950, p. 195). Only later does the insight gradually develop in Toulmin's writings that rhetoric is more than the strategic promotion of one's interests; that in fact rhetoric is legitimate and necessary in debating ethical and deliberative issues.

One important reason why this is so, and one which—had he considered it—might have led Toulmin to embrace the term rhetoric and the rhetorical tradition earlier, is precisely the multidimensionality of the warrants invoked in practical argumentation and the resultant lack of a common measure to help us decide which is the weightiest. Since no logical inference or calculation can tell us how incommensurate dimensions should be weighted in deliberation, the result is that two opposite standpoints on a deliberative issue may both be legitimate (or 'optional', as Raz has it); and this again implies that the use of rhetoric to win adherence for one's standpoint becomes not only legitimate but necessary.

Rhetoric comes into the picture not just because people want to sway and persuade each other but because people may legitimately have different views of the same matter and prefer different courses of action. When people use rhetoric to try to win each other's adherence, they do so not just because they want others to comply at any cost (this is the 'strategic' definition of rhetoric), but because they may be legitimately convinced that the view they represent is not only an *optional* one but the *preferable* one; and their opponents may have the same legitimacy in thinking likewise of *their* standpoint. So rhetoric exists because it may be legitimate to hold several different views on a matter and because those holding each of these views may legitimately wish to win the adherence of the others.

Philosophers have been slow to acknowledge, let alone explain, that this is so. Why it is so has to do, as I have tried to show, with multidimensionality. This concept implies 1) that different warrants may be invoked in a debate which are incommensurate with each other; and 2) that different people, or the same person at two different times, may assign different weights to arguments belonging to different dimensions.

Both these facts, again, have to do with the fact that on the one hand there is no rational, necessary and certain way to weigh arguments invoking incommensurate warrants on the same scale; on the other hand people who have to make practical decisions have to weigh them on the same scale somehow. Rhetoric helps them do this, but not in a rational way, i.e., not in a way that can pretend to be necessary and certain. So the existence of rhetoric helps explain how there can be, on the one hand, choices where no one alternative is required, yet where some people, on reasoning, find one alternative preferable and some the other.

This kind of situation is well known to us all, and the more thoughtful textbooks on argumentation are aware of it as well:

> In many ethical judgments, you and your audience might agree on certain values, but not necessarily rank them in the same way. ... most of the time weighting will be the crucial issue for your audience. People are quite likely to agree about the relevance of a set of criteria, but they often disagree about which particular ones are most important in a given situation. (Fahnestock and Secor, 2004, p. 249)

Rhetorical theory and textbooks ever since antiquity have been acutely aware of the same fact. As the *Rhetorica ad Alexandrum* exemplifies, they have been aware of the incommensurate warrants in practical argumentation, so that they can help us correct this scarcity of concepts in one part of Toulmin's system. Also, they are aware of the means we still have of weighing alternatives, including the topical tools of similarities, differences, and paradigmatic examples, as well as the numerous devices of 'amplification' and 'diminution', with the aid of which we may add to or detract from the weight of any given argument.

Such 'sophistic' argumentation theory antagonized Plato and is still by many seen as cynical, relativist and opportunist. Indeed, some of the major classical rhetoricians, including Aristotle, did what they could to reduce the warrants invoked in practical argumentation to one single dimension (that of expediency, *sumpheron*, cf. *Rhetoric*, 1358b).

However, the earliest rhetorical theorists, I suggest, had it right. They knew that practical reasoning has several dimensions, which is why decisions cannot be found on a merely rationalist basis. For example, they would have dismissed current pretensions to 'prioritize' objectively between policies for the improvement of the world's predicament on the basis of the single warrant of economic cost-benefit. Yet they did point to resources for reason to use where rationality fails. The type of multidimensional theory represented by the *Rhetorica ad Alexandrum* has, even now, a realism and practical applicability which argumentation theory, along Toulmin's lines or otherwise, would do well to attend to.

So practical reasoning in situations characterized by multidimensionality and incommensurability becomes the realm of rhetoric? Some might object here that while the displacement of the rationalist paradigm with its demand for universal and necessary forms of argument does open space for a conception of rhetoric as a legitimate mode of ethical and political inquiry, it also tempts rhetoricians to rush too quickly into this space and lay claim to occupy more of it than they can justify. Instead of making the strong claims that the practical reason is the province of rhetoric and that rhetoric is necessary to it, should we not make the more modest and more easily sustained claim that rhetoric is one legitimate dimension of practical reason? Ethics, for one, would certainly seem to be another.

A reply to this concern would be that while ethical considerations and arguments undeniably are and should be involved in practical reasoning, including policy debates, that still does not imply that the part played by rhetoric is, by the same token, diminished. The two categories are not mutually exclusive. That is to say, we might perhaps define them so that they are; but such a definition would be, as far as rhetoric is concerned, misleading. Rhetoric, I suggest, should be understood as the totality of resources at the disposal of arguers who wish to increase adherence to their standpoint in debates where choices are, as Raz has it, 'optional'. They are optional because individuals may legitimately opt for one or the other.

Philosophy ends here, because philosophy is, in its very nature, about finding solutions that hold with equal validity for all. Ethics, as a branch of philosophy, is about answering ethical questions in ways that hold equally for all.

Rhetoric, by contrast, is not about finding answers that hold equally for all. And rhetoric is not complementary to ethics (which would make the two mutually exclusive). Rather, rhetoric can be defined as the means we have to influence the standpoints of *individuals* on 'optional' issues. They are usually optional because there is incommensurability involved. Ethical considerations may indeed enter into the rhetorical efforts of one individual to win the adherence of others, perhaps in conflict with other ethical considerations, or with considerations of, say, expediency. The point is that on optional issues, individuals may opt differently, and be differently influenced, and even be moved to change their minds—individually. All this is what rhetoric is there to do. Philosophy can only state that incommensurability and the resultant optional issues exist—a rather recent philosophical insight that many philosophers still hotly deny, possibly because it seems to leave them at a dead end.

But the dead end is only apparent, an appearance caused by the philosophical presumption to find solutions holding equally for all. The road sign at this point might read, 'Incommensurability ahead'. Beyond it is the realm of rhetoric. We can bring all our reasonings there, including ethics. Thanks to rhetoric, we are not, even in that realm, stuck with unsolvable dilemmas. We may actually find solutions to the quandaries we meet, and with rhetoric we can perhaps win the adherence of other individuals for those solutions; but because of incommensurability, the adherence of individuals is all that our reasoning may achieve.

CHAPTER 17

TXETXU AUSÍN

THE QUEST FOR RATIONALISM WITHOUT DOGMAS IN LEIBNIZ AND TOULMIN

Institute of Philosophy, Spanish National Research Council CSIC, Pinar 25, 28006 Madrid, Spain
E-mail: ausin@ifs.csic.es

ABSTRACT: The aim of this paper is to connect Leibniz's and Toulmin's conceptions about practical and deliberative rationality. When trying to rationally justify contingent judgments Leibniz, like Toulmin, defends a weighing argumentative method. Thus, in Leibniz we can discern the balance between the legitimate demands of formal models of rationality and the lessons of a practice "situated" on a historical, social, and evaluative context (*theoria cum praxi*).

KEYWORDS: Leibniz; Stephen E. Toulmin; reasonableness; scales of reason; *theoria cum praxi*

1. INTRODUCTION

Usually, G.W. Leibniz has been considered as a typical example of rationalist thinkers of the 17th century, joined to 'new science' and deep trust in human reason, as if one of his main concerns in philosophy was to oppose the epistemology of Locke with a system where all knowledge would be deduced *a priori* from first principles. 'Nothing happens without a sufficient reason', as the well-known principle of his philosophy says. This is also Toulmin's first approach to the philosopher of Leipzig, as pointed out, for example, in his excellent book *Cosmopolis* (1990 [2001]). Indeed, the few references Stephen Toulmin makes to Leibniz in his classic *The Uses of Argument* (1958/2003) are to Leibniz as a representative of the modern view of logic he was there opposing, where logic is represented as a calculus in which the validity of arguments is decided solely formally. However, Leibniz was far from the classical model of rationalist, à la Descartes, but a rationalist with a lot of tones and shades. Stephen Toulmin himself regards Leibniz as what could be called a 'qualified rationalist':

> . . . although he continued to advocate Unity as a general program, Leibniz saw the world as made up of multiple levels of units: not all of them had the same theoretical status as 'particles' in Newton's dynamics. Instead, he recognized differences of

D. Hitchcock and B. Verheij (eds.), Arguing on the Toulmin Model: New Essays in Argument Analysis and Evaluation, 261–272.

of 'monads' within his overall System of the World. (Toulmin, 2001[2003], p. 136)

In Leibniz, we cannot establish a clear-cut distinction between his life and his public activities, on the one hand, and his thought and his philosophical reflections, on the other. This issue has been also remarked on by Toulmin, since Leibniz's 'rationalist dream' is the outcome of an age characterized by theological disputes, religious wars, and political upheavals (Toulmin, 1990[2001], pp. 145 ff.).

At this point it is beneficial to recall that, in Leibnizian thought, theory and praxis are strongly tied, and mutually co-involved, according to his well-known motto 'theoria cum praxi'. This means that the theoretical reason is guided by the necessities of the practical reason in the same way that the practical reason clarifies its goals with the developments and the imperatives of the theoretical reason. That is the case with Toulmin's philosophical standpoints too (Toulmin, 2001[2003], p. 247).

Furthermore, the universe of human praxis is headed by the *factum* of the contingent, those that could be in another way;[1] that is, the realm of liberty, morals, politics and, in sum, of history. Starting from Aristotelian practical philosophy, Leibniz clearly objects to determinism, as pointed out in his criticism of Spinoza's *Ethics*: 'If all things exist necessarily ... moral philosophy would be destroyed'. In short, contingency is not only a metaphysical principle but also basically a moral one, since it makes possible the freedom of individuals and, thus, the non-forecast of their actions. In Leibniz's opinion, human action is not only free but is expressed in a great variety of ways (pluralism), and human history, individual and social, is up to it, constituting the contingent *par excellence*.[2] Besides, this sphere of the contingent, of free human action, manifested in history, is characterized by conflict, contradiction of interests, and difference. This complex approach to reality is what Leibnizian rationalism copes with.

In the following, I present some of the key elements of Leibniz's conceptions about practical and deliberative rationality and their connection to Toulmin's ones. Both uphold a type of rationality in which principles must be joined to the particular and contingent, to what is characteristic of the case and its circumstances. That is, it is a 'situated' rationality, namely, a historical one, linked to differing interests and values, and bonded to practice and experience (*reasonableness* in Toulmin's terms).

---

[1] This Leibnizian support of contingency occurs when theological controversies about free will and predestination are changing into polemics on liberty and natural determinism. Scientific developments revealed a universe tied to general laws that allow forecasting of natural facts. So, if a human being is a part of the natural world, his actions have to be subject to the same causal determinism. Leibniz adopts mechanicism, up to a point, but strongly rejects absolute determinism in any form.

[2] Leibniz affirms, criticizing art. 6 of Descartes' *Principia*: "We have free will not when we perceive, but when we act" (GP IV, 357).

10. THE MAXIM PROJECT OF LEIBNIZ

Faced with the challenge of scepticism, Leibniz suggests a two-way solution. The first and best known is a rigorous and strict formalization of thought, which Fernando Gil calls 'the maxim project'. It involves the idea of a *Characteristica univeralis*, a conceptual logic—which was later to inspire Frege's *Begriffsschrift*—that would allow for only one valid solution from the premises under consideration: "instead of discussing, let's calculate".[3] It is the working model for geometry and arithmetic; and the method of deductive logic, which is the art of reason in the domain of the necessary—where principles, such as that of non-contradiction, applied to the possible or to essences, work (*NN.EE.* I, ch. 1, §5; *Monadology* 31; *Theodicy* 44, 169). It is also the dream of Rationalism, which aspires to a universal method, a perfect language and a unitary system of Nature, with the model of mathematics as its starting point:

> But there are also other cases in which a judge of controversies other than reason is equally unnecessary, since truth can be clearly found by precise paths and commonly known ways, as it is the case with geometric and arithmetical issues about the magnitude of things. Certainly, there is no need of a judge in calculus; it is enough to carefully enumerate without omitting anything for the conclusion to follow necessarily, in all evidence, as in the case of Geometry.[4]

In this approach, the search for a universal and perfect language plays a prominent role, as Toulmin has highlighted in his works. That is, the development of a universal language by means of symbols and words that drive reason and where mistakes are merely faults of calculation.

However, this research was not original to Leibniz, since there was an important tradition of that kind. We must not forget Toulmin's viewpoint that Leibniz was a product of his age. In fact, Leibniz knew the works of the forerunners in the search for a perfect language: Ramon Llull, John Dee, Pedro Bermudo, George Dalgarno, Atanasio Kircher or John Wilkins (Eco, 1993). In Leibniz, the project of a universal or rational language would have the advantage that the symbol, the *Characteristica*, does not only represent directly ideas and cognitive contents (like Egyptian ideograms or Chinese writing), but allows reasoning in a way similar to arithmetical calculation: 'Cum Deus calculate et cogitationem exercet, fit mundus'.[5]

---

[3] In this regard, Leibniz shows himself to be the clearest precursor of modern formal logic, which becomes the dominant conception in many contemporary readings of this philosopher. On the one hand, the idea of a *Characteristica universalis* is a precedent of symbolic logic; and, on the other, his *ratiocinator* calculus is a precedent of contemporary conceptions of mathematic-algebraic logic.

[4] *Brief commentaries on the judge of controversies or the balance of reason and norm of the text* § 58 (A, VI, 1).

[5] *Dialogue de la connexion entre les mots et les choses*, 1677 (A VI, 4, 22).

As pointed out by Marcelo Dascal, the cognitive role of language as an instrument of reason is a precedent of modern theses about the identification of language and thought (Fodor, Dretske). Clearly, Leibniz affirms that thought is basically symbolic (Dascal, 1978; 1987; Rutherford, 1995).

Nevertheless, Leibniz recognizes the great gnoseological and moral value of natural languages as proven by his important etymological studies. One of the principles of his thought is the positive appraisal of diversity and plurality—as commented further on.

As remarked by Concha Roldán in her excellent work 'Pluralité des langues et éthique universelle' (2005), the plurality of languages is not only unavoidable but necessary from the perspective of the ethical Leibnizian project which wants to show the complexity and metaphysical richness of individuals.

Thus, from a pluralist Leibnizian perspective, the diversity of natural languages is richness, with an enormous value, and the *Characteristica* would be an auxiliary language in order to help our comprehension of the world and our understanding of others[6]: "... cuius auxilio diversae nationes animi sensa comunicare et quae scripsit alter in sua quisque lingua legere queat ..."[7]

Summarizing, the 'maxim project' does not finish Leibnizian 'theoria cum praxi'. Specifically, the formal-calculistic model is clearly insufficient for contingent matters (moral, juridical, political, etc.), and Leibniz himself acknowledges this:

> Thus the form of disputation has been shown to be necessary in necessary matters where eternal truths occur but not in contingent matters where the most probable must be chosen ... For the common saying is true enough, *rationes non esse numerandas sed ponderandas*; arguments are not to be counted but weighed.[8]

According to Leibniz, there are two realms of truths, that of necessary truths and that of contingent truths. And since we humans have no access to the complete individual notions of substances, as Rescher (2003, p. 117) explains, we therefore "cannot penetrate the realm of contingent fact by means of calculation and reasoning from general principles . . . Reasoning alone cannot carry us beyond the sphere of the necessary truths". So we are constrained to adopt "the conjectural method a priori", which "proceeds by hypotheses, assuming certain causes, perhaps without proof, and showing that the things which actually happen follow from these assumptions".[9]

---

[6] *La place d'autrui* principle is a main rule of Leibnizian practical reason: put yourself in the place of others (*La place d'autrui*, 1679. A VI, 3, 903904). Some authors like Dale Jacquette (2005) and Wouter H. Slob (2005) have explored the crucial role of the others' position in argumentation on the grounds that considering both sides of any issue makes one more likely to arrive at the truth and that Toulmin's understanding of the rebuttal suggests a way to incorporate such a substantial role of the opponent.

[7] *De numeris characteristicis ad linguam universalem constituendam* (A VI, 4, 264).

[8] *Letter to Gabriel Wagner on the value of logic*, 1696 (L 467).

[9] *De Elementis Physicae*, 1678 (L 283).

11. LEIBNIZIAN MINIMAL METHOD

In Leibniz we also find a 'minimal method' when trying to rationally justify contingent judgments. In a passage quoted by Rescher (2003, p. 121), Leibniz likens this method to deciphering a cryptograph:

> A hypothesis of this kind is like the key to a cryptograph, and the simpler it is, and the greater the number of events that can be explained by it, the more probable it is. But just as it is possible to write a letter intentionally so that it can be understood by means of several different keys, of which only one is the true one, so the same effect can have several causes. Hence no firm demonstration can be made from the success of hypotheses.[10]

As pointed out by Ezequiel de Olaso (1995), Leibniz was the philosopher of diversity, pluralism and tolerance, and always considered controversies positively, on the condition that they would be regulated by means of a method. It seems without a doubt that debate and controversy are basic, extended, and typical ways of human interaction. Controversies are a type of polemics that holds an intermediate position between discussion and dispute, but which should not be reduced to mere unsolvable conflicts of preferences.

At this point a dialogic perspective of analysis is required; one that does not unleash wild rhetoric, and one that serves to justify rationality in contingent judgments, especially in situations of conflict—the method mentioned by Olaso. There is no doubt that dialogue (among churches, states, philosophers, and cultures) is a key to Leibniz's theoretical and practical enterprises—the so-called Leibnizian 'linguistic turn'. Similarly, contemporary debate about moral problems dealing with scientific-technical research, with professions, with the clash among cultures, etc. stirs up concern about practice, moving us away from abstract moral theories and closer to the case method. This issue approximates Leibniz to Jonsen and Toulmin's theses about 'new casuistry' (Jonsen and Toulmin 1988), a kind of moral reasoning related to circumstances and situations, as a reaction against the oversimplification of the moral realm and against the 'tyranny of principles' (Toulmin, 1981). They reject 'moral geometry' but rather prefer 'practical wisdom'. The new casuistry does not offer 'prescriptions' or 'recipes' but upholds the necessity of analysis, weighing and valuation of circumstances; it is, basically, 'prudent'. In the case of Leibniz, justice, for example, is inconceivable apart from prudence. Justice, in this sense, would be no more than a form of prudence that avoids hurting others and fosters the Common Good (the basic principle of his ethical-political thought).[11]

So, neither a mechanical application of principles nor abandonment to passions in judgment serves as a valid instrument for this type of analysis. Leibnizian practical reasoning—and also that of Jonsen and Toulmin—is rather a proposal, like

---

[10] *De Elementis Physicae*, 1678 (L 283).
[11] *Elementa Juris Naturalis* (A VI, 1, 459-465; L 134, 137).

Aristotle's *phronesis*, which is placed on an intermediate or pragmatic level, i.e., non-rigid forms of reasoning which are crucial in most of Leibniz's theoretical and practical enterprises, without a clear line between them:

1. The importance of presumption and interpretation in the legal domain.
2. The gradualist approach to religious differences and the search for a re-unification of the churches (Irenism).
3. The idea of 'defensibility' (reasonableness) in *Theodicy* versus naïve Lutheran literalism.
4. The understanding of science as a guided, cooperative and institutionalized activity.
5. Ethical consequentialism, close to some utilitarian approaches.
6. Political pragmatism, etc.

Therefore, Leibniz does not consider a mere calculistic method (the mere sum of probabilities, for example)[12] to be a suitable instrument for the analysis of contingent matters—in the way that classical deductive logic is for necessary things.

Thus Leibniz would be an example of a 'flexible rationalist', who has abandoned an arrogant and totalitarian approach to reason. In Leibniz, we can discern, using Toulmin's terms, the balance between the legitimate demands of formal models of rationality and the lessons of a practice 'situated' in a historical, social and evaluative context.

This weighing 'method' would include:

1. rules of a heuristic type (such as presumptions);[13]
2. the determination of the *status quaestionis* in an argumentative process;
3. paying attention to the descriptive terms of the other's position;
4. considering the epistemic reliability of premises;

---

[12] There is a tension, even some confusion, in Leibniz between the concept of probability, linked to juridical tools as presumption, and the notion of prudence. The former has an algorithmic character, as a mathematical model, to deal with uncertainty; whereas the latter has more to do with the relational and gradual ideas of proportionality and similarity. Somehow, prudence would be characterized by 'utility', weighed with probability, without being reduced to it.

[13] Like any other type of inference, a presumption leads us from a certain amount of already proven, or at least accepted, premises to a conclusion, which constitutes the assumed fact. What is characteristic of presumptions is that we reach certain conclusions from certain factual information for want of other data, but we have the possibility to modify the conclusion if more information is provided. That is to say, it involves a dispensable or revisable conclusion, which is the outcome of a weakened type of inference (in which the deductive property of monotonicity does not appear). Presumptions are, in general, fundamentally, although not exclusively, based on a probability or normality judgment that is the outcome of experience, upon the relation between certain fact (trace-fact or base-fact) and a fact that is taken to be true (presumptive fact).

5. assessing the relevance of the elements of discourse;[14]
6. taking into account analogies and comparisons;
7. specifying the burden of proof.

This picture of an argumentative weighing method fits with Toulmin's criticism—in *The Uses of Argument*—of considering arguments as merely formal-deductive inferences, and his reaction against narrow and classical logical approaches to ordinary reasoning. This way we can make *reasonable*, although *defeasible*, decisions, which are non-definite and non-stringent. Thus, returning to the question in relation to moral dilemmas or conflicts: given certain circumstances (with specific particular elements, with different agents involved), the choice at a particular moment of a certain precept or principle over another does not cancel the one being rejected. Even if it weakens it, the now rejected norm can be adopted under different circumstances.[15] In other words, the non-applied norm still holds a degree of normativity that will fade only insofar as it is not being used or in dialectical relation with its use or lack of use in ethical practice—inviting a gradualist analysis of moral principles and concepts.

In Leibniz's work, the 'scales of reason' metaphor emerges as the essential weighing element for rational argumentation in the domain of the contingent, praxis, and the particular case; scales which, as Dascal says, would no longer have a digital or metrical character (the algorithmic project), but would *also* have a dialectic and comparative character. We say 'also' because, for Leibniz, these two projects are not incompatible or in opposition. Rather, they are complementary.[16] This is precisely Toulmin's central thesis in *Return to Reason*; namely, to restore the balance between the rationalist ideal of necessity and certainty, on the one hand, and ordinary practice and experience, on the other. It would involve a re-equilibrium between rhetoric and logic, the case and moral theory (Toulmin 2001[2003], pp. 250-251).

Unlike the calculistic model (the classic logical-deductive one), which gives rise to definitive and stringent conclusions (i.e., certainties), the weighing model, as represented by the scales of reason, would not provide absolute certainties. In this approach there is a weighing of hypotheses and judgments by reference to their success in accounting for phenomena (in the context of science), by the aid of principles of comprehensiveness, simplicity, coherence, and so forth, or by means of the *claims* relevant to the *field* in question, to use two of Toulmin's terms. However

---

[14] The notions of 'epistemic reliability' as well as that of 'relevance' are elements of contemporary theories on pragmatics and belief change (Sperber and Wilson; Gärdenfors). In both cases 'qualitative' and not merely 'quantitative' or 'enumerative' elements of discourse are emphasized.

[15] This is especially contemplated in the case of legal norms, in which the jurist's interpretation in favor of a norm and against an incompatible one does not eliminate conflict, since it does not necessarily cause its revision or derogation.

[16] Nowadays there is a debate among Leibnizian scholars about the 'nature' of Leibnizian rationalism, more calculistic or more pragmatic. We opt in this paper for an inclusive disjuntion of both sides of the polemic. (About the discussion, see the works of Heinrich Schepers and Marcelo Dascal in *The Leibniz Review* 14 (2004) and the topics of the International Congress "Leibniz: What Kind of Rationalist?", held in Israel in June 2005).

it would provide reasonable 'justified inclinations' in favor of one of the pans of the scale or one of the points of view at issue; this amounts to an inclination that is consistently non-definitive, non-conclusive, and revisable (*incliner sans necessiter*). This idea of unbalance plays a fundamental role in Leibniz's metaphor, since to balance would be to concur with the skeptic, just as is the case with Buridan's ass.[17]

The concept of weighing, of the balance of reasons, is clearly inspired by the activities of the jurists, particularly in their jurisprudential doings,[18] to the extent that Leibniz refers to it as 'inventive and juridical logic' or as 'the art of plausible consequences':

> I want to introduce the scales of Law, a new type of instrument with which one cannot estimate wealth and precious stones, but, what is more valuable, the weight of reasons. Usually it is said that the one who has the supreme faculty of deciding in his hands after pondering all elements must not count, but *weigh* the arguments of those deciding, the stances of the authors, the expressions of those deliberating ... In this manner, we finally reach the matter—outstandingly useful throughout life—of the tabernacle of jurisprudence, where it was so hidden that it could scarcely be recognized. In view of this discovery, it should indeed be considered that *just as mathematicians have exercised logic, that is, the art of reason in necessary things in an optimum way and to a greater extent than anyone else, also juriconsultants have practiced it in contingent matters.*[19]

This is another agreement between Leibniz and Toulmin, since the latter has upheld the parallel between logic and jurisprudence, as a starting point of his study of ordinary argumentations:

> Arguments can be compared with law-suits, and the claims we make and argue for in extra-legal contexts with claims made in the courts, while the cases we present in making good each kind of claim can be compared with each other. A main task of jurisprudence is to characterise the essentials of the legal process: the procedures by which claims-at-law are put forward, disputed and determined, and the categories in terms of which this is done. Our own inquiry is a parallel one: we shall aim, in a similar way, to characterise what may be called 'the rational process', the

[17] *Brief commentaries on the judge of controversies or the balance of reason and norm of the text* § 65a (A, VI, 1).

[18] It is practical wisdom that justifies and decides on juridical matters of experiential and, most of the times, complex character; due to the multiplicity of legal sources, the protection of interests in conflict, the indetermination and graduality of concepts, gaps, etc. Recall that the young Leibniz starts his intellectual activity precisely in the domain of Law.

[19] *For a balance of Law* (C 210). See likewise the above-mentioned *Letter to Gabriel Wagner*, where Leibniz states that nobody has been closer to pondering the balance of reasons than the jurists.

> procedures and categories by using which claims-in-general can be argued for and settled ... the 'jurisprudential analogy' in mind: our subject will be the *prudential*, not simply for *jus*, but more generally of *ratio* (Toulmin, 1958, pp. 7-8; 2003, pp. 7-8).

12. PRAGMATISM, PLURALISM, AND GRADUALISM

These three characteristics of Leibnizian philosophy are the logical complements to his idea of reasonableness.

We have also mentioned the strong tie between theory and praxis in Leibnizian thought. This issue is going to incline Leibniz to an ethical-legal-political consequentialism, far from the ethical foundationalism, formalism, and abstraction defended by Kant. For Leibniz, the utility and the results of knowledge will be the fundamental principles of sciences in general, so he maintains an ordering of the sciences by means of their results (*effectus*) instead of their subjects (*subjecta*).[20]

> The last work of all will be "On Happiness, or on the Science of Life", in which will be shown the use of all the remaining things, and the problems that can be constructed with their help will be arranged in the order of the effects, not of the subjects.[21]

Thus, praxis does not reduce to a marginal aspect of knowledge or only refer to the realm of applications, but it is an element that governs and marks out cognitive activities. Consequently, Leibniz is a gnoseological anti-foundationalist; in order to justify knowledge, we have to see to the coherence of the belief system, or the coherence between the system and a heap of empirical confirmations (coherentism), or to see to the set of results obtained by applying the theory (pragmatism). Against Cartesian intuitivism and the worship of the distinct and clear idea, Leibniz advocates an approach usually called 'formalism', but whose main axis is that the system of known truths has to be under the test of internal coherence and coherence with experienced facts too (Rescher, 1986, p. 130). As suggested by Richard T.W. Arthur (in his comments on a previous version of this article), the above remarks about hypotheses that deserve the highest praise are reminiscent of Lakatos' about the criteria for evaluating progressive research programmes. Consistently with such a Popperian outlook, Leibniz concludes in an earlier piece on the nominalist Nizolius that "Perfect certainty can clearly never be hoped for from induction, even with the addition of any aids whatever" (Rescher, 2003, p. 123).

Leibniz is aware of the complexity, diversity, and plurality of the world, in the historical and contingent side as well as in the natural and necessary one. However, this fact is not a problem, but a richness, since his principle of plenitude states that the better world is, in any case, the 'fuller' world and, therefore, nothing or almost nothing

---

[20] *De arte inveniendi* (C 169).
[21] *De arte inveniendi* (C 169).

has to be rejected and all or almost all can be integrated and harmonize. In sum, Leibniz is interested in the positive and enrichment aspects present in all rational reasoning.

The ultimate rationale of Leibnizian pluralism is his perspectivism. In the same way that each monad reflects the universe from a perspective, each culture represents its own view of the world, i.e., a perspective of the same reality:

> Just as the same city regarded from different sides offers quite different aspects, and thus appears multiplied *by the perspective*, so it also happens that the infinite multitude of simple substances creates the appearance of many different universes. Yet they are but perspectives of a single universe, varied according to the *points of view*, which differ in each monad.[22]

So Leibnizian universalism cannot be assimilated to a cosmopolitanism without a face, since Leibniz foresees that different cultures will preserve their individual character (like monads), at the same time that they make up a more complex order that will put an end to human discords.

Finally, the Leibnizian method of rationality, based on comparison and weighing, has been interpreted as a typically pragmatic resource (in the sense of linguistic analysis). Therefore, heuristic rules, epistemological considerations, and other resources of practical reasoning would constitute a type of para-logical theory, which is added to logic in order to offer an account of a non-rigorous domain, namely that of argumentation on contingent matters. This is Marcelo Dascal's interpretation, and it stands in opposition to other views that take Leibniz's model of flexible rationality as an invitation to 'widen' logic. It is this latter approach that I defend.[23]

Beyond appealing to weighing, comparison, and analogy—all of which are mechanisms of an indubitably gradual character—some basic principles of Leibniz's metaphysics, such as the principle of continuity, deal in detail with the gradualist perspective that I defend. There are many texts in which we can find this gradualist or continuistic metaphysical approach.[24] One of the characteristics of this approach is the exclusion of defined leaps, breaks, or cuts in the domain of the real: *natura non facit saltus*. Although Leibniz called this general principle of physics and mathematics '*lex iustitiae*', he did not explicitly apply it to the normative domain; and, in logic, he always adopted the bivalent classic deductive model. Only in some fragments (e.g., *NN.EE.* IV, ch. 16) does he appeal to the need to build a type of logic that accounts for degrees of plausibility.

It is also interesting to highlight that Leibniz's metaphysical idea of graduality (a term, which among other things, he also called: a principle of transition, a law of

---

[22] *Monadology* §57 (GP VI, 616).

[23] In this context I understand logic in a 'minimal' way, as the mere representation of certain arguments by means of schematizations which help to better understand, even visually, what are the inferentially important points and stamp more rigor on a certain set of argumentations. Therefore, logic is not something exclusive to mathematics or the hard sciences, such as physics, but applies to all domains in which an argumentative process is involved (that is, all questions of a practical type).

[24] *Monadology, Letter to Varignon, Letter to Rémond, Theodicy, NN.EE.*

continuity, or a principle of change without leap) appears in his mature philosophy, whereas his interest in jurisprudence is, as has been already pointed out, rather early. Maybe this chronological discordance is part of the reason why Leibniz did not consider this principle in the normative and logical domains.

In any case, I will here dare to establish a connection between these metaphysical principles and Leibniz's approach to practical rationality. The notions of weighing as well as those of comparison and similarity take place in a gradual manner, by means of transitions instead of leaps or breaks.

What has been said serves as an invitation to logically implement Leibniz's gradualism by a fuzzy calculus in which propositions take their truth-value in the interval [0, 1]. Consequently, the notion of 'truth' can be 'modulated', as happens in ordinary experience and argumentation, so that 'true' and 'false' have lost their static and abstract character.[25]

Fuzzy logic does not benefit relativism in any way, but it makes manifest truth's relational character. Thereby the opposition between 'truth' and 'opinion', which has been a matter of concern in Western thought since pre-Socratic times, is rejected as irrelevant and confusing (Trillas, Alsina, and Terricabras, 1995, p. 40).

The same is the case with normative notions, which, from the point of view of practical deliberation, are of special interest. Deontic descriptions of licitness, prohibition and duty, in this spirit, are treated as gradual notions. From this perspective, a particular action can have more or less licitness and, to the extent that it is not completely licit, it will have some degree of illicitness. This would be an example of 'working logic', field-connected and field-dependent, in Toulmin's terms. The core of this type of analysis is the principle of graduation, according to which, when two facts are similar, their juridical treatment must also be similar. This idea is clearly due to the above-mentioned Leibnizian principle of transition or continuity (*lex iustitiae*).

As we have said above, consistently espousing the rejection of leaps calls for a gradualistic non-Aristotelian logic, a logic of degrees of truth or existence.[26] However, Leibniz himself always embraced classical, two-valued, Aristotelian logic, with its two polarly opposed values of pure, and complete, truth and pure, and utter, falsity. Leibniz is envisaging a new gradualistic logic, but a logic of degrees of probability, not of truth. When it comes to truth, he hangs on to the hard and old dichotomy of 1/0. In any case, Leibniz anticipated many contemporary thoughts and research-lines—including some philosophical motivations for fuzzy logic. Neither Leibniz nor Toulmin advocate a non-classical logic to cope with graduality in argumentation, but this way for logic to become more and more working,

[25] The relational notion of truth is closely similar to the ontological and moral views of Dewey's pragmatism.

[26] From this approach, we needn't waive the principle of excluded middle—to the effect that either an entity is so-and-so or else it isn't. What we need is to jettison the result of prefixing to the principle of excluded middle the particle 'completely'. Since the operator 'completely' distributes over disjunction ("Entirely (p-or-q)" is equivalent to "Entirely p or entirely q"), what we are in effect rejecting is the alternative between a certain fact existing altogether and its complete failure to exist.

experimental, and applied and not idealized, is close to the spirit of Toulmin's reflections.

13. LEIBNIZ AND TOULMIN: RATIONALISM WITHOUT DOGMAS

Concluding, Leibniz and Toulmin would share a kind of soft and tinged rationalism, open to difference, plurality and controversy. When trying to rationally justify contingent judgments Leibniz and Toulmin defend a weighing and qualified argumentative method. Thus, in both of them we can discern the balance between the legitimate demands of formal models of rationality and the lessons of a practice 'situated' in a historical, social, and evaluative context (*theoria cum praxi*). That is, a way to cope with complexity of life and with its contingency and uncertainty; in sum, a rationalism without dogmas.

Acknowledgements

This paper adapts material from Ausín and Roldán (2005). I thank for their helpful comments Richard T.W. Arthur, Armando Menéndez, Lorenzo Peña, Concha Roldán, and members of the research project 'Practical wisdom, balance and education' (Luis Arenas, Jesús de Garay, Ricardo Parellada, Lourdes Rensoli, Vicente Serrano, David Teira and Juan Antonio Valor).

References to Leibniz's texts

A: German Academy of Sciences (ed.). *G.W. Leibniz: Sämtliche Schriften und Briefe*. Akademie Verlag, Berlin, 1923-. (References are to series and volume).

GP: C.I. Gerhardt (ed.): 1960, *Die Philosophischen Schriften von G.W. Leibniz*, Olms, Hildesheim.

C: L. Couturat (ed.): 1961, *Opuscules et fragments inédites de Leibniz*, Olms, Hildesheim. Originally printed: 1903, Alcan, Paris.

Gr: G. Grua (ed): 1948, *G.W. Leibniz: Textes inédites d'après des manuscrits de la Bibliothèque provincial d'Hanovre*, PUF, Paris.

L: L.M. Loemker (ed.): 1969, *G.W. Leibniz: Philosophical Papers and Letters*, Reidel, Dordrecht.

CHAPTER 18

JOHN FOX[1] AND SANJAY MODGIL[2]

FROM ARGUMENTS TO DECISIONS: EXTENDING THE TOULMIN VIEW

Advanced Computation Lab, Cancer Research UK
E-mail: [1]john.fox@cancer.org.uk, [2]sm@acl.icnet.uk

ABSTRACT: In his 1958 essays Toulmin criticises "scientific" views of logic and probability, suggesting that these philosophical and theoretical frameworks have failed to accommodate features of everyday dispute and debate. He offers an alternative perspective, summarised by his famous argumentation schema. He draws primarily on legal and regulatory examples, but we have found that medicine and science also provide rich sources of argumentation examples and many of these fit the Toulmin schema. However the decision-making elements of clinical judgement suggest the need for extensions to the standard layout. This paper presents a view of argumentation based decision making that preserves the essence of the Toulmin model but in an extended form.

1. INTRODUCTION

> Some philosophers ... have an ineradicable suspicion of our everyday forms of thought ... In their view, the development of science, and the displacement of all our ordinary, pre-scientific ideas by the more refined notions of the theoretical sciences, hold out the only hope of salvation for incoherence, fallacy and intellectual confusion. (Toulmin, 1958, p. 92)

Toulmin's philosophical interest in developing his layout of argument was "the contrast between the standards and values of practical reasoning and the abstract and formal criteria relied on in mathematical logic and much of twentieth-century epistemology". Rather than being concerned with disembodied mathematical proofs, Toulmin wanted to understand everyday disputes, viewing argument as a social dialectic of claim, rebuttal and counter-claim. His rejection of "a conception of 'deductive inference' which many recent philosophers have accepted without hesitation as impeccable" is now being echoed well beyond the domain of philosophy, from artificial intelligence and software engineering to theories of legal reasoning and, in our own work, decision-making and planning.

The standard Toulmin example of argumentation discusses a claim that "Harry is presumably a British citizen" and its rebuttal (Toulmin, 1958, p. 101). The

D. Hitchcock and B. Verheij (eds.), Arguing on the Toulmin Model: New Essays in Argument Analysis and Evaluation, 273–287.

example is concerned with a small problem in the rules of citizenship but is taken to be paradigmatic. He argued that the preoccupation with formal logic has misled us into thinking of argument strictly in terms of soundness, completeness and other properties that have little to do with natural patterns. Recent writers influenced by Toulmin, such as (Walton, 1989), see their task as one of understanding natural argument structures and inter-personal argument dialogues like negotiation and persuasion (Walton and Krabbe, 1995), rather than providing a formal account of how arguments ought to be constructed.

The motivation for our work on argumentation has been different from Toulmin's and many of his successors, being stimulated by problems in the theory and practice of clinical reasoning and decision-making. On the face of it there is a significant difference between argumentation in human affairs and argumentation in scientific fields like medicine. Whether a woman does or does not have breast cancer or whether a particular treatment is or is not best for her are not subjective matters of rhetoric and persuasion; objectivity, evidence and real outcomes of real diseases are the prime concerns. Yet structures and patterns of argument are just as recognisable in medicine as in the world of jurisprudence, and it turns out that the Toulmin layout takes us a part of the way towards understanding these structures and patterns. However, in science and medicine we have to confront questions which have not been given as much attention in legal and political argument, such as how to compare the strength of arguments and how to evaluate collections of arguments in deciding between competing claims.

Our wider interests are in how 'agents' (whether human or artificial) can, do and ought to argue when they reason about problems, make decisions or construct plans. Our research adopts a more eclectic methodology than is usual in discussions of these matters, drawing on systematic observation (e.g. doctors making decisions in the clinic); designing and testing software agents which can support clinical work (e.g. to carry out complex decisions and plans) and engaging in natural language dialogues with humans, as well as foundational work in argument theory. Toulmin's views have been very influential, and rightly so, but understanding the roles of argument in risk assessment, prediction, decision-making, planning, learning and other practical tasks that people routinely engage in needs a larger canvas. Our aim is a theory of argument that can illuminate many tasks that human professionals routinely carry out and which can guide the design and construction of artificial agents with comparable abilities.

2. THE RIGHT WAY TO MAKE A DECISION

How should human or artificial agents make decisions in the face of uncertainty and different points of view about what is true or what is important? The need for a formal solution has been recognised as a major scientific and technical challenge for at least 400 years. In the years since Toulmin's essays, discussions have been further stimulated by problems arising in the cognitive and computer sciences. Mathematical probability and statistical decision theory have provided the orthodox foundation for addressing this problem, with many seeing them as providing standards of rationality against which we should "bring human judgement under the authority of mathematics" (Johnstone, 2000). The decision theorist Dennis Lindley observes:

> ... there is essentially only one way to reach a decision sensibly. First, the uncertainties present in the situation must be quantified in terms of values called probabilities. Second, the consequences of the courses of actions must be similarly described in terms of utilities. Third, that decision must be taken which is expected on the basis of the calculated probabilities to give the greatest utility. The force of 'must' used in three places there is simply that any deviation from the precepts is liable to lead the decision maker in procedures which are demonstrably absurd. (Lindley, 1985, p. vii)

Notwithstanding the strength of Lindley's convictions, expected utility models of decision-making have substantial practical limitations. One that has been widely discussed is the difficulty of estimating precise probabilities and utilities in real-world settings. In medicine, for example, quantitative epidemiological knowledge about the patterns of symptoms that indicate the presence or herald the onset of diseases is surprisingly sparse. The kinds of statistics that Lindley identifies are not generally known with any precision and most doctors don't even have a basis for estimating these things for the community in which they live. Yet as the economist J. M. Keynes observed "As living and moving beings, we are forced to act ... [even when] our existing knowledge does not provide a sufficient basis for a calculated mathematical expectation" (Keynes, 1921). The question is how can decisions be taken when quantitative data required for the calculation are not available, rough or unreliable?

This question led us to a different approach to decision-making from the orthodox one. We viewed the decision process in terms of the formulation of arguments for and against options, and the combination of arguments in such a way as to yield an overall assessment of each alternative and hence an order of preference (Fox *et al.*, 1990). However, we retained a conventional view in the sense that some of the formal constraints arising from classical logic and probability theory are still relevant to a theory of argument-based decision making. For example, while people are not always apparently bound by the rule that an argument for taking an action implies an argument against taking some alternative action, a rational agent should (arguably) accept this implication. The position we developed was that arguments can take the form of traditional deductive proofs but do not necessarily have the force or semantic import of such proofs. Arguments do not determine the absolute truth or falsity of propositions, but represent reasons for or against accepting particular beliefs or adopting particular plans of action (Fox *et al.*, 1992).

This view extends the traditional view of logic to accommodate uncertainty about the state of the world or the likely outcomes of actions without having to quantify uncertainty in probabilistic terms, as "fuzzy" values or in some other way. It accepts the idea that in everyday settings a single line of argument (which would traditionally be a proof) may be insufficient to arrive at a firm conclusion and an agent may need to consider a number of arguments for and against each competing belief or action and weigh them in the balance in coming to a decision. It accommodates the idea that arguments can have different strengths, which can be captured with qualitative schemes (e.g. the distinction between supporting and conclusive arguments) and quantitative frameworks in which conventional measures of probability and utility are used to provide a measure of an argument's force (Fox *et al.*, 1993; Krause *et al.*, 1995). The key response to Lindley is that quantification is an option in decision making, it is not a necessity.

We also introduced the common sense idea that lines of argument for a decision (e.g. lines of argument for/against a breast lump being benign or one treatment being preferred to another) have to be justified in some way and the credibility of the justification influences the force of the argument. In a medical setting justifications can include, in decreasing order of credibility: general medical knowledge and scientific principles; objective evidence from clinical observations and trials; the authority of professional organizations; a local hospital policy, or the 'clinical judgement' of an individual doctor.

The formal framework that was intended to accommodate these ideas was our Logic of Argument (LA) (Fox *et al.*, 1992; Krause *et al.*, 1995, Fox, 2003). In LA, arguments are terms containing 3 elements: one describes the claim (e.g. a decision option) that the argument refers to; one the grounds or justification of the argument (an explicit representation of the assumptions of and steps in the argument), and lastly a label representing the strength of, or confidence conferred by, the argument. LA provides a qualitative alternative to quantitative decision theory, makes more natural use of human conceptions of knowledge and is easily understood by doctors and patients. Yet it has a clear interpretation with respect to standard probability and decision theory and a sound and complete semantics (Krause *et al.*, 1995; Fox and Das, 2000). Fox (2003) provides a more detailed review of the approach.

3. ARGUMENT IN PRACTICE

This section briefly reviews a selection of medical applications of this approach to provide sufficient context for the current presentation, and show how the argumentation involved is similar to, but also different from, the Toulmin form.

Assessment of Suspected Breast Cancer

'Triple Assessment' of patients with symptoms of possible breast cancer is a process which aims to achieve a provisional diagnosis, and an assessment of the grade and spread of the disease, if any. Triple assessment includes: 1) Clinical examination; 2) Various forms of imaging (mammography, ultrasound, etc.); 3) Biopsy and tissue pathology. The assessment process includes a number of tasks, starting with finding out about the patient's general medical background and specific complaints and symptoms. The process then goes on to identify possible explanations for the patient's problem and involves making decisions about the appropriate tests and investigations to be carried out, which will provide evidence for a final diagnosis. One of the decisions to be taken during this process will be whether an X-ray of the breast (mammogram) is needed and/or an ultrasound-scan, or no imaging is required. Figure 1 shows a software system that has been developed to support

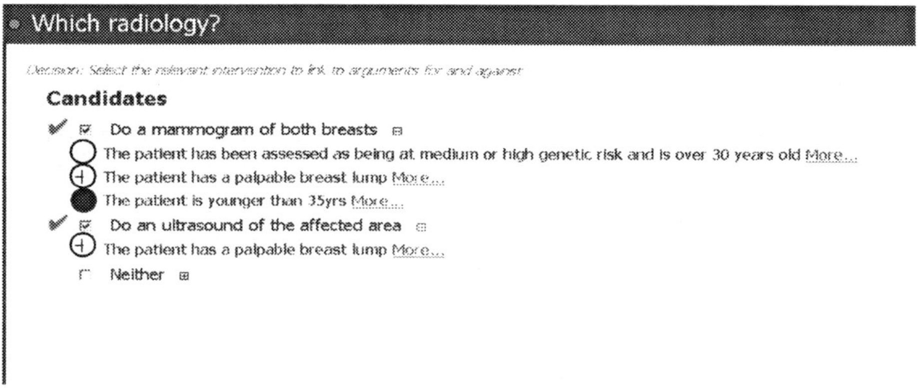

Figure 1. Summary of argumentation for imaging tests in breast cancer assessment[1].

this process (Hurt, Patkar *et al.*, 2005). This display appears when the decision about imaging is being taken and shows three possible options together with summaries of the arguments for and against them.

The arguments about mammography and ultrasound represent the justifications pro and con each investigation. Although the pros and cons are shown informally here in the form of text, the reasoning is carried out by an inference engine which tests logical conditions that are evaluated over the information that has been recorded about the patient. For example, the first argument for mammography in

[1] Plus signs on the left indicate arguments that support the claims that mammography or ultrasound are appropriate for this patient, and the minus sign indicates an argument against mammography (colour is used in the original display). The large tick indicates a possible option on the basis of the argumentation, and the small tick in the box is the final decision taken by the doctor (more than one in this case). The "More..." text is a button that is used to display the backing for the argument (see Figure 2).

Figure 1 is a paraphrase of the condition ((brca_risk = moderate OR brca_risk = high) AND age_of_patient > 30). We shall call the English form of this the 'Toulmin warrant'.

In Toulmin's scheme, a warrant has itself to be justified by an appropriate 'backing'. In a medical setting there are several accepted forms of backing, ranging from strong evidence-based backing in which the argument is grounded in a peer reviewed scientific article which reports an objective study in a controlled clinical trial to relatively weak justifications based on expert opinion or 'normal practice'. Figure 2 shows the same display as in Figure 1, but now expanded to show backing material in the form of summaries of relevant articles and references. The backing for an argument is revealed in the software by clicking on 'More...' in the display shown in Figure 1.

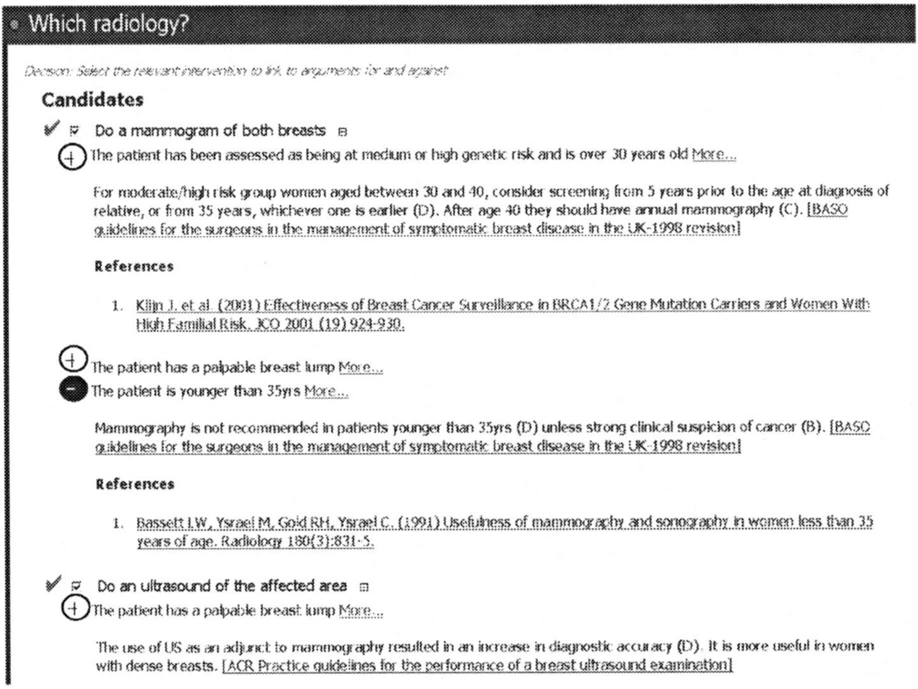

Figure 2. Extending Toulmin warrants to show their backing.

Although Figure 2 shows the backing in terms of titles of research publications, a further level of backing can be provided. Since this is a web application the user can call up a further level of background material by clicking on the reference, and this will then link to the original publication, where citations and further links can be pursued. Unlike the usual "Harry is a British citizen" example of the Toulmin schema, a backing is viewed as the beginning of an indefinitely long chain of documents and other explanatory and justificatory material.

Prescribing Drugs for Common Conditions

Probably the most frequent type of decision that doctors take is drug prescribing. This is a decision in which classical decision theory is surprisingly difficult to use because of the difficulty of quantifying the objective probabilities and subjective benefits and costs associated with many medical interventions. CAPSULE was developed to assist general practitioners in routine prescribing based on the use of qualitative argument schemas (Walton *et al.*, 1997). CAPSULE has a database of information about drugs, and a set of schemas for reasoning about the attributes of medications that may be considered for the patient, formalised in first-order logic. Put informally a typical schema might be "if a treatment that is being considered could have a harmful side-effect for the patient then this argues against use of the treatment for that patient". When CAPSULE is invoked the logical argumentation schemas are instantiated with information about the drugs that are being considered, data from the patient record and knowledge from the drug database.

Suppose CAPSULE is considering drug A. The fact that drug A is relatively cheap by comparison with the alternatives being considered, is an argument in favour of A. On the other hand if the patient is already taking drug B and B is known to have an undesirable interaction with A then this is an argument against A. CAPSULE's decision criteria cover 9 argument schemas, dealing with the efficacy of a drug for a problem, the past effectiveness of the drug for this patient if this is known, possible interactions with other drugs the patient may be taking, as well as clinical contra-indications, side effects and financial cost. In order to establish the order of preference over the candidate drugs for recommending a decision, CAPSULE simply counts up the arguments for and against each drug and presents the set of candidates in an order based on the ratio of pros to cons. This rudimentary aggregation function is surprisingly effective (Fox and Glasspool, 2001) but can be substituted by other functions which take into account the relative strength of arguments, both quantitatively and qualitatively (Fox, 2003).

Assessing Genetic Risk of Cancer

RAGs (Risk Assessment in Genetics) was designed to help general physicians to advise healthy people with a family history of cancer, such as breast cancer, whether to seek advice from specialist clinical geneticists. RAGs helps to acquire and record information about an individual and any family members who are believed to have contracted particular kinds of cancer, assemble a family tree, and formulate arguments for and against the person having a genetic predisposition to the cancer (Coulson *et al.*, 1999). RAGs acquires relevant information about the woman seeking advice and her relatives, determining who had cancer and what their approximate age was at diagnosis and so on. It then applies rules like "If the person has two or more first-degree relatives diagnosed with breast cancer and both relatives were diagnosed under the age of 40 then this is a strong risk factor for genetic predisposition to the disease".

Unlike Triple assessment and CAPSULE, rules in RAGs are 'weighted' to represent the relative importance of different risk factors, and hence the relative force of the arguments. In this case the scheme is ad hoc; an integer between 1 and 3 represents the strength of the risk factor, and the overall risk for the woman is determined by establishing which rules are true in her case and adding up the associated numbers. Despite the simplicity of this method the risk classifications generated by the RAGs software for 50 families with known genetics were identical to the classifications made by a leading statistical risk assessment package (Emery *et al.*, 2000).

4. MODELLING ARGUMENTATION IN DECISION-MAKING

A Schema for Decision Making and Knowledge Representation

Toulmin's layout of arguments has served the argumentation research community well, but it was primarily intended to model inference rather than more general tasks like making decisions among competing claims. Consequently we need a more elaborate picture than that offered by the standard Toulmin layout. Figure 3 is intended to extend the classical "chaining" view of inference to a cyclical process of reasoning and decision-making, in which an agent applies its general knowledge to particular settings. In this view the agent starts with a collection of beliefs and goals about the situation, uses its background knowledge to argue for and against possible decision options in the situation (e.g. possible hypotheses or treatments), assesses the collections of arguments for competing options to determine which is currently the best, and may finally commit a provisionally preferred option as a firm belief or intention.

We take an orthodox view of a decision-maker's knowledge base as a collection of sentences in some language such as first order logic. Such a knowledge base may include beliefs about specific situations (e.g. "this patient is suffering from breast cancer") as well as general knowledge organized into fields such as immunology, physiology, anatomy, biochemistry, genetics, epidemiology and so on. Toulmin distinguishes between field-dependent and field-invariant argumentation. The kinds of arguments seen in the above medical examples draw heavily on field-dependent

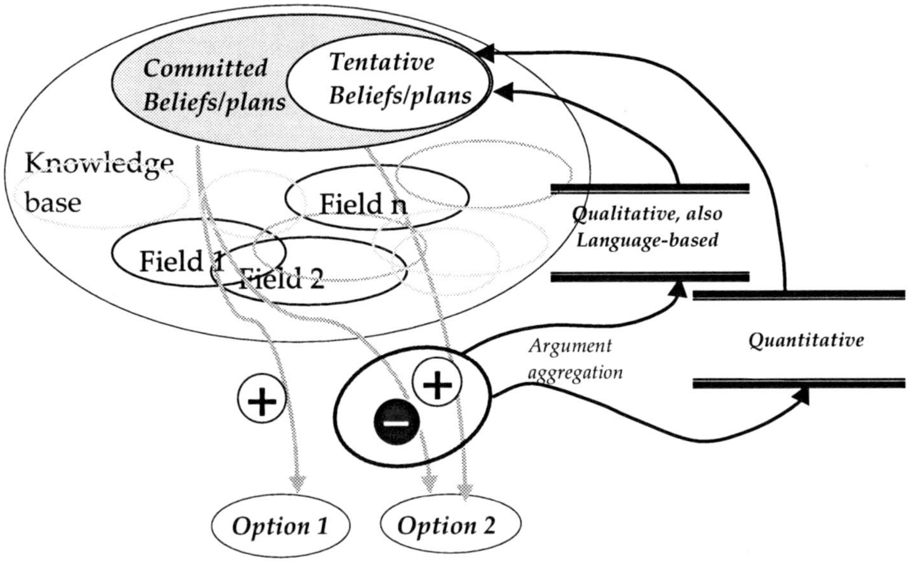

Figure 3. A general argument scheme that extends the Toulmin layout into the domain of decision-making and the representation of knowledge and belief.

patterns. However, we also have a large pool of general and 'common sense' knowledge, about physical objects and their properties, time and space etc. which can participate in field invariant argument patterns. We can also apply different modes of reasoning, which lie somewhere between strictly field-dependent and field-invariant patterns, as when we reason statistically rather than causally when arguing about risk, reasoning about normal or abnormal observations when taking a diagnosis decision, or deontically, when planning a treatment.

Suppose that a medical decision-maker (DM), whether human or artificial, comes to believe that a mammogram is abnormal. We assume that such a DM adopts the general goal in such circumstances of finding the most likely cause of the abnormality (the diagnosis). The DM might formulate several candidate explanations for this, including the possibilities that the abnormality is a cyst or a tumour. The process of constructing arguments around these possibilities may draw upon knowledge from different fields and involve different modes of argument leading to arguments for a claim from knowledge of one field but arguments against the claim based on knowledge of other fields. Despite differences in content such arguments can be viewed as similar in form to conventional proofs, in which we evaluate logical conditions that support one or other of the competing possibilities. However, most arguments do not by themselves have the force of a proof, indicated by the same symbols in Figure 3 as were used in Figures 1 and 2: + (meaning 'supporting') and – (meaning 'opposing').

The Logic of Argument — Constructing Arguments

The Logic of Argument (LA) provides a formal model for argument construction consistent with the above interpretation. LA starts with a more or less conventional deductive model of argument but extends this with a few basic ideas that bring it to a form close in spirit to Toulmin's model. 2 We summarize the basic structure of LA with the following consequence relation:

$$\text{Knowledge base} \cup \text{Beliefs} \vdash_{LA} (\text{Claim} : \text{Justification} : \text{Qualifier})$$

We start with a knowledge base, a collection of formal sentences: propositions (facts), specific rules and general schemas, and a set of beliefs concerning a particular situation. A knowledge base might be a body of general medical knowledge, for example, and the beliefs are about a particular patient's clinical problem. The turnstyle $\vdash$ represents axioms or inference rules of some base logic which can be used to construct valid steps in an argument about a claim based on current knowledge and beliefs. The argument term on the right is a triple of elements consisting of:

1. The Claim which the argument refers to (an option, in a decision-making context)
2. The Justification of the argument; the formal grounds of the informal Toulmin warrant. (The justification could be the specific sequence of logical steps made in constructing the argument, a proof tree in some normalised form, or a set of assumptions from which the argument could be reconstructed)
3. A Qualifier that represents the confidence that is warranted by the argument in the claim.

Note that the conventional choice of axioms for the base logic can be that of classical logic, though in practice a weaker logic may be more natural. Classical logics include the axiom of the excluded middle; an argument for a claim is implicitly an argument against every competing claim. However, in everyday settings like clinical decision-making, we often find this axiom is violated. Arguing

---

[2] This summary is based on material taken from Fox and Das (2000) chapter 2, which provides a relatively non-technical introduction to LA, but Krause *et al.* (1995) and Fox and Parsons (1998) provide more formal treatments.

that a patient has the flu on the basis of a temperature does not necessarily imply an argument that the patient does not have glandular fever, though we might construct a quite separate argument that the presence of both diseases at the same time is unlikely. Intuitionistic logic drops the axiom and we find it is more flexible and natural for representing informal medical reasoning.

Qualifiers may take a number of possible forms. For example, a qualifier can simply say that an argument supports a claim or opposes it, meaning that the argument increases or decreases the DM's confidence in the claim but without indicating by how much. A delta argument is indicated with a + or a –. Qualifiers can also represent degrees of strength as in the genetic risk assessment example, or real numbers drawn from the [0,1] interval so that probabilistic measures of confidence may be represented where this is appropriate. We may also use linguistic qualifiers, such as the word "presumably" from Toulmin's example, if we can give a clear definition for such terms (see below).

The Logic of Argument — Evaluation of Arguments

Having addressed the issue of argument construction, we now address evaluation of the preferred set of arguments. Figure 3 illustrates a case where there are two competing claims and three arguments (there can of course be any number of claims and any number of arguments for and against each claim). Given a set of arguments for and against competing claims, how may we select the most plausible, probable or otherwise preferred alternative? In standard decision theory we would do this by calculating the relative probabilities of alternative beliefs and expected utilities in order to decide the most preferred action. However, as we have seen above, in many decisions we do not know what these parameters are, and ordinary logic cannot help because it does not have any way of representing degrees of belief or value at all.

LA provides an alternative to these contrasting approaches because it allows us to assess relative confidence in the competing claims by comparing the balance of arguments for and against them. This leads to a simple decision procedure. If we have several independent arguments for one claim, but only one argument for the other, then even if we cannot assign strengths to individual arguments it is reasonable to have more confidence in the first claim than in the second. This process of argument aggregation allows us to assess the overall persuasiveness of the competing claims even if we cannot establish the absolute strength of individual arguments. As we saw in the cancer genetics example, we can also associate weights with individual arguments and take these weights into account with appropriate numerical aggregation functions.

There are various methods of argument aggregation other than those based on combining weights. Some are based on qualitative rather than quantitative methods and we view these as providing an interpretation of Toulmin's famous qualifiers. As natural language users we routinely use such qualifiers. We don't just say "I'm starting a cold" but also "it is {conceivable, possible, likely, pretty certain, …} that I'm starting a cold". Similarly a doctor doesn't just say "you've got athlete's foot".

S/he will just as often say "I {assume, suspect, doubt, believe, am certain/uncertain} that you {have, may have, could have} athlete's foot" and so on. This vocabulary is further augmented by hedges (e.g. {quite, very, highly ...}), conventional elaborations (e.g. "it appears to be the case that...", "there are persuasive reasons to think that..."), the lexical and affixal negative forms of English (e.g. not possible, impossible), and many other everyday constructions.

The existence of such a large sub-language for talking about the status of our claims in most if not all natural languages has long puzzled linguists, psychologists, philosophers and others. Logicians, and Toulmin himself, view such terms as modal operators, while others see them as mere stylistic decorations of no formal significance. However, Toulmin also seems to have been inclined to see them in a conversational context, as they signal a particular emphasis or serve an auxiliary social or pragmatic function to convey the status of our beliefs. If I say "it's possible that (I'm starting a cold)" I intend to communicate something like "I have grounds to think I may be getting a cold (such as a sore throat, sneezing etc.) but there is also at least some reason to believe that I may not (e.g. (1) I already had a cold just last week; (2) I had the same symptoms yesterday but nothing happened, (3) my throat is only slightly sore)". In everyday communication we haven't the time to go into detail so if our language allows us to communicate our epistemic state with a built in summary of the reasons for that state so much the better.

We see exactly this kind of phenomenon in medical and other texts. For example a guideline published by the International Agency for Research on Cancer, sets out a standard terminology for talking about categories of risk associated with chemical compounds, in that the claim "chemical X causes cancer" can be classified with one of seven qualifying terms:

confirmed:	there is epidemiological data and/or an established causal relationship
possible:	a potential hazard is recognised
probable:	there is better evidence than merely recognition of possible carcinogenic activity
improbable:	possible carcinogenic activity, but strong evidence against
equivocal:	hazard recognised and both evidence for and evidence against
open:	no information regarding potential hazard is available
not:	test case data or direct chemical analysis disconfirms carcinogenic activity

In short, we suspect (sic!) that our large repertoire of uncertainty expressions has a practical communicative function. This might be nothing more than a set of arbitrary conventions, like the IARC set, with little formal interest. However, Toulmin developed his ideas about qualifiers of claims on just such observations of common language use and it would be interesting to understand what these words "really" mean. From a more technical point of view we are also interested in being able to modalise propositions in a natural way. If modalities can be included in logical expressions, within the premises of inference rules or the preconditions of decision rules, to represent levels of confidence, the existence of suspicion or doubt and so forth, this increases the expressiveness of a formal language.

This possibility has drawn us to the idea that the meaning of such terms might be based on patterns of argument (as in "P is possible if there is an argument that supports P and no argument that rebuts it", (Fox, 1990)). Elvang-Gøransson *et al.* (1993a; 1993b) formalised this idea by defining a set of logical 'acceptability classes' for talking about belief, basing these classes solely on the logical properties of the set of arguments for and against the claim. These acceptability classes define a completely ordered set of modalities for expressing confidence in a proposition P, from low to high:

open P:	if P is any well formed formula in the language of the logic
supported P:	if an argument, possibly using inconsistent data, can be constructed for P
plausible P:	if a consistent argument can be constructed (we may also be able to construct a consistent argument against)
probable P:	An argument can be constructed for P, and no consistent argument can be constructed against it.
confirmed P:	if P satisfies the conditions of being probable and, in addition, no consistent arguments can be constructed against any of the premises used in its supporting argument
certain P:	if P is a tautology of the logic (meaning that its validity is not contingent on any data in the knowledge base).

The particular interpretations of modal terms proposed by Elvang-Gørannson *et al.* seem debatable. For example, the meaning attributed to the term "supported" allows an argument to support a claim even if it is inconsistent; readers may have their own intuitions about use of these words in common parlance. However, the specific assignments are not the crucial point here. The important contribution of the work is that it shows that we can in principle construct a useful set of descriptive modalities in a way that is clear and consistent, and which provides us with a way of signaling that a claim is tentative in some respect, and even provides a simple scale for ordering the competing claims. We believe that Toulmin's qualifiers are just such modalities, introduced into everyday language and conversation for practical purposes as needed.

Any discussion of the evaluation of arguments would not be complete without referencing Dung's account of a 'calculus of opposition' (Dung, 1995). Dung's work abstracts from the structure of arguments to consider a principled approach to evaluation of the status of arguments on the basis of how they interact. Our work on argumentation-based decision making suggests a number of issues currently un-addressed by the Dung framework. Dung's focus is on the acceptability of arguments, where an acceptable argument is one that is supported and is not attacked by another argument, or if it is attacked the attacking argument can be defeated. The main difference with LA, is that in Dung an argument can be acceptable or not acceptable and can have no other status. A rational agent will accept an argument according to whether or not a successful attack can be mounted against it. In LA, however, arguments can have a certain force (which can be represented qualitatively or quantitatively). The idea of force implies that arguments can be aggregated: a rational agent can assign a degree of acceptability to a claim based on the aggregated force of the arguments for and against the claim, and claims can be ordered based on the overall level of acceptability of the arguments for and against it. Furthermore, in the LA framework arguments and claims can be attacked with the result that they are weakened but not completely refuted.

This is consistent with ideas from decision theory and clarifies important relationships between argumentation theory and more classical notions of inference. Verheij (1996) is also interested in this relationship and has independently suggested that arguments "accrue"—two arguments are stronger than one—though others question whether this should be part of the logic (Pollock, 1987). Our idea of a separate aggregation function within the decision argumentation cycle (Figure 3) may clarify this issue. Neither quantitative nor qualitative aggregation are found in the Dung framework; arguments are defeated or they are not. Prakken (personal communication) believes that the Dung model can be extended to deal with aggregation and accrual and if this proves to be the case it may help to strengthen the claims by some theorists that Dung semantics could provide the most general foundation for different theories of argumentation dialectics.

The Logic of Argument: Arriving at Conclusions and Making Commitments

The Dung account may also be incomplete in another respect, in that it does not address what is called in decision theory the "stopping problem": when do we stop arguing and arrive at a conclusion? From the perspective of non-monotonic logic this notion is confused. There is no such thing as a final conclusion; a claim is simply acceptable until such time as the argument for it is defeated. Even this outcome is tentative, however, because at some later time the defeater of the defeated argument may itself be successfully attacked, thereby reinstating the original claim. From the point of view of the decision theorist however this just won't do: the essence of a decision process is a commitment to action (or to a belief that has implications for action) and in the real world action may be needed urgently. The idea of leaving all competing claims tentative is absurd if one must act immediately. This is why we make the distinction between tentative and committed beliefs/plans in the final steps of the decision cycle in Figure 3.

The stopping rule is a significant theoretical challenge to both decision theory and argument theory in that we need to identify principled criteria that determine when it is safe—and in medicine this may really mean safe—to make commitments. At some point the balance of argument might be strongly in favour of one option, but if we wait a while before committing to it more information may become available on which we can base further arguments that will change the order of preference over the competing claims. This applies whether we think in terms of defeasible argumentation or aggregation of arguments in the LA framework. What is needed is some stronger condition than simply the current belief that such and such an action or hypothesis is the best of the available alternatives. We need to satisfy some sort of stability condition that says, essentially, there is no point in looking for further information that might alter the main preference—it is time to stop arguing and make a choice. We are aware of two conditions that embody general stopping rules:

Stopping rule 1 (epistemic): there are no unknown sources of information in the context of our current knowledge that could provide the grounds for further arguments that would lead to a different preference ordering over the competing claims or options.

Stopping rule 2 (utilitarian): even if there is significant missing information the expected costs of seeking it would exceed the costs of incorrectly committing to the current most preferred option.

If either of these conditions is satisfied then the decision-maker can terminate the decision process and commit to the most preferred option with confidence that the choice is stable. If neither is satisfied the 'principle of least commitment' applies: if a decision is not absolutely necessary then it is ok to wait, otherwise toss a coin.

5. CONCLUSIONS

To summarise, the basic characteristics of the Toulmin model of argument are retained in our account. Lines of argument which assert or rebut a claim appear unchanged, though weaker forms of argument which merely support or oppose claims are also introduced. Lines of argument are warranted in much the same spirit as Toulmin intended but half a century after his essays we are able to articulate his concept of a warrant in terms of contemporary ideas about logic and knowledge based reasoning. The backing also appears in a clearly recognisable form as a mixture of general background knowledge, documentary support and so on, though a backing may be just the recursive introduction of another argument structure. The idea of competing claims, however, entails a need for decision-making which requires some developments that Toulmin did not investigate, notably the idea of weighting arguments and aggregating them in order to arrive at an ordering over decision options. We have also suggested that modal qualifiers, which are left rather vague in Toulmin's discussion, can be interpreted as predicates over sets of arguments rather than operators. Such modalities can be used to summarise the relative persuasiveness of a claim without requiring a quantitative scale of belief, force etc. Modalities can also be used to increase the expressiveness of the logical language used for reasoning and decision-making. The main points to have emerged in the context of decision-making are the need to understand the "force" or strength of arguments, the importance of combining as well as attacking arguments in weighing up options, and the theoretical issues surrounding the stopping problem.

CHAPTER 19

JOHN ZELEZNIKOW

USING TOULMIN ARGUMENTATION TO SUPPORT DISPUTE SETTLEMENT IN DISCRETIONARY DOMAINS

School of Information Systems, Victoria University Melbourne 8001, Australia
E-mail: john.zeleznikow@vu.edu.au

ABSTRACT: Our goal is to model reasoning in discretionary legal domains. To do so, we have used Knowledge Discovery from Database Techniques. However there are obstacles to this approach, including difficulties in generating explanations once conclusions have been inferred, difficulties associated with the collection of sufficient data from past cases and difficulties associated with integrating two vastly different paradigms. Toulmin's treatise on the uses of argument can be gainfully employed to construct legal decision support systems in discretionary domains. We show how we can use Toulmin's approach to build such systems with examples taken from the domains of eligibility for legal aid, evaluation of eyewitness evidence, family law, refugee law and sentencing.

Since the principal institution of the law is not trial, but settlement out of court, we show how Toulmin Argument Structures can be developed to construct an Online Dispute Resolution environment that allows for supporting interest based dispute settlement. Our environment involves the determination of BATNAs, allowing exchanges of opinions between the disputants and providing advice about tradeoffs.

KEYWORDS: Argumentation; Stephen E. Toulmin; legal decision support systems; discretionary reasoning; alternative dispute resolution; online dispute resolution

1. MODELING LEGAL DISCRETION

Our research over the past fifteen years has focussed upon building decision support systems that can be used in legal practice. Zeleznikow (2003) has observed that most commercial legal decision support systems have been rule-based. The major reasons for this occurrence include that it is easy to model rules and there are many tools for building rule-based systems.

Users of rule-based legal decision support systems accept a positivist view of decision-making.[1] Our goal is to model discretionary decision-making.

[1] The German Conceptualist movement assumes that judges are almost totally constrained by rules. Every attempt is made by adherents to this theory to determine one single correct meaning for every term in every rule in a legal system. Once this is achieved, legal reasoning reduces to the logical application of facts to rules. However, few legal academics or professionals accept this view of law today. Legal positivists believe that a legal system is a *closed logical system* in which correct decisions may be

D. Hitchcock and B. Verheij (eds.), Arguing on the Toulmin Model: New Essays in Argument Analysis and Evaluation, 289–301.

Flick (1979) defines discretionary domains as those in which a judicial decision-maker has the freedom to select one interpretation or outcome from a number of permissible options. According to Dworkin, discretionary reasoning arises when a decision-maker is free to select one from a number of plausible outcomes (Dworkin, 1986). Barak (1989) states that *"Dworkin and those who share his view believe that each legal problem has one lawful solution"* (p. 28).

However, we believe that there is no concept of *one correct answer*, it is possible and sometimes probable for two decision makers to arrive at a different decision based on the same facts. This is a result of reliance upon factors described as induction and intuition as well as the capacity to assess the social impact of decisions (see Sourdin, 2002).

Dworkin (1977) presents a systematic account of discretion by proposing two basic types of discretion, which he calls strong and weak discretion. Weak discretion describes situations where a decision-maker must interpret standards in his own way whereas strong discretion characterises those decisions where the decision-maker is not bound by any standards and is required to create his or her own standards.

Zeleznikow (2004) claims that there are levels of discretion depending on the domain. There are many domains in which the exercise of discretion cannot be explained by the application of rules and principles. They hold this view because there exist domains such as property division in Australian family law, in which two decision makers may be applying identical rules and principles to facts interpreted in the same way, yet both arrive at different, yet legally valid outcomes. Typically, the statute that underlies these domains presents a list of factors to be considered by the decision-maker, but does not indicate the relative weighting of each factor. Christie (1986) calls these types of statutes shopping list acts. Judges, in such domains, exercise discretion by assigning a relative importance to each factor.

Few automated legal reasoning systems have been developed in domains of law in which a judicial decision maker has extensive discretion in the exercise of his or her powers. Discretionary domains challenge existing artificial intelligence paradigms because models of judicial reasoning are difficult, if not impossible, to specify.

In investigating how Australian Family Court judges distribute marital property following divorce, Stranieri *et al.* (1999) demonstrated that systems for reasoning in discretionary domains can be built by integrating rule sets with neural networks trained with data collected from standard past cases. However there are obstacles to this approach, including difficulties in generating explanations once conclusions have been inferred, difficulties associated with the collection of sufficient data from past cases and difficulties associated with integrating two vastly different paradigms.

We claim that connectionism[2] can be useful in law if a series of smaller, interconnected networks are used instead of one larger network and if explanations

---

deduced from predetermined rules by logical means alone. Hart (1961) is a major proponent of legal positivism.

[2] A neural network receives its name from the fact that it resembles a nervous system in the brain. It consists of many self-adjusting processing elements cooperating in a densely interconnected network. Each processing element generates a single output signal which is transmitted to the other processing

are generated independently of the process used to infer a conclusion. This is in keeping with the legal realist philosophy.[3] The aim is to discover a knowledge representation that assists in the decomposition of a task into smaller sub-tasks and which also enables an independent generation of explanations. The knowledge representation we present that achieves this goal is based on the structure of arguments proposed by Toulmin (1958).

2. THE SPLIT-UP SYSTEM

That section of the Family Law Act (1975) of Australia which is concerned with distributing marital property is regarded as a discretionary Act, in that it makes explicit a number of factors that must be taken into account by a judge in altering the property interests of parties to a marriage but is silent on the relative importance of each factor. Different judges may, and do, reach different conclusions, even when they agree on facts, because each judge assigns different relative weights to factors.

Section 79 (1) of the *Family Law Act (1975)* empowers judges of the Family Court to make orders altering the property interests of parties to the marriage but does not lay down procedural guidelines for judicial decision makers. In practice, judges of the Family Court follow a five-step process in order to arrive at a property order:

1. Ascertain the property of the parties.
2. Value all property of both parties.
3. Determine which assets will be paramount in property considerations. This is referred to as common pool property distribution.
4. Determine a percentage of the property to be awarded to each party. This is referred to as percentage split determination.
5. Create an order altering property interest to realize the percentage.

The Split-Up system (Stranieri *et al.*, 1999) implements steps 3 and 4 above; the common pool determination and the prediction of a percentage split. According to domain experts, the common pool determination task (Step 3) does not greatly involve the exercise of discretion, in stark contrast to the percentage split task (Step 4).

The aim of the approach used in developing Split-Up was to identify, with domain experts, relevant factors in the distribution of property under Australian family law. They assembled a dataset of values on these factors from past cases that

---

elements. The output signal of a processing element depends on the inputs to the processing element: each input is gated by a weighting factor that determines the amount of influence that the input will have on the output. The strength of the weighting factors is adjusted autonomously by the processing element as data is processed.

[3] Legal realists are jurisprudes for whom the reliance on rules is anathema. They argue that judges make decisions for a range of reasons that cannot be articulated or at least are not apparent on the face of the judgement given.

can be fed to machine learning programs such as neural networks. In this way, the manner that judges weighed factors in past cases could be learnt without the need to advance rules. The legal realist jurisprudence movement inspired this approach.

For legal realists exemplified by Llewellyn (1962), rules and principles may be invoked after a decision has been reached in order to ensure that a decision is just, moral and legally correct. Rules and principles are invoked to explain a decision but there is no need to assume they are used to reach the decision.

Ninety-four variables were identified as relevant for a determination of the distribution of marital property. The way the factors combine was not elicited from experts as rules or complex formulas. Rather, values on the ninety-four variables were to be extracted from cases previously decided, so that a neural network could learn to mimic the way in which judges had combined variables.

However, according to neural network rules of thumb, the number of cases needed to identify useful patterns given ninety-four relevant variables is in the many tens of thousands. Data from this number of cases is rarely available in any legal domain. Furthermore, few cases involve all ninety-four variables. For example, childless marriages have no values for all variables associated with children so a training set would be replete with missing values. In addition to this, it became obvious that the ninety-four variables were in no way independent. Thus, in the Split-Up system, the relevant variables were structured as separate arguments following the argument structure advanced by Toulmin (1958).

For the philosopher Stephen Toulmin, practical reasoning, as distinct from analytical reasoning, involves the construction of an argument. Arguments, regardless of the domain, have a structure, which consists of six basic invariants: claim, data, modality, rebuttal, warrant and backing. Every argument makes an assertion based on some data. The assertion of an argument stands as the claim of that argument. A warrant justifies why the claim follows from the data. The backing supports the warrant and in a legal argument is typically a reference to a statute or a precedent case. The rebuttal component specifies an exception or condition that obviates the claim.

The Toulmin Argument Structure has been used by a number of researchers in various fields to model reasoning. However, a survey by Stranieri *et al.* (2001) illustrates that the majority of researchers vary the structure to suit their particular use. The variation that we used aimed to facilitate Knowledge Discovery from Databases. The structure is illustrated in Figure 1.

We see from figure 1 that there are three data items (contributions, resources, level of wealth). Each of these is the claim item of other arguments leading to a tree of arguments (Zeleznikow, 2004, p. 160) where the ultimate claim of the system is the root of the tree (percentage split determination).

Our variation on Toulmin's theory of argumentation does not include either modality or rebuttal. Whilst these are important components of legal disputation, it was not felt worthwhile to include these invariants, given the programming difficulties involved in representing them.

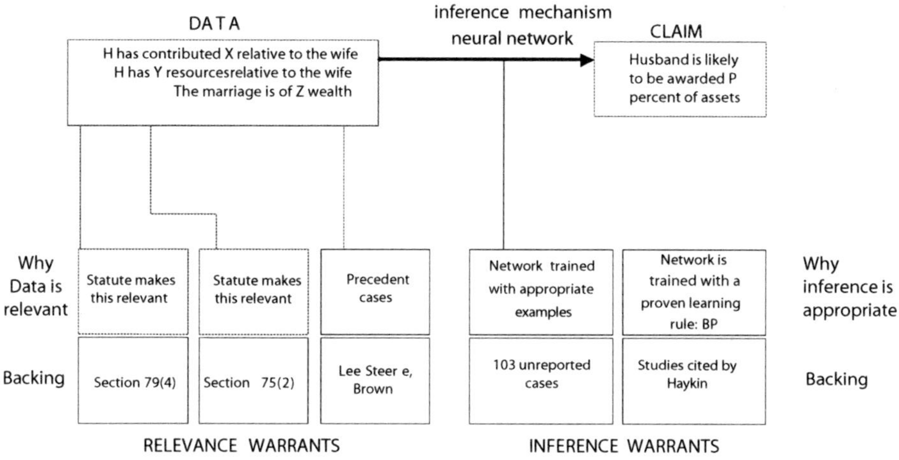

Figure 1. Toulmin argument structure for one of the Split-Up arguments.

Our research shows a more accurate percentage split prediction can be made when using sixteen of the ninety-four variables. This was observed through the application of feature selection techniques using genetic search to the data used to determine percentage split in the Split-Up system (Skabar *et al.*, 1997). An interpretation of this result is that Family Court judges when distributing property rarely use the other seventy-eight attributes. However, because we were concerned with simulating the explanations of family court judges, we decided to focus upon emulating the decision-making process rather than developing the most efficient system.

3. LEGAL DECISION SUPPORT SYSTEMS CONSTRUCTED USING TOULMIN'S THEORY OF ARGUMENTATION

The Toulmin structure has been used to structure knowledge in many studies. The representation facilitated the organisation of complex legal knowledge for information retrieval by Dick (1987), Marshall (1989) and Ball (1994). Clark (1991) represented the opinions of individual geologists as Toulmin structures so that his group decision support system could identify points of disagreement between experts. Johnson *et al.* (1993) identified different types of expertise using this structure, Bench-Capon *et al.* (1991) used Toulmin Argument Structures to explain logic programming conclusions, and Matthijssen (1999) represented user-defined tasks with Toulmin Argument Structures. Branting (1994) expands Toulmin Argument Structure warrants as a model of the legal concept *ratio decidendi*.

Toulmin proposed his views on argumentation informally and never claimed to have advanced a theory of argumentation. He does not rigorously define key terms such as warrant and backing. He only loosely specifies how arguments relate to other arguments and provides no guidance as to how to evaluate the best argument or identify implausible ones. Although there are substantial examples of benefits with the use of the Toulmin structures that conform to the original formulation, the majority of applications vary the structure.

In our implementation of Toulmin Argument Structures we include:

1. A variable-value representation of claim and data items;
2. A certainty value slot associated with each variable-value to represent the degree of confidence that the value assigned to the variable is correct;
3. Reasons for relevance of the data items;
4. A list of inference procedures that could be used to infer a claim value from data values;
5. Reasons for the appropriateness of each inference procedure;
6. Context variables to represent the context of the possible uses of the argument.

Having adapted Toulmin's work on Argumentation to build a decision support system in the domain of Australian Family Law, we next wanted to investigate whether there are certain generic principles involved in constructing web-based legal decision support systems. Given the interests of our industry, government and university partners,[4] we have been developing systems in the domains of:

a) Eligibility for Legal Aid – GETAID (Hall *et al.*, 2002) – 8 arguments;
b) Computer copyright – RIGHTCOPY (Stranieri and Zeleznikow, 2001a) – 50 arguments;
c) Refugee decision-making – EMBRACE (Yearwood and Stranieri, 1999) – 200 arguments;
d) Evaluation of eyewitness evidence - ADVOKATE (Bromby and Hall, 2002) – 23 arguments;
e) Scottish Family Law – (Kingston *et al.*, 2002);
f) Sentencing – (Hall *et al.*, 2005) – 23 arguments.

[4] Phillips and Wilkins, Software Engineering Australia, JUSTSYS, Victoria Legal Aid, Australian Refugee Review Tribunal, University of Edinburgh and Glasgow Caledonian University.

Get Aid

When an applicant for legal aid approaches Victoria Legal Aid (VLA), their application is assessed to determine their eligibility for legal aid. If the applicant satisfies a financial test, the application undergoes a merits test. The merits test involves a prediction about the likely outcome of the case. A web-based system GetAid has been developed which advises solicitors and their clients as to whether the client is eligible for legal aid (Stranieri and Zeleznikow, 2001b). GetAid has captured the reasoning of VLA grants assessors.

Knowledge about an applicant's prospects for acquittal could not readily be represented by experts as a decision tree as was the case for knowledge regarding statutory guidelines. This motivated us to model the decision as a tree of Toulmin arguments.

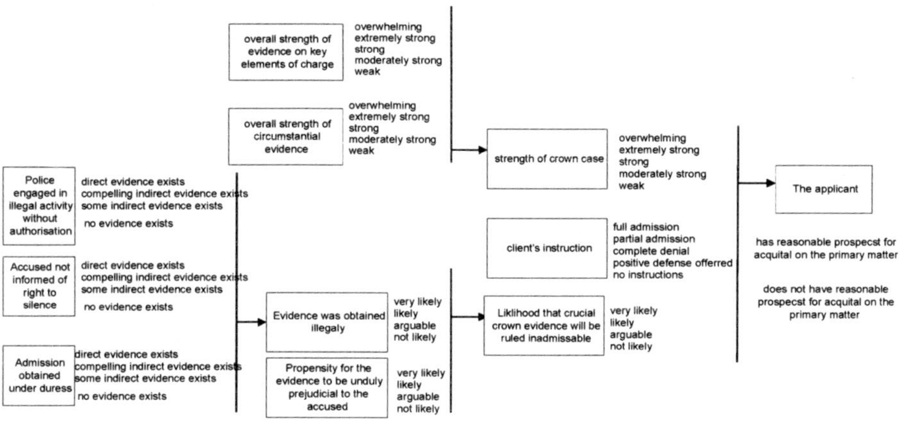

Figure 2. Argument tree for acquittal prospects.

EMBRACE

The Refugee Review Tribunal of Australia determines the refugee status of applicants. Ensuring that the decision-making is as consistent as possible and transparent in this complex and discretionary domain is critical. Toward that end, Yearwood and Stranieri (1999) have modeled reasoning in Australian refugee law as two hundred generic arguments that have been used by members of the Refugee Review Tribunal or applicants for refugee status. No inference mechanism has been specified for any generic arguments as no machine inferences can be entertained in this politically sensitive domain. However, even without machine inferences, the argument structures have proven to be useful in modeling refugee decisions.

Furthermore, they have shown that the process of automatically generating a document that represents the reasoning made toward a decision is facilitated if the knowledge is represented as a series of actual arguments instantiated from generic templates.

Sentencing Decision Support Systems

Hall *et al.* (2005) reports on a project undertaken to provide decision support in discretionary legal domains by referring to a recently created model that involves the interplay and weighting of relevant rule-based and discretionary factors used in a decision-making process. The case study used in the modeling process is the Criminal Jurisdiction of the Victorian Magistrate's Court (Australia), where the handing down of an appropriate custodial or non-custodial sentence requires the consideration of many factors. Tools and techniques used to capture relevant expert knowledge

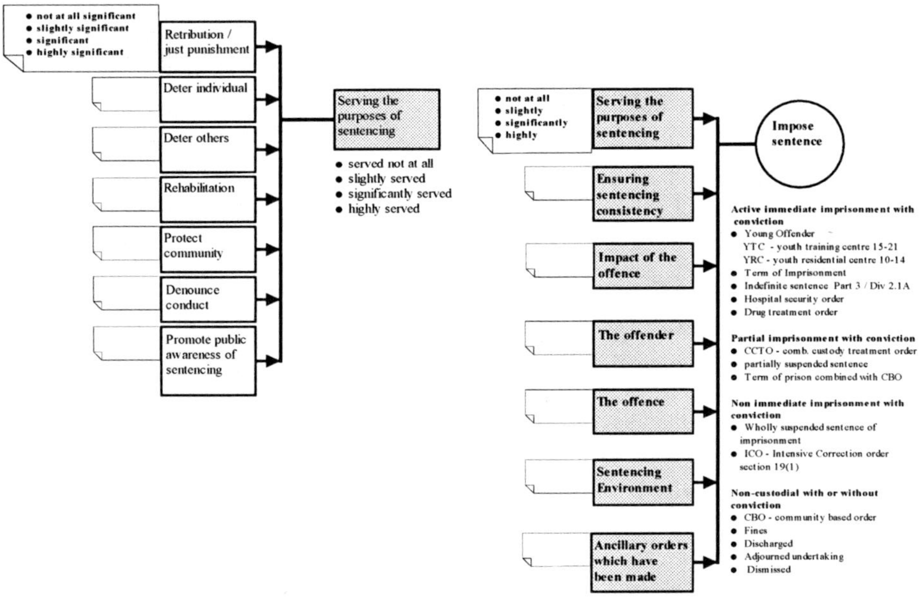

Figure 3. Top-level sentencing argumentation model with expansion of first node.

and to display it both as a paper model and as an online prototype application are discussed. Models of sentencing decision-making with rule-based and discretionary elements are presented and analyzed.

The goal is to provide training support for novice lawyers at Victoria Legal Aid. It has 23 arguments. An example of the top-level Toulmin Argument is given in figure 3.

ADVOKATE

ADVOKATE is a web-enabled knowledge-based decision support application designed for use in criminal investigations, civil litigation or as a teaching aid for investigative training. ADVOKATE provides an indicative assessment of the credibility of eyewitness testimony.

The detailed determination of witness' suitability and reliability are not rule-based inferences but rather discretionary decisions where the decision maker, taking account of several input factors, chooses from one of several possible outcomes. Decision-makers may arrive at different outcomes, depending on how they choose to inference from their understanding of the input factors. Thus the ADVOKATE domain can be categorised as a bounded discretionary domain (Zeleznikow, 2000). The factors to be taken into account are known but no norms specified, leaving the decision-maker free to weight the factors as they wish.

ADVOKATE, implemented as a browser accessible application, was made available to forensic experts, lawyers and police who provided feedback to the designers. The knowledge model was iteratively refined and enhanced and is available at http://cfslr.gcal.ac.uk/ advokate/advkstn.php.[5]

4. USING TOULMIN'S THEORY OF ARGUMENTATION TO SUPPORT DISPUTE RESOLUTION

Dispute Resolution Fundamentals

Ross (1980) states *the principal institution of the law is not trial; it is settlement out of court.* To support this argument, Williams (1983) notes that whilst the figures may vary in different jurisdictions, of all the cases listed before the courts only about 5% of the cases are ever heard by the court and only 1% of the cases result in judicial decision-making. A survey in The Netherlands (Velthoven and Ter Voert, 2004) indicates that about 48% of all disputes were settled out of court and just 4% is decided by litigation. Thus, a major goal of useful legal advice should be to avoid litigation.

---

[5] Accessed January 4, 2006.

Alternative Dispute Resolution (ADR) refers to procedures for settling disputes by means other than litigation – such as arbitration and mediation. Arbitration is a process of dispute resolution in which a neutral third party (the arbitrator) renders a decision after a hearing at which both parties have an opportunity to be heard. Mediation is a private, informal dispute resolution process in which a neutral third party (the mediator) helps disputing parties to reach an agreement. The mediator has no power to impose a decision on the parties. Such procedures, which are usually less costly and more expeditious than litigation, are increasingly being used in civil, commercial, family and labour disputes.

Online Dispute Resolution (ODR), the application of Internet technology to ADR, has become an alternative method for resolving disputes that arise both from online transactions and in the offline context.

It is our goal to build an Online Dispute Resolution environment to provide support for parties to a dispute. But what are the essential features of such an environment?

The Harvard Negotiation Project introduced the concept of principled negotiation, which advocates separating the problem from the people (Fisher and Ury, 1981). Fundamental to the concept of principled negotiation is the notion of *Know your best alternative to a negotiated agreement (BATNA)*. The reason you negotiate with someone is to produce better results than would otherwise occur. If you are unaware of what results you could obtain if the negotiations are unsuccessful, you run the risk of:

1. Entering into an agreement that you would be better off rejecting; or
2. Rejecting an agreement you would be better off entering into.

One of our aims is to provide litigants with information about the expected outcome of court proceedings. Data mining techniques or Semantic Web Technology can be used to determine a BATNA. At this moment there is no generic tool available for determining BATNAs. The BEST project (*B*ATNA *E*stablishment using *S*emantic Web *T*echnology) is attempting to address this problem.[6]

Thus, the first stage of our integrated tool is the provision of a decision support system that advises upon appropriate BATNAs. For example, Split-Up advises upon property distribution following divorce in Australia and can be used to determine one's BATNA. Split-Up shows both litigants what they would be expected to be awarded by a court if their relative claims were accepted. It gives them relevant advice as to what would happen if some or all of their claims were rejected. Users are then able to have dialogues with the system to explore hypothetical situations to establish clear ideas about the strengths and weaknesses of their claims.

Split-Up does provide disputants with their respective BATNAs. However, more is required of negotiation support systems. Namely they should model the structure of an argument and also provide useful advice on how to sequence the negotiation and propose solutions.

---

[6] For a discussion of the BEST project see http://www.best-project.nl/index.shtml; accessed January 1, 2006.

Using Argumentation in an Online Dispute Environment

Zeleznikow and Bellucci (2003) have integrated game theory and artificial intelligence to advise upon structuring the mediation process and advising disputants upon possible trade-offs. Lodder (1999) developed argumentation tools that support disputants communicating about their conflict. The negotiation systems of Zeleznikow and Bellucci do not facilitate discussion, whilst the dialogue tools of Lodder do not suggest solutions. Both systems are useful in what they offer to the user, but the weakness of one application is the strength of the other. We therefore propose to combine the dialogical reasoning of Lodder with the game-theoretic based negotiation techniques of Zeleznikow and Bellucci to construct an online dispute resolution environment.

When initiating a two-party dispute, one of the parties introduces her grievances and the remedies she requires. Her opponent responds with counterarguments and her own proposed remedies. Our argument support tool makes explicit how the statements of the parties support their arguments.

The argument tool used in our proposed ODR environment is based on research about dialogical models of legal reasoning, in particular on DiaLaw (Lodder, 1999), a dialogical model of justification. A dialogue in DiaLaw starts when a player introduces a statement she wants to justify. The dialogue ends if the opponent accepts the statement (justified) or if the statement is withdrawn (not justified). The rules of the game are rigid and the language used in the game is formal.

Influenced by John Nash's significant research on game theory (Nash, 1953) and Raiffa's work on using game theory for negotiation support (Raiffa, 1982), Zeleznikow wished to integrate artificial intelligence and game theory techniques to develop intelligent negotiation support systems. He saw that an important way in which mediators encouraged disputants to resolve their conflicts was through the use of compromise and trade-offs (Bellucci and Zeleznikow, 2005). Once the trade-offs have been identified, other decision-making mechanisms must be employed to resolve the dispute.

To construct our environment,[7] we have set forth three basic stages for the effective resolution of online disputes:

1. Determining a BATNA, which helps the disputing parties determine what will happen if the dispute is not resolved (this task is context-dependent);[8]
2. Allowing parties to communicate among themselves using dialogue techniques (this task is generic); and

---

[7] See Lodder and Zeleznikow (2005) for a detailed discussion of our Online Dispute Resolution Environment.

[8] We cannot build a generic decision support system that advises upon BATNAs in all negotiation domains because, for example, family law disputes are very different from disputes about international treaties. Knowing about the context of the dispute is essential. It is possible, however, to build systems that allow disputants to communicate with each other and to build systems that advise upon trade-offs. See Bellucci and Zeleznikow (2006) for further details.

3. Using game theory techniques that employ compensation/trade-off strategies to attempt to resolve remaining issues in dispute (this task is generic).

Steps 2 and 3 are repeated recursively until either the dispute is resolved or a statemate is reached. Steps 1 and 2 have been successfully supported using Toulmin's theory of argumentation. Whilst step 3 uses game theory rather than argumentation, we are developing a platform based on Toulmin's theory that supports the development of trade-offs and compromises.

5. CONCLUSIONS AND FUTURE RESEARCH

We have shown how Toulmin's treatise on the uses of argument can be gainfully employed to construct legal decision support systems. This is particularly so in discretionary domains.

We have decided to model reasoning in such domains using knowledge discovery techniques. Such techniques do not provide adequate explanations or arguments. This utilisation of Toulmin Argument Structures allows one to use a hybrid of different inferencing techniques. We have applied Toulmin's theory in disparate domains such as family law, eligibility for legal aid, copyright, refugee law, evaluation of eyewitness evidence and sentencing.

To support the development of our systems, we have established an Australian, not-for-profit start up company JUSTSYS (www.justsys.com.au). JUSTSYS is currently building generic tools for constructing web-based legal decision support systems.

Given that current legal practice focuses upon the avoidance of litigation, we have discussed how we are using Toulmin Argument Structures to develop dispute resolution software. In particular we have developed an Online Dispute Resolution environment that allows for determining BATNAs, exchanging opinions and providing advice about tradeoffs.

The use of BATNAS and trade-offs, assumes all parties are involved in interest-based or integrative negotiations. Such negotiations focus on developing mutually beneficial agreements based on the interests of the disputants. However there are some scenarios where the concept of justice based negotiation must take precedence over integrative negotiation.[9] Further, Bush and Folger (1995) argue that the point of mediation as a dispute resolution process is "not" to replicate the processes of the courts, but rather to adopt a very different world view of disputing, one based as they say on 'empowerment and recognition'. They term this process as transformative mediation. Whilst transformative mediation has the potential to transform disputes, we have primarily focused upon an integrative negation solution.

[9] For example, in Australian Family, the interests of the children are paramount. So a Family Law judge can override a negotiated settlement between the parents if she does not believe the agreement meets the need of the children. This issue is discussed in further detail in Bellucci and Zeleznikow (2006).

Keeping this in mind, we are using the environment to provide negotiation support for:

1. Plea bargaining – using our sentencing decision support system to learn how to determine BATNAs in the domain, defence lawyers at Victoria Legal Aid can hold discussions with the Office of Public Prosecutions (Vincent and Zeleznikow, 2005);
2. Family Law – parties to a family dispute can receive advice about possible outcomes, exchange arguments and receive mediation advice about how best they can attain their objectives. Together with Relationships Australia (Queensland Branch) we are developing a system that incorporates justice and integrative bargaining to support divorcing couples to resolve their disputes;
3. Interest Based Negotiation – we are building a general purpose web-based advisory system to advise upon appropriate trade-offs in a dispute;
4. Negotiations about the Outsourcing of Information Technology Agreements.

CHAPTER 20

JAMES F. VOSS

TOULMIN'S MODEL AND THE SOLVING OF ILL-STRUCTURED PROBLEMS

Learning Research and Development Center, 3939 O'Hara Street, Pittsburgh, PA 15260, USA
E-mail: voss@pitt.edu

ABSTRACT: Toulmin's (1958) model of argument was employed in the analysis of verbal protocols obtained during the solving of ill-structured problems. The participants were experts in the domain under study. For the analysis the Toulmin model was extended in order to enable description of lines of argument found in protocols as long as 10 paragraphs. Results included: 1) The analysis provided for tracing a solver's line of argument. 2) On occasion datum and backing were difficult to distinguish. 3) Warrants were essentially not stated, although substantial backing was provided. Conclusions included: That while the Toulmin model provided for description of lines of argument, it did not provide for delineation of components of the problem solving process. A second analysis assumed a "higher level" solving structure and a "lower level" argument structure that supported and provided detail to the "higher" process, thus producing an integrated problem solving specific argumentation structure depicting how reasoning is used in relation to particular task goals. Finally, at a more general level, the overall problem solving process was considered as a Toulmin-type argument structure.

KEYWORDS: Problem solving; protocol; ill-structured; expertise; descriptive

1. INTRODUCTION

My colleagues and I have employed the Toulmin (1958) model of argument in a number of psychological studies. These include research on argumentation by children (Means and Voss, 1996), the mental processing of arguments (Voss, Fincher-Kiefer, Wiley, and Silfies, 1993), the argumentation of the 1991 US Senate debate on the Gulf Crisis (Voss, Wiley, Kennet, Schooler, and Silfies, 1998), and teaching reasoning via the use of argumentation (Voss and Means, 1991). In most of these studies the Toulmin model was employed as a descriptive tool for delineating and discussing argument components. Our most challenging use of the model and the subject of the present paper involved research on the solving of ill-structured problems (defined later), in which we used a modified Toulmin model to delineate lines of argument as found in solver-generated verbal protocols as long as 10

D. Hitchcock and B. Verheij (eds.), Arguing on the Toulmin Model: New Essays in Argument Analysis and Evaluation, 303–311.

paragraphs (Voss, Tyler, and Yengo, 1983). Discussing this application requires a preliminary statement of the problem solving research context in which we were working.

2. THE INFORMATION PROCESSING MODEL OF PROBLEM SOLVING

In the first half of the 20th Century, psychological research on problem solving was dominated by two theoretical approaches, stimulus-response behaviorism, emphasizing utilization of appropriate associations, and Gestalt theory, emphasizing mental reorganization manifesting itself as insight. In the middle of the 20th Century, with the emergence of cognitive psychology, a partial rapprochement of these views occurred, but more importantly, computer simulation of problem solving was taking root, which gave rise to the information processing model. This model was stated in its most complete form in the classic work of Newell and Simon, *Human Problem Solving* (1972).

3. WELL-STRUCTURED PROBLEMS

The general information processing model frequently is described via a spatial metaphor. The term task environment refers to the problem statement and its context, and is outside of the individual. All remaining components are in the problem space, (a metaphor, not a neurological place or system). These components include the constraints of the problem, the possible states of the problem, and the operators of the problem. During the solving of the problem, the solver moves from one state to another via the use of an operator, beginning in the initial state and finishing in the goal state.

As an example, assume the problem is to find the sum of a column of three numbers. The initial state contains the goal and the number 5, let us assume, and the operator "Add" adds the next number, 6 for example, to the initial number, making the sum 11. Taking this sum and applying the operator "Add" to the next number, such as 3, the goal state is 14. As suggested by this example, the operators used in a problem are a function of the particular problem.

While the above problem is simple, essentially the same principles hold when solving more complex problems. The solving process however also becomes more complex. One move is the solver likely employing sub-goals. In playing chess, for example, the solver may set the sub-goal of capturing an opponent's bishop, and this may serve as a possible means to capture the opponent's queen. In addition to developing sub-goals, solvers, especially experts, sometimes solve problems in two phases. In the first, a physics expert initially may study the problem to categorize it, determining for example it is a problem in kinetics. Upon making this identification, the individual then solves the problem. The first phase of this solving process is termed developing a representation of the problem and the second is termed the solution phase. Indeed, results in the domain of physics indicate that appropriate representation development is a way by which experts perform better than novices (Chi, Feltovich, and Glaser, 1981).

Problems described to this point are termed well-structured in that 1) the goal is well-defined, and generally the solution is agreed upon by the members of the respective community, as physicists. 2) Constraints are usually stated in the problem statement or are readily apparent, and the constraints employed by different individuals dealing with the same problem are the same or quite similar. 3) Operators are frequently mathematical, logic-based, or in the case of some games, object moves. 4) Well-structured problems lend themselves to computer simulations because the number of states of a problem, the constraints, and the operators is readily within computer simulation capabilities.

4. ILL-STRUCTURED PROBLEMS

We became interested in the solving of ill-structured problems, in part because solving such problems had received little attention (Reitman, 1965; Simon, 1978), and they posed a number of challenges not found in well-structured problems. Moreover, they occur in virtually all disciplines and in everyday life. Three examples would be how to develop a US exit strategy in Iraq, how to improve education in your school system, and when you should start to think about retiring.

While the distinction of well-structured and ill-structured problems involves a weakly defined continuum, there are a substantial number of examples at each extreme. As opposed to well-structured problems, ill-structured problems usually have 1) a vaguely stated goal that requires analysis and refinement in order to define the particular issue clearly. For example, if you wanted a US exit strategy for Iraq or wanted to improve education, how would you define your more specific goals? 2) The constraints of the problem typically are not in the problem statement; instead, the solver needs to retrieve and examine the constraints ("posting") when appropriate during the solving process. 3) In most cases, the solver's solution is divided into a representation and a solution phase, as previously discussed. However, in contrast to well-structured problems, different solvers may vary considerably in the nature and contents of each of the phases. This is because ill-structured problems may be approached in different ways, according to the solver's knowledge, beliefs, attitudes, and other factors. 4) Solutions to ill-structured problems typically are not right or wrong, and not valid or invalid; instead, solutions usually are regarded in terms of some level of plausibility or acceptability. 5) When a solution is stated, it usually is justified by verbal argument that indicates why the solution will work and perhaps providing a rebuttal by attacking a particular constraint or barrier to the solution or by attempting to refute an anticipated opposing position. The solver's defining the problems via the representation phase and presenting its solution and its justification demonstrates that this solution process is rhetorical in nature. 6) Because there usually are no right or wrong answers with ill-structured problems, evaluation of a solution typically is worded in terms of agreement or disagreement, acceptability or the lack thereof, or some level of plausibility. The evaluator of course may disagree with the solver's justification, the extent to which the justification supports the solution offered, or the evaluator may offer a better solution. 7) The solutions of ill-structured problems are not "final", in the sense that a solver may generate an exit plan for Iraq, and the problem asked for is "solved", but to know if it would "really work", it would require implementation and subsequent evaluation. When to terminate discussion of the solution is thus somewhat arbitrary. 8) The size of the database required for most ill-structured problems and the difficulties in accessing it make simulation difficult.

The reader may have noted that given the differences in the operators of well-structured and ill-structured problems, problems in domains such as mathematics and physics are well-structured. However, in such domains, problems arising on the "cutting edge" frequently are ill-structured. Evidence is shown by Tweney's (1985) study of Michael Faraday's notebooks during the course of Faraday's discovery of electromagnetic induction. The solution process quite substantially followed the course of solving ill-structured problems.

5. USING TOULMIN'S MODEL

The research we conducted involved experts on the Soviet Union indicating how they would improve the USSR's poor agricultural productivity (Voss, Greene, Post, and Penner, 1983). (The work was conducted while the Soviet Union was in existence.) Each expert was asked to assume he or she was Head of the Soviet Ministry of Agriculture and was asked how the agricultural productivity could be improved. Each person responded orally, thus providing a "think aloud" protocol, the account being tape-recorded. The expert protocols were approximately 10 paragraphs in length. (We compared expert and novice performance but only expert data are considered here.) The purpose of the research was to determine the nature of the solving process from both the form and content of the protocols. Toward this end, we thought the descriptive/analytic use of the Toulmin model could tell us about the solving process, especially in tracing the solver's lines of argument. The upper part of Figure 1 presents the Toulmin (1958) model.

The model consists of the Datum or grounds and the Claim, that is, the basic argument, the Warrant, which relates the Datum and Claim, and the possible Backing for the Datum-Claim argument. In addition, the model contains the opportunity to constrain the argument, the Qualifier, and the opportunity to object to the argument, the Rebuttal.

Initially we observed that the model did not provide for the relatively highly developed arguments found in many of our protocols. We therefore devised six extensions that allowed us to analyze the more complex text (Voss, Tyler, and Yengo, 1983). The extensions are essentially generalizations of the Toulmin model components and are presented in the remaining section of Figure 1. The first listed allows the claim of one argument to be the datum of a second argument, thus permitting argument continuity. For example, there may be the argument that "We will become dependent on the West because we do not produce enough food" followed by "Our regime will become unstable because we will be dependent on the West." The second assumes that a warrant is implied in each argument, although, more correctly, the warrant is implicit. This is effectively a restatement of the existence of the warrant in Toulmin's model but indicated as implicit because participants virtually never stated an argument's warrant. The third allows the backing to be an argument, which also permits argument continuity. For example, a statement that "Agriculture productivity is low because the aristocracy did not fend for itself" may be followed by the statement "The aristocracy did not develop modern agricultural methods because it was dependent on the czar." The backing in this case, the second statement, indicates how the aristocracy did not fend for itself. It did not develop modern methods, and the support for this claim indicates why they did not develop such methods, because they were supported by the czar. The fourth allows for a rebuttal statement to have backing, as "Agricultural productivity is poor only because there is so little arable land. In the USSR only 10% of the land is arable." The fifth permits the rebuttal of Toulmin's model to be an argument. A rebuttal argument is given above, "Agricultural productivity is poor because the USSR has so little arable land." The sixth permits a qualifier to be an argument. While the use of a qualifier usually is suggested by terms such as 'maybe', 'perhaps', or 'except for', which constrain the range of operation of a claim, our protocols included a broader use. For example after making a statement to the effect that, although the Soviet government had normally maintained its ideological agricultural policy, it had allowed families to have private plots, a person continued with the clause "even though the private plot was thought to be a less progressive means of agricultural production". The qualifier statement introduced by "even though" is regarded as a qualifier with the argument that the private plot is regarded as a less historically progressive means of agricultural production. It should be noted that this coding of the protocols was conducted over 20 years ago, and that if the argument analysis were repeated today, improvement would no doubt be obtained. Nevertheless, the work did constitute the application of the Toulmin model to highly complex text, and as noted later, served to provide connectivity between argumentation and problem solving processes.

We turn now to one expert's protocol, Expert A in Voss, Tyler, and Yengo (1983) and Voss, Greene, Post, and Penner (1983), as analyzed via the modified Toulmin model. (While both the representation and solution phases of the protocol were analyzed, for reasons of brevity only the analysis of part of the solution is presented.)

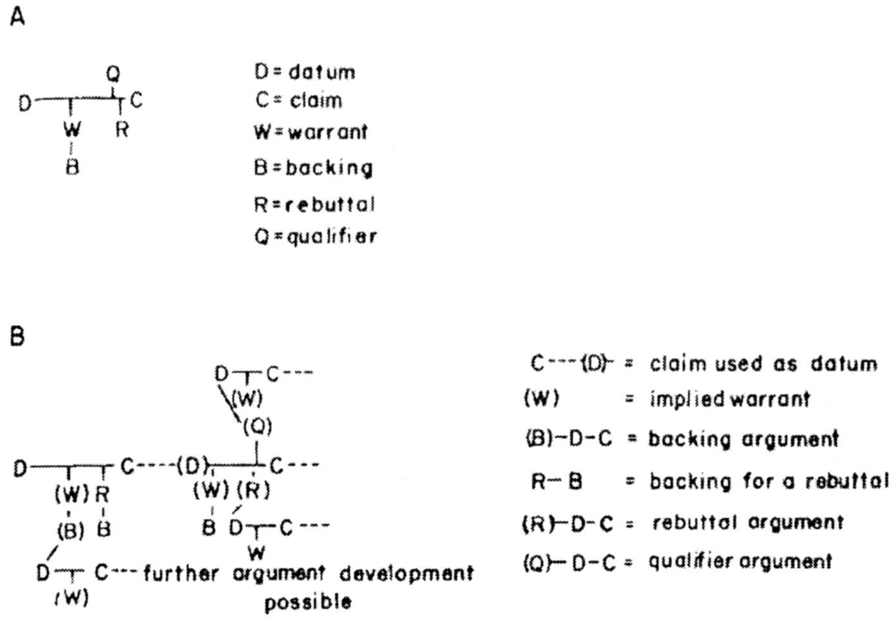

FIGURE 1. Diagram of Toulmin's model of argument (**A**) and diagram of problem-solving adaptation of toulmin's model (**B**).

Figure 1. The original Toulmin argument diagram (A) and the modifications of the Argument, as taken from Voss, Tyler, and Yengo (1983, Figure 1).

In the problem representation phase the expert stated that Russia has the constraints of a poor climate and only 10% of the land being arable, largely in the Ukraine, and that the agricultural problem has been Russia's "Achilles heel" since the time of the czars, when the aristocracy was supported by the czars and a Middle Class did not develop as in England.

Then, continuing with the problem history, he noted that the Soviet regime has used three methods to increase crop production. One was exhortation, ideological campaigns telling peasants and other agricultural workers to increase their effort. But this did not work. A second way was constant reorganization, which led to confusion, mismanagement, and the peasants taking a "this too will pass" attitude. The solver noted that some of these changes involved state farms and collectives, while also pointing out that families in the USSR have had private plots and while regarded ideologically as primitive in the USSR, 40% of the crop productivity comes from the private plots. The third way has been to attempt to mechanize.

This solver continued by suggesting his solution to the problem, namely, increased modernization via agricultural investment, including the use of scientific technology. In the remainder of the protocol the solver supported his position by showing how investment in modernization would improve agricultural productivity via indicating how particular components of poor productivity would be improved. In addition, he attacked some of the problem's constraints.

The solver, in Statements 35-40 of Figure 2, indicated that investment would provide for needed tractor repair parts, would increase transportation facilities to move crops, In addition, use of fertilizer and crop rotation needs to be increased, with such shortcomings making agriculture quite labor intensive.

From Statements 41-57 the solver indicated that the economic decision makers of the Soviet Union need to be convinced that some industrial development money needs to be placed in agricultural development, arguing that with demands going up and the food supply below demand, it means being vulnerable to the West for supplies. Given this, socialism should involve self-sufficiency and you need to avoid dependence on potential adversaries. The money, he maintained, would permit the development of an infrastructure so the USSR could develop a plastics industry, adding that 50% of the fertilizer is lost because it is put in paper bags that get wet and similarly, the transportation system could be improved.

In Statements 59-68 the solver indicated the need for educational program development among agricultural workers and managers of collectives and state farms, pointing out that these positions have always been in the hands of people who have strong party credentials but know nothing about agriculture. An institute would be needed to train the people for these positions. This argument thus was attacking the constraint of ill-prepared party members serving as agriculture experts.

Stopping at this point with consideration of the contents, some conclusions of our analyses are considered. The overall analysis showed that the Toulmin analysis described the lines of argument of the solver (Voss, Tyler, and Yengo, 1983). Furthermore, the analysis showed how the solver justified his solution of investment in modernization, that is, by indicating the things that could be done or would need to be done, and by attacking particular constraints.

While lines of argument were provided by the Toulmin analysis, it should be recognized that a problem solution protocol such as that described constitutes an argument in itself. Specifically, the solver is faced with a question or problem and the representation phase essentially involves an analysis aimed at providing a statement of the cause(s) of that problem, with problem history often being part of this analysis. A solution is then proposed (usually experts prefer an overall solution whereas novices tend to list specific sub-problem solutions) and the remainder of the solution phase consists of justification of that solution. Thus, the solution is the claim, the datum consists of the causal factors, and the solution development constitutes backing. In agreement with Toulmin, this solving process places emphasis upon justification (cf. van Eemeren, Grootendorst, and Snoeck Henkemans, 1996, p. 129).

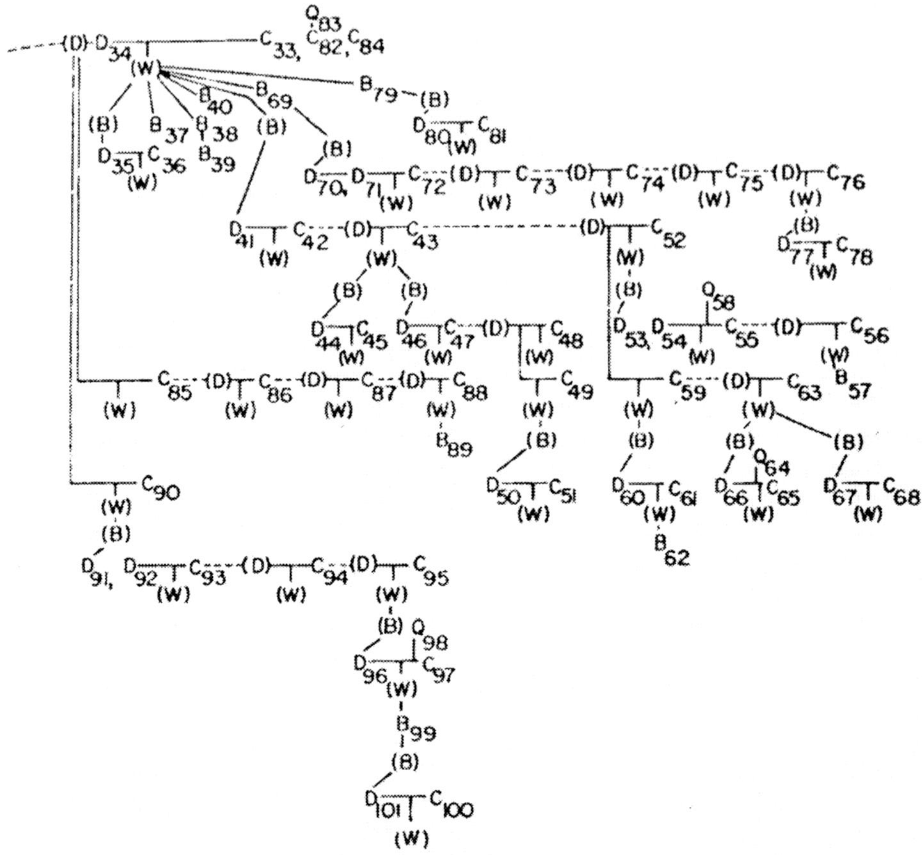

FIGURE 4. Diagram of problem solution of Expert A. (See Figure 2 legend for key.)

Figure 2. Part of an expert's protocol taken from Voss, Greene, Post, and Penner (1983, Figure 4).

With respect to the actual coding of the protocols, the following points are noted. First, there can be difficulty distinguishing whether a given statement is datum or backing, especially when a signal word such as "because" does not occur. A second finding is that within our scoring system, the warrant of an argument is almost never stated. Following Toulmin (1958) as well as Hample (1977) and Govier (1987), statement of the warrant would make the argument logically valid. But the solver of course is interested in providing support for the argument and will thus provide backing, not deductive purity. However, in many cases, the degree of support or the acceptability provided by the particular backing for the argument likely will be a function of the evaluator's knowledge and beliefs.

A shortcoming we found of the Toulmin model relates to our goal of studying solving ill-structured problems. While providing a means to isolate lines of argument, the Toulmin model did not provide information concerning the problem solving process. The second analysis we performed was designed to remove this deficiency (Voss, Greene, Post, and Penner, 1983).

We assumed the existence of a "higher level" problem solving structure that included the elements of the previously described information processing model. The protocol data were analyzed in relation to this structure, and the argument structure then became "lower level" with respect to the problem solving structure. Moreover, two sets of operators were used in the analysis, one in reference to the problem solving structure and the other in relation to the reasoning or argument structure. The operators for the former were state constraint, state sub-problem, state solution, interpret problem statement, evaluate, and summarize. For the latter the operators were state argument, state assertion, state fact, present specific case, state reason, state outcome, compare and/or contrast, elaborate and/or clarify, state conclusion, and state qualifier. This analysis provided an integration of an argumentation analysis being integrated into and facilitating an analysis of complex problem solving. As noted, however, the analysis may also be viewed as showing components lines of argument as found in a more extensive argument.

CHAPTER 21

MANFRED KRAUS

ARGUING BY QUESTION: A TOULMINIAN READING OF CICERO'S ACCOUNT OF THE ENTHYMEME

Philologisches Seminar, Universität Tübingen, Wilhelmstraße 36, D-72074 Tübingen, Germany
E-mail: manfred.kraus@uni-tuebingen.de

ABSTRACT: In his *Topics* (§§ 54-55) Cicero discusses a type of argument which he calls enthymeme, and which he states is based on the third type of 'undemonstrated' syllogism of Stoic logic (not both p and q; but p; therefore not q). From Cicero's examples, however, it is clear that this kind of argument is meant to be regularly phrased as a rhetorical question. An analysis of this argumentative pattern according to Stephen Toulmin's model of argument structure reveals that its weak point is the unsubstantiated presupposition of some 'incompatibility' that serves as the argumentative warrant. It is argued that instead of providing appropriate argumentative backing the form of the rhetorical question is employed in order to secure acceptance of the warrant by putting strong psychological or moral pressure upon the audience by way of shifting the burden of proof or arguing *ad hominem*. An analysis of a selection of arguments of this kind from both Cicero's philosophical writings and his speeches further demonstrates that the persuasive force of the warrants implied can be reduced to various standard topical arguments (such as analogies, *e contrario*, correlations, cause-to-effect, *a minore* etc.), from which appropriate rebuttals may be easily derived.

KEYWORDS: Enthymeme; syllogism; incompatibility; Stoic logic; Toulmin model; warrant; backing; rhetorical question; tactical maneuverings; burden of proof; topical argument

1. INTRODUCTION

Ever since Aristotle's times the enthymeme has been a central feature in rhetorical argumentation. It is strange, therefore, that in Latin rhetoric we have to wait until Cicero's latest years for the first discussion of this means of persuasion in terms of logic and argumentation. Only in his *Topics*, written in 44 B.C.E., one year before his death, does Cicero give a formal analysis of the enthymeme, which, however, differs both from the Aristotelian account and from what is the standard modern understanding of the term, i.e. a syllogism with one premiss suppressed.

In what follows I shall present Cicero's account of what he calls an enthymeme and analyse its traditional logical background as well as its standard outward

D. Hitchcock and B. Verheij (eds.), Arguing on the Toulmin Model: New Essays in Argument Analysis and Evaluation, 313–325.

linguistic appearance as a rhetorical question. It will be demonstrated, however, that the peculiar way this kind of argument works is best revealed by an analysis according to Stephen Toulmin's model of the structure of an argument, from which it will become apparent that in arguments of this kind the step from data to claim is usually only poorly warranted by an alleged, but generally insufficiently substantiated incompatibility of the data and the contradictory of the claim, a logical weakness which is to be compensated, however, by the persuasive phrasing as a rhetorical question.

2. CICERO'S ACCOUNT

Context

Within his list of *loci*, especially the *loci* 'from consequents', 'from antecedents' and 'from incompatibles', Cicero devotes an entire section of his *Topics* (§§ 53-57) to the presentation of a number of "modes of inference" that may provide the underlying structure for such arguments. These "modes of inference" turn out to be a set of different types of syllogisms, strictly speaking Stoic syllogisms. They can be identified as the so-called 'indemonstrable' (*anapódeiktoi*) or rather ' undemonstrated' (Mates, 1953, p. 67; Hitchcock, 2005b, p. 239, note 3) syllogisms of Stoic dialectics (Diogenes Laertius 7.79; Sextus Empiricus, *Against the Logicians* 2.223), which form a set of basic syllogisms, to which all valid arguments within the Stoic system are reducible (Mates, 1953, pp. 67-74; Frede, 1974, pp. 127-167; Bobzien, 1996, pp. 134-141). According to the best sources (Diogenes Laertius 7.79-81; Sextus Empiricus, *Pyrrhonian Hypotheses* 2.157-158), their regular number is five. But Cicero adds two more types (see p. 316).

Definition

Cicero describes the third type of argument as follows:

> But when you deny a conjunction of propositions, and take as posited one or more constituent propositions of this conjunction so that that which is left is to be refuted, this is called the third type of argument. From this spring the rhetoricians' arguments concluded from contraries which they themselves call enthymemes. (*Topics* 54-55; Reinhardt, 2003, p. 143)

A few lines later he affirms that this type of argument "is more the province of the philosophers" and that it "is called third mode by the dialecticians, enthymeme by the rhetoricians" (*Topics* 56; Reinhardt, 2003, p. 145).

Logical Background

A third Stoic indemonstrable is usually described by the following mode: "Not both the first and the second; but the first; therefore, not the second" (O'Toole and

Jennings, 2004, p. 476), or, in formal language: $\neg (p \wedge q); p \rightarrow \neg q$ (see Sextus, *Against the Logicians* 2.226; *Pyrrhonian Hypotheses* 2.158; Diogenes Laertius 7.80; Galen, *Institutio Logica* 14.4). The standard example given by the Stoics is: "Not both it is day and it is night; but it is day; therefore not it is night". What Cicero presents is thus not, strictly speaking, a mode of the third indemonstrable (a mode being a scheme of an argument, in which propositions are represented by ordinal numbers), but an account or definition of it (Bobzien, 1996, pp.134-136).

It needs to be pointed out that a negated conjunction in the Stoic sense is not equivalent to an exclusive disjunction. (The problem of the Stoic understanding of disjunction is discussed at some length in O'Toole and Jennings (2004, pp. 497-520).) For as a conjunction is true, if and only if both its conjuncts are true, a negated conjunction will be true, if at least one of its conjuncts is false. But they may as well both be false, as in the following example: "Not both Dion is in Rome and Dion is in Athens" (for he may be in a third place). Consequently, nothing follows from the negation of one of the conjuncts. A negated conjunction may thus be truth-functionally described by the truth-table 0111.

In addition to this truth-functional relation of "incompossibility", as O'Toole and Jennings (2004, p. 490) prefer to call it, it is further required for a third indemonstrable to serve as a starting point for sensible proof that the conjuncts be somehow 'in conflict' with each other, i.e. that it be logically or physically impossible that they can both be true. Otherwise this pattern of argument would be completely useless for proof. O'Toole and Jennings (2004, p. 490) may well be right in stating that this is the true sense of the Stoic concept of *mákhē* ('conflict'), usually translated as 'incompatibility'. The importance of this additional requirement was first pointed out by Galen (*Institutio Logica* 14.32-34) in the 2nd century C.E. (Burnyeat, 1994, pp. 43-44; Reinhardt, 2003, p. 316), but it seems to be already presupposed by Cicero (or his source).

Some Peculiarities

Cicero's presentation of the third indemonstrable has several peculiarities. First, if the text we read is reliable (there is a variant reading which has "the first" instead of "one or more" (Di Maria, 1994, p. 94; Reinhardt, 2003, p. 318)), he describes an extended model, which allows for conjunctions with more than two conjuncts. This is not unusual, though, as Philoponus also offers a version with multiple conjuncts (*In Aristotelis Analytica Priora Commentaria* 245,20-24 = Hülser, 1987-1988, fr. 1133), the difference being that in Cicero the second premiss asserts all but one of the conjuncts so that the conclusion denies the remaining one, whereas in Philoponus the added premiss asserts only one conjunct and the conclusion denies the remaining ones. Both versions are logically equivalent. There is thus no reason for maintaining that a multiplicity of conjuncts makes the argument invalid (as in Bayer, 1993, p. 149). Nor does Reinhardt's objection apply that multiple conjuncts would not allow for incompatibility, as "the case of *plura* would then yield a false compound minor premiss" (Reinhardt, 2003, p. 313); for it is not required that each conjunct be incompatible with each one of the others, but only that two clearly defined subsets (one of which may be a conjunction itself) be incompatible with each other. Furthermore, it has been demonstrated that a generalized truth-functional description of a negated conjunction with more than two conjuncts is possible (O'Toole and Jennings, 2004, p. 504).

Second, in some manuscripts, there is an additional clause to the effect that one of the conjuncts should be also negated (Di Maria, 1994, pp. 92-94). Although this would fit with the majority of Cicero's examples, it is very probably an intrusion from Boethius' commentary on the passage (Boethius, *In Ciceronis Topica Commentaria* 1142 C-1144 B, Stump, 1988, pp. 149-152) and is thus best ignored, the more so since any of the propositions may be affirmative or negative without disturbing the overall pattern of the argument (Reinhardt, 2003, pp. 317-318).

Third, Cicero adds a sixth and seventh mode, both also based on negated conjunctions (*Topics* 57; Reinhardt, 2003, p. 145). As mode seven ("Not both this and that; but not this; therefore that") will not be valid unless the negated conjunction is interpreted as equivalent to an exclusive disjunction (O'Toole and Jennings, 2004, pp. 510-512), both modes six and seven appear to be later additions either by Cicero or his source (Kneale and Kneale, 1962, pp. 179-181), based on a later Stoic redefinition of the truth-functional value of a negated conjunction as 0110.

Examples

Cicero himself does not give a detailed analysis of his account of the enthymeme, nor does he specify how exactly it is related to a third Stoic indemonstrable. Instead he chooses to illustrate his concept by a number of examples, as follows (*Topics* 55; see Reinhardt, 2003, p. 145):

(1) To fear this, and not to be afraid of the other!
(2) Do you condemn the woman whom you accuse of nothing?
(3) Do you assert that the woman you say has deserved well deserves ill?
(4) What you do know does no good; does what you don't know do harm?

All the examples are in iambic verse and thus clearly picked from some lost Roman tragedy or tragedies. The arguments contained are all stated in extremely succinct form, as is typical of enthymemes. A thorough analysis of their syllogistic structure as third indemonstrables, however, is given by Boethius in his commentary (see above). Expanded to full syllogistic form, (1) would read: "Not both fearing this and not being afraid of the other; but you fear this; therefore you should also be afraid of the other". Burnyeat (1994, pp. 41-42) is surely mistaken in taking this, by virtue of the exclamation mark, to be a double imperative ("Fear this, and do not get into a panic about the other!"). The sense of this line as an indignant exclamation is attested beyond doubt, as it is one of Cicero's favourite quotations, which he employs twice in letters to Atticus to support his respective claims that it would be foolish to worry about one's loss of dignity but not about one's financial difficulties, or to have feared Caesar, but not to be afraid of Antony (*Letters to Atticus* 12.51,3; 14.21,3). Thus the exclamation is tantamount to a rhetorical question which implies the denial of the second conjunct (Schmidt-Radefeldt, 1977, p. 378; Abdullaev, 1977, p. 268).

In like manner, (2) would read: "Not both no accusation and condemnation; but no accusation; therefore no condemnation". (3): "Not both saying the woman has deserved well and asserting she deserves ill; but you say she has deserved well; therefore you must not assert she deserves ill". (4): "Not both what you do know does no good and what you don't know does harm; but what you do know does no good; therefore what you don't know cannot do any harm".

In each case, in accordance with the pattern of a third indemonstrable, a conjunction of two propositions is denied and the first conjunct asserted, so that, as a consequence, the second conjunct is denied. The outward syllogistic form of these arguments is thus impeccable. Nevertheless they all have a decidedly probabilistic ring. One instantly feels that it will be quite easy to raise serious objections or rebuttals. As for (2), lots of examples from history testify to the fact that it is highly debatable whether having nothing to reproach a person of is strictly incompatible with condemning that person (in any sense like its being day is incompatible with its being night). And if (1) were to draw on, say, the incompatibility of fearing a dog and not dreading a lion, lots of exceptions can be conceived of. What if the dog is a trained bloodhound and the lion just a kitten? Or else the lion may be safely behind bars, but the dog at large.

Obviously the conclusiveness of such arguments vitally depends upon the kinds of incompatibilities involved. Whereas the standard examples of Stoic logic are all based on strictly exclusive logical or physical incompatibilities (day/night, in Rome/in Athens), Cicero's enthymemes clearly are not. The alleged incompatibilities they draw on, on closer inspection turn out to hold only in general or for the most part or in the absence of exceptional conditions. This is where the weak point of these arguments is to be found that separates them from proper syllogisms. Even Cicero himself does not maintain that enthymemes *are* third indemonstrables, but only that they "spring from" that particular argumentative pattern.

On the other hand, it cannot be denied either that in real practice arguments of that type can have a highly persuasive effect, which of course is of primary importance in a rhetorical argument. In this respect, it is important to note that Cicero's examples are all phrased as rhetorical questions (or, similarly, as an indignant exclamation), a striking feature Cicero does not address at all in his analysis.

For an appropriate assessment of both the conclusiveness and persuasiveness of the kind of enthymemes Cicero describes, thus, Cicero's account in purely syllogistic terms apparently proves insufficient and needs to be supplemented, if not replaced by a more detailed model of the structure and function of arguments.

3. APPLYING THE TOULMIN MODEL

Toulmin's Model

In his book *The Uses of Argument* (1958/2003) Stephen E. Toulmin expounds a model of the layout of arguments that seems to have much better prospects to offer with respect to the type of argument Cicero calls an enthymeme than Stoic syllogistics. Toulmin describes an argument as a step from given *data* (1958, p. 97) or *grounds* (Toulmin, Rieke and Janik, 1984, p. 38) to a proposed *claim*. That step, however, needs to be authorised by what he calls a *warrant*, i.e. a general rule licensing the transition from data to claim (Toulmin, 1958, pp. 98,143; Toulmin, Rieke and Janik, 1984, p. 46; see Hitchcock, 2003a, esp. p. 70). Warrants often are, but need not necessarily be implicit (Toulmin, 1958, p. 100). The concept of warrants, which replaces the classical reading in terms of premisses, is the central piece of Toulmin's model.

Toulmin repeatedly criticizes Aristotelian syllogistics for its formalism, inflexibility and over-simplicity (1958, pp. 96, 108-109, 143-145). His criticism would just as much apply to Stoic syllogistics. Toulmin denies that the validity of an argument can be judged from purely formal criteria. Instead, he affirms, it is the warrants that have to be looked at primarily when it comes to evaluating arguments. Warrants, however, according to Toulmin's theory, are not field-invariant but field-dependent, which is to say that their validity can only be evaluated with respect to and within the context of a certain field of argument. If the validity of a warrant is not self-evident and is called in doubt by an opponent, some further substantial *backing* will be called for. Any such backing, however, will also be highly field-dependent (1958, pp. 103-104). If serious objections can be raised, these *rebuttals* need to be made explicit in the argument, lest the argument should be inconclusive (1958, p. 101).

Toulmin thus also accounts for arguments, which he terms "quasi-syllogistic" (1958, pp. 109-111, 131-134, 139-141), in which, due to imperfect backing or to the existence of substantial rebuttals, the validity of the warrant (and consequently of the conclusion) is weakened or qualified by a *modal qualifier* such as "probably", "generally", "almost certainly" or the like (1958, pp. 100-101).

The pattern of data, claim and warrant may be termed Toulmin's *simple model*, whereas the pattern additionally involving backing, rebuttals and/or qualifiers can be called his *extended model* (van Eemeren, Grootendorst and Kruiger, 1987, pp. 176-178).

The Petersen Example

To illustrate his models of the layout of arguments, Toulmin uses several standard examples. The example most appropriate for demonstration of the extended model and the one that comes closest to the pattern of Cicero's enthymemes is the Petersen example. The claim that a certain Petersen will not be a Roman Catholic is defended based on the datum that the said Petersen is a Swede. The warrant required to justify the step from datum to claim will then be something like "A Swede can be taken almost certainly not to be a Roman Catholic" (Toulmin, 1958, p. 98). As this step is "not trivial" and the warrant thus "not self-authenticating" (1958, p. 98), some additional backing will be needed, which may for instance be provided by the statistical observation that "the proportion of Roman Catholic Swedes is less than 2%" (1958, p. 108-109). As this statistical evidence does not account for a universal warrant, the modal qualifier "almost certainly" has to be inserted.

Yet, as Toulmin himself points out (1958, pp. 108-109), both warrant and backing can alternatively be formulated by the sentence "Scarcely any Swedes are Roman Catholics", which may appear as a major premiss in a syllogistic argument: "Petersen is a Swede; Scarcely any Swedes are Roman Catholics; So, almost certainly, Petersen is not a Roman Catholic". But Toulmin points out that, by virtue of the modal qualifier, this will at best be a "quasi-syllogism", which he contrasts with the corresponding syllogism proper: "Petersen is a Swede; *No* Swede is a Roman Catholic; So, *certainly*, Petersen is not a Roman Catholic" (1958, p. 131-133).

This latter syllogism, however, can be rephrased as a third indemonstrable: "Not both Petersen is a Swede and Petersen is a Roman Catholic; but Petersen is a Swede; therefore he is not a Roman Catholic." Following Cicero, this can be further transformed into an enthymeme such as: "(How) can Petersen, being a Swede, be a Roman Catholic?" It is evident that the proper syllogisms are unsound, as they rely on warrants without sufficient backing. For the proportion of Catholic Swedes is *not* zero, but about 1.0 to 1.5%. There is, as Toulmin states, "no positive contradiction in the supposition of Petersen's being a Swede, scarcely any Swedes being Roman Catholic, and yet Petersen's being a Roman Catholic" (1958, p. 139, cf. p. 133). Thus to make the above third indemonstrable sound, it would require either explicit rebuttals such as "unless he was born from Roman Catholic parents or has been converted to Catholicism" or a modal qualifier such as "almost certainly". Yet if the indemonstrable is unsound without rebuttals or modal qualifier, so will be the corresponding enthymeme.

Cicero's Examples Read in Toulminian Terms

We can now return to Cicero's examples and try to evaluate them using Toulmin's model as a guiding concept. In each case there is a clearly defined claim: "You should also be afraid of the other", "You cannot condemn this woman", "You cannot assert that this woman deserves ill", "What you don't know does no harm". To defend those claims, if challenged, we will ask: "What have we got to go on?" As a response, we can present the respective data: "You fear this", "You accuse this woman of nothing", "You say this woman has deserved well", "What you do know does no good". But the all-important question will be: "How do we get there?" In other words: What can we produce as a warrant to justify the step from data to claims? Due to the abbreviated form of the enthymemes, none of the warrants is explicitly stated, but they can be reconstructed.

In each example, at least two implicit assumptions are made that serve as warrants. The first one is purely formal. It is the formal validity of the syllogistic pattern of a third indemonstrable as such, which may be granted off-hand. If one accepts this as a warrant, it will indeed be a field-invariant type of warrant. In spite of Toulmin's general reluctance to accept an overall Principle of the Syllogism as a warrant (1958, pp. 128-135, reconfirmed explicitly by himself during the discussion of the present paper), it has been suggested by others that purely formal warrants should be accepted and that Toulmin's thesis of the field-dependency of warrants would need some qualification in that respect (Hitchcock, 2003a, pp. 79-81).

The second presupposition is more intricate. In every single example, to make the argument work properly, it needs to be accepted that the respective datum is in fact incompatible with the contradictory of the corresponding claim. These substantial warrants, however, are very clearly field-dependent. For it is only with respect to knowledge in a particular field of argument that it is possible to assess whether two propositions are or are not in fact incompatible with each other (unless they are related to each other in a purely logical way, such as e.g. affirmation and denial of the very same proposition).

Something of that kind is indeed implied in each of Cicero's examples. Fearing this is presupposed to be incompatible with not being afraid of the other, default of accusation with condemnation, saying somebody has deserved well with asserting that the same person deserves ill, and the uselessness of what one knows with the harmfulness of what one does not know. Yet, as we observed earlier, apart from the fact that they are strongly field-dependent, none of those 'incompatibilities' are logical truisms or proven facts. They are not even universally valid, but allow for various exceptions and rebuttals. They can at best be said to hold in general or for the most part. This is also made evident by contrast with Cicero's example for a proper third indemonstrable (*Topics* 53; Reinhardt, 2003, p. 143): "It is not the case both that silver is bequeathed and that money in coins is not bequeathed; but silver is bequeathed; therefore, money in coins is bequeathed." It is crucial to know that coined money in this example is simply presupposed to be a subclass of silver by virtue of its also being called *argentum*, which (like *argent* in French) is basically the word for "silver"; this makes the argument valid: provided that "silver" includes not only silverware, but also coined money by definition, if "silver" is bequeathed to a certain person in a will, then any coined money left in the estate will also be bequeathed to that person; for any exclusion of coined money from the legacy will be incompatible with the fact that silver is bequeathed.

Analysis in Toulminian categories thus reveals that in Cicero's enthymemes, as a rule, in spite of the formal validity of a third indemonstrable the inference is poorly warranted substantially, which is the crucial weak point of this type of argument. Just as in Toulmin's Petersen example, the argument would thus strongly require qualification by explicit enumeration of potential rebuttals or by insertion of a modal qualifier. But there is nothing of that kind. In fact, there can't be in an enthymeme, lest the argument lose much of its pungency.

In support of the deficient substantial warrants we would at least expect some appropriate argumentative backing to make them acceptable to the audience. But no such backing seems to be provided either.

4. ARGUING BY RHETORICAL QUESTIONS

Rhetorical Questions as Statements

We will remember the striking fact that Cicero's examples are all phrased as rhetorical questions. Yet a rhetorical question can be regarded as an indirect speech act (Searle, 1975; Anzilotti, 1982), whose true function is not, as in real questions, to elicit information, but to make a statement or exhortation. There is thus a discrepancy between outward form and illocutionary function (Ilie, 1994, pp. 45-51). The statement implied in a rhetorical question is identical with the contradictory of its propositional content. This is what Cornelia Ilie calls the "polarity shift" between question and implied statement (1994, pp. 45, 51-52). "Can you condemn this woman?" implies "You cannot condemn her" (see Schmidt-Radefeldt, 1977, p. 384; Abdullaev, 1977, pp. 266-268; Grésillon, 1980, pp. 277-280; Conrad, 1982, pp. 420-421; Meibauer, 1986, p. 128).

Persuasive Force

But rhetorical questions can do much more than that. They can display a strong persuasive force. Ilie has convincingly demonstrated that rhetorical questions are basically multifunctional and that eliciting agreement from the addressee is one of their major functions (1994, pp. 59-60). Rhetorical questions often are what one might call "loaded" or "leading" questions. They provoke the addressee to infer and thereby to somehow agree on the one and only answer intended by the proponent. At the same time they convey the impression of a strong commitment of the proponent to this statement (Ilie, 1994, pp. 53-59). Clearly, in an argumentative context, the effect of the employment of rhetorical questions will be not so much "to communicate doubt, perplexity, uncertainty" (Schmidt-Radefeldt, 1977, p. 389), but the "strengthening [of] persuasive effects" (Frank, 1990, p. 737). Frank even goes so far as to assert that "the primary function of [rhetorical questions] is to persuade" (1990, p. 737). The claim that arguments are strengthened by rhetorical questions is also clearly supported by recent research in cognitive psychology (Zillman, 1972, 1974; Petty, Cacioppo and Heesacker, 1981; Cacioppo and Petty, 1982).

This most certainly is exactly the reason why Cicero's enthymemes are phrased as rhetorical questions. Instead of proper argumentative backing the rhetorical questions are used in order to compensate the weakness of the respective warrants implied. The form of the rhetorical question ("How can you ...?") puts strong psychological and moral pressure on the audience in order to make them accept without protest what is highly debatable, but vitally needed for the argument to work.

Tactical Maneuverings and Fallacies

This persuasive force of rhetorical questions in Ciceronian enthymemes is ultimately assured or enhanced by a number of tactical maneuverings which, from a pragma-dialectical point of view, can be regarded as fallacious.

Shifting the Burden of Proof

It is an iron rule of critical discussion that whoever advances an argument has to accept the burden of proof. If an argument is phrased as a rhetorical question, however, the burden of proof may fallaciously appear to be shifted onto the side of the respondent, who, if not convinced by the argument, will now feel obliged to defend his or her conflicting standpoint, especially so with questions exerting strong moral pressure such as the "How can you ...?" type, as the respondent will literally feel being asked for evidence ("On what reasons can you ...?") (see van Eemeren and Houtlosser, 2002, esp. pp. 22-23).

Evading the Burden of Proof

Whoever advances a Ciceronian enthymeme in a rhetorical question, may be guilty of evading the burden of proof in a twofold sense: first, because he or she obviously refuses to produce appropriate arguments, but replaces them by a rhetorical device instead (cf. Walton, 1996a); second, because the proponent may, if he or she were to meet with unexpectedly fierce resistance from the part of the respondent, easily deny commitment and withdraw to the excuse that after all he or she only wanted to ask a question (Grésillon, 1980, p. 275; but see Meibauer, 1986, pp. 168-169).

Argumentum ad hominem

In certain cases, rhetorical questions may also result in an *argumentum ad hominem*, particularly so in aggressively put second person questions of the "How can you ...?" type, by which the addressee may with good reason feel personally attacked (Ilie, 1994, pp. 167-168, 206-208), as he or she may feel accused of logical (or moral) inconsistency and thus of intellectual (or, for that reason, moral) inferiority. Although this may be found to presuppose a rather broad concept of *argumentum ad hominem*, it can hardly be denied that aggressive rhetorical questions of this kind at least can be felt to be aimed at the personal self of the opponent as a whole.

Begging the Question

Rhetorical questions of the kind used in Ciceronian enthymemes may even be said in a sense to beg the question. For any such question may be taken to imply both warrant and conclusion at a time. An expression such as "How can you condemn this person whom you accuse of nothing?" may on the one hand be interpreted as logically equivalent to the warrant "You can't both not accuse and yet condemn any person", but on the other hand also as a way of asserting the conclusion itself: "You can't condemn this particular person" (see Walton, 1991, pp. 234-235, 310-311).

It is these and similar tactical maneuverings and fallacies inherent in the kind of rhetorical questions used in Ciceronian enthymemes that account for much of the persuasive force and moral pressure they exert on their audiences.

5. HIDDEN BACKINGS

Cicero explicitly states that the type of argument in question is as popular with philosophers as it is with orators (*Topics* 56; Reinhardt, 2003, p. 145), a statement for which both his philosophical writings and his speeches offer ample evidence. This, fortunately, considerably broadens the basis for an analysis of practical examples. Such a sample analysis, with special attention paid to the individual character of the 'incompatibility' warrants implied in each case, yields that the alleged incompatibilities involved turn out to be ultimately based on a comparatively small variety of standard argumentative patterns.

By far the most popular type appears to be the one based on what one would call an *argumentum a minore*, such as in Cicero's first example in the *Topics*. "If you fear this, you should also be afraid of the other (as it is even more frightful)". Another fine example of this type is found in *Tusculan Disputations* 2.34: "Can boys do this and shall men prove unable?" Similarly in *Pro Roscio Amerino* 113: "If in a matter of very little importance a man who has neglected his trust cannot escape condemnation ..., in a case so grave as the present ... shall he be reckoned among honourable men?" Or, most celebrated, in *Philippics* 2.86: "What is more shameful than that he should be living who set on the diadem, while all men confess that he was rightly slain who flung it away?" The list could be as long as desired.

Conversely, an *argumentum a maiore* may also be used, such as in *Pro Caecina* 43: "Shall not that which is called 'force' in war be called the same in peace?"

In other cases the argument is based on some parallelism or analogy, such as in *De finibus* 2.13: "If these gentlemen can understand what Epicurus means, cannot I?" Or in *Tusculan Disputations* 2.39: "Shall the veteran soldier be able to act like this, and the trained philosopher be unable?"

An *argumentum e contrario* is involved e.g. in Cicero's fourth example in the *Topics*: If what one knows does no good, what one does not know cannot do any harm. This veritable pattern of *e contrario*, of course, is not to be confused with the popular appellation of the entire type of argument as *contrarium* e.g. in the *Rhetoric to Herennius* (4.25-26) or Quintilian (5.10,2).

Sometimes, if rarely, an argument is produced from semantically correlated terms, such as in *Orator* 142: "Why is it shameful to learn what is honourable to know? Why is it not glorious to teach that which it is most excellent to know?"

An even more sophisticated type of argument is the one from parts to whole employed in *De natura deorum* 2.87: "When you see a statue or painting, you recognize the exercise of art ... how then can it be consistent to suppose that the world, which includes the works of art in question ... can be devoid of purpose and of reason?"

Lastly, there are also arguments from cause to effect, as (tentatively) in Cicero's second example in the *Topics* (if there is no accusation, there can't be any condemnation either), or, conversely, from effect to cause, such as in *Pro Caecina* 44: "Can you deny the cause when you admit the effect?"

Evidently, it is these argumentative patterns that constitute the real substantial warrants Cicero's enthymemes are ultimately based on. These are the potential backings that one might produce on demand in support of Cicero's incompatibility warrants. They are, however, simple common sense arguments without any syllogistic structure, which may only account for inferences of a certain limited probability. To rhetoricians they are known by the name of topical arguments.

It now becomes clearer, why Cicero's arguments from incompatibilities appear so poorly warranted and why it is necessary to hide those ultimate backings as best one can, if one argues by a Ciceronian enthymeme. For once the topical pattern is unveiled, any opponent will easily detect the appropriate rebuttals needed to counter or rebuke the respective argument. Viewed from this angle, Cicero's whole incompatibility theory appears to be a quasi-syllogistic construct devised to conceal the basic weak point of arguments of that type and to make them appear logically sound, as in fact Stoic rhetorical theory would demand. But on the other hand, it would also appear that, after all, this theory is not really badly placed in a work such as the *Topics*.

6. CONCLUSION

By our analysis of Cicero's account of the enthymeme on the basis of Stephen Toulmin's model of the layout of arguments we hope to have successfully demonstrated that arguments of this type, in spite of their syllogistic appearance, are, as a rule, rather poorly warranted, which is explained by the fact that they are ultimately based on topical arguments. We have also tried to make plausible that the ultimate reason for the standard phrasing of such arguments as rhetorical questions lies in the fact that the persuasive force of rhetorical questions, by way of several kinds of tactical maneuverings, will put strong psychological or moral pressure on the audience so as to make them accept the implicit warrants without any need of argumentative backing.

7. POSTSCRIPT: AN ACID TEST BY SURPRISE

Immediately after the preceding paper had been delivered at the Conference of the Ontario Society for the Study of Argumentation at Hamilton, Ontario, Canada in May 2005, Professor Jeanne Fahnestock approached me in what seemed a state of excitement to ask me: "How in the world can you say that topical arguments are weak?" I instantly felt somewhat affronted and did not fail for a second first to bolster up and defend my point by way of various sorts of backing arguments, then eventually even to partly give in to her apparent disagreement by moderately toning down my statements, saying among other things that I had not really wanted to say that they were *that* weak, but only that they were relatively weak or weak in a certain sense etc., when, all of a sudden, she burst out laughing and said: "Didn't you realize what I just did to you? I put your theory to a test at your own self, and you perfectly proved it." Although I had just presented a paper dealing with the subtle persuasive mechanisms at work in rhetorical questions, I had fallen into the same trap myself only a minute later when tackled by an aggressively put rhetorical question. I had felt challenged personally, and I had felt the immediate need to back up my view with further arguments; I had even begun to feel doubtful about my own convictions. This, if anything, seems to be convincing proof of the validity of the theory expounded above, and I am thus exceedingly thankful to Professor Fahnestock for hoaxing me the way she did.

CHAPTER 22

ANDREW ABERDEIN

THE USES OF ARGUMENT IN MATHEMATICS

Humanities and Communication, Florida Institute of Technology, 150 West University Blvd, Melbourne, Florida 32901-6975, U.S.A.
E-mail: aberdein@fit.edu

ABSTRACT: Stephen Toulmin once observed that 'it has never been customary for philosophers to pay much attention to the rhetoric of mathematical debate' (Toulmin *et al.*, 1979, p. 89). Might the application of Toulmin's layout of arguments to mathematics remedy this oversight?

Toulmin's critics fault the layout as requiring so much abstraction as to permit incompatible reconstructions. Mathematical proofs may indeed be represented by fundamentally distinct layouts. However, cases of genuine conflict characteristically reflect an underlying disagreement about the nature of the proof in question.

KEYWORDS: Euclid, mathematical argumentation, proof, rebuttal, Stephen Toulmin, undercutter

Modern formal logic's earliest successes were in the analysis of mathematical argument. However, formal logic has long been recognized as useful elsewhere, and is now the dominant means of logical analysis in all fields of discourse. Informal logicians claim that this mathematical success has been bought at the cost of broader application. They have proposed methods of argument analysis complementary to that of formal logic, providing for the pragmatic treatment of features of argumentation which cannot be reduced to logical form. Most informal logicians have conceded mathematics to formal logic, while stressing the superiority of their own systems as analyses of argumentation in natural language. My contention is that this is an unnecessary concession: both systems provide complementary insights into mathematics, just as they do into natural language argumentation.

In this paper I exhibit some aspects of mathematical argumentation which can best be captured by informal logic.[1] Specifically I investigate the applicability of Toulmin's layout of arguments to mathematics. I demonstrate how the layout may be used to represent the structure of both 'regular' and 'critical' arguments in mathematics. Mathematical proof is typically regular argumentation, and it is this which I address most closely.

---

[1] I considered other applications of informal logic to mathematics in (Aberdein, 2005).

D. Hitchcock and B. Verheij (eds.), Arguing on the Toulmin Model: New Essays in Argument Analysis and Evaluation, 327–339.

1. TOULMIN'S LAYOUT

Toulmin's *The Uses of Argument* is perhaps the single most influential work in modern argumentation theory (Toulmin, 1958). Especially widely cited is the general account it offers of the structure of arguments. Toulmin begins with the thought that an argument is a claim (*C*) derived from data (*D*) in accordance with a warrant (*W*). While this is superficially similar to the treatment of arguments in deductive logic, greater generality is achieved through additional components of the layout. The argument may have a modal qualifier (*Q*), such as 'necessarily' or 'presumably', which explicates the force of the warrant. If the warrant does not provide necessity, its conditions of exception or rebuttal (*R*) may be noted. We may also keep track of the backing (*B*) which supports the warrant. The overall layout is often set out graphically, as in Figure 1.

While philosophers attacked *The Uses of Argument* as 'Toulmin's anti-logic book', rhetoricians, communication theorists and subsequently computer scientists have found its account of argumentation deeply insightful (Shapin, 2002). Although it traduces Toulmin to characterize him as 'anti-logic', his motivation was indeed to critique formal logic, specifically its claim to represent all the significant content of

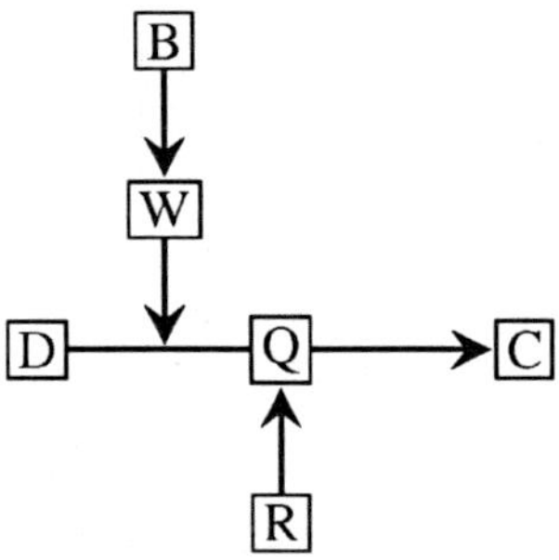

Figure 1. Toulmin's layout (Toulmin, 1958, p. 104).

non-mathematical argument. Mathematics, as the discourse for which formal logic is best suited, was exempt from this critique. Nevertheless, Toulmin's layout is intended to encompass all forms of argument, mathematics included, as he makes clear in a later work (Toulmin *et al.*, 1979, p. 89). In the remainder of this paper we will see how well it accomplishes this task, and whether it has advantages over formal logic alone in this discourse too.

Criticism of the Toulmin layout has largely focused on its representation of argument in everyday communication, complaining for example that 'argument diagrams necessarily abstract arguments from the phenomenal world of the social actor' (Willard, 1976, p. 309). Most criticism of this sort would seem to be substantially less telling against the use of the layout to diagram mathematical argument. However, one important objection remains outstanding: that the layout is perniciously ambiguous, making different, incompatible, reconstructions possible. Use of the layout would thus risk distorting the original argument to an unacceptable degree. I shall explore whether this criticism undermines the application of Toulmin's layout to mathematics below, but first I must address an important distinction.

2. REGULAR AND CRITICAL ARGUMENTS

In discussing scientific arguments, Toulmin distinguishes between arguments that are conducted within, or as applications of, a scientific theory and arguments which challenge a prevailing theory or seek to motivate an alternative (Toulmin *et al.*, 1979, p. 247). The former he terms 'regular arguments', the latter 'critical arguments'. This distinction echoes the familiar one between normal and revolutionary science promoted by Thomas Kuhn, although Toulmin rejects Kuhn's hard and fast distinction between these two modes (Toulmin, 1970). Hence critical arguments are always available to scientists, not just in revolutionary phases, although they may not always have cause to use them. Moreover, critical arguments are more broadly conceived than scientific revolutions, since they do not necessarily require the overthrow of the prior theory in order to succeed. As Toulmin observes, '[c]omplete immutability in our rational procedures and standards of judgment is not to be found even in . . . pure mathematics. The standards of rigour relied on in the judging of mathematical arguments have had their own history' (Toulmin *et al.*, 1979, p. 133). Even commentators who deny that there can be revolutions in mathematics on the grounds that it is a purely cumulative discipline concede that there can be revolutions in mathematical rigour.[2] Thus even the most conservative history of mathematics must consider mathematical critical arguments. Furthermore, when we apply Toulmin's layout to regular mathematical argumentation, we shall see how it may be used to keep track of the changing standards of rigour to which critical argumentation can give rise.

A good example of a mathematical critical argument is that offered by Ernst Zermelo and others for admitting the Axiom of Choice as one of the axioms of set theory. This is discussed by Jesús Alcolea Banegas, one of the few people to specifically address the application of informal logic to mathematics (Alcolea, 1998).[3] I have reproduced his reconstruction of the layout of this argument as Figure 2. However, mathematical critical arguments are arguments *about* mathematics, not arguments *in* mathematics. For this reason, mathematical critical arguments are much like the critical arguments of any other discipline: there is nothing specifically mathematical about the warrant invoked, or any other aspect of their structure. Indeed, there cannot be, since they are appealing to the extra-mathematical in order to settle a dispute which cannot be resolved by purely mathematical means.

---

[2] For example, (Crowe, 1975). Positions for and against mathematical revolutions are explored at length in (Gillies, 1992).

[3] I am grateful to Miguel Gimenez of the University of Edinburgh for translating this paper from the original Catalan.

The characteristic content of mathematics is mathematical proof. Proofs are regular arguments—they may inspire criticism of underlying principles, but the criticism must take place outside the proof itself. In the next section we will examine how closely Toulmin's layout models the work of mathematical proof.

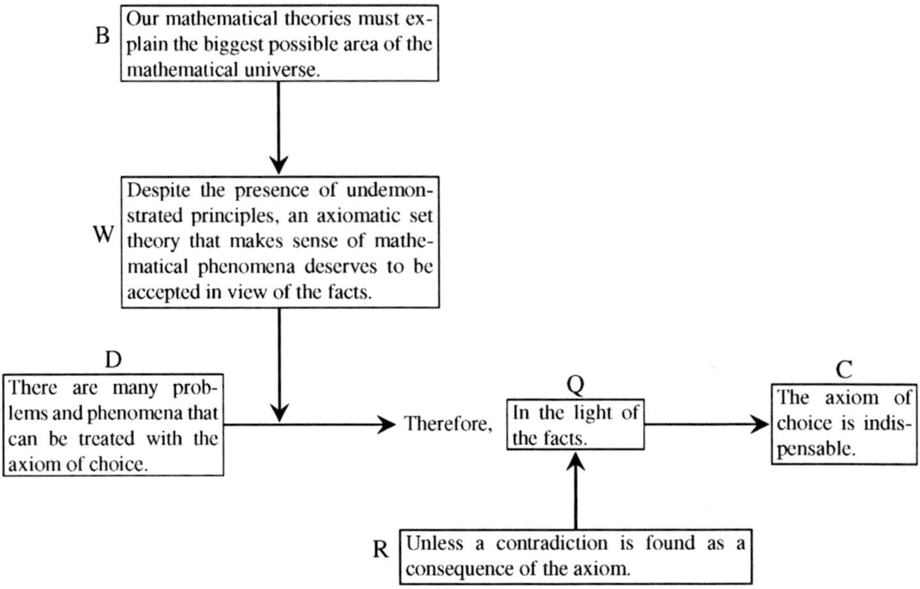

Figure 2. Alcolea's analysis of Zermelo's argument for the adoption of the axiom of choice (Alcolea, 1998, p. 143).

3. PROOFS

Toulmin's own example applying his layout to mathematics is Theaetetus's proof that there are exactly five platonic solids. This result is recorded by Euclid as the final proposition of Book XIII of his *Elements*, where the proof reads:

> I say next that *no other figure, besides the said five figures, can be constructed which is contained by equilateral and equiangular figures equal to one another*.
>
> For a solid angle cannot be constructed with two triangles, or indeed planes.
>
> With three triangles the angle of the pyramid is constructed, with four the

angle of the octahedron, and with five the angle of the icosahedron; but a solid angle cannot be formed by six equilateral and equiangular triangles placed together at one point, for, the angle of the equilateral triangle being two thirds of a right angle, the six will be equal to four right angles: which is impossible, for any solid angle is contained by angles less than four right angles [XI.21].

For the same reason, neither can a solid angle be constructed by more than six plane angles.

By three squares the angle of the cube is contained, but by four it is impossible for a solid angle to be contained, for they will again be four right angles.

By three equilateral and equiangular pentagons the angle of the dodecahedron is contained; but by four such it is impossible for any solid angle to be contained, for, the angle of the equilateral pentagon being a right angle and a fifth, the four angles will be greater than the four right angles: which is impossible.

Neither again will a solid angle be contained by other polygonal figures by reason of the same absurdity.

Q.E.D. (Heath, 1956, Vol. 3, pp. 507 f.)

Toulmin's layout of this proof, slightly adapted for consistency of notation, is reproduced as Figure 3. We can see that it is an essentially faithful reproduction of Euclid's argument, but it will be profitable to compare the two more closely. Firstly, there is a harmless simplificiation, but slight loss of rigour, in Toulmin's omission of the statement that a solid angle cannot be constructed from two planes (a consequence of Euclid's Def. 11, Book XI). Most of the remainder of Euclid's proof becomes Toulmin's data, *D*, the claim, *C*, is essentially the same in both presentations, and Toulmin's warrant, *W*, combines the definition of a regular convex polyhedron with the essential prior result on which the proof depends, Euclid's Prop. 21, Book XI. Other parts of the layout are more novel: *Q*, a characterization of the rigour of the proof, makes explicit something implicit in Euclid, and *R* is not there at all, since on Toulmin's account the proof cannot be rebutted. All of these identifications seem reasonable, and there does not seem to be any scope for pernicious ambiguity. However, this is an elementary proof—problems may yet arise in more complicated cases.

One obvious way in which Theaetetus's proof is untypical of mathematical proofs is that it has only one step. Most proofs, indeed most proofs in Euclid, contain many steps, from the initial premisses through various intermediate results to the eventual conclusion. How might Toulmin's layout be applied to these multi-step proofs? The most thorough method would be to diagram each step of the proof separately, perhaps linking them together in a sort of sorites.[4] If the fine detail of the

[4] As suggested in (Toulmin *et al.*, 1979, p. 79). More complex structures will be required to represent some sorts of proof, such as proof by contradiction. Although Toulmin only discusses linked and sequential arguments, it is possible to assemble his layouts into convergent, divergent and nested combinations, although the details are beyond the scope of this paper. See Aberdein 2006.

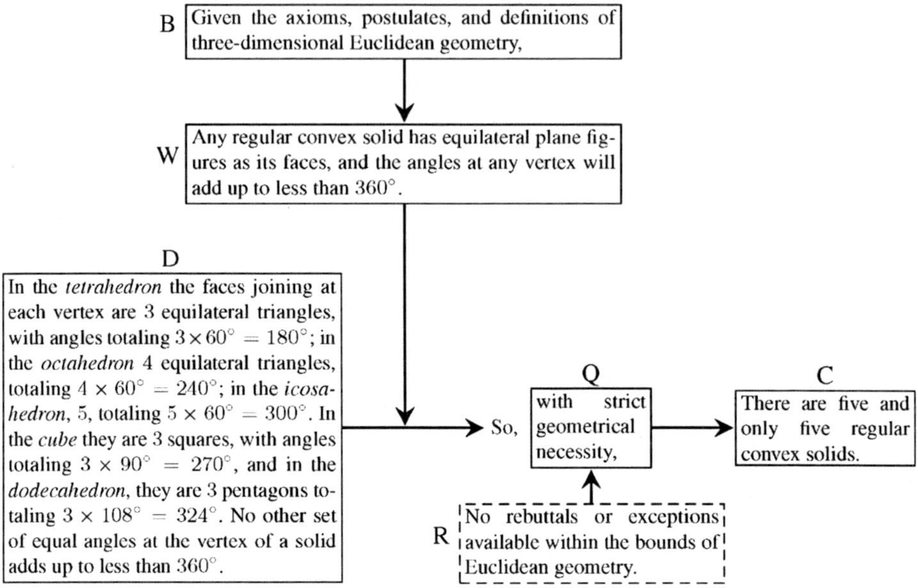

Figure 3. Toulmin's analysis of Theaetetus's proof that the platonic solids are exactly five in number (Toulmin *et al.*, 1979, Fig. 7.4, p. 89).

proof is of particular interest this would be the best approach, but typically we would prefer something more coarse-grained. A useful maxim that applies to any modeling process is that a model should be as detailed as we need it to be, *but no more so.* In most multi-step mathematical proofs the qualifier (and rebuttal) will be the same at every step. This allows us to merge the layouts for the separate steps into one, by combining the given components of the data, the warrants (and if necessary the backing) of each step to produce a single layout for the whole proof.[5] Where different steps have different qualifiers, the qualifier for the whole proof would represent the degree of certainty of the least certain step.

One source of examples of this phenomenon is the class of constructively invalid classical proofs. Characteristically, most of the steps of these proofs *are* constructively valid, making it important to identify the ones that are not. Here a fine-grained application of Toulmin layouts can make the guilty steps explicit, unlike a single layout in which the qualifier for the whole proof would merely indicate that the result is classically, but not constructively, valid. For instance, Figure 4 lays out a familiar classical proof that there are irrational numbers α and β such that α^β is rational. (The rebuttal components have been omitted for simplicity.) This decomposition of the proof into its separate steps clearly exhibits the dependencies

[5] This is a simplification, but more technical details are not required to establish this point.

of each step: whereas the second step relies on the constructively acceptable inference rule of constructive dilemma (CD), the first step employs the non-constructive law of excluded middle (LEM). We can see immediately that the proof could be transformed into a constructive proof if a constructive derivation of C_1 from D_1 could be found to replace the first step. This can be done, since there is a constructive proof that $\sqrt{2}^{\sqrt{2}}$ is irrational: substituting this statement for W_1, and its proof for B_1, yields a wholly constructive proof.[6] The Intermediate Value Theorem, which states that if f is a continuous real-valued function, $u < v$ and $f(u) < m < f(v)$, then there must be a number w such that $u < w < v$ and $f(w) = m$, provides

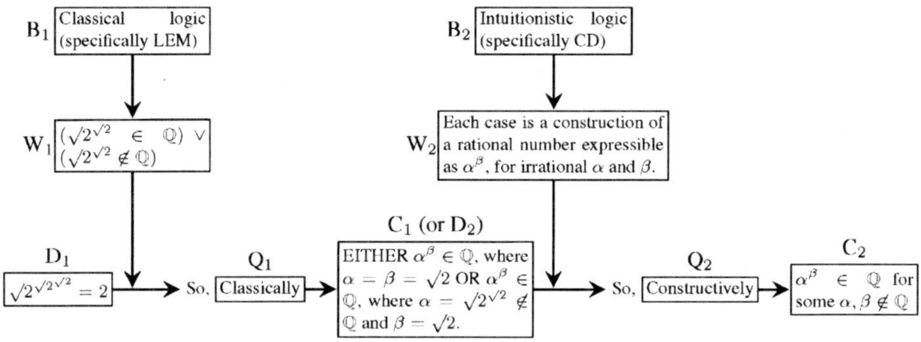

Figure 4. Classical proof that there are irrational numbers α and β such that α^β is rational.

a more protracted example of a non-constructive classical proof. The sketch of this proof laid out in Figure 5, has four steps, of which three are constructive. However, the last step, that of Trichotomy, is irredeemably classical. The constructivist has to choose between strengthening the hypotheses of the proof to rule out Brouwerian counterexamples to Trichotomy, and accepting a weaker result, that $f(w)$ and m are arbitrarily close, rather than equal (George & Velleman, 2002, p. 140 f.). These examples suggest that, providing individual proof steps may be represented unambiguously, longer sequences of steps, whether represented separately or in combination, should also be unambiguous.

However, there are circumstances where ambiguity of layout would seem to be a genuine risk. To begin with we shall look at another example from Euclid. In 1879, Charles Dodgson, better known as Lewis Carroll, produced a diagram exhibiting the logical interdependency of the propositions of Book I (Carroll, 1973, frontispiece).

[6] Albeit a rather cumbersome proof, since the constructive proof that $\sqrt{2}^{\sqrt{2}}$ is irrational relies on the deep Gelfond-Schneider Theorem. There are much simpler constructive proofs that α^β may be rational for irrational α, β.

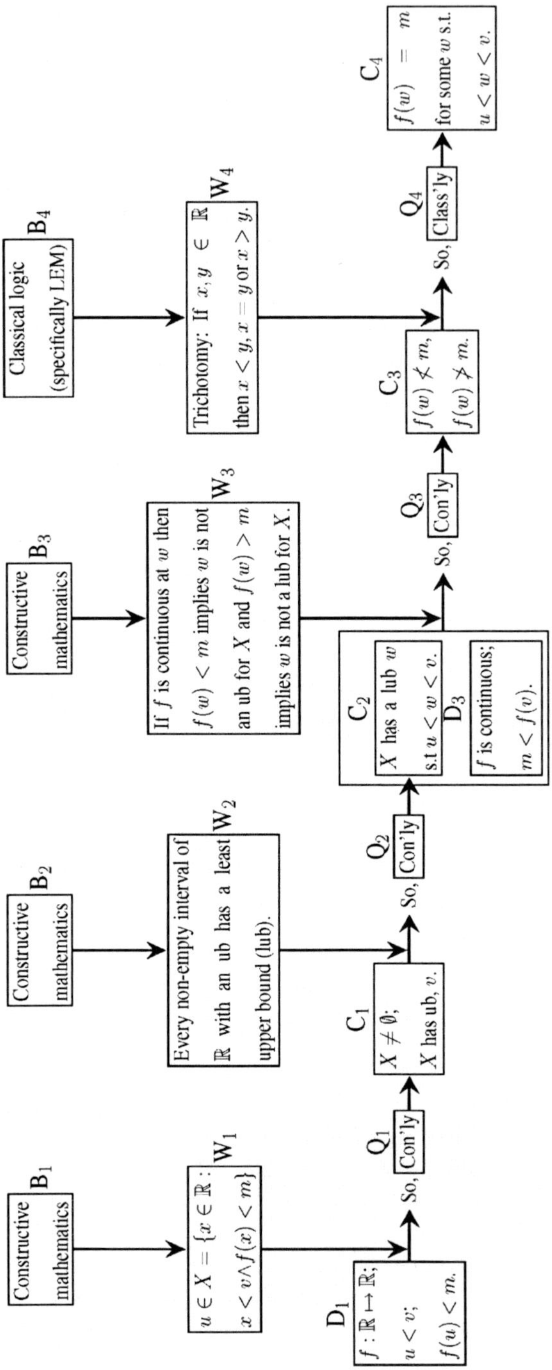

Figure 5. Classical proof of the Intermediate Value Theorem.

A similarly motivated but distinct diagram for Book I (and diagrams for the other books, all inspired by the work of Ian Mueller (Mueller, 1981)) is provided in the most recent scholarly edition of the *Elements* (Vitrac, 1990, p. 518). Both diagrams omit some detail to maintain readability, and most of the differences between the two can be explained as contrasted editing choices. However, there are some points at which they are explicitly at odds. For example, for Mueller and Vitrac Proposition I.12 follows from I.8 and I.10, whereas for Carroll I.12 follows from I.9 alone. However the previously established propositions in the proof of I.12 are employed, whether as data or warrant, two distinct layouts would follow from these differing analyses. One possible explanation for the difference would be that Carroll was in error, or was working from a corrupt text: Johan Ludvig Heiberg's much improved edition of the *Elements* only became available in Greek in 1883 and in English in 1908. This text supports Mueller/Vitrac over Carroll (Heath, 1956, Vol. 1, pp. 270 ff.). If the difference can be resolved in this way it will be obvious which layout is correct.

However, there are more persistent types of disagreement, one of which may provide an alternative account of this difference. Any modeling process will make explicit ambiguities which had been ignored in the original context. For example, propositional logic forces us to choose between $A \wedge (B \vee C)$ and $(A \wedge B) \vee C$ as formalizations of English sentences of the form "A and B or C". We should be astonished to find an ambiguity of this kind in the *statements* of a mathematical proof, since it would compromise the proof in a fashion any mathematician should be expected to spot. Much less attention has been paid to the *dialectic* of mathematical proofs. In rendering it explicit through the formalism of the Toulmin layout we should not be surprised if we occasionally uncover a dialectical ambiguity: an argument which bears reconstruction in two distinct ways. Where such ambiguities have gone uncorrected it is likely that they are sound arguments both ways. This difference would be interesting, but benign. If one or even both of the resolutions of a dialectical ambiguity is unsound, then the close reading required for the application of the Toulmin layout has performed a genuine service in demonstrating that the proof is at best poorly phrased and at worst fallacious.

A more profound sort of disagreement may arise where there is no dispute over what the proof says, but there is a dispute over what it ought to say. Some of the best known propositions of Euclid, such as I.5, the *pons asinorum*, and I.47, Pythagoras's theorem, have many independent proofs, of which Euclid's is not necessarily the most rigorous, or the clearest. Presumably, the different proofs will have different layouts, but there is no inconsistency in this. A more fundamental example from the *Elements*, is the proof of Proposition I.4, that two triangles are equal if they have two sides and the enclosed angle equal, which makes use of the principle of superposition. This principle, expressed in one of Euclid's axioms, Common Notion 4, as 'things which coincide with one another are equal to one another', is used sparingly by Euclid, and has long been suspected as too empirical in character for geometrical proof (Heath, 1956, Vol. 1, pp. 224 ff.). Many modern axiomatizations of geometry take I.4 as an axiom, not a theorem (Heath, 1956, Vol. 1, p. 249).

All of the sources of conflict considered so far reflect an ambiguity in the proof under analysis, either because the text of the proof is in dispute, or is ambiguously expressed, or because there are multiple distinct proofs of the same proposition. All of these cases may give rise to a choice of different layouts, but in so doing they are faithfully reproducing an ambiguity in the source material. This is a useful service, especially if a concealed ambiguity is brought to light. Could a mathematical proof be represented by fundamentally distinct layouts in some other, harmful way?

4. THE FOUR COLOUR THEOREM

Alcolea, whose analysis of a critical mathematical argument I reproduced in Section 2, also has a case study of a regular mathematical argument, Kenneth Appel and Wolfgang Haken's computer assisted proof of the Four Colour Conjecture. The conjecture states that four colours may be assigned to the regions of any planar map in such a way that no adjacent regions receive the same colour. A partial proof published by Alfred Kempe in 1879 was taken as decisive for a decade until the discovery of counterexamples demonstrating its limitations. The conjecture has proved resistant to straightforward methods of proof, and in 1976 was confirmed by a computer assisted proof, which remains controversial in some quarters since the full details are too protracted for human inspection. Alcolea reconstructs the central argument of the proof as a derivation from the data $D_1 - D_3$

(D_1) Any planar map can be coloured with five colours.
(D_2) There are some maps for which three colours are insufficient.
(D_3) A computer has analyzed every type of planar map and verified that each of them is 4-colourable.

of the claim C, that

(C) Four colours suffice to colour any planar map.

by employment of the warrant W,

(W) The computer has been properly programmed and its hardware has no defects.

which has backing B

(B) Technology and computer programming are sufficiently reliable. (Alcolea, 1998, pp. 142f.)

We can see at a glance that the warrant and backing of this proof are very different from those of Theaetetus's proof. The dependence on apparently extra-mathematical methods is made explicit. Alcolea draws the moral that the proof lacks mathematical rigour, and may even hide an unforeseen counterexample (Alcolea, 1998, p. 143).

However, as I have argued elsewhere, this is not the only way of representing Appel and Haken's proof within Toulmin's layout (Aberdein, 2005). We might also represent it as:

> Given that (*D*) the elements of the set *U* are reducible, we can (*Q*) almost certainly claim that (*C*) four colours suffice to colour any planar map, since (*W*) *U* is an unavoidable set (on account of (*B*) conventional mathematical techniques), unless (*R*) there has been an error in either (i) our mathematical reasoning, or (ii) the hardware or firmware of all the computers on which the algorithm establishing *D* has been run.

This analysis requires some unpacking. I have gone further into the details of the proof than Alcolea, in the hope of making the nature of its dependency on the computer precise. The concepts of unavoidability and reducibility originate with Kempe's first, unsuccessful attempt to prove the conjecture. An unavoidable set is a set of configurations—regions or clusters of neighbouring regions—such that every planar map must contain at least one member. A configuration is reducible if it can be shown that all planar maps containing that configuration are four-colourable. Kempe correctly demonstrated that the two-sided, three-sided, four-sided and five-sided regions together constitute an unavoidable set. He also believed that he had shown all of these configurations to be reducible, which would have proved the conjecture. Unfortunately, the five-sided region is not reducible. Appel and Haken's proof is similar in nature to Kempe's, but much greater in scale: they derived an unavoidable set of reducible configurations with 1,482 members. Although the set was found by a computer search, its unavoidability could be verified by hand. However, confirmation of the reducibility of each of its members is too formidable a task for human proof checking. Our confidence in the proof rests on the reliability of the methods programmed into the computer.

5. REFUTATIONS

The fundamental difference between these two layouts of the Four Colour Theorem lies in the rebuttal component, *R*. Alcolea does not offer one, in accordance with Toulmin's injunction that 'a mathematical inference . . . leaves no room for "exceptions" or "rebuttals"; and indeed to raise the question of possible rebuttals would be to challenge the status of the entire argument' (Toulmin *et al.*, 1979, p. 254). On my reconstruction, the rebuttal forms the largest part of the layout. What has happened here?

As the second part of this quotation from Toulmin makes clear, his account of rebuttal is not intended to permit challenges to the soundness of the argument, but rather to index possible exceptions allowed for by the choice of qualifier. This distinction between the different ways in which an argument may be defeated has been developed at length in various places, often as a distinction between rebuttals and undercutters.[7] Intuitively, an argument may be rebutted by offering independent

[7] What follows is loosely derived from John Pollock's account. He offers a general definition of a defeater as "If *P* is a reason for *S* to believe *Q*, *R* is a defeater for this reason if and only if *R* is logically consistent

reasons to disbelieve its conclusion, or undercut by challenging its soundness. Most species of argument may be rebutted, undercut, or both. In empirical science both defeaters occur, but as the result of very different work: an empirical study could be rebutted by an independent study, or undercut by a challenge to its methodology. A paper which does the former might also do the latter, but need not. Mathematics is different: proofs may be rebutted and undercut or just undercut, but not just rebutted. Kempe's failed proof of the Four Colour Conjecture was undercut when counterexamples to it were discovered, but not rebutted since the counterexamples did not challenge the conjecture, which eventually turned out to be true. Other failed proofs have been undercut and rebutted, when it has transpired that the 'theorem' in question is not merely unproven but false. But this is the only way a proof can be rebutted. While we could accept that two empirical studies had conflicting results, despite both having sound methodologies, we could not accept that a mathematical conjecture could be independently proven to be both true and false: at least one of the 'proofs' must fail.

Toulmin, however, does not admit undercutters into his layout. Hence, the only sort of defeater he can accept is rebuttal without undercutting, which is precisely the sort of defeater which mathematical proofs cannot have. In the light of his own definitions, Toulmin is right to say that mathematical proofs cannot be rebutted. But should we accept these definitions? Toulmin's motivation seems to be the thought that an undercutter cannot be part of a regular argument, but must instead reopen the issue 'from a new, critical standpoint' (Toulmin *et al.*, 1979, p. 254). Is this what happens when a proof is undercut?

Undercutters for mathematical proofs have been described as 'inferential gaps' (Fallis, 2003, p. 51). In terms of my application of Toulmin's layout to multi-step proofs, an inferential gap would be a step in the proof in which the data and warrant do not support the claim. The data represents the point the proof had reached when the (first) gap arises, the claim the point from which the remainder of the proof proceeds, and the warrant contains the mathematical results and definitions used to derive the claim from the data. The failure of this inferential step might be attributable to the failure of the warrant. Something like this happens when standards of rigour change, as in the criticism of Euclid's proposition I.4 discussed in Section 3. This would indeed open up a new critical argument. However, what is far more typical of inferential gaps is that there is nothing wrong with the warrant—it just does not warrant the claim on the basis of the data. It may be that the warrant needs to be supplemented, or that the claim is false, because the proof has been rebutted

---

with P and $(P \wedge R)$ is not a reason for S to believe Q", and then defines rebutting and undercutting defeaters as:

> If P is a *prima facie* reason for S to believe Q, R is a *rebutting* defeater for this reason if and only if R is a defeater (for P as a reason for S to believe Q) and R is a reason for S to believe not-Q;
> If P is a *prima facie* reason for S to believe Q, R is an *undercutting* defeater for this reason if and only if R is a defeater (for P as a reason for S to believe Q) and R is a reason to deny that P would not be true unless Q were true (Pollock, 1986, pp. 38 f.).

and undercut, or has simply taken a wrong turning. These are not grounds for a critical argument 'challeng[ing] the credentials of current ideas', but evidence of human error in the conduct of a regular argument. In the light of this observation, it seems more helpful to treat all defeaters alike, and admit them all into Toulmin's layout, generalizing his conception of 'rebuttal'.[8]

We can now understand the difference between the two reconstructions of the Four Colour Theorem. Alcolea sticks to Toulmin's narrow account of rebuttal, and produces a reconstruction with an emphatically non-mathematical warrant. I offered instead a layout with a mathematical warrant, but a slightly more cautious qualifier than normal, admitting of two sources of rebuttal: human error and computer error. I have argued elsewhere that in this case the likelihood of the former is orders of magnitude greater than the likelihood of the latter, and that this is why mathematicians are right to regard the proof with as much confidence as they do more orthodox proofs (Aberdein, 2005).

The underlying problem here is that of rational reconstruction, a familiar one in the history and philosophy of mathematics. Mathematical textbooks unself-consciously rewrite the proofs of past mathematicians, happily introducing anachronistic notation and standards of rigour. Historians try to be more sensitive, but there is often a tension between doing justice to the context of discovery, by reproducing the twists and turns which led to the result, and doing justice to the context of justification by providing a sound proof (Pólya, 1968, p. 159). This tension provides sufficient room for substantive disagreement about how best to reconstruct contentious proofs. Toulmin's layout may bring these disagreements into sharper focus, but it can hardly be blamed for them. As with the simpler sources of ambiguity discussed in Section 3, the layout's capacity to represent proofs in different ways turns out not to be a handicap, but perhaps its most valuable feature.[9]

---

[8] Several contemporary applications of Toulmin's work take this step.

[9] I am grateful for the helpful comments that I received from two anonymous reviewers and from participants in OSSA 2005 at McMaster University, especially Peter Asquith and Stephen Toulmin.

CHAPTER 23

CHRIS REED[1] AND GLENN ROWE[2]

TRANSLATING TOULMIN DIAGRAMS: THEORY NEUTRALITY IN ARGUMENT REPRESENTATION

Division of Applied Computing, University of Dundee, Dundee DD1 4HN, Scotland, UK
E-mail: [1]*chris@computing.dundee.ac.uk,* [2]*growe@computing.dundee.ac.uk*

ABSTRACT: The Toulmin diagram layout is very familiar and widely used, particularly in the teaching of critical thinking skills. The conventional box-and-arrow diagram is equally familiar and widespread. Translation between the two throws up a number of interesting challenges. Some of these challenges (such as the relationship between Toulmin warrants and their counterparts in traditional diagrams) represent slightly different ways of looking at old and deep theoretical questions. Others (such as how to allow Toulmin diagrams to be recursive) are diagrammatic versions of questions that have already been addressed in artificial intelligence models of argument. But there are further questions (such as the relationships between refutations, rebuttals and undercutters, and the roles of multiple warrants) that are posed as a specific result of examining the diagram inter-translation problem. These three classes of problems are discussed. To the first class are addressed solutions based on engineering pragmatism; to the second class, are addressed solutions drawn from the appropriate literature; and to the third class, fuller exploration is offered justifying the approaches taken in developing solutions that offer both pragmatic utility and theoretical interest. Finally, these solutions are explored briefly in the context of the *Araucaria* system, showing the ways in which analysts can tackle arguments either using one diagrammatic style or another, or even a combination of the two.

KEYWORDS: Argument analysis; argument diagramming; argument software; computational models of argument; Toulmin diagrams

1. INTRODUCTION

The analysis of arguments is often hard, not only for students, but for experts too. As a result, a variety of tools and techniques have emerged from the theory of argumentation and the theory of argument/informal logic/critical thinking pedagogy that aim to help in the task of analysis. One of the most common and intuitive of these tools is diagramming, by which the abstract form of an argument can be identified and seen at a glance, and according to which it is then possible to analyse

D. Hitchcock and B. Verheij (eds.), Arguing on the Toulmin Model: New Essays in Argument Analysis and Evaluation, 341–358.

more closely the relationships between an argument's parts. The utility of argument diagramming is seen in its almost universal adoption in the teaching of critical thinking and argumentation skills, as well as its deployment in various practical tools employed where complex argumentation is part of a profession (most notably in legal domains). There are a wide range of diagramming techniques, some very general, some tailored to particular domains. But there are two that are perhaps most well known through the various pedagogic and professional applications of argumentation theory.

The first technique is the conventional "box-and-arrow" approach of identifying atomic components of an argument, and then indicating links between them with arrows. One of the first proponents of the approach in a pedagogic context was Beardsley (1950), and little has changed since then. In addition to identifying relationships of support between atoms in an argument, the scheme has become refined to also identify four distinct ways in which compounds can be formed: as serial argument (in which one statement supports another, which in turn supports a third); convergent argument (in which two or more statements independently support a third); linked argument (in which two or more statements jointly support a third) and divergent argument (in which two or more statements are supported by a third). Complex argumentation can be constructed through arbitrarily complex combinations of these forms. As it is so familiar to many, and by analogy to the terminology used in fallacy theory, we here refer to this "box-and-arrow" approach as the *standard treatment* of diagrammatic argument analysis.

But almost contemporaneously with the development of the standard treatment, a second approach, which sprang from quite different concerns, has developed into an equally successful, well known and widely used method for diagramming, viz. the Toulmin schema (Toulmin, 1958). Rather than viewing arguments as essentially just more or less complex binary relationships of support, Toulmin sees arguments as six-part complexes, comprising the familiar Data, Warrant, Claim, Backing, Rebuttal, Qualifier. Though the starting point was jurisprudential, the resulting theory and its subsequent application are very general, and a Toulmin-style approach, replete with appropriate diagrams is commonplace in current undergraduate curricula.

An important observation is that both the standard treatment and the Toulmin schema are, of course, much more than just ways of drawing pictures. There is more to the standard treatment than p. 2 of (Freeman, 1991), in just the same way that there is more to Toulmin than p. 104 of (Toulmin, 1958). Both systems embody many theoretical assumptions and conclusions, and work as a way of packaging up substantial theories into practical tools that are simple and easy to understand—and produce analyses that are the products of those background theories. The motivation that drives the remainder of this paper is a challenge initiated through the apparently innocuous desire to allow diagrams in one form to be translated into another. The challenge lies in the fact that for a variety of reasons, such translation demands coherence and interaction between the two approaches at a deep, theoretical level. For if an analysis embodies the theory by which it has been constructed, then transmutation of that analysis into one constructed according to a different theory demands some sort of tying together of the two theories.

2. THE COMPUTATIONAL ANGLE

Recently, there have been an increasing number of applications of argumentation in computational sciences, including computational linguistics, artificial intelligence and distributed computing (Reed and Norman, 2003). These different applications have used different accounts of argument: some, such as (Bench-Capon, 2003) have been rhetorical in style, using models from Perelman and Olbrechts-Tyteca (1969); others (perhaps rather surprisingly) have involved predicate calculus interpretations of Toulmin, (e.g. Fox and Das, 1996). Many have developed intuitive models that are closest to the standard treatment: Dung (1995) offers a particularly influential example.

One area in which computing has contributed back to the theory, and particularly pedagogic practice, of argument is in the design and implementation of software tools to support diagramming. There are many dozens of such systems each with different strengths and weaknesses: Kirschner *et al.* (2003) offer a review of many of them. Interestingly, most of these systems adopt the standard treatment, rather than a Toulmin structure, as the basis for diagramming (though there are exceptions: Chryssafidou and Sharples (2002) is a Toulmin-based diagramming tool, and a number of those described by Kirschner *et al.* use models from decision making such as IBIS (Rittel and Webber, 1973)).

With this exciting and rapid proliferation in computational applications and diagramming tools, has come an interest in standardisation and interoperability. To our knowledge, the only application to date that aims to tackle argumentation representation within different theoretical frameworks is *Araucaria* (Reed and Rowe, 2001; 2004). *Araucaria* is a software tool designed to support the manual analysis of argument, and the subsequent storage of that argument for a variety of computational and pedagogic purposes. Though the software has enjoyed relatively widespread use in universities and colleges, it was until recently severely hampered, simply because many instructors value the clarity and other pedagogic virtues of the Toulmin model. From an entirely pragmatic perspective, then, the development of a Toulmin model in *Araucaria* has practical classroom utility.

Working in the context of *Araucaria*, the aim is to develop both the theory and implementation (in software) of diagramming tools that are "theory neutral". Specifically, therefore, there are several objectives:

(i) It should be possible for diagrams to be constructed in more than one theoretical framework.
(ii) Resulting analyses should be stored in a common format or interlingua.

(iii) Partly as a result of (ii), it must be possible to convert, in software, from a diagram in one theoretical framework to an equivalent in another.
(iv) Conversion according to (iii) must be consistent and deterministic, and should not require additional input from the user.
(v) Analysts working solely within one theoretical framework should not be impacted at all by features, contrivances or idiosyncrasies from other theoretical frameworks.

Perhaps surprisingly, simple image processing software, that is not specialised to argument at all, fares well against these objectives, with the exception of (iii) and (iv). It is these that make the task one that is specialised to argumentation. Together, then, these five objectives for software development frame a research project that tackles both theoretical and practical strands of work. The two strands are intimately connected, with practical, classroom needs dictating the remit of the more abstract work, and the equivalences developed theoretically tested in practice in software with real examples.

3. TRANSLATION

Atoms

A variety of initial translation "building blocks" are relatively unproblematic. The first concerns atomicity. The notion of what constitutes an argument or an atomic component of an argument (Katzav and Reed, 2004; Parsons, 1996; Wreen, 1998) is highly contentious. There is an enormous range of opinions on what might reasonably stand as a premise or a conclusion. Yet the theoretical framework in which such analysis might take place is for the most part independent of such differences: whether one analyses according to the standard treatment, to the Toulmin schema, to the pragma-dialectical model, or to some other system has relatively little impact on the size and character of the stretches of lexical material from which the argument is constructed. In textbook presentations, there are canonical examples (e.g. of warrants, or conclusions, etc.) that simplify the picture and sharpen contrasts between theoretical apparatus, but when analysing real world examples of argument, textual complexity brings atomic concepts of one theory into direct correspondence with those of another. Our conclusion, then, is that atoms in one theory are not substantially different from another: a Toulmin datum might be associated with a standard treatment premise, for example.

Warrants

The second building block concerns the simplest structural translation: from a Data-Warrant-Claim (henceforth, DWC) complex of a Toulmin analysis, to a linked argument in the standard treatment. Linkage expresses some need for both components to be present (explicitly or implicitly) in order for the argument to go through. Sometimes, moving from one linked premise to another functions as a way of delivering or manifesting relevance between premise and conclusion. Freeman (1991) offers a dialectical analysis, such that a linked premise is elicited by asking, "Why is that [first premise] relevant [to that conclusion]?" Freeman's discussion is tabled in the context of the Toulmin warrant, and although he identifies many problems with explications of the latter, we are not here trying to critique either of the theories involved. Instead, the aim is to adopt them "warts and all", and provide mechanisms for those that adhere to one or the other (or both) to work within their frameworks. There seems, in this context, to be good reason therefore for identifying the DWC complex with a linked argument in which a single conclusion is supported by two linked premises. In combination with the direct mapping of argument atoms, the intertranslation presented in Figure 1 is reasonable.[1] (The example is from Hansard, and is taken from the *AraucariaDB* online corpus). It is important not to read too much in to Figure 1. Specifically, it is not making ontological claims about the interpretation of one language for expressing argument *by* another (though it is providing interpretation of one language *in* another). For some authors, presumably including Toulmin, the warrant is most certainly not a premise (Hitchcock, 2003b): the Toulminian framework is simply and deeply richer than that. Yet in the standard treatment, there are no other ontological categories. With a Toulminian analysis of some argument that yields a DWC complex, how might a standard treatment analyst go about performing the same analysis? Without a concept of warrant, it seems reasonable that the analyst might view two components of the argument as linked premises—and one of those would happen to correspond to what the Toulminian identified as a warrant. In this way, there is no implicit claim that either analysis is right, or more right, or more basic, but merely that the analysis conducted in one framework might be rendered in such a way as to make sense to an analyst from another framework. This is what Figure 1 is depicting.

---

[1] All the figures in this paper have been produced using *Araucaria* which is available for download from http://araucaria.computing.dundee.ac.uk

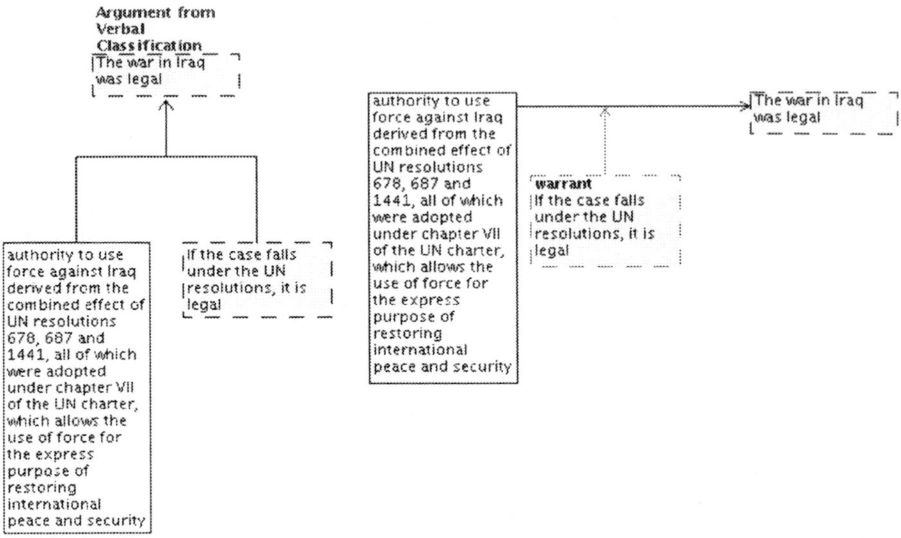

Figure 1. A linked argument as a single DWC complex.

Figure 1 also highlights a closely related point of correspondence in the translation. In the standard analysis, the example has been marked as an instance of a particular argumentation scheme. Toulmin analyses do not usually employ such devices. However, as both Walton (1996b) and Katzav and Reed (2004) have pointed out, argumentation schemes can be seen as analytic devices for handling warrants. So perhaps Toulmin warrants are best translated as instances of particular schemes. There is unfortunately a practical problem with this solution. Where Toulmin analyses identify a warrant explicitly, and can therefore mark any number of different warrants as such, models of argumentation schemes are in their infancy and are consequently limited. Though efforts at taxonomic work have begun (*vide* Walton, and Katzav and Reed, *ibid*), coherent and wide-ranging systems of argumentation schemes are simply not available. Worse, it is far from clear that a single, uncontentious, field-independent system might ever be produced. If there is no way of guaranteeing the schemes that might be available, it is difficult to use those schemes in translation. There is, however, a way forward. With recent proposals for seeing argumentation schemes as (at least in part) "shorthand" for a number of characteristic implicit premises or sets of implicit premises (Bex *et al.*, 2003), the explicit warrant of a Toulmin analysis might be seen as one of the linked premises associated with a scheme in a standard analysis. This leaves scope for the analyst to identify a scheme from those that are available, but does not necessitate such identification in the automated translation process. We return to the issue again in the context of rebutting, below.

One challenge remains. In the standard treatment, a linked argument can have any number of premises; a Toulmin analysis on the other hand typically has a single datum and a single associated warrant. How then, can many-premised, linked arguments be faithfully represented in Toulmin schema? One possibility is simply to ignore linked premises beyond the first two—i.e. a Toulmin analysis recognises exactly one D, W and C in each DWC complex. This is unattractive because it fails to preserve information between frameworks. Perhaps, then, an additional premise in a linked argument might be seen as a fulfilling one of the other roles in the Toulmin model. Unfortunately, there are no other roles that could be filled in a consistent way: the relationship between backing and warrant is most closely similar to the relationship of support in the standard treatment—and not the relationship holding between "sibling" premises. The only alternative left open is to broaden what Toulmin diagrams can handle, either by allowing more than one datum in an argument, or allowing more than one warrant. Permitting more than one datum in a single DWC complex requires extension to the Toulmin model that is unnecessary (multiple data, each with corresponding warrants, all supporting the same claim is a different problem, tackled below). A single datum seems to offer a single basis from which to build an argument to support a claim. The final option—to permit multiple warrants—is a little strange, but not downright offensive to the Toulminian theoretical framework, particularly given more recent exegesis: "The question [for a warrant] is not 'How do you get there?' but 'How might you get there?' And then: 'Is one of the ways you might get there a reliable route?'" (Hitchcock, 2003b, §4).

So, perhaps the best (default) Toulminian interpretation of a standard treatment analysis involving more than two linked premises is of an argument with more than one warrant. Though taking liberties with the Toulmin picture, this meets objectives (iii) and (iv) from the introduction, and most importantly, means that as described in objective (v), analysts working in either tradition needn't worry about the foibles of the other (just because Toulmin diagrams can be constructed in which more than one warrant supports the move from datum to claim does not mean that such analyses will be at all common for those working in the Toulmin framework).

Complex Arguments

A similar approach is required with another general problem. The standard treatment allows the construction of analyses of arbitrary complexity and depth. In this respect it is like most methods for analysing, synthesising and representing argument, including Wigmore's (1931) method of analysing legal argument, Pollock's (1995) argumentation based reasoning system, and so on. Toulmin was unconcerned with such larger scale structures, and focused therefore upon the simple, individual argument with its six components. The simplest solution to this problem is to see each of the components as points for expansion. That is, if a given argument, A, for some claim comprises a datum, a warrant, a backing, a rebuttal and a qualifier, then each of those five components might stand as a claim in some other argument, B. In this way, Toulmin arguments can be glued together. From a computational point of view, this is extremely attractive, as it allows a simple recursive definition that supports Toulmin diagrams of arbitrary complexity. Partly as a result of this attraction, and partly because the solution seems for the most part to remain true to the spirit of the original work, this recursive definition has been adopted in most computational uses of the Toulmin model, such as Krause *et al.*'s (1995) implementation of automated Toulmin-esque reasoning, and Bench-Capon's (1998) dialectical system called simply, the Toulmin Dialogue Game. The same approach is followed by *Araucaria*. Figure 2a shows an example taken from a standard critical thinking textbook that is there used to illustrate serial argumentation (Hoaglund, 1999, p. 122). The guidance in the textbook would yield the three unshaded boxes in the standard treatment diagram. In anticipation of the translation, two further premises have been inserted by the analyst to form two linked arguments. (Of course, the analysis is arguable: the aim here is simply to ensure a faithful interpretation.)

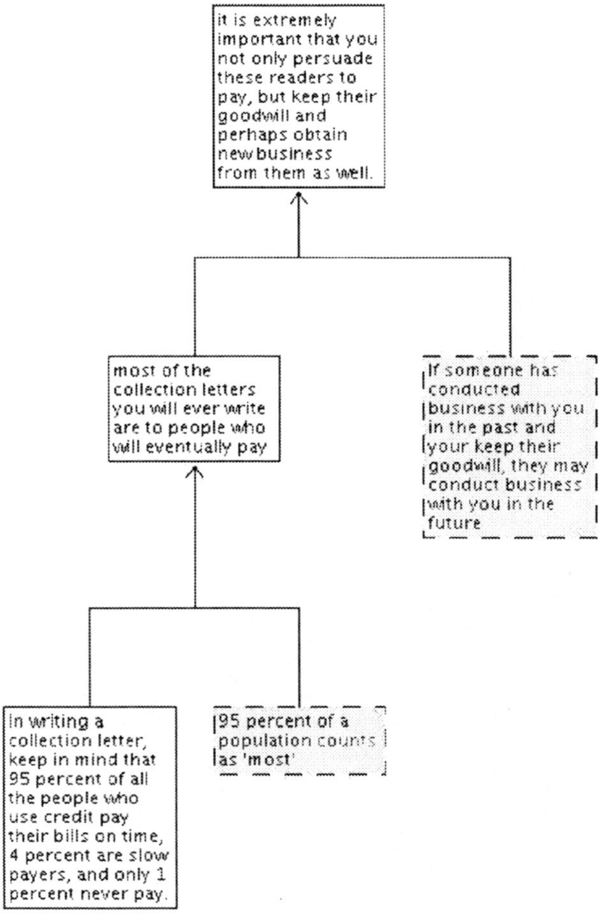

Figure 2a. Serial (linked) arguments in the standard treatment.

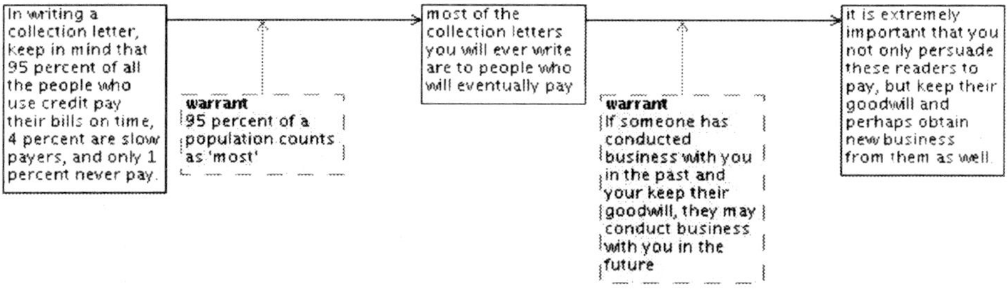

Figure 2b. Serial arguments in Toulmin form.

Its conversion to a Toulmin diagram is then quite straightforward, with the datum of the right-hand argument forming the claim of the left-hand, as depicted in Figure 2b.

In a similar fashion, computational approaches usually allow multiple instantiations of Toulmin schema to support a single claim, as in Figure 3, which shows a large example from the *AraucariaDB* online corpus. Each horizontal arrow represents a single DWC complex, sometimes with warrants present, sometimes not, and with reconstructed components in shaded boxes.

Qualifiers

In fact, for various reasons, all Toulmin-based computational systems adapt the original model somewhat to their own purposes. One of the effects of such adaptations is that not all of the five components that form an argument for a claim are able to stand as claims in other arguments. In *Araucaria*, the only exception is the qualifier. In the standard treatment, qualifiers (called "evaluations" in the standard treatment tools in *Araucaria*) are rarely included in analyses and diagrams: when they are, they are identified with support relations. Thus, qualifiers work as a modality or modifier, expressing the degree of support captured by an arrow between two argument components. This role is very similar to that carried out by the qualifiers in the Toulmin approach, so a mechanism for exchange suggests itself, as in Figure 4. Here, we use Toulmin's introductory example.

If there are multiple evaluations in a standard analysis, it is the one attached to the warrant (i.e. the premise that stands in the Toulmin "warrant" role) that is identified as the qualifier. Most of Toulmin's examples suggest that the qualifier modifies the scope of the warrant, or is picking out the defeasibility, plausibility or presumptive nature of the warrant (so, in the example above, it is the "generally" of the warrant that seems to require qualification of the claim with "presumably"). Toulmin points this out explicitly in introducing qualifiers: "Warrants are of different kinds, and may confer different degrees of force on the conclusions they justify" (Toulmin, 1958, p. 100).

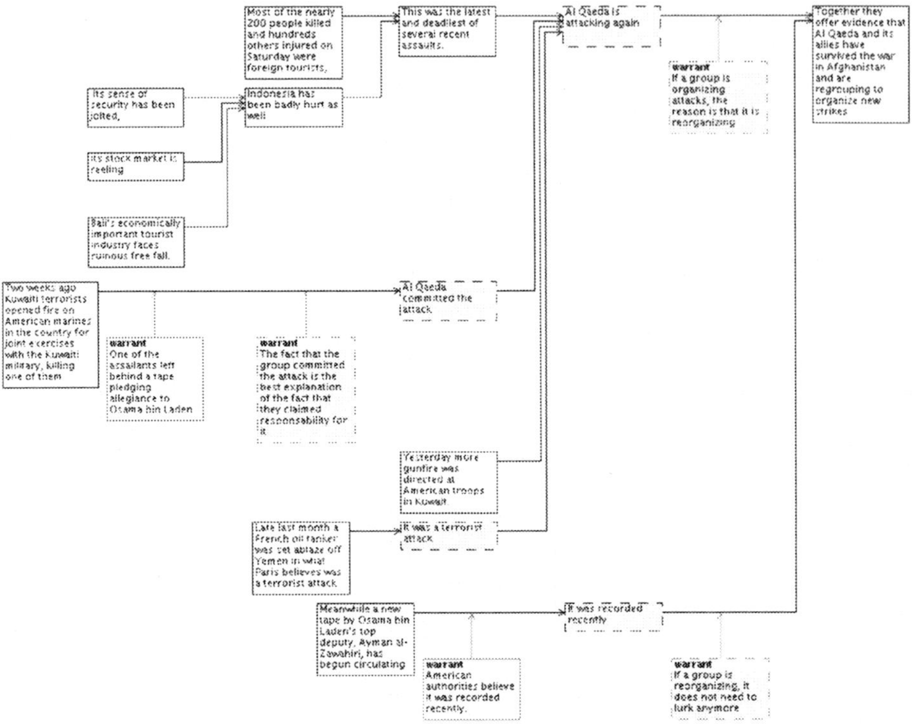

Figure 3. Large Toulmin analysis.

Backings

The penultimate translation issue, backing, is interesting in that a number of computational interpretations of Toulmin omit the category entirely. Backings are perhaps the clearest indication of the jurisprudential heritage of the Toulmin model, indicating links to legal precedents, case law and so on. Though these are adapted in some work (so, for example, Fox and Das (1996), use backings to indicate links into the medical literature in their Toulmin model of oncological reasoning), the challenge is often that the relationship between backing and warrant is identical, ontologically and formally, to the relationship between a warrant in one DWC complex that is standing as a claim in another, and the datum in that other complex. Referring to Figure 5, if we permit the recursivity conditions that allow arguments of arbitrary complexity, as discussed above, then we must permit diagrams such as the one on the left. But in that case, it is difficult to see how it differs in any important way from the analysis on the right.

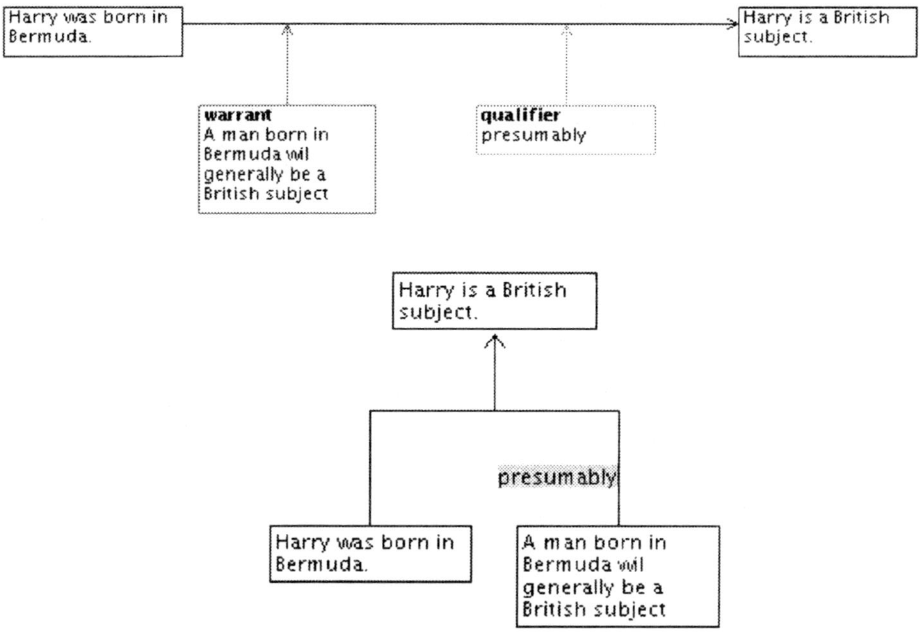

Figure 4. Mapping evaluations and qualifiers between Toulmin (upper) and Standard Treatment (lower).

The argument from a Toulmin perspective would undoubtedly turn upon the nature of the material that constitutes the "on account of" component in Figure 5. And that determination may be context-dependent: in some circumstances one may want to ask of the leap from backing to warrant, "How did you get there?"—and if so, perhaps the left-hand approach is analytically clearer. Alternatively, if one is focusing upon the data-claim link, and the backing is merely an anchor in the literature of the field, then the relationship between the backing and the warrant may be self-evident and the right hand analysis is more appropriate. Similarly, if the literature (case law, medical scholarship, etc.) is itself inconsistent and contestable, then perhaps there will be call for analysis between those components—in that case, the recursive structure of either the left hand picture, or even the more complex structure of Figure 6, is more appropriate.

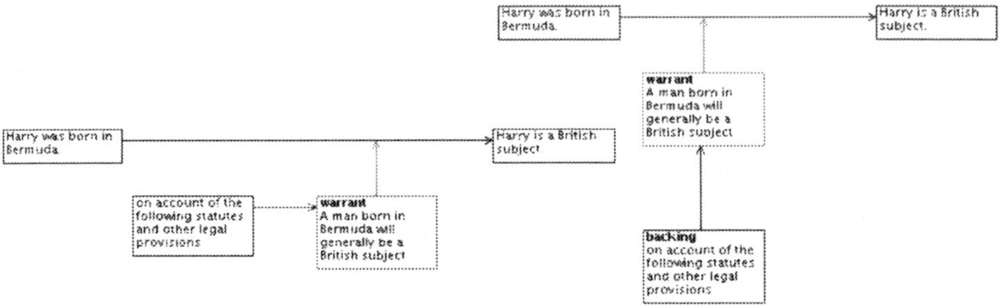

Figure 5. Two ways of supporting a warrant.

The conclusion is that there are good reasons why an analyst might use any one of these structures in a given case, so it is neither the job of theoretical structure nor software tools to proscribe any of them. Each is permissible in *Araucaria*. The default is the conventional DWBC structure, but changing to either alternative is a simple matter. The decision as to which of the two diagrams in Figure 5 (or alternatively the one in Figure 6) should apply in a given situation is a decision that only has meaning within the Toulmin framework. Without the ontological difference (and rather slippery ontological difference at that) between backing and data-supporting-a-warrant, the standard treatment cannot and should not distinguish between the two approaches. As a result, the two analyses in Figure 5 should be rendered identically under the standard treatment. In order to meet the objectives listed in the introduction however, it is important that (a) any analytical decision taken under the Toulmin view is tacitly preserved even under the standard treatment, and (b) there is a deterministic way of identifying an appropriate Toulmin interpretation of the Toulmin-ambiguous standard treatment analysis. The solution to (a) lies in a general approach which is also employed in the data/warrant distinction, where there is an analogous problem of under-specification in one theoretical framework with respect to the distinctions that can be made in another. Each theoretical framework has various roles that it identifies for the atoms of argument. Those roles can be characterised by restrictions upon how they interact. A Toulmin backing, for example, cannot stand to support a qualifier. The identification of which components stand in which roles can only be carried out within the appropriate theoretical framework: identifying a component as a backing can only be carried out in the context of a theory, such as Toulmin's, that has

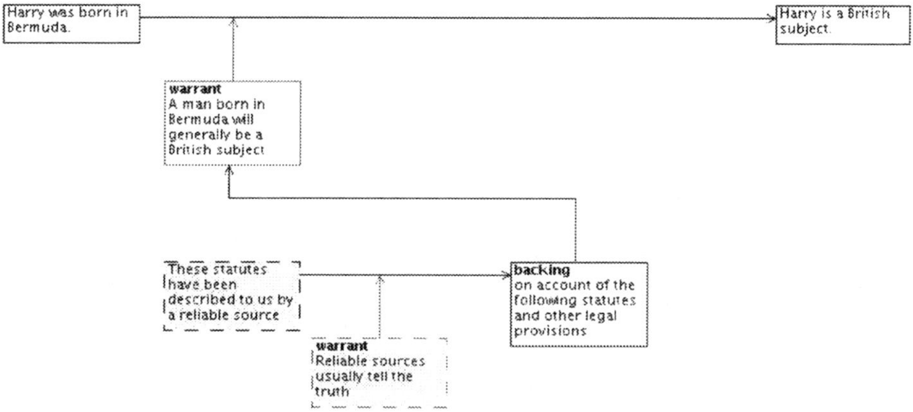

Figure 6. Supporting a backing.

backings. These role-assignments, by their very nature, cannot easily be represented in some lowest common denominator of an argument theory: any technique for translation must simply respect the differences in the target theories. But on the other hand, the mechanisms for translation must nevertheless be principled and well defined to avoid a combinatorial explosion in the effort of translating either large arguments, or arguments between large numbers of theoretical frameworks (that is, we do not want to have to build $n - 1$ new translation mechanisms on encountering the nth theory). The approach taken in *Araucaria* is to allow theory-specific roles to be identified, represented, and stored explicitly in the underlying language. So, in that language, a single component of an argument may simultaneously instantiate a backing role in the Toulmin theory, and a premise role in the standard treatment theory. Equally, if the analyst has not specified a role for a component in a given theory, then that role is simply undefined—or, more accurately is defined implicitly and by default through the semantics implemented in software. This is the solution to (b), in that a default translation is applied. Here, that default is to interpret support for warrants as a new DWC complex rather than as a backing—though in this case and in general, such defaults can be overridden by the analyst.

Rebuttals

The final component of the Toulmin picture is perhaps the single most troublesome—and most interesting from a theoretical point of view: rebuttals. Most standard treatment systems involve some mechanisms for identifying conflicts: propositional negations, counter-positions, incompatibilities, etc. For some reason, there does not seem to have emerged a consensus on how best to deal with the issue diagrammatically. This has transferred directly into software implementations of diagramming methods: Reason!Able, for example uses coloured arrows (van Gelder, 2003), Argue! has lines terminated in diamonds (Verheij, 2003a) and so on. *Araucaria*'s solution is to use double-headed horizontal lines, and to restrict any given proposition to a single conflicting proposition (though that proposition in turn may have an additional conflicting proposition that is not the first, and so on). Whatever the exact mechanism for handling and representing these conflicts, the challenge is the same: is it possible to construe Toulmin rebuttals in terms of standard treatment refutations?

There seem to be (at least) four possible standard treatment interpretations of the Toulminian notion of rebuttal, summarised in Figure 7.

The first candidate is that a rebuttal refutes its claim (we use *rebuttal* to refer specifically to that Toulmin role, and *refutes* to refer specifically to the countering relationship expressed by a horizontal line in *Araucaria*'s implementation of the standard treatment). The single largest problem with this approach is that it seems to fail to capture accurately the function of the Toulmin rebuttal. Not only the examples in Toulmin (1958), but even the very diagrams that label rebuttals with "unless", suggest that rebuttals function not to refute the claim, but to capture exceptions, objections or ways in which the argument may not apply (and may perhaps not apply in the case at hand). In this way, rebuttals are functioning in a manner akin to undercutters in Pollock's (1995) terminology.[2] Undercutters take on the role of defeating an argument by attacking the inference, the way by which a conclusion was derived. Of course, in the Toulmin framework, the "way by which a conclusion was derived" is captured specifically by the warrant. Perhaps then, a second possible interpretation is more favourable: the rebuttal refutes the warrant. Again, though, this perverts the explication laid out by Toulmin. In the initial example, used in Figure 4, above, the warrant is "A man born in Bermuda will generally be a British subject". It is surely not the case that the rebuttal, "Both his [Harry's] parents were aliens" refutes this general statement. Even if the rebuttal is true in a specific circumstance, the general presumptive rule might nevertheless hold true. It might be argued that what the rebuttal does serve to do in this case is to lend implicit support to the conclusion that (in this case) Harry is not a British subject. This, then, offers a third possibility: that a rebuttal supports a refutation of the claim. The claim, C, has some counterposition which might be expressed loosely with the gloss, "it is not the case that C". This component itself is then supported directly by the rebuttal. Though this seems to work in the Harry case, it captures our intuitions poorly since the rebuttal is now interpreted as being entirely distinct from the data and warrant—under this interpretation a rebuttal is interacting only with the claim, and not with the

[2] It is an unfortunate feature of terminology that Pollock contrasts these undercutters with direct counters that he calls rebutters. We re-emphasise that here we use the term rebuttal strictly in its Toulminian sense.

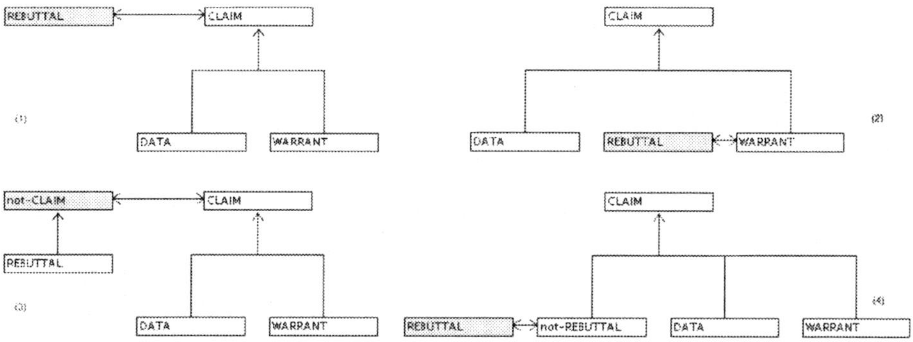

Figure 7. Four candidate standard treatment interpretations of Toulmin rebuttals.

way in which the claim is being derived. Furthermore, if the relationship between rebuttal and Pollock-style undercutter is close, then Pollock's analysis is in direct conflict with this third option, for, crucially, undercutters do not offer support for any counter to the conclusion. Pollock offers the example shown in Figure 8.

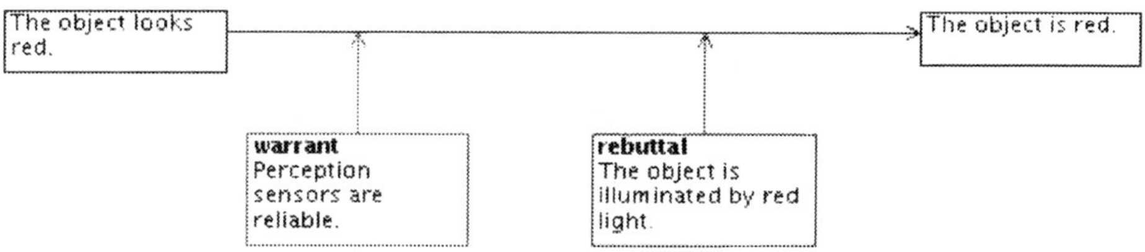

Figure 8. Pollock-style undercutters as Toulmin rebutters.

Here, the fact that an object is illuminated by red light offers no support whatsoever for concluding that the object is not red. But it certainly casts doubt on the inference from its looking red to its actually being red.

Is there, therefore, a way of capturing this undercutting style of attack that seems so close to the Toulminian notion that a rebuttal serves to identify objections or exceptions to the way in which the conclusion has been reached using the warrant? There are two ways of achieving such a representation that are structurally identical, but semantically quite different. The first is to reify the inference. In this way, the DWC complex implicitly includes another component—represented, perhaps, by the horizontal line. The inference then runs, roughly, given the datum and the warrant, it is reasonable to conclude the claim. It is this implicit premise, that the rebuttal refutes. The approach has a direct counterpart in more traditional models of inference. A conventional approach to first order logic uses the principle of *modus ponens* to get from premises A and (A $\rightarrow$ B) to conclusion B. But it is just as reasonable to extract the leap of faith or "inference rule" and identify it explicitly, as a premise: A, (A $\rightarrow$ B), (A $\wedge$ (A $\rightarrow$ B)) $\rightarrow$ B. The Carrollian regress looms instantly, and threatens the Toulmin model in an identical way if we go down this path. In addition to being a sly way of "deductivising" any non-deductive theoretical framework, a further problem is that it is far from clear that having the rebuttal refute this implicit premise is any better than having it refute the warrant. It may well be that the datum and warrant do still plausibly support the claim, even if the rebuttal holds.

The final alternative then, is to introduce an implicit premise, but have that premise represent nothing more than the counter of the rebuttal. This implicit premise might be seen (by the analyst) as an additional warrant. It could be that it is an attack on the entire inference scheme. It could be a specialisation of the warrant that is expressed. But perhaps the most common and accessible interpretation will be that this missing premise is some kind of implicit assumption. In this way, it is very similar to the implicit components expressed in argumentation schemes (Walton, 1996b; Katzav and Reed, 2004). The approach taken in *Araucaria* (partly because it is designed also to handle such theoretical structures) is to use this scheme-like approach in implementation (cf. Bex *et al.*, 2003). This approach naturally handles "conditions of exception or rebuttal" (Toulmin, 1958, p. 101) and "circumstances in which the general authority of the warrant [should] be put aside" (*ibid.*) as well as the full range of interpretations of rebutting used by analysts based on Toulmin's brief and ambiguous presentation. It also means that there is a clear relationship between components of argumentation schemes in the standard treatment and their (automatic) characterisation in Toulmin diagrams.

There remains a problem. The function of a rebuttal in a Toulmin diagram is, on our understanding of it, one of challenging an inference. The function of standard treatment refutation, at least as implemented in *Araucaria*, is one of representing some sort of dissonance between statements. These two theoretical frameworks thus manifest a fundamental difference in the way they handle inference: essentially, the former has a metaphysical basis that identifies multiple forms of inference, whilst the latter is cast in the deductivist mould. The only straightforward way in which translation between them might be accomplished is to reify the inference types of the former, so that they can be represented explicitly as statements in the latter. The problem then, is that it might be argued that the richer model is weakened by its translation to the more formal model. The first observation to make in response to such a challenge is that it is interesting and perhaps surprising that an apparently simple diagramming translation problem is intimately tied to the great deductivist debate that is still going strong (witness, e.g. Groarke (1999) and its responses). We do not here seek any kind of resolution of that debate, but rather seek to build a pluralistic approach that allows analysts and researchers to work within their many theoretical frameworks, allows work conducted in one to be re-used in another, and, perhaps, allows research exploring the differences between frameworks to have practical support.

4. A COMMON INTERLINGUA

From a technical point of view, translation between two importantly different approaches requires an interlingua, or generic representation, that is very broad. Though clearly just two theories do not guarantee immediate generalisation to all structural theories of argument, the discussions in the previous section demonstrate that many key issues have been tackled. Initial work into the approaches of Pollock (1995) (which in many ways is similar to Toulmin) and Wigmore (1931) (which has been compared with both Toulmin and standard treatment theories in (Bex *et al.*, 2003)) suggests that extensions to the interlingua itself are likely to be relatively minor.

Reed and Rowe (2004) describe AML, the Argument Markup Language in which analyses (such as those in the corpus) can be stored. AML encapsulates a relatively straightforward markup scheme, in which statements of an argument are individualised, and the relationships between them stored explicitly. AML, then, is the "deep structure" from which standard treatment, Toulmin, or, in the future, other diagrammatic or linguistic "surface structures" can be automatically generated. Thus, for each new theory there are two translation processes, one from AML to that theory, and one from that theory to AML. Each translation process must meet the objectives (iii) through (v) discussed above, but once in place, it is possible to translate from any one theory to any other in two steps, via AML. To ensure the precision of such translation, it is crucial that any theory-specific analysands are preserved through AML. Thus if two theories A and B are the only two that make use of some feature, X, it is important that X is preserved in AML, regardless of whether or not any other theory recognises X. Given that it is, in general, impossible to determine all the possible instances of such features *a priori*, AML instead offers a generic mechanism for representing theory-specific features. On each analysed statement, any number of *role* tags can added. Each *role* tag indicates a *class* and an *element*: the former for a theory identifier, the latter for a theory-specific feature. So, for example, where a Toulmin backing only makes sense in the context of a Toulmin analysis, the underlying AML stores the statement of the backing along with a role tag specifying the *class*: *toulmin element*: *backing*. Translation processes are then composed predominantly of a mapping to and from "vanilla", generic AML, with a small part of theory specific intertranslation. This approach avoids the combinatorial problems whilst still supporting theory-specific features, both in and between theories.

5. CONCLUSIONS

We have presented mechanisms for translation between the standard treatment of box-and-arrow diagrams and the Toulmin model of analysis. The translation presented is consistent, deterministic and requires no user intervention. Information loss during translation is limited to those features that are only expressible in one theory or the other; such information is preserved in a deep structure and is recoverable. Such intertranslation makes possible a single piece of software that can support teaching, diagramming, storage and manipulation of argument structures in the two frameworks. But more than that, it offers a mechanism for interchange and reuse between communities. As an example, *Araucaria* has been used to develop a corpus of natural argument, comprising over 500 analysed extracts from a wide variety of sources in several languages from around the world. The work was carried out as part of a project investigating argumentation schemes, and as a result adopted the standard treatment for its primary method of analysis. That corpus is currently being employed in a variety of research work, but is also available for teaching. With mechanisms for translation, a rich resource is now available not only to educators who use the argumentation scheme techniques, but also those who use the Toulmin model in the classroom. Future empirical work is required to explore how well automatically translated material fits the needs of professionals and educators.

This work has shown that theory neutrality in designing tools is a goal that can be met, and that solutions that do so are implementable in software that is still simple enough to use that students working within any of the supported theoretical frameworks find little challenge in working with the software. Inevitably, as with any translation, some of the subtlety or nuances that can be captured in one theory or language might be rendered imperfectly in another. But what has been demonstrated here is that such translation can be carried out with a sound theoretical basis to support both scholarly research into argument structure and practical application of such research in specific domains.

Acknowledgements

The authors would like to acknowledge the support of the Leverhulme Trust under grant F/00 143/C for a part of this work, and to thank both Doug Walton for ongoing discussions on closely related topics, and the anonymous reviewers who provided very detailed and helpful comments.

CHAPTER 24

FABIO PAGLIERI[1, 3] AND CRISTIANO CASTELFRANCHI[2]

THE TOULMIN TEST: FRAMING ARGUMENTATION WITHIN BELIEF REVISION THEORIES

[1]*Department of Communication Sciences, University of Siena, Piazza S. Francesco 8, 53100 Siena, Italy*
[2]*Institute for Cognitive Sciences and Technologies ISTC-CNR, Via S. Martino della Battaglia 44, 00185 Roma, Italy*
[3]*E-mail: paglieri@media.unisi.it*

ABSTRACT: Persuasive argumentation is a dialogical attempt to bring about a desired change in the beliefs of another agent – that is, to trigger a specific belief revision process in the mind of such agent. However, so far formal models of belief revision widely neglected any systematic comparison with argumentation theories, to the point that even the simplest argumentation structures cannot be captured within such models. In this essay, we endeavour to bring together argumentation and belief revision in the same conceptual framework, and to highlight the important role played by Toulmin's layout of argument in fostering such integration.

KEYWORDS: Argumentation; belief revision; Toulmin's layout of argument; data structures; computational models; multi-agent systems

1. INTRODUCTION

This research aims to bring together two separate threads in the study of doxastic change: *belief revision* and *argumentation theories*. Belief revision describes the way in which an agent is supposed *to change his own mind* in the face of new information, while argumentation deals with persuasive strategies employed *to change the mind of other agents*, by providing reasons for such change:[1] hence

[1] Here we intend argumentation as 'persuasion to believe' (possibly as a means for 'persuading to do'), in opposition to both (i) forceful coercion via threats and promises, and (ii) other conversational contexts in which arguments may be employed. This restricted definition of argumentation serves to make more explicit the connection with belief revision. Nonetheless, it should be noticed that belief revision is a pervasive phenomenon in *every* instance of persuasion, i.e. not only in argumentation, but in coercion as well. Even when an agent is forced to do the bidding of another by means of threats or promises, such incentives are effective only if the agent believes they are enforceable. Putting a gun to my head is not enough to force me to do something: I must also believe that the person who holds the gun is ready to pull the trigger – and I must prefer life under coercion to violent death. Therefore, even coercion requires belief change, although only to a limited extent, and the distinction is more subtle: while threats and

D. Hitchcock and B. Verheij (eds.), Arguing on the Toulmin Model: New Essays in Argument Analysis and Evaluation, 359–377.

belief revision and argumentation can be seen as two sides (*cognitive* and *social*) of the same epistemic coin. Argumentation theories remain incomplete, if they cannot be grounded in belief revision models: they describe interesting dialogical patterns and their effects, but cannot explain *why and how such effects are produced.* Without an underlying model of belief dynamics, argumentation theories are forced to remain 'out of the black box'.

In spite of the vast literature on belief change in epistemology (Rescher, 1976; Harman, 1986; Levi, 1991; Pollock and Gillies, 2000), logic (Alchourrón *et al.*, 1985; Gärdenfors, 1988; Rott, 2001) and Artificial Intelligence (Doyle, 1992; Boutilier, 1998; Dragoni and Giorgini, 2003), so far the formal treatment of belief revision avoided systematic comparison with argumentation theories. Conversely, current argumentation theories (Toulmin, 1958/2003; Perelman and Olbrechts-Tyteca, 1969; van Eemeren and Grootendorst, 1992; 2004; Walton and Krabbe, 1995; Walton, 1996b; 1998; Tindale, 1999; Johnson, 2000) have not yet been integrated with belief revision dynamics of the arguing agents.

Our basic claim is that such *lack of integration* poses severe limitations to our understanding of both doxastic change and argumentation, so that *more comprehensive models should instead be devised* (Pollock and Gillies, 2000; Falappa *et al.*, 2002; Paglieri and Castelfranchi, 2005a; 2005b). As a preliminary step in this direction, here current belief revision formalisms are tested against Toulmin's layout of argument (Toulmin, 1958/2003), to check whether or not they are able to express the basic features of argumentation. The test consists in trying to represent Toulmin's layout of argument within a given belief revision formalism: the underlying assumption is that, if such formalisms fail to capture Toulmin's scheme (here taken as one of the more general frames of analysis for argumentation), then they cannot be expected to account for more sophisticated models, such as pragma-dialectics (van Eemeren and Grootendorst, 1992; 2004), argumentation schemes (Walton, 1996b; 1998), and rhetorical theories (Tindale, 1999). We submit two different belief revision models to the "Toulmin test": the classical set-theoretical approach of the *AGM theory* (Alchourrón *et al.*, 1985; Gärdenfors, 1988), and *Data-*

---

promises can be used in 'persuasion to do' (provided they are actually believed), they cannot be used in 'persuasion to believe', i.e. argumentation. This depends on the *non negotiability of beliefs* (Stalnaker, 1984; Bratman, 1992; Castelfranchi, 1996), i.e. the fact that agents cannot deliberately decide to believe or disbelieve something just because it is convenient to do so. As for other conversational contexts in which argumentation is used not necessarily to foster persuasion, such as inquiry, deliberation, negotiation, etc. (Walton and Krabbe, 1995; Walton, 1998), belief change is nevertheless involved. For instance, *inquiry* can be characterized as an attempt to gather new information on a certain issue and to test against each other alternative hypotheses, which more often than not will result in a change in the agent's beliefs, and that will certainly produce a change in the underlying data structure (cf. 3); as for *deliberation*, we can argue about our decisions and our motives only by supporting or challenging the beliefs underlying each of them (for instance, when we argue that a certain action is not worth the effort, we are actually handling a complex argument that involves beliefs about means-end relations, perceived values and expected costs, and alternative lines of action available to the agent). More generally, to the extent that the function of argumentation is to increase or decrease the acceptability of a controversial standpoint (van Eemeren *et al.*, 1996, p. 5), this will usually results in a corresponding belief change.

oriented Belief Revision (DBR from now on; Castelfranchi, 1996; Paglieri, 2004; 2005), a cognitive theory of doxastic processing based on critical assessment of available information (cf. 3). While the AGM approach fails to capture even the most basic features of argumentation (cf. 2), the DBR framework provides an effective mapping for several facets of Toulmin's model (cf. 4). So Toulmin's layout is first shown to act as a *litmus test* for assessing the expressive power of belief revision formalisms: failure in integrating such layout in the formal description of belief revision reveals a lack of structural analysis, which in turn prevents more comprehensive accounts of doxastic dynamics. In addition, Toulmin's model itself is argued to be improved in some relevant respects by a close comparison with the DBR framework (cf. 5).

2. THE AGM MODEL: BELIEF REVISION WITHOUT ARGUMENTATION?

The AGM paradigm (Alchourrón *et al.*, 1985; Gärdenfors, 1988) has been the most influential model of belief revision so far, serving as a frame of reference for both refinements and criticisms of the original proposal. Roughly summarizing (for details, see Gärdenfors, 1988; Rott, 2001), this model is conceived as an idealistic theory of rational belief change: belief states are characterized as *sets of propositions* (infinite and deductively closed), three basic types of change are described (*expansion*, *contraction*, *revision*), and rationality is expressed by a set of postulates binding these operators.[2] To decide between different outcomes of the revision process (i.e. different sets of propositions consistent with the rationality postulates), an ordering criterion is introduced in the original belief state, ranking propositions according to their relative importance (*epistemic entrenchment*): hence, different epistemic entrenchments would result in different outcomes of the same revision process. The basic aim of this framework is to explain how an agent might change her belief set, while (1) effectively avoiding contradictions and (2) minimizing the loss of information (Harman, 1986).

[2] An important rationality postulate in the original AGM approach, and one of the most debated in subsequent works on belief revision, is the so called *success postulate*: this principle states that new incoming information is always to have priority over previous beliefs – in AGM terminology, the new evidence is always maximally entrenched, hence taken as valid by the receiver. This requirement is not only unrealistic, it also makes the original AGM belief revision very ill-suited to address argumentation, since the main point of every argument is precisely to assess whether or not a given claim should be accepted, and for what reasons. If we simply postulate priority of new information over old beliefs, this crucial dimension is lost. This is also the reason why more recent works on belief revision have successfully improved the AGM framework, by keeping intact the general set-theoretical approach, but relaxing some of its most idealistic assumptions (for an interesting review, see Wassermann, 2000). The success postulate was one of the first axioms to be relaxed, giving rise to the sub-field of *non-prioritized belief revision* (Hansson, 1999), i.e. AGM models of belief change in which incoming information is not necessarily preferred over older convictions (see also Pagnucco, 1996, for connections with abduction).

However, what remains out of the picture in the AGM approach is an account of the *reasons behind epistemic entrenchments*: why and how should a given belief become more important (i.e. entrenched) than another one – besides, why and how should a proposition come to be believed at all? The AGM model, and more generally all *coherence theories* of belief revision, as opposed to *foundations theories*[3] (Doyle, 1992), do not take in account such 'reasons to believe' – and that is precisely the reason why they cannot capture argumentation structures effectively.

In fact, AGM belief revision fails to integrate with argumentation theories because (1) it does not make any predictions or assumptions about how and why some propositions come to be believed, rather than others, and how and why some of them happen to be held more dearly than others by the agent; (2) there is a deliberate lack of structural properties in the AGM characterization of doxastic states. Argumentation theories capture the ways in which a desired change in the audience's beliefs is brought about by the arguer: therefore, without an explicit theory of *the reasons to believe something*, the main point of argumentation is lost. Moreover, structural properties of doxastic states play a crucial role in accounting for argumentative strategies, as we will discuss in 4 and 5. AGM-style belief revision simply lacks the necessary internal structure to describe such strategies, since it relies on an over-simplified conceptual model of belief dynamics (Figure 1).

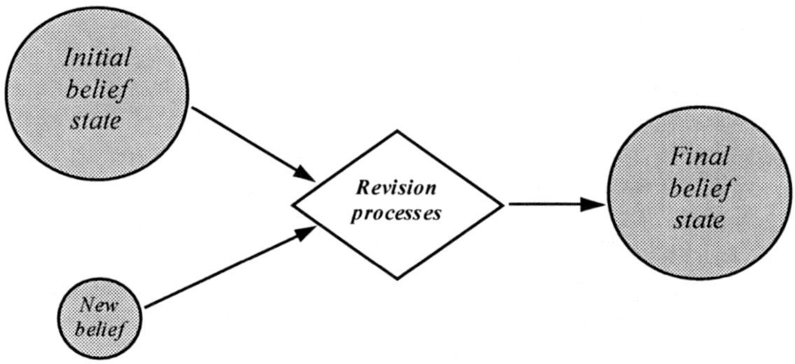

Figure 1. Belief dynamics in AGM: an oversimplification.

If we now turn to consider Toulmin's layout of argument (Figure 2), it is evident there is no way of capturing even its simple structure within the AGM framework. The functional relations between different parts of an argument (its 'physiology', according to Toulmin's metaphor; 1958, p. 94; 2003, p. 87) cannot be

[3] The so called *foundations theories* of belief revision exactly aims to provide a precise account of the reasons supporting a given belief, either using Truth Maintenance Systems (Doyle, 1992) or probabilistic models (Boutilier, 1998). Recently, similar proposals have also been advanced in the field of multi-agent systems (Dragoni and Giorgini, 2003). Although a closer comparison between the model presented here and foundations theories of belief revision is a future goal of our research (cf. 6), it is a fact that none of these theories explicitly addresses argumentation so far.

expressed by an ordering criterion such as epistemic entrenchment, nor by simple inferential rules – in fact, it was mainly to contrast the logical-mathematical analysis of arguments in terms of syllogisms that Toulmin conceived his alternative proposal (1958, pp. 96, 107-113; 2003, pp. 89, 100-105). Hence, an in-depth analysis of supporting and conflicting relations among different information is required to cope with the Toulmin's layout (cf. 4).

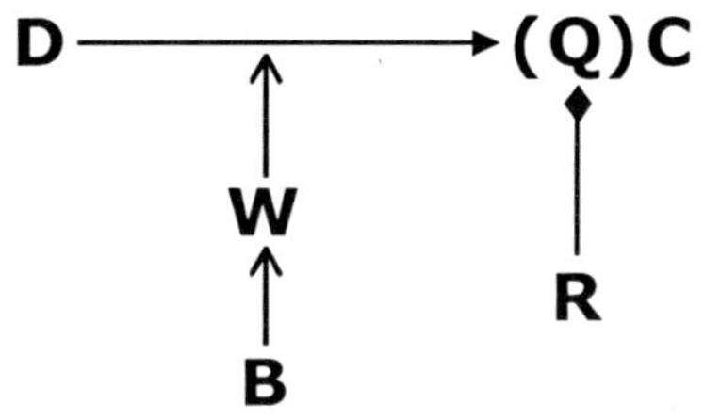

Figure 2. Toulmin's layout of argument.

3. DATA-ORIENTED BELIEF REVISION (DBR)

The following sections outline very shortly a model of belief dynamics alternative to the AGM approach: *Data-oriented Belief Revision (DBR)*. This introduction to DBR is meant to provide only the basic features needed to frame argumentation structures within the model: a more comprehensive overview of DBR can be found in Castelfranchi (1996) and Paglieri (2004).

Data and Beliefs: Properties and Interactions

Two basic informational categories, *data* and *beliefs* (Rescher, 1976; Castelfranchi, 1996; Cantwell, 1998; Paglieri, 2004), are put forward in this model, to account for the distinction between pieces of information that are simply *gathered and stored* by the agent (data), and pieces of information that the agent considers (possibly up to a certain degree) *truthful representations of states of the world* (beliefs) – hence taking them as a reliable basis for action, decision, and specific reasoning tasks, e.g. prediction and explanation. Clearly, the latter are a subset of the former: the agent might well be aware of a datum that he does not believe (i.e. he does not consider reliable enough); on the other hand, the agent should not be forced to forget (i.e. to lose as a datum) a piece of information which he temporarily rejects as a belief (Castelfranchi, 1996).

The distinction between data and beliefs yields a number of consequences for the formal study of doxastic dynamics: to start with, it leads to conceive *belief change as a two-step process*. Whenever a new piece of evidence is acquired through perception or communication, it affects *directly* the agent's data structure, and only *indirectly* his belief set. In other words, the effects (if any) of the new datum on the agent's beliefs depend (1) on its effects on the other data, and (2) on the process of belief selection applied by the agent over such data (cf. the next subsection). More generally, data and beliefs define two basic cognitive layers of doxa stic processing, as summarized in Figure 3.

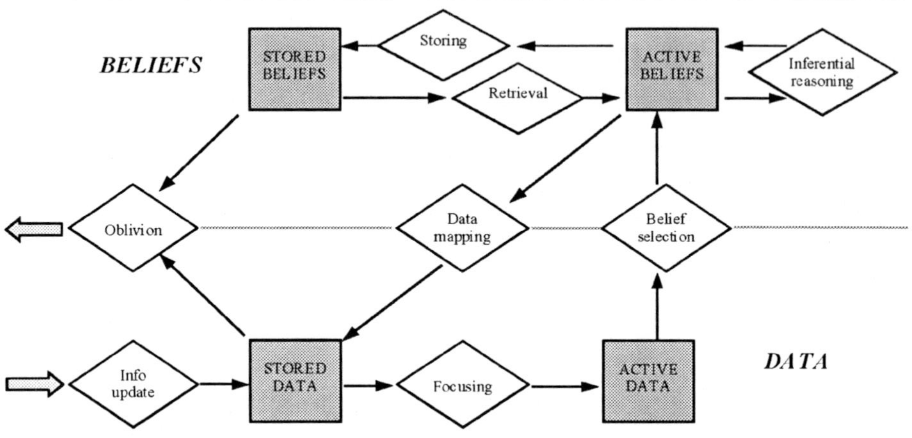

Figure 3. Doxastic processing in Data-oriented Belief Revision.

In this model data are selected (or rejected) as beliefs on the basis of their properties, i.e. the *cognitive reasons to believe* them (Castelfranchi, 1996; Paglieri, 2004), such as:

1. *Relevance*: a measure of the pragmatic utility of the datum, i.e. the number and values of the (pursued) goals that depends on that datum;
2. *Credibility*: a measure of the number and values of all supporting data, contrasted with all conflicting data, down to external and internal sources;
3. *Importance*: a measure of the epistemic connectivity of the datum, i.e. the number and values of the data that the agent will have to revise, should he revise that single one;
4. *Likeability*: a measure of the motivational appeal of the datum, i.e. the number and values of the (pursued) goals that are directly fulfilled by that datum.

The assessment of such properties in DBR is detailed elsewhere (Paglieri, 2004; 2005; Paglieri and Castelfranchi, 2005a). As for their function in belief dynamics, credibility, importance and likeability determine the outcomes of belief selection (cf.

3.2); relevance instead is crucial in pre-selecting the sub-set of active data (focusing), i.e. determining which data in the agent's data base are useful/appropriate for the current task, and should therefore be taken in consideration as candidate beliefs. While relevance and likeability depend on a comparison between data and goals, credibility and importance basically *depend on structural relations between data* (Castelfranchi, 1996). In fact, in DBR data bases are highly structured domains, best conceived as *networks*: data are represented as *nodes*, interconnected through functional relations (cf. the sub-section after the next one), i.e. *links* in the network. In contrast, beliefs are characterized by a given *strength*, which reflects their implicit ordering after the selection process (cf. the next sub-section): hence beliefs are organized in *ordered sets*, rather than networks (Gärdenfors, 1988).

Belief Selection in DBR

Once the informational values of the active data are assessed (Paglieri, 2004; 2005), a *selection* over such data is performed, to determine the subset of reliable information (i.e. beliefs) and their degree of *strength*. When new relevant information is gathered by the agent, modifying his data network and the subset of active data, the belief selection takes place anew, possibly (but not necessarily) changing the agent's belief set.

This process of belief selection regulates the interaction from data to beliefs, determining (1) what data are to be believed, given the current informational state, and (2) which degree of strength is to be assigned to each of them. The outcome of belief selection is determined by the informational values of the candidate data (credibility, importance, likeability) and by the nature of the agent's selection process.

In DBR the agent's belief selection is represented by a mathematical system, including a *condition* C, a *threshold* k, and a *function* F. Condition C and threshold k together express the minimal informational requirements for a datum to be selected as belief. The function F assigns a value of strength to the accepted beliefs. Both C and F are mathematical functions with credibility and/or importance and/or likeability as their arguments. Given a datum ϕ, c^{ϕ}, i^{ϕ}, l^{ϕ} are, respectively, its credibility, importance, and likeability. Let $\boldsymbol{B}$ represent the set of the agent's beliefs, and $B^{s}\phi$ represent the belief ϕ with strength s, while the notation s^{ϕ} indicates the strength of belief ϕ. The general form of the selection process is:

$$\text{if } C(c^{\phi}, i^{\phi}, l^{\phi}) \leq k \text{ then } \quad B^{s}\phi \notin \boldsymbol{B}$$

$$\text{if } C(c^{\phi}, i^{\phi}, l^{\phi}) > k \text{ then } \quad B^{s}\phi \in \boldsymbol{B} \text{ with } s^{\phi} = F(c^{\phi}, i^{\phi}, r^{\phi})$$

The setting of C, F and k is an individual parameter, which might vary in different agents. Here we provide just few examples of different individual policies in belief selection, while their impact on argumentation is discussed more thoroughly in Paglieri and Castelfranchi (2005a).

$C: c^{\phi} > k$	$k: 0.5$	$F: c^{\phi}$
$C: c^{\phi} > k$	$k: 0.6$	$F: (c^{\phi} + i^{\phi} + l^{\phi}) / 3$
$C: c^{\phi} > k \times (1 - l^{\phi})$	$k: 0.8$	$F: c^{\phi} \times (i^{\phi} + l^{\phi})$

All these parametrical settings assign to data credibility the main role in determining belief selection, but they do so in widely different ways. The first parametrical setting expresses a thoroughly realistic attitude towards belief selection, regardless of any considerations about importance or likeability. At the same time, the minimal threshold is set at a quite tolerant level of credibility (0.5). The threshold is slightly higher in the second parametrical setting, and the condition is identical: on the whole, this reflects a more cautious acceptance of reliable data. But once a datum is indeed accepted as belief, its strength is now calculated taking in account also importance and likeability, in contrast to the previous setting. The same happens in the third parametrical setting, although along different lines. Here the threshold is extremely high (0.8), but the condition is influenced by likeability as well: assuming that likeability ranges in the interval **[0, 1]**, here the minimal threshold over credibility is conversely proportional to the likeability of the datum (e.g. it is 0.08 for a datum with likeability 0.9 vs. 0.72 for a datum with likeability 0.1). That expresses a systematic bias towards the acceptance of likeable (i.e. pleasant) data, in spite of their credibility. In other words, these parametrical settings define three agents with different 'personalities', with respect to belief selection: a *tolerant full realist* (the first), a *prudent open-minded realist* (the second), and a *wishful thinking agent* (the third).

Allowing several parametrical settings in belief selection (as well as in other features of DBR: see Paglieri, 2004; 2005; Paglieri and Castelfranchi, 2005a) serves to capture *individual variation in doxastic dynamics*, i.e. specifying different strategies of belief change for different agents and/or for different contexts and tasks.[4] It also shows that, although the selection process in DBR is just a mathematical simplification of the cognitive process of belief formation, it is quite flexible and expressive, since we can manipulate condition, function and threshold in such a way as to express different selection strategies, with a high degree of sophistication. Moreover, a mathematically straightforward treatment of individual variation will prove essential for investigating evolutionary dynamics in shaping belief revision dynamics and argumentation strategies in multi-agent systems (Parsons *et al.*, 2003; Reed and Norman, 2004; Rahwan *et al.*, 2005), e.g. applying genetic algorithms over population of agents with randomized internal settings (cf. 6).

---

[4] Individual variation in MAS is a major concern also for argumentation studies, e.g. as a way of framing a theory of personality in multi-agent platforms (see for instance Kakas and Moraïtis, 2003).

Information Update and Data Structure

Belief revision is often triggered by *information update* either on a fact or on a source: the agent receives a new piece of information, rearranges his data structure accordingly, and possibly changes his belief set. Information update specifies how new evidences are integrated in the agent's data structure (Castelfranchi, 1997; Cantwell, 1998).

Data structures are conceived as networks of nodes (data), linked together by characteristic relations. For the purposes of the present discussion, it will suffice to define three different types of data relations: support, contrast, and union.

1. *Support*: ϕ supports ψ ($\phi \Rightarrow \psi$) iff $c^{\phi} \propto c^{\psi}$, the credibility of ϕ is directly proportional to the credibility of ψ.
2. *Contrast*: ϕ contrasts ψ ($\phi \perp \psi$) iff $c^{\phi} \propto 1/c^{\psi}$, the credibility of ϕ is inversely proportional to the credibility of ψ.
3. *Union*: ϕ and ψ are united (ϕ & ψ) iff c^{ϕ} and c^{ψ} jointly (not separately) determine the credibility of another datum γ.

As we shall discuss in 4 and 5, data relations and their dynamics are the key to representing argumentation in DBR. Moreover, they are also needed to account for information update, since a new input generates not only a datum concerning its *content*, but also data concerning *source attribution* and *source reliability*, and the *structural relations* among them. More precisely, information update brings together:

1. a datum concerning the content (object datum, *O-datum*);
2. a datum identifying the information source (*S-datum*);
3. a datum concerning the reliability of the source (*R-datum*).

These data are closely related, since the credibility of the new information depends on the joint credibility of the other two data (Castelfranchi, 1997): i.e. the union of the S-datum and the R-datum supports the O-datum (Figure 4). Once an agent has been told by x that ϕ holds, his confidence in ϕ will depend on the reliability he assigns to x (*rel(x)* in Figure 4), provided he is sure enough that the source of ϕ was indeed x (*src(x, ϕ)* in Figure 4). The environmental input is characterized by a content ϕ (e.g. its propositional meaning), a source x (e.g. another agent), and a noise n (affecting both source identification and content understanding). In Figure 4, as well as in all following diagrams, support relations are represented by arrows, contrast relations are indicated by crossed lines, and union relations are represented by ovals including data-nodes (portrayed as circle with content-labels).

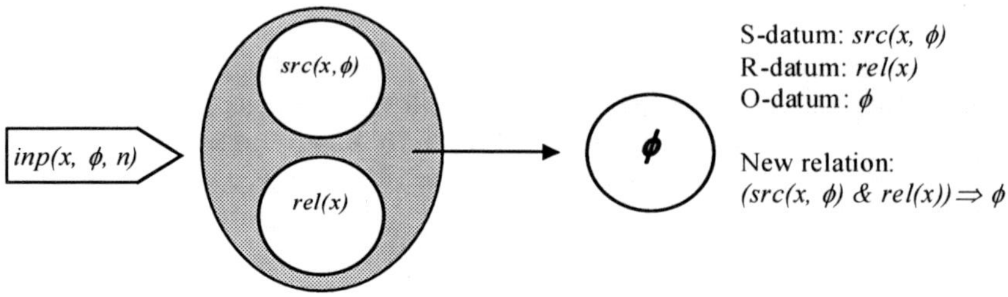

Figure 4. Information update: integrating new external data.

4. TOULMIN'S LAYOUT OF ARGUMENT IN DBR

Grounding Toulmin's Layout in Data Networks

Toulmin's layout (Figure 2) distinguishes and analyzes six features of an argument: data, claim, warrant, backing, qualifier, and rebuttal. *Data* are the facts (e.g. 'John loved his wife') which support the arguer's *claim* (e.g. 'John did not murder her'), while the *warrant* ensures the connection between data and claim (e.g. 'people do not murder the ones they love'), on the basis of some *backing* (e.g. statistical evidences); the *qualifier* specifies to what extent the warrant applies (e.g. 'usually'), and the *rebuttal* describes exceptions to the warrant (e.g. 'John aimed to benefit from her insurance').

This schema is liable of immediate implementation in DBR, since it defines a specific data structure (Figure 5). The *union* of data and warrant *supports* the claim, and the warrant is in turn *supported* by its backing and *contrasted* by the rebuttal, i.e. supports to the rebuttal make the warrant less reliable. The qualifier is represented by the *degree of credibility* assigned to the claim by this data structure.

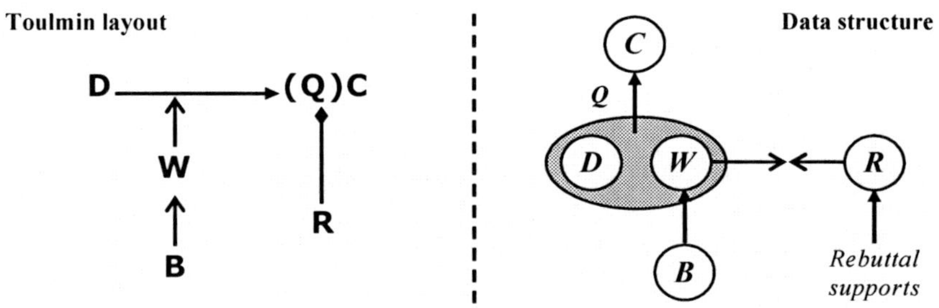

Figure 5. Toulmin's layout in data structure.

Assessing Defeasible Reasoning in DBR

Argumentation is often modelled in the framework of *defeasible reasoning* (Pollock and Gillies, 2000; Falappa *et al.*, 2002), distinguishing between two kinds of defeaters, i.e. possible counterarguments against a reason-schema: *rebutting* vs. *undercutting defeaters*. Applying to defeasible reasoning the terminology proposed by Toulmin (1958/2003), a rebutting defeater is any reason which directly denies the claim of the argument, while an undercutting defeater is a reason which undermines the validity of the relevant warrant. Actually, in strictly Toulminian terminology, the expression 'rebutting defeaters' is rather misleading, since "conditions of rebuttal (R) indicat[e] circumstances in which the general authority of the warrant would have to be set aside" (Toulmin, 1958, p. 101; 2003, p. 94). Hence rebuttals are in fact undercutting defeaters. To avoid confusion, we propose the expression *direct defeaters*, instead of rebutting defeaters, as a less ambiguous term to indicate defeaters which directly affect the claim.

In DBR, different defeaters are effectively shown to target different nodes in the data network (Figure 6): direct defeaters are data which contrast the claim-node (in the previous example, 'John was seen shooting his wife'), while undercutting defeaters are data contrasting the warrant-node (e.g. 'jealousy can make you kill the ones you love most'). Moreover, a third category of defeaters can be expressed: *premise defeaters*, i.e. reasons which contrast the data-node (e.g. 'John did not love his wife'). Undercutting and premise defeaters have similar function but different targets: the former attack the connection between data and claim, while the latter question the statement of fact supporting the conclusion.

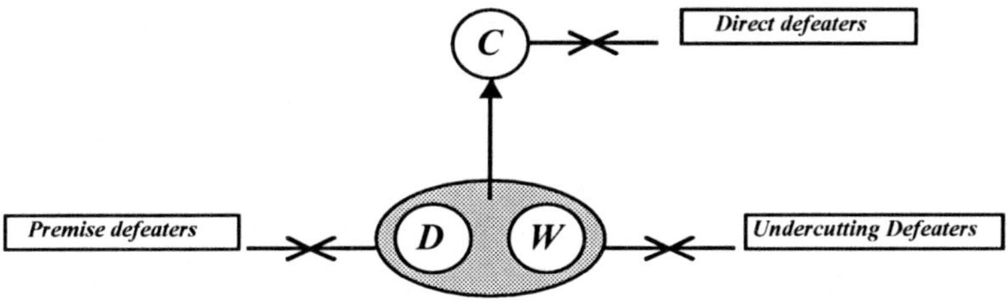

Figure 6. Defeasible reasoning in data structure.

Recursion in Argumentation and Belief Change

Toulmin was well aware of possible *recursion* in argumentation. He explicitly mentioned this issue with reference to, respectively, data and warrants:

> [I]f the claim is challenged, it is up to us to appeal to these facts [i.e. data], and present them as the foundation upon which our

> claim is based. Of course we may not get the challenger even to agree about the correctness of these facts, and in that case we have to clear his objection out of the way by a preliminary argument: only when this prior issue or 'lemma', as geometers would call it, has been dealt with, are we in a position to return to the original argument. (1958, p. 97; 2003, p. 90)

> Indeed, if we demanded the credentials of all warrants at sight and never let one pass unchallenged, argument could scarcely begin. Jones puts forward an argument invoking warrant W_1, and Smith challenges that warrant; Jones is obliged, as a lemma, to produce another argument in the hope of establishing the acceptability of the first warrant, but in the course of this lemma employs a second warrant W_2; Smith challenges the credentials of this second warrant in turn; and so the game goes on. (1958, p. 106; 2003, p. 98)

Therefore, Toulmin's layout of argument is not a finite and self-sustaining structure – and the same applies to any other structural account of argumentation. Recursive processes are always possible: all features supporting or challenging a claim can be supported or challenged in turn, hence becoming the (disputed) claim of a specific sub-argument. This holds not only for data and warrants, but also for backings, rebuttals, and even qualifiers. All these recursive processes are liable of representation in DBR.

Consider again the example introduced in the previous two sub-sections, and imagine I am determined to prove John guilty of the murder of his wife, defeating the plea for innocence argued for by my opponent, John's lawyer. I might decide to challenge the backing of such argument, i.e. statistical evidences, by questioning their accuracy, since they refer only to crimes of passion and not to premeditated homicides, henceforth being biased and *ad hoc*; to which the opponent might reply that John stands accused to have murdered his wife out of jealousy, hence statistics on passion crimes are absolutely relevant for the issue; and so on. In this specific case, the backing becomes the claim of a sub-argument aimed to assess its validity, with its own data, warrant and rebuttal (Figure 7).

Alternatively, I might attack the qualifier of the original argument ('usually'), by pointing at specific circumstances, such as jealousy, in which the very fact that John did love his wife might have been a motive to kill her – hence concluding that loving one's own wife does not 'usually' entail not being ready to kill her. For the structural analysis of argumentation, this case is less obvious than the previous one: since the qualifier is not an independent node in the structure, but rather a specification of the triadic relation between data, warrant and claim, it cannot be attacked by opposing to it some counter-argument. To challenge the qualifier, I must show that the *same data* presented by my opponent, considered in the light of a *different warrant*, do not support the conclusion he wanted to draw, or support it to a minor extent, or even contrast it (as in our example). In this way, I indirectly argue that the original qualifier overestimated the bearing of data and warrant on the claim (Figure 7).

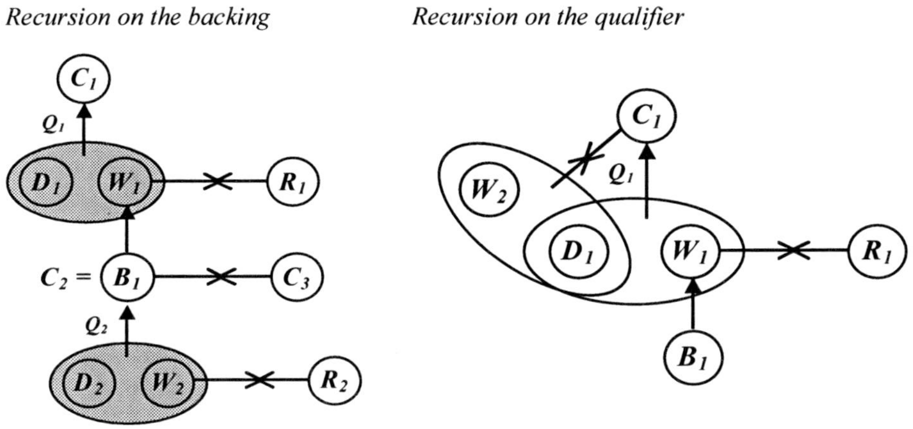

Figure 7. Two cases of recursion: Backing and qualifier.

A similar analysis applies also to recursion on data, warrants and rebuttals. The explanation of such a precise and 'natural' mapping between recursive arguments and data structures is straightforward: arguments are dialogical devices to provide reasons to believe a given claim – but rational belief is not born in isolation, i.e. it always requires a network of mutual support to be formed and maintained. Isolated beliefs are mere matters of faith – and even in this case, the human mind strenuously struggles to provide some rational foundation to its conviction, and it is not by chance that some of the most famous philosophical arguments of all times were concerned with religious issues (e.g. St Anselm's demonstration of God's existence and Pascal's wager). Structural integration of available information is a basic cognitive feature of our mind, which constraints both belief dynamics and argumentative persuasion.

A final interesting point on recursion is that it has to *stop* somewhere – and, indeed, it does. As remarked by Toulmin, without some arbitrary limitation to recursive arguments, argumentation itself would be a pointless (and endless) occupation.

> Some warrants must be accepted provisionally without further challenge, if argument is to open to us in the field in question: we should not even know what sort of data were of the slightest relevance to a conclusion, if we had not at least a provisional idea of the warrants acceptable in the situation confronting us. The existence of considerations such as would establish the acceptability of the most reliable warrants is something we are entitled to take for granted. (1958, p. 106; 2003, pp. 98-99)

Exactly the same might be said of belief: we would never believe anything, nor we would decide anything, without first taking some background knowledge for granted (Stalnaker, 1984; Bratman, 1992). In order to reason at all, we must reason finitely,[5] and much of whatever goes on in our mind, it goes on unchallenged and unchecked – although usually it *could* be challenged and checked, should the need arise. So the fact that argumentation conforms to the limitations of our recursive reasoning is neither surprising nor very inspiring for speculation. But what *is* inspiring, as we shall see in 5, are rather the specific ways in which these very limitations can actively be exploited to achieve persuasion. While the mere fact that we need to start somewhere, both in believing and arguing, is trivial, *where we decide to start* is not trivial at all.

5. BEYOND TOULMIN'S MODEL

The utility of DBR in understanding argumentation is not limited to representing some features of Toulmin's layout. In the next sections we aim to show that representing argumentation structures in DBR sheds light on some problems that were left unsolved, vague, or simply unnoticed in Toulmin's account of arguments.[6]

Implicitness vs. Explicitness of Arguments and Beliefs

We argued (cf. 4) that any argument, as any belief, is developed against a background of claims that are taken for granted (Burke, 1985; Gough and Tindale, 1985), i.e. which are not in themselves to be disputed and settled – although they might be. However, how each opponent chooses and manipulates such background is an important part of argumentation, which relates to the process of *focusing* in DBR (cf. 3.1).

Arguing is not only a matter of supporting or challenging specific claims, but also a struggle to *conveniently direct the attention of our opponent*, to make him focus on the strengths of our arguments, while letting pass unnoticed their weaknesses.[7] We often hide some of our premises exactly because we would have no sound reasons to support them, should they be challenged explicitly. Consider again the example in 4: when I, trying to convict John for murdering his wife, argue

---

[5] This is exactly why we become so annoyed, and yet vaguely uncomfortable, whenever faced by the everlasting question of any curious child: "Yes, but *why* is it so?". In principle, the child is perfectly right in raising the question – actually, we are not annoyed by any lack of rationality on her behalf, but rather by her being so damnably rational. In contrast, what we want her to understand is just a matter of practical wisdom, not a theoretical law: that it is pointless to spend the rest of your life, or even a small part of it, going on to chain one 'why' to another.

[6] Additional results in integrating DBR and argumentation have already been discussed in Paglieri and Castelfranchi (2005a), in particular with reference to the impact of individual variation over argumentation–a point also discussed in Kakas and Moraïtis (2003).

[7] The connection between the DBR understanding of *focusing strategies* and the pragma-dialectic notion of *strategic maneuvering* (van Eemeren and Houtlosser, 1999) is bound to be deep and insightful. However, detailed analysis of this issue is left to future work (cf. 6), due to space constraints.

that the very fact he loved her might be a motive for the crime, since jealousy can make us kill the ones we love most, I am grounding this argument on the implicit premise that John was indeed jealous of his wife – which is not the same as to say he loved her. In fact, loving her was just a possible (not sufficient) reason to be jealous of her, and much more would be needed to effectively support my suggestion of a passion crime: e.g. John should be proved to be inclined to violent passion, and ready to act on it; and I should also show that there were indeed such overt hints in John's wife behaviour as to ignite his alleged jealousy. By hiding the premise 'John was jealous of his wife', I am just trying to dispense with all this complex (and slippery) sub-argument. If the opponent lets go this step unchallenged, my strategy is successful, since I will have forced him to cope with a counter-argument that he might have easily disposed of – which is somehow similar to the mechanism exploited in the straw-man fallacy.

Nor do we want to provide our opponent with fuel for his own arguments, i.e. hints and suggestions that might help him supporting his claim or challenging ours. So we try to avoid giving away information that might be harmful for the case we want to make, and we actively attempt to distract the opponent's attention from information he might already possess, but whose salience he has not yet realized. Imagine our friend John has an elderly mother, of whom he is incredibly fond, who in turn cherished John's wife as the apple of her eye. My opponent, John's lawyer, is perfectly aware of this issue, but he has not yet raised it, nor does he seem likely to do so in the future: he might possibly underestimate the impact of such emotional argument on the jury (e.g. 'John would have never risked breaking the heart of his dear mother by killing her beloved daughter-in-law!'), or he is simply missing the point. In any case, I shall pay great attention to avoid mentioning John's mother in my own arguments, lest my opponent be reminded of such potential counter-argument and decide to use it.

Toulmin mentioned only in passing the parts of an argument that are left untold, i.e. *implicit*, and claimed that implicitness should be considered a distinctive feature of warrant, in contrast with data (1958, p. 100; 2003, pp. 92-93). Although it might be true that warrants are more frequently taken for granted than data, this is not a necessary rule: the same argument can easily, and sometimes effectively, be presented by stating explicitly the warrant rather than the data, as we have just seen ('It is because jealousy can make you kill your most beloved ones, that I suspect John to be the murderer of his wife').

Here two different issues influence each other: (1) whether given information is *assessed* (i.e. claimed to be or not to be the case) or *not assessed*; and (2) the fact that this happens *explicitly* or *implicitly*, i.e. within or outside the scope of the agent's attention. Integrating these independent distinctions, we obtain a taxonomy of four *degrees of focusing*: whenever information is explicitly assessed, it is *argued for*, i.e. it is submitted to full scrutiny by the arguer, focusing both the claim and its supporting structure; in contrast, a claim is *presupposed* whenever some commitment on its value is assumed but left implicit, i.e. the claim itself is focused by the arguers, but not the structural relations that might verify or falsify it.[8] In parallel, some claims are not assessed but just left aside: they are either available in principle to the arguer, but not explicitly focused (i.e. *passed under silence*), or they are utterly *unknown* to the arguer.

Such taxonomy yields a topological representation of focusing, in relation to the data available to the agent (Figure 8). A claim which is argued for is directly under the spotlight of the arguers' attention, while a presupposed fact is (literally) a borderline case: the claim itself is under consideration, but not the doxastic structure behind it, i.e. its supports and contrasts. A fact passed under silence stands in a shadow zone, where it remains available within the mind of the arguers, but it is not being currently focused; finally, an unknown fact is simply represented as falling out of the agent data structure.

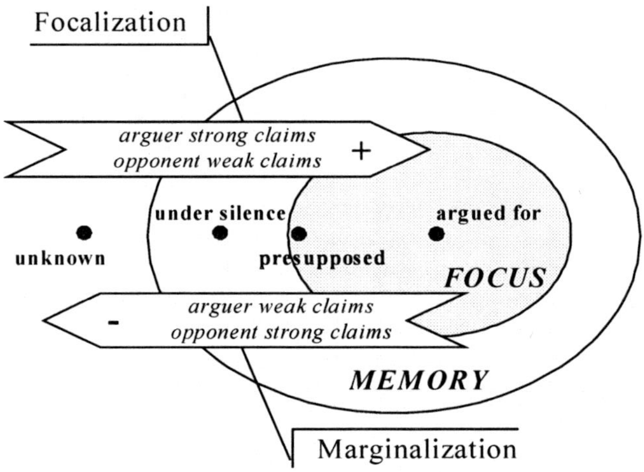

Figure 8. Degree of focusing: topological and dynamical model.

This results in an elementary prescriptive model of *focusing dynamics* in argumentation (represented by the arrows in Figure 8), depending on the perceived soundness of a claim according to the arguer. Whenever she considers one of her claims to be strong and well-founded, she will try to make it more central in the debate; conversely, she will try to marginalize her weakest claims, and to keep out of the field of discussion facts that she thinks might endanger her own case. As for the claims of her opponent, the overall strategy is simply reversed: she will try to focus on the weakest spots in the opponent's arguments, while putting aside the strongest claims. In practice, this is not achieved by 'moving the claims', but rather

[8] Verheij (2002) would say that statements which are argued for are *issues*, while presupposed statements are *assumptions*: although here we use a different terminology, the notions are basically synonymous.

by *shifting the focus of the opponent's attention* from a certain set of issues to a different one: a procedure in which the surface form of our arguments, i.e. how they are phrased, plays a crucial role.

Plausibility: The Role of Importance in Argumentation

In DBR, one of the crucial factors in determining whether a new piece of information will be accepted or rejected as belief is its *importance* (Gärdenfors, 1988; Paglieri, 2004), i.e. the degree of connectivity (integration) of the new datum in the audience's data structure. An effective argument does not only present new information to the audience, but also provides the relevant connections with data already available to, and possibly believed by, that particular audience (Hunter, 2004). Such connections vouch for the *plausibility* of the new datum (Rescher, 1976; Castelfranchi, 1996) and are crucial in persuading the audience to accept it. In data networks, we distinguish two cases of argumentation through plausibility:

1. *Self-evident data*: the new datum is presented as following from what the audience already knew – the datum had not yet been inferred, but it might have been, and the audience is likely to remark: "Sure! Of course! Obviously!" etc.;
2. *Explanatory data*: the new datum is presented as supporting and explaining data already available – since such explanation was missing so far, it produces reactions like: "Now I see! That's why! I knew it!" etc.

This distinction is easily represented by a structured data-domain: in our model, self-evident data are data with a high number of supports, while explanatory data in turn support many other data (Figure 9). Different degrees of self-evidence and explanatory power are expressed by the epistemic importance of the node (cf. 3).

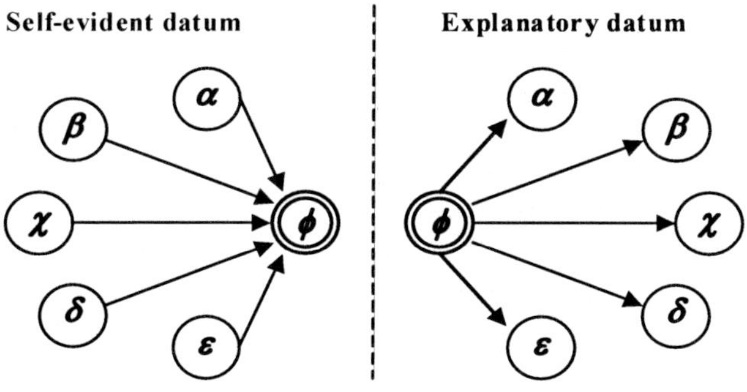

Figure 9. Two plausibility arguments: self-evident and explanatory data.

Toulmin did not focus much on the role of plausibility in argumentation, since his account was mainly devoted to articulating the *premises* supporting a given claim rather then its *consequences* (and their role in the acceptance of the claim itself). However, whenever we aim to persuade a given audience of a certain claim, its degree of *integration* in the audience's beliefs is extremely relevant, not only 'upstream' (self-evidence), but also 'downstream' (explanatory power). For instance, I can try to convince a jury that John is guilty of murdering his wife by pointing out that such guilt would explain several strange habits John acquired recently, such as waking up in the middle of the night screaming and sweating, paying frequent visits to his confessor Father Brown, and wandering aimlessly in the streets with a remorseful countenance.

6. CONCLUSIONS AND FUTURE WORK

The main implication of this preliminary proposal is to initiate a systematic effort of integrating research areas necessarily connected with each other, i.e. argumentation and belief revision, but that only rarely have been so far modelled within the same framework (Pollock and Gillies, 2000; Falappa *et al.*, 2002; Paglieri, Castelfranchi, 2005a; 2005b). To this purpose, DBR constitutes a first step towards formal and computational models of epistemic change (both intra- and inter-agents) to express the complex socio-cognitive dynamics involved in belief change, in contrast with the idealistic approach which dominated this field so far (Castelfranchi, 1996; Pollock and Gillies, 2000; Paglieri, 2004).

With reference to Toulmin's layout of argument, our analysis emphasizes its relevance for understanding not only argumentation, but belief dynamics as well. Toulmin's theory turns out to be crucial both for a critical assessment of the existing formalisms of doxastic change (cf. 2), and as an inspiring frame of reference for new models (cf. 4 and 5). However, while Toulmin's layout was ideal to preliminarily check the convergence between belief change and argumentation, more sophisticated theories of argumentation will have to be discussed within the DBR framework, such as pragma-dialectics (van Eemeren and Grootendorst, 1992; 2004) and argumentation schemes (Walton, 1996b) – with special emphasis on the impact on computational models of argumentation (Falappa *et al.*, 2002; Parsons *et al.*, 2003; Reed and Norman, 2004; Rahwan *et al.*, 2005).

Finally, the DBR model itself requires refinements and fine-tuning: in current and future works, we aim to extend the computational treatment of data properties to motivational and emotional features, i.e. relevance and likeability (Castelfranchi, 1996; Frijda *et al.*, 2000; Paglieri, 2005), to explore the interaction between Truth-Maintenance Systems (Doyle, 1992), DBR and belief structures, and to move towards implementation in agent-based cognitive and social simulation, by exploiting random parametrical variation to study evolutionary dynamics in belief change and argumentation strategies (Paglieri and Castelfranchi, 2005a). As a starting point, we plan to use argumentation tasks as testing ground for belief revision algorithms, and vice versa – building on the general results discussed here.

Acknowledgements

A preliminary version of some parts of this article was published in Paglieri and Castelfranchi (2005b). The comments that we received on this draft from Eric Krabbe, Douglas Walton, and Wouter Slob during the OSSA Conference in Hamilton, Canada (18-21 May 2005), greatly helped us to improve the current version. We are also thankful for the insightful remarks of two anonymous reviewers, and we wish to express our gratitude to David Hitchcock and Bart Verheij for their excellent editorial work in putting together this volume. The first author received financial support from the ESF EUROCORES Program *The Origin of Man, Language, and Languages*, while the second author was supported by the European Project *MindRACES*, n°511931, EU FP6.

CHAPTER 25

JOHN WOODS

EIGHT THESES REFLECTING ON STEPHEN TOULMIN

Department of Philosophy, University of British Columbia, 1866 Main Mall, Vancouver, B.C. V6T1Z1, Canada
E-mail: jhwoods@interchange.ubc.ca

ABSTRACT: Examination of theses either expressly espoused by Stephen Toulmin or suggested by his writings reveals a general scepticism about the applicability of received theories to the real-life practice of individual agents. Chief among these theories are the logics of deduction and induction, notably probability theory. Key to Toulmin's reservations are the contextual conditions that both animate and constrain the performance of beings like us. On their first appearance, Toulmin's heterodoxies were met with stiff resistance, or they were simply ignored. Developments in computer science, cognitive psychology and logic itself in the past forty years have produced a research record that is much more welcoming to Toulmin's views. In this essay, I attempt to add to this welcome. I do so in a spirit of repentance of my own earlier resistance, and in confirmation of the adage that later is sometimes better than never.

KEYWORDS: Logic; validity; deduction; induction; inductive strength; probability; probability theory; plausibility; possibility; quantum logic; domain-specificity; models; theoretic progress; conceptual change; cognitive targets; cognitive standards; ideal models; normativity; *Can Do Principle; Make Do Principle*

My title harbours an engaging ambiguity. In one sense, it suggests theses which Stephen Toulmin himself espouses or is committed to. In another, it suggests theses held by others, but occasioned by reflecting on Toulmin's writings. Of course, the two are not strictly disjoint. My principal purpose here is to lend these propositions some degree of favour, if not in every case theses of Toulmin's *making*, then perhaps of his *example*. The eight that I shall be discussing are:

1. Validity is nearly always the wrong standard for real-life reasoning.
2. The probability calculus distorts much of probabilistic reasoning.
3. Scant resources have a benign influence on human reasoning.
4. Theoretical progress and conceptual change are linked.
5. Logic should attend to the cognitive aspects of reasoning and arguing.
6. Ideal models are unsuitable for determining normativity.

D. Hitchcock and B. Verheij (eds.), Arguing on the Toulmin Model: New Essays in Argument Analysis and Evaluation, 379–397.

7. The *Can Do Principle* should be applied with caution.
8. Domain-specific logics are as welcome as they are unavoidable.

1. VALIDITY IS NEARLY ALWAYS THE WRONG STANDARD FOR REAL-LIFE REASONING

It is widely assumed that among the argumentative and ratiocinative virtues, validity ranks highest except for soundness, inductive strength comes next, and trailing along in third place, is a motley group of attributes loosely collected under the name of plausibility. It takes little reflection to see that nothing whatsoever in competent human practice supports such a ranking. The idea that strictest is best is a dogma, as deeply dug in as it is untrue.

Argument and reasoning succeed or fail only in relation to an agent's *targets*. Such targets are cognitive in nature, typified by a desire to know what to believe and what to do. Targets are usually contextually cued and implicit in an agent's behaviour. They are for the most part presumed rather than declared. This matters in two ways. Not only are targets themselves open to judgements of appropriateness and inappropriateness, they are also liable to misattribution. Judging a person's behaviour as bad requires a finding that it does not attain a certain target. But any such finding collapses if the target on which it pivots has been misattributed.

It is clear that validity itself is never a realistic target. If your desire is simply to possess a valid argument, then '*P*, therefore *P*' will always do the trick. Even if you have it in mind to give someone an illustrative *example* of a valid argument, some validities are better than others, and some are no good at all ('*P*, therefore *P*' again).

The more accurate thing to say is that targets embed attainment-*standards* and that sometimes this is precisely what validity is: not a target, but a target's standard. If, for example, someone's target were to have a truth-preserving demonstration of a proposition of set theory, validity would indeed be a standard that the argument must meet.

Although truth-preservation is sometimes an appropriate and attainable target for beings like us, for the most part it is neither. Given our constitution and situatedness, cognitive aims are prosecuted for the most part under what is loosely called conditions of uncertainty. "Uncertainty" here is a technical term, denoting the absence of the conditions that make for truth-preservation. When someone postpones her decision about whether to buy a given stock until she has a deductively sound proof that it will yield at least 8% per annum, she has made two mistakes. She has set herself the wrong target. And, right or wrong, it is a target that cannot be attained.

That validity is hardly ever the right standard for real-life reasoning carries an important consequence for attribution and assessment. On the attribution side,

1. The correct default position is that an agent's target does not embed the validity standard.

On the assessment-side,

2. The correct default position is that in the failure to meet the validity standard there is nothing to criticize in a person's behaviour.

Accordingly,

3. By and large, the invalidity of a person's argument or reasoning is grounds not to attribute to him a validity-demanding cognitive target.

In other words,

4. An argument's invalidity is typically no basis for judging it negatively.

Why, then, for all its 2,400-year history have logicians concentrated on what is mainly the wrong standard? Perhaps it is little else than that it is the only standard that logicians have had substantial theoretical success with. Nothing succeeds like success. (I shall return to this point when we discuss the *Can Do Principle*.)

Even when an argument attains it, validity is a rather passive standard. It can be rendered impotent with a single disruption of the reasoner's knowledge-set. On receipt of new information *K* that contradicts a desired-to-be-proved *P*, the reasoner's present valid argument remains valid, but the proof is lost. Axiomatic approaches to mathematics owe a good deal of their motivation to an interest in dealing with the passivity of validity. For if the inputs to the theory's deductive apparatus could carry assurances of their truth, no *K* would emerge to contradict any *P* for which a valid argument currently exists. But now, long since, such optimism about axiomatics has been driven by well-known paradoxes into the waiting harbours of system-relativity or other forms of *ad hoc* sanctuary.

Validity's station ensures that proof is a *brittle* accomplishment. Validity is wholly indifferent to new information. The premissory extension of a valid argument is a valid argument. This means that if ever we were ill-advised enough to set validity as the *target* of our reasoning, achieving it would constitute wholly adequate grounds for shutting the enquiry down. This makes us see how wrong it is to think of validity as the goal of good argument. Of course, a proof-of-*P* is (sometimes) the goal of good argument. But it is an expensive goal. In a proof-context for which a *K* exists, not only must *P* be abandoned, but the proof-principles that abetted its derivation have to be revised, or precious theorems surrendered. This is expensive work in the cognitive economy. Although sometimes the costs have to be paid, as in the aftermath of the valid argument that toppled intuitive set theory,[1] and remained valid after it did so, very often this is work of a kind that we haven't time for.[2]

---

[1] In 1902, Russell communicated to Frege a proof that intuitive set theory sanctions the existence of a set that is a member of itself if and only if it is not a member of itself (Russell, 1967).

[2] A minority opinion is a version of dialetheism according to which it is less costly to "fix" logic than to "fix" mathematics. See Priest (1987) and Woods (2005b).

If the argument here displayed is taken classically:

1) Ocelots are four-legged.
2) Ozzie is an ocelot.
3) Therefore, Ozzie is four-legged.

then (3) is defeated if Ozzie is three-legged, and *so is (1)*. But if, instead of being seen as a universally quantified conditional, (1) is taken as a *generic* claim (Carlson and Pelletier, 1995), then Ozzie's three-leggedness defeats (3) but leaves (1) standing. Re-writing (1) as a universally quantified conditional that is impervious to Ozzie's discouragement is notoriously difficult business, as the whole literature on *ceteris paribus* clauses makes clear (Gabbay and Woods, 2005). But take it generically (and re-write "therefore" as a default operator), we achieve two advantages. We avoid the cost of exceptionalizing (1), and we conform to how we reason about such things anyway. This is not to say that a proof-of-*P* target is always wrong for us. Far from it. But it is brittle, that is, easy to wreck; and expensive, that is, difficult to fix.

Although a part of the proof standard in mathematics, validity has no purchase in any reasoning that aims (however tentatively) at conclusions carrying information not fully conveyed by the premisses. One of the first tasks of deductivism is to establish that the divide between truth-preservation and ampliation is not as chasmatic as usually supposed. I lack time for deductivists here. I will say only that I wish them luck. They will need it.

Perhaps this would be a good place to repeat our general point about targets. It is that in the situations in which real-life participants actually find themselves, targets are usually contextually-cued. Rather than simply announcing themselves, they have to be attributed. Very often such attributions are made in conditions of uncertainty. When this basic fact is laid beside a second general fact, interesting consequences ensue. This second fact is that, by and large, beings like us are cognitive adepts. We tend to get most of the right things right enough, enough of the time. So we survive, we prosper, and occasionally build great civilizations. Taken together, this pair of facts suggests that in most situations we should hesitate to attribute to other parties cognitive targets that their behaviour then and there runs foul of. This is a major lesson of the Charity Principle (Scriven, 1976). Of course, it's got nothing to do with charity.

2. THE PROBABILITY CALCULUS DISTORTS MUCH OF PROBABILISTIC REASONING

In 1953, Stephen Toulmin writes as follows:

> Starting with a study of the syllogism, the probability calculus and the calculus of classes, and then coming to the physical sciences, logicians have been misled by their earlier preoccupations and

> interests, vested as they are in formal systems of considerable refinement and elaboration, into looking for the wrong things.

Later in the same work he expands upon this point.

> The mathematical theory of probability has some place in the process of theory-establishing, certainly; but it is a more restricted one than logicians have thought. It has a central place only in limited branches of theory, such as statistical mechanics and parts of quantum mechanics . . . . The application of the calculus of probability in this sort of way raises no general questions of a philosophical kind, but only particular questions of statistical technique: questions to be answered in terms of the theory of curve-fitting, significant deviations and so on. (Toulmin,1953, pp. 112-113)

If the behaviour of individual agents is anything to go on, standard accounts[3] of inductive inference constitute a significant distortion of the actual record. Can the same be said for the linked issue of probabilistic reasoning in the here-and-now? James Franklin (2001) sees in probability an interesting parallel with the concepts of continuity and perspective. All three of these things took a long time before yielding to mathematical formulation and, before that happened, judgements of them tended to be unconscious and (he says) mistaken.

I have a somewhat different version of this story to suggest. Sometimes a conceptually inchoate idea is cleaned up by a subsequent explication of it. Sometimes these clarifications are achieved by modelling the target notion mathematically. Sometimes the clarification could not have been achieved save for the mathematics. We may suppose that something like this proved to be the case with perspective and continuity. To the extent that this is so, anything we used to think of these things which didn't make its way into the mathematical model could be considered inessential if not just mistaken. It is interesting to reflect on how well this line of thought fits the case of probability.

In raising the matter, we are calling attention to two questions. (1) What was probability like before Pascal? (2) How do we now find it to be? Concerning the first of this pair of questions, I think that we may say that, in their judgements under conditions of uncertainty, people routinely smudged (and still do) such distinctions as may have obtained between 'it is probable that', 'it is plausible that', and 'it is possible that' (the *P*-idioms). In fact, in some of their usages the *P*-idioms are freely interchangeable. One person's judgement of considerable *unlikelihood* could, without semantic loss, be another person's judgement of the hardly *possible*, and yet another's of striking *implausibility*. This too is important. It tells us that whether an agent has put in play a *concept* of probability (or possibility or plausibility) is usually underdetermined *lexically*. This plain fact of ordinary speech has been

---

[3] See, for example, Skyrms (1966). For a different kind of reservation about inductive logic, see Popper (1959/1935).

ignored by theorists, who see the *P*-concepts as strictly disjoint. So taken this way, probability is what the probability calculus axiomatizes, possibility is what standard modal logics such as S5 axiomatize (or weird ones such as S2)[4] and, although still in its theoretical infancy comparatively speaking, plausibility is what plausibility logics in the manner of Rescher (1976) try to make it out to be – in Rescher's case, another effort at axiomatization.

No doubt there are contexts in which it is reasonable to suppose that an interlocutor has indeed put a concept of probability in play. But even here underdetermination retains its bite. Whether or not it is the Pascalian, or what Jonathan Cohen calls the "aleatory" concept of probability, is also lexically underdetermined.[5] If what we sometimes intend by `probability' fails to find a welcome in the probability calculus, then unlike what appears to have been the case with perspective and continuity, we must take care not to say without further ado that those inferences that don't make the aleatory cut are *mistakes*.

Accordingly, our probability assessments require some guidance, as follows:

5. Probabilistic idioms are not a wholly reliable indicator of probabilistic conceptualization. It is possible to say "probable" and mean "plausible" (or "possible").

Even so,

6. Whenever one does determine that an interlocutor is reasoning or arguing probabilistically, it may be assumed that her behaviour embeds some concept or other of probability.

However,

7. In the general case, probabilistic behaviour leaves the identity of the embedded concept of probability underdetermined.

This being so,

8. One's default position should be not to attach to an interlocutor's target a notion of probability for which the present behaviour is defective.

Let us take it that, unlike perspective and continuity, idioms of probability (or probability/plausibility/possibility) that don't cut the Pascalian mustard leave residues of philosophically interesting usage. If this were so, there might well be

---

[4] S5 and S2 are two of the earliest axiomatizations of the modal operators, by C.I. Lewis. A good introduction to modal logic is Girle (2000).

[5] "Aleatory" derives from the Latin word for game of chance. Pascalian or aleatory probability is the concept of probability captured by the axioms and theorems of the calculus of probability. The name commemorates Blais Pascal, the principal founder of the calculus. A good discussion can be found in Cohen (1977).

philosophically important issues, the successful handling of which requires the wherewithal of this conceptual residue. To take a well-known example, standard solutions to Kahneman-Tversky problems don't make the grade of aleatory probability, but they might well comport with other conditions on non-demonstrative reasoning.[6] What, then, are we to say? That these bright, well-educated subjects are Pascalian misfits or that they are more comfortably at home (though unconsciously) with an alternative construal of their assigned tasks? If we say the second, we take on an onus we might not quite know how to discharge. It is the task of certifying the conditions under which these non-Pascalian manoeuvres are well-justified. In lots of cases, we won't have much of a clue as to how to achieve these elucidations. Small wonder, then, that the *Can Do Principle* beckons so attractively (Woods, 2003). This is the principle that bids the theorist who is trying to solve a problem *P* to stick with what he already knows and, if possible, to adapt what he knows to the requirements of *P*. One of the great attractions of Pascalian probability is that we know how to axiomatize it. *Can Do* is right to emphasize the advantage to be gained if we could somehow bend the probability calculus to the task at hand. But sometimes the connection can't be made without a vitiating conceptual distortion.

How, then, after the initial experiment, did Tversky and Kahneman know that their subjects were working with an *aleatory* conception of probability (and making a bad fist of it)? The received answer is that they instructed their subjects to do so, after pointing out the error embedded in their original majority decision. Given the further experimental results, their subjects turned out to be either insubordinate or aleatory misfits. But there is an alternative story that begs for a hearing.

Whenever – as in the Linda case – propositions *P* and *Q* have non-integral values, and neither proposition logically implies the other, it is demonstrable that the aleatory probability of their conjunction is always less than the probability of either conjunct. What is more, the quite general fact that conjunction is a probability-depressor holds in the face of any set-up information (or none). What Linda did as a student and what she is like now is irrelevant to whether a conjunction of further propositions about her is more or less probable than either of the conjuncts. The very fact that Kahneman and Tversky include the set-up information in their experiments carries an unmistakable presumption of its relevance. While it is not relevant to the subjects' probability determinations, it would certainly be relevant if the task they were performing were to determine the hypothesis of greater *plausibility*. I lack the space to develop this point in detail here. Suffice it to say that (2) together with the set-up information does well on the score of *explanatory coherence* (Thagard, 1992;

---

[6] Subjects were given the following information about Linda. Linda is 31 years of age, single, outspoken and extremely intelligent. As a student she majored in philosophy and was deeply involved in movements for anti-discrimination and social justice. She was also active in the anti-war campaign. Call this information *set-up information*. Subjects are now required to pick the proposition below that strikes them as the more probable.

(1) Linda is a bank-teller.

(2) Linda is a bank-teller active in the feminist movement.

Although (2) is less probable than (1) according to the probability calculus, a majority judged otherwise (Kahneman and Tversky, 1974).

2000), whereas (1) does not. Since it is clear that the subjects took relevant notice of the set-up, the safer conclusion to draw is not that they tried and failed to solve a probability problem, but that they tried and succeeded in solving a plausibility problem. If, then, in the follow-up experiments they were "guilty" of anything, it was that of giving greater heed to the presumption of relevance as regards the set-up information than to the instruction to be guided by the probability calculus. If so, this confirms what we might already have expected, namely, that

9. While "probability" tasks are wholly common in the cognitive lives of individual agents, it is less natural than not for competent individual cognitive agents to seek to meet the Pascalian standards in performing them.

3. SCANT RESOURCES HAVE A BENIGN INFLUENCE ON HUMAN REASONING

St. Augustine speaks of "the *eros* of the mind". Here is Peirce to the same effect, though with less passion, in which love is demoted to an itch:

> The action of thought is excited by the irritation of doubt and ceases when belief is attained; so that the production of belief is the sole function of thought. (Peirce, 1931-1958)

This is a salutary reminder. In a way, it is so obvious as to be effortlessly forgettable that reasoning is wholly without point or value except as facilitating something else. When Leibniz proposed *Calculemus*, the last thing he had in mind was calculation for its own sake. In the main, we value reasoning for the role it plays in belief-fixation and decision-making. Accordingly, reasoning is judgeable only in relation to an agent's cognitive agenda and the cognitive resources available for him in advancing it. Reasoning is also sometimes involved in more purely dialectical or rhetorical ends. Argumentation theorists are quite right to take note of this; and quite wrong to give it so central a place in their speculations. In its most basic employment, reasoning is an aid to cognition. In contexts of cognitive *disagreement,* it is unavoidable that various dialectical constraints be honoured, if only to discourage question-begging and what Aristotle called "babbling". But these constraints flow not from the nature of reasoning but rather from the nature of conflict management. Not all reasoning is conflictual. Not all reasoning is conversational.

Agents of all stripes, ourselves as well as NASA and MI5, operate under press of scant resources. These include *information, time* and *computational capacity* and, often enough, infrastructural and cultural support, and, of course, money. There is however, a marked difference between individual and institutional agents. In most matters, institutional agents command resources in quantities that individuals could not begin to achieve or manage. Agents tend to set their targets in light of the resources available for their attainment. This serves to mark off a further difference between individual and institutional agents. Given the comparative scantness of his cognitive resources, an individual agent will set targets of concomitantly comparable *modesty*. Accordingly,

10. With regard to most of their cognitive targets, individuals fall short of the standards championed by mainstream logicians.

Even so,

11. It is a considerable mistake to equate shortfalls from mainstream logic with the cognitively subpar, still less with a failure of rationality.

In large measure, the reason for saying so is that in most things the standards of deductive and inductive logic are embedded in cognitive agendas that would be unreasonable for the individual to set for himself. J.S. Mill was on to something important when he observed in *A System of Logic* (Mill, 1959) that inductive reasoning is the proper preserve of societies rather than individuals. Yet it seems that we simply cannot forbear to tell our students, year in and year out, that their ampliative reasonings are subpar to the extent that they fall below the standard of inductive strength, that is, of high conditional (Pascalian) probability.

Reasoning facilitates cognition. Cognition succeeds when certain conditions are met. One has only to look at actual – and largely successful – human practice to see that our cognitive behaviour implies a fallibilist epistemology. That being so, it is part of a human reasoner's rationality that he reason with a circumspection appropriate to his recognition *going in* that his procedures embed the practical certainty of occasional error.[7] If logic is a science of reasoning, it must take into account – indeed it must honour – the fallibility of the human reasoner when reasoning as he should. However,

12. The two mainstream logics leave this duty largely unperformed. Deductive logic embeds an epistemology of Cartesian error-elimination, and inductive logic embeds an epistemology of scientific rectitude that attends such things as drug trials by Health Canada.

It cannot be surprising, therefore, that these logics are in the main massively wrong for cognitive beings like us. Pascalized inductive strength may be fine for some of what NASA and MI5 do, but the individual who is presently seized with an on-rushing tiger experience would be well-advised to forgo the experimental method.

---

[7] For present purposes, let's say that an error is something that its committer has an implied interest in reversing himself on. One of the great virtues of fallibilism is the pressure that it puts on theorists to pay serious attention to the multiple things that collect under the name of "error". Fallacy theorists have a considerable stake in this.

4. THEORETICAL PROGRESS AND CONCEPTUAL CHANGE ARE CONNECTED

Now that the Humanities are awash in the various scepticisms of what laughably is called "post-modernism", Stephen Toulmin's heterodoxies about conceptual change may strike us as small beer. The trouble with post-modernism is not its relativities and its constructivisms; the trouble rests with the naïfs in English Departments, Faculties of Law and Education, and elsewhere, who construct such rotten arguments on their behalf. If there is a "fallacy of understatement", it could not better be instanced than by the assertion that Stephen Toulmin is no naïf. In Toulmin's hands, and later in Paul Thagard's (Thagard, 1992), a central idea is that scientific advancement is driven by conceptual change. This is a principal thesis of Toulmin's *The Philosophy of Science* (1953), where it is defended with subtlety and power. In Toulmin's telling, conceptual change comes with new ways of modelling correlations. Modelling is inherently abductive, a way of seeing things; and how one sees things is a function of what one is able to see, and what one is interested in seeing. These are a large part of what makes for the disciplined historicism that flavours Toulmin's epistemology.

When *The Philosophy of Science* made its brazen, cocky appearance, the philosophical mainstream was scandalized. It wasn't that the book didn't receive some good reviews (all of Toulmin's books have found receptive critics), but rather that the book's doctrines remained decidedly a minority position among philosophers of science.[8] This is decidedly odd. At mid-century, English-speaking philosophy – especially its more technical branches – was agog over revolutionary advances in arithmetic, semantics and physics. In each case, the prime movers of these transformations were quite aware of the conceptual changes that drove their theories forward – Cantor's "infinite", Tarski's "truth", and Heisenberg's "particle". Among the more interesting possibilities that arise from these facts is that

13. Conceptual changes that arise from modelling phenomena in new ways constitute a form of ambiguation.

Ambiguation is meaning-change on purpose. Logicians and argumentation theorists of all stripes are determinedly hostile to ambiguity, a lingering influence of Aristotle no doubt. Perhaps the most common complaint against those who make progress by changing the subject is a kind of red herring fallacy. But the trouble, if trouble there is, is not with the meaning-changer's reasoning; the trouble rests with the fallacy theorist's affection for naive realism. If the history of science has anything of metaphysical moment to tell us, it can only be the incompatibility of scientific progress with that kind of realism. Argumentation theorists, accordingly, should lighten up and give their attention to the subtleties of reasonings that both occasion and flow from this creative kind of ambiguation.

[8] When I was a Ph.D student in the early 1960s, Toulmin gave a standing-room-only lecture at the University of Michigan. He was introduced by William Alston, who banteringly averred that our visitor was the most refuted philosophical writer of the day.

Perhaps it may also be said that logicians would do well to give renewed attention to one of their subject's more dramatic instances of meaning-change-on-purpose in the last half-century. Ever since the founding of logic as a systematic discipline, logicians have understood the concept fallacy in ways that comport well with Aristotle's original conception of it. In *On Sophistical Refutations,* Aristotle describes fallacies as arguments which appear to be *syllogisms* but are not in fact.[9] In other places, he generalizes on this; fallacies are arguments which appear to be good in a certain way and are not good in that way.[10] This was a conception that set a twofold task for fallacy theorists.[11] One was to give a principled account of argument goodness. The other was to give a principled account of the property of *appearing*-to-be-good-while-being-in-fact-bad. While logicians could claim some headway with the first task, they could claim none at all with the second. (Doubtless, one of the reasons for this is two century's worth of anti-psychologism in logic. See the thesis to follow.)

Hamblin's *Fallacies* (1970) is the founding document of present-day fallacy theory, and of much else in the theory of argument. Its *cri de coeur* was that logicians had failed to bring the study of fallacies to anything resembling theoretical maturity. Among the several researchers who were stirred into action by Hamblin's call for theoretical renewal are those who make up the Dutch Pragma-Dialectical approach (*PDA*), in which we find two developments of particular note. One is that the *PDA* followed Hamblin's exhortation to dialectify logic. The other is that it utterly re-conceptualized fallacies. In the hands of van Eemeren and Grootendorst and their colleagues and students, a fallacy is simply a move in a critical discussion that violates any rule that governs it. Given the great gap – a difference of kind – between *breaking* a Dutch rule and *being* an argument that looks good but isn't, this is conceptual change of the first order.[12] It is a change motivated in large part by the *PDA* acceptance of Hamblin's suggestion that the Aristotelian conception of fallacy had proved to be theoretically intractable. Accordingly, the thinking in Amsterdam was that

14. If theoretical headway is to be made with the fallacies, we must have a new concept of fallacy.

This is not the place to judge the fruits of the *PDA* revolution in fallacy theory.[13] Suffice it to say that it now has many adherents beyond the ambit of Amsterdam.

---

[9] In chapter 4 of *On Sophistical Refutations,* Aristotle discusses fallacies "dependent on language". Chapter 5 of the same work deals with fallacies "independent of language".

[10] See Hitchcock (2000).

[11] In one variation, a fallacy is an *invalid* argument which seems *valid.* Hans Hansen has shown that this is certainly not the standard *wording* of the standard view (Hansen, 2002).

[12] For attempts to eliminate this *kind* of gap see Hintikka (1987). A critique of Hintikka is Woods and Hansen (1997). Hintikka replies in Hintikka (1997).

[13] For reservations see Woods (2004). A good example of general support for the *PDA* is Walton (1995).

5. LOGIC SHOULD ATTEND TO THE COGNITIVE ASPECTS OF REASONING AND ARGUING

If what we have said about reasoning as a facilitator of cognition is so, and if logic retains (or re-engages with) its historic mission as a science of reasoning, then logic must take account of what cognitive agents are like, what they are interested in and what they are capable of. Given that beings like us come rigged with psychologies as standard equipment, the hostility of logic to psychologism is risibly inapposite. Of course, speaking of ambiguity, psychologism has attracted its own hefty multivocality, ably sorted out in Jacquette (2003).[14] Not everything that "psychologism" has meant or might come to mean is right for the logic of cognitive systems. But it can be said with some confidence that logic's toleration of psychologism must embrace the idea of reasoning in the service of cognition and take due notice of reasoners as performers of cognitive tasks. Frege's contempt was another thing. He associated psychologism with two (inequivalent) views that he detested. One is the "Millean" doctrine that the principles of logic are empirical generalizations.[15] The other asserts that the principles of logic can attain no greater degree of objectivity than that rendered by "intersubjective agreement". We find ourselves oddly positioned. At first blush, we would have thought Frege (1950) right in his insistence that there is no place for psychology in the theory of sets. Tarski (1956) could say the same for model theory, Post (1944) for recursion theory, and Gentzen (1935) for proof theory. If, as a great many mainline logicians assume, this is all there is to logic, then logic has no room for psychology because these theories make no room for cognitive agents. But, upon reflection, given what he actually takes psychologism to be, it is striking how difficult it has become in the last fifty years to sustain Frege's claims with confidence and assurance. In the one case, Frege has Putnam to contend with, in his insistence that quantum theory has given to logic an empirical cast (Putnam, 1975). In the second, Russell and Hilbert demand a hearing, each urging (for somewhat different reasons) the theoretical legitimacy of stipulations once they are accepted by the requisite research communities (Russell, 1903; Hilbert, 1935).

Whatever may be said about the four princely domains of mathematical logic – set theory, model theory, proof theory and recursion theory – the past forty years has seen the re-engagement by logic of agent-based reasoning. Logic proper has had a role in this transformation, what with the emergence of belief dynamics, situation logics, dialogue logics, time and action logics, and logics of practical reasoning, among many others.[16] A second source of change is computer science and artificial

[14] See also Godden (2005).

[15] The quotation marks are a necessary admonition. Mill did give serious consideration to the idea that the laws of arithmetic are empirical generalizations. But it was left to Frege to make this out to be a thesis about logic. So it would be were logicism true. But Mill was no logicist. Logicism is the view that all of arithmetic reduces to pure logic.

[16] We might note in passing that the papers of the so-called Woods-Walton Approach to the fallacies were set largely in this sector of logic's own transformations (Woods and Walton, 1989). In those earlier days,

intelligence, what with their emphasis on non-monotonicity, default and defeasible reasoning. A third has been informal logic, and argumentation theory more generally.[17] A theme that runs through all these developments is that theories of reasoning must attend to how human beings actually do reason. Where disagreement exists, it turns on the problem (or anyhow the challenge) of validating those norms of reasoning which nearly everyone seems to agree are from time to time violated in actual practice. I shall return to this important issue when we examine our next thesis, just below. For now, it suffices to say that

15. The admissibility of psychological factors into any logic that is serious about individual cognitive agency is a no-brainer.

More generally,

16. It is helpful to conceive of a cognitive agent as a being, or a device, that executes a certain cognitive psychology. An open question is the extent to which normative considerations could be handled by a requisite epistemology.

6. IDEAL MODELS ARE UNSUITABLE FOR DETERMINING NORMATIVITY

Writing at mid-century, Toulmin allows that

> [i]n practice, of course, we do not always adopt the most satisfactory methods of argument – we generalize hastily, ignore conflicting evidence, misinterpret ambiguous observations and so on. We know very well that there are reliable standards of evidence to be observed, but we do not always observe them. In other words, we are not always rational; for to be 'rational' is to employ always these reliable, self-consistent methods of forming one's scientific beliefs, and to fail to be 'rational' is to entertain the hypothesis concerned with a degree of confidence out of proportion to its 'probability' (Toulmin, 1950b, p. 164).[18]

Walton and I would repose the burdens of *petitio principii* on Kripke models for intuitionistic logic. We would take it as given that relevant logic *à la* Pittsburgh and Canberra would suffice for irrelevancies of inference on the ground. And so on. The two of us have since wised up, and now pursue different, and more comprehensive, methodological ends, concerning which it is unlikely that we are both right (Walton, 1995; Woods, 2004).

[17] Other important sources are cognitive psychology and empirical economics. Case-based analyses of administrative and corporate decision-making have been with us for a hundred years. The common law is centuries old. Logicians are just starting to take note of these. Stephen Toulmin is an exception. They have been in his sights, one way or another, since *The Place of Reason in Ethics* (Toulmin, 1950b). See also *The Abuse of Casuistry* (Jonsen and Toulmin, 1988) and *Return to Reason* (Toulmin, 2001).

[18] It is not wholly clear whether Toulmin's quotation marks are intended to be admonitory rather than merely emphatic.

Here is Toulmin in his first book, *The Place of Reason in Ethics*, making a point that to this day is gospel among theorists of human behaviour, although Cohen (1982) and Gigerenzer and Selten (2001) are important exceptions. This is the idea that when humans reason in ways that fail to comport with the relevant theories – deductive and inductive logic, probability theory, decision theory, among others – they perform irrationally.[19] Perhaps we might agree that just three years later, Toulmin had wisely modified his position. (See again the quotations from *Philosophy of Science* at the beginning of our discussion of thesis two). What Toulmin was saying in 1953 is that when a piece of human reasoning fails to honour the requisite theory, then *two* possibilities are open for consideration. One is that the defections reveal a lack of rationality. The other is that the theory whose principles are defected from doesn't apply to the cases in question. Much of our discussion so far has it that

17. It is a theme of Toulminian import that in the case of first-order logic, inductive logic, the probability calculus and rational decision theory, it is typically a mistake to suppose that on pain of irrationality individual human reasoning must conform itself to their theorems.

Against this is the insistence by a great many practitioners of these disciplines that the defected-from principles are normatively valid, and that it follows from this that a failure to comport with them is indeed rationally subpar. If this is right, it embodies a hugely important insight into human rationality, one that sustains a pessimism that runs roughshod over the Charity Principle, which "requires that we make the best, rather than the worst possible interpretation" (Scriven, 1976, p. 71). This is something to pause over. It convicts us all of widespread irrationality, and it makes us massive cognitive misfits.

Still, these theorists have reasons for their view of the matter, the two most prominent of which are: first, that the principles of these disciplines are articulable in ideal models in which they are *analytic*; and, second, that their normative force is guaranteed by a kind of *reflective equilibrium*. Both of these claims are problematic (Gabbay and Woods, 2003b). The analyticity claim is beggared by question-begging. If, for example, someone says that it is not true that belief is closed under consequence, it is dialectically unavailing to counter with the assurance that there is an ideal model in which the opposite is analytically true. Not only does "analytically true" not work as a *rejoinder* to "not true", but being true-in-a-model makes no claim, just as it stands, to being true in the world. So, again, imagine that someone says that various would-be normative principles don't hold, and that someone else responds that there is a model M in which they do. This might be so, but it is of no matter.

---

[19] Even more emphatic is Reichenbach in *The Rise of Scientific Philosophy* (1951, p. 308): What gives priority to science? (he asks). "Who can judge about the theory of knowledge if he has not seen knowledge in its most successful form?" Malcolm, reviewing the book, thought this "primitive nonsense".

18. Anything true-in-a theorist's model M might actually be false.

The reflective equilibrium defence of the normativity of ideal models falters at the starting gate. It may be true that by and large the cognitive behaviour of beings like us is in reflective equilibrium with what could with justice be called the principles of right reasoning. But

19. There is not a jot of support in the assumption of the reflective equilibrium of practice and principle for the assertion that the principles privileged by standard ideal models – that is to say, principles of deductive and inductive logic, the probability calculus and rational decision theory – are invariably or even typically those principles of right reasoning with which our cognitive practices are in reflective equilibrium.

Accordingly, we may think it best to abandon these defences, and direct our quest for the normative elsewhere. On one approach a good place to look is indeed, our general practice, but not because it is in reflective equilibrium with the proffered ideal models, but, again, rather more because our run-of-the-mill reasoning doesn't kill us: Again, we survive, we pass on our ratiocinative devices to our descendant class, we prosper, and occasionally we build great civilizations. Either we do these things on the basis of such knowledge as our cognitive processes are capable of attaining for us, or in the absence of it. If the former is true, the pessimism of the ideal model approach is unjustified. If the latter is true, the value of knowledge is debased (Woods, 2005a).

7. THE CAN DO PRINCIPLE SHOULD BE APPLIED WITH CAUTION

In most things cognitive,

20. The Can Do Principle bids the individual cognitive agent to try to tailor the advancement of his agendas to principles he is already at home with and to problem-solving techniques over which he already has attained a certain mastery.

Can Do requires the problem-solver not to start from scratch if he can help it. *Can Do* is one of the principal canons of the cognitive economies in which agents of all types operate. But there are limits. A hammer's usefulness in pulling nails gives it no leg up in the removal of paint from walls of one's dining room. Using a valuable and versatile tool for a task for which it is unsuited is a misbegotten, false economy. When the misapplication is inadvertent, there is room to postulate the presence of the *Make Do Principle*. *Make Do* is a degenerate case of *Can Do*. It has a twofold appeal. It allows the cognitive agent the comfort of doing something rather than nothing. It is also abetted by the ideal model methodology for normativity, for which it is tailor-made. In his more composed moments, the reasoner will see the disutility of methods and applications of principles that have no standing in the problem-space at hand. But not only is this something that he sometimes cannot see but, in not seeing it, *Make Do* is given a degree of encouragement by the attractive example of scientific progress via conceptual change.

Any probability theorist who knows his onions will be aware that, after Pascal, probability *changed.* This presents us with a fundamental question: When something is a new conception of something, does it extinguish its predecessor-concept, or does it foster a new ambiguity which leaves the old concept standing? The probability theorists's inclination is to see the axioms of probability theory on the analogy of the principle of rectilinear propagation, after which the scientific concept of light both changed *and* was laid open to an improved scientific understanding. Why could we not proclaim a similar law for probability – the principle of Pascalian compounding – thanks to which the concept of probability both changed *and* was made susceptible to a better theoretical (i.e. mathematical) understanding? Perhaps we could, but doing so does not answer this fundamental question. Certainly we don't expect an individual's ordinary reasoning about light to comport with the rectilinear propagation principle. An individual who managed to live his life wholly innocent of the disclosures of optical geometry might well run up an error-free record in his reasonings about light and shadow in rainy Vancouver. This tells us that the laws of optical geometry are not normative for ordinary reasoning about light.[20] But probability theory (and deductive logic and decision theory) are quite different in their normative presumptions. They *do* purport to bind an individual's actual practice. I wonder about this. Granted that the aleatory theorems are binding on certain patterns of reasoning "in statistical mechanics and parts of quantum mechanics … [or concerning] particular questions of statistical technique: questions to be answered in terms of the theory of curve-fitting, significant deviations and so on", it is left wide open as to which principles apply to individual agents when they estimate the probability of Linda being a bank-teller who works on feminist issues. Unreflective resort to the calculus of probability gives Toulminian offence for its procrusteanism (Toulmin, 1953, p. 126).[21] By my lights, and to the same effect, it is a matter of *Make Do*. It is "looking for the wrong things".

Although they never put it in these terms, one of the central accomplishments of advancers of the informal logic research programme, which *The Uses of Argument* did so much to motivate and shape, is the stiff resistance they have shown to procrusteanism and *Make Do* in the analysis of human reasoning and argument.[22] It is a welcome turning in the human sciences, but not as yet one graced by a place in the mainstream. More needs to be done.

---

[20] Perhaps it will be countered that the principles of optical geometry are normative for everyday reasoning about light and shadow at least in the sense that such reasoning not transgress the theory. I haven't the space to take up this challenge here, beyond saying that much of ordinary reasoning about light and shadow is not directed at getting the physical nature of light right. It is directed at getting right such things as setting the aperture of a camera.

[21] To be clear, Toulmin's target in this instance is Eddington, not Pascal.

[22] Mind you, in giving validity so free a rein, Pragma-Dialectics is something of a hold-out.

8. DOMAIN-SPECIFIC LOGICS ARE AS WELCOME AS THEY ARE UNAVOIDABLE

Aristotle was a master reductionist, and a strategically adroit compacter of complexity. In *On Interpretation* Aristotle asserted that everything stateable in Greek is stateable without relevant loss in the language of (what we know as) categorical propositions (17^9 13, 18^a 24). In the *Analytics,* Aristotle said, and repeated, that all correct reasoning reduces to syllogistic.[23] Had Aristotle been right in the first instance, he would have achieved a striking economy in logical grammar. Had he been right in the second instance, he would have had – thanks to the perfectability proof of the *Prior Analytics* (A1, 24^b 27; A23, 40^b 20) – something approaching effective recognizability for all reasoning. But not even Aristotle thought that correct reasoning could be detached from the protocols of premiss-selection, concerning which he would insist on what he called premissory "appropriateness".

In one strain of universalism espoused by more recent logicians, an argument's validity owes nothing to the propositional content of premisses. This topic-neutrality of modern formal logic is strictly a matter of the uninterpretedness of the atomic elements of the language. This is, by the way, is a huge encumbrance for any logic that seeks a regulatory role in reasonings transacted in human languages. (The principal reason is that the atomic components of any natural language often stand in logical relations to one another.) Logicians seek to minimize the gap between its uninterpreted derivations and natural language reasoning by supplementation of logical particles, which do admit of interpretation after a fashion. The upshot is a proliferation of systems, concomitant with the growth of logical particles; and although valid arguments remain valid under any valuation of atomic components, the validity now threatens to be system-relative, not universal.

Before and after Stephen Toulmin's heretical insistence that logically correct reasoning be made sensitive to disciplinary peculiarities, post-Fregean logicians could hardly have been unaware that the purported *reductive* universality of pure logic would be of scant use to the deductive sciences.[24] Arising therefrom was the idea that set theory was part of logic. Well, either it is or it isn't. If it is, pure logic is not universal even in the sense of system-relative topic-neutrality. If it isn't, pure logic can't capture all the deductions even of mathematics, and so must abandon any pretence of being the *über-theorie* of the deductive sciences.

One might think that there is an attenuated sense in which something like first-order logic does achieve a kind of universality. This is the sense in which the analyses it makes of its target properties – validity, entailment, logical truth, consistency – are correct for any context in which these properties are either invoked

[23] However, Aristotle also recognized counterexamples to this claim (see, e.g. *Prior Analytics* 41^b 36-42^a 5; 53^b 12 ff; and 34^a 5 ff).

[24] "No more than any other science can mathematics be founded by logic alone; rather . . . something must already be given to us in our faculty of representation . . ." (Hilbert, 1967/1927, p. 464).

or attributed. On this view, entailment is entailment, whether in macroeconomics or biochemistry or politics. But no one who has even a nodding acquaintance with the sheer scope of today's rivalrous pluralism in logic can make this claim for universality with any prospect of serenity. Every one of these properties is the subject of unsettled land claims; and even on those few occasions when treaties have been signed, they all take the low road (by universalists' lights) of domain-relativity.

One might think that there is a systematic tie between, on the one hand, what a logic counts as its logical particles and the interpretation it gives of them and, on the other, the account it is able to give of its target properties. Taking entailment as our example, one view is that any change to one's logical particles will result, however slightly, in an altered conception of entailment. This is sometimes disputed on grounds that concept-identity is an intensional notion, that the entailment-changes wrought by changes to a system's logical vocabulary are often just changes to its former extension, and that, up to a point, extensional change is compatible with intensional persistence. A case in point is a basic intuitionist system in which entailment retains its standard definition as not admitting a valuation in which an antecedent is true and its consequent false, yet in which certain classical entailment-statements fail.[25]

Perhaps it is all a matter of how extensive the revisions of the logical vocabulary turn out to be. The model theory of quantum languages is an instructive case. Classical model theory postulates a domain of well-individuated individuals, whose pairwise distinctness is sharp enough to enable strict enumerability. Classical truth in turn pivots on these features. But one of the chief respects in which quantum mechanics is both conceptually and technically challenging is that the objects it postulates are not well-individuated; rather they are probabilistic blurs. This being so, quantum sentences about such objects are ineligible for classical truth. And that being so, every quantum deduction whose premisses contain such a sentence is classically valid. For there will be no valuation that makes all the premisses classically true and the conclusion false (Woods and Peacock, 2004). Clearly this is an exuberance of validity on the scale of absolute inconsistency. So we must allow that classical validity cannot serve as the validit y required by quantum mechanics' strict deductions. Accordingly, if validity is to be allowed as a standard for quantum deductions, it is not a property that classical logic can capture. A Toulminian response would be to call for a purpose-built quantum logic. It is the right response.

[25] An even more interesting case is provided by certain systems of relevant logic in which entailment is non-classical while the logical particles stay firmly classical. See, for example, Tennant (1992).

In the spring of 2005 there occurred in Montreux the first international conference on Universal Logic. Part of what the organizers sought to achieve was some indication of the kind of all-embracing logical architecture that might offer, however guardedly, promise of universalizing logic's pluralistic sprawl. Judging from the papers read there, including my own, the organizers will have been left with no alternative but to trudge home and kick the cat.[26, 27]

[26] As it has arisen of late, the term "universal logic" has taken on a certain ambiguity. In one sense, it is a research programme whose aim is to reconfigure logic on the model of universal algebra (Béziau, 2005). In its other meaning, universal logic is a type of logical system that applies to all contexts, including contradictory ones (Brady, 2005). It helps to emphasize their difference to point out that universal logic (the research programme) cannot be understood as the study of universal logic (the all-contexts system of logic).

[27] The present essay is a somewhat extended version of a paper of the same name presented at a Conference on The Uses of Argument at McMaster University in May 2005, ably organized by David Hitchcock. The Conference honoured the huge contributions that Stephen Toulmin has made to an appropriately humanized logic, and it took its title from that of Toulmin's third, and one of his most important, books. I wish to warmly thank Michael Scriven, who commented wisely on my talk, and the several others who participated helpfully in the discussion that followed. They are Stephen Toulmin, Harvey Siegel, Manfred Kraus, Thomas Goodnight, Ralph Johnson, Donald Hatcher and Rolf George. I am especially in debt to David Hitchcock for his astute suggestions for improving the present version. For welcome instruction before and after the conference I would like to express my gratitude to Bas van Fraassen, Dov Gabbay, Andrew Irvine, Ori Simchen, Jonathan Adler, Johan van Benthem, Alvin Goldman, Peter Bruza, Luis Lamb and Michael Woolridge.
For financial support, I am obliged to the Engineering and Physical Sciences Research Council of the United Kingdom and the Social Sciences and Humanities Research Council of Canada. For invaluable technical support I am most grateful to Carol Woods.

CONTRIBUTORS

Andrew Aberdein is Assistant Professor of Logic and Humanities at Florida Institute of Technology. Before coming to Florida he taught at the University of Edinburgh. He graduated with a Ph.D. in Logic & Metaphysics from the University of St. Andrews in 2001. Dr Aberdein's principal research is concerned with the interplay between logic and the philosophy of science. He is particularly interested in the contribution that argumentation theory can make to the understanding of the formal sciences.

Txetxu Ausín is Contract Researcher at the Institute of Philosophy, Spanish National Research Council CSIC (www.ifs.csic.es). He holds a PhD in Philosophy and a BA in Advanced Studies in Logics and Foundations of Computer Science and Cognitive Science. He has been Assistant Professor of Professional Ethics of Communication, Logic, and Argumentation at the European University of Madrid. He is a member and Secretary-Treasurer of the Spanish Leibniz Society (www.leibnizsociedad.org). His research is focused on deontic logics and argumentation with norms, applied ethics and human rights, and the legal and political writings of Leibniz. His most recent publication is the book, in Spanish, *Between Logics and Law: Paradoxes and Normative Conflicts* (2005).

Lilian Bermejo-Luque holds a PhD in Philosophy from the University of Murcia in Spain. She works on the integration of the logical, rhetorical and dialectical aspects of argumentation.

Cristiano Castelfranchi is full professor of Cognitive Sciences at the University of Siena, and director of the Institute for Cognitive Sciences and Technologies of the National Research Council in Rome. He is a cognitive scientist, with a background in linguistics and psychology, who is active in several scientific communities, including cognitive sciences, Multi-Agent Systems and social simulation. He is a Fellow of ECCAI, program chair of AAMAS-2002, chair of several international workshops, and an advisory member of several international conferences and societies (e.g. Cognitive Science; IFMAS). He participated in a number of research networks under the FP4, FP5 and FP6. His research interests include cognitive agent theory and architecture; multi-agent systems; agent-based social simulation; argumentation theories; social cognition and emotions; trust and deception. He has extensively published on all these topics, and he has been invited speaker at IJCAI'97 and in several other conferences on AI, logics, and cognitive sciences. He is member of the editorial board of the *Journal of Autonomous Agents and MAS* and *Cognitive Science Quarterly*, and of the MIT *CogNet*.

Robert H. Ennis received his PhD from the University of Illinois, UC and now is Professor Emeritus at the same institution, and Immediate Past-President of the Association for Informal Logic and Critical Thinking. He has been a Fellow at the Center for Advanced Study in the Behavioral Sciences at Stanford, California, President of the Philosophy of Education Society, a Post-Doctoral Fellow at the

University of California, Berkeley, a full professor at Cornell University, and a physical-science teacher at the Oakwood Twp. High School in Illinois. Ennis is the author of three books, *Ordinary Logic, Logic in Teaching,* and *Critical Thinking*; co-author of one book, *Evaluating Critical Thinking*; co-editor of two books, *Language and Concepts in Education* and *Philosophy of Educational Research*; and co-author of three critical thinking tests: *Cornell Critical Thinking Test Level X*, *Cornell Critical Thinking Test Level Z*, and *Ennis-Weir Critical Thinking Essay Test*. He is author of over fifty articles, co-author of six articles, and editorial-board member for three journals: *Informal Logic*, *Inquiry*, and *Teaching Philosophy*. His academic web site is http://faculty.ed.uiuc.edu/rhennis, where more details can be found.

James B. Freeman is Professor of Philosophy at Hunter College of The City University of New York, where he has taught since 1978. His main area of research is informal logic and argumentation theory. His informal logic text, *Thinking Logically: Basic Concepts for Reasoning* (Englewood Cliffs, NJ: Prentice Hall, 1988, 1993), presents a method of diagramming argument structure integrating elements of the Toulmin model with the "standard" approach, familiar from the texts of Stephen N. Thomas and others. His monograph, *Dialectics and the Macro-structrue of Arguments: A Theory of Argument Structure* (Berlin and New York: Foris Publications, 1991), critically appraises the Toulmin model and argues for incorporating various aspects of the model into the standard approach as presented in *Thinking Logically*. His latest book, *Acceptable Premises: An Epistemic Approach to an Informal Logic Problem* (Cambridge: Cambridge University Press, 2005), calls upon the Toulmin model to explicate certain issues concerning the acceptability of basic premises. Besides the paper presented in this volume, he discusses explicating relevance through Toulmin's notion of warrant in "Relevance, Warrants, Backing, Inductive Support," *Argumentation* **6** (1992), 219-235. He is currently concerned with the problem of connection adequacy in arguments, specifically with assaying relevance and ground adequacy.

John Fox was educated at Durham and Cambridge Universities in the UK, and then carried out research in AI and cognitive science at Carnegie-Mellon and Cornell Universities in the USA. At Cancer Research UK he leads the Advanced Computation Laboratory whose research straddles computer science, artificial intelligence and software engineering with a particular focus on medicine (see www.acl.icnet.uk). Fox has published widely in AI and cognitive science and biomedical engineering, and was founding editor of the *Knowledge Engineering Review* (Cambridge University Press). Recent publications include *Safe and Sound: Artificial Intelligence in Hazardous Applications* (AAAI and MIT Press, July 2000), which deals with many aspects of the theory and use of argumentation within the context of autonomous agents. In 1996 the ACL received the 20th Anniversary Gold Medal of the European Federation of Medical Informatics for its work on PROforma, a declarative agent specification language, and an associated suite of application development tools. Among the applications of PROforma are decision support and workflow management, many of which have been developed and validated for medical use (www.openclinical.org/gmm_proforma.html). He is scientific coordinator of the ASPIC project (Argumentation Service Platform with Integrated Components), which is funded by the EU (see www.argumentation.org).

G. Thomas Goodnight is Professor of Communication and Director of the Doctoral Program, the Annenberg School for Communication, at the University of Southern California in Los Angeles, California. Professor Goodnight writes in the areas of controversy, public argument, the rhetoric of science, and rhetorical theory and criticism. He has published works on these topics in the *Quarterly Journal of Speech*, *Informal Logic*, and *Argumentation.*

David Hitchcock is Professor of Philosophy at McMaster University in Hamilton, Canada. He is the author of *Critical Thinking: A Guide to Evaluating Information* (Toronto: Methuen, 1983) and (with Milos Jenicek, MD) of *Evidence-Based Practice: Logic and Critical Thinking in Medicine* (Chicago: AMA Press, 2005). He has published scholarly papers on non-deductive (enthymematic, conductive, inductive and analogical) inference; on a variety of other topics in the theory of argumentation (constraints on formal systems of inquiry dialogues, deliberation dialogue (with Peter McBurney), practical reasoning (with Rod Girle, Peter McBurney and Bart Verheij), the fallacy of denying the antecedent); on Plato, Aristotle and the Stoics; and on Tarski's conception of logical consequence. He is currently at work on a monograph on the concept of consequence (the inferential concept, not the causal one).

James F. Klumpp is Professor of Communication at the University of Maryland. He has written extensively in contemporary rhetorical theory and particularly in argumentation theory, and studies contemporary and historical discourse as a rhetorical critic. He has edited the journal *Argumentation and Advocacy* and has been the Director of the NCA/AFA Summer Conference in Argumentation.

Christian Kock is Professor of Rhetoric in the Department of Media, Cognition, and Communication at the University of Copenhagen. He was co-founder of the Academic Writing Centre at that institution and has been a Visiting Professor of English at Indiana University, Bloomington. His research interests include argumentation theory and pedagogy, public debate, writing pedagogy, literary and musical aesthetics, and the history of rhetoric. He is author or co-author of a number of monographs, textbooks and articles across these fields, in Danish and English. He is a member of the Humanities Subcommittee of the Research Council of Norway.

Manfred Kraus is lecturer for Classics at the University of Tübingen, Germany. He studied Classics and German Language and Literature in Munich and Oxford and took his degree of Dr. phil. in 1984 at the University of Munich. The title of his doctoral thesis is *Name und Sache. Ein Problem im frühgriechischen Denken* (Amsterdam: B.R. Grüner 1987). He has written various articles on topics concerning Greek and Latin literature, ancient philosophy, the history of rhetoric and the theory of argumentation, and has contributed a number of major articles to the *Historisches Wörterbuch der Rhetorik* edited at Tübingen. His main scholarly interests are early Greek philosophy, the philosophy of Plato and Aristotle, philosophy of language, poetics and aesthetics of Greek tragedy, history of education, theory and history of rhetoric from antiquity to modern times, and the theory of argumentation (with special emphasis on the theory of the enthymeme). He is currently a member of the Council of the International Society for the History of Rhetoric (ISHR) and co-editor of the journal *Rhetorica*.

Ronald P. Loui holds a joint Computer Science and Philosophy doctoral degree from the University of Rochester, and studied intellectual history and applied mathematics at Harvard. He is currently an Associate Professor in Computer Science and Engineering at Washington University in St. Louis. A recognized innovator in artificial intelligence, logic, and the mathematical foundations of social science, he has been studying citation counts in his field for fifteen years.

Sanjay Modgil was educated at Imperial College London, where he completed an MSc in Computer Science and a PhD in logic. He is currently a senior research fellow employed on the EU 6th framework ASPIC project (Argumentation Service Platform with Integrated Components). His current research interests are in non-monotonic reasoning, logical argumentation systems, and applications of this work in a medical domain. Previous research has focused on logic programming techniques and Description Logics and applications of this work in medical expert systems and medical planning.

Fabio Paglieri is a researcher in Cognitive Science, with a strong background in philosophical epistemology, cognitive and social psychology, formal logic, and Artificial Intelligence. His research interests are focused on the cognitive dynamics of doxastic and motivational states (belief formation and revision, practical reasoning, goal-oriented behaviour, motivated reasoning, intention processing, anticipatory mechanisms), their integration in social practices (argumentation, coordination, cooperation, altruism, emergence and evolution of social institutions), and the formal modelling of these phenomena in BDI logics, multi-agent systems and game-theoretical models, plus several foundational issues, such as the nature of mental representations and the distinction between implicit and explicit mental states. He is currently working at the University of Siena and at the Institute for Cognitive Sciences and Technologies of the CNR in Roma: in the recent past, he has been a visiting student at the Institute for Logic, Language and Computation at the University of Amsterdam. The discussion of his PhD dissertation in Cognitive Science at the University of Siena is due in July 2006, title *Belief dynamics: From cognitive architectures to formal models, and back again*. For further information and a full list of publications, see http://www.media.unisi.it/cirg/fp/paglieri.html.

Robert C. Pinto is Professor Emeritus at the University of Windsor, where he has taught since 1963. He holds a Ph.D. in philosophy from the University of Toronto, and is a member of the editorial boards of *Argumentation* and *Informal Logic*. His publications include *Argument, Inference and Dialectic* (Kluwer, 2001); with J.A. Blair, *Reasoning:* A *Practical Guide* (Prentice-Hall, 1993); and with Hans V. Hansen, *Fallacies: Classical and Contemporary Readings* (Pennsylvania State Press, 1995).

Henry Prakken is a lecturer in the Intelligent Systems Group (http://www.cs.uu.nl/ groups/IS/) of the computer science department at Utrecht University, and professor of Law and ICT at the Law Faculty (http://www.rug.nl/law/index) of the

University of Groningen. He holds master's degrees in law (1985) and philosophy (1988) from the University of Groningen. In 1993 Henry Prakken obtained his PhD degree at the Free University Amsterdam with a thesis titled *Logical Tools for Modelling Legal Argument*. He is interested in logical foundations of common-sense reasoning, and in the application of Artificial Intelligence and advanced IT to legal reasoning, dispute resolution, group decision making and negotiation.

Chris Reed is Lecturer and Assistant Head of Research in the Division of Applied Computing at the University of Dundee in Dundee, Scotland. Since acquiring his PhD in 1998, he has focused his research on the interdisciplinary area lying between artificial intelligence and the theory of argumentation. He has published about 50 papers in refereed conference proceedings and journals, and has attracted both government and industrial funding, in the United Kingdom and internationally. In 2000 he organized the Symposium on Argument and Computation, an international meeting and collaborative authoring effort that helped to kick-start interdisciplinary work between argumentation and AI. From 2001 to the present, he has co-organized with Floriana Grasso a series of workshops on computational models of natural argument.

Glenn Rowe is a lecturer in Applied Computing at the University of Dundee in Scotland. His research interests include computer-based learning and computer-based assessment, particularly in the teaching of programming. He is also interested in the application of biologically inspired techniques such as ant swarm models and genetic algorithms to practical problems such as optimizing heat exchange in chemical plants. In the argumentation field, he is the main software developer in the Araucaria project (in collaboration with Chris Reed). He and Chris are currently putting the finishing touches on Araucaria version 3.1, which includes Wigmore diagrams in addition to the standard and Toulmin diagrams featured in version 3.0.

Wouter H. Slob received his PhD from the University of Groningen in 2002. A revised version of his dissertation was published as *Dialogical Rhetoric; an essay on truth and normativity after postmodernism*, Kluwer, Dordrecht (2002). His fields of interest are logic, argumentation, theology, and philosophy of history. Presently, he works as a minister in the Dutch Reformed Church and teaches at the Department of Theology in Groningen.

Olaf Tans is a legal philosopher and political scientist working as post-doctoral researcher at the legal faculty of the University of Amsterdam. In 2003 he defended his PhD thesis, which analyses the function of constitutional norms in political communities from a discourse perspective. More generally his research interests are: processes of constitutional ordering, the development of European democracy, evolution of law, and practical reasoning.

Stephen Edelston Toulmin is a University Professor and Adjunct Professor of Anthropology, International Relations, and Religion at the University of Southern California. He is the author of *An Examination of the Place of Reason in Ethics* (1950), *Philosophy of Science: An Introduction* (1953), *The Uses of Argument* (1958), *Foresight and Understanding: An Enquiry into the Aims of Science* (1961), *Human Understanding* (1972), *Knowing and Acting: An Invitation to Philosophy*

(1976), *The Return to Cosmology: Postmodern Science and the Theology of Nature* (1982), *Cosmopolis: The Hidden Agenda of Modernity* (1990), and *Return to Reason* (2001). He is also the co-author of *The Fabric of the Heavens: The Development of Astronomy and Dynamics* (1961, with June Goodfield), *The Architecture of Matter* (1965, with June Goodfield), *The Discovery of Time* (1965, with June Goodfield), *Wittgenstein's Vienna* (1973, with Alan Janik), *An Introduction to Reasoning* (1979 and 1984, with Richard Rieke and Alan Janik), and *The Abuse of Casuistry: A History of Moral Reasoning* (1988, with Albert R. Jonsen).

Bart Verheij is assistant professor at the Artificial Intelligence department of the University of Groningen, the Netherlands. His research has focused on defeasible argumentation, legal argumentation, argumentation support software and argumentation schemes, often using formalism as a tool of analysis. In his future work, the perspective of multi-agent systems will be emphasized, e.g. by studying arguing agents and artificial societies. Bart Verheij's dissertation is entitled *Rules, Reasons, Arguments. Formal studies of argumentation and defeat* (1996). He is the author of the book *Virtual Arguments. On the Design of Argument Assistants for Lawyers and Other Arguers* (2005). Further information is available at http://www.ai.rug.nl/~verheij/.

James F. Voss is Emeritus Professor of Psychology and Political Science of the University of Pittsburgh and former Associate Director and Senior Scientist of the Learning Research and Development Center of the same institution. He has published in a variety of research areas including the role of knowledge in subsequent learning, expert and novice differences in social science problem solving, psychological processes in argumentation including the use of narrative as argument, argumentation as a factor in the learning of history, and expert performance in history.

Mark Weinstein is Professor and Chair of the Department of Educational Foundations at Montclair State University in New Jersey. His chapter in the present volume combines his original interest in logic and philosophy of science with his more recent concern with applied epistemology as the foundation for critical thinking and argument.

John Woods is Director of the Abductive Systems Group at the University of British Columbia and the Charles S. Peirce Professor of Logic in the Group on Logic and Computation at King's College London. He has written extensively on philosophical logic and fallacy theory, concerning which latter Woods is co-originator, with Douglas Walton, of the so-called Woods-Walton Approach. His *Logic of Fiction* (Mouton, 1974) is widely recognized as one of the pioneering works in the formal semantics of non-denoting terms. Woods' recent books include *Paradox and Paraconsistency* (Cambridge, 2003), which is an exploration of conflict resolution in the absence of empirical checkpoints, and *The Death of Argument* (Kluwer, 2004), a collection of articles on fallacies. Woods is also co-author, with Dov Gabbay, of *Agenda Relevance* (2003) and *The Reach of Abduction* (2005), both from Elsevier. Work in progress includes a co-authored book on dialetheic logic under the working title, *True Contradictions.*

John Zeleznikow is a full Professor of Information Systems at Victoria University, Melbourne, Australia. Prior to this, he spent two and a half years at the University of Edinburgh, Scotland, UK, where he was the Director of the Joseph Bell Centre for Forensic Statistics and Legal Reasoning at the University of Edinburgh Law School. Professor Zeleznikow has successfully supervised ten PhD students, published two research books, forty refereed journal articles and one hundred refereed conference articles. Professor Zeleznikow's current research focus is upon Information Technology applications in law, including Web-based decision support, knowledge discovery and data-mining, negotiation and dispute resolution.

REFERENCES

Abdullaev, S.: 1977, 'Zu den Möglichkeiten der Transposition der Satzarten im Deutschen – Die Grundstrukturen der rhetorischen Frage und des imperativischen Ausrufs', *Deutsch als Fremdsprache* **14**, 263-270.

Aberdein, A.: 2005, 'The Informal Logic of Mathematical Proof', in R. Hersh (ed.), *18 Unconventional Essays on the Nature of Mathematics*, Springer-Verlag, New York, pp. 56-70.

Aberdein, A.: 2006, 'Managing informal mathematical knowledge: Techniques from informal logic', *Lecture Notes in Artficial Intelligence* **4108**, 208-221.

Alchourrón, C., P. Gärdenfors and D. Makinson: 1985, 'On the Logic of Theory Change: Partial Meet Contraction and Revision Functions', *Journal of Symbolic Logic* **50**, 510-530.

Alcolea Banegas, J.: 1998, 'L'Argumentació en Matemàtiques', in E. Casaban i Moya (ed.), *XIIè Congrés Valencià de Filosofia,* València, pp. 135-147. Translation at http://my.fit.edu/~aberdein/Alcolea.pdf.

Aleven, V.: 1997, *Teaching Case Based Argumentation Through an Example and Models*, PhD Thesis, The University of Pittsburgh.

Alexy, R.: 1989, *A Theory of Legal Argumentation. The Theory of Rational Discourse as Theory of Legal Justification*, Clarendon Press, Oxford.

Anscombe, G.E.M.: 1957, *Intention*, Basil Blackwell, Oxford.

Anzilotti, G.I.: 1982, 'The Rhetorical Question as an Indirect Speech Device in English and Italian', *Canadian Modern Language Review* **38**, 290-302.

Apostel, L.: 1960, 'Toward the Formal Study of Models in the Formal and Non-formal Sciences', *Synthèse* **12**, 125-161.

Aristotle: 1926, *The Art of Rhetoric*, in J.H. Freese (trans.), Loeb Classical Library 193, Harvard University Press, Cambridge.

Aristotle: 1937, *Problems*, books 22-38, *Rhetorica ad Alexandrum*, in W.S. Hett and H. Rackham (trans.), Loeb Classical Library 317, Harvard University Press, Cambridge.

Aristotle: 1989, *Topica*, in E.S. Forster (trans.), Loeb Classical Library 391, Harvard University Press, Cambridge.

Ashley, K.D.: 1990, *Modeling Legal Argument: Reasoning with Cases and Hypotheticals*, MIT Press, Cambridge.

Ashley, K.D.: 2004, 'Capturing the Dialectic Between Principles and Cases', *Jurimetrics* **44**, 229-279.

Atkinson, K., T.J.M. Bench-Capon and P. McBurney: 2005, 'Arguing about Cases as Practical Reasoning', in *Proceedings of the Tenth International Conference of Artificial Intelligence and Law*, ACM Press, New York, pp. 35-44.

Ausín, T. and C. Roldán: 2005, 'Leibnizian Basis for Intercultural Dialogue', in F. Triki, T. Ausín, R. Parellada and V. Serrano (eds.), *Formes de Rationalité et Dialogue Interculturel*, Hildesheim, Olms, pp. 83-102.

Austin, J.L., 1946, 'Other Minds', *Proceedings of the Aristotelian Society*, Supplementary Volume XX, 148-187.

Austin, J.L.: 1962, *How to Do Things with Words*, Harvard University Press, Cambridge.

Austin, J.L.: 1970, 'Other Minds', in J.O. Urmson and G.J. Warnock (eds.), *Philosophical Papers*, 2nd. ed., Oxford University Press, London, pp. 76-116.

Ball, W.J.: 1994, 'Using Virgil to Analyse Public Policy Arguments: A System Based on Toulmin's Informal Logic', *Social Science Computer Review* **12**, 26-37.

Barak, A.: 1989, *Judicial Discretion,* Y. Kaufmann (trans.), Yale University Press, New Haven.

Barth, E.M. and E.C.W. Krabbe: 1982, *From Axiom to Dialogue: A Philosophical Study of Logics and Argumentation*, Walter de Gruyter, Berlin/New York.

Bates, B.R., J.A. Lynch, J.L. Bevan and C.M. Condit: 2005, 'Warranted Concerns, Warranted Outlooks: A Focus Group Study of Public Understandings of Genetic Research', *Social Science and Medicine* **60**, 331-344.

Bayer, K. (ed.): 1993, *M. Tullius Cicero, Topica. Die Kunst, richtig zu argumentieren. Lateinisch und deutsch*, Artemis & Winkler, München.

Beardsley, M.C.: 1950, *Practical Logic*, Prentice Hall, Englewood Cliffs.
Bellucci, E. and J. Zeleznikow: 2005, 'Trade-off Manipulations in the Development of Negotiation Decision Support Systems', *Proceedings of the Thirty-Eighth Hawaii International Conference on System Sciences*, IEEE Computer Society, Los Alamitos, pp. 36-42.
Bellucci, E. and J. Zeleznikow: 2006, 'Developing Negotiation Decision Support Systems that Support Mediators: A Case Study of the Family Winner System', to appear in *Artificial Intelligence and Law*.
Bench-Capon, T.J.M.: 1997, 'Argument in Artificial Intelligence and Law', *Artificial Intelligence and Law* **5**, 249-261.
Bench-Capon, T.J.M.: 1998, 'Specification and Implementation of Toulmin Dialogue Game', in J.C. Hage, T.J.M. Bench-Capon, A.W. Koers, C.N.J. de Vey Mestdagh and C.A.F.M. Grűtters (eds.), *Legal Knowledge Based Systems. JURIX: The Eleventh Conference*, Gerard N oodt Institute, Nijmegen, pp. 5-20.
Bench-Capon, T.J.M.: 2003, 'Persuasion in Practical Argument Using Value-based Argumentation Frameworks', *Journal of Logic and Computation* **13**, 429-448.
Bench-Capon, T.J.M., D. Lowes and A.M. McEnery: 1991, 'Argument-based Explanation of Logic Programs', *Knowledge Based Systems* **4**, 177-183.
Bench-Capon, T.J.M. and G. Sartor: 2003, 'A Model of Legal Reasoning with Cases Incorporating Theories and Values', *Artificial Intelligence* **150**, 97-143.
Bengoetxea, J.: 1993, *The Legal Reasoning of the European Court of Justice, Towards a European Jurisprudence*, Clarendon Press, Oxford.
Bergman, P.: 1997, *Trial Advocacy in a Nutshell*, 3rd. ed., West Publishing Co., St. Paul.
Berlin, I.: 2002, 'Two Concepts of Liberty', in H. Hardy (ed.), *Liberty, Incorporating Four Essays on Liberty*, Oxford University Press, Oxford, pp. 166-217.
Berman, D.H. and C.D. Hafner: 1987, 'Indeterminacy: A Challenge to Logic-based Models of Legal Reasoning', in *Yearbook of Law, Computers and Technology*, Vol. 3, Butterworths, London, pp. 1-35.
Bermejo-Luque, L.: 2004, 'Rhetorical Criteria for Argument Evaluation?', in T. Suzuki (ed.), *Proceedings of the 2nd Tokyo Conference on Argumentation and Social Cognition*, Japan Debate Association, Tokyo, pp. 147-151.
Bex, F.J., H. Prakken, C. Reed and D.N. Walton: 2003, 'Towards a Formal Account of Reasoning about Evidence: Argumentation Schemes and Generalisations', *Artificial Intelligence and Law* **11**, 125-165.
Béziau, J.Y. (ed.): 2005, *Logica Universalis*, Birkhäuser Verlag, Basel.
Blair, J.A.: 1999, 'Presumptive Reasoning/Argument, an Overlooked Class', *Protosociology* **13**, 46-60.
Blair, J.A.: 2001, 'Walton's Argumentation Schemes for Presumptive Reasoning: A Critique and Development', *Argumentation* **15**, 365-379.
Blair, J.A.: 2003, 'Towards a Philosophy of Argument', in J.A. Blair, D. Farr, H.V. Hansen and R.H. Johnson (eds.), *Informal Logic at 25: Proceedings of the Windsor Conference* (CD-ROM), OSSA, Windsor.
Bobzien, S.: 1996, 'Stoic Syllogistic', *Oxford Studies in Ancient Philosophy* **14**, 133-192.
Boutilier, C.: 1998, 'A Unified Model of Qualitative Belief Change: A Dynamical Systems Perspective', *Artificial Intelligence* **98**, 281-316.
Brady, R.: 2005, *Universal Logic,* CSLI, Stanford.
Brandom, R.: 1994, *Making It Explicit*, Harvard University Press, Cambridge.
Brandom, R.: 2000, *Articulating Reasons: An Introduction to Inferentialism*, Harvard University Press, Cambridge.
Brandom, R.: 2002, *Tales of the Mighty Dead: Historical Essays in the Metaphysics of Intentionality*, Harvard University Press, Cambridge.
Branting, L.K.: 1994, 'A Computational Model of Ratio Decidendi', *Artificial Intelligence and Law* **2**, 1-31.
Branting, L.K.: 2003, 'An Agenda for Empirical Research in AI and Law', in L.K. Branting and S. Brüninghaus (eds.), *Proceedings of the Workshop on the Evaluation of Legal Reasoning and Problem-Solving Systems*, 9th International Conference on Artificial Intelligence and Law (ICAIL-03), Edinburgh, pp. 28-35.
Bratman, M.: 1992, 'Practical Reasoning and Acceptance in a Context', *Mind* **101**, 1-15.
Brewer, S.: 1996, 'Exemplary Reasoning: Semantics, Pragmatics, and the Rational Force of Legal Argument by Analogy', *Harvard Law Review* **109**, 923-1028.

Brockriede, W. and D. Ehninger: 1960, 'Toulmin on Argument: An Interpretation and Application', *Quarterly Journal of Speech* **46**, 44-53.
Brockriede, W. and D. Ehninger: 1963, *Decision by Debate*, Harper and Row, New York.
Bromby, M.C. and M.J. Hall: 2002, 'The Development and Rapid Evaluation of the Knowledge Model of ADVOKATE: An Advisory System to Assess the Credibility of Eyewitness Testimony', in T.J.M. Bench-Capon, A. Daskalopulu and R.G.F. Winkels (eds.), *Legal Knowledge and Information Systems. JURIX 2002: The Fifteenth Annual Conference*, IOS Press, Amsterdam, pp. 143-152.
Burke, M.: 1985, 'Unstated Premises', *Informal Logic* **7**, 107-118.
Burks, A.W.: 1951, 'The Logic of Causal Propositions', *Mind* **60**, 363-382.
Burleson, B.R.: 1979, 'On the Analysis and Criticism of Arguments: Some Theoretical and Methodological Considerations', *Journal of the American Forensic Association* **15**, 137-147.
Burnyeat, M.: 1994, 'Enthymeme: Aristotle on the Logic of Persuasion', in D.J. Furley and A. Nehamas (eds.), *Aristotle's Rhetoric: Philosophical Essays*, Princeton University Press, Princeton, NJ, pp. 39-46.
Burton, G.O.: 2004, Stasis, in *Silva Rhetoricae: The Forest of Rhetoric*. http://rhetoric.byu.edu/; accessed 31 March 2005.
Bush, R.A.B. and J.P. Folger: 1995, *The Promise of Mediation: Responding to Conflict through Empowerment and Recognition*, The Jossey Bass Conflict Resolution Series, Wiley, San Francisco.
Cacioppo, J.T. and R.E. Petty: 1982, 'Language Variables, Attitudes, and Persuasion', in E.B. Ryan and H. Giles (eds.), *Attitudes Towards Language Variation: Social and Applied Contexts*, Edward Arnold, London, pp. 189-207.
Calhoun, G.: 1988/1989, 'Social Theory and the Law: Systems Theory, Normative Justification, and Postmodernism', *Northwestern University Law Review* **83**, 398-460.
Cantwell, J.: 1998, 'Resolving Conflicting Information', *Journal of Logic, Language and Information* **7**, 191-220.
Carlson, G.N. and F.J. Pelletier (eds.): 1995, *The Generic Book*, The University of Chicago Press, Chicago.
Carroll, L.: 1895 'What the Tortoise Said to Achilles', *Mind* **4**, 278-280.
Carroll, L.: 1973, *Euclid and His Modern Rivals*, Dover, New York.
Castelfranchi, C.: 1996, 'Reasons: Belief Support and Goal Dynamics', *Mathware & Soft Computing* **3**, 233-247.
Castelfranchi, C.: 1997, 'Representation and Integration of Multiple Knowledge Sources: Issues and Questions', in V. Cantoni, V. Di Gesù, A. Setti and D. Tegolo (eds.), *Human and Machine Perception: Information Fusion*, Plenum Press, New York, pp. 235-254.
Chesñevar, C.I., A.G. Maguitman and R.P. Loui: 2000, 'Logical Models of Argument', *ACM Computing Surveys* **32**, 337-383.
Chi, M.T.H., P.J. Feltovich and R. Glaser: 1981, 'Categorization and Representation of Physics Problems by Experts and Novices', *Cognitive Science* **5**, 121-125.
Chisholm, R.: 1957, *Perceiving: A Philosophical Study*, Cornell University Press, Ithaca.
Chisholm, R.: 1966, *Theory of Knowledge*, Prentice-Hall, Englewood Cliffs.
Chisholm, R.: 1977, *Theory of Knowledge*, 2nd. ed., Prentice-Hall, Englewood Cliffs.
Christie, G.: 1986, 'An Essay on Discretion', *Duke Law Journal* **35**, 747-778.
Chryssafidou, E. and M. Sharples: 2003, 'Computer-supported Planning of Essay Argument Structure', in F.H. van Eemeren, J.A. Blair, C.A. Willard and A.F. Snoeck Henkemans (eds.), *Proceedings of the Fifth Conference of the International Society for the Study of Argumentation*, Sic Sat, Amsterdam, pp. 189-194.
Churchland, P.: 1988, *Matter and Consciousness*. MIT Press, Cambridge.
Clark, P.: 1991, *A Model of Argumentation and Its Application in a Cooperative Expert System*, PhD thesis. Turing Institute, Department of Computer Science, University of Strathclyde, Glasgow.
Clarke, D.S., Jr.: 1989, *Rational Acceptance and Purpose: An Outline of a Pragmatist Epistemology*, Rowan and Littlefield, Totawa.
Coady, C.A.J.: 1992, *Testimony: A Philosophical Study*, Clarendon Press, Oxford.
Cohen, L.J.: 1982, 'Are People Programmed to Commit Fallacies? Further Thoughts about the Interpretation of Experimental Data and Probability Judgement', *Journal of Theory and Social Behavior* **12**, 251-274.
Cohen, L.J.: 1997, *The Probable and the Provable*, Clarendon Press, Oxford.

Conrad, R.: 1982, 'Rhetorische Fragen', *Zeitschrift für Slawistik* **27**, 420-428.
Coulson A.S., D.W. Glasspool, J. Fox and J. Emery: 2001, 'RAGs: A Novel Approach to Computerized Genetic Risk Assessment and Decision Support from Pedigrees', *Methods of Information in Medicine* **40**, 315-322.
Crowe, M.: 1975, 'Ten "Laws" Concerning Patterns of Change in the History of Mathematics', *Historia Mathematica* **2**, 161-166.
Dascal, M.: 1978, *La Sémiologie de Leibniz*, Aubier Montaigne, Paris.
Dascal, M.: 1987, *Leibniz. Language, Signs and Thought*, John Benjamins, Amsterdam/Philadelphia.
Dascal, M.: 2001, 'Nihil sine Ratione → Blandior Ratio', in *VII. Internationaler Leibniz-Kongress: Nihil sine Ratione: Mensch, Natur und Technik im Wirken von G. W. Leibniz*, Technische University, Berlin, pp. 276-280.
Dick, J.: 1987, 'Conceptual Retrieval and Case Law', *Proceedings of the First International Conference on Artificial Intelligence and Law*, ACM Press, Boston, pp. 106-115.
Douglas, M. and A. Wildavsky: 1983, *Risk and Culture*, University of California Press, Berkeley.
Doyle, J.: 1992, 'Reason Maintenance and Belief Revision: Foundations vs. Coherence Theories', in P. Gärdenfors (ed.), *Belief Revision*, Cambridge University Press, Cambridge, pp. 29-51.
Dragoni, A. F. and P. Giorgini: 2003, 'Distributed Belief Revision', *Autonomous Agents and Multi-Agent Systems* **6**, 115-143.
Dung, P.M.: 1995, 'On the Acceptability of Arguments and Its Fundamental Role in Nonmonotonic Reasoning, Logic Programming and *n*-Person Games', *Artificial Intelligence* **77**, 321-357.
Dworkin, R.: 1977, *Taking Rights Seriously*, Harvard University Press, Cambridge.
Dworkin, R.: 1986, *Law's Empire*, Duckworth, London.
Eberle, R.: 1971, 'Replacing One Theory by Another under Preservation of a Given Feature', *Philosophy of Science* **38**, 486-500.
Eco, U., 1993, *La Ricerca della Lingua Perfetta nella Cultura Europea*, Laterza, Roma et Bari.
Eemeren, F.H. van, J.A. Blair, C.A. Willard and A.F. Snoeck Henkemans (eds.): 2003, *Anyone Who Has a View: Theoretical Contributions to the Study of Argumentation*, Kluwer, Dordrecht.
Eemeren, F.H. van and R. Grootendorst: 1992, *Argumentation, Communication, and Fallacies: a Pragma-Dialectical Perspective*, Lawrence Erlbaum Associates, Hillsdale.
Eemeren, F.H. van and R. Grootendorst: 2004, *A Systematic Theory of Argumentation: The Pragma-dialectical Approach*, Cambridge University Press, Cambridge.
Eemeren, F.H. van, R. Grootendorst, S. Jackson and S. Jacobs: 1993, *Reconstructing Argumentative Discourse*, The University of Alabama Press, Tuscaloosa.
Eemeren, F.H. van, R. Grootendorst and T. Kruiger: 1984, *The Study of Argumentation*, Irvington.
Eemeren, F.H. van, R. Grootendorst and T. Kruiger: 1987, *Handbook of Argumentation Theory: A Critical Survey of Classical Backgrounds and Modern Studies*, Foris Publications, Dordrecht.
Eemeren, F.H. van, R. Grootendorst, A.F. Snoeck Henkemans, J.A. Blair, R.H. Johnson, E.C.W. Krabbe, C. Plantin, D.N. Walton, C.A. Willard, J. Woods and D. Zarefsky: 1996, *Fundamentals of Argumentation Theory: A Handbook of Historical Backgrounds and Contemporary Developments*, Lawrence Erlbaum Associates, Mahwah.
Eemeren, F.H. van and P. Houtlosser: 1999, 'Strategic Maneuvering in Argumentative Discourse', *Discourse Studies* **1**, 479-497.
Eemeren, F.H. van and P. Houtlosser: 2002, 'Strategic Maneuvering with the Burden of Proof', in F.H. van Eemeren (ed.), *Advances in Pragma-Dialectics,* Sic Sat, Amsterdam/Vale Press, Newport News, pp. 13-28.
Elvang-Gøransson M., P.J. Krause and J. Fox: 1993a, 'Acceptability of Arguments as Logical Uncertainty', in M. Clarke, R. Kruse and S. Moral (eds.), *Symbolic and Quantitative Approaches to Reasoning and Uncertainty; Proc. European Conference ECSQUARU 93*, Berlin, Springer, pp. 79-84.
Elvang-Gøransson M., P.J. Krause and J. Fox: 1993b, 'Dialectic Reasoning with Inconsistent Information', in D. Heckerman and A. Mamdani (eds.), *Uncertainty in Artificial Intelligence. Proceedings of the 9th Conference*, Morgan Kaufman, San Mateo, pp.114-121.
Emery J., R. Walton, M. Murphy, J. Austoker, P. Yudkin, C. Chapman, A. Coulson, D. Glasspool and J. Fox: 2000, 'Computer Support for Interpreting Family Histories of Breast and Ovarian Cancer in Primary Care: Comparative Study with Simulated Cases', *British Medical Journal* **321**, 28-32.

Ennis, R.H.: 1962, 'A Concept of Critical Thinking: A Proposed Basis for Research in the Teaching and Evaluation of Critical Thinking Ability', *Harvard Educational Review* **31**, 81-111.
Ennis, R.H.: 1969, *Ordinary Logic,* Prentice-Hall, Englewood Cliffs.
Ennis, R.H.: 1981, 'A Conception of Deductive Logic Competence', *Teaching Philosophy* **4**, 337-385.
Ennis, R.H.: 1982, 'Identifying Implicit Assumptions', *Synthese* **51**, 61-86.
Ennis, R.H.: 1996, *Critical Thinking*, Prentice-Hall, Upper Saddle River.
Ennis, R.H.: 2001, 'Argument Appraisal Strategy: A Comprehensive Approach', *Informal Logic* **21**, 97-140.
Ennis, R.H.: 2004, 'Applying Soundness Standards to Qualified Reasoning', *Informal Logic* **24**, 23-39.
Fahnestock, J. and M. Secor: 2004, *A Rhetoric of Argument*, 3rd. ed., McGraw-Hill, Boston.
Falappa, M.A., G. Kern-Isberner and G. Simari: 2002, 'Explanations, Belief Revision and Defeasible Reasoning', *Artificial Intelligence* **141**, 1-28.
Fallis, D.: 2003, 'Intentional Gaps in Mathematical Proofs', *Synthese* **134**, 45-69.
Feteris, E.T.: 1997, 'A Survey of 25 Years of Research on Legal Argumentation', *Argumentation* **11**, 355-376.
Finocchiaro, M.A.: 1994, 'Two Empirical Approaches to the Study of Reasoning', *Informal Logic* **16**, 1-21.
Fisher, R. and W. Ury: 1981, *Getting to YES: Negotiating Agreement Without Giving In*, Houghton Mifflin, Boston.
Flick, G.A.: 1979, *Natural Justice. Principles and Practical Application*, Butterworths, Sydney.
Fox J.: 1990, 'Decision Support for Safety Critical Decisions', *Philiosophical Transactions of the Royal Society B* **327**, 555-567.
Fox J.: 2003, 'Logic, Probability and the Cognitive Foundations of Rational Belief', *Journal of Applied Logic* **1**, 197-224.
Fox, J., D.A. Clark, A.J. Glowinski and M.J. O'Neil: 1990, 'Using Predicate Logic to Integrate Qualitative Reasoning and Classical Decision Theory', *IEEE Transactions on Systems, Man, and Cybernetics* **20,** 347–357.
Fox, J. and S. Das: 1996, 'A Unified Framework for Hypothetical and Practical Reasoning', in D.M. Gabbay and H.J. Ohlbach (eds.), *Proceedings of the 1st International Conference on Formal and Applied Practical Reasoning (FAPR'96),* Springer, Berlin, pp. 58-72.
Fox J. and S. Das: 2000, *Safe and Sound: Artificial Intelligence in Hazardous Applications*, MIT Press, Cambridge.
Fox, J. and D. Glasspool: 2001, 'REACT - A Decision-support System for Medical Planning', in S. Bakken (ed.), *Proceedings of the American Medical Informatics Association Symposium 2001*, Hanley and Belfus, Philadelphia, pp. 911.
Fox J., P.J. Krause and S. Ambler: 1992, 'Arguments, Contradictions, and Practical Reasoning', in B. Neumann (ed.), *Proceedings of the Tenth European Conference on Artificial Intelligence. August 3-7, 1992*, John Wiley & Sons, New York, pp. 623-626.
Fox J., P.J. Krause and M. Elvang-Goransson: 1993, 'Argumentation as a General Framework for Uncertain Reasoning', in D. Heckerman and E.H. Mamdani (eds.), *Proceedings of the 9th Annual Conference on Uncertainty in Artificial Intelligence (UAI-93),* Morgan Kaufman, Washington, pp. 428-434.
Fox J. and S. Parsons: 1998, 'Arguing about Beliefs and Actions', in A. Hunter and S. Parsons (eds.), *Applications of Uncertainty Formalisms*, Springer, Berlin, pp. 266-302.
Fraassen, B. van: 1971, *Formal Semantics and Logic*, MacMillan, New York.
Frank, J.: 1990, 'You Call That a Rhetorical Question? Forms and Functions of Rhetorical Questions in Conversation', *Journal of Pragmatics* **14**, 723-738.
Franklin, J.: 2001, *The Science of Conjecture: Evidence and Probability before Pascal,* The Johns Hopkins University Press, Baltimore.
Frede, M.: 1974, *Die stoische Logik*, Vandenhoeck & Ruprecht, Göttingen.
Freeman, J.B.: 1991, *Dialectics and the Macrostructure of Arguments: A Theory of Argument Structure*, Foris, Berlin.
Freeman, J.B.: 1992, 'Relevance, Warrants, Backing, Inductive Support', *Argumentation* **6**, 219-235.
Freeman, J.B.: 2000, 'What Types of Statements Are There?' *Argumentation* **14**, 135-157.
Freeman, J.B.: 2003, 'The Pragmatic Dimension of Premise Acceptability', in F.H. van Eemeren, J.A. Blair, C.A. Willard and A.F. Snoeck Henkemans (eds.), *Anyone Who Has a View, Theoretical Contributions to the Study of Argument*, Argumentation Library, Vol. 8, Kluwer Academic Publishers, Dordrecht/ Boston/London, pp. 17-26.

Freeman, J.B.: 2005a, *Acceptable Premises: An Epistemic Approach to an Informal Logic Problem*, Cambridge University Press, Cambridge.
Freeman, J.B.: 2005b, 'Systematizing Toulmin's Warrants: An Epistemological Approach', in D. Hitchcock (ed.), *The Uses of Argument. Proceedings of a Conference at McMaster University, 18-21 May, 2005*, OSSA, Hamilton, pp. 101-110.
Frege, G.: 1950, *The Foundations of Arithmetic. A Logico-Mathematical Enquiry into the Concept of Number*, J.L. Austin (trans.), Blackwell, Oxford.
Frijda, N.H., A.S.R. Manstead and S. Bem (eds.): 2000, *Emotions and Beliefs: How Feelings Influence Thoughts*, Cambridge University Press, Cambridge.
Fuhrmann, M.: 1984, *Die antike Rhetorik: eine Einführung*, Artemis-Verlag, München.
Gabbay, D.M., C.J. Hogger and J.A. Robinson (eds.): 1994, *Handbook of Logic in Artificial Intelligence and Logic Programming. Volume 3. Nonmonotonic Reasoning and Uncertain Reasoning*, Clarendon Press, Oxford.
Gabbay D.M. and J. Woods: 2003a, *Agenda Relevance: A Study in Formal Pragmatics*, North Holland, Amsterdam.
Gabbay D.M. and J. Woods: 2003b, 'Normative Models of Rationality: The Disutility of Some Approaches', *Logic Journal of IGPL* **11**, 597-613.
Gabbay D.M. and J. Woods: 2005, *The Reach of Abduction: Insight and Trial*, North Holland, Amsterdam.
Gabbay D.M. and J. Woods: 2006, 'Fallacies as Cognitive Virtues', in O. Majer, A. Pietarinen and T. Tulenheimo (eds.), *Logic, Games, and Philosophy: Foundational Perspectives*, Springer, Berlin, forthcoming.
Gärdenfors, P.: 1988, *Knowledge in Flux: Modelling the Dynamics of Epistemic States*, MIT Press, Cambridge.
Gardner, A. vdL.: 1987, *An Artificial Intelligence Approach to Legal Reasoning*, MIT Press, Cambridge.
Garssen, B.: 2001, 'Argument Schemes', in F.H. van Eemeren (ed.), Crucial Concepts in Argumentation Theory, Amsterdam University Press, Amsterdam, pp. 81-99.
Gasper, D.R.: 1996, 'Analysing Policy Arguments', *European Journal of Development Research* **8**, 36-62.
Gasper, D.R. and R.V. George: 1998, 'Analyzing Argumentation in Planning and Public Policy: Assessing, Improving, and Transcending the Toulmin Model', *Environment and Planning B: Planning and Design* **25**, 367-390.
Gelder, T.J. van: 2003, 'Enhancing Deliberation through Computer-supported Argument Visualization', in P.A. Kirschner, S.J. Buckingham Shum and C.S. Carr (eds.), *Visualizing Argumentation: Software Tools for Collaborative and Educational Sense-Making*, Springer, London, pp. 97-115.
Gentzen, G.: 1935, 'Untersuchungen über das logische Schliessen', *Mathematische Zeitschrift* **39**, 176-210, 405-431.
George, A. and D.J. Velleman: 2002, *Philosophies of Mathematics*, Blackwell, Oxford.
George, R.: 1972, 'Enthymematic Consequence', *American Philosophical Quarterly* **9**, 113-116.
George, R.: 1983, 'Bolzano's Consequence, Relevance, and Enthymemes', *Journal of Philosophical Logic* **12**, 299-318.
Gigerenzer, G. and R. Selten: 2001, 'Rethinking Rationality', in G. Gigerenzer and R. Selten (eds.), *The Adaptive Toolbox*, MIT Press, Cambridge, pp. 1-12.
Gillies, D. (ed.): 1992, *Revolutions in Mathematics*, Clarendon, Oxford.
Girle, R.: 2000, *Modal Logics and Philosophy*, McGill-Queen's University Press, Montreal and Kingston.
Girle, R., D.L. Hitchcock, P. McBurney and B. Verheij: 2003, 'Decision Support for Practical Reasoning: A Theoretical and Computational Perspective', in C. Reed & T.J. Norman (eds.), *Argumentation Machines. New Frontiers in Argument and Computation*, Kluwer Academic Publishers, Dordrecht, pp. 55-84.
Godden, D.M.: 2005, 'Psychologism in the Logic of John Stuart Mill: Mill on the Subject Matter and Foundations of Ratiocinative Logic', *History and Philosophy of Logic* **26**, 115-143.
Goldman, A.: 1988, *Epistemology and Cognition*, Harvard University Press, Cambridge.
Goldman, A.: 1999, *Knowledge in a Social World*, Oxford University Press, Oxford.
Goldman, A.: 2002, 'The Unity of the Epistemic Virtues', in A. Goldman (ed.), *Pathways to Knowledge: Private and Public*, Oxford University Press, Oxford, pp. 51-70.
Goodman, N: 1965, *Fact, Fiction and Forecast*, Bobbs-Merrill, Indianapolis.

Goodnight, G.T.: 1982, 'The Personal, Technical and Public Spheres of Argument: A Speculative Inquiry into the Art of Public Deliberation', *Journal of the American Forensic Association* **18**, 214-227.
Goodnight, G.T.: 1991, 'Controversy', in D.W. Parson (ed.), *Proceedings of the Seventh SCA/AFA Conference on Argumentation*, Speech Communication Association, Washington DC, pp. 1-11.
Goodnight, G.T.: 1993, 'Legitimation Inferences: An Additional Component for the Toulmin Model', *Informal Logic* **15**, 1-15.
Gordon, T.F.: 1995, *The Pleadings Game. An Artificial Intelligence Model of Procedural Justice*, Kluwer Academic Publishers, Dordrecht/Boston/London.
Gordon, T.F.: 2003, 'Artificial Intelligence Models of Legal Argumentation', Tutorial notes, Ninth International Conference on Artificial Intelligence and Law, Edinburgh.
Gough, J. and C. Tindale: 1985, 'Hidden or Missing Premises', *Informal Logic* **7**, 99-106.
Govier, T.C.: 1985, *A Practical Study of Argument*, Wadsworth, Belmont.
Govier, T.C.: 1987, *Problems in Argument Analysis and Evaluation*, Foris, Providence.
Govier, T.C.: 1995, 'Reply to Massey', in H.V. Hansen and R.C. Pinto (eds.), *Fallacies: Classical and Contemporary Readings*, Pennsylvania State University Press, University Park, pp. 172-180. Revised version of Chapter 9, 'Four Reasons Why There are no Fallacies', of Govier (1987).
Grennan, W.: 1997, *Informal Logic: Issues and Techniques*, McGill-Queen's University Press, Montreal and Kingston.
Grésillon, A.: 1980, 'Zum linguistischen Status rhetorischer Fragen', *Zeitschrift für Germanistische Linguistik* **8**, 273-289.
Griffin, J.: 1977, 'Are There Incommensurable Values?', *Philosophy and Public Affairs* **7**, 39-59.
Groarke, L.: 1999, 'Deductivism within Pragma-dialectics', *Argumentation* **13**, 1-16.
Haack, S.: 1978, *Philosophy of Logics*, Cambridge University Press, Cambridge.
Habermas, J.: 1981, *The Theory of Communicative Action. Volume 1 Reason and the Rationalization of Society*, T. McCarthy (trans.), Beacon Press, Boston.
Hage, J.C.: 1997, *Reasoning with Rules. An Essay on Legal Reasoning and Its Underlying Logic*, Kluwer Academic Publishers, Dordrecht.
Hage, J.C.: 2000, 'Dialectical Models in Artificial Intelligence and Law', *Artificial Intelligence and Law* **8**, 137-172.
Hall, M.J., A. Stranieri and J. Zeleznikow: 2002, 'A Strategy for Evaluating Web-Based Discretionary Decision Support Systems', in Y. Manolopoulos and P. Návrat, *Proceedings of ADBIS2002 - Sixth East-European Conference on Advances in Databases and Information Systems*, Slovak University of Technology, Bratislava, pp. 108-120.
Hall, M.J., D. Calabro, T. Sourdin, A. Stranieri and J. Zeleznikow: 2005, 'Supporting Discretionary Decision Making with Information Technology: A Case Study in the Criminal Sentencing Jurisdiction', *University of Ottawa Law and Technology Journal* **2**, 1-36.
Hamblin, C.L.: 1970, *Fallacies*, Methuen, London.
Hambrick, R.S.: 1974, 'A Guide for the Analysis of Policy Arguments', *Policy Sciences* **5**, 469-478.
Hample, D.: 1977, 'The Toulmin Model and the Syllogism', *Journal of the American Forensic Association* **14**(2), 1-9.
Hansen, H.V.: 2002, 'The Straw Thing of Fallacy Theory', *Argumentation* **16**, 133-155.
Hansen, H.V. and R.C. Pinto: 1995, *Fallacies: Classical and Contemporary Readings*, Pennsylvania State University Press, University Park.
Hansson, S.: 1999, 'A Survey on Non-prioritized Belief Revision', *Erkenntnis* **50**, 413-427.
Hardcastle, G. and A. Richardson (eds.): 2003, *Logical Empiricism in North America*, University of Minnesota Press, Minneapolis.
Hare, R.M.: 1952, *The Language of Morals,* Oxford University Press, Oxford.
Harman, G.: 1986, *Change in View: Principles of Reasoning*, MIT Press, Cambridge.
Hart, H.L.A.: 1961, *The Concept of Law*, Clarendon Press, Oxford.
Hartshorne, C. and P. Weiss: 1960, *The Collected Papers of Charles Sanders Pierce*, Harvard University Press, Cambridge.
Hastings, A.C.: 1963, *A Reformulation of the Modes of Reasoning in Argumentation*, Ph.D. Thesis, Northwestern University, Evanston.
Heath, T.: 1956, *The Thirteen Books of Euclid's Elements.* Dover, New York.

Heidt, R.J.:1968, *Stephen Toulmin's Argument Model as a Critical Device for Speech*, Thesis, San Jose State College, San Jose.

Hilbert, D.: 1935, *Gesammelte Abhandlungen, Band III*, Springer, Berlin and Heidelberg.

Hilbert, D.: 1967, 'The Foundations of Mathematics', in J. van Heijenoort (ed.), *From Frege to Gödel*, Harvard University Press, Cambridge, 464-479, German original published in 1927.

Hintikka, J.: 1969, *Models for Modalities*, D. Reidel, Dordrecht.

Hintikka, J.: 1987, 'The Fallacy of Fallacies', *Argumentation* **1**, 211-238.

Hintikka, J.: 1997, 'What Was Aristotle Doing in His Early Logic, Anyway? A Reply to Woods and Hansen', *Synthese* **113**, 241-249.

Hitchcock, D.L.: 1985, 'Enthymematic Arguments', *Informal Logic* **7**, 83-97.

Hitchcock, D.L.: 1992, 'Reasoning by Analogy: A General Theory', in S.P. Norris (ed.), *The Generalizability of Critical Thinking: Multiple Perspectives on an Educational Ideal*, Teachers College Press, New York, pp. 109-124.

Hitchcock, D.L.: 1994, 'Validity in Conductive Arguments', in R.H. Johnson and J.A. Blair (eds.), *New Essays in Informal Logic*, Informal Logic, Windsor, pp. 58-66.

Hitchcock, D.L.: 1998, 'Does the Traditional Treatment of Enthymemes Rest on a Mistake?', *Argumentation* **12**, 15-37.

Hitchcock, D.L.: 2000, 'Fallacies and Formal Logic in Aristotle', *History and Philosophy of Logic* **21**, 207-221.

Hitchcock, D.L.: 2002, 'Sampling Scholarly Arguments: A Test of a Theory of Good Inference (plus appendix)', in H.V. Hansen, C.W. Tindale, J.A. Blair, R.H. Johnson and R.C. Pinto (eds.), *Argumentation and Its Applications* (CD-ROM), OSSA, Windsor.

Hitchcock, D.L.: 2003a, 'Toulmin's Warrants', in F.H. van Eemeren, J.A. Blair, C.A. Willard and A.F. Snoeck Henkemans (eds.), *Anyone Who Has a View, Theoretical Contributions to the Study of Argument*, Argumentation Library, Vol. 8, Kluwer Academic Publishers, Dordrecht/Boston/London, pp. 69-82.

Hitchcock, D.L.: 2003b, 'Toulmin's Warrants', in F.H. van Eemeren, J.A. Blair, C.A. Willard and A.F. Snoeck Henkemans (eds.), *Proceedings of the 5th International Conference of Argumentation*, Sic Sat, Amsterdam, pp. 485-490.

Hitchcock, D.L.: 2005a, 'Good Reasoning on the Toulmin Model', in D.L. Hitchcock (ed.), *The Uses of Argument: Proceedings of a Conference at McMaster University, 18-21 May, 2005*, OSSA, Hamilton, pp. 199-208.

Hitchcock, D.L.: 2005b, 'The Peculiarities of Stoic Propositional Logic', in K.A. Peacock and A.D. Irvine (eds.), *Mistakes of Reason: Essays in Honour of John Woods*, University of Toronto Press, Toronto, pp. 224-242.

Hitchcock D.L., P. McBurney and S. Parsons: 2002, 'A Framework for Deliberation Dialogues', in H.V. Hansen, C.W. Tindale, J.A. Blair and R.H. Johnson (eds), *Argumentation and its Applications.* (CD-ROM), OSSA, Windsor.

Hoaglund, J.: 1999, *Critical Thinking*, 3rd. ed., Vale Press, Newport News.

Hofstadter, D.: 1980, *Gödel, Escher, Bach: an Eternal Golden Braid*, Vintage Books, New York.

Horty, J.F.: 2001, 'Nonmonotonic Logic', in L. Goble (ed.), *The Backwell Guide to Philosophical Logic*, Blackwell Publishers, Oxford, pp. 336-361.

Houtlosser, P.: 2002, 'Indicators of a Point of View', in F.H. van Eemeren (ed.), *Advances in Pragma-dialectics*, Sic Sat, Amsterdam. pp. 169-184.

Hülser, K.: 1987-1988, *Die Fragmente zur Dialektik der Stoiker*, 4 vols. Friedrich Frommann, Stuttgart/ Bad Cannstatt.

Hunter, A.: 2004, 'Towards high impact argumentation', in *Proceedings of NMR2004*, Whistler, Canada, pp. 227-232.

Hurt, C.N., V. Patkar, R. Steele, S. Love, M. Williams, R. Thomson and J. Fox: 2005, 'A Quantitative and Qualitative Evaluation of the Effect of Computerised Decision Support for the Triple Assessment of Women Referred to Specialist Breast Cancer Units', Submitted for publication to Advanced Computation Laboratory Publications, London.

Ilie, C.: 1994, *What Else Can I Tell You? A Pragmatic Study of English Rhetorical Questions as Discursive and Argumentative Acts*, Almqvist & Wiksell, Stockholm.

Jacquette, D. (ed.): 2003, *Philosophy, Psychology and Psychologism: Critical and Historical Readings on the Psychological Turn in Philosophy*, Kluwer, Dordrecht and Boston.

Jacquette, D.: 2005, 'Two Sides of Any Issue', in D.L. Hitchcock (ed.), *The Uses of Argument: Proceedings of a Conference at McMaster University, 18-21 May, 2005*, OSSA, Hamilton, pp. 209-217.

Janik, A. and S.E. Toulmin: 1973, *Wittgenstein's Vienna*, Simon and Schuster, New York.

Jenicek, M. and D.L. Hitchcock: 2005, *Evidence-Based Practice: Logic and Critical Thinking in Medicine*, AMA Press, Chicago.

Johnson, P.E., I.A. Zualkernan and D.W. Tukey: 1993, 'Types of Expertise: An Invariant of Problem Solving', *International Journal of Man Machine Studies* **39**, 641-665.

Johnson, R.H.: 1995, 'Informal Logic and Pragma-dialectics: Some Differences', in F.H. van Eemeren, R. Grootendorst, J.A. Blair and C.A. Willard (eds.), *Perspectives and Approaches. Proceedings of the Third ISSA Conference on Argumentation*, II, Sic Sat, Amsterdam, pp. 237-245.

Johnson, R.H.: 1996, *The Rise of Informal Logic*, Vale Press, Newport News.

Johnson, R.H.: 2000, *Manifest Rationality: A Pragmatic Theory of Argument*, Lawrence Erlbaum Associates, Mahwah.

Johnson, R.H. and J.A. Blair: 1977, *Logical Self-Defense*, McGraw-Hill Ryerson, Toronto.

Johnson, R.H. and J.A. Blair: 1983, *Logical Self-Defense*, 2nd edition. McGraw-Hill Ryerson, Toronto.

Johnston, I.: 2000, *And Still We Evolve: A Handbook on the History of Modern Science*, http://www.mala.bc.ca/~johnstoi/darwin/sect4.htm.

Jonsen, A. and S.E. Toulmin: 1988, *The Abuse of Casuistry: A History of Moral Reasoning*, University of California Press, Los Angeles.

Kadane, J.B. and D.A. Schum: 1996, *A Probabilistic Analysis of the Sacco and Vanzetti Evidence*, John Wiley & Sons, New York.

Kahneman, D. and A. Tversky: 1974, 'Judgement under Uncertainty: Heuristics and Biases', *Science* **185**, 1124-1131.

Kakas, A. and P. Moraïtis: 2003, 'Argumentation Based Decision Making for Autonomous Agents', in *Proceedings of AAMAS 2003*, ACM, Melbourne, pp. 883-890.

Katzav, J. and C. Reed: 2004, 'On Argumentation Schemes and the Natural Classification of Arguments', *Argumentation* **18**, 239-259.

Keynes J.M.: 1921, *Treatise on Probability*, Macmillan and Cambridge University Press, London.

Kienpointner, M.: 1992, *Alltagslogik: Struktur und Funktion von Argumentationsmustern*, Frommann-Holzboog, Stuttgart/Bad Cannstatt.

Kingston, J., L. Edwards and M.J. Hall: 2002, 'Prototyping a Legal Decision Support System: A Case Study', in *Proceedings of the 3rd International Conference on Law and Technology*, IASTED, Calgary, pp. 200-204.

Kirschner, P.A., S.J. Buckingham-Shum and C.S. Carr: 2003, *Visualizing Argument*, Springer, London.

Klayman, J.: 1995, 'Varieties of Confirmation Bias', in J. Busemeyer, R. Hastie and D.L. Medin (eds.), *Decision Making from a Cognitive Perspective (Psychology of Learning and Motivation* 32), Academic Press, New York, pp. 365-418.

Kleene, S.: 1950, *Introduction to Metamathematics*, Van Nostrand, Princeton.

Klumpp J.F.: 1981, 'A Dramatistic Approach to Fields', in G. Ziegelmueller and J. Rhodes (eds.), *Dimensions of Argument: Proceedings of the Second Summer Conference on Argumentation*, Speech Communication Association, Annandale, pp. 44-55.

Klumpp, J.F.: 2005, 'The Three Arguments of Iraq', in C.A. Willard (ed.), *Critical Problems in Argumentation*, National Communication Association, Washington, pp. 726-732.

Klumpp, J.F.: 2006, 'Facts, Truth and Iraq: A Call to Stewardship of Democractic Argument', in P. Riley (ed.), *Engaging Argument*, National Communication Association, Washington, pp. 1-12.

Kneale, W. and M. Kneale: 1962, *The Development of Logic*, Clarendon Press, Oxford.

Kock, C.: 2003, 'Multidimensionality and Non-Deductiveness in Deliberative Argumentation', in F.H. van Eemeren, J.A. Blair, C.A. Willard and A. F. Snoeck Henkemans (eds.), *Anyone Who Has a View: Theoretical Contributions to the Study of Argumentation*, Kluwer Academic Publishers, Dordrecht/Boston/London, pp. 157-171.

Kornblith, H.: 1993, *Inductive Inference and Its Natural Ground: An Essay in Naturalistic Epistemology*, MIT Press, Cambridge.

Kosso, P.: 1992, *Reading the Book of Nature: An Introduction to the Philosophy of Science*, Cambridge University Press, New York.

Kosso, P.: 2001, *Knowing the Past: Philosophical Issues of History and Archeology*, Humanity Books, Amherst.

Krause, P., S. Ambler, M. Elvang-Goransson and J. Fox: 1995, 'A Logic of Argumentation for Reasoning under Uncertainty', *Computational Intelligence* **11**, 113-131.

Krause, P. and D. Clark: 1993, *Representing Uncertain Knowledge: An Artificial Intelligence Approach*, Intellect Books, Oxford.

Kruger, A.N.: 1975, 'The Nature of Controversial Statements', *Philosophy & Rhetoric* **8**, 137-158.

Kuhn, T.S.: 1962, *The Structure of Scientific Revolutions*, University of Chicago Press, Chicago.

Langford, C. and R. Beebe: 1969, *The Development of Chemical Principles*, Addison-Wesley, Reading.

Levi, I.: 1991, *The Fixation of Belief and its Undoing*, Cambridge University Press, Cambridge.

Lindley, D.V.: 1985, *Making Decisions*, John Wiley and Sons, London.

Llewellyn, K.: 1962, *Jurisprudence*, University of Chicago Press, Chicago.

Lodder, A.: 1999, *DiaLaw - on Legal Justification and Dialogical Models of Argumentation*, Kluwer Academic Publishers, Dordrecht.

Lodder, A. and J. Zeleznikow: 2005, 'Developing an Online Dispute Resolution Environment: Dialogue Tools and Negotiation Systems in a Three Step Model', *The Harvard Negotiation Law Review* **10**, 287-338.

Loftus, E.F.: 1979, *Eyewitness Testimony*, Harvard University Press, Cambridge.

Loftus, E.F. and J.M. Doyle: 1992, *Eyewitness Testimony, Civil and Criminal*, Michie, Charlottesville.

Loui, R.P.: 1995, 'Hart's Critics on Defeasible Concepts and Ascriptivism', in *Proceedings of the Fourth International Conference on Artifical Iintelligence and Law (ICAIL-95)*, ACM Press, College Park, pp. 21-30.

Loui, R.P.: 1998, 'Process and Policy: Resource-Bounded Non-Demonstrative Reasoning', *Computational Intelligence* **14**, 1-38.

Loui, R.P. and J. Norman: 1995, 'Rationales and Argument Moves', *Artificial Intelligence and Law* **3**, 159-189.

Lundgren, R. and A. McMakin: 1998, *Risk Communication*, Batelle Press, Columbus.

Lutomski, L.S.: 1989, 'The Design of an Attorney's Statistical Consultant', in *Proceedings of the Second International Conference on Artificial Intelligence and Law*, ACM Press, New York, pp. 224-233.

MacCormick, N., 1978, *Legal Reasoning and Legal Theory*, Oxford University Press, Oxford.

Magnani, L.: 2001, *Abduction, Reason and Science*, Kluwer, New York.

Maria, G. Di (ed.): 1994, *Marci Tulli Ciceronis Topica*, L'Epos, Palermo.

Marshall, C.: 1989, 'Representing the Structure of Legal Argument', *Proceedings of the Second International Conference on Artificial Intelligence and Law*, ACM Press, New York, pp. 121-127.

Mates, B.: 1953, *Stoic Logic*, University of California Press, Berkeley/Los Angeles.

Matthijssen, L.: 1999, *Interfacing Between Lawyers and Computers. An Architecture for Knowledge based Interfaces to Legal Databases,* Kluwer Law International, Dordrecht.

McBurney, P. and S. Parsons: 2000, 'Tenacious Tortoises: A Formalism for Argument over Rules of Inference', *Computational Dialectics (ECAI 2000 Workshop)*, Berlin.

McKerrow, R.: 1990, 'The Centrality of Justification: Principles of Warranted Assertability', in D.C. Williams and M.D. Hazen (eds.), *Argumentation Theory and the Rhetoric of Assent*, University of Alabama Press, Tuscaloosa, pp. 17-32.

Means, M. and J.F. Voss: 1990, 'Who Reasons Well? Two Studies of Informal Reasoning among Children of Different Grade, Ability, and Knowledge Levels', *Cognition and Instruction*, **4**, 139-178.

Medin, D.L. and A. Ortony: 1989, 'Comments on Part I: Psychological Essentialism', in S. Vosniadou and A. Ortony (eds.), *Similarity and Analogical Reasoning*, Cambridge University Press, Cambridge, pp. 179-95.

Meibauer, J.: 1986, *Rhetorische Fragen*, Max Niemeyer, Tübingen.

Mendelson, E.: 1964, *Introduction to Mathematical Logic*, Van Nostrand, Princeton.

Mill, J.S.: 1959, *A System of Logic*, Longman's Green, London.

Mostowski, A.: 1966, *Thirty Years of Foundational Studies*, Barnes and Noble, New York.

Mueller, I.: 1981, *Philosophy of Mathematics and Deductive Structure in Euclid's Elements*, MIT Press, Cambridge.
Nagel, E.: 1961, *The Structure of Science*, Harcourt, Brace and World, New York.
Nash, J.: 1953, 'Two Person Cooperative Games', *Econometrica* **21**, 128-140.
Newell, A. and H.A. Simon: 1972, *Human Problem Solving*, Prentice-Hall, New Jersey.
Norris, S.P.: 1979, *The Dependability of Observation Statements*, Rational Thinking Reports Number 8, Bureau of Educational Research, Urbana, ERIC document 183590.
Norris, S.P.: 1981, 'A Concept of Observation Statements', *Philosophy of Education* **37**, 132-142.
Norris, S.P.: 1984, 'Defining Observational Competence', *Science Education* **68**, 129-142.
Norris, S.P.: 1985, 'The Philosophical Basis of Observation in Science and Science Education', *Journal of Research in Science Teaching* **22**, 817-833.
Norris, S.P. (ed.): 1992, *The Generalizability of Critical Thinking: Multiple Perspectives on an Educational Ideal*, Teachers College Press, New York.
Norris, S.P. and R. King: 1984, 'Observation Ability: Determining and Extending its Presence', *Informal Logic* **6**(3), 3-9.
Nussbaum, M.: 1991, *Love's Knowledge: Essays on Philosophy and Literature*, Oxford University Press, New York.
Olaso, E. de: 1995, 'Cómo Discutir con los Escépticos? El Caso de Leibniz', in J.A. Nicolás and J. Arana (eds.), *Saber y Conciencia. Homenaje a Otto Saame*, Comares, Granada, pp. 323-332.
Omer, I.A.: 1970, 'On the D-N Model of Scientific Explanation', *Philosophy of Science* **37**, 417-33.
O'Toole, R.R. and R.E. Jennings: 2004, 'The Megarians and the Stoics', in D.M. Gabbay and J. Woods (eds.), *Handbook of the History of Logic, Vol. 1: Greek, Indian and Arabian Logic*, Elsevier North Holland, Amsterdam, pp. 397-522.
Paglieri, F.: 2004, 'Data-oriented Belief Revision: Towards a Unified Theory of Epistemic Processing', in E. Onaindia and S. Staab (eds.), *Proceedings of STAIRS 2004*, IOS Press, Amsterdam, pp. 179-190.
Paglieri, F.: 2005, 'See What You Want, Believe What You Like: Relevance and Likeability in Belief Dynamics', in L. Cañamero (ed.), *Proceedings AISB'05 Symposium 'Agents that Want and Like: Motivational and Emotional Roots of Cognition and Action'*, AISB, Hatfield, pp. 90-97.
Paglieri, F. and C. Castelfranchi: 2005a, 'Revising Beliefs through Arguments: Bridging the Gap between Argumentation and Belief Revision in MAS', in I. Rahwan, P. Moraïtis and C. Reed (eds.), *Argumentation in Multi-Agent Systems*, Springer, Berlin, pp. 78-94.
Paglieri, F. and C. Castelfranchi: 2005b, 'Arguments as Belief Structures: Towards a Toulmin Layout of Doxastic Dynamics?', in D.L. Hitchcock (ed.), *The Uses of Argument: Proceedings of a Conference at McMaster University, 18-21 May, 2005*, OSSA, Hamilton, pp. 356-367.
Pagnucco, M.: 1996, *The Role of Abductive Reasoning within the Process of Belief Revision*, PhD Thesis, Department of Computer Science, University of Sydney, Sydney.
Parsons, S., M. Wooldridge and L. Amgoud: 2003, 'Properties and Complexity of some Formal Inter-agent Dialogues', *Journal of Logic and Computation* **13**, 347-376.
Parsons, T.: 1996, 'What is Argument?', *Journal of Philosophy* **93**, 164-185.
Patterson, D.: 1996, *Law and Truth*, Oxford University Press, Oxford.
Peirce, C.S.: 1931-1958, *Collected Works*, C. Hartshorne and P. Weiss (eds.), Harvard University Press, Cambridge.
Peirce, C.S.: 1955, *Philosophical Writings of Peirce*, J. Buchler (ed.), Dover Publications, New York.
Perelman, C. and L. Olbrechts-Tyteca: 1958, *La Nouvelle Rhétorique: Traité de l'argumentation*. Presses Universitaires de France, Paris.
Perelman, C. and L. Olbrechts-Tyteca: 1969, *The New Rhetoric*, University of Notre Dame Press, Notre Dame.
Petty, R.E., J.T. Cacioppo and M. Heesacker: 1981, 'Effects of Rhetorical Questions on Persuasion: A Cognitive Response Analysis', *Journal of Personality and Social Psychology* **40**, 432-440.
Pinto, R.C.: 1999, 'Argument Schemes and the Evaluation of Presumptive Reasoning: Some Reflections on Blair's Account', *Protosociology* **13**, 61-69.
Pinto, R.C.: 2001, *Argument, Inference and Dialectic*, Kluwer Academic Publishers, Dordrecht.
Pinto, R.C.: 2002, 'Truth and Premiss Adequacy', in H.V. Hansen, C.W. Tindale, J.A. Blair, R.H. Johnson and R.C. Pinto (eds.), *Argumentation and its Applications* (CD-ROM), OSSA, Windsor.

Pinto, R.C.: 2003a, 'Reasons', in F.H. van Eemeren, J.A. Blair, C.A. Willard and A.F. Snoeck Henkemans (eds.), *Anyone Who Has a View: Theoretical Contributions to the Study of Argumentation*, Kluwer, Dordrecht, pp. 3-15.

Pinto, R.C.: 2003b: 'The Uses of Arguments in Communicative Contexts', in J.A. Blair, D. Farr, H.V. Hansen and R.H. Johnson (eds.), *Informal Logic at 25: Proceedings of the Windsor Conference* (CD-ROM), OSSA, Windsor.

Pinto, R.C., J.A. Blair and K.E. Parr: 1993, *Reasoning: A Practical Guide for Canadian Students*, Prentice Hall Canada, Scarborough. A U.S. edition was published the same year as Pinto, R.C. and J.A. Blair, *Reasoning: A Practical Guide*, Prentice Hall, Englewood Cliffs.

Pollock, J.L., 1970, 'The Structure of Epistemic Justification', *American Philosophical Quarterly* monograph series **4**, 62-78.

Pollock, J.L.: 1986, *Contemporary Theories of Knowledge*, Rowman and Littlefield, Totowa.

Pollock, J.L.: 1987, 'Defeasible Reasoning', *Cognitive Science* **11**, 481-518.

Pollock, J.L.: 1995, *Cognitive Carpentry: A Blueprint for How to Build a Person,* MIT Press, Cambridge.

Pollock, J.L.: 2001, 'Defeasible Reasoning with Variable Degrees of Justification', *Artificial Intelligence* **133**, 233-282.

Pollock, J.L. and A.S. Gillies: 2000, 'Belief Revision and Epistemology', *Synthese* **122**, 69-92.

Pólya, G.: 1968, *Mathematics and Plausible Reasoning, Vol. 2: Patterns of Plausible Inference*, Princeton University Press, Princeton.

Popper, K.: 1959, *The Logic of Scientific Discovery,* Hutchinson, London. German original first published in 1935.

Post, E.L.: 1944, 'Recursively Enumerable Sets of Positive Integers and Their Decision Problems', *Bulletin of the American Mathematical Society* **50**, 305-357.

Prakken, H.: 1997, *Logical Tools for Modelling Legal Argument. A Study of Defeasible Reasoning in Law*, Kluwer Academic Publishers, Dordrecht.

Prakken, H.: 2002, 'An Exercise in Formalising Teleological Case-based Reasoning', *Artificial Intelligence and Law* **10**, 113-133.

Prakken, H.: 2004, 'Analysing Reasoning about Evidence with Formal Models of Argumentation', *Law, Probability & Risk* **3**, 33-50.

Prakken, H., C. Reed and D.N. Walton: 2003, 'Argumentation Schemes and Generalisations in Reasoning about Evidence', in *Proceedings of the Ninth International Conference on Artificial Intelligence and Law*, ACM Press, New York, pp. 32-41.

Prakken, H. and G. Sartor: 1996, 'A Dialectical Model of Assessing Conflicting Arguments in Legal Reasoning', *Artificial Intelligence and Law* **4**, 331-368.

Prakken, H. and G. Sartor: 1998, 'Modelling Reasoning with Precedents in a Formal Dialogue Game', *Artificial Intelligence and Law* **6**, 231-287.

Prakken, H. and G. Sartor: 2002, 'The Role of Logic in Computational Models of Legal Argument: A Critical Survey', in A. Kakas and F. Sadri (eds.), *Computational Logic: Logic Programming and Beyond. Essays In Honour of Robert A. Kowalski, Part II.* Springer Lecture Notes in Computer Science 2048, Berlin, pp. 342-380.

Prakken, H. and G.A.W. Vreeswijk: 2002, 'Logics for Defeasible Argumentation', in D.M. Gabbay and F. Guenthner (eds.), *Handbook of Philosophical Logic, Second Edition*, Vol. 4, Kluwer Academic Publishers, Dordrecht, pp. 218-319.

Priest, G.: 1987, *In Contradiction: A Study of the Transconsistent,* Kluwer, Dordrecht.

Putnam, H.: 1975, 'The Logic of Quantum Mechanics', *Mathematics, Matter and Method*, Cambridge University Press, Cambridge, pp. 174-197.

Putman, H.: 1983, *Realism and Reason: Philosophical Papers,* Vol. 3, Cambridge University Press, Cambridge.

Quine, W. van O.: 1953, *From a Logical Point of View*, Harvard University Press, Cambridge.

Quine, W. van O.: 1960, *Word and Object*, MIT Press, Cambridge.

Quine, W. van O. and J.S. Ullian: 1978, *The Web of Belief*, Random House, New York.

Rahwan, I., P. Moraïtis and C. Reed (eds.): 2005, *Argumentation in Multi-Agent Systems*, Springer, Berlin.

Raiffa, H.: 1982, *The Art and Science of Negotiation*, Harvard University Press, Cambridge.

Raz, J., 1990, *Practical Reason and Norms*, Oxford University Press, Oxford.

Raz, J.: 2000, *Engaging Reason: On the Theory of Value and Action*, Oxford University Press, Oxford.
Reed, C. and T.J. Norman (eds.): 2003, *Argumentation Machines. New Frontiers in Argument and Computation*, Kluwer Academic Publishers, Dordrecht.
Reed, C. and G.W.A. Rowe: 2001, 'Araucaria: Software for Puzzles in Argument Diagramming and XML', in Department of Applied Computing, University of Dundee Technical Report.
Reed, C. and G.W.A. Rowe: 2004, 'Araucaria: Software for Argument Analysis, Diagramming and Representation', *International Journal of AI Tools* **14**, 961-980.
Reichenbach, H.: 1951, *The Rise of Scientific Philosophy*, University of California Press, Berkeley and Los Angeles.
Reinhardt, T.: 2003, *Marcus Tullius Cicero, Topica*, Oxford University Press, Oxford.
Reiter, R.: 1980, 'A Logic for Default Reasoning', *Artificial Intelligence* **13**, 81-132.
Reitman, W.: 1965, *Cognition and Thought*, Wiley, New York.
Renn, O.: 1992, 'Concepts of Risk: A Classification', in S. Krimsky and D. Golding (eds.), *Social Theories of Risk*, Praeger, Westport, pp. 53-82.
Rescher, N.: 1976, *Plausible Reasoning: An Introduction to the Theory and Practice of Plausible Inference*, van Gorcum, Assen, Amsterdam.
Rescher, N.: 1978, *Dialectics: A Controversy-Oriented Approach to the Theory of Knowledge*, State University of New York Press, New York.
Rescher, N.: 1986, *Leibniz: An Introduction to his Philosophy*, University Press of America, Lanham.
Rescher, N.: 1988, *Rationality*, Clarendon Press, Oxford.
Rescher, N.: 2003, *On Leibniz*, University of Pittsburgh Press, Pittsburgh.
Rittel, H.W. and M.M. Webber: 1973, 'Dilemmas in a General Theory of Planning', *Policy Sciences* **4**, 155-169.
Robbin, J.: 1969, *Mathematical Logic: A First Course*, Benjamin, New York.
Roldán, C.: 1997, 'Theoria cum praxi: la vuelta a la complejidad. Apuntes para una filosofía práctica desde el perspectivismo leibniziano', *Isegoria* **17**, 85-105.
Roldán, C.: 2005, 'Langue naturelle et éthique rationnelle', in D. Berlioz and F. Nef (eds.), *Leibniz et les Puissances du Langage*, Vrin, Paris, pp. 325-339.
Ross, H.L.: 1980, *Settled Out of Court*, Aldine, Chicago.
Rott, H.: 2001, *Change, Choice and Inference: A Study of Belief Revision and Nonmonotonic Reasoning*, Oxford University Press, Oxford.
Rowland, R.C.: 1982, 'The Influence of Purpose on Fields of Argument', in *Journal of the American Forensic Association* **18**, 228-245.
Russell, B.: 1903, *The Principles of Mathematics*, George Allen and Unwin, London.
Russell, B.: 1967, 'Letter to Frege', in J. Heijenoort (ed.), *From Frege to Gödel*, Harvard University Press, Cambridge. Written in 1902, but previously unpublished.
Rutherford, D.: 1995, 'Philosophy and Language in Leibniz', in N. Jolley (ed.), *The Cambridge Companion to Leibniz*, Cambridge University Press, Cambridge.
Schacter, D.L. (ed.): 1995, *Memory Distortion: How Minds, Brains, and Societies Reconstruct the Past*, Harvard University Press, Cambridge.
Schacter, D.L.: 2001, *The Seven Sins of Memory: How the Mind Forgets and Remembers*, Houghton Mifflin, Boston.
Schauer, F.: 1991, *Playing by the Rules. A Philosophical Examination of Rule-Based Decision-Making in Law and in Life*, Clarendon Press, Oxford.
Schmidt-Radefeldt, J.: 1977, 'On So-called "Rhetorical" Questions', *Journal of Pragmatics* **1**, 375-392.
Schroeder, C.: 1997, 'Knowledge and Power, Logic and Rhetoric, and Other Reflections in the Toulmin Mirror: A Critical Consideration of Stephen Toulmin's Contributions to Composition', in *Journal of Advanced Composition* **17**, 95-107.
Scriven, M.: 1976, *Reasoning*, McGraw-Hill, New York.
Scriven, M.: 2003, 'The Philosophy of Critical Thinking and Informal Logic', in D. Fasko, Jr. (ed.), *Critical Thinking and Reasoning*, Hampton Press, Cresskill, pp. 21-45.
Searle, J.R.: 1969, *Speech Acts: An Essay in the Philosophy of Language*, Cambridge University Press, Cambridge.
Searle, J.R.: 1975, 'Indirect Speech Acts', in P. Cole and J.L. Morgan (eds.), *Syntax and Semantics, Vol. 3: Speech Acts*, Academic Press, New York, pp. 59-82.

Searle, J.R.: 1979, *Expression and Meaning: Studies in the Theory of Speech Acts*, Cambridge University Press, Cambridge.
Sellars, W.: 1948, 'Concepts as Involving Laws and Inconceivable without Them', *Philosophy of Science* **15**, 287-315.
Sellars, W.: 1953, 'Inference and Meaning', *Mind* **62**, 313-338.
Sellars, W.: 1963, *Science, Perception and Reality*, Routledge & Kegan Paul, London.
Sellars, W.: 1964, 'Induction as Vindication', *Philosophy of Science* **31**, 197-231.
Sellars, W.: 1968, *Science and Metaphysics: Variations on Kantian Themes*, Routledge & Kegan Paul, London.
Shapere, D.: 1982, 'The Concept of Observation in Science and Philosophy', *Philosophy of Science* **49**, 485-525.
Shapin, S.: 2002, 'Dear Prudence' [Review of S.E. Toulmin's *Return to Reason*], *London Review of Books* **24**, no. 2 (14 January 2002), pp. 25-27.
Siegel, H.: 1987, *Relativism Refuted*, D. Reidel, Dordrecht.
Siegel, H.: 1988, *Educating Reason: Rationality, Critical Thinking and Education*, Routledge, London and New York.
Siegel, H.: 1996, 'Instrumental Rationality and Naturalized Philosophy of Science', *Philosophy of Science* **63**, Proceedings, S116-S124.
Simon, H.A.:1973, 'The Structure of Ill-structured Problems', *Artificial Intelligence* **4**, 181-201 .
Simonton, D.K.: 1999, *Origins of Genius: Darwinian Perspectives on Creativity*, Oxford University Press, Oxford.
Simosi, M.: 2003, 'Using Toulmin's Framework for the Analysis of Everyday Argumentation: Some Methodological Considerations', *Argumentation* **17**, 185-202.
Simpson, J.A. and E.S.C. Weiner (eds.), 1991, *The Oxford English Dictionary*, 2nd ed., Clarendon Press, Oxford.
Skabar, A., A. Stranieri and J. Zeleznikow: 1997, 'Using Argumentation for the Decomposition and Classification of Tasks for Hybrid System Development', *Progress in Connectionist Based Information Systems. Proceedings of the 1997 International Conference on Neural Information Processing and Intelligent Information Systems*, Springer, Singapore, pp. 814-818.
Skalak, D.B. and E.L. Rissland: 1992, 'Arguments and Cases: An Inevitable Intertwining', *Artificial Intelligence and Law* **1**, 3-44.
Skyrms, B.: 1966, *Choice and Chance*, Dickenson Publishing, Belmont.
Slob, W.H.: 2002a, *Dialogical Rhetoric: An Essay on Truth and Normativity after Postmodernism*, Kluwer, Dordrecht.
Slob, W.H.: 2002b, 'How to Distinguish Good and Bad Arguments: Dialogico-Rhetorical Normativity', *Argumentation* **16**, 179-196.
Slob, W.H.: 2005, 'The Voice of the Other: A Dialogico-rhetorical Understanding of "Opponent" and Toulmin's "Rebuttal"', in D.L. Hitchcock (ed.), *The Uses of Argument: Proceedings of a conference at McMaster University, 18-21 May, 2005*, OSSA, Hamilton, pp. 423-432.
Snoeck Henkemans, A.F.: 1997, *Analysing Complex Argumentation*, Sic Sat, Amsterdam.
Snoeck Henkemans, A.F.: 2002, 'Clues for Reconstructing Symptomatic Argumentation', in F.H. van Eemeren (ed.), *Advances in Pragma-dialectics*, Sic Sat, Amsterdam, pp. 185-196.
Sosa, E.: 1991, *Knowledge in Perspective: Selected Essays in Epistemology*, Cambridge University Press, Cambridge.
Sourdin, T.: 2002, *Alternative Dispute Resolution*, Law Book Company, Sydney.
Stalnaker, R.C.: 1984, *Inquiry*, MIT Press, Cambridge.
Stranieri, A. and J. Zeleznikow: 2001a, 'Copyright Regulation with Argumentation Agents', *Information and Communications Technology Law* **10**, 109-123.
Stranieri, A. and J. Zeleznikow: 2001b, 'WebShell: The Development of Web Based Expert Systems', in M. Bramer, F. Coenen and A. Preece (eds.), *Research and Development in Expert Systems XVIII. Proceedings of ES2001- The Twenty-first SGES International Conference on Knowledge Based Systems and Applied Artificial Intelligence*, Springer, London, pp. 245-258.
Stranieri, A., J. Zeleznikow, M. Gawler and B. Lewis: 1999, 'A Hybrid-neural approach to the Automation of Legal Reasoning in the Discretionary Domain of Family Law in Australia', *Artificial Intelligence and Law* **7**, 153-183.

Stranieri, A., J. Zeleznikow and J. Yearwood: 2001, 'Argumentation Structures that Integrate Dialectical and Monolectical Reasoning', *Knowledge Engineering Review* **16**, 331-348.

Strawson, P.F.: 1949, 'Truth', *Analysis* **9**, 83-97.

Stump, E.: 1988, *Boethius's In Ciceronis Topica*, Cornell University Press, Ithaca/London.

Sunstein, C.R.:1993, 'On Analogical Reasoning', *Harvard Law Review* **106**, 741-749.

Suppes, P.: 1969, *Studies in Methodology and Foundations of Science*, Humanities Press, New York.

Tarski, A.: 1956, 'The Concept of Truth in Formalized Languages', in J.H. Woodger (trans.) *Logic, Semantics, Metamathematics*, Clarendon Press, Oxford, pp. 152-278.

Tennant, N.: 1992, *Autologic*, Edinburgh University Press, Edinburgh.

Thagard, P.: 1992, *Conceptual Revolutions*, Princeton University Press, Princeton.

Thagard, P.: 2000, *Coherence in Thought and Action*, MIT Press, Cambridge.

Thomas, S.N.: 1977, *Practical Reasoning in Natural Language*, Prentice-Hall, Englewood Cliffs.

Tindale, C.W.: 1999, *Acts of Arguing: A Rhetorical Model of Argument*, SUNY Press, Albany.

Toulmin, S.E.: 1950a, 'Probability', in *Proceedings of the Aristotelian Society*, Supplementary Vol. XXIV, The Aristotelian Society, London, pp. 27-62.

Toulmin, S.E.: 1950b, *The Place of Reason in Ethics*, University of Cambridge Press, Cambridge.

Toulmin, S.E.: 1953, *The Philosophy of Science: An Introduction*, The Hutchinson University Library, London.

Toulmin, S.E.: 1958, *The Uses of Argument*, Cambridge University Press, Cambridge.

Toulmin, S.E., 1964, *The Uses of Argument*, Cambridge University Press, Cambridge. Paperback edition of Toulmin (1958).

Toulmin, S.E.: 1970, 'Does the Distinction between Normal and Revolutionary Science hold Water?', in I. Lakatos and A. Musgrave (eds.), *Criticism and the Growth of Knowledge*, Cambridge University Press, Cambridge, pp. 39-47.

Toulmin, S.E.: 1972, *Human Understanding*, Harper and Row, New York.

Toulmin, S.E.: 1981, 'The Tyranny of Principles', *The Hasting Center Report* **6**, 31-39.

Toulmin, S.E.: 1990[2001], *Cosmopolis: The Hidden Agenda of Modernity*, Spanish ed., B. Moreno (trans.), Península, Barcelona.

Toulmin, S.E.: 2001, *Return to Reason*, Harvard University Press, Cambridge.

Toulmin, S.E.: 2001[2003], *Return to Reason*, Spanish ed., I. González-Gallarza (trans.), Península, Barcelona.

Toulmin, S.E.: 2003, *The Uses of Argument*, 2nd. ed., Cambridge University Press, Cambridge.

Toulmin, S.E. and J. Goodfield: 1961, *The Fabric of the Heavens*, Harper and Row, New York.

Toulmin, S.E. and J. Goodfield: 1962, *The Architecture of Matter*, Harper and Row, New York.

Toulmin, S.E. and J. Goodfield: 1965, *The Discovery of Time*, Chicago University Press, Chicago.

Toulmin, S.E., R.D. Rieke and A. Janik: 1979, *An Introduction to Reasoning*, Macmillan, New York.

Toulmin, S.E., R.D. Rieke and A. Janik: 1984, *An Introduction to Reasoning*, 2nd ed., Macmillan, New York.

Trent, J.D.: 1968, 'Toulmin's Model of an Argument: An Examination and Extension', *Quarterly Journal of Speech* **54**, 252-259.

Trillas, E., C. Alsina and J.M. Terricabras: 1995, *Introducción a la Lógica Borrosa*, Ariel, Barcelona.

Tuomela, R.: 2000, 'Belief versus Acceptance', *Philosophical Exploration* **2**, 122-137.

Tweney, R.D.: 1985, 'Faraday's Discovery of Induction: A Cognitive Approach', in D. Gooding and F. James (eds.), *Faraday Rediscovered: Essays on the Life and Work of Michael Faraday: 1791-1867*, Stockton Press, New York.

Urdang, L. (ed.): 1968, *The Random House Dictionary of the English Language*, Random House, New York.

Velthoven, B.C.J van and M.J. ter Voert: 2004, *Geschillenbeslechtingsdelta 2003. Over verloop en afloop van (potentieel) juridische problemen van burgers*, Den Haag, Ministerie van Justitie, WODC, serie Onderzoek en beleid nr. 219.

Verheij, B.: 1996, *Rules, Reasons, Arguments. Formal Studies of Argumentation and Defeat*, Doctoral Dissertation, University of Maastricht, The Netherlands.

Verheij, B.: 1999, 'Logic, Context and Valid Inference. Or: Can There be a Logic of Law?', in H.J. van den Herik, M.F. Moens, J. Bing, B. van Buggenhout, J. Zeleznikow and C.A.F.M. Grütters (eds.),

Legal Knowledge Based Systems. JURIX 1999: The Twelfth Conference, Gerard Noodt Instituut, Nijmegen, pp. 109-121.
Verheij, B.: 2001, 'Legal Decision-making as Dialectical Theory Construction with Argumentation Schemes', *The 8th International Conference on Artificial Intelligence and Law. Proceedings of the Conference*. ACM, New York. The full paper is available at http://www.ai.rug.nl/~verheij/publications.htm.
Verheij, B.: 2002, 'Evaluating Arguments based on Toulmin's Scheme', in H.V. Hansen, C.W. Tindale, J.A. Blair, R.H. Johnson and R.C. Pinto (eds.), *Argumentation and Its Applications* (CD-ROM), OSSA, Windsor.
Verheij, B.: 2003a, 'Artificial Argument Assistants for Defeasible Argumentation', *Artificial Intelligence* **150**, 291-324.
Verheij, B.: 2003b, 'DefLog: On the Logical Interpretation of Prima Facie Justified Assumptions', *Journal of Logic and Computation* **13**, 319-346.
Verheij, B.: 2003c, 'Dialectical Argumentation with Argumentation Schemes: An Approach to Legal Logic', *Artificial Intelligence and Law* **11**, 167–195.
Verheij, B.: 2005a, 'Evaluating Arguments Based on Toulmin's Scheme', *Argumentation* **19**, 347-371.
Verheij, B.: 2005b, *Virtual Arguments. On the Design of Argument Assistants for Lawyers and Other Arguers*, T.M.C. Asser Press, The Hague.
Vincent, A. and J. Zeleznikow: 2005. 'Towards a Plea Bargaining Decision Support System for Legal Aid Lawyers in Victorian Lower Courts', *Proceedings of Second International ODR Workshop,* Wolf Legal Publishers, Nijmjegen, pp. 47-58.
Vitrac, B.: 1990, *Euclide d'Alexandrie: Les Éléments*, Vol. 1, Presses Universitaires de France, Paris.
Voss, J.F., R. Fincher-Kiefer, J. Wile and L.N. Silfies: 1993, 'On the Processing of Arguments', *Argumentation* **7**, 165-181.
Voss, J.F., T.R. Greene, T.A. Post and B.C. Penner: 1983, 'Problem Solving Skill in the Social Sciences', in G.H. Bower (ed.), *The Psychology of Learning and Motivation: Advances in Research and Theory*, Vol. 17, pp. 165-213.
Voss, J.F. and M. Means: 1991, 'Learning to Reason via Instruction in Argumentation', *Learning and Instruction* **1**, 337-350.
Voss, J.F., S.W. Tyler and L. Yengo: 1983, 'Individual Differences in the Solving of Social Science Problems', in R. Dillon and R. Schmeck (eds.), *Individual Differences in Cognition*, Academic Press, New York, pp. 205-232.
Voss, J.F., J. Wiley, J. Kennet, T.E. Schooler and L.N. Silfies: 1998, 'Representations of the Gulf Crisis as Derived from the US Senate Debate', in D.A. Sylvan and J.F. Voss (Eds.), *Problem Representation in Foreign Policy Decision Making*, Cambridge University Press, Cambridge, pp. 279-302.
Vreeswijk, G.A.W.: 1997, 'Abstract Argumentation Systems', *Artificial Intelligence* **90**, 225-279.
Walker, G.B. and J. DiP. Congalton: 1987, 'Generic Argument and Argument Fields', *Journal of the American Forensic Association* **23**, 125-135.
Walton D.N.: 1989, *Informal Logic. A Handbook for Critical Argumentation,* Cambridge University Press, New York.
Walton, D.N.: 1991, *Begging the Question: Circular Reasoning as a Tactic of Argumentation*, Greenwood Press, New York/Westport/ London.
Walton, D.N.: 1995, *A Pragmatic Theory of Fallacy*, University of Alabama Press, Tuscaloosa.
Walton, D.N.: 1996a, 'Plausible Deniability and Evasion of Burden of Proof', *Argumentation* **10**, 47-58.
Walton, D.N.: 1996b, *Argumentation Schemes for Presumptive Reasoning*, Lawrence Erlbaum Associates, Mahwah.
Walton, D.N.: 1998, *The New Dialectic: Conversational Contexts of Argument*, University of Toronto Press, Toronto.
Walton, D.N.: 2003, 'Is There a Burden of Questioning?', *Artificial Intelligence and Law* **11** 1-43.
Walton, D.N. and E.C.W. Krabbe: 1995, *Commitment in Dialogue: Basic Concepts of Interpersonal Reasoning*, SUNY Press, Albany.
Walton, D.N. and C. Reed: 2003, 'Diagramming, Argumentation Schemes and Critical Questions', in F.H. van Eemeren, J.A. Blair, C.A. Willard and A.F. Snoeck Henkemans (eds.), *Anyone Who Has a View: Theoretical Contributions to the study of Argumentation*, Kluwer, Dordrecht, pp. 195-211.

Walton R., C. Gierl, P. Yudkin, H. Mistry, M.P. Vessey and J. Fox: 1997, 'Evaluation of Computer Support for Prescribing (CAPSULE) Using Simulated Cases', *British Medical Journal* **315**, 791-795.

Wassermann, R.: 2000, *Resource-bounded Belief Revision*, ILLC DS-2000-01, Universiteit van Amsterdam, Amsterdam.

Weinstein, M.: 1990, 'Towards a Research Agenda for Informal Logic and Critical Thinking', *Informal Logic* **12**, 121-143.

Weinstein, M.: 1991, 'Entailment in Argumentation,' in F.H. van Eemeren, R. Grootendorst, J.A. Blair and C.A. Willard (eds.), *Proceedings of the Second International Conference on Argumentation*, Vol. 1B, Sic Sat, Amsterdam, pp. 226-235.

Weinstein, M.: 2002a, 'Exemplifying an Internal Realist Model of Truth', *Philosophica* **69**, 20-49.

Weinstein, M.: 2002b, 'Critical Review of Robert C. Pinto's *Argument, Inference and Dialectic*', *Informal Logic* **22**, 161-180.

Wenzel, J.W.: 1982, 'On Fields of Argument as Propositional Systems', *Journal of the American Forensic Association* **18**, 204-213.

Wigmore, J.H.: 1931, *The Principles of Judicial Proof*, 2nd. ed., Little, Brown and Co., Boston.

Willard, C.A.: 1976. 'On the Utility of Descriptive Diagrams for the Analysis and Criticism of Arguments', *Communication Monographs* **43**, 308-319.

Willard, C.A.: 1981, 'Argument Fields and Theories of Logical Types', *Journal of the American Forensic Association* **17**, 129-145.

Willard C.A.: 1982, 'Argument Fields', in J.R. Cox and C.A. Willard (eds.), *Advances in Argumentation Theory and Research*, Southern Illinois University Press, Carbondale, pp. 24-77.

Willard, C.A.: 1983, *Argumentation and the Social Grounds of Knowledge*, University of Alabama Press, Alabama.

Willard, C.A.: 1989, *A Theory of Argumentation*, University of Alabama Press, Tuscaloosa.

Williams, G.R.: 1983, *Legal Negotiation and Settlement*, West Publishing Co., St. Paul.

Woods, J.: 2003, *Paradox and Paraconsistency: Conflict Resolution in the Abstract Sciences*, Cambridge University Press, Cambridge and New York.

Woods, J.: 2004, *The Death of Argument: Fallacies in Agent-Based Reasoning*, Kluwer, Dordrecht and Boston.

Woods, J.: 2005a, 'Epistemic Bubbles', in Artemov, S., H. Barringer, A.S.d'A. Garcez, L.C. Lamb and J. Woods (eds.), *We Will Show Them: Essays in Honour of Dov Gabbay*, Vol. 2, College Publications, London, pp. 732-771.

Woods, J.: 2005b, 'Dialectical Considerations on the Logic of Contradiction', *Logic Journal of the IGPL* **13**, 231-266.

Woods, J. and H.V. Hansen: 1997, 'Hintikka on Aristotle's Fallacies', *Synthese* **113**, 217-239.

Woods J and K. Peacock: 2004 'Quantum logic and the unity of science', in S. Rehman, J. Symons, D.M. Gabbay and J.P. van Bendegem (eds.), *Logic, Epistemology and the Unity of Science*', Kluwer, Dordrecht and Boston, pp. 257-287.

Woods, J. and D.N. Walton: 1989, *Fallacies: Selected Papers 1972-1982*, Foris de Gruyter, Berlin and New York.

Wreen, M.J.: 1998, 'A Few Remarks on the Individuation of Arguments', in F.H. van Eemeren, R. Grootendorst, J.A. Blair and C. Willard (eds.), *Proceedings of the 5th International Conference of Argumentation*, Sic Sat, Amsterdam, pp. 883-888.

Yearwood, J. and A. Stranieri: 1999, 'The Integration of Retrieval, Reasoning and Drafting for Refugee Law: A Third Generation Legal Knowledge Based System', *Proceedings of the Seventh International Conference on Artificial Intelligence and Law*, ACM, Oslo, pp. 117-126.

Zarefsky, D.: 1982, 'Persistent Questions in the Theory of Argument Fields', *Journal of the American Forensic Association* **18**, 191-203.

Zeleznikow, J.: 2000, 'Building Judicial Decision Support Systems in Discretionary Legal Domains', *International Review of Law, Computers and Technology* **14**, 341-356.

Zeleznikow, J.: 2003, 'An Australian Perspective on Research and Development required for the Construction of Applied Legal Decision Support Systems', *Artificial Intelligence and Law* **10**, 237-260.

Zeleznikow, J.: 2004, 'The Split-Up Project: Induction, Context and Knowledge Discovery in Law', *Law, Probability and Risk* **3**, 147-168.

Zeleznikow, J. and E. Bellucci: 2003, 'Family Winner: Integrating Game Theory and Heuristics to Provide Negotiation Support', in D. Bourcier (ed.), *Proceedings of the Sixteenth International Conference on Legal Knowledge Based Systems*, IOS Publications, Amsterdam, pp. 21-30.

Zillman, D.: 1972, 'Rhetorical Elicitation of Agreement in Persuasion', *Journal of Personality and Social Psychology* **21**, 159-165.

Zillman, D.: 1974, 'Rhetorical Elicitation of Concession in Persuasion', *The Journal of Social Psychology* **94**, 223-236.

INDEX

The index contains references to subjects discussed thematically in the chapters, as well as to names of persons. It has been compiled on the basis of chapter indexes provided by their authors.